# Azure Data Engineer Associate Certification Guide

## *Second Edition*

Ace the DP-203 exam with advanced data engineering skills

**Giacinto Palmieri**

**Surendra Mettapalli**

**Newton Alex**

‹packt›

# Azure Data Engineer Associate Certification Guide

## *Second Edition*

**Authors**: Giacinto Palmieri, Surendra Mettapalli, and Newton Alex

**Reviewer**: Anindita Basak

**Publishing Product Manager**: Anindya Sil

**Senior-Development Editor**: Megan Carlisle

**Development Editor:** M Keerthi Nair

**Presentation Designer**: Shantanu Zagade

**Editorial Board**: Vijin Boricha, Megan Carlisle, Simon Cox, Ketan Giri, Saurabh Kadave, Alex Mazonowicz, Gandhali Raut, and Ankita Thakur

First Published: February 2022

Second edition: May 2024

Production Reference: 1220524

Published by Packt Publishing Ltd.
Grosvenor House
11 St Paul's Square
Birmingham
B3 1RB

ISBN: 978-1-80512-468-9

www.packtpub.com

# Contributors

## About the Authors

**Giacinto Palmieri** has been working in the IT sector for more than 35 years (initially in his native Italy and then in London, where he moved 23 years ago) as a trainer, software developer, data engineer, and consultant. In the past three years, he has been focusing mostly on his activity as a Microsoft Certified Trainer with particular focus on Azure data services, Azure development, and the Power Platform. Outside of IT, he holds an MA in Philosophy and a PhD in Translation Studies and sometimes performs as a stand-up comedian, even bringing several shows to the Edinburgh Fringe Festival (a fact he tends to hide from his IT course participants, lest they expect a laugh per minute experience).

> *"I want to thank my lovely wife Alison for putting up with me*
> *while I was working on this book, and with me in general."*

**Surendra Mettapalli** is a Principal Data Engineer/Scientist with over 12 years of experience leading Data teams in the UK and India. He specializes in designing and implementing innovative data solutions in large and complex environments. His team's expertise spans Microsoft Fabric, Azure Data Factory, Azure Synapse Analytics, Databricks, and Power BI.

With a deep understanding of Data Engineering, Cloud Architecture, and AI-driven applications, he has successfully collaborated with diverse clients across technology, finance, retail, and government sectors. His contributions have been instrumental in delivering some of the largest and most impactful data projects and empowering organizations to leverage Azure's full potential and optimize their business operations.

Surendra holds various certifications from Microsoft Azure in data engineering, data science, and AI streams, as well as certifications from Databricks. His notable contribution to "Optimizing COVID-19 Interventions with Evolutionary AI" has gained positive recognition within the industry.

Beyond his professional endeavors, he is passionate about sharing his knowledge and experience with the community. He regularly contributes to industry events and forums, guiding others through the complexities of the data landscape.

> *"I want to extend my heartfelt thanks to my family, whose endless encouragement and belief in me*
> *have been the cornerstone of my journey. To my parents, who have shaped me into the person I am*
> *today, my loving wife Gowthami, and our precious little one, Vihika, You are my greatest blessings."*

**Newton Alex** was the Group Engineering Manager for several Azure Data Analytics projects in Microsoft, India. He led the teams that developed Azure technologies like Azure Synapse, Azure Databricks, Azure HDInsight working deeply with open-source projects like Apache YARN, Apache Spark, Apache Hive etc. He started his Big Data career with the early versions of Hadoop, PIG and Oozie while at Yahoo, USA, where he helped create the very first batch processing pipelines for Yahoo's ad serving team. After Yahoo, he led the Big Data teams at Pivotal Inc., USA, where he was responsible for the Open-Source stack of Pivotal Inc. He later moved to Microsoft and started the Azure Data team in India. Newton now leads several Data Analytics teams at Google. He has helped several Fortune 500 companies to build their data systems in his career.

# About the Reviewer

**Anindita Basak** is a Principal Cloud Architect primarily helping enterprises with hybrid cloud journey and digital transformation. She has over 15+ years of industry experience and has delivered more than ten successful cloud migration and modernization of enterprise applications on Microsoft Azure. She worked with Microsoft as a cloud consultant and in various other roles, accelerating the cloud digital journey for businesses in the BFSI, healthcare, retail, and FMCG sectors.

She co-authored two books on Azure Stream Analytics and Machine Learning and has technically reviewed more than fifteen books on Cloud, Data, and AI with DevSecOps on AWS, and the Azure platform.

# Table of Contents

## Part 3:
## Data Processing

# 4

## Ingesting and Transforming Data

# 5

## Developing a Batch Processing Solution 177

# 6

## Developing a Stream Processing Solution 229

# 7

# 10

## Optimizing and Troubleshooting Data Storage and Data Processing     435

## 11

# Preface

Azure is one of the foremost cloud providers in the world, providing numerous services for data hosting and data processing. As more companies transition toward cloud-native solutions, the demand for data engineering expertise has skyrocketed. Companies are increasingly relying on cloud-based solutions for their data needs, and this has led to an explosion of data engineering jobs and an increasingly competitive landscape for aspiring and experienced professionals looking to fill those positions.

Gaining the **DP-203: Azure Data Engineer Associate certification** is a surefire way of showing potential employers that you have what it takes to become an Azure data engineer, and the *Azure Data Engineer Associate Certification Guide (DP-203), Second Edition* will help you prepare for the **DP-203** examination in a structured way, covering all the topics specified in the syllabus with detailed explanations and exam tips.

This book will first cover the fundamentals of Azure and walk you through the various stages of building data engineering solutions using an example of a hypothetical company. Throughout the book, you will learn about the various Azure components involved in building data systems and explore them using a wide range of real-world use cases. Finally, you will work on example questions and answers to familiarize yourself with the exam pattern.

By the end of this Azure book, you will have gained the confidence you need to pass the **DP-203** exam with ease and land your dream job in data engineering.

## Second Edition

More than two years have passed since the first edition of this *Azure Data Engineer Associate Certification Guide*. There have been a lot of changes to Microsoft's Azure platform and the Microsoft cloud ecosystem in that time.

The overall scope of the exam remains focused on data engineering on the **Microsoft Azure** platform, including questions relating to data storage, data processing, data exploration, and data security. However, the specific topics and their weightings have been updated to reflect the evolution of Azure Data Services and technologies.

To address this, the second edition will provide updated exam materials and additional notes, hints, tips, and tricks to help you navigate the current exam and the certification process in the ever-evolving world of Microsoft Azure. It will give thorough coverage of the exam topics, spanning fundamental concepts and advanced strategies for Azure as well as introducing new areas of focus.

The key exam-related topics covered in this book are as follows:

- Partitioning strategies for **Azure Synapse Analytics** and **Azure Data Lake Storage Gen2 (ADLS Gen2)**

- Ingesting and transforming data using **Azure Synapse Pipelines** or **Azure Data Factory (ADF)** and **Azure Databricks (ADB)**

- Handling late-arriving data and managing duplicate data

- Exploring data using SQL Serverless and **Spark clusters** in **Azure Synapse**

- Integrating **Azure Purview** for data lineage and metadata management

- The basics of Azure Data Services and architecture

- Leveraging Azure data storage and management and implementing a partitioning strategy

- Designing and implementing data processing solutions using **ADF**, **Azure Synapse Analytics**, and **ADB**

- Utilizing **Azure Synapse Analytics** and **Azure Stream Analytics** for Big Data and real-time analytics workloads

- Implementing security, monitoring, and troubleshooting strategies for Azure data solutions

- Optimizing and troubleshooting data storage and data processing

This book organizes this material in accordance with exam objectives, including both relevant theory and knowledge application through practical guidance and exam-related practice questions. Some topics have also been updated to align with the revised exam and incorporate the latest innovations and advancements in the Microsoft cloud ecosystem.

The new edition will give you unlimited access to the online practice resources platform. Here, you will engage with the **mock exams** and **flashcards** and perform **practical exercises** to let you practice what you learned in the book from any device. You will get access to specially designed **flashcards** and **exam tips** to help you memorize key topics and be fully prepared to ace the exam.

## Online Practice Resources

With this book, you will unlock unlimited access to the online exam-prep platform (*Figure 0.1*). This is your place to practice everything you learn in the book.

> **How to access the resources**
>
> To learn how to access the online resources, refer to *Chapter 11, Accessing the Online Resources*, at the end of this book.

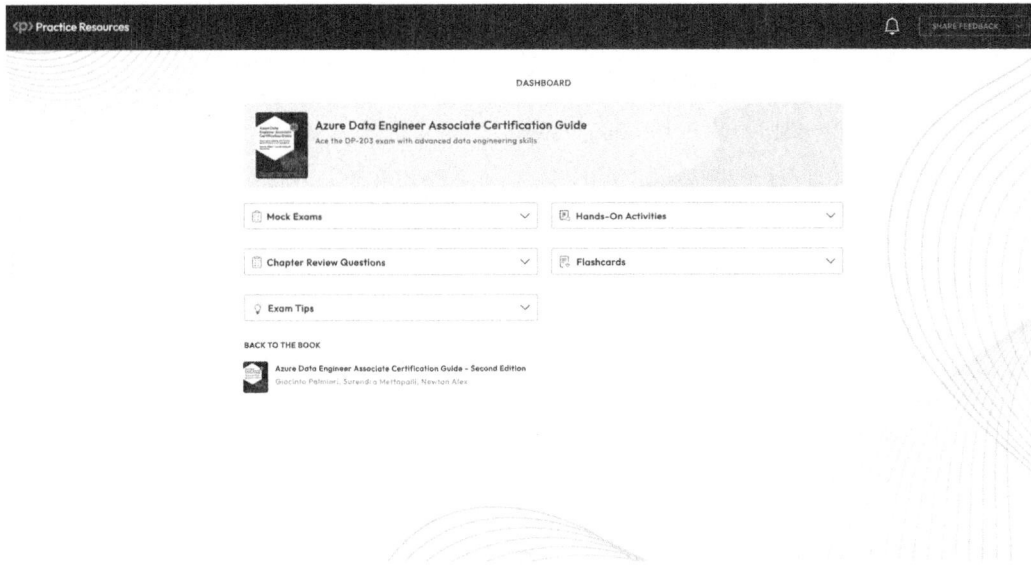

Figure 0.1 – Exam DP-203: Azure data engineer Associate online exam-prep platform

Sharpen your knowledge of **DP-203** concepts with multiple sets of mock exams, interactive flashcards, and practical exercises that are accessible from all modern web browsers. If you get stuck, you can raise your concerns with the author directly through the website. Before doing that, go through the list of resolved questions as well. These are based on questions asked by other users. Finally, review the exam tips on the website to ensure you are well prepared.

## Who This Book Is For

This book is intended for data engineers, data architects, cloud architects, solution architects, and DataOps professionals who are just beginning to work with cloud-based solutions and services or are new to Azure. It is designed for those who want to pass the **DP-203: Azure Data Engineer Associate** exam and are looking to gain more in-depth knowledge of the Azure Cloud stack. No specific knowledge is assumed or required.

This book will also help engineers and product managers who are new to Azure or who will be interviewed by companies that work with Azure technologies to acquire effective hands-on experience with Azure data technologies. A basic knowledge of cloud technologies, **Extract, Transform, and Load** (ETL), and databases is expected to help you get the most out of this book.

You can learn more about the certification and exam at https://packt.link/arKva.

# What This Book Covers

This book is aligned with the revised syllabus of **Exam DP-203: Azure Data Engineer Associate Certification** and comprises the following chapters:

*Chapter 1, Introducing Azure Basics*, will introduce you to Azure and explains its capabilities. This is a refresher chapter designed to renew your knowledge of some of the core Azure concepts, including VMs, data storage, compute options, the **Azure portal**, accounts, and subscriptions. You will be building on top of these technologies in future chapters.

*Chapter 2, Implementing a Partition Strategy*, will explore the implementation of partition strategies for efficient data management. You will delve into strategies for optimizing analytical workloads through data partitioning and discuss approaches to improve performance for streaming workloads. Additionally, you will examine the utilization of partitioning within **Azure Synapse Analytics** for enhanced data processing, and identify scenarios where partitioning is necessary in **ADLS Gen2** for improved data organization and processing.

*Chapter 3, Designing and Implementing the Data Exploration Layer*, will focus on creating and executing queries using **SQL** Serverless and Spark cluster technologies. You will also review database templates in **Azure Synapse Analytics** and their implementation as part of this exploration. Additionally, you will learn to push new or updated data lineage to **Microsoft Purview** and explore the importance of searching and browsing metadata in the Microsoft Purview data catalog for effective data management.

*Chapter 4, Ingesting and Transforming Data*, will focus on designing and implementing incremental loads for efficient data ingestion. You will utilize **Apache Spark**, **Transact-SQL (T-SQL)** in **Azure Synapse Analytics**, **Stream Analytics**, and **ADF** for data transformations. You will also look into the various aspects of data pipelines, such as cleansing data, parsing data, encoding, and decoding data, and **normalizing** and **denormalizing** values. Additionally, you will focus on configuring error handling for transformations, including handling duplicate, missing, and late-arriving data. Finally, you will delve into performing exploratory analysis for effective data analysis.

*Chapter 5, Developing a Batch Processing Solution*, will utilize a combination of **Azure Data Lake Storage**, **ADB**, **Azure Synapse Analytics**, and **ADF**. You will use PolyBase to load data into an SQL pool and implement **Azure Synapse Link** for efficient data loading. Additionally, you will learn how to create and test data pipelines, integrate notebooks, and configure batch retention as part of your data pipeline development. Error handling is examined as well, including managing upserted data, reverting data to a previous state, and configuring exception handling for robust data processing.

*Chapter 6, Developing a Stream Processing Solution*, will focus on creating solutions using **Stream Analytics** and **Azure Event Hubs** for real-time data processing. You will use Spark Structured Streaming for data processing. Additionally, you will address schema management, including handling schema drift and managing time series data effectively. Finally, you will learn about pipeline optimization techniques, such as configuring checkpoints, watermarking, and optimizing pipelines for analytical and transactional purposes.

*Chapter 7, Managing Batches and Pipelines*, will cover triggering and handling failed batch loads to ensure data integrity. For pipeline management, you will focus on managing and scheduling data pipelines using **ADF** and **Azure Synapse Pipelines**. Additionally, you will learn how to implement version control for pipeline artifacts to track changes effectively and explore managing Spark jobs within a pipeline for efficient Spark job management.

*Chapter 8, Implementing Data Security*, will explore strategies for data masking and encryption to ensure data protection and focuses on how to design and implement data encryption, both at rest and in transit, data auditing, data masking, and data retention. You will implement security controls such as row-level, column-level security, and **Azure RBAC** to restrict access effectively. Additionally, you will cover access management, including managing POSIX-like **Access Control Lists** (**ACLs**) for **Data Lake Storage Gen2** and securing endpoints to control data access. Finally, you will address sensitive data management, including handling sensitive information within DataFrames and managing encrypted data for enhanced security.

*Chapter 9, Monitoring Data Storage and Data Processing*, covers the implementation of logging used by **Azure Monitor**, focusing on setting up and utilizing its features to track the activities and health of Azure services effectively. You will explore the performance of data movement processes within Azure services and monitor and update statistics about data across a system to reflect its current state accurately. You will delve into monitoring data pipeline performance, identifying bottlenecks and ensuring smooth data flow, and you will learn how to interpret Azure Monitor **metrics** and **logs** to make informed decisions. Finally, you will implement a pipeline alert strategy for prompt responses to potential issues.

*Chapter 10, Optimizing and Troubleshooting Data Storage and Data Processing*, will explore strategies for compacting small files to improve processing efficiency and system performance. You will review techniques for handling skew in data distribution to mitigate processing delays, explore ways to manage data spillage and optimize resource management to maximize performance, use indexers to reduce data search times, and use caching to speed up query execution. Additionally, you will learn about troubleshooting failed **Spark jobs**, diagnosing, and resolving issues that cause them to fail, troubleshooting failed pipeline runs (including activities executed in external services), and providing insights on identifying and fixing problems to ensure smooth pipeline execution.

## Minimum Hardware Requirements

For an optimal experience, the following hardware configuration is recommended:

- **Processor**: Dual-core or better

- **Memory**: 4 GB RAM

- **Storage**: 10 GB available space

## Minimum Software Requirements

You must have the following software installed:

| Chapter | Software Required | OS Required |
|---------|-------------------|-------------|
| 1–10 | Azure account (free or paid) | Windows, macOS, and Linux |
| 1–10 | Azure Command-Line Interface (CLI) | Windows, macOS, and Linux |
| 1–10 | Visual Studio Code (VS Code) | Windows, macOS, and Linux |

> **Note**
>
> You can find the Azure CLI installation link in GitHub as part of *Chapter 1, Introducing Azure Basics*, at `https://packt.link/muMNE`.

# Download the Example Code Files

You can download the example code files for this book from GitHub at `https://packt.link/HMJ10`. If there's an update to the code, it will be updated in the GitHub repository. Download all the folders and data files from GitHub (*Figure 0.2*) or download individual chapter files separately as needed:

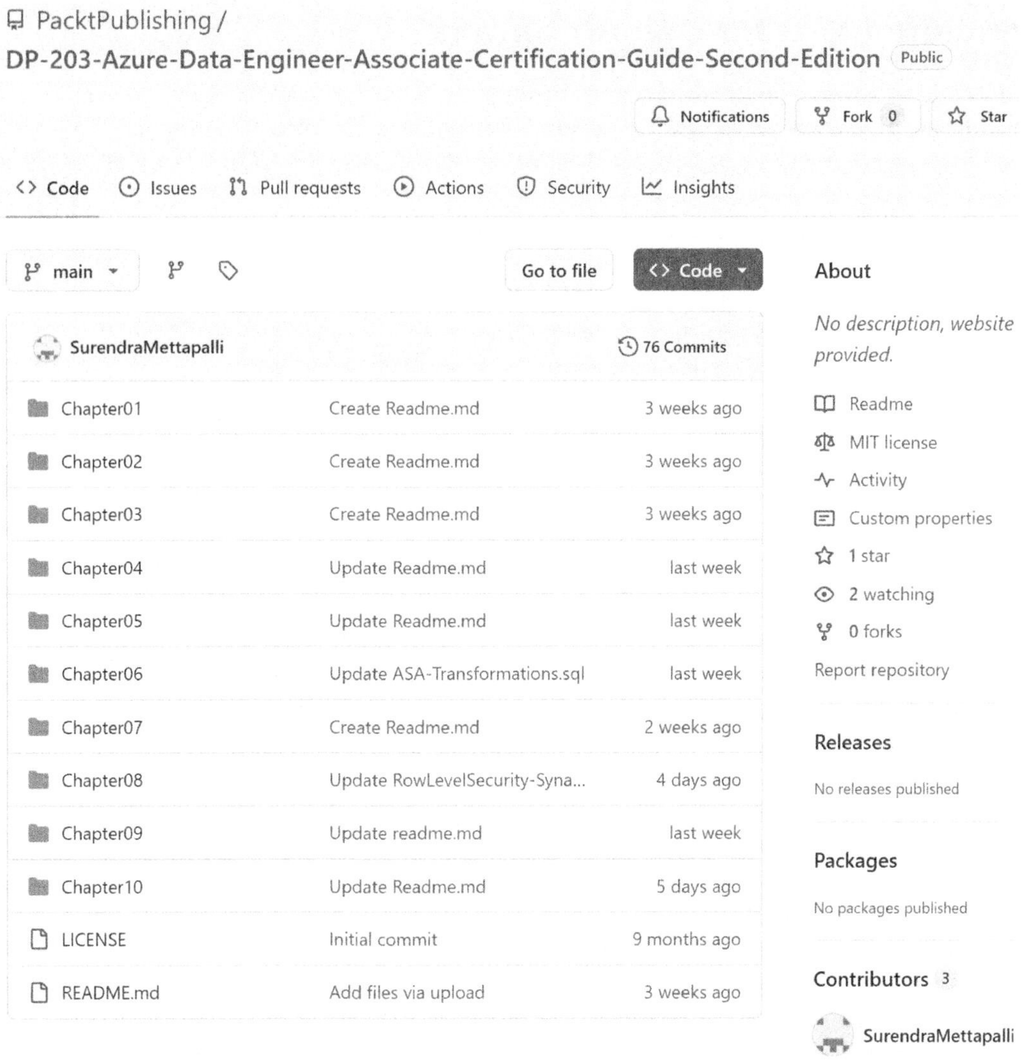

🖥 PacktPublishing /

DP-203-Azure-Data-Engineer-Associate-Certification-Guide-Second-Edition  Public

| | |
|---|---|
| 🔔 Notifications | 🍴 Fork 0    ☆ Star |

<> Code    ⊙ Issues    ⭧ Pull requests    ▷ Actions    ⊘ Security    ⟋ Insights

| ⑂ main ▾    ⑂   ◇ | Go to file | <> Code ▾ |
|---|---|---|

| 🐱 SurendraMettapalli | | 🕙 76 Commits |
|---|---|---|
| 📁 Chapter01 | Create Readme.md | 3 weeks ago |
| 📁 Chapter02 | Create Readme.md | 3 weeks ago |
| 📁 Chapter03 | Create Readme.md | 3 weeks ago |
| 📁 Chapter04 | Update Readme.md | last week |
| 📁 Chapter05 | Update Readme.md | last week |
| 📁 Chapter06 | Update ASA-Transformations.sql | last week |
| 📁 Chapter07 | Create Readme.md | 2 weeks ago |
| 📁 Chapter08 | Update RowLevelSecurity-Syna... | 4 days ago |
| 📁 Chapter09 | Update readme.md | last week |
| 📁 Chapter10 | Update Readme.md | 5 days ago |
| 📄 LICENSE | Initial commit | 9 months ago |
| 📄 README.md | Add files via upload | 3 weeks ago |

**About**

*No description, website provided.*

📖 Readme

⚖ MIT license

〰 Activity

▤ Custom properties

☆ 1 star

⊙ 2 watching

⑂ 0 forks

Report repository

**Releases**

No releases published

**Packages**

No packages published

**Contributors** 3

🐱 SurendraMettapalli

Figure 0.2 – GitHub code files for DP-203 certification

We also have other code bundles from our rich catalog of books and videos available at
`https://packt.link/xi324`. Check them out!

## Requirements for Online Content

The online content includes interactive elements such as mock exams, flashcards, exam tips, and hands-on labs practical exercises. For an optimal experience, it is recommended that you use the latest version of a modern desktop (or mobile) web browser, such as Edge, Chrome, Safari, or Firefox.

## How to Get the Most Out of This Book

To carry out any tasks to further your learning using the Microsoft Azure Cloud platform, you will require the following:

- Access to an internet browser

- A Microsoft account; if you do not have one, you can create a free account at this URL: `https://packt.link/sRKgo`

- An Azure subscription that has access to create and delete resources in it; if you do not have an Azure subscription, you can create a free Azure account at this URL: `https://packt.link/hMtqw`

## Download the Color Images

We also provide a PDF file that has color images of the screenshots and diagrams used in this book. You can download it here: `https://packt.link/graphics`.

## Conventions Used

There are a few text conventions used throughout this book:

**Code in text:** These elements refer to code snippets, table names in databases, folder and file names, extensions, file paths, placeholder URLs, user inputs, and references to Twitter handles. Here is an example: "Select `Azure SQL Service` from the Azure dashboard. Create a new Azure SQL instance if you don't already have one."

**Code block within paragraphs:** A block of code is set as follows:

```
az vm extension set \
  --resource-group <YOUR_RESOURCE_GROUP> \
  --vm-name <VM_NAME> \
  --name OmsAgentForLinux \
  --publisher Microsoft.EnterpriseCloud.Monitoring \
  --protected-settings '{«workspaceKey»:»<YOUR_WORKSPACE_KEY>»}' \
  --settings '{«workspaceId":"<YOUR_WORKSPACE_ID>"}'
```

**Code block within steps:** When a code block is part of a step, it is presented as follows:

1. Insert the following dummy values into this table:

```
INSERT INTO [dbo].[FactTrips] values (100, 200, CURRENT_
TIMESTAMP);
INSERT INTO [dbo].[FactTrips] values (101, 201, CURRENT_
TIMESTAMP);
INSERT INTO [dbo].[FactTrips] values (102, 202, CURRENT_
TIMESTAMP);
```

**Bold:** This indicates a definition or an important word or words that you see on screen. Here is an example: "Azure is one of the major hyperscalers in the industry, offering **Infrastructure as a Service (IaaS), Platform as a Service (PaaS), the Internet of Things (IoT), Artificial Intelligence (AI), and Software as a Service (SaaS).**"

**Supplementary details:** Important or additional information is provided as a **Note** or **Further knowledge**. They appear as follows:

> Note/Further knowledge
> Notes or Further knowledge appear in the book like this.

# Get in Touch

Feedback from our readers is always welcome.

- **General feedback**: If you have questions about any aspect of this book, email us at customercare@packt.com and mention the book title in the subject of your message.

- **Errata**: Although we have taken every care to ensure the accuracy of our content, mistakes do happen. If you have found a mistake in this book, we would be grateful if you would report this to us. Please visit https://packt.link/vFgzz and fill in the form. We ensure that all valid errata are promptly updated in the GitHub repository, with the relevant information available in the Readme.md file. You can access the GitHub repository at https://packt.link/HMJ1O.

- **Piracy**: If you come across any illegal copies of our works in any form on the internet, we would be grateful if you would provide us with the location address or website name. Please contact us at copyright@packt.com with a link to the material.

- **If you are interested in becoming an author**: If there is a topic that you have expertise in and you are interested in either writing or contributing to a book, please visit authors.packtpub.com.

## Share Your Thoughts

Once you've read *Azure Data Engineer Associate Certification Guide, Second Edition*, we'd love to hear your thoughts! Scan the QR code below to go straight to the Amazon review page for this book and share your feedback.

https://packt.link/r/1805124684

Your review is important to us and the tech community and will help us make sure we're delivering excellent quality content.

# Download a Free PDF Copy of This Book

Thanks for purchasing this book!

Do you like to read on the go but are unable to carry your print books everywhere?

Is your eBook purchase not compatible with the device of your choice?

Don't worry, now with every Packt book you get a DRM-free PDF version of that book at no cost.

Read anywhere, any place, on any device. Search, copy, and paste code from your favorite technical books directly into your application.

The perks don't stop there, you can get exclusive access to discounts, newsletters, and great free content in your inbox daily.

Follow these simple steps to get the benefits:

1.  Scan the QR code or visit the link below:

https://packt.link/free-ebook/9781805124689

2.  Submit your proof of purchase.
3.  That's it! We'll send your free PDF and other benefits to your email directly.

# Part 1:
# Azure Basics

The **Azure Basics** domain in the **DP-203: Data Engineering on Microsoft Azure** exam is a basic component focusing on foundational elements of Microsoft Azure, cloud computing, Azure architecture, and management and governance in Azure environments.

The chapters under this domain will explore these fundamentals, including cloud concepts such as **Infrastructure as a Service (IaaS)**, **Platform as a Service (PaaS)**, and **Software as a Service (SaaS)**, as well as different deployment models, such as public, private, and hybrid clouds. You will delve into Azure's architectural components, such as regions, availability zones, and resource groups, and how they support Azure infrastructure, as well as various Azure services and how they can be integrated to create comprehensive solutions. Finally, you will be introduced to tools for managing Azure resources, governance features such as policies and RBAC, and cost management techniques to optimize Azure costs.

In this section of the book, you'll find *Chapter 1, Introducing Azure Basics.*

# 1

# Introducing Azure Basics

This chapter introduces you to the basics of Azure and explains its general capabilities. It covers several core Azure concepts, including **Virtual Machines (VMs)**, data storage, compute options, the Azure portal, accounts, and subscriptions, which future chapters will build upon.

Azure is one of the major hyperscalers in the industry, offering **Infrastructure as a Service (IaaS)**, **Platform as a Service (PaaS)**, the **Internet of Things (IoT)**, **Artificial Intelligence (AI)**, and **Software as a Service (SaaS)**. It provides several cloud, hybrid, and on-premises services, such as VMs, networks, compute, databases, messaging, and **Machine Learning (ML)**, while focusing on security and compliance. You could use these services to build anything from web pages to mobile apps, and from Data Analytics solutions to IoT solutions.

In Azure, users have the flexibility to choose from completely hosted no-code solutions to completely build-your-own solutions. The latter of these can be built from the ground up using basic building blocks such as VMs and **Virtual Networks (VNets)**, allowing users full control over every aspect of the system. Most of these technologies come prebaked with cloud advantages, such as geo-replication, high availability, data redundancy, scalability, and elasticity.

## Making the Most Out of this Book – Your Certification and Beyond

This book and its accompanying online resources are designed to be a complete preparation tool for your **DP-203 exam**.

The book is written in a way that you can apply everything you've learned here even after your certification. The online practice resources that come with this book (*Figure 1.1*) are designed to improve your test-taking skills. They are loaded with timed mock exams, hands-on activities, interactive flashcards, and exam tips, to help you work on your exam readiness from now till your test day.

**Before You Proceed**

To learn how to access these resources, head over to *Chapter 11, Accessing the Online Resources,* at the end of the book.

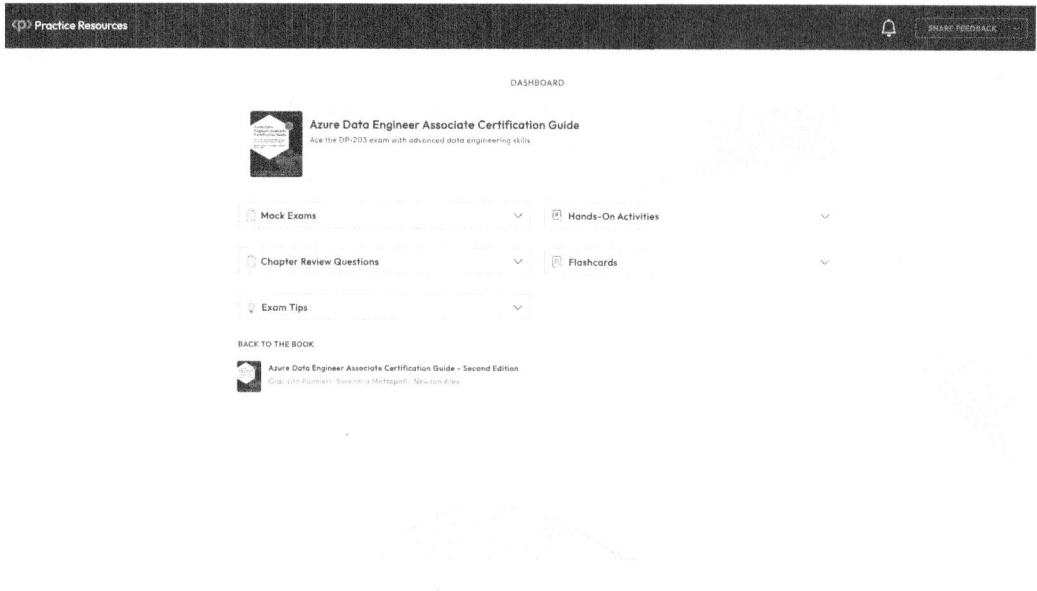

Figure 1.1: Dashboard interface of the online practice resources

Here are some tips on how to make the most out of this book so that you can clear your certification and retain your knowledge beyond your exam:

1. Read each section thoroughly.

2. **Make ample notes**: You can use your favorite online note-taking tool or use a physical notebook. The free online resources also give you access to an online version of this book. Click the BACK TO THE BOOK link from the Dashboard to access the book in Packt Reader. You can highlight specific sections of the book there.

3. **Chapter Review Questions**: At the end of this chapter, you'll find a link to review questions for this chapter. These are designed to test your knowledge of the chapter. Aim to score at least **75%** before moving on to the next chapter. You'll find detailed instructions on how to make the most of these questions at the end of this chapter in the *Exam Readiness Drill - Chapter Review Questions* section. That way, you're improving your exam-taking skills after each chapter, rather than doing it at the end.

4. **Flashcards**: After you've gone through the book and scored 75% more in each of the chapter review questions, start reviewing the online flashcards. They will help you memorize key concepts.

5. **Mock Exams**: Solve the mock exams that come with the book till your exam day. If you get some answers wrong, go back to the book and revisit the concepts you're weak in.

6. **Hands-on Labs – Practical Exercises**: After completing this book, complete the Practical exercises online to improve your practical experience.

7. **Exam Tips**: Review these from time to time to improve your exam readiness even further.

This chapter begins with a quick review of the basics of Azure, and the following sections will focus on brushing up on the fundamentals. If you already have a working knowledge of Azure and know how to spin up resources, then you can safely skip this chapter and go directly to the next one.

In this first chapter, you will find an overview of Azure, including some common Azure services. This way, you will get an effective grounding in the basics, such as accounts, VMs, storage, compute, and networking. You will also walk through ways to spin up services using both the Azure portal and the CLI.

By the end of this chapter, you will be able to answer questions on the following confidently:

- The Azure portal
- Azure accounts, subscriptions, and resource groups
- Azure services
- Azure VMs
- Azure Storage
- Azure Networking (VNets)
- Azure compute

> **Note**
> Your journey in Azure starts here: `https://packt.link/QNL4m`.

The first section starts with an introduction to the Azure portal.

## Technical Requirements

To follow along with this chapter, you will need an Azure account (free or paid) and should have installed the Azure **Command Line Interface** (**CLI**) on your workstation.

# Introducing the Azure Portal

The Azure portal (`https://packt.link/MPYKB`) is the starting page for all Azure developers, functioning as a comprehensive dashboard that offers curated pathways to every Azure service, ensuring developers have immediate access to the entire spectrum of Azure offerings. *Figure 1.2* shows the home page of the Azure portal:

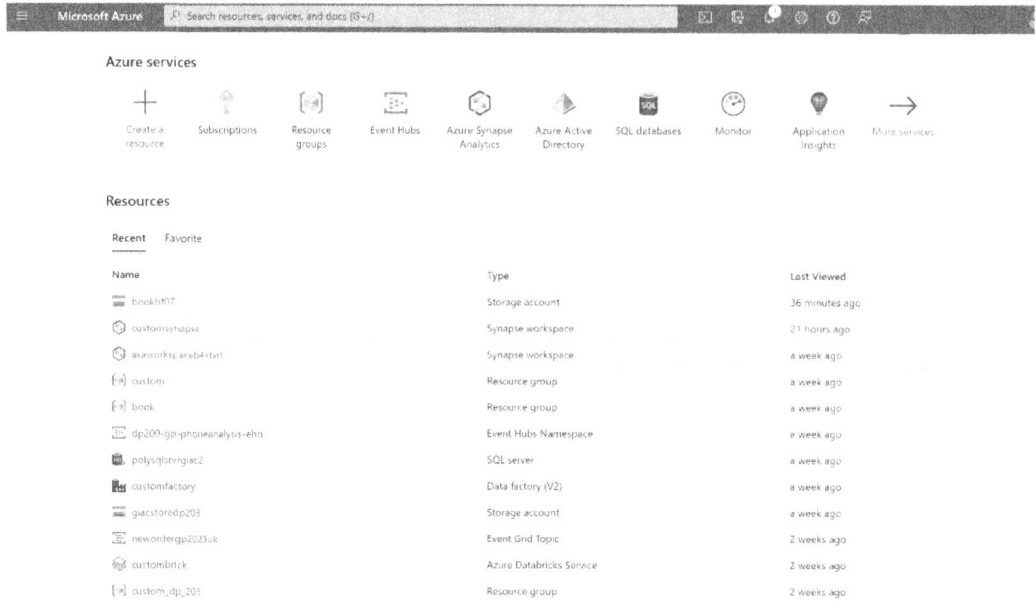

Figure 1.2 – The Azure portal home page

You can browse through all the services available in Azure or quickly search for them using the search box. Once you click on a service, the corresponding service web page will appear. These service-specific pages are also known as **blades** in Azure.

Azure maintains strong consistency in terms of blade design. All the service blades will look very similar. So, if you are familiar with one, you should be able to easily navigate the others. You will be exploring a few of the service blades in this chapter.

# Exploring Azure Accounts, Subscriptions, and Resource Groups

You can explore Azure with or without an account. If you are just exploring Azure and are planning to run a few sandbox experiments, you don't need to create an Azure account. But if you are planning on investing more time in Azure, then it is recommended to create an account. Azure provides 200 USD of free credits for the first 30 days which you can use for the practice exercises for this certification. You can enroll for a free account here: `https://packt.link/jO2dW`.

> **Note**
>
> Azure requires a valid credit card number to create the account, but it doesn't charge the credit card for free accounts. Once the 200 USD credit is exhausted, it will notify you and then delete the resources.

The following are some important services that you can use for free:

- **Azure VMs**: You can use Windows or Linux VMs for free for up to 750 hours each of B1s, B2pls V2 (Arm-based), and B2ats V2 (Arm-based) burstable VMs for 12 months from the date you create your Azure account.

- **Azure SQL Database**: You can use up to 100,000 vCore seconds of SQL database serverless usage per month with 32 GB of storage for free.

- **Azure Blob Storage**: You can use a 5 GB **Locally Redundant Storage** (**LRS**) hot block with 20,000 read and 10,000 write operations for free.

- **Azure Cosmos DB**: You can use 1,000 request units per second provisioned throughput with 25 GB storage for free.

- **Azure App Service**: You can create 10 web, mobile, or API apps with 1 GB storage for free for 1 hour per day.

- **Azure Functions**: You can use 1 million requests for free.

> **Note**
>
> There are many other services that are free for you to use in the first 12 months and others that are always free. You can find more information about free services offered by Azure at `https://packt.link/O20B8`.

You will start by learning about Azure accounts.

## Azure Account

An **Azure account** refers to the Azure Billing account. It is mapped to the email ID that you use to sign up for Azure. An account can contain multiple subscriptions. Each of these subscriptions can have multiple resource groups, and the resource groups, in turn, can have multiple resources. The billing is done at the level of subscriptions. So, one account could have multiple invoices raised per subscription.

## Azure Subscription

Every resource (VMs, VNets, databases, and so on) that you create in Azure is tied to a subscription. A **subscription** is a container for all the resources that are created for applications and solutions under that subscription. A subscription contains the details of all the VMs, networks, storage, and other services that were used during that month that will be used for billing purposes. Azure creates a default subscription when you create an account. But you could choose to have multiple subscriptions based on your teams (dev, test, sales, marketing, finance, and so on), regions (North America, EMEA, Asia Pacific, and so on), or other logical divisions that you feel are appropriate for your use case.

## Resource Groups

**Resource groups** are logical groups of resources belonging to an application or a team. You can think of them as the equivalent of folders in a filesystem, which allows you to group together all the resources that belong to a specific application or department so that you can easily query, monitor, and manage the collection of resources as one. For example, you could create a resource group called a **sandbox** for the Azure practice sessions. At the end of the day, you can delete all the resources that were created under that resource group in one go, instead of going through every resource and deleting them. You can have multiple resource groups under a single subscription. On the other hand, a resource can only belong to a single resource group. If you need multiple ways to organize your sources, you can combine resource groups with **tags**, which are name/value couples such as `Department: Sales` or `Department: Accounting`. A resource can be associated with as many tags as you want, or none (while the resource is mandatory) and tags can be used as criteria in the search box.

### Resources

Resources refer to all the VMs, stores, databases, functions, and so on that can be created in Azure.

Before you move on to the next topic, it will be helpful to consider a practical example utilizing the material covered so far. In the following section, you will set up an example use case of an imaginary company that will be used as a real-world use case across all chapters throughout this book as you build your data solutions.

## Establishing a Use Case

Pretend that there is a company called **Imaginary Airport Cabs (IAC)**. IAC wants to build a cab booking portal. They have an engineering team and a marketing team that needs applications to be hosted on Azure. The engineering team is planning to build a scalable web server with an Azure SQL backend. The frontend and the backend are segregated using two different VNets for isolation and security reasons, while the marketing team requires only an Azure SQL Database to store their customer information.

If you plot this requirement against the accounts, subscriptions, resource groups, and resources, it might look something like the one shown in *Figure 1.3*:

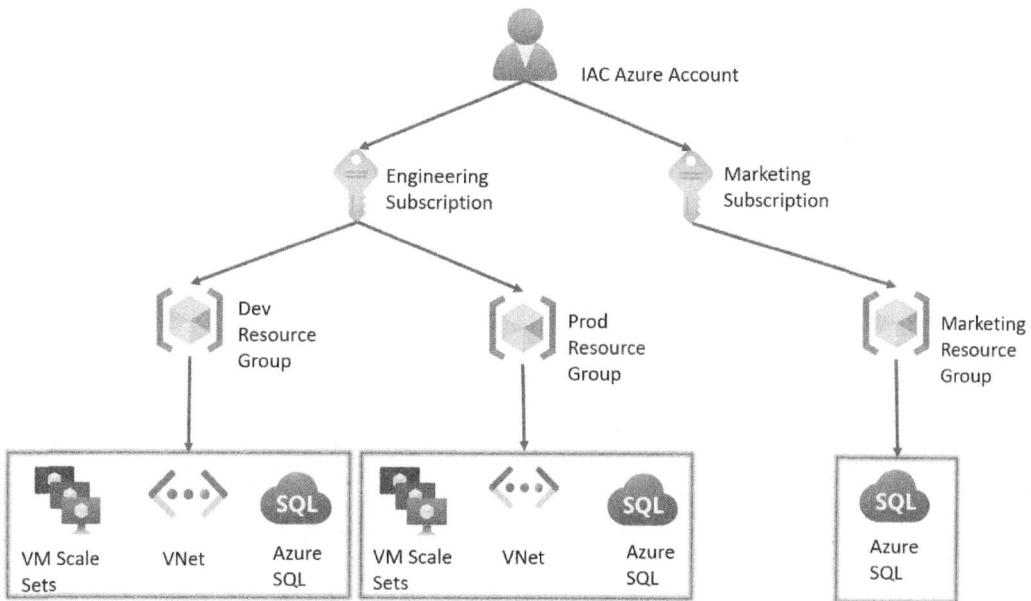

Figure 1.3 – Relationship between accounts, subscriptions, resource groups, and resources

You will be returning to IAC and using Azure to solve their IT needs throughout this book. In addition to that, you will solve more complicated use cases for IAC in the following chapters so that you can grasp the Azure concepts with real examples in preparation for your certification exam.

You have now learned how to identify and navigate all the objects in Azure that are above the level of services, specifically the management group/subscription/resource group hierarchy. Moving further down in the hierarchy, Azure offers a variety of services that might be useful to IAC, some of which you will learn about in the following section.

# Introducing Azure Services

Azure provides a wide array of services and technologies that can easily fulfill most real-world use cases. The services provided by Azure are categorized and detailed in the following sections.

## Infrastructure as a Service (IaaS)

In IaaS, you get the bare infrastructure (that is, VMs, VNets, and the storage provided by the disks mounted on VMs), and you need to build the rest of the application stack yourself. This option gives the most flexibility for developers in terms of OS versions, library versions, custom patches, and so on.

For example, if you want to run SQL Server on Azure while maintaining control of which version of SQL Server to run, the only option is to create an Azure VM and install SQL Server on it. This makes IaaS the ideal solution for so-called "lift-and-shift" scenarios, where an existing on-premises application needs to be moved to the cloud with minimal changes. However, the trade-off is that IaaS still requires high levels of administrative effort. For instance, while you can maintain full control of the SQL Server backups, you will still need to manually schedule them, manage their storage, their retention and deletion, and so on. Equally, if you run a web application on a VM you can install all the runtimes you want, while if you use App Service, you are limited to those supported.

IaaS is therefore recommended for the following purposes:

- **Customization and control**: Choose IaaS when you require full control over the underlying infrastructure and need to customize the environment extensively. For complex data engineering workflows that demand specific configurations, IaaS provides the flexibility to manage and maintain VMs, storage, and networking components according to your requirements.

- **Legacy applications and migration**: Choose IaaS if you have legacy applications that cannot be easily refactored or require specific OS configurations. It's suitable for lifting and shifting existing on-premises applications to the cloud, providing a consistent environment for applications that are not yet cloud-ready.

## Platform as a Service (PaaS)

In PaaS, you agree to delegate more to the cloud provider and relinquish more control (the software platforms are pre-installed and preconfigured). These are managed services in the sense that Azure manages the life cycle of this software for you. Continuing with the previous example, this means creating an instance of the Azure SQL Service, instead of installing SQL Server on a VM. By doing so, you will relinquish the freedom to choose the version of the SQL Server engine (the latest stable version is chosen for you) and backup policy. Among other things, the version will always be the latest stable version of SQL Server and the frequency of backups will be chosen for you. The advantage is that the administration effort required is reduced.

Other examples of PaaS offerings include Azure Storage Account, Azure Databricks, and **Azure Kubernetes Service** (**AKS**). You will still be able to tune the software to some level, but you might not have the flexibility of choosing particular versions, patches, and so on.

PaaS is recommended for the following:

- **Simplified development and deployment**: Choose PaaS when you prioritize streamlined development, deployment, and scalability. PaaS offerings, such as **Azure Data Factory** (**ADF**), **Azure Databricks** (**ADB**), and **Azure SQL Database**, abstract away the underlying infrastructure complexities. This allows your team to focus on building data pipelines, analytics, and applications without worrying about managing servers and resources, leading to faster development cycles and easier maintenance.

- **Scalability and cost efficiency**: Choose PaaS when you need automatic scaling and want to optimize costs. PaaS services automatically scale resources based on demand, ensuring optimal performance without the need for manual intervention. Additionally, you pay for the specific resources you use, allowing for cost-efficient operations as your data engineering workloads fluctuate in size and complexity.

## Software as a Service (SaaS)

What other platforms call **SaaS**, Azure refers to as **Function as a Service** (**FaaS**). In SaaS or FaaS, you don't get to see any of the software installation details. You usually have a notebook-like user interface or an API interface for directly submitting your jobs; the cloud service provider takes care of instantiating the service, scaling the service, and running the jobs for you. This is the easiest and quickest way to get started, but it is also the most restrictive in terms of software setup.

In SaaS, you use a prebuilt software application running on the cloud. An example is the Azure portal itself; you can use it to manage your IaaS or PaaS resources, but in doing so you are using a software tool that is prebuilt and preconfigured for this purpose. Other obvious examples include online email or calendar services.

*Figure 1.4* illustrates these concepts of IaaS, PaaS, and SaaS services:

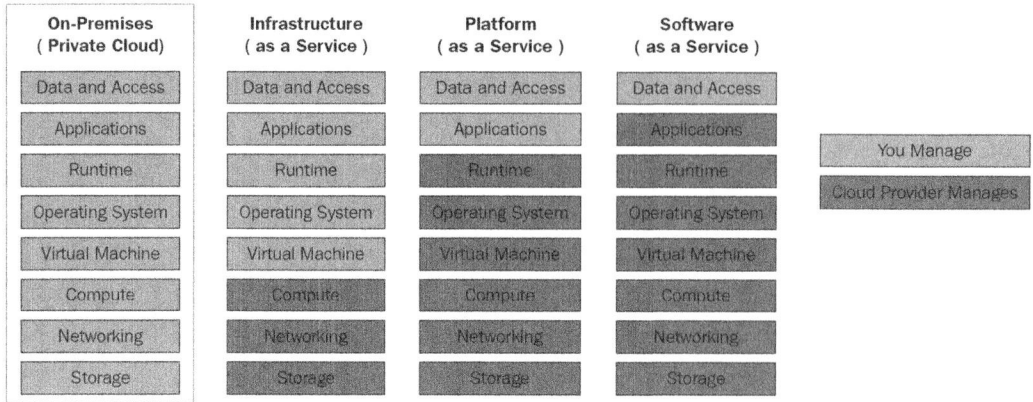

Figure 1.4 – Breakdown of Azure services

For the purpose of preparing for the DP-203 exam, you will spend most of your time in the realm of PaaS, which will consequently represent the main focus of the chapters to follow. At the other extreme, SaaS by its nature describes the type of applications that are predeveloped for you, so not much needs to be said about them. Now that you know what SaaS is, you will look at the most typical case of IaaS on Azure: Azure VMs.

## Exploring Azure VMs

VMs are software abstractions of physical hardware. They can emulate the computer hardware for the applications running on it. You can have multiple VMs running on a single machine. Each VM will have a portion of the host machine's CPU, memory, and storage allocated to it.

Azure VMs are the most common resources that are spun up in Azure. You can use VMs to set up virtually any application that you want. They are like plain vanilla servers that can be used to install any software that you need, except the OS upgrades and security patches, which are taken care of by Azure. Azure VMs provide the advantage of faster deployments, scalability, security isolation, and elasticity. Azure provides both Windows and Linux VMs. There is a huge collection of OS flavors and versions available in the Azure Marketplace that can be used to spin up the VMs.

Here are some of the VM types available:

- General-purpose
- Compute-optimized
- Memory-optimized
- Storage-optimized
- GPU
- High performance

> **Note**
>
> You can find more up-to-date information at `https://packt.link/wi663`.

In the following subsections, you will walk through the process of creating a VM.

## Creating a VM Using the Azure Portal

First, you must learn how to create a VM using the Azure portal and then using the CLI. Perform the following steps to create the VM using the portal:

1. Go to the **Azure portal** screen.
2. At the portal, click `Create a resource` from the left pane.

> **Note**
>
> Before you proceed to create a new resource in Azure, ensure you have access to the Azure portal. If you don't have access, go to the portal (`https://packt.link/PmbKU`) and sign in to proceed.

3. Under **Compute**, choose `Virtual machines` (under **Services**) from the searches in the search box.
4. Click on the `+ Create` button.
5. Select `Virtual Machines`.

A **Create a virtual machine** screen will be displayed, as shown in *Figure 1.5*:

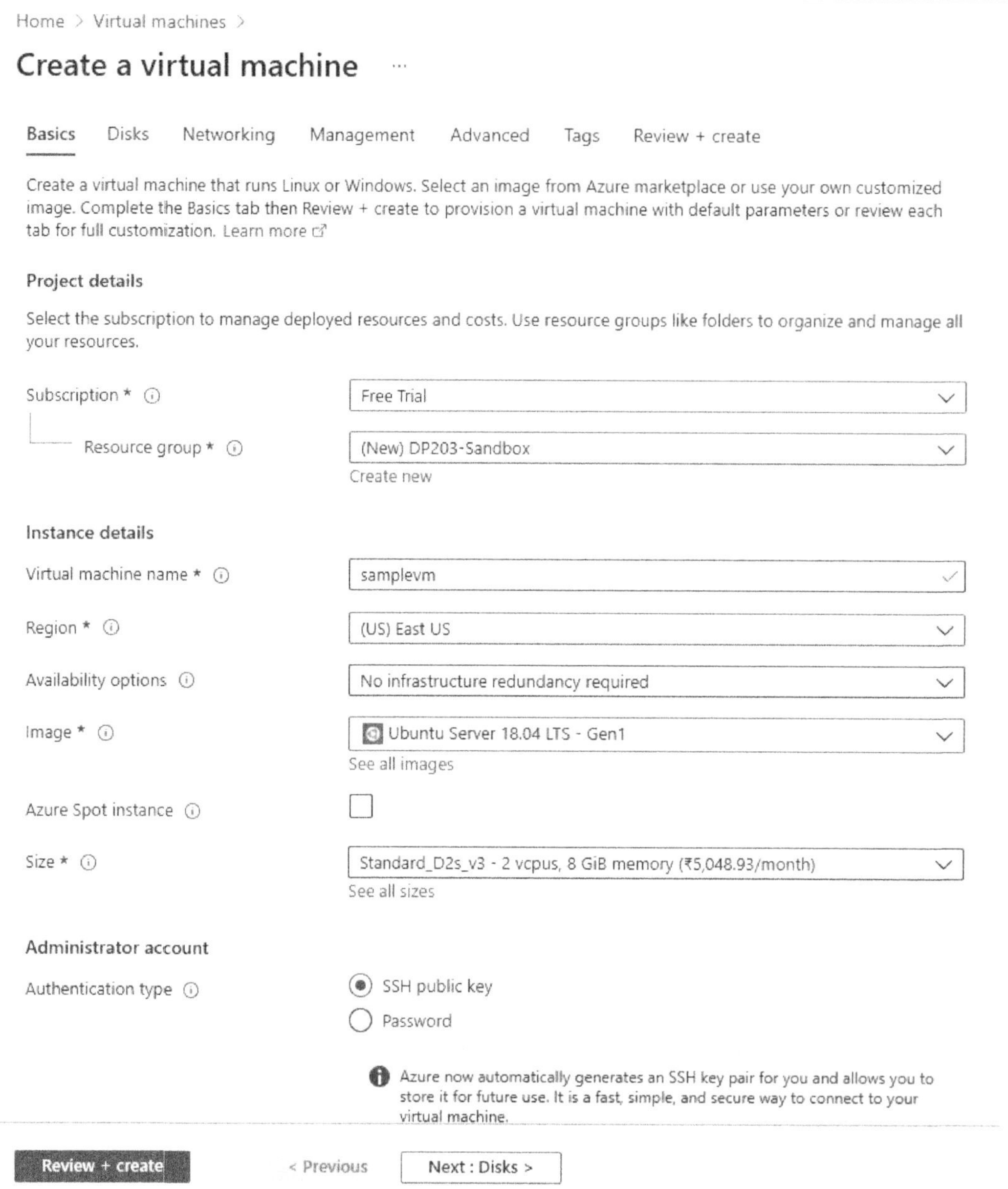

Home > Virtual machines >

# Create a virtual machine    ...

Basics    Disks    Networking    Management    Advanced    Tags    Review + create

Create a virtual machine that runs Linux or Windows. Select an image from Azure marketplace or use your own customized image. Complete the Basics tab then Review + create to provision a virtual machine with default parameters or review each tab for full customization. Learn more ☐

### Project details

Select the subscription to manage deployed resources and costs. Use resource groups like folders to organize and manage all your resources.

| | |
|---|---|
| Subscription * ⓘ | Free Trial ⌄ |
| Resource group * ⓘ | (New) DP203-Sandbox ⌄ |
| | Create new |

### Instance details

| | |
|---|---|
| Virtual machine name * ⓘ | samplevm ✓ |
| Region * ⓘ | (US) East US ⌄ |
| Availability options ⓘ | No infrastructure redundancy required ⌄ |
| Image * ⓘ | ◉ Ubuntu Server 18.04 LTS - Gen1 ⌄ |
| | See all images |
| Azure Spot instance ⓘ | ☐ |
| Size * ⓘ | Standard_D2s_v3 - 2 vcpus, 8 GiB memory (₹5,048.93/month) ⌄ |
| | See all sizes |

### Administrator account

| | |
|---|---|
| Authentication type ⓘ | ◉ SSH public key |
| | ◯ Password |
| | ⓘ Azure now automatically generates an SSH key pair for you and allows you to store it for future use. It is a fast, simple, and secure way to connect to your virtual machine. |

Review + create    < Previous    Next : Disks >

Figure 1.5 – Creating VMs using the Azure portal

6. Create a new resource group.

   *Figure 1.5* shows the resource group as **DP-203-Sandbox**.

7. Fill in **Virtual machine name**, in this case using `samplevm`.

8. Fill in **Region**, in this case with `East US`.

9. Next, fill in **VM Image**, in this case with `Ubuntu Server 18.04 LTS - Gen1`.

10. Set **Size** for the VM, in this case as `Standard_D2s_v3 - 2 vcpus, 8 GiB memory`.

11. Set **Authentication type**, in this case as `SSH public key`.

12. Then, click on the `Review + create` button.

13. Finally, click `Create`. You should see a popup with the `Generate new key pair` option.

14. Click on the `Download` button and save the private key in a safe location. You will need this key to log in to your VM.

    You can also configure the **Advanced** options tab shown in *Figure 1.5*. These include the following:

    - **Disks**: Azure VMs have one OS disk and a temporary disk for short-term storage. Under **OS Disks**, you can configure the OS disk size (the default is `30 GiB`) and OS disk type (`Premium SSD locally-redundant storage`), which determines the type of storage and size you can use.

    - **Networking**: The Networking section in the interface configures network settings for a VM. It either allows users to define network connectivity by public IP to communicate VMs from outside the VNet or deny the inbound/outbound traffic from and to the VMs by configuring the **Network Interface Card** (**NIC**) settings.

    - **Management**: The Management options are used to manage VMs, such as **Role-Based Access Control** (**RBAC**) role assignment, enabling auto-shutdown, backups, and OS updates.

    - **Advanced**: You can add an advanced additional configuration script to the VM, such as post-deployment scripts, which contain application files that are securely downloaded on your VM after deployment. In addition to that, you can easily add or remove applications on your VM after creating.

    - **Tags**: Tags are value pairs that enable you to categorize resources and view consolidated billing by applying the same tag to multiple resources and resource groups. You can add tags to resources such as VMs and storage accounts. For example, you can use tags to identify all the resources that belong to a specific department or project, and this can also be used to view billing information for all resources with a specific tag.

You have now created a VM using the Azure portal. You'll next create a VM using the Azure CLI.

## Creating a VM Using the Azure CLI

Using the portal is the easiest way to create and edit resources. But there are cases where you might want to use a script instead—for instance, to make it part of a repeatable release process.

For this purpose, Azure offers two imperative languages and one declarative language. Generally speaking, imperative language means specifying a set of instructions to be executed in sequence, while declarative language means describing the desired result, leaving it to the language interpreter to produce the required set of actions. An example of declarative language you are probably familiar with is SQL, while programming languages such as C# or JavaScript are primarily declarative.

Regarding the creation and management of Azure resources, the declarative approach is represented by ARM templates. There are two imperative options available: the Azure CLI and Azure PowerShell.

The difference is mostly syntactical, as the latter is a derivation of the Unix/Linux family of shell languages, while the former uses a syntax that is probably more familiar to Windows users. For this reason, this will be discussed first. Since you will be using the CLI for the first time, the next section will help you get started.

### Installing the CLI

There are two ways you can use the CLI. First, you can use the Azure CLI option directly from the Azure portal, as shown in *Figure 1.6*:

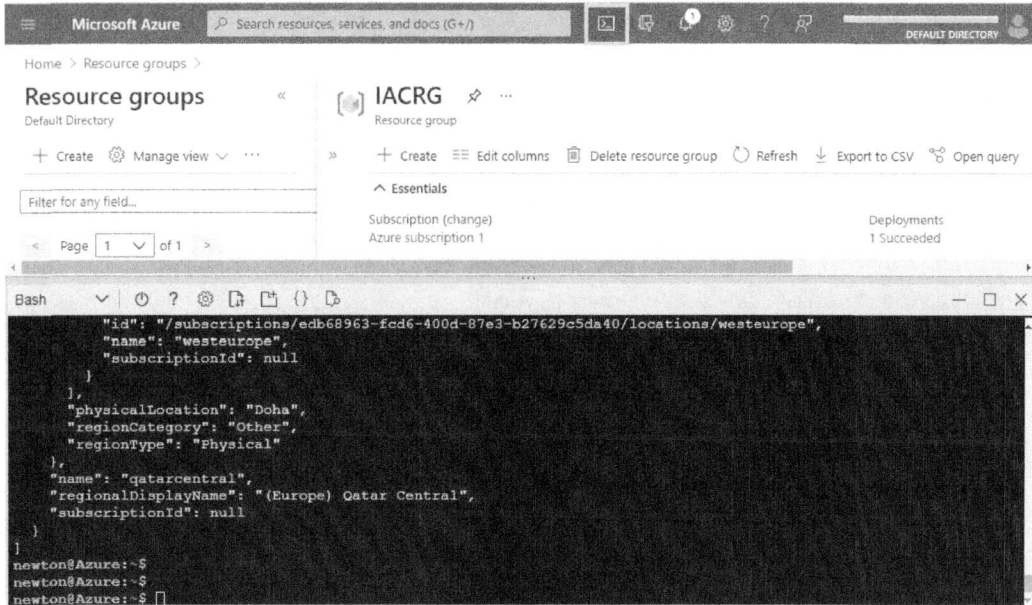

Figure 1.6 – Using the CLI directly from the Azure portal

Alternatively, you can choose to install the Azure CLI client on your local machine and run the commands from there.

> **Note**
>
> You can learn how to download and install the Azure CLI client at https://packt.link/bnYrx.

To create a VM using the Azure CLI, a set of steps need to be followed.

> **Note**
>
> All these commands and scripts are available in the GitHub link that is provided along with this book so that you can easily copy, paste, and try the commands.

Perform the following steps to create an Ubuntu VM:

1.  Find all the Ubuntu images that are available using the vm image list option:

    ```
    az vm image list --all --offer Ubuntu
    ```

2.  Next, find the Azure regions where it is to be deployed with the following command:

    ```
    az account list-locations --output table
    ```

    You can choose a region that is closest to you.

    Next, you can either create a new resource group or use an existing one to associate this VM with.

3.  To create a new resource group called IACRG use the following command:

    ```
    az group create --name 'IACRG' --location 'eastus'
    ```

> **Note**
>
> You can skip *Step 3* if the group you will refer to when creating the VM (in *Step 4*) already exists. You can utilize the code script to configure your subscription within the corresponding GitHub repository at https://packt.link/OpzgJ.

4.  Finally, create a VM using the information from the preceding commands. In this case, the eastus location is chosen to deploy this VM to:

    ```
    az vm create --resource-group 'IACRG' --name 'sampleVM' --image
    'UbuntuLTS' --admin-username '<your username>' --admin-password
    '<your password>' --location 'eastus'
    ```

    Here, all the non-mandatory fields will default to the Azure default values. This command will create a VM named sampleVM under the resource group named IACRG.

That should have given you a sound idea of how the CLI works in Azure.

> **Note**
>
> You can learn more about Azure VMs at `https://packt.link/Rim8y`. You can find the complete code in the accompanying GitHub repository at `https://packt.link/zMkKB`.

In this section, you learned how to create VMs using both the portal and the CLI. You can explore the storage options that are available in Azure in the next section.

# Exploring Azure Storage

Azure has multiple storage options that can suit a wide range of applications and domains. You will explore the most common ones in the following sections.

## Azure Blob Storage

Blob Storage is the most common storage type in Azure. It can be used to store unstructured data such as videos, audio, metadata, log files, text, and binary. It is also a highly scalable and cost-effective storage solution. It provides support for tiered storage, so the data can be stored at different tiers based on their access pattern and usage frequency. Highly used data can be kept at hot tiers and not-so-used data in cold tiers. Historical data can be archived.

The data in Blob Storage can be easily accessed via **Representational State Transfer** (**REST**) (one way of implementing web services) endpoints, as well as client libraries available in a wide set of languages, such as .NET, Java, Python, Ruby, PHP, and Node.js.

Go ahead and create a storage account now if you don't already have one. You will need this storage account throughout this book to store all the sample data, scripts, and more.

To create a storage account from the Azure portal home page, you need to click on the usual `Create a resource` link and choose `Storage Account` as the resource type. This will result in the screen shown in *Figure 1.7*:

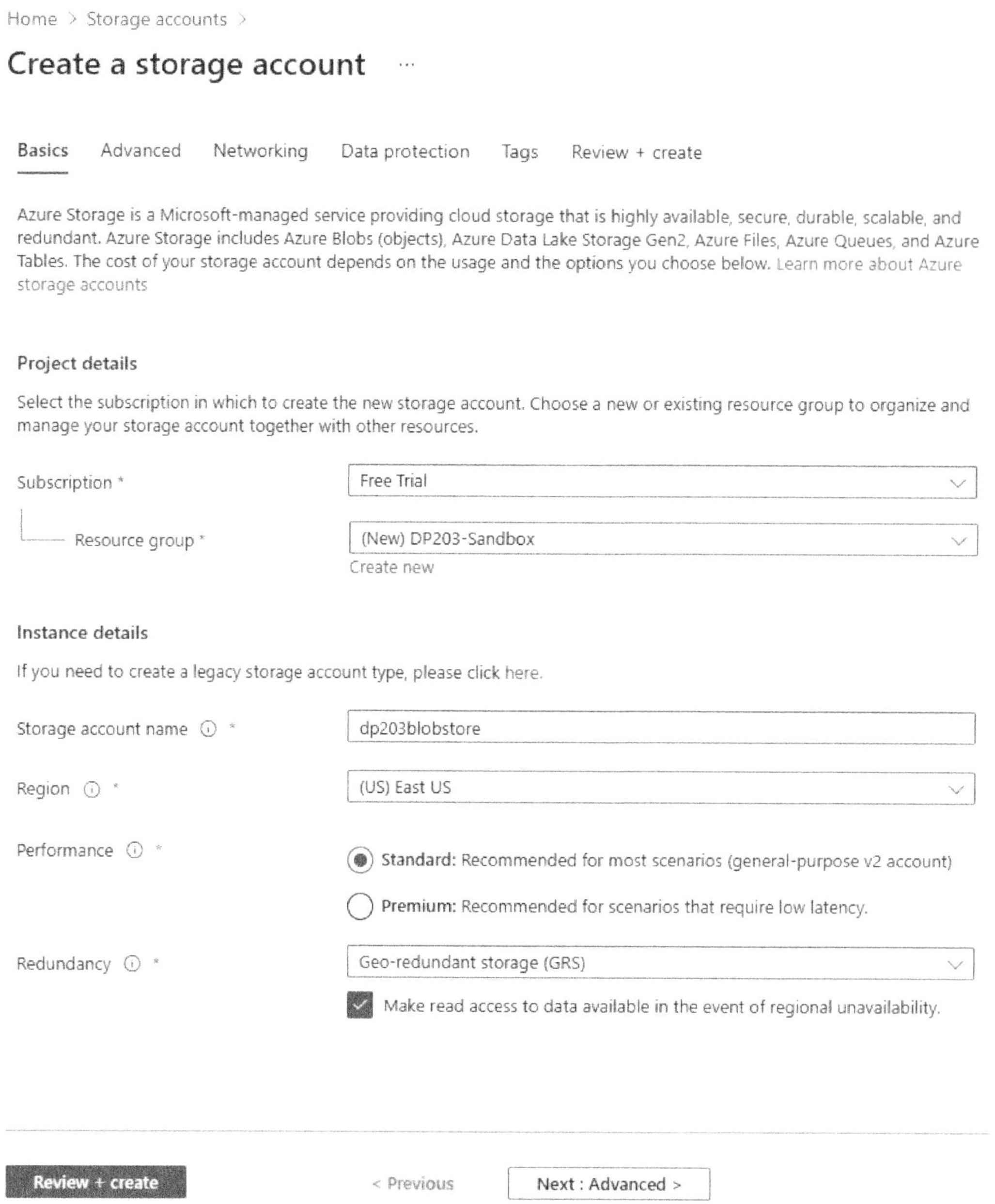

Home > Storage accounts >

# Create a storage account    ...

Basics    Advanced    Networking    Data protection    Tags    Review + create

Azure Storage is a Microsoft-managed service providing cloud storage that is highly available, secure, durable, scalable, and redundant. Azure Storage includes Azure Blobs (objects), Azure Data Lake Storage Gen2, Azure Files, Azure Queues, and Azure Tables. The cost of your storage account depends on the usage and the options you choose below. Learn more about Azure storage accounts

### Project details

Select the subscription in which to create the new storage account. Choose a new or existing resource group to organize and manage your storage account together with other resources.

| Subscription * | Free Trial | ⌄ |
|---|---|---|
| └─ Resource group * | (New) DP203-Sandbox | ⌄ |
| | Create new | |

### Instance details

If you need to create a legacy storage account type, please click here.

| Storage account name ⓘ * | dp203blobstore |
|---|---|
| Region ⓘ * | (US) East US    ⌄ |
| Performance ⓘ * | ⦿ **Standard:** Recommended for most scenarios (general-purpose v2 account) |
| | ◯ **Premium:** Recommended for scenarios that require low latency. |
| Redundancy ⓘ * | Geo-redundant storage (GRS)    ⌄ |
| | ☑ Make read access to data available in the event of regional unavailability. |

| Review + create | < Previous | Next : Advanced > |
|---|---|---|

Figure 1.7 – Creating a storage account using the Azure portal

Once created, you can access your Blob Storage from `https://<storage-account>.blob.core.windows.net`. After learning how to create a storage account, the next section will focus on another important storage option provided by Azure that will be used extensively for data lakes: **Azure Data Lake Storage** (**ADLS**) Gen2.

## Azure Data Lake Gen2

Azure Data Lake Gen2 or **Azure Data Lake Storage Gen 2** (**ADLS Gen2**) is a superset of Blob Storage that is optimized for Big Data Analytics. ADLS Gen2 is the preferred option for data lake solutions in Azure. It provides hierarchical namespace support on top of Blob Storage. **Hierarchical namespace support** means that all the directories within a storage account will contain metadata describing their structure and content, which will improve operations such as moving an entire directory structure to a different parent directory, as only the metadata will need to be updated. While this improvement is purely related to performance, the other advantage of hierarchical namespace support is functional, and it is related to controlling access to the directories.

Unlike Blob Storage, ADLS Gen2 provides real support for directories with **Portable Operating System Interface** (**POSIX**) compliance and **Access Control List** (**ACL**) support. This makes operations such as renaming and deleting directories atomic and quick. For example, if you have 100 files under a directory in Blob Storage, renaming that directory would require 100 metadata operations. But in ADLS Gen2, just one metadata operation will need to be performed at the directory level. ADLS Gen2 also supports **RBAC**, just like Blob Storage does.

Another important feature of ADLS Gen2 is that it is a Hadoop-compatible filesystem. So, building any open source analytics pipeline on top of ADLS Gen2 is a breeze. Since ADLS Gen2 is discussed here, you might be curious to learn about ADLS Gen1.

ADLS Gen1, as its name suggests, was the first generation of highly scalable and high-performing data lake storage that was built for Data Analytics. It is still available but will be deprecated in February 2024. ADLS Gen1 is optimized for large files, so it works best for file sizes of 256 MB and above.

The features of Gen1 are also available in Gen2, though Gen2 has some additional advantages, such as better regional availability, meaning that it is available in all Azure regions, compared to a select few regions where Gen1 is available. Gen2 also supports LRS, **Zone-Redundant Storage** (**ZRS**), and **Geo-Redundant Storage** (**GRS**) for data redundancy and recovery, while Gen1 only supports LRS.

> **Note**
> The syntax of an ADLS Gen2 URL is as follows: `https://<storage-account>.dfs.core.windows.net`.

To create an ADLS Gen2 account, you need to click the `Enable hierarchical namespace` checkbox placed in the `Advanced` tab on the `Create a storage account` screen (*Figure 1.8*):

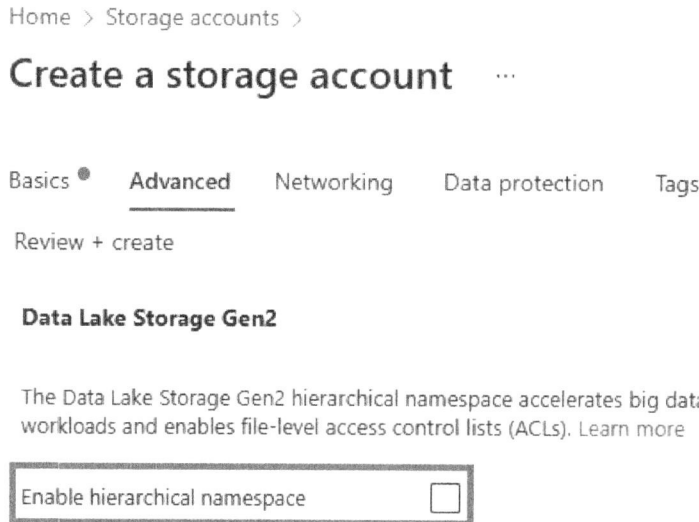

Home > Storage accounts >

# Create a storage account    ...

Basics ●     **Advanced**     Networking     Data protection     Tags

Review + create

### Data Lake Storage Gen2

The Data Lake Storage Gen2 hierarchical namespace accelerates big data analytics workloads and enables file-level access control lists (ACLs). Learn more

| Enable hierarchical namespace | ☐ |
|---|---|

Figure 1.8 – Enable hierarchical namespace in Azure Storage for an ADLS Gen2 account

> **Note**
>
> You can find the complete code in the accompanying GitHub repository at `https://packt.link/BZn6L`.

After exploring hierarchical namespaces, ACLs, and both Gen1 and Gen2 of data lakes, the next section introduces another Azure Storage technology, called Azure Files.

## Azure Files

Azure Files provides remote file shares that can be mounted using the **Server Message Block** (**SMB**) or **Network File Share** (**NFS**) protocol. These are great storage options for anyone planning to migrate on-premises workloads to the cloud with a lift-and-shift model, for instance, without having to invest in redevelopment for the cloud-based model. Azure Files can easily be mounted both from cloud servers and on-premises servers.

Azure Files is particularly useful for cases that need shared data, shared configurations, and shared applications across multiple users, teams, or regions. Now read through some example commands for creating file shares in Azure.

## Creating Azure File Shares with the Azure CLI

As you have already seen a few prior examples of Azure portal usage, the aim of this next example will be to use the Azure CLI so that you become familiar with the command-line options as well. You will continue to use the IAC example here so that you can grasp how the CLI is used with real examples. It should also give you an idea of how Azure Files commands are structured.

For the following example, you will need to create a resource group and a storage account. You can reuse the IACRG resource group, which you created in the *Creating a VM Using the Azure CLI* section. For the storage account, easily create one using the following commands:

```
az storage account create --resource-group IACRG --name iacstorage
--location eastus --kind StorageV2 --sku Standard_LRS
```

This will create a storage account named iacstorage. The storage account names must be unique, so you might have to find a name that is not already used.

Once you have created the storage account, you can visit the storage account page in the Azure portal. From the Access keys tab, copy Primary Key (Key1), which will be required to perform any activity on this storage account. *Figure 1.9* shows how you can find and copy the access key:

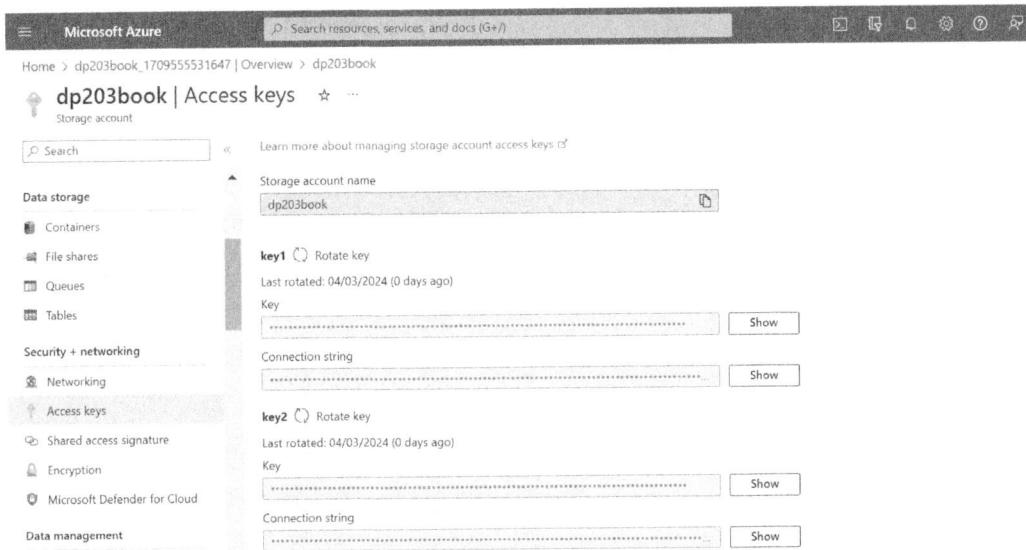

Figure 1.9 – Locating access keys for a storage account

> **Note**
>
> Using the primary key is an easy way to access the storage but not a recommended option to use in production systems. The book will discuss more secure options in *Chapter 8, Implementing Data Security.*

Once the primary key is copied, export the following two variables from your CLI screen using the following commands:

```
export AZURE_STORAGE_ACCOUNT=<your storage account name>
export AZURE_STORAGE_KEY=<your storage primary key>
```

> **Note**
>
> If you are using a Windows machine, please refer to this book's GitHub link (`https://packt.link/apMuF`) to find examples of exporting variables in Windows.

Perform the following steps to create a new Azure file share for IAC using the `share-rm create` option:

1.  Type the following command to create a file share named `iacfileshare` under `iacstorage`:

    ```
    az storage share-rm create --resource-group IACRG --storage-
    account iacstorage --name iacfileshare
    ```

2.  List the file shares using the `share list` option:

    ```
    az storage share list --account-name iacstorage
    ```

3.  Place the file into your file share using the `file upload` command:

    ```
    az storage file upload --share-name iacfileshare --source ./
    testfile.txt
    ```

4.  View the files in your file share using the `file list` command:

    ```
    az storage file list --share-name iacfileshare
    ```

5.  Finally, download the file that you had previously uploaded using the `file download` command:

    ```
    az storage file download --share-name iacfileshare -p testfile.
    txt --dest ./testfile.txt
    ```

As you can see, Azure provides a very easy and intuitive set of commands for interfacing with the various Azure services that are available.

> **Note**
>
> You can find the complete code in the accompanying GitHub repository at https://packt.link/n0bea.

An Azure file share is a **Server Message Block (SMB)**/**Network File System (NFS)** mounted managed file share that allows mounting from both Windows and Linux platforms. The file share is provisioned with Azure Storage Account V2 or the premium File Share Tier. Next, you will look at Azure Queues.

## Azure Queues

Azure Queues are used to store a large number of messages that can be accessed asynchronously between the source and the destination. This helps in decoupling applications so that they can scale independently. Azure Queues can be used across applications that are running in the cloud, on-premises, on mobile devices, and more. The two types of queues are as follows:

- Storage queues
- Service Bus

Storage queues can be used for simple asynchronous message processing. They can store up to 500 TB of data (per storage account) and each message can be up to 64 KB in size. If a simple async queue is insufficient and your application needs advanced features such as pub-sub models, strict ordering of messages, and blocking and non-blocking APIs, then Service Bus is a better option. With Service Bus, the message sizes can be up to 1 MB, but the overall size is capped at 80 GB.

> **Note**
> The syntax of an Azure Queues URL is `https://<storage account>.queue.core.windows.net/<queue>`.

The next section will demonstrate how to create queues in Azure using a few example commands.

### Creating Azure Queues Using the CLI

This section will show some sample CLI commands for creating and using an Azure Queue. Here, it is assumed that the `AZURE_STORAGE_ACCOUNT` and `AZURE_STORAGE_KEY` environment variables have already been set. Perform the following steps:

1. Type the `storage queue create` command to create a new Azure Queue:

    ```
    az storage queue create --name iacqueue --account-name
    iacstorage
    ```

    This command will create a queue named `iacqueue` under `iacstorage`.

2. List the queues under a storage account using the `storage queue list` command:

    ```
    az storage queue list --account-name iacstorage
    ```

3.  Add a new message to the newly created queue using the `storage message put` command:

```
az storage message put --queue-name iacqueue --content "test"
```

4.  Finally, use the `storage message peek` command to view the message:

```
az storage message peek --queue-name iacqueue
```

This command retrieves one or more messages from the front of the queue but does not alter the visibility of the message.

> **Note**
>
> You can find the complete code in the accompanying GitHub repository at `https://packt.link/Vznd7`.

Now that you know the basics of Azure Queues, head to the next section to read up on Azure tables.

## Azure Tables

Azure tables refers to key-value stores provided by Azure. They are reliable for storing structured non-relational data. There are two solutions available in Azure for table stores. They are as follows:

- Azure Table storage
- Cosmos DB

Both of these features provide the same table model and **Create, Read, Update, and Delete (CRUD)** features, but the difference lies in their scale, **Service-Level Agreements** (SLAs), and availability. **Cosmos DB** is the premium form of table storage and can provide more than 10 million operations per second, whereas **Azure Table** storage has a scaling limit of 20,000 operations per second.

Cosmos DB also provides several additional advantages, such as five flexible levels of consistency, up to 99.999% read availability on multi-region databases, serverless mode, and global presence.

> **Note**
>
> Cosmos DB deserves a complete chapter on its own. You will explore Cosmos DB in more detail in *Chapter 2, Implement a Partition Strategy, Chapter 8, Implementing Data Security*, and *Chapter 10, Optimizing and Troubleshooting Data Storage and Data Processing*, later in this book. The syntax of an Azure Table URL is `http://<storage account>.table.core.windows.net/<table>`.

As with the other storage options you came across earlier in the chapter, it will be helpful to consider some example CLI commands to become familiar with this technology. You can just glance through these examples for now.

> **Note**
>
> You will find the detailed steps for implementing the examples required for the certification later in this book.

### Creating Azure Tables Using the CLI

This section will show you how to use the Azure CLI to create and use an Azure Table. Here, it is assumed that you will have to export the two env variables (AZURE_STORAGE_ACCOUNT and AZURE_STORAGE_KEY) before running the commands. Perform the following steps to do so:

1.  Create a new Azure Table for the example company, IAC, by using the storage table create command:

    ```
    az storage table create --name iactable --account-name
    iacstorage
    ```

    The following command will create a table named iactable under the iacstorage storage account.

2.  List the tables under a storage account using the storage table list command:

    ```
    az storage table list --account-name iacstorage
    ```

3.  Insert an entity into the newly created table using the storage entity insert command:

    ```
    az storage entity insert --table-name iactable --entity
    PartitionKey=testPartKey RowKey=testRowKey Content=testContent
    ```

4.  Finally, use the storage entity show command to view the entry:

    ```
    az storage entity show --table-name iactable --partition-key
    testPartKey --row-key testRowKey
    ```

> **Note**
>
> You can find the complete code in the accompanying GitHub repository at https://packt.link/Yb2Go.

With that, you have covered the core storage options provided by Azure. Next, you'll look at Azure managed disks, which are required for managing disk/**Solid-State Drive** (**SSD**) storage for VMs.

## Azure Managed Disks

Azure managed disks are virtual hard disks that are mounted to an Azure VM. As the name suggests, these disks are completely managed by Azure. So, you don't need to worry about OS upgrades, security patches, and so on. Unlike physical disks, Azure managed disks offer 99.999% availability. They achieve such a high availability score by storing three different replicas of the data on different servers.

Managed VMs can also be allocated to availability sets and availability zones (that is, distributed across racks and data centers) to increase their survivability in cases of server, rack (stamp), or data center outages. The managed disks also provide options for data encryption at rest and disk-level encryptions. There are different types of managed disks available, such as standard HDD, standard SSD, premium SSD, and ultra disks.

### Creating and Attaching Managed Disks to a VM Using the CLI

This section will focus on using the CLI to create and attach managed disks to `sampleVM`. For that type this one-line command for creating a new disk and attaching it to an existing VM:

```
az vm disk attach --resource-group IACRG --vm-name sampleVM --name
IACmgdisk --size-gb 64 –new
```

Please do remember that you also have the option to specify more advanced configuration parameters as part of the CLI command itself that, when not specified, would assume default values.

> **Note**
>
> You can learn more about Azure Storage technologies at `https://packt.link/3hREV`.

Azure Storage is a managed object, file, disk, and messaging data storage platform. It is a highly available, scalable, and cost-effective storage option available on the Azure platform. Now it is time to explore another core Azure technology, known as Azure Networking.

## Exploring Azure Networking (VNet)

Like Azure VMs, Azure VNet is another core component of Azure that you should be aware of. A VNet ties all resources, such as VMs, storage accounts, and databases, together securely in a private network. It is used to encapsulate the cloud or on-premises services together within a secure boundary by controlling who can access these services and from which endpoints.

Azure Networking provides the following four main services:

- **Security**: This provides secure connectivity within Azure resources using the basic VNet, VNet Peering, and Service endpoints.

- **Networking**: This provides networking beyond the Azure Cloud and into the internet and hybrid clouds using express routers, private endpoints, and point-to-site and site-to-site VPNs.

- **Filtering**: This provides network filtering, in other words firewall rules, that can be implemented either via network or app security groups. There are options to implement the same using network appliances, which are ready-made servers available for specialized networking scenarios.

- **Routing**: It provides network routing abilities that allow you to configure network routes using route tables and Border Gateway Protocol.

Now, you will learn about creating a VNet using the Azure CLI.

### Creating an Azure VNet Using the CLI

You will work on a simple example of how to create a VNet and assign a VM to it. For that, you will reuse the IACRG resource group that you used in the earlier examples in this chapter. Perform the following steps to do so:

1.  First, create a VNet by specifying the necessary IP ranges and subnet prefixes:

    ```
    az network vnet create --address-prefixes 10.20.0.0/16 --name
    iacvnet --resource-group IACRG --subnet-name iacsubnet --subnet-
    prefixes 10.20.0.0/24
    ```

    The command creates a VNet named iacvnet under the IACRG resource group.

2.  Then, create a public IP to access the VM from the internet:

    ```
    az network public-ip create --resource-group IACRG --name
    iacpubip --allocation-method dynamic
    ```

3.  Next create a NIC, which will be the network interface between the VM and the outside world, with the previously created VNet and public IP:

    ```
    az network nic create --resource-group IACRG --vnet-name iacvnet
    --subnet iacsubnet --name iacnic --public-ip-address iacpubip
    ```

    You now have all the components required to create a VM within your new VNet, iacvnet.

4.  Reuse the UbuntuLTS image that was used in the earlier VM creation example to create a new VM within the new VNet:

    ```
    az vm create --resource-group IACRG --name sampleVMwithinVNET
    --nics iacnic --image UbuntuLTS --generate-ssh-keys
    ```

You have now learned how to create networking components such as VNets and public IPs.

> **Note**
>
> You can learn more about Azure Networking at https://packt.link/LMVEs.

## Summary

With that, you have completed the first chapter. For those with some experience of Azure, this overview has hopefully offered a useful recap. For those of you who are completely new to Azure, it might have felt a bit overwhelming. Don't worry; as you complete the next few chapters, your confidence will grow.

In this chapter, you learned how to navigate the Azure portal and observed the relationship between Azure accounts, subscriptions, resource groups, and resources. You also learned how to create new VMs, storage instances, VNets, and so on using both the Azure portal and the CLI. You are also aware of the major compute services that are available in Azure. With this foundational knowledge in place, you can move on to more interesting and certification-oriented topics.

In the next chapter, you will explore the concept of a partition strategy and how to implement it.

# Exam Readiness Drill – Chapter Review Questions

Apart from a solid understanding of key concepts, being able to think quickly under time pressure is a skill that will help you ace your certification exam. That is why working on these skills early on in your learning journey is key.

Chapter review questions are designed to improve your test-taking skills progressively with each chapter you learn and review your understanding of key concepts in the chapter at the same time. You'll find these at the end of each chapter.

> **How to Access These Materials**
>
> To learn how to access these resources, head over to the chapter titled *Chapter 11, Accessing the Online Resources*.

To open the Chapter Review Questions for this chapter, perform the following steps:

1.  Click the link – `https://packt.link/DP203E2_CH01`.

    Alternatively, you can scan the following **QR code** (*Figure 1.10*):

Figure 1.10 – QR code that opens Chapter Review Questions for logged-in users

2.    Once you log in, you'll see a page similar to the one shown in *Figure 1.11*:

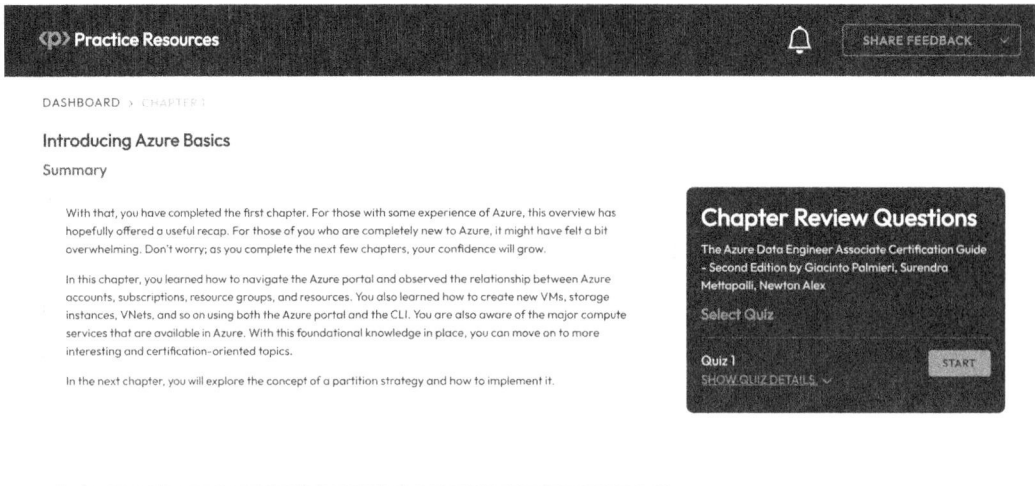

Figure 1.11 – Chapter Review Questions for Chapter 1

3.    Once ready, start the following practice drills, re-attempting the quiz multiple times.

## Exam Readiness Drill

For the first 3 attempts, don't worry about the time limit.

### *ATTEMPT 1*

The first time, aim for at least **40%**. Look at the answers you got wrong and read the relevant sections in the chapter again to fix your learning gaps.

### *ATTEMPT 2*

The second time, aim for at least **60%**. Look at the answers you got wrong and read the relevant sections in the chapter again to fix any remaining learning gaps.

## *ATTEMPT 3*

The third time, aim for at least **75%**. Once you score 75% or more, you start working on your timing.

> **Tip**
>
> You may take more than **three** attempts to reach 75%. That's okay. Just review the relevant sections in the chapter till you get there.

# Working On Timing

Target: Your aim is to keep the score the same while trying to answer these questions as quickly as possible. Here's an example of how your next attempts should look like:

| Attempt | Score | Time Taken |
|---------|-------|------------|
| Attempt 5 | 77% | 21 mins 30 seconds |
| Attempt 6 | 78% | 18 mins 34 seconds |
| Attempt 7 | 76% | 14 mins 44 seconds |

Table 1.1 – Sample timing practice drills on the online platform

> **Note**
>
> The time limits shown in the above table are just examples. Set your own time limits with each attempt based on the time limit of the quiz on the website.

With each new attempt, your score should stay above **75%** while your "time taken" to complete should "decrease". Repeat as many attempts as you want till you feel confident dealing with the time pressure.

# Part 2:
# Data Storage

The **Design and Implement Data Storage** domain in the **DP-203: Data Engineering on Microsoft Azure** exam is a critical component that focuses on the foundational aspects of data storage in Azure environments.

In this domain, you will delve into strategies for effectively partitioning data to manage large datasets by dividing them into discrete, manageable pieces, which can significantly improve performance and scalability. You will also review different partitioning techniques and evaluate these strategies according to your date workloads, best practices, and the efficiency of data organization and retrieval to prepare you to make the most appropriate choice for your specific needs.

Additionally, you will explore the creation of a data layer that facilitates the exploration and analysis of data stored in Azure. This includes designing data models that enable easy access and analysis of data and implementing exploration services such as **Azure Synapse Analytics**. These services will provide powerful capabilities for data exploration and generate meaningful insights.

This section of the book comprises the following chapters:

- *Chapter 2, Implementing a Partition Strategy*
- *Chapter 3, Designing and Implementing the Data Exploration Layer*

# 2

# Implementing a Partition Strategy

In *Chapter 1, Introducing Azure Basics*, you gained foundational knowledge on the Azure portal, subscriptions, Resource groups, and resources. You also learned how to create **Virtual Machines** (**VMs**), storage instances, and **Virtual Networks** (**VNets**) using both the Azure portal and the **Command-Line Interface** (**CLI**). From this chapter onward, you will be following the exact sequence of the DP-203 syllabus.

> **Note**
>
> Following the August 2023 update, the first topic listed is the **Implement a Partition Strategy** topic (left unchanged after a further update in November 2023). You can find the MSFT official DP-203 certification syllabus updates for reference at `https://packt.link/wT0ay`.

**Partitioning** represents, above all, an optimization strategy. This means that you first need to clarify what it is exactly that you will try to optimize and why the topic of partitioning has so much come to the fore.

Before delving into the partition strategy, it's essential to grasp the fundamentals discussed in *Chapter 1, Introducing Azure Basics*: Azure services, database fundamentals, **Structured Query Language** (**SQL**), and data modeling.

Data partitioning refers to the process of dividing data and storing it in physically different locations. You partition data mainly for performance, scalability, manageability, and security reasons. These considerations were already important in the **on-premises** world but become even more important in the world of cloud computing.

This chapter will focus on data partitioning and why it is important, the different types of data partitioning, ways to choose the right data partitioning strategy, and how data partitioning in different systems (files, **Azure Data Lake Storage Gen2** (**ADLS Gen2**), and Azure Synapse Analytics) can be implemented.

This chapter will prepare you to answer questions on the following confidently:

- Partitioning

- Partition strategy for files, analytical and streaming workloads, efficiency/performance, and Azure Synapse Analytics

- Partitioning needed in ADLS Gen2

## Technical Requirements

To follow along with this chapter, you will need an Azure account (free or paid) and should have installed the Azure CLI on your workstation.

## Benefits of Partitioning

Pick up a marketing presentation of any cloud service, and you can be sure to see the word "scalability" and (with only slightly weaker certainty) that it will include something about **parallelism** or parallel execution.

There is some justification for the marketing hype: cloud platforms such as Azure indeed make it much easier to allocate and deallocate new instances of services (not only the VMs that you create explicitly, in the case of **Infrastructure-as-a-service (IaaS)** but also the VMs that are created for you behind the scenes, in the case of PaaS). In turn, this means that you are offered a great opportunity to optimize your SQL queries, for example, by splitting them into specific tasks that can be executed in parallel.

This brings us to an important and potentially tricky terminological distinction: the difference between partition and **distribution** strategies. Similar to many other terminological differences, there appears to be a clear distinction; however, exceptions often make it unclear. The clear line is that **partitioning** is about the vertical splitting of data across different "files within the same machine," while distribution is about the horizontal splitting of "data across different machines."

Partitioning and distribution strategies play a pivotal role in the context of cost optimization strategy:

- **Resource utilization**: Partitioning optimizes resource utilization within a machine, ensuring that storage and processing power are efficiently used. This efficiency translates to cost savings, especially in cloud environments where resources are billed based on usage.

- **Scaling efficiency**: Distribution strategies in cloud platforms allow for efficient scaling. By distributing data across multiple nodes, cloud resources can be scaled up or down based on demand. This elasticity ensures that you only pay for the resources you need at any given time, minimizing costs.

- **Query performance**: Optimized partitioning and distribution lead to improved query performance. Faster queries mean less processing time and, consequently, reduced costs, as you are billed based on the resources used during computation.

With on-premises SQL Server, you would have already implemented a partitioning strategy, as splitting data across multiple files is always possible with no requirement for a cluster of machines to run your service in parallel. If you move from SQL Server to an Azure Synapse dedicated SQL pool, you will find yourself in a familiar environment from a functional point of view. However, there will be **one** major difference: you will deal with a pool or cluster of multiple machines.

With this change, the concern that arises is how the data can be split across multiple machines in such a way that every subtask your query can be split into could run on a single node of the cluster. For this reason, when creating a table on a Synapse dedicated SQL pool, you will be able to choose a distribution (across multiple nodes of the cluster) strategy, on top of the partition (across multiple files of the same node) strategy.

The already mentioned February 2023 update of the syllabus resulted in the removal of the topic previously entitled *Design a Distribution Strategy*. Knowing about distribution and its relationship with partitioning, however, is still important to prevent confusion, so a brief introduction to distribution strategies will be offered later.

Outside of Synapse Analytics, however, the distinction between portion and distribution strategies can be fuzzy or even disappear altogether. This is the case for Cosmos DB—a cloud-native service with clustering, scalability, and parallelism built-in from the start in its own design—as opposed to Synapse dedicated SQL pools with their roots in on-premises SQL Server.

As such, Cosmos DB documentation uses the word "partition" to mean probably something more akin to what would be called "distribution" in Synapse. Moreover, in Cosmos DB, the distinction essentially loses its significance. This is because of the service's cloud-oriented nature, which shields users from the intricate details of where their data is physically stored. More generally speaking, terminological hurdles like this one can at first sound like moot points; but Microsoft exams are very strong on terminological distinctions, so trying to avoid terminological confusion becomes an important part of preparing for them.

Almost all the major Azure Storage and Azure Analytics Services support partitioning in one way or another, but you will be going through only those services that are relevant to the exam.

> **Note**
>
> You can learn more about partitioning in the other Azure services at
> `https://packt.link/M9rga`.

By now, you have already grasped the main benefits of partitioning and why they become particularly relevant in the world of cloud computing. The next sections will cover each of them in detail.

## Improving Performance

Partitioning helps improve the parallelization of queries by splitting massive monolithic data into smaller, easily consumable chunks. As already mentioned, partitioning allows a query to be split into subtasks so that they can be executed in parallel, such that every subtask will ideally find all the data needed for its execution on the same file and/or machine.

Apart from parallelization, partitioning also improves performance via **data pruning**. Data pruning is the process of ignoring unnecessary data during querying and thereby reducing **Input/Output (I/O)** operations.

Partitions are also beneficial when it comes to archiving or deleting older data. Imagine you need to remove all data that is older than 12 months. By partitioning the data into monthly units, you can delete an entire month's data with just one DELETE command. This is much more efficient than deleting individual files or rows from a table.

## Improving Scalability

In the world of big data processing, there are two types of scaling: **vertical** and **horizontal**. Vertical scaling refers to the technique of increasing the capacity of individual machines by adding more memory, CPU, storage, or network to improve performance. This usually helps in the short term, but it eventually hits a limit beyond which you cannot scale.

The second type of scaling is called **horizontal scaling**. This refers to the technique of increasing processing and storage capacity by adding more and more machines to a cluster, with regular hardware specifications that are easily available in the market (commodity hardware). As and when the data grows, you just need to add more machines and redirect the new data to the new machines. This method theoretically has no upper bounds and can grow forever. Data lakes are based on the concept of horizontal scaling.

The following are some best practices and recommendation strategies for scaling data analytics on Azure using horizontal scaling:

- **Azure Data Services**: Use ADLS Gen2 as it is designed for storing large volumes of data and offers high throughput for data warehousing needs. Synapse Analytics can handle massive amounts of data and supports both provisioned and serverless on-demand query processing.

- **Autoscaling**: Use **Virtual Machine Scale Sets** (**VMSSs**) to automatically scale the number of VM instances based on demand. Enable cluster autoscaling to automatically adjust the number of nodes in an **Azure Kubernetes Service** (**AKS**) cluster on resource requirements and constraints.

- **Serverless computing**: Utilize **Azure Functions** and **Azure Logic Apps**, which automatically scale based on demand, automate workflows, and integrate with other Azure services.

- **Data partitioning and sharding**: Use Cosmos DB, which provides automatic and instant scalability, along with global distribution and low-latency capabilities. Implement proper data partitioning techniques to distribute data across different nodes, ensuring efficient use of resources.

- **Cost optimization**: Azure Cost Management + Billing continuously monitors your usage and costs. Utilize these tools, especially when dealing with large volumes of data.

**Data partitioning** (or distribution in the context of Synapse SQL pools) naturally helps with horizontal scaling. Assume that you store data at daily intervals in partitions. You will then have about 30 partitions per month. Now, if you need to generate a monthly report, you can configure the cluster to have 30 nodes so that each node can process one day's worth of data. If the requirement increases to process quarterly reports (that is, reports every three months), you can just add more nodes—that is, 60 more nodes to your original cluster size of 30 to process 90 days of data in parallel. Hence, if you could design your data partition strategy in such a way that you split the data easily across new machines, it would help us scale faster.

## Improving Manageability

In many analytical systems, you will have to deal with data from a wide variety of sources, and each of these sources might have different data governance policies assigned to them. For example, some data might be confidential that requires access restriction; some might be transient data that can be regenerated at will; some might be logging data that can be deleted after a few months; some might be transaction data that needs to be archived for years; and so on. Similarly, there might be data that needs faster access so you might choose to persist it on premium **Solid-State Drive** (**SSD**) stores or on a **Hard Disk Drive** (**HDD**) to save on costs.

If you store such different sets of data in their own storage partitions, then applying separate rules (such as access restrictions, or configuring different data life cycle management activities, such as deleting or archiving data, and so on) for the individual partitions becomes easy. Thus, partitioning reduces the management overhead, especially when dealing with multiple different types of data such as in a data lake.

The following is an example of the storage data lifecycle policy with the **Azure Blob Storage** data lifecycle policy:

- Azure Blob Storage's data lifecycle policy is a rule-based policy. You can use the lifecycle policy to transition Blob data to the appropriate access tiers or to expire data at the end of the data lifecycle. You can create one or more rules to define a set of actions to take on a condition being met.

  For example, you could create a rule to tier blobs to the cool tier 30 days after the last modification and then archive them 90 days after the last modification. You could also create a rule to delete blobs 2,555 days (seven years) after the last modification. The following is a JSON script outlining the storage lifecycle policy tailored for this scenario:

  ```
  {
    "rules": [
      {
        "name": "TransitionToCoolAfter30Days",
  ```

```json
      "enabled": true,
      "type": "Lifecycle",
      "definition": {
        "actions": {
          "baseBlob": {
            "tierToCool": {
              "daysAfterModificationGreaterThan": 30
            }
          }
        },
        "filters": {
          "blobTypes": ["blockBlob"]
        }
      }
    },
    {
      "name": "ArchiveAfter90Days",
      "enabled": true,
      "type": "Lifecycle",
      "definition": {
        "actions": {
          "baseBlob": {
            "tierToArchive": {
              "daysAfterModificationGreaterThan": 90
            }
          }
        },
        "filters": {
          "blobTypes": ["blockBlob"]
        }
      }
    },
    {
      "name": "DeleteAfter2555Days",
      "enabled": true,
      "type": "Lifecycle",
      "definition": {
        "actions": {
          "baseBlob": {
            "delete": {
              "daysAfterModificationGreaterThan": 2555
            }
          }
```

```
        },
        "filters": {
          "blobTypes": ["blockBlob"]
        }
      }
    }
  ]
}
```

> **Note**
>
> You can find the complete code in the accompanying GitHub repository at `https://packt.link/wacC7`.

## Improving Security

As you saw in the previous section about improving manageability, confidential datasets can have different access and privacy levels. Customer data will usually have the highest security and privacy levels. On the other hand, product catalogs might not need very high levels of security and privacy.

Enhancing security on the **Azure Data Analytics** platform involves implementing various strategies and features:

- **Dynamic data masking**: It implements **Dynamic Data Masking (DDM)** in Azure SQL Database to mask sensitive data in query results and define masking rules on columns containing sensitive information. For example, the following code shows how you can mask customer phone numbers to show only the last few digits:

```
ALTER Customer
ALTER COLUMN PhoneNumber ADD MASKED (FUNCTION = 'partial(2,
"XXX-XXX-", 4)')
```

- **Encryption of data at rest**: It enables **Azure Disk Encryption** to encrypt data at rest for Azure VMs and Azure-managed disks. This ensures that data stored on disks is encrypted to protect against unauthorized access.

- **Row-level security**: It implements **Row-Level Security (RLS)** policies in Azure Synapse Analytics to control access to rows in a table based on the characteristics of the user executing a query. For example, the following code shows how you can define security predicates to filter rows based on user attributes:

```
CREATE SECURITY POLICY SalesFilterPolicy
Add FILTER PREDICATE dbo.fn_securitypredicate(UserID) ON Sales
```

- **Transparent data encryption**: Enable **Transparent Data Encryption** (**TDE**) to automatically encrypt the database, associated backups, and transaction log files. This protects data at rest. Decryption is automatic when data is accessed by authorized users. The following is the syntax for the same:

```
ALTER DATABASE [DatabaseName] SET ENCRYPTION ON
```

So, by partitioning the data based on security requirements, you can isolate the secure data and apply independent access control and audit rules to those partitions, thereby allowing only privileged users to access such data.

## Improving Availability

If your data is split into multiple partitions that are stored in different machines, applications can continue to serve at least partial data even if a few partitions are down. Only a subset of customers whose partitions went down might get impacted, while the rest of the customers will not see any impact. This is better than the entire application going down. In this way, physically partitioning the data helps improve the availability of services. In general, if you plan your partition strategy correctly then the returns could be significant. This is shown as follows:

- **Increased availability**: Partitioning data can help to improve the availability of services by reducing the impact of failures. If a single partition goes down, only the subset of customers whose data is stored on that partition will be affected. The rest of the customers will continue to be able to access their data.

- **Improved performance**: Partitioning data can also improve the performance of queries and other data processing operations. This is because the database can focus on processing the data that is relevant to the query, rather than having to scan the entire dataset.

- **Reduced costs**: Partitioning data can also help to reduce costs by making it easier to manage and scale your storage. For example, you can partition your data by time and then archive older data to cheaper storage tiers.

This section talked about enhancing performance by optimizing query processing, boosting scalability by enabling efficient distribution of data, and improving manageability through simplified maintenance. Additionally, you learned how to enhance security by enabling access control and data protection while ensuring high availability by enabling fault tolerance and parallel processing.

The next section explores optimized techniques for organizing and managing files within the Azure services. It provides in-depth insights into structuring data, leveraging partition keys, and implementing efficient file partitioning strategies tailored for Azure Blob Storage and ADLS Gen2.

# Designing a Partition Strategy for Files

The Azure Storage services are generic and very flexible when it comes to partitioning. You can implement whatever partition logic you want using the same **Create, Read, Update, Delete (CRUD) Application Programming Interfaces (APIs)** that are publicly available. There are no special APIs or features available for partitioning. With that background, you'll now explore the partitioning options available in Azure Blob Storage and ADLS Gen2 in the following sections.

> **Note**
>
> This section primarily focuses on the **Implement a partition strategy for files** concept of the DP-203: Data Engineering on Microsoft Azure exam.

## Azure Blob Storage

**Azure Blob Storage** is a popular Azure service used for storing data in folders as **blobs**, regardless of the content or file structure. This feature makes it suitable for storing raw data, commonly used as a source for future data transformations.

In Azure Blob Storage, you first create Azure Storage Accounts. Then, within these accounts, you create Blob Containers (and maybe queues, file shares, and unstructured tables, which are the other types of contents supported; a single Azure Storage Account can hold any combination of these types of storage).

Within containers, you create actual storage blobs. These **containers** are logical entities. Even when you create data blobs within containers, there is no guarantee that the data will land within the same partition. But there is a trick to enhance your chances of storing the blobs in the same partition, and *Table 2.1* details them:

| Storage Tier | Description | Use Cases |
| --- | --- | --- |
| Standard Tier (GPv2) | The default storage tier for Azure Blob Storage. This is an effective choice for most general-purpose workloads. | Storing website files, images, and videos, data for backup and recovery, and data for archiving. |
| Premium Tier Blob | Designed for high-performance workloads. | Streaming video and audio, online gaming, and high-performance data processing. |
| Premium Tier File Share | Designed for high-performance file-sharing workloads. | Storing and accessing shared files for applications, high-performance file sharing for collaboration, and high-performance file sharing for Data Analytics. |

| Storage Tier | Description | Use Cases |
|---|---|---|
| Premium Storage Tier | Designed for high-performance workloads that require low latency and high throughput. | Mission-critical applications, high-performance data processing, and workloads that need to process large amounts of data quickly. |

Table 2.1 – Scenarios to use different tiers of an Azure Storage Account

Azure uses something called **range partitioning** for storing blobs. In a range partition, files that are in a lexical sequence end up together in a partition.

For example, if you have filenames such as `Cab1-20211220`, `Cab1-20211221`, `Cab1-20211222`, and `Cab1-20211223`, these files will mostly end up in the same partition. Similarly, filenames such as `IAC-Cabs`, `IAC-Routes`, `IAC-Customers`, and `IAC-Drivers` will mostly end up within the same partition.

Azure Storage uses `<account name + container name + blob name>` as the partition key. It continues to store blobs in the same partition until it reaches the partition's internal limit. At that point, Azure Storage repartitions and rebalances the data and spreads it evenly among the partitions. This entire process of repartitioning and rebalancing will be taken care of automatically by Azure Storage, without intervention from the user.

If the amount of data stored is large and Azure Storage starts repartitioning and rebalancing the data, the latency of the CRUD APIs will be impacted. You can avoid or delay such repartitions by adding a three-digit hash value (random value) to your filenames. This will cause the data to be distributed across multiple partitions. For example, your filenames could use the following format:

```
New York/cabs/cab1234/customers/{XYZYYYYMMDD}
```

Here, `XYZ` could be the random hash value.

## Azure Data Lake Storage Gen2

The term **data lake** is used to describe a data store that contains raw data, which are potentially heterogeneous in format and structure, typically used as the starting point for further data transformation and refining. If you think this sounds very much like what was mentioned previously with reference to Blob Storage, you are right.

Indeed, while ADLS Gen1 used to be offered as a separate service, you will not find a service called ADLS Gen2 in the Azure Marketplace. Instead, ADLS Gen2 is offered a specific flavor of Azure Blob Storage, obtained by enabling the **Hierarchical Namespace** option at the time of creating a specific storage account. This option results in both performance (some sort of folder indexing) and security (the ability to create Access Control Lists at the folder and even the file level) improvements, which make this type of storage account optimized to play the role of a data lake.

Considering the variety and volume of data that will land in a data lake, it is very important to design a flexible, but maintainable, folder structure. Poorly designed or ad hoc folder structures will become a management nightmare and will render the data lake unusable. Some points to keep in mind while designing the folder structure are as follows:

- **Human readability**: Human-readable folder structures will help improve data exploration and navigation.

- **Representation of organizational structure**: Aligning the folder structure according to the organizational structure helps segregate the data for billing and access control. Such a folder structure will help restrict cross-team data access.

- **Sensitive data distinction**: The folder structure should be such that it can separate sensitive data from general data. Sensitive data will require higher levels of audit, privacy, and security policies, so keeping it separate makes it easy to apply the required policies.

- **Manageability of ACLs**: ACLs are used to provide control over which users have read, write, or execute permissions on files and folders. You should design the folders in such a way that you apply ACLs only at the top levels of the folders and not at the leaf folders. This approach prevents the need to constantly update ACLs whenever a new subfolder is automatically generated, like timestamp folders for streaming inputs.

- **Optimization for faster and evenly distributed reads**: If you can distribute the data evenly, then workloads can access the data in parallel. This will improve query performance. Also, think of support for pruning, which was discussed in the *Improving Performance* section.

- **Subscription limits**: Azure has per-subscription limits on the size of data, the network ingress/egress, parallelism, and so on. So, if the data is going to be huge, you need to plan to split it at a subscription level.

Apart from the folder structure, you can also partition data for the benefits that were discussed in the *Benefits of Partitioning* section, including performance, scalability, manageability, security, and availability. The process of segregating data into partitions could be done manually. It could also be automated using **Azure Data Factory** (**ADF**).

---

Note

You will delve deeper into automation using ADF in the later implementation-oriented *Chapter 4, Ingesting and Transforming Data*, and *Chapter 5, Developing a Batch Processing Solution*.

---

Now that you have a fairly sound idea about Blob storage and file-based partitioning optimizations, and how to effectively structure and manage data within Azure Blob Storage and ADLS Gen2, the next section will talk about designing sophisticated partitioning strategies that align with Azure's analytical services. By knowing about the horizontal, vertical, and functional partitioning techniques, data engineers can optimize data storage, retrieval, and processing, enabling faster and more efficient analytical workloads in the Azure cloud environment.

# Designing Partition Strategy for Analytical Workloads

The syllabus of the DP-203 exam is heavily skewed towards analytical workloads, as opposed to transactional workloads. While the latter is concerned with the creation, updating, or deletion of **live** production data, the former is concerned with trying to extract meaningful lessons from historical data (which mainly deals with data that is read only). The primary objective is to extract insights from historical data with data refresh and transformation activities for analytical purposes. In this context, the term "historical" could mean data from just last month or even last week.

> **Note**
>
> This section primarily focuses on the **Implement a partition strategy for analytical workloads** concept of the DP-203: Data Engineering on Microsoft Azure exam.

There are three main types of partition strategies for analytical workloads. These are as follows:

- Horizontal partitioning (also known as sharding)
- Vertical partitioning
- Functional partitioning

Read on to explore each of them in detail.

## Horizontal Partitioning

In a **horizontal partition**, you divide the table data horizontally with subsets of rows stored in different data stores. Each of these subsets of rows (with the same schema as the parent table) is called a **shard**. Essentially, each of these shards is stored in different database instances.

You can see an example of a horizontal partition in *Figure 2.1*:

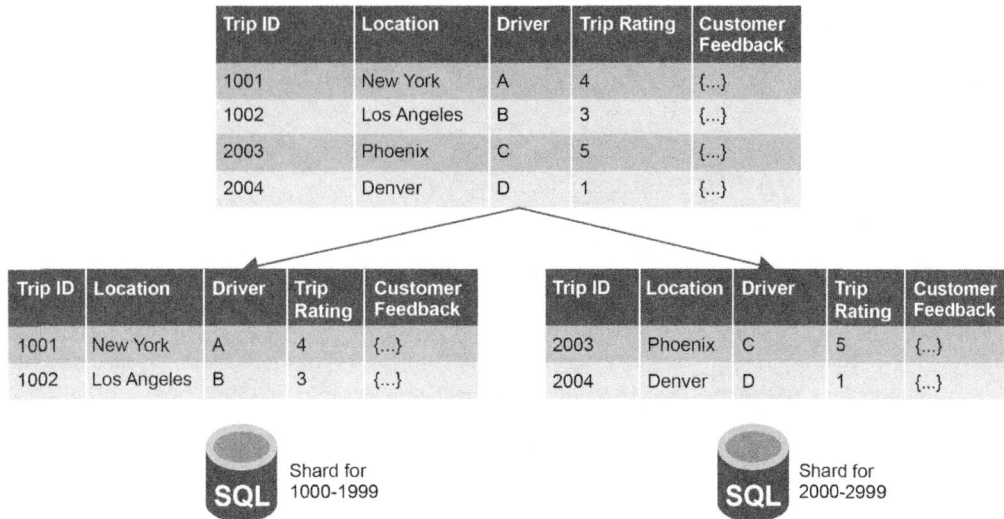

Figure 2.1 – An illustration of horizontal partitioning in action

In the preceding example, you can see that the data in the top table is distributed horizontally based on the `Trip ID` range. The shard for 1000-1999 contains data for taxi trips with `Trip ID` ranging from `1000` to `1999`. Any trip with `Trip ID` falling within this range will be stored in this specific shard. For instance, if there is a trip with Trip ID `2500`, its details, including `Location`, `Driver`, `Trip Rating`, and `Customer Feedback`, will be stored within the 2000-2999 shard.

## Selecting the Right Shard Key

It is important to select the right shard key (also called a **partition key**) for partitioning the data, as changing it later will be a very expensive operation. Here, "expensive" refers to the time, computational power, and resources needed to perform. The following guidelines will help you with selecting the right partition key:

- Select a key that spreads the data in such a way that the application traffic to the data partitions is evenly distributed.

- Select a key that doesn't change too often. Best keys are static and widespread—that is, the range of that key should neither be too small nor too large. As a rule, a key that can generate hundreds of partitions is effective. Avoid keys that generate too few partitions (tens of partitions) or too many partitions (thousands of partitions).

Don't try to balance the data to be evenly distributed across partitions unless specifically required by your use case because, usually, the most recent data will get accessed more than older data. Thus, the partitions with recent data will end up becoming bottlenecks due to high data access.

You will learn more about the sharding pattern in the *Partition Strategy for Efficiency and Performance* section.

## Vertical Partitioning

In a vertical partition, you divide the data vertically, and each subset of the columns is stored separately in a different data store. In the case of vertical partitioning, you partially normalize the table to break it into smaller tables (that is, with fewer columns).

This type of partitioning is ideal in cases where a table might have a subset of data that is accessed more frequently than the rest. Vertical partitioning can help speed up queries as only the required subset of data can be selectively retrieved, instead of reading entire rows. This is ideal for column-oriented data stores such as HBase and Cosmos DB.

You can see an example of a vertical partition in *Figure 2.2*:

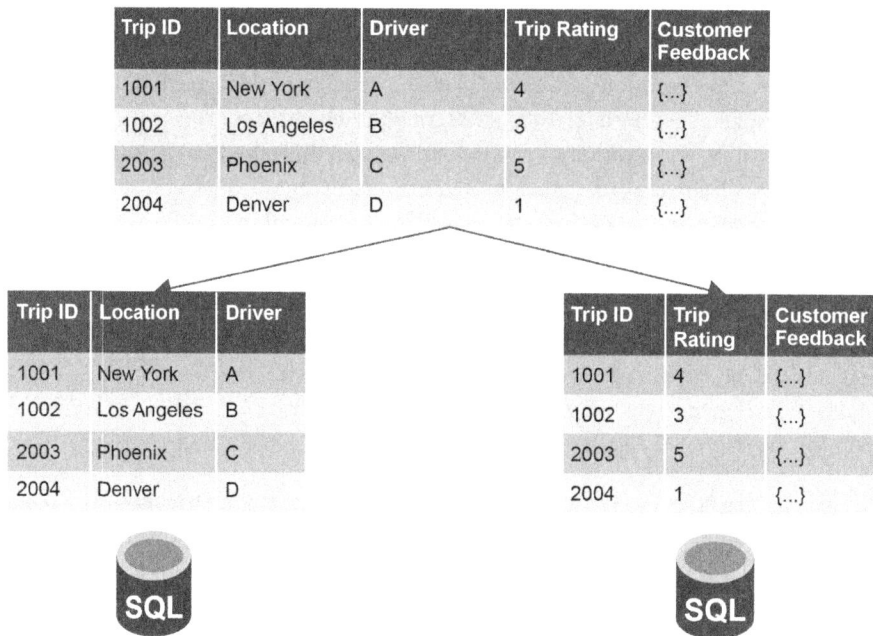

Figure 2.2 – An illustration of Vertical partitioning in action

In *Figure 2.2*, you can see that the columns such as `Trip Rating` and `Customer Feedback`, which might not be used frequently, are split into separate partitions. This will help reduce the amount of data being read for queries.

## Functional Partitioning

Functional partitions are similar to vertical partitions, except that, here, you store entire tables or entities in different data stores. They can be used to segregate data belonging to different organizations, frequently used tables from infrequently used ones, read-write tables from read-only ones, sensitive data from general data, and so on.

You can see an example of a functional partition in *Figure 2.3*:

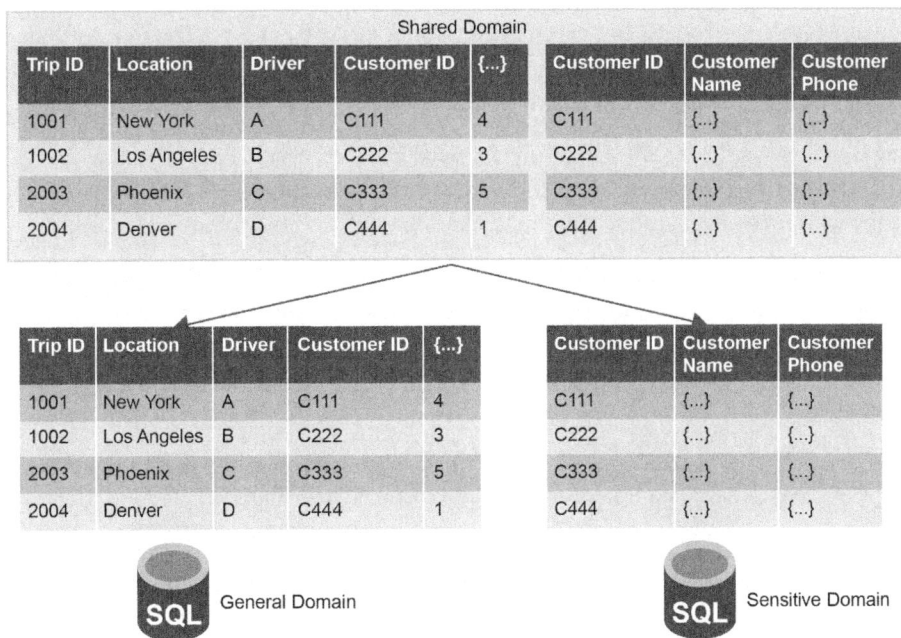

Figure 2.3 – Example of a functional partition

In *Figure 2.3*, you can see how the customer data is moved into its own partition. Here, data is divided into partitions based on specific functions or business logic, rather than just arbitrary ranges or discrete values. This segregation is often used in scenarios where data needs to be grouped logically according to its usage. You can see the `Customer ID`, `Customer Name`, and `Customer Phone` data grouped logically and stored in the Sensitive Domain partition, and this will help apply different privacy and security rules for the different partitions accordingly.

Azure services such as Azure SQL and Azure Synapse dedicated pool support all the partitioning formats discussed in this section.

By now, you have learned about the various partitioning options for analytical workloads such as horizontal and vertical partitioning, selecting the right partition key to distribute the data across partitions, and finally, using functional partitioning to distribute the data based on business logic. In the next section, you will learn about partition strategy for streaming workloads to explore different strategies for partitioning streaming data and selecting the right one for your specific workload using **Event Hubs**, **Stream Analytics**, and **Azure Databricks**.

# Implementing Partition Strategy for Streaming Workloads

In this section, you will explore the world of data streaming and how to effectively manage it. **Data streaming** is a big deal in today's fast-paced digital world. It involves the "continuous transfer of data at high speed" and you see it in action when you watch videos online, play multiplayer games, or even when you use real-time apps on your smartphone.

Managing this constant flow of data efficiently is crucial in the context of data streaming. It means you can "divide the data into smaller streams" that can be processed independently. This can significantly improve the efficiency of data processing and make your system more robust and scalable.

Now, you will explore different strategies for partitioning streaming data. Selecting the right one for your specific workload depends on factors such as the volume of your data and the processing speed you require.

> **Note**
>
> This section primarily focuses on the **Implement a partition strategy for streaming workloads** concept of the DP-203: Data Engineering on Microsoft Azure exam.

Azure provides a range of services and features designed to help you partition your streaming workloads efficiently. You will gain knowledge of a few essential components and techniques to create a successful partition strategy in the coming sections.

## Event Hubs

**Azure Event Hubs** is a super-scalable service that is all about processing events in real time. Think of it as a hub where all your streaming data goes and provides the built-in feature called **partitioning**. Basically, it helps you to handle huge streams of data by splitting them into smaller chunks when you set up an Event Hub, and you can decide how many partitions you want based on the workload. Here, more partitions mean you can process the data faster and handle even more data at once.

The following code is a series of Azure CLI commands to create and configure Azure resources related to Azure Event Hubs:

```
# Create a resource group (if you haven't created already)
az group create --name StreamingResourceGroup --location UKSouth
# Create an Event Hubs namespace with 10 partitions
az eventhubs namespace create --name StreamingNamespace --resource-
group StreamingResourceGroup --location UKSouth --sku Standard
--capacity 10
```

The preceding code snippet creates an Azure Resource group named `StreamingResourceGroup` in the `UKSouth` location with a standard **Stock Keeping Unit** (**SKU**) and a capacity of `10` partitions.

> **Note**
>
> You can find the complete in the accompanying GitHub repository at `https://packt.link/CHmTz`.

The following code snippet creates an Event Hub named `StreamingEventHub` within the previously created `StreamingNamespace` Event Hubs namespace and the `StreamingResourceGroup` specified Resource group:

```
# Create an Event Hub within the namespace
az eventhubs eventhub create –name StreamingEventHub –namespace-name
StreamingNamespace –resource-group StreamingResourceGroup
```

> **Note**
>
> You can learn more about creating Event Hubs at `https://packt.link/fpI2P`.

## Stream Analytics

**Azure Stream Analytics** is a real-time analytics service designed to help you analyze and visualize streaming data in real time. It is like a "super-smart filter" that takes in partitioned data for processing. You can use stream analytics to monitor data, trigger alerts, or drive real-time reporting.

Assume the input data stream contains data to be partitioned based on the `DeviceId` column and you define the partitioning function and use it in a Stream Analytics query. The following is an example of a **Stream Analytics partition strategy**:

```
#Create a user-defined function to partition the data
CREATE FUNCTION MyPartitioningFunction()
RETURNS @result TABLE
(
PartitionKey nvarchar(100),
```

```
PartitionId int
)
WITH SCHEMABINDING
AS
BEGIN
INSERT INTO @result
SELECT
DeviceId As PartitionKey, -- your partition key column
HASHBYTES('MD5', CAST(DeviceId AS nvarchar(100))) % 10    AS
PartitionId -- Assuming 10 partitions
FROM
input
RETURN;
END
#you would use the partition function in your query to process the
data:
SELECT
DeviceId,
AVG(Temparature) AS AvgTemparature,
COUNT(*) AS MessageCount
INTO
output
FROM
input
PARTITION BY
MyPartitioningFunction().PartitionId
GROUP BY
DeviceId,
TumblingWindow(minute,5)
```

> **Note**
>
> You can find the complete code in the accompanying GitHub repository at `https://packt.link/Qyazg`.

In this example, the following can be observed:

- The `MyPartitioningFunction` function takes `DeviceId` from each message in the input data stream

- It applies the MD5 hash function to the `DeviceId`

- It assigns a `PartitionId` between 0 and 9

- It calculates the average `Temperature` and counts the number of messages for each device over a five-minute Tumbling Wacceindow

> **Note**
> You can learn more about creating Azure Stream Analytics at `https://packt.link/GU1MH`.

## Azure Databricks

**Azure Databricks** is a powerful cloud platform for big data analytics and processing, and it offers robust capabilities for dealing with your streaming operations. Here, one of the key considerations is how to efficiently partition the data so that it can be processed in parallel and help you to enhance query performance and reduce latency.

Partitioning in the context of Azure Databricks streaming refers to dividing a large dataset into smaller, more manageable pieces called **partitions**, which can be processed concurrently. This strategy is crucial for handling high-throughput workloads and is particularly beneficial when dealing with real-time data streams.

Azure Databricks leverages **Structured Streaming**, an engine built on top of the Spark SQL engine for processing the streaming data. This allows for a high level of abstraction and ease of use, as you can express streaming computations as standard batch-like queries.

Here is a scenario where you have an Azure Databricks job that reads streaming data from an Event Hub, processes it, and then writes the result back to another Event Hub. The data consists of messages from various sensors, and you can partition the output based on `sensorId`.

The following is the code for the same:

```
from pyspark.sql.functions import col
# Load data from Event Hub using Spark
df = spark.readStream \
.format("eventhubs") \
.option("eventhubs.connectionString",
"<YourEventHubConnectionString>") \
.option("eventhubs.partitionCount", "8") \
.option("eventhubs.consumerGroup", "$Default") \
.load()


# Assuming the incoming data has a column 'sensorId' which is used as
a partition key
partitionColumn = "sensorId"


# Add a column 'partitionKey' that will be used for partitioning in
the output Event Hub
```

```
df_with_partition = df.withColumn("partitionKey",
col(partitionColumn))

# Write data to partitions based on the 'partitionKey'
query = df_with_partition.writeStream \
.format("eventhubs") \
.option("eventhubs.connectionString",
"<YourOutputEventHubConnectionString>") \
.option("eventhubs.partitionKey", "partitionKey") \
.outputMode("update") \
.option("checkpointLocation", "/path/to/checkpoint/dir") \
.start()

query.awaitTermination()
```

> **Note**
>
> You will explore these streaming options in detail in the upcoming *Chapter 6, Developing a Stream Processing Solution*.
>
> You can find the complete code in the accompanying GitHub repository at `https://packt.link/bV2Qi`. You can also utilize the Azure Databricks storage setup code block within the corresponding GitHub repository at `https://packt.link/EVoLO`.

By now, you have learned about the various storage and analytical partitioning options. In the next section, you will recap the points you learned about performance and efficiency and learn about some additional performance patterns.

## Partition Strategy for Efficiency and Performance

In the *Benefits of Partitioning* section, you learned how partitioning helps with performance, scale, security, availability, and so on.

The following are some strategies to be kept in mind while designing for efficiency and performance:

- Partition datasets into smaller chunks that can be run with optimal parallelism for multiple queries.

- Partition the data so that queries don't end up requiring too much data from other partitions—that is, minimize cross-partition data transfers.

- Design effective folder structures to improve the efficiency of data reads and writes. The following is the sample directory structure that you can create within ADLS Gen2 (*Figure 2.4*):

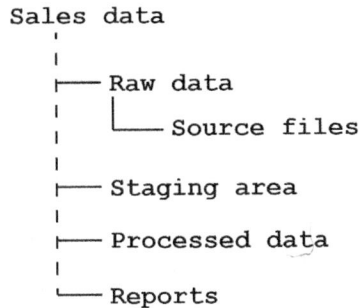

```
Sales data
 |
 |
 ├── Raw data
 |    └── Source files
 |
 ├── Staging area
 |
 ├── Processed data
 |
 └── Reports
```

Figure 2.4 – The directory structure within ADLS Gen2

- Use descriptive names for files, reflecting their content, date, or purpose; for example, "sales_data_2024_q1.csv." Also consider using a prefix, such as "raw_," "processed_," or "report_" to distinguish file types. Suffixes such as "_data" or "_report" can also help with quick identification.

- Assign ACL permissions based on roles (e.g., read, write, execute, etc.) to directories and files. Use **Azure Active Directory** (**Azure AD**) identities for user- and group-based access control. Partition data so that a significant amount of data can be pruned while running queries.

- Partition in units of data that can be easily added, deleted, swapped, or archived. This helps improve the efficiency of data lifecycle management.

- File sizes in the range of 256 **megabytes** (**MB**) to 100 **gigabytes** (**GB**) perform well with analytical engines, such as HDInsight and Azure Synapse. So, aggregate the files to these ranges before running the analytical engines on them.

- For I/O-intensive jobs, try to keep the optimal I/O buffer sizes in the range of 4 MB to 16 MB; anything too big or too small will become inefficient.

- Run more containers or executors per virtual machine (such as Apache Spark executors or Apache **Yet Another Resource Negotiator** (**YARN**) containers).

Remember the preceding sound practices while designing your next partition strategy. Next, you'll learn how to find the right data to partition and how much data to partition.

## Iterative Query Performance Improvement Process

The following are the high-level iterative processes to improve query performance:

1.  List business-critical queries, the most frequently run queries, and the slowest queries.

2.  Check the query plans for each of these queries using the EXPLAIN keyword and see the amount of data being used at each stage.

> **Note**
>
> You will learn about viewing query plans in *Chapter 5, Developing a Batch Processing Solution*, and *Chapter 9, Monitoring Data Storage and Data Processing*.

3.  Identify the joins or filters that are taking the most time. Also, identify the corresponding data partitions.

4.  Try to split the corresponding input data partitions into smaller partitions or change the application logic to perform isolated processing on top of each partition and later merge only the filtered data.

5.  Try to see whether other partitioning keys would work better and whether you need to repartition the data to get better job performance for each partition.

6.  If any particular partitioning technology doesn't work, explore using more than one piece of partitioning logic. For example, you could apply horizontal partitioning within functional partitioning.

7.  Monitor the partitioning regularly to check whether the application access patterns are balanced and well distributed. Try to identify hot spots early on.

8.  Iterate this process until you hit the preferred query execution time.

You will be using these guidelines in the examples presented in *Chapter 5, Developing a Batch Processing Solution*, and *Chapter 9, Monitoring Data Storage and Data Processing*.

> **Note**
>
> *Chapter 9, Monitoring Data Storage and Data Processing*, will explain the monitoring and observability strategy with examples, such as Azure SQL DB query optimization, data sharding monitoring through Azure monitor, performance tuning, and the query optimizer.

By now, you have learned about advanced techniques and best practices for optimizing your data partitioning strategy and improving query performance. In the next section, you will learn about distribution techniques and performance improvement techniques while loading data and effectively filtering queries within Azure Synapse Analytics.

# Designing Partition Strategy for Azure Synapse Analytics

Azure Synapse Analytics is the premium analytics service that Azure is investing in quite heavily. When Azure Synapse Analytics is mentioned, you might think of it as an SQL Data Warehouse; however, in reality, Synapse Analytics is a complete suite of integrated analytical services.

> **Note**
>
> This section primarily focuses on the **Implement a partition strategy for Azure Synapse Analytics** concept of the DP-203: Data Engineering on Microsoft Azure exam.

Synapse Analytics has integrated support for several Azure Storage services, compute technologies such as SQL Data Warehouse and Synapse Spark, orchestration engines such as ADF, specialized stores such as Cosmos DB, cloud-based **Identity and Access Management** (**IAM**) services such as Azure AD, data governance support via Azure Purview, and more.

Azure Synapse Analytics also doubles as the analytics store for the serving layer as it has a highly scalable SQL Warehouse store at its core. This can be used to store processed data that is reduced in size to be used for analytical queries, data insights, reporting, and so on.

Synapse Analytics contains two compute engines. These are as follows:

- An SQL pool that consists of serverless and dedicated SQL pools (previously known as SQL Data Warehouse)
- A Spark pool that consists of Synapse Spark pools

But when people refer to Azure Synapse Analytics, they are usually referring to the dedicated SQL pool option. This section will look at the partition strategy available for a Synapse dedicated SQL pool.

> **Note**
>
> You have already briefly encountered partitioning in Spark as part of the Data pruning in the *Benefits of Partitioning* section. The same concepts apply to Synapse Spark, too.

But before you can explore the partitioning options, you need to grasp the data distribution techniques of a Synapse dedicated as this will play an important role in your partition strategy. The following defines distribution:

> *A dedicated SQL pool is a Massively Parallel Processing (MPP) system that splits the queries into 60 parallel queries and executes them in parallel. Each of these smaller queries runs on something called a distribution. A distribution is a basic unit of processing and storage for a dedicated SQL pool.*

> **Note:**
> You can find the definition of a dedicated SQL pool at `https://packt.link/EejMx`.

There are three different ways to distribute (i.e., shard) data among distributions, as listed here:

- **Round-robin tables**: In a round-robin table, the data is serially distributed among all the distributions. It is the simplest of the distributions and is the default when the distribution type is not specified. This option is the quickest to load data but is not the best for queries that include joins. Use round-robin tables for staging data or temporary data, where the data is mostly going to be read.

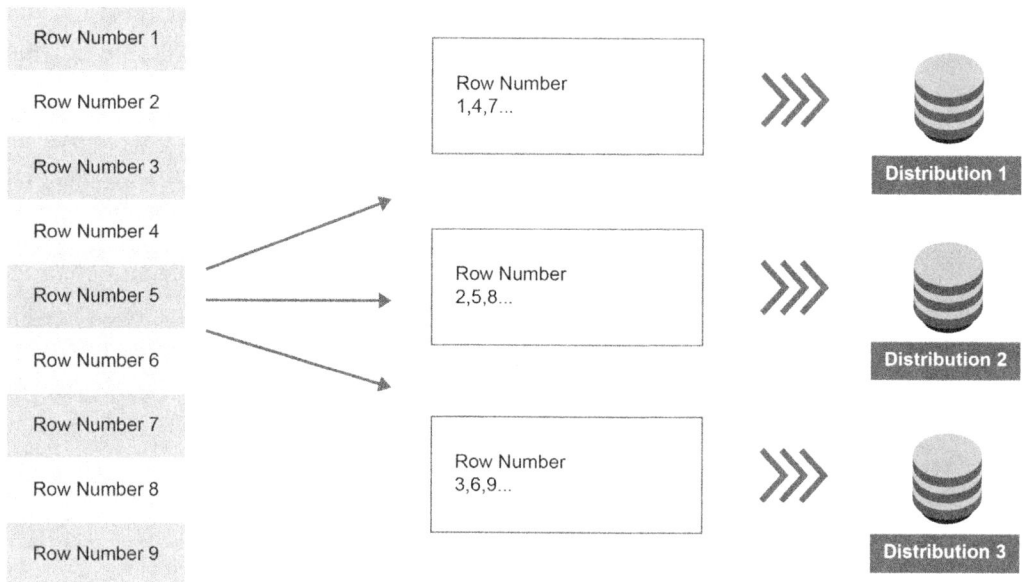

Figure 2.5 – Round-robin table distribution showing the distribution of data

In the `RoundRobinTable` example shown in *Figure 2.5*, when you insert the data into this table, the rows will be distributed evenly across all nodes in a round-robin manner, allowing for a relatively even distribution of data storage and processing load.

The following code snippet is employed for generating a table named `RoundRobinTable` containing two columns: `ID` characterized as an integer type, and `NAME` characterized as a variable character string with a maximum length of 50 characters:

```
--Create table with round-robin Distribution
CREATE TABLE RoundRobinTable
(
    ID INT,
```

```
        NAME VARCHAR(50)
)
WITH
(
DISTRIBUTION=ROUND_ROBIN
);
```

> **Note**
>
> You can find the complete code in the accompanying GitHub repository at `https://packt.link/q4x5F`.

The following are the two different distribution strategies in the context of database management systems.

- **Hash tables**: In a hash table, the rows are distributed to different nodes based on a hash function. The hash key is usually one of the columns in the table. Hash tables are best for queries with joins and aggregations. They are ideal for large tables. When the size of the table is greater than 2 GB, columns have a large number of distinct values, and the table has more frequent insert/update/delete operations.

> **Note**
>
> You can find the complete code in the accompanying GitHub repository at `https://packt.link/eJLBQ`.

- **Replicated tables**: With replicated tables, the table data is copied over to all the distributions. These are ideal for small tables where the cost of copying the data over for the query joins outweighs the storage costs for these small tables. Use replicated tables for storing quick **LookUp Tables (LUTs)**.

> **Note**
>
> You can find the complete code in the accompanying GitHub repository at `https://packt.link/dKDhd`.

Partitioning is supported on all the distribution types in the preceding list. Apart from the distribution types, the dedicated SQL pool also supports the following three types of tables:

- Clustered column store tables
- Clustered index tables
- Heap tables

Partitioning is supported in all these types of tables, too.

> **Note**
>
> You will explore these table options in detail in *Chapter 5, Developing a Batch Processing Solution*, and *Chapter 6, Developig a Stream Processing Solution*.

In a dedicated SQL pool, data is already distributed across its 60 distributions. So, you need to be careful while deciding whether to further partition the data. The clustered column store tables work optimally when the number of rows per table in a distribution is around 1 million.

For example, if you plan to partition the data further by the months of a year, you have the following sub-divisions:

```
12 partitions x 60 distributions = 720 sub-divisions
```

Each of these divisions needs to have at least 1 million rows—that is, the table (usually a fact table) needs to have more than 720 million rows. So, you will have to be careful to not over-partition the data when it comes to dedicated SQL pools.

That said, partitioning in Synapse dedicated pools has two distinct advantages, which are as follows:

- There is performance improvement while loading data
- There is also performance improvement for filtering queries

## Performance Improvement while Loading Data

Partitioning helps load data for queries in dedicated SQL pools. This is a technique that you learned in the *Benefits of Partitioning* section of this chapter. If you can group the data belonging to a particular time frame together in a partition, then adding or removing that data becomes as simple as running a simple ADD or DELETE command.

For example, assume that you need to generate a rolling 12-month report. At the end of every month, you remove the oldest month and add a new month to the report. If you partition the data with the granularity of months, then you can easily delete the old data and add the new data using a partition-switching technique in a dedicated SQL pool.

## Performance Improvement for Filtering Queries

Partitioning can also help improve query performance by being able to filter the data based on partitions. Partitions help with the WHERE clause in queries. For example, if you have partitioned the data based on the months of a year, you can specify which exact month to look for in your queries, thereby skipping the rest of the months.

By now, you have learned about distribution and performance improvement techniques while loading data and effectively filtering queries within Azure Synapse Analytics. It is time to move to the next section which talks about when to start partitioning data in ADLS Gen2. The section focuses on the circumstances in which partitioning your data becomes necessary for efficient storage and its limitations.

## Recognizing Partitioning Needs in ADLS Gen2

As mentioned in the *Benefits of Partitioning* section, you can partition data according to your requirements such as performance, scalability, security, operational overhead, and so on. However, there is another reason why you might end up partitioning your data: the various I/O bandwidth limits that are imposed at subscription levels by Azure. These limits apply to both Blob Storage and ADLS Gen2.

> **Note**
>
> This section primarily focuses on the **Identify when partitioning is needed in Azure Data Lake Storage Gen2** concept of the DP-203: Data Engineering on Microsoft Azure exam.

The rate at which you ingest data into an Azure Storage system is called the **ingress** rate, and the rate at which you move the data out of the Azure Storage system is called the **egress** rate.

*Table 2.2* shows a snapshot of some of the limits enforced by Azure Blob Storage:

| Resource | Limit |
| --- | --- |
| Number of storage accounts per region per subscription, including standard and premium storage accounts. | 250 by default, 500 by request (with a quota increase). |
| Default maximum storage account capacity. | 5 PiB (can be increased by calling Azure Support). |
| A maximum number of Blob containers, blobs, file shares, tables, queues, entities, or messages per storage account. | No limit. |
| Default maximum request rate per storage account. | 20,000 requests per second (can be increased by calling Azure Support). |
| Default maximum ingress for general-purpose V1 storage accounts (all regions). | 10 Gbps (can be increased by calling Azure Support). |
| Maximum egress for general-purpose storage accounts (US regions). | 20 Gbps if RA-GRS/GRS is enabled, 30 Gbps for **Locally Redundant Storage (LRS)/Zone Redundant Storage (ZRS)** |
| Maximum egress for general-purpose v1 storage accounts (non-US regions). | 10 Gbps if RA-GRS/GRS is enabled, 15 Gbps for LRS/ZRS. |

| Resource | Limit |
|---|---|
| Maximum number of IP address rules per storage account. | 200. |
| Maximum number of VNet rules per storage account. | 200. |
| Maximum number of resource instance rules per storage account. | 200. |
| Maximum number of private endpoints per storage account. | 200. |

Table 2.2 – Default limits for Azure Blob Storage accounts

*Table 2.2* gives you an idea of the limits that Azure Storage imposes. When you design your data lake applications, you need to take care of such restrictions as part of your design itself.

So, for example, if your egress rate is beyond 50 Gbps for your data lake, you will have to create multiple accounts and partition your data among those accounts.

> **Note**
>
> You can find complete and up-to-date Azure Storage limits at `https://packt.link/8hqPx`.

Some of the limits in the table (such as ingress rates and storage capacity limits) are soft limits, which means you can reach out to Azure Support to increase them to some extent; however, you will eventually hit the hard limits for each option. Other resources, such as **Internet Protocol** (**IP**), addresses, and VNets, are hard limits, so you need to plan the partitions with these numbers in mind.

Remember that if you are using a hybrid setup of on-premises and on-cloud systems and transfer data between such systems often, you need to ensure that your source/destination machines and the actual public network can support the level of ingress and egress data transfer rates provided by Azure Storage. If you are moving data from on-premises sources, consider using Azure ExpressRoute.

> **Note**
>
> The higher ingress/egress requirements could also come from the applications running on top of Azure Storage and not just via direct data uploads and downloads into the Azure store. For example, if you have an Azure SQL or Azure Synapse dedicated pool (data warehouse) that has a very busy shard, it might exceed the read (egress) limits of that storage account. In such cases, you will have to repartition that shard to divide the data among multiple accounts.

In general, for any Azure service, do keep an eye on the resource limits so that it doesn't come as a surprise when your product is deployed to production.

## Summary

With that, you have come to the end of the second chapter. In this chapter, you learned about the different partitioning techniques available in Azure. You started with the basics of partitioning and its benefits of partitioning, before moving on to partitioning techniques for storage and analytical workloads. You next explored the best practices to improve partitioning efficiency and performance and reviewed the concept of distribution tables and how they impact the partitioning of Azure Synapse Analytics. Finally, you studied storage limitations, which play an important role in deciding when to partition for ADLS Gen2.

This covers the syllabus for the *Implement a Partition Strategy* topic for the DP-203 exam. You will reinforce the learnings from this chapter via implementation details and tips in *Chapter 6, Developing a Stream Processing Solution*.

The next chapter, *Chapter 3, Designing and Implementing the Data Exploration Layer*, will explore the concepts of Azure Synapse Analytics database templates, executing queries by compute solutions that leverage the SQL serverless and Spark clusters, and search metadata and data lineage in Microsoft Purview.

# Exam Readiness Drill – Chapter Review Questions

Apart from a solid understanding of key concepts, being able to think quickly under time pressure is a skill that will help you ace your certification exam. That is why working on these skills early on in your learning journey is key.

Chapter review questions are designed to improve your test-taking skills progressively with each chapter you learn and review your understanding of key concepts in the chapter at the same time. You'll find these at the end of each chapter.

> **How to Access These Materials**
>
> To learn how to access these resources, head over to the chapter titled *Chapter 11, Accessing the Online Resources*.

To open the Chapter Review Questions for this chapter, perform the following steps:

1. Click the link – `https://packt.link/DP203E2_CH02`.

   Alternatively, you can scan the following **QR code** (*Figure 2.6*):

Figure 2.6 – QR code that opens Chapter Review Questions for logged-in users

2. Once you log in, you'll see a page similar to the one shown in *Figure 2.7*:

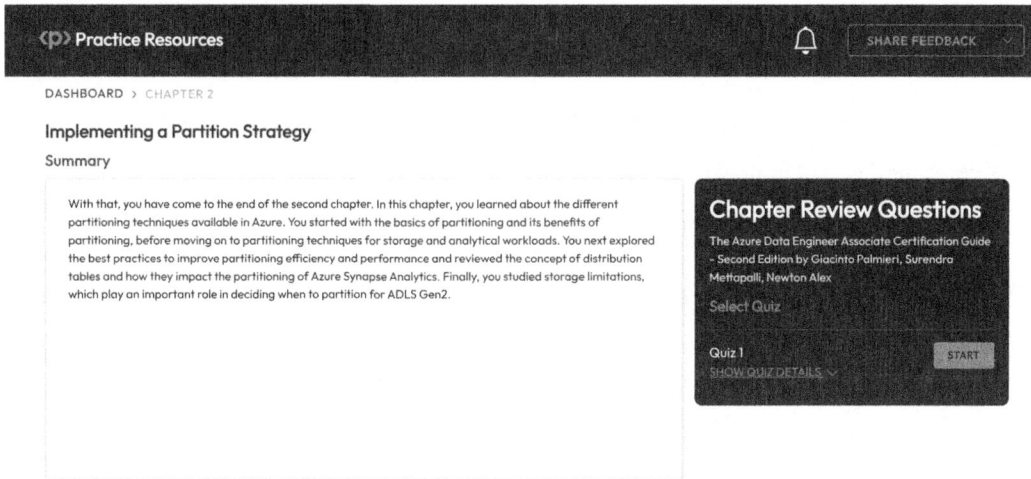

Figure 2.7 – Chapter Review Questions for Chapter 2

3. Once ready, start the following practice drills, re-attempting the quiz multiple times.

## Exam Readiness Drill

For the first three attempts, don't worry about the time limit.

### ATTEMPT 1

The first time, aim for at least **40%**. Look at the answers you got wrong and read the relevant sections in the chapter again to fix your learning gaps.

### ATTEMPT 2

The second time, aim for at least **60%**. Look at the answers you got wrong and read the relevant sections in the chapter again to fix any remaining learning gaps.

*ATTEMPT 3*

The third time, aim for at least **75%**. Once you score 75% or more, you start working on your timing.

> Tip
>
> You may take more than **three** attempts to reach 75%. That's okay. Just review the relevant sections in the chapter till you get there.

# Working On Timing

**Target**: Your aim is to keep the score the same while trying to answer these questions as quickly as possible. Here's an example of how your next attempts should look like:

| Attempt | Score | Time Taken |
|---------|-------|------------|
| Attempt 5 | 77% | 21 mins 30 seconds |
| Attempt 6 | 78% | 18 mins 34 seconds |
| Attempt 7 | 76% | 14 mins 44 seconds |

Table 2.3 – Sample timing practice drills on the online platform

> Note
>
> The time limits shown in the above table are just examples. Set your own time limits with each attempt based on the time limit of the quiz on the website.

With each new attempt, your score should stay above **75%** while your "time taken" to complete should "decrease". Repeat as many attempts as you want till you feel confident dealing with the time pressure.

# 3
# Designing and Implementing the Data Exploration Layer

In *Chapter 2, Implementing a Partition Strategy*, you learned to implement a partition strategy for different types of data and workloads in Azure, how to partition files based on their format, size, and frequency of access, and how to use tools such as **Azure Data Factory** (**ADF**) and Azure Databricks to perform partitioning operations. Additionally, you learned how to partition data for Azure Synapse Analytics, a unified analytics platform that combines data warehousing and big data processing. Finally, you learned how to identify when partitioning is needed in Azure Data Lake Storage Gen2, a scalable and secure data lake service to determine the optimal partitioning strategy for your data lake.

This chapter primarily focuses on the **Design and implement the data exploration layer** topic of the **DP-203: Data Engineering on Microsoft Azure** exam and covers the techniques and technologies involved in exploring and documenting your data.

By the end of this chapter, you will be able to answer questions on the following confidently:

- SQL serverless
- Spark clusters
- Azure Synapse Analytics database templates
- Pushing data lineage to Microsoft Purview
- Metadata in the Microsoft Purview data catalog

Now it is time to delve into the topics. Before proceedings, review the technical requirements.

## Technical Requirements

For this chapter, you will need an Azure account (free or paid).

## Introduction to Data Exploration

Data exploration is often the first step needed in designing and developing a data warehouse solution, as it allows you to grasp the nature of your raw data and plan for the transformations needed. To explore your data effectively, you need to know not only what your data contains but also how the data is organized and stored. You also need to know what tools and methods you can use to access and analyze your data. This is why you need a **data catalog**. A data catalog is a document that describes the sources, locations, formats, and features of your data, helping you to find, know, and use your data consistently and efficiently.

Later in the data exploration process, making changes to the structure of a table in a data source, for instance, will require knowing what tasks and data structures will be impacted by this change. This refers to modifications made to the way data is organized within your Database or Data Warehouse and this could involve actions such as the following:

- **Adding or removing columns**: Adding new fields can help you store additional information. You can remove existing fields that are no longer needed.

- **Modifying data types**: Sometimes, you may need to change the data type of a column to better accommodate the type of data being stored or to improve efficiency.

- **Renaming tables or columns**: Renaming tables or columns can help improve clarity and consistency within the database schema.

- **Changing relationships**: If your data model includes relationships between tables, then modifying these relationships may be necessary to reflect changes in business requirements.

- **Restructuring indexes**: You can use indexes to optimize query performance. Adjusting or adding indexes may be necessary to improve the efficiency of data retrieval.

Also, you need a tool to visualize the data lineage. Finally, you need to verify and document data compliance with the rules and regulations pertinent to your business sector, company policies, and geopolitical area.

Many tools in Azure can help you with these tasks, but in this chapter, you will focus on Synapse Analytics for data exploration and Microsoft Purview for documentation and compliance.

## SQL Serverless and Spark Clusters

Data exploration often consists of running a series of queries against raw data to grasp its structure and content, keeping in mind the need to plan the transformations required to make it feasible for data analysis. Azure offers many tools that can be used for this purpose, particularly **Synapse Analytics Serverless SQL pool** and the various implementations of Apache Spark, such as **Synapse Spark** and **Databricks**.

> **Note**
>
> This section primarily focuses on the **Creating and executing queries by using a compute solution that leverages SQL serverless and Spark cluster** topic of the DP-203: Data Engineering on Microsoft Azure exam.

Starting with Synapse Analytics Serverless pool, the easiest way to introduce the Serverless SQL pool is by comparing and contrasting it with the other options available in Synapse to run SQL pools – for example, **dedicated SQL pools**. The SQL server instances consist of clusters (**pool** and **cluster** can be considered synonyms, with Synapse preferring the first and Databricks preferring the second), and these clusters of SQL Server instances need to be explicitly created with a pre-allocated set of resources that will be consistently available, which will be billed regardless of whether or not they are actually used.

The advantage is the predictability of performance, with the obvious disadvantage being a lack of flexibility, particularly in terms of "billing." If you create a dedicated SQL pool, it is important that you remember to pause it when those resources are not needed to avoid incurring potentially very high costs. Conversely, having dedicated resources not only means predictable performance but also permanent storage. Dedicated SQL pools are the only Synapse SQL pools that can hold a physical database, and hence, they are normally used to provide the **serving layer**.

In the case of the **exploration** layer (the subject of this chapter), however, all this predictability of performance and permanence of storage is not really required. Indeed, data exploration is an activity that is normally performed only once at the start of a data engineering project, requiring a one-off spike in the demand for resources and producing results that are often interactively observed by the data engineer and acted upon straight away, instead of being stored permanently.

Synapse Analytics offers its serverless SQL pool to provide this flexibility. The shift from the plural "pools" to the singular "pool" was not by chance; in a Synapse workspace, there is exactly one "built-in" serverless pool, and only that. This is because creating new ones or deleting the existing ones would not make any sense, as no resource is ever permanently allocated or deallocated. The only thing you will need to do is write your query, specifying that you want to run it on the **built-in pool**, and Synapse will automatically allocate resources for it, deallocating them at the end of the query executions.

Consequently, the cost will also be exclusively based on "consume." The main limitation is that no data can be stored in a serverless pool, but it can be used to store a logical database. A **logical database** stores views and external tables, providing access to data that is physically stored somewhere else, such as a dedicated SQL pool, an external database, or a data lake. The data lake example shown in *Figure 3.1* is particularly pertinent to the case of data exploration. Usually, the data lake is where you store the raw data that you need to explore in terms of the content and structure of its files.

To see this for yourself, create an external table from within the Synapse SQL query editor that points to the **Parquet** files on the Azure Storage.

> **Note**
>
> Parquet is an open source type of storage format that is built to handle large amounts of data. It's great for saving space and making data queries run quickly. Instead of arranging your data in rows, Parquet puts it in columns, which helps to shrink the size of the data and makes it faster to complete the search. This is especially useful for tasks where you analyze lots of data and need quick results.
>
> You can learn more about the Parquet file format at `https://packt.link/wXDPb`.

*Figure 3.1* shows an example of creating an external table:

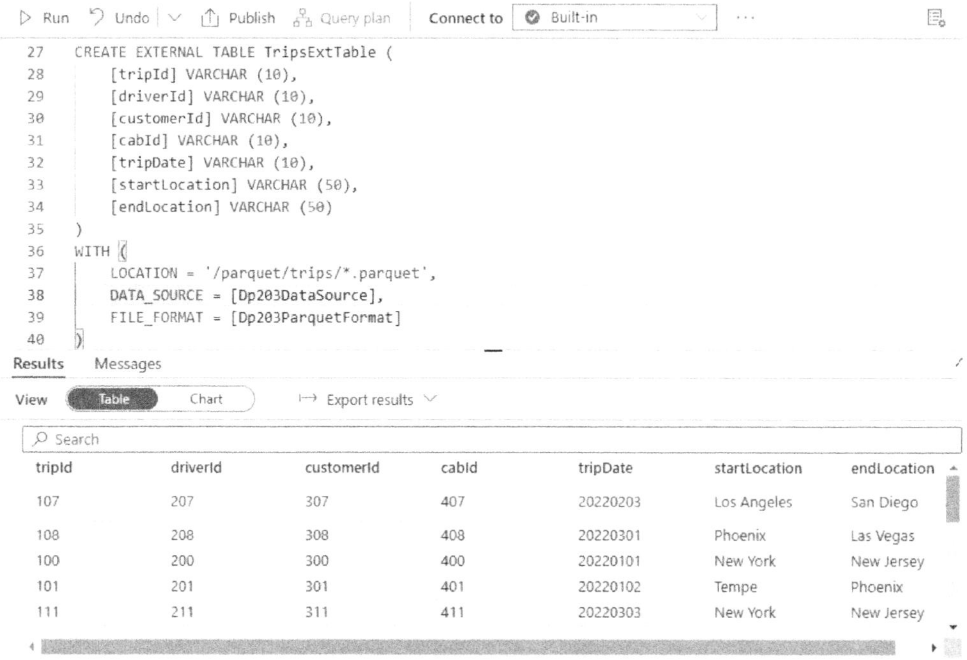

Figure 3.1 – Creating a SQL pool external table

> **Note**
>
> You can find the complete code in the accompanying GitHub repository at `https://packt.link/tluGE`.

Now, run a sample query to see how it works – for example, how a BI tool would access this data. Now learn how BI tools work.

## BI Tools

Imagine you have got a gold mine of data but need to figure out where the gold is – that's where BI tools come in. BI tools are like the high-tech gear that helps you dig through mountains of information to find valuable insights. These tools collect and tidy up data from different places, analyze it to spot trends and peculiarities, and then turn all those numbers and stats into cool charts and graphs so that you can see what's happening at a glance. In short, BI tools are uniquely effective in enabling businesses to make sense of their data and make impactful decisions.

*Figure 3.2* shows the number of trips per location from the data loaded in *Figure 3.1* and displays it as a chart:

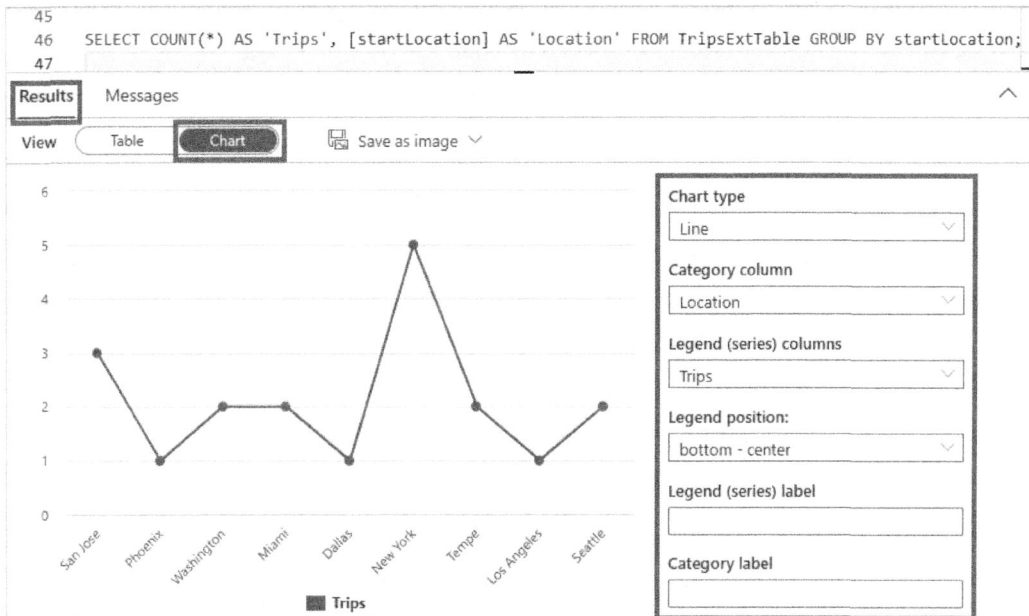

Figure 3.2 – Sample query on Parquet data visualized as a chart

To view charts, select the `Chart` option in the **Results** screen. Synapse SQL provides several options to configure the charts. The right-hand side of *Figure 3.2* shows the following options:

- **Chart type**
- **Category column**
- **Legend (series) columns**
- **Legend position**
- **Legend (series) label**
- **Category label**

As you can see, reading and serving data from Parquet files is as simple as defining an external table and querying it.

> **Note**
>
> You can learn more about using external tables in Synapse SQL at `https://packt.link/u1gTz`.

The other main option for data exploration is offered by the multiple implementations of Azure's **Synapse Spark**, which is an open source architecture for clustering. As is always the case with open source, you can choose between running your own implementation, such as on Azure **Virtual Machines** (**VMs**), or relying on a commercial product built on top of the open source architecture, which offers you support, a level of service agreement, and a more user-friendly interface.

If you opt for the latter option, in Azure you can choose between **HDInsight**, **Databricks**, and **Synapse Spark**, which is an "implementation of Spark" available as part of Synapse Analytics. Regardless of the product you choose, using **Spark** means first creating a cluster and secondly running a notebook written in Python, Scala, or SQL (plus R in the case of Databricks and C# in the case of Synapse Spark).

Now, it is time to try the same set of tasks you accomplished through serverless SQL pools, but this time executed utilizing Spark, first on Synapse and then on Databricks.

## Synapse Spark

In a Synapse Spark Notebook, you can read Parquet files using the following command:

```
spark.read.load('path/to/parquet/files', format='Parquet')
```

*Figure 3.3* shows an example of using Spark to query Parquet files:

```
1    df = spark.read.load('abfss://                    .dfs.core.windows.net/parquet/trips/*.parquet'
2        format='parquet')
3    spark.sql("CREATE DATABASE IF NOT EXISTS TripsDatabase")
4    df.write.mode("overwrite").option("overwriteSchema", "true").saveAsTable("TripsTable")
5    sqldf = spark.sql("""
6        SELECT COUNT(*) AS Trips,
7        startLocation AS Location
8        FROM TripsTable
9        GROUP BY startLocation """)
10   display(sqldf)
```

✓ 3 min 54 sec - Apache Spark session started in 2 min 58 sec 614 ms. Command executed in 55 sec 882 ms by newton.pac...

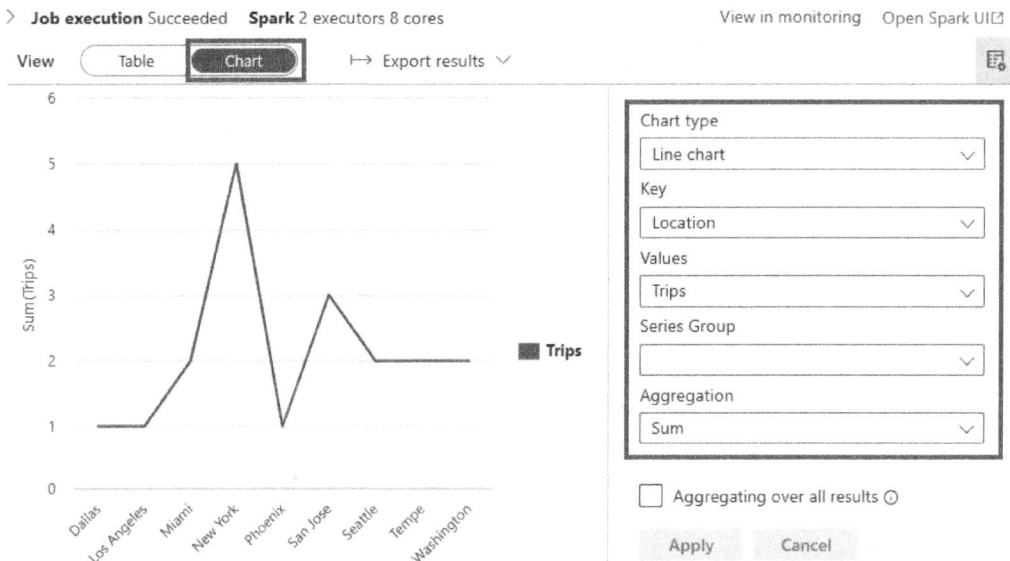

Figure 3.3 – Using Spark to query Parquet files

Spark also provides charting options (such as the one shown for Synapse SQL). These include the following, as shown on the right-hand side of *Figure 3.3*:

- **Chart type**
- **Key**
- **Values**
- **Series Group**
- **Aggregation**

The next section will explore how you can accomplish the same using Azure Databricks.

## Azure Databricks

Azure Databricks is a fast, easy, and collaborative Apache Spark-based analytics platform optimized for Azure. Azure Databricks is a cloud-based big data and analytics service provider by Microsoft Azure, developed in collaboration with Databricks. Azure Databricks combines the capabilities of Apache Spark and Databricks to help users with data engineering and data science tasks.

Before you explore and run the queries (the set of tasks you completed with serverless SQL pool and Synapse Spark) on Azure Databricks, you must first create an Azure Databricks service and a Spark cluster in Azure Databricks.

### Azure Databricks Service

Creating an **Azure Databricks service** is a prerequisite to running queries. An **Azure Databricks service** establishes the foundation for your Data Analytics workflows and provides the necessary infrastructure, management tools, and collaborative features required to effectively run your queries, analyze data, and derive insights from your datasets. Without this service, your ability to work with data at scale and leverage the capabilities of Spark would be significantly limited.

Perform the following steps to create an Azure Databricks service using the Azure portal:

4.   From the Azure portal menu, select + `Create a resource`, as shown in *Figure 3.4*:

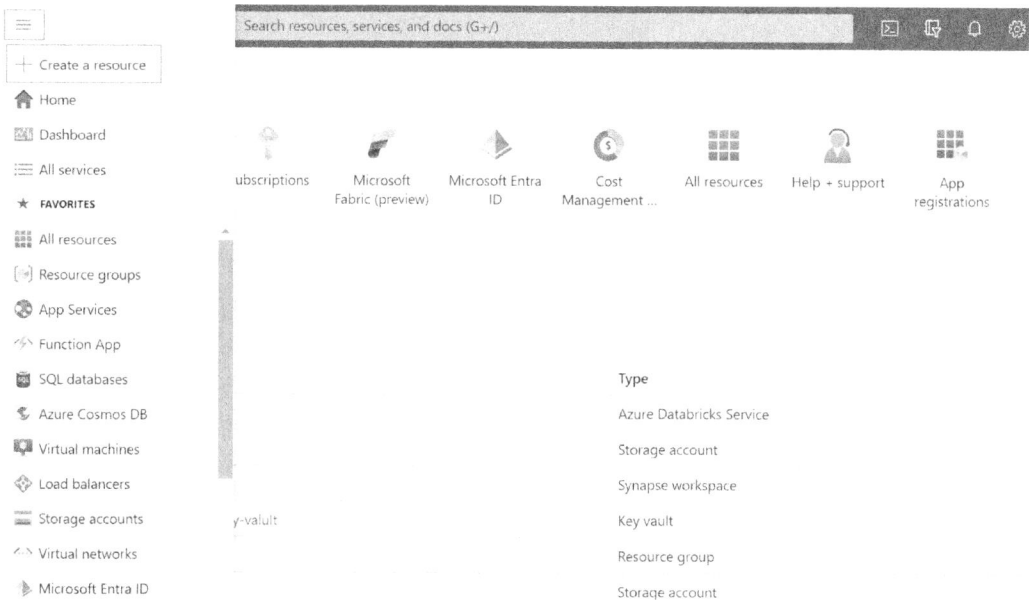

Figure 3.4 – Creating a resource in the Azure portal

5.   Select `Analytics`.

6.  Choose `Azure Databricks`, as shown in *Figure 3.5*:

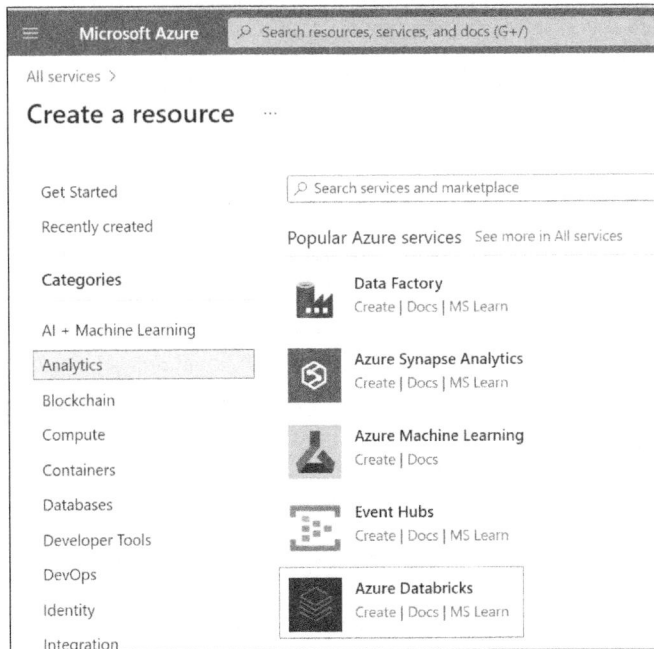

Figure 3.5 – Azure Databricks resource creation

7.  Create an Azure Databricks workspace by choosing the property. *Table 3.1* shows the description of each property:

| Property | Description |
| --- | --- |
| **Subscription** | From the dropdown, select your Azure subscription. In this case, it is `Azure subscription`. |
| **Resource group** | Specify whether you want to create a new resource group or use an existing one. For instance, here a new resource group is created, `rg-dp203-databricks`. |
| **Workspace name** | Provide a name for your Databricks workspace – for example, `DP-203-databricks-workspace`. |
| **Region** | From the list of available regions in the dropdown, select the region where you want to deploy your Databricks workspace. For instance, here the region chosen is `UK South`. |
| **Pricing tier** | From the dropdown, select the pricing tier for your workspace based on your needs. For example, here the Pricing tier chosen is `Standard (Apache Spark, Secure with Microsoft Entra ID)`. |

Table 3.1 – Describing each property in the Azure Databricks workspace

*Figure 3.6* shows how to create an Azure Databricks workspace with the preceding properties entered:

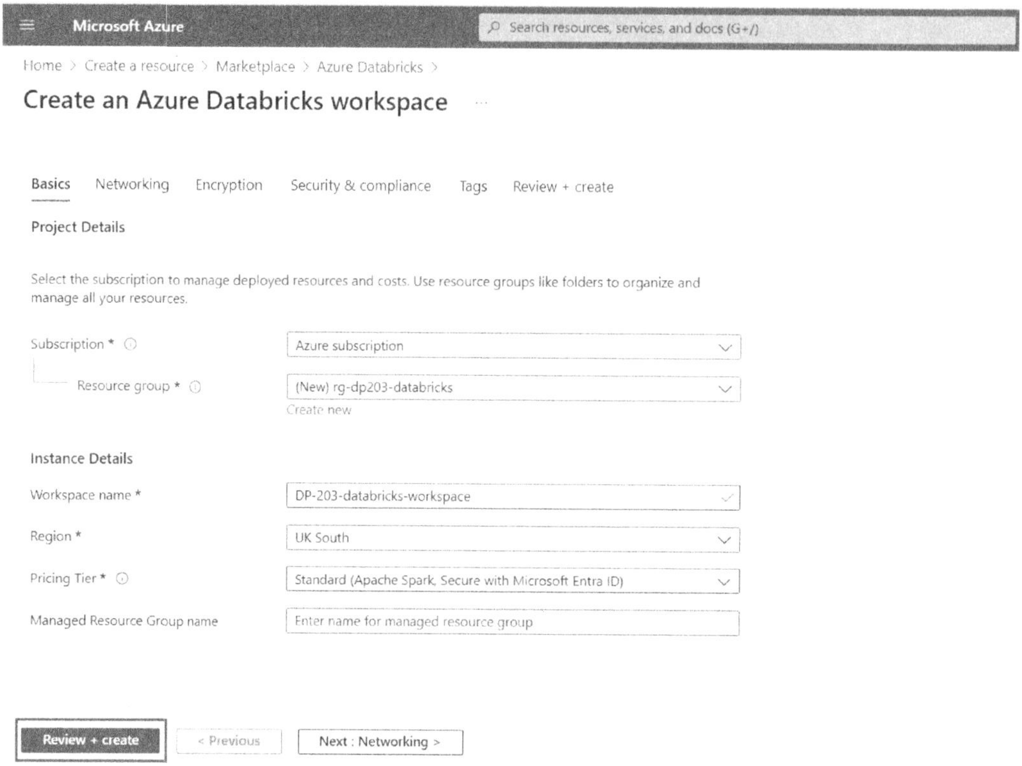

Figure 3.6 – Creating an Azure Databricks workspace

8.  Once you have provided the required property values, click Review + create to create the workspace in the Azure Databricks service.

*Table 3.2* provides a brief overview of the Azure Databricks pricing tiers that cater to various use cases and requirements. You can choose the Pricing tier for your workspace based on your needs.

| Feature | Standard tier | Premium tier |
| --- | --- | --- |
| Suitability | General-purpose workloads | The workloads require enhanced security and compliance |
| Apache Spark | Included | Included |
| Job scheduling | With libraries and notebooks | With libraries and notebooks |
| Azure integration | Yes | Yes |

| Feature | Standard tier | Premium tier |
|---|---|---|
| Databricks Delta | Not included | Included |
| Interactive clusters | Not included | Included |
| Collaboration tools | Not included | It has notebooks, collaboration, and ecosystem integrations |
| Security and compliance | Basic | It is enhanced, with compliance add-ons |
| Pricing (all-purpose) | $0.40 per DBU/hour | $0.55 per DBU/hour |
| Pricing (jobs compute) | $0.15 per DBU/hour | $0.30 per DBU/hour |
| Pricing (light jobs) | $0.07 per DBU/hour | $0.22 per DBU/hour |

Table 3.2 – Azure Databricks pricing tiers

> **Note**
> You can find more detailed information on Azure Databricks pricing tiers at https://packt.link/2QHYV.

With the completion of workspace creation in Azure Databricks, you are now equipped to embark on the next phase – creating a Spark cluster. This pivotal step will empower you to harness the full potential of Azure Databricks, which enables efficient data analysis. Now, move forward and dive into the exciting world of Spark cluster creation in Azure Databricks.

## Spark Cluster in Azure Databricks

After completing the creation of your workspace in Azure Databricks, the next step is to set up a cluster. A **cluster** is essential because it provides the computing resources necessary to process and analyze data within your workspace efficiently. By creating a cluster, you enable parallel processing, which allows for faster execution of tasks such as data transformations, machine learning model training, and complex analytics. In simpler terms, the cluster acts as the engine that powers your data operations. Without it, your workspace would lack the computational muscle needed to handle large datasets or perform resource-intensive tasks effectively. Therefore, setting up a cluster is a critical step in maximizing the capabilities of your Azure Databricks environment and guaranteeing optimal performance for your data processing workflows.

Perform the following steps to create a Spark cluster in Azure Databricks:

1. In the Azure portal, go to the Databricks service that you created in the previous exercise.

2. Select Launch Workspace. You will be redirected to the Azure Databricks portal.

3. From the portal, select New Cluster, as shown in *Figure 3.7*:

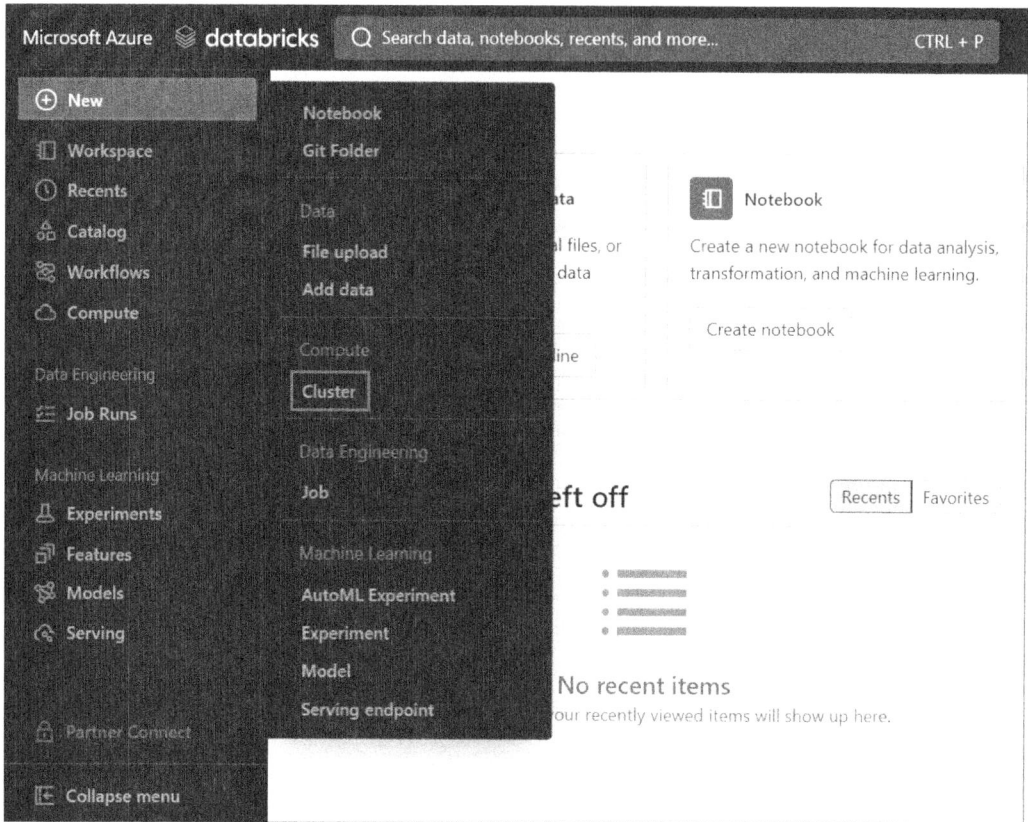

Figure 3.7 – Cluster creation in an Azure Databricks workspace

4.  On the **New Cluster** screen, provide the required property values to create a cluster. *Table 3.3* shows the description of the values:

| Property | Description |
|---|---|
| **Cluster name** | Provide the cluster name. In this case, it is DP-203 Cluster. |
| **Access mode** | From the list of available access mode options, select the access mode for how you run SQL, Python, R, and Scala workloads. In this case, it is Single user, and by default, the administrator of the account is selected. |
| **Databricks runtime version** | Select the version that will be used to create the cluster. For instance, here, the runtime version chosen is Runtime: 14.3 LTS (Scala 2.12, Spark 3.5.0). |
| **Use Photon Acceleration** | Select Photon, which accelerates modern Apache Spark, if you want to reduce your total cost per workload. Here, the checkbox is selected. |
| **Worker type** | From the list of available options, select the worker type depending on your needs. The worker type includes instance types with local **Solid Stage Drives** (**SSDs**) to take advantage of disk caching. For instance, here the worker type chosen is Standard_DS3-v2, keeping **Min workers** as 2 and **Max workers** as 8. |
| **Spot instances** | Use spot instances to save costs. If spot instances are evicted due to unavailability, on-demand instances will be deployed to replace evicted instances. Here, spot instances are not enabled. |
| **Driver type** | From the list of available options, select the driver type instance or choose the recommended type, which is the same as the worker type. For example, here the driver type chosen is Same as worker (Standard_DS3-v2 was chosen as Worker type). |
| **Enable autoscaling** | Check the Enable autoscaling option so that compute instances automatically scale between the minimum and maximum number of nodes, based on load. Here, the checkbox is selected. |
| **Terminate after** | The compute will terminate after the specified time interval of inactivity (i.e., no running commands or active job runs). This feature is best supported in the latest Spark versions and cost-saving options when you are inactive for a specified time. Here, the value input is 120. |
| **Tags** | The tags (**Vendor**, **Creator**, **ClusterName**, and **ClusterId**) are automatically added to cluster instances to track usage. Here, the Environment tag key and its development **Value** can be added. |

Table 3.3 – Property values and their description to create a cluster in the DP-203 cluster

*Figure 3.8* shows the DP-203 cluster with the preceding property values entered:

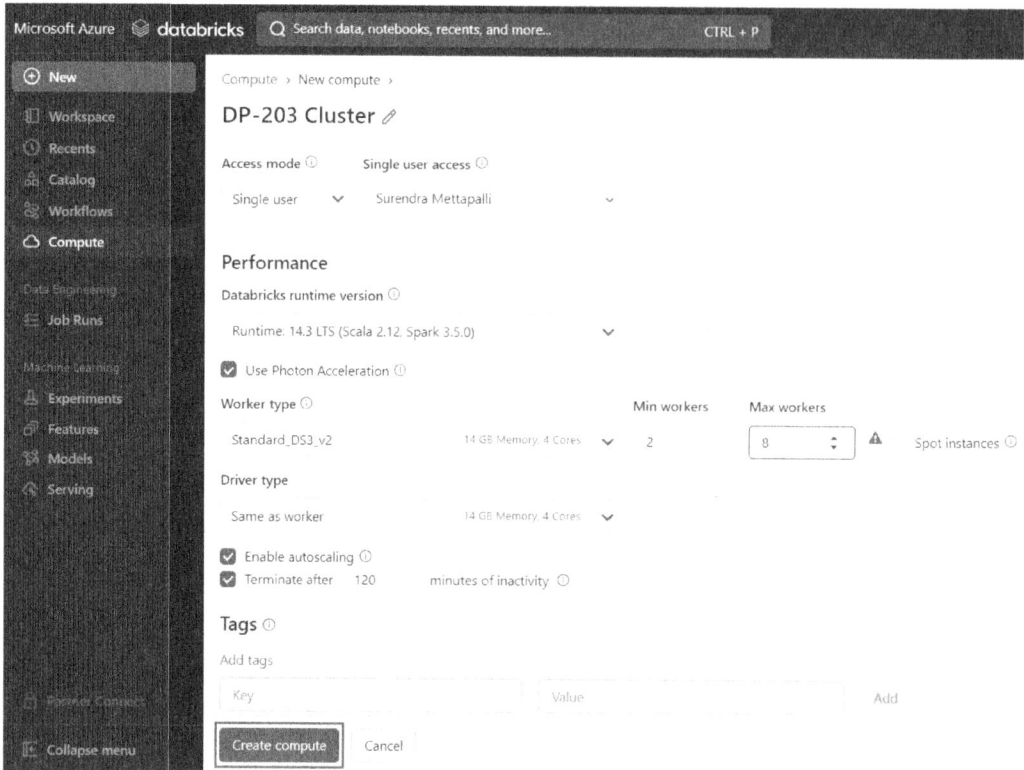

Figure 3.8 – Providing values to create a cluster in Azure Databricks

5.   Once you have provided the property values, click Create compute to create a new cluster.

Now you can explore and run your queries on an Azure Databricks workspace. Azure Databricks' Spark examples are similar to the Synapse Spark examples. In the case of Azure Databricks, you will need to define a service principal for Azure Databricks to talk to Azure Data Lake Storage Gen2.

> **Note**
>
> You can find more detailed information on setting up the service principal at `https://packt.link/avAoz`.

Once you have the cluster session ready, you can use the same Spark syntax that you used in the *Synapse Spark* section:

```
spark.read.load('path/to/parquet/files', format='Parquet')
```

*Figure 3.9* shows an example where all the contents of all the Parquet files in the `parquet/trips` folder are viewed:

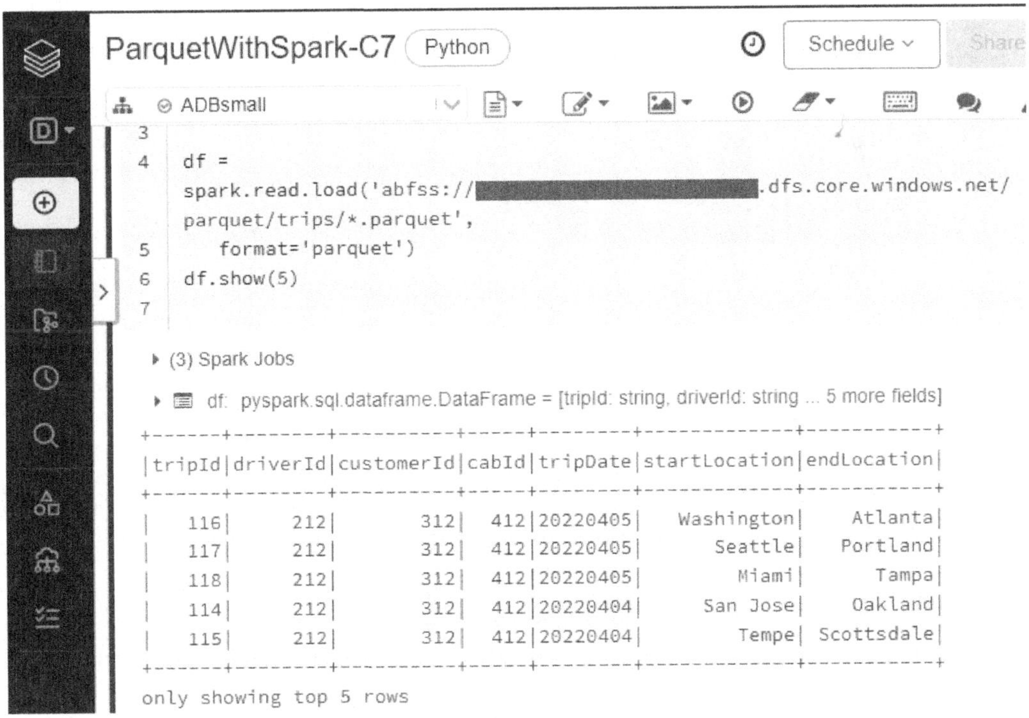

Figure 3.9 – An Azure Databricks notebook query to read Parquet files

Here is an example of the same transformation query that you ran earlier in the *Synapse Spark* section, but in Databricks (*Figure 3.10*):

```python
1   df = spark.read.load('abfss://███████████████.dfs.core.windows.net/parquet/trips/*.parquet',
2       format='parquet')
3   spark.sql("CREATE DATABASE IF NOT EXISTS TripsDatabase")
4   df.write.mode("overwrite").option("overwriteSchema", "true").saveAsTable("TripsTable")
5   sqldf = spark.sql("""
6       SELECT COUNT(*) AS Trips,
7       startLocation AS Location
8       FROM TripsTable
9       GROUP BY startLocation """)
10  display(sqldf)
```

▶ (7) Spark Jobs

▶ 🖻 df   pyspark.sql.dataframe.DataFrame = [tripId: string, driverId: string ... 5 more fields]

▶ 🖻 sqldf   pyspark.sql.dataframe.DataFrame = [Trips: long, Location: string]

Chart    Data Profile

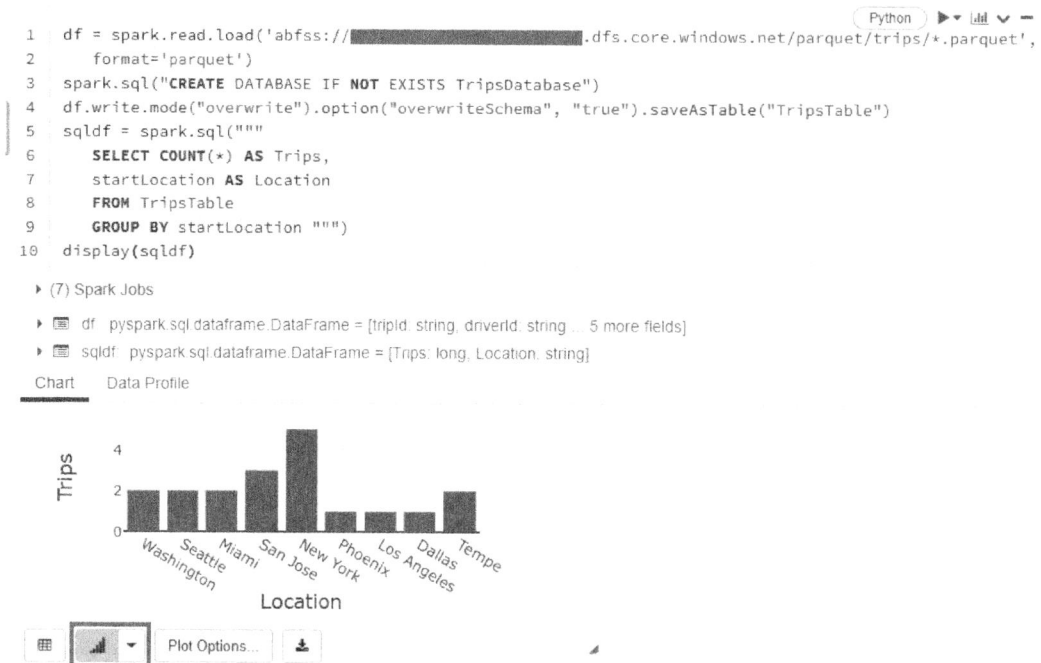

Figure 3.10 – A simple Spark query on Parquet data in Databricks

Azure Databricks also provides a rich set of charting options that can be used to visualize data. You can access the chart options by clicking on the chart icon below the results screen.

You have now explored and analyzed data in Azure using serverless SQL and Spark clusters. You learned how to query raw data, leverage Synapse Analytics (serverless & Spark), explore Parquet data, visualize insights, and set up Databricks for efficient analysis. The next section will focus on a cloud-based version of SQL Server tailored for analytical workloads.

# Azure Synapse Analytics Database Templates

**Azure Synapse Analytics** is the most feature-rich of the Azure Data Services. Its origin lies in a project once called **SQL Datawarehouse**, with its foundation rooted in the aim to deliver a cloud-based version of SQL Server tailored for analytical workloads. This is achieved primarily through strong support for clustering and the parallel execution of queries.

> **Note**
>
> This section primarily focuses on the **Recommend and implement Azure Synapse Analytics database templates** concept of the DP-203: Data Engineering on Microsoft Azure exam.

For this initial purpose of providing a cloud-based version of SQL Server specifically designed for analytical workloads, Synapse has progressively added an increasing number of features, such as support for pipelines, borrowed from **ADF** for Apache Spark, and more recently, integration with Purview, Data Explorer, and the **Kusto** query language. The impression is that Microsoft is positioning Synapse as some sort of "one-stop shop" for data services. The advantage of this type of approach is that integrating all these services becomes much "easier" when they all belong to the "same workspace." The disadvantage is that the added complexity of the platform can grow, making it more challenging for you to navigate and grasp all the available functionalities.

To compensate for this possible disadvantage, Microsoft has added a series of database templates available from Synapse. In particular, these templates can be used to create a **lake database**, in which data is stored in a data lake of text files on a storage account. There are templates available for a wide range of business sectors, such as retail or mining, and each result in the creation of a series of database objects, including **tables** and **views**. *Figure 3.11* shows the list of available templates:

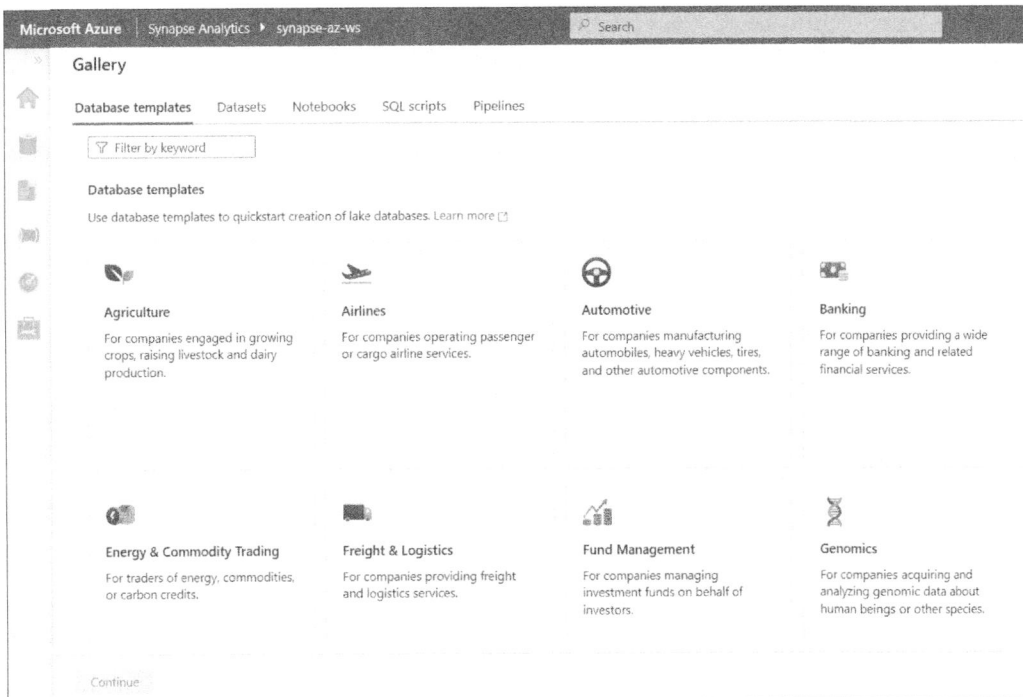

Figure 3.11 – A Synapse database showing the available templates

The concept of a lake database needs some clarification. Traditional data warehouse processes, such as **Extract, Load, and Transform (ELT)**, utilize a data lake as the destination to ingest data from multiple sources. The data lake, being file-based, format-agnostic, and easy to manage, serves as the starting point for transformations that lead to the creation of a relational data warehouse, which is typically a **relational database**.

The problem with this architecture is that the data warehouse will need to be periodically refreshed to reflect the updated content of the data lake, which might result in data statelessness between refreshes and can be very demanding in terms of resources. The alternative is to use the data lake itself as the data warehouse by adding a layer or relational tables on top of the data lake files, allowing the use of the SQL language, and considering other advantages such as support for transactions.

Creating external tables in Synapse Analytics is an example of adding a relational table-type of approach, but it requires the data lake and its files to already be in place. With the more recent addition of lake database templates, however, users can create the data lake structure and the external tables associated with them at the same time. You can choose a template and specify which of the tables from that template you want to use, and the system then creates the files and tables for you.

The following is an example that demonstrates how to incorporate a lake database template into your workspace:

1. Navigate to the **Gallery** screen, as shown in *Figure 3.11*, and select the database templates.

2. Within the Gallery, choose the `Airlines` and `Banking` templates to accelerate the setup of your lake databases.

3. Once selected, click on `Create database`. These databases will be readily available in your workspace, conveniently listed under the section titled **Lake databases**.

4. *Figure 3.12* shows the list of lake database templates that you created:

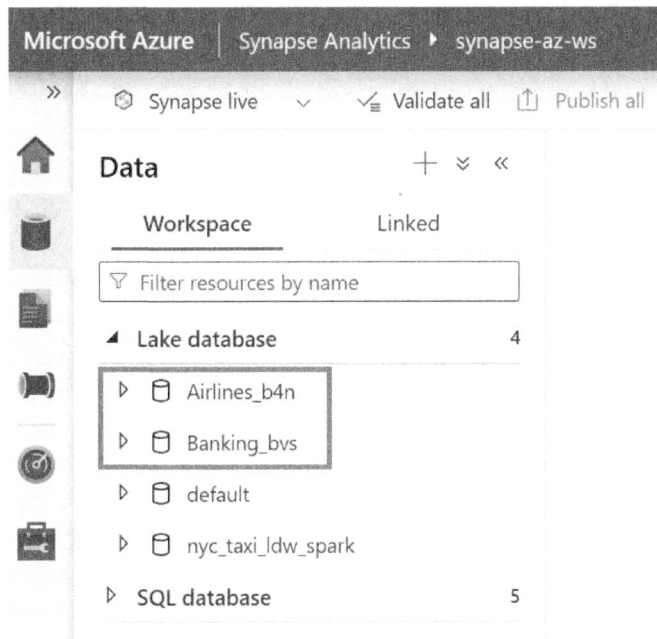

Figure 3.12 – The Synapse workspace showing the lake database templates

Now that you have created a lake database, you will learn how to push new or updated data lineage to Microsoft Purview.

# Microsoft Purview

**Microsoft Purview** is the most recently added service covered by the DP-203 exam. Its focus is on data documentation, particularly to verify and enforce regulatory compliance.

---

**Note**

This section primarily focuses on the **Push new or updated data lineage to Microsoft Purview** concept of the DP-203: Data Engineering on Microsoft Azure exam.

---

Even if you are not interested or involved in compliance, having a centralized place to collect and access information about your data services can offer other important advantages. A particularly important one is the ability to track **data lineage** – "what depends on what." For instance, you might have developed a Data Factory pipeline that "copies" files from a **data lake**, which then calls a **Spark notebook** that creates "staging tables" in a Synapse Analytics dedicated **SQL pool**, which then calls a **data flow** that calculates aggregations and stores them in another dedicated SQL pool. The danger of such a distributed system is losing track of this tree of dependency. Microsoft Purview can help document this tree of dependencies, thereby minimizing the risk of breaking it by mistake.

> **Note**
> Microsoft Purview was added to the scope of the exam in the February 2023 update.

The first step to leverage Microsoft Purview to document the tree of dependencies in the distributed system, after creating an instance of Microsoft Purview within your subscription, is to register your data sources in the service instance's **Data Map**. Just like with other forms of service registration, the type of information needed will depend on the type of data source. Registering a database service such as Azure SQL, for instance, will require connection details and credentials, while registering a file will require indicating its path and structure. This and the following tasks are all performed using a tool called the **Microsoft Purview governance portal**, which can be opened from the **Overview** panel of the service instance. *Figure 3.13* shows the registration window for a Synapse workspace:

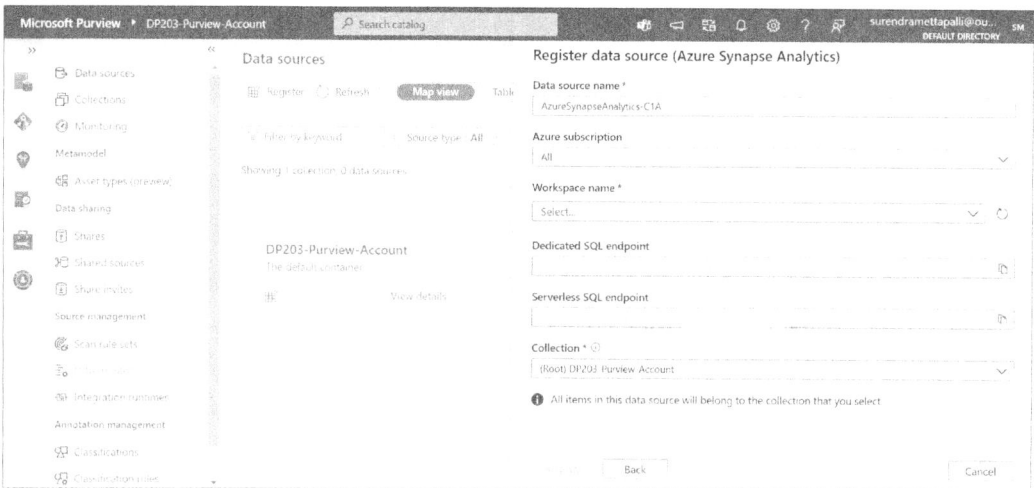

Figure 3.13 – Registering a data source in the Microsoft Purview governance portal

When the registration is successful, a Data Map is updated. *Figure 3.14* shows an example of a Data Map with two registered resources – a **Synapse workspace** and a **Storage Account Gen2 data lake**:

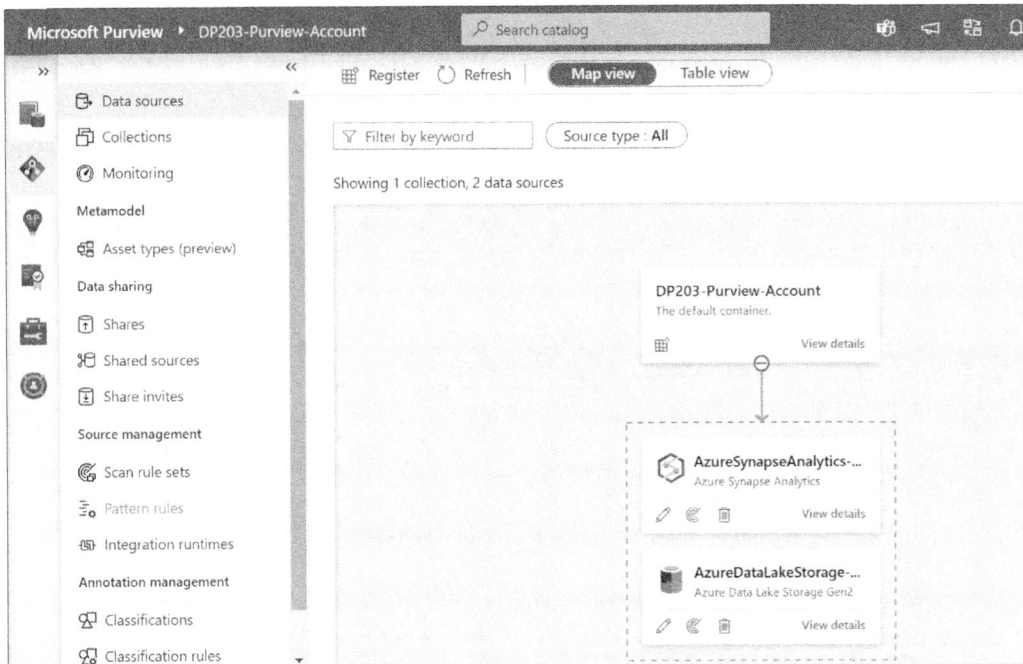

Figure 3.14 – Visualizing a Data Map in a Synapse workspace and Data Lake Storage Gen2 Account

Note, however, that the granularity of the information collected and displayed so far as part of the Data Map is limited to the data sources in their totality, which are still black boxes with regards to their content, and so the next step will be to perform a scan of these data sources. Scans can be scheduled and executed according to either the default **scan rule** set for that data source or according to a user-created rule set, specifying, for instance, the file types and the paths that you want to include when scanning a storage account.

The assets discovered by this scan will then appear in the data catalog after the scanning is successful. If the scanning is unsuccessful, the most common source of problems is probably permissions. If you want Purview to be able to scan the content of a Blob container in a storage account, for example, you will need to assign the **Storage Blob Data Reader** role for that account to your instance of Purview. However, if you want it to be able to scan the content of a **Synapse Analytics workspace**, you will need to assign the Reader role.

Using **Role Based Access Control (RBAC)** in the latter case is not enough, however, as Synapse Analytics uses a **hybrid authentication** model that also relies on **SQL authentication** (that is, on users and roles stored in the security tables in that specific workspace). As an example, if you want your Purview instance to be able to scan the contents of a dedicated SQL pool, you will have to create a SQL authentication user for it to impersonate and add it to the predefined db_datareader SQL authentication role.

If you manage to satisfy these requirements and run the scan successfully, you can select one of the assets discovered and click on the **Lineage** tab. This will provide a visual representation of what other assets within the catalog this asset depends on and what other assets, in turn, depend on it, with lines and arrows representing these dependencies. An example of data lineage for a Power BI asset in this specific case is shown in *Figure 3.15*:

Figure 3.15 – An example of data lineage for Power BI

One important aspect of this lineage service offered by Microsoft Purview is the ability to track new dependencies, provided that they appear within the boundaries of the Data Map. For example, if the Data Map contains a reference to a workspace of Synapse Analytics and a new pipeline is created on this workspace with a reference to a **CSV file** that is also part of the Data Map, the next time the lineage is displayed for this file, the new pipeline will appear in the diagram, with a line indicating that the pipeline depends on the CSV file. For this feature to work, however, the instance of Purview also needs to be registered within the Synapse workspace, by means of the **Manage hub** in Synapse Studio.

## Searching Feature in Microsoft Purview Data Catalog

In the previous section, you briefly reviewed the Microsoft Purview data catalog from the point of view of tracing and tracking dependencies between assets.

> **Note**
>
> This section primarily focuses on the **Browse and search metadata in Microsoft Purview Data Catalog** concept of the DP-203: Data Engineering on Microsoft Azure exam.

Following the structure of the DP-203 exam documentation, you will now add an additional aspect, specifically referencing the utilization of the search feature. Indeed, creating a potentially vast **data catalog of objects** is only helpful if searching across it is made significantly easier than it would be to browse for the file or data source itself on your network or cloud. For this purpose, note a search box, similar to the Azure portal search box, at the top of the data catalog where users can not only type asset names (or part of them) but also data types, classification labels, and glossary terms. Once the list of results is returned, you can then refine it by using both facets and filters.

## Refining Search Results Using Facets and Filters

One way of refining results is offered by facets on the left-hand side of the results list, as shown in *Figure 3.16*:

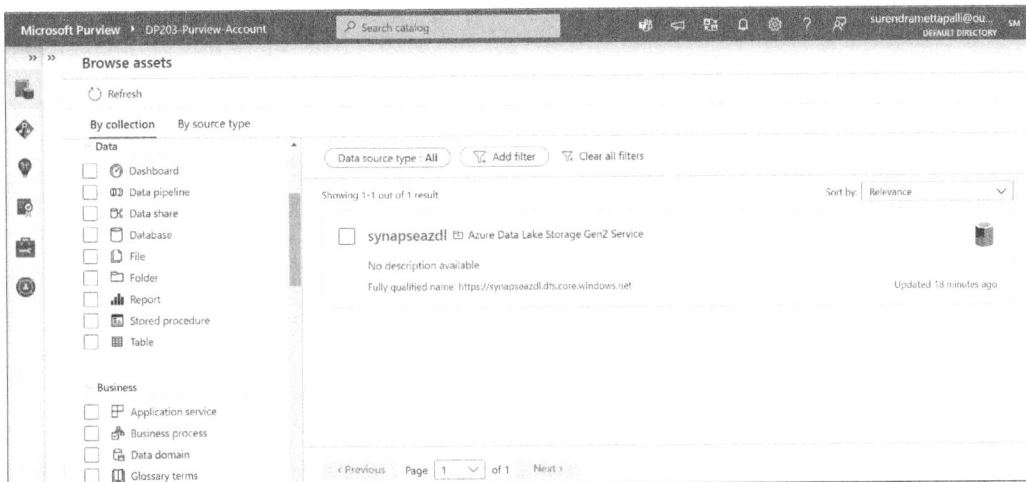

Figure 3.16 – Filtering search results with facets

The results can be filtered by **data object type**, such as table, stored procedure, or pipeline. Another way they can be filtered is by the **organization** or **department** they belong to, the **business object** they represent (**Product** or **Process**, for instance), and any **label** or **classification** that was previously assigned to them. This allows the **data catalog** to be used as an effective database of metadata. As with any database, the quality and effectiveness of the search depend on the quality and extensiveness of the indexing. However, the very possibility of running this type of search should stimulate better practices in cataloging and documenting data objects.

Further filters can be applied based on the creation or update time of the objects and on the tags assigned to them. For instance, tags can classify resources according to the development stage environment (Dev, Test, or Prod, for instance). *Figure 3.17* shows how a filter is created to include only the assets created within the last 24 hours:

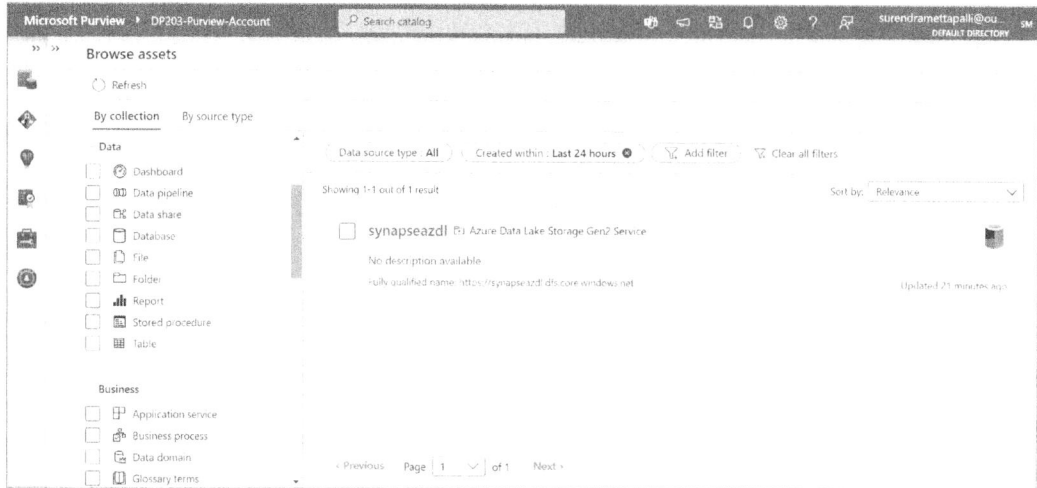

Figure 3.17 – Filtering search results with date filters

Thus, Microsoft Purview search simplifies data discovery by quickly finding relevant assets and revealing details about their structure, metadata, and origin.

In this section, you learned to leverage Microsoft Purview effectively with the first step being to register data sources in its Data Map, providing necessary connection details or paths along with permissions for roles like Storage Blob Data Reader or db_datareader. You then progressed towards cataloging the assets so that the data lineage could be visualized for knowing the dependencies between assets in addition to integration with other services like Synapse Analytics to further enhance its capabilities, facilitate seamless data lineage tracking across Azure services.

You explored the search feature in Microsoft Purview data catalog to find out how it simplifies data discovery by quickly locating relevant assets and providing details about their structure, metadata, and origin, and how results can be further refined using facets and filters, enabling users to narrow down results based on object type, organization, business object representation, classification labels, creation/update time, and tags.

# Summary

This chapter helped you to develop your expertise in navigating **Azure Data Services** effectively, such as mastering queries with Serverless SQL and Spark clusters and utilizing Azure Synapse Analytics templates for efficient database management, enabling you to focus on data analysis. Additionally, it emphasized the importance of keeping track of data lineage with Microsoft Purview to know about data's origins, transformation, and destination, ensuring transparency and traceability. Furthermore, you now have a sound knowledge of exploring and managing metadata, making it easier for you to locate and govern your datasets using the Microsoft Purview data catalog.

All these topics complete the syllabus for DP203 – **Design and implement the data exploration layer**, and with the completion of this chapter, you have now learned how to design your own serving layer in Azure.

In *Chapter 4, Ingesting and Transforming Data*, you will develop data processing systems that include reading data using different file formats, encoding, performing data cleansing, handling duplicate and missing data, error handling, and running transformations using services such as Spark, SQL, ADF, and Azure Synapse Analytics.

# Exam Readiness Drill – Chapter Review Questions

Apart from a solid understanding of key concepts, being able to think quickly under time pressure is a skill that will help you ace your certification exam. That is why working on these skills early on in your learning journey is key.

Chapter review questions are designed to improve your test-taking skills progressively with each chapter you learn and review your understanding of key concepts in the chapter at the same time. You'll find these at the end of each chapter.

> **How to Access These Materials**
>
> To learn how to access these resources, head over to the chapter titled *Chapter 11, Accessing the Online Resources*.

To open the Chapter Review Questions for this chapter, perform the following steps:

1.  Click the link – `https://packt.link/DP203E2_CH03`.

    Alternatively, you can scan the following **QR code** (*Figure 3.18*):

Figure 3.18 – QR code that opens Chapter Review Questions for logged-in users

2.  Once you log in, you'll see a page similar to the one shown in *Figure 3.19*:

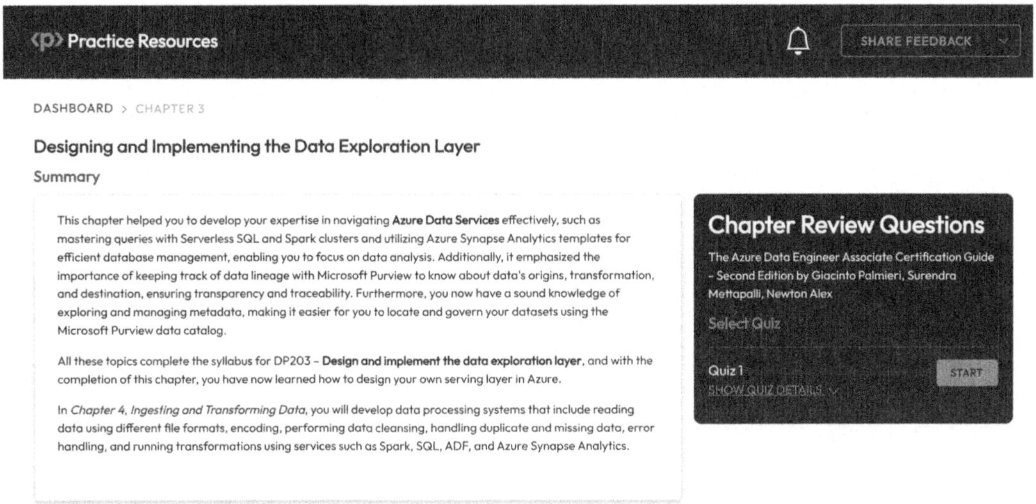

Figure 3.19 – Chapter Review Questions for Chapter 3

3.  Once ready, start the following practice drills, re-attempting the quiz multiple times.

## Exam Readiness Drill

For the first three attempts, don't worry about the time limit.

### ATTEMPT 1

The first time, aim for at least **40%**. Look at the answers you got wrong and read the relevant sections in the chapter again to fix your learning gaps.

## ATTEMPT 2

The second time, aim for at least **60%**. Look at the answers you got wrong and read the relevant sections in the chapter again to fix any remaining learning gaps.

## ATTEMPT 3

The third time, aim for at least **75%**. Once you score 75% or more, you start working on your timing.

> **Tip**
> You may take more than **three** attempts to reach 75%. That's okay. Just review the relevant sections in the chapter till you get there.

# Working On Timing

**Target**: Your aim is to keep the score the same while trying to answer these questions as quickly as possible. Here's an example of how your next attempts should look like:

| Attempt | Score | Time Taken |
| --- | --- | --- |
| Attempt 5 | 77% | 21 mins 30 seconds |
| Attempt 6 | 78% | 18 mins 34 seconds |
| Attempt 7 | 76% | 14 mins 44 seconds |

Table 3.4 – Sample timing practice drills on the online platform

> **Note**
> The time limits shown in the above table are just examples. Set your own time limits with each attempt based on the time limit of the quiz on the website.

With each new attempt, your score should stay above **75%** while your "time taken" to complete should "decrease". Repeat as many attempts as you want till you feel confident dealing with the time pressure.

# Part 3:
# Data Processing

In the dynamic landscape of data engineering, efficient data processing lies at the heart of success. Whether you're a seasoned professional or just embarking on your data journey, the **Develop Data Processing** domain in the **DP-203: Data Engineering on Microsoft Azure** exam is your gateway to unlocking powerful skills.

In this domain, you will explore various aspects of data processing and pipeline management in Azure. This includes knowing about different methods for data ingestion into Azure Data Services, utilizing Azure tools to transform raw data into suitable formats for analysis, and integrating data from diverse sources and formats into a coherent data store. Additionally, you will explore batch processing concepts and their relevance in data engineering, a knowledge of which will enable you to leverage Azure services such as **Azure Data Factory (ADF)** and **Azure Databricks (ADB)** to design efficient and scalable batch processing pipelines according to best practices.

You will also delve into stream processing fundamentals and real-time data handling, implementing stream processing using **Azure Stream Analytics** and **Azure Event Hubs** for processing streaming data and performing real-time analytics to derive actionable insights. Furthermore, you will learn how to orchestrate and manage data pipelines, ensuring smooth data flow and processing while implementing strategies for monitoring batch and stream processing pipelines to maintain optimal performance and troubleshoot common issues to ensure reliability and efficiency.

This section of the book comprises the following chapters:

- *Chapter 4, Ingesting and Transforming Data*
- *Chapter 5, Developing a Batch Processing Solution*
- *Chapter 6, Developing a Stream Processing Solution*
- *Chapter 7, Managing Batches and Pipelines*

# 4

# Ingesting and Transforming Data

Welcome to the next major section of the book. In *Chapter 3*, *Designing and Implementing Data Exploration Layer*, you learned about implementing the serving layer and saw how data is shared between services such as **Synapse SQL** and **Spark**.

In this chapter, you will focus on designing and developing data processing systems. This will include an examination of **data transformation**—that is, the process of transforming your data from its raw format to a more useful format that can be used by downstream tools and projects utilizing services such as Spark, SQL, and **Azure Data Factory** (**ADF**), reading data using different file formats and encodings, and data cleansing.

> **Note**
> This chapter primarily focuses on the **Ingest and transform** topic within **Develop data processing** concept of the DP-203: Data Engineering on Microsoft Azure exam.

By the end of this chapter, you will be able to answer questions on the following confidently:

- Incremental loads and Apache Spark Transact-SQL
- Azure Synapse Pipelines or Azure Data Factory
- Stream Analytics
- Cleansing data, and handling duplicate, missing , and late-arriving data
- Splitting data and shredding JSON
- Encoding and decoding data
- Error handling for a transformation
- Normalizing and denormalizing values, data exploratory analysis

It is now time to learn about incremental loads. But first, you must know the technical requirements.

## Technical Requirements

For this chapter, you will need an Azure account (free or paid), an active Synapse workspace, and an active ADF workspace.

It is time to get started on the process of implementing incremental loads.

## Designing and Implementing Incremental Loads

**Incremental loading** (or **delta loading**) refers to the process of loading smaller increments of data into a storage solution. For example, you could have daily data that is being loaded into a data lake or hourly data flowing into an **Extract, Transform, Load** (**ETL**) pipeline, and so on. During data-ingestion scenarios, it is very common to do a bulk upload followed by scheduled incremental loads.

> **Note**
> This section primarily focuses on the **Design and implement incremental loads** concept of the DP-203: Data Engineering on Microsoft Azure exam.

Azure has a very versatile service called **ADF**, which can help with incremental loading. Since this is the first time you are using ADF in this book, you need to learn a little more about it now, as the information will come in handy in future chapters.

ADF is a managed cloud service that can be used to coordinate and orchestrate complex cloud- or hybrid- (a mixture of cloud and on-premises) based pipelines. ADF allows you to build **ETL** and **Extract, Load, Transform** (**ELT**) pipelines through the following tasks:

- Ingesting data from a wide variety of sources such as databases, file shares, **Internet of Things** (**IoT**) hubs, **Amazon Web Services** (**AWS**), **Google Cloud Platform** (**GCP**), and more

- Building complex pipelines using variables, parameters, branches, and so on

- Transforming data by using compute services such as Synapse, HDInsight, Cosmos DB, and so on

- Scheduling and monitoring ingestions, control flow, and data flow operations

The ADF workspace looks as follows:

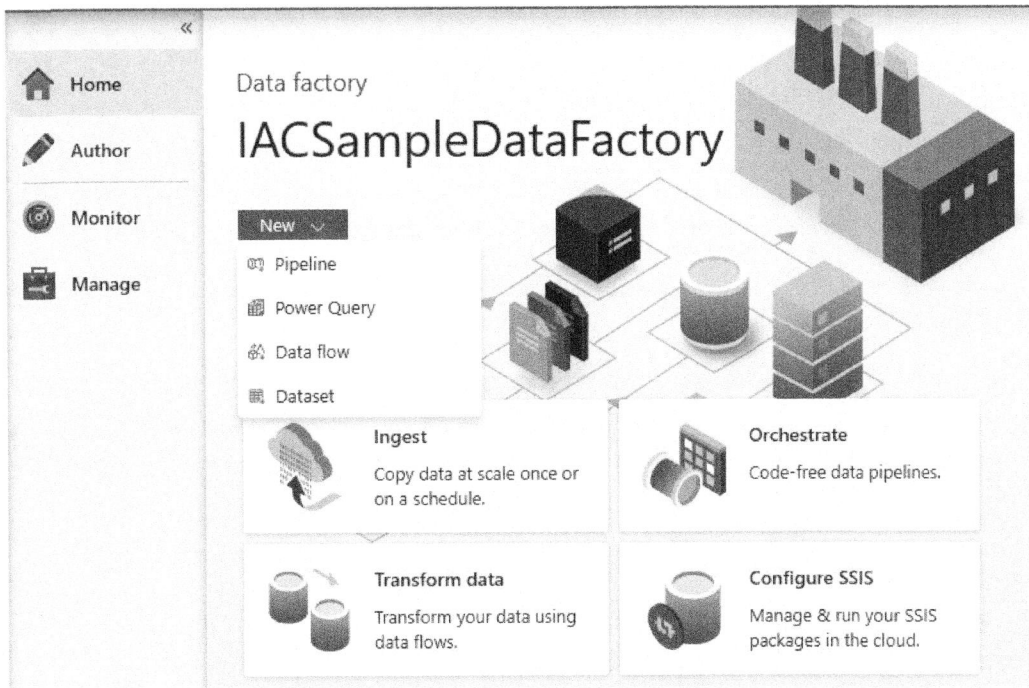

Figure 4.1 – The Data factory workspace landing screen showing a range of ADF activities

ADF is built of a basic set of components, the most important of which are the following:

- **Pipelines**: A pipeline is a collection of activities that are linked together to perform some control flow or data transformation.

- **Activities**: Activities in ADF refer to steps in the pipeline, such as copying data and running a Spark job.

- **Datasets**: This is the data that your pipelines or activities operate on.

- **Linked services**: Linked services are connections that are utilized by ADF to link with a variety of data stores and resources in Azure. They are like connection strings that let you access data from external sources.

> **Note**
>
> Connection strings will be discussed in *Chapter 5*, *Developing a Batch Processing Solution*.

- **Triggers**: Triggers are events used to start pipelines or activities.

To utilize these components, you can establish an ADF service directly from the Azure portal. Perform the following steps to do so:

1.  From the **Azure portal** menu, select + Create a resource, as shown in *Figure 4.2*:

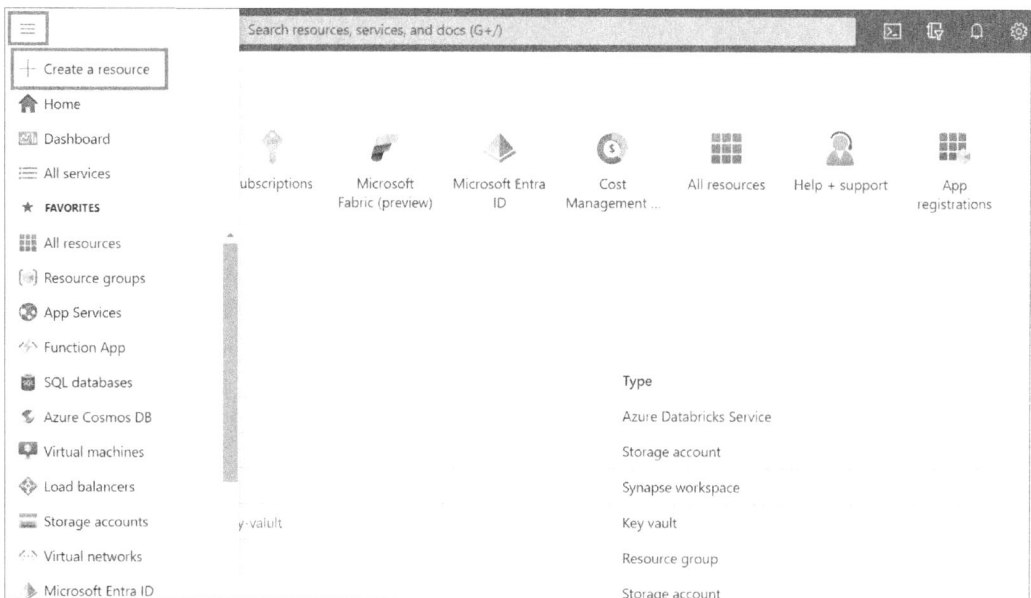

Figure 4.2 – Creating a ADF resource in the Azure portal

2. Select `Analytics` and then choose `Data Factory`, as shown in *Figure 4.3*:

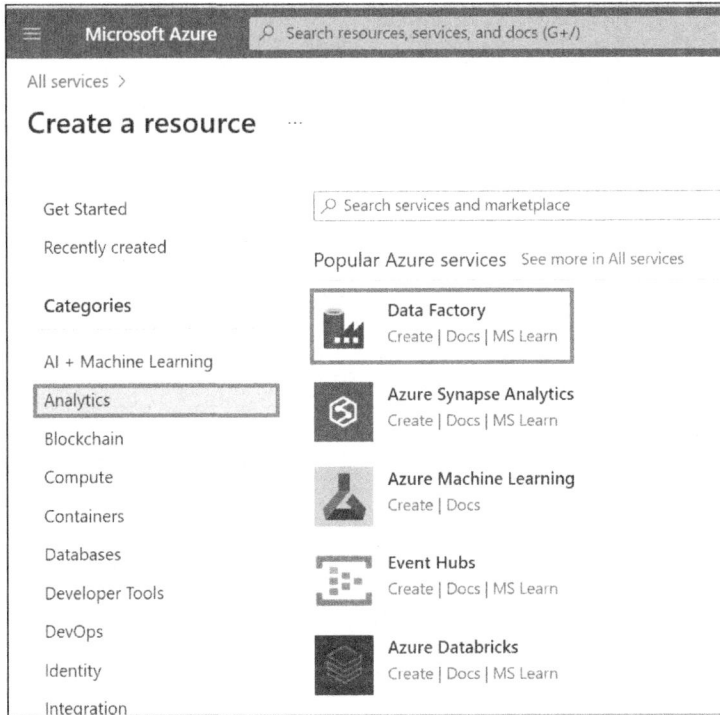

Figure 4.3 – ADF resource creation

3. Create an ADF resource by choosing a property. *Table 4.1* shows the description of each property:

| Property | Description |
| --- | --- |
| Subscription | From the dropdown, select your Azure subscription. In this case, it is `Azure subscription`. |
| Resource group | Specify whether you want to create a new resource group or use an existing one. For instance, here, a new resource group is created, `rg-dp203-datafactory`. |
| Name | Provide a name for your ADF instance – for example, `IACSampleDataFactory`. |
| Region | From the list of available regions in the dropdown, select the region where you want to deploy your ADF resource. For instance, here, the region chosen is `UK South`. |
| Version | Proceed with the default version, `V2`. |

Table 4.1 – Description of each property in ADF

*Figure 4.4* shows an ADF resource being created with the preceding properties entered:

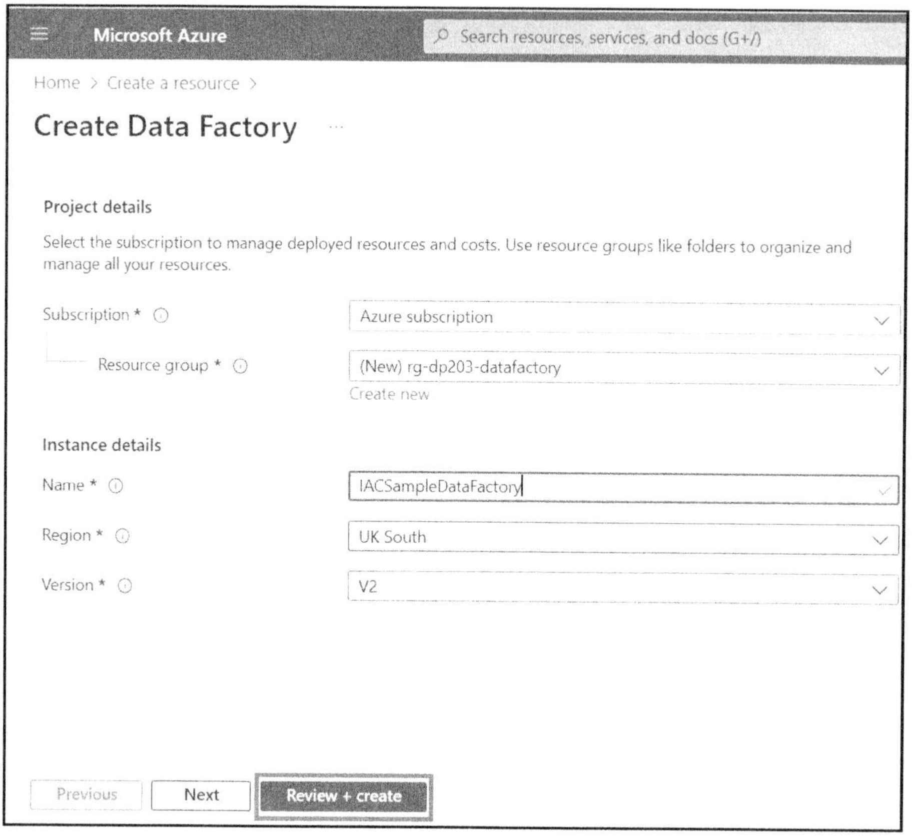

Figure 4.4 – Creating an ADF resource

4.  Once you have provided the required property values, click Review + create to create
    the ADF resource.

The next step is to create source datasets. So, launch ADF Studio, as shown in *Figure 4.5*:

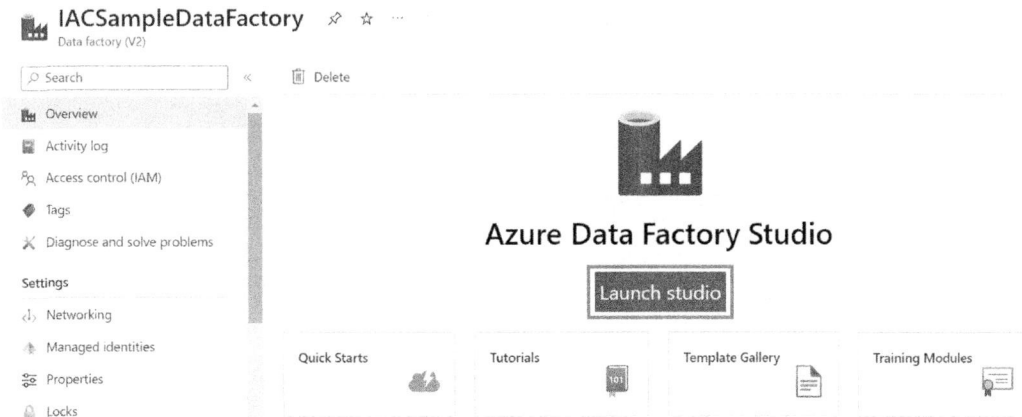

Figure 4.5 – ADF prompting to open the workspace and start building pipelines

This will open the ADF workspace, where you can build your pipelines (*Figure 4.6*):

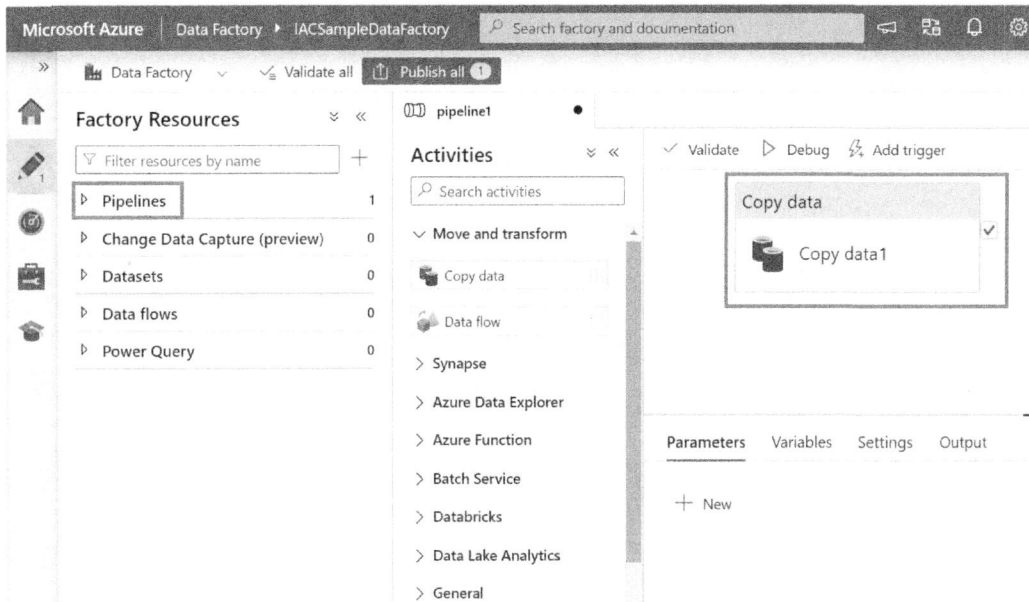

Figure 4.6 – ADF Studio to build the pipeline activities

Remember that all ADF transformations happen on datasets. So, before you can do any transformation, you will have to create datasets of the source data.

5.  Click on the plus (+) symbol and choose `Dataset` to create a new dataset (*Figure 4.7*):

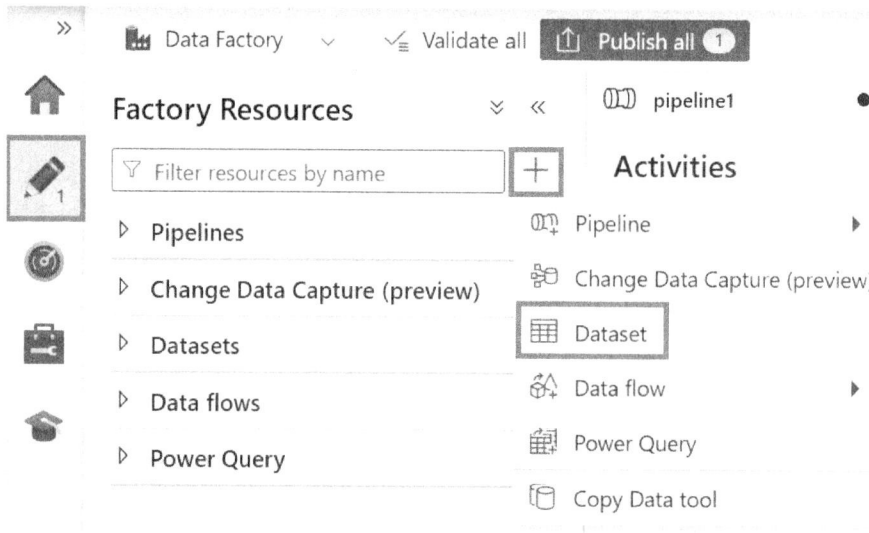

Figure 4.7 – Creating a new dataset in ADF

The **New dataset** screen will be displayed. ADF provides a wide range of Azure and non-Azure data sources, as shown in *Figure 4.8*:

## New dataset

In pipeline activities and data flows, reference a dataset to specify the location and structure of your data within a data store. Learn more ☐

Select a data store

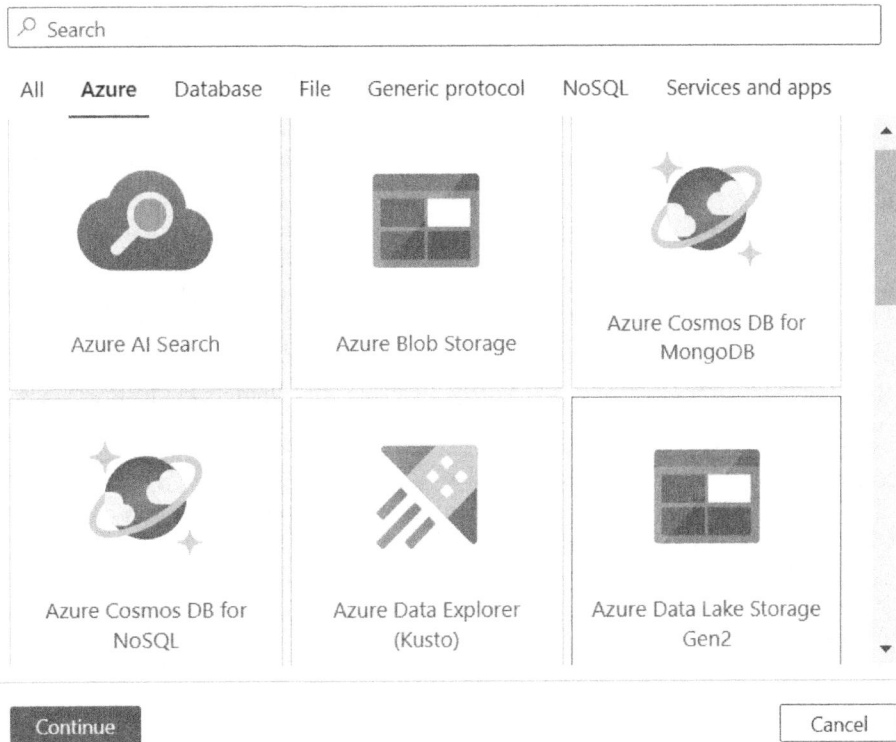

Figure 4.8 – Dataset source options in ADF

6.  Select the appropriate data source and click Continue.

7.  Add the location of the source data files or folders that need to be transformed.

You have now created source datasets and are ready to perform various activities, such as incremental loading and transforming data using ADF.

ADF allows you to design incremental loading using several techniques, based on the type of data source. These include the following:

- **Watermarks**: This technique is used when the data source is a database or relational table-based system.

- **File timestamps**: This method is used if the source is a filesystem or Blob Storage.

- **Partition data**: If the source is partitioned based on time, this technique is used.

- **Folder structure**: This practice is used when the source is divided based on time.

The following sections will explore each of these techniques in detail.

## Watermarks

**Watermarking** is a very simple technique in which you keep track of the last record loaded (your watermark) and load all the new records beyond the watermark in the next incremental run.

In relational storage technologies, such as SQL databases, you can store the watermark details as just another simple table and automatically update the watermark with stored procedures. The stored procedure should trigger every time a new record is loaded, which will update your watermark table. The next incremental copy pipeline can use this watermark information to identify the new set of records that need to be copied.

To implement the following example watermark design with ADF using Azure SQL as a source, you can create a simple table named `FactTrips` that will be incrementally loaded into an Azure SQL table. Perform the following steps to do so:

1.  Select `Azure SQL Service` from the **Azure dashboard**. Create a new Azure SQL instance if you don't already have one.

2.  Create a simple `FactTrips` table using the following code:

    ```
    CREATE TABLE FactTrips (
    TripID INT,
    customerID INT,
    LastModifiedTime DATETIME
    );
    ```

3.  Insert the following dummy values into this table:

    ```
    INSERT INTO [dbo].[FactTrips] values (100, 200, CURRENT_
    TIMESTAMP);
    INSERT INTO [dbo].[FactTrips] values (101, 201, CURRENT_
    TIMESTAMP);
    INSERT INTO [dbo].[FactTrips] values (102, 202, CURRENT_
    TIMESTAMP);
    ```

*Figure 4.9* shows the values inserted into the **Query editor** and the table displayed on the **Results** screen:

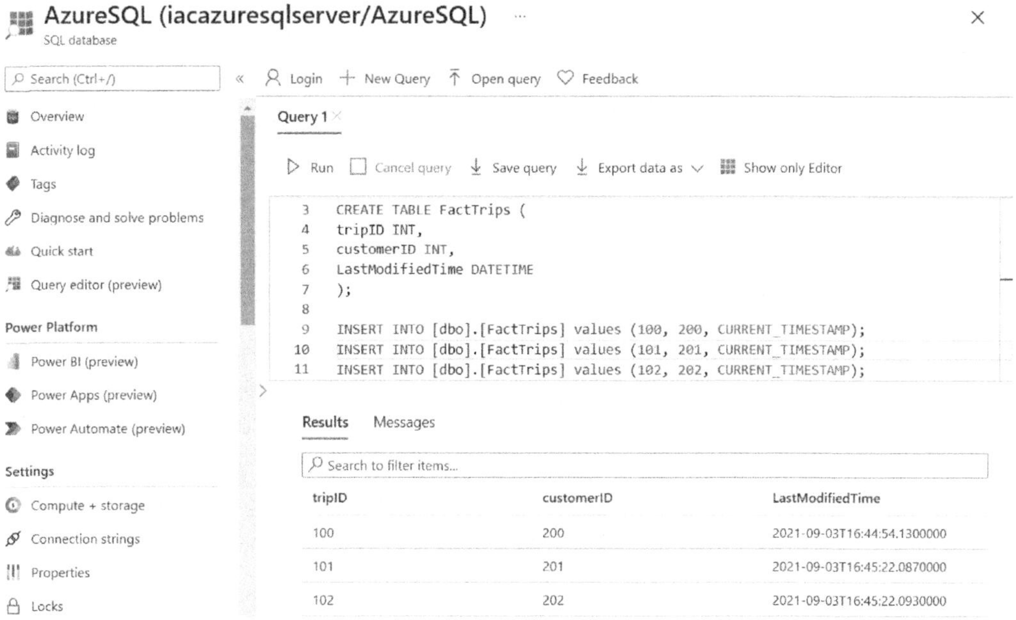

Figure 4.9 – Creating a simple table using the Query editor in Azure SQL

4.  Create a watermark table using the following code by selecting the +New Query option, as shown in *Figure 4.9*:

```
CREATE TABLE WatermarkTable
(
   [TableName] VARCHAR(100),
   [WatermarkValue] DATETIME,
);
```

5.  Create a stored procedure with + New Query and use the following code to automatically update the watermark table whenever there is new data:

```
CREATE PROCEDURE [dbo].uspUpdateWatermark @LastModifiedtime
DATETIME, @TableName VARCHAR(100)
AS
BEGIN
UPDATE [dbo].[WatermarkTable] SET [WatermarkValue] = @
LastModifiedtime WHERE [TableName] = @TableName
END
```

Now, on the ADF side, you need to create a new pipeline to identify the difference between the old and new watermarks and subsequently initiate an incremental copy process.

6. From the **Pipeline** page in ADF, create two lookup activities by first clicking the `Activities` option and then choosing `General | Lookup`, as shown in *Figure 4.10*:

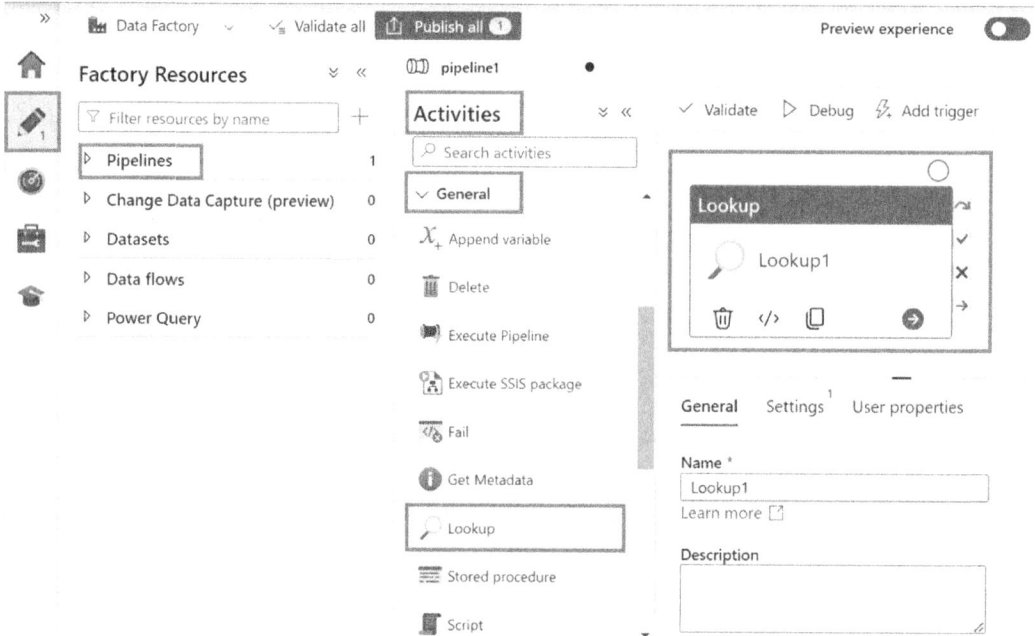

Figure 4.10 – The ADF authoring page

Here, you added the lookup transformation from the ADF activities list, which is `Lookup1`.

7.  Configure the first lookup activity to look up the previous watermark table entry, as shown in *Figure 4.11*. The `Watermark` dataset has been configured to point to `WatermarkTable`.

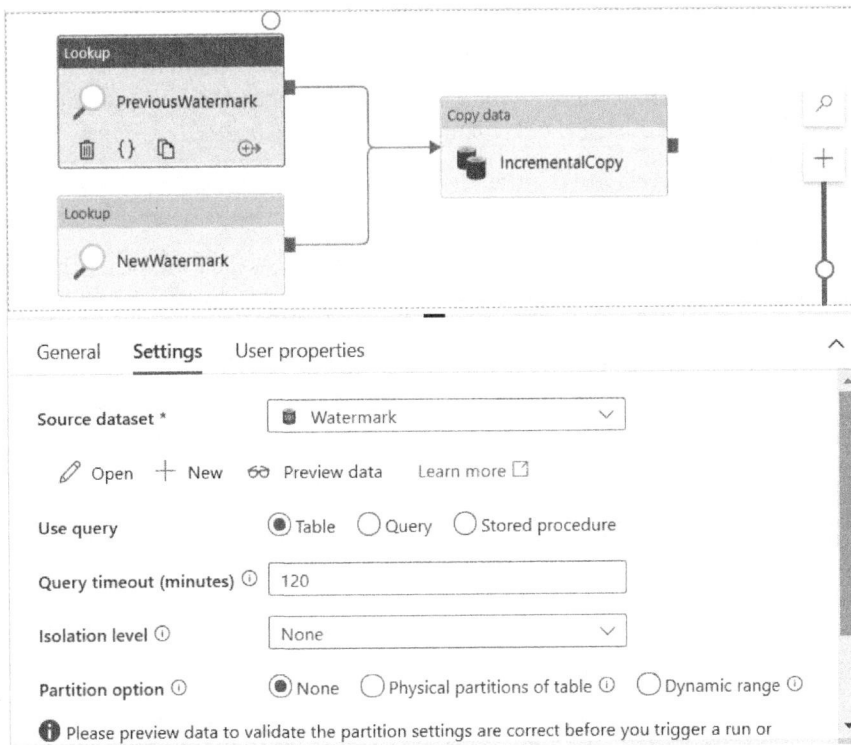

Figure 4.11 – The lookup activity configuration using the Watermark table

Here, you applied the settings on `Lookup1`, which is named `PreviousWatermark`. This represents the `Watermark` dataset that points to the `Watermark` table.

8.  Configure the next lookup activity to look at the latest file's modified time in the source table. In this case, the source dataset is the `FactTrips` table.

9.  Enter the following query in the `Query` textbox under the **Settings** tab (*Figure 4.12*):

```
SELECT MAX(LastModifiedTime) AS NewWatermarkValue FROM
FactTrips;
```

The following is a quick overview of the other options on the `Settings` tab:

- `Use query`: This will allow you to specify a SQL query to fetch data instead of selecting the entire table or view, which provides more control over the data you want to process.

- `Query timeout (minutes)`: You can define the maximum time a query should run before timing out. By default, it will be `120` minutes, and this can be customized to prevent long-running queries that could potentially hang the system.

- `Isolation level`: You can set the transaction isolation level, which determines how transaction changes are visible to other transactions and helps maintain data integrity.

- `Partition option`: This allows you to choose how data will be partitioned during processing. Partitioning can help improve performance by parallelizing the workload.

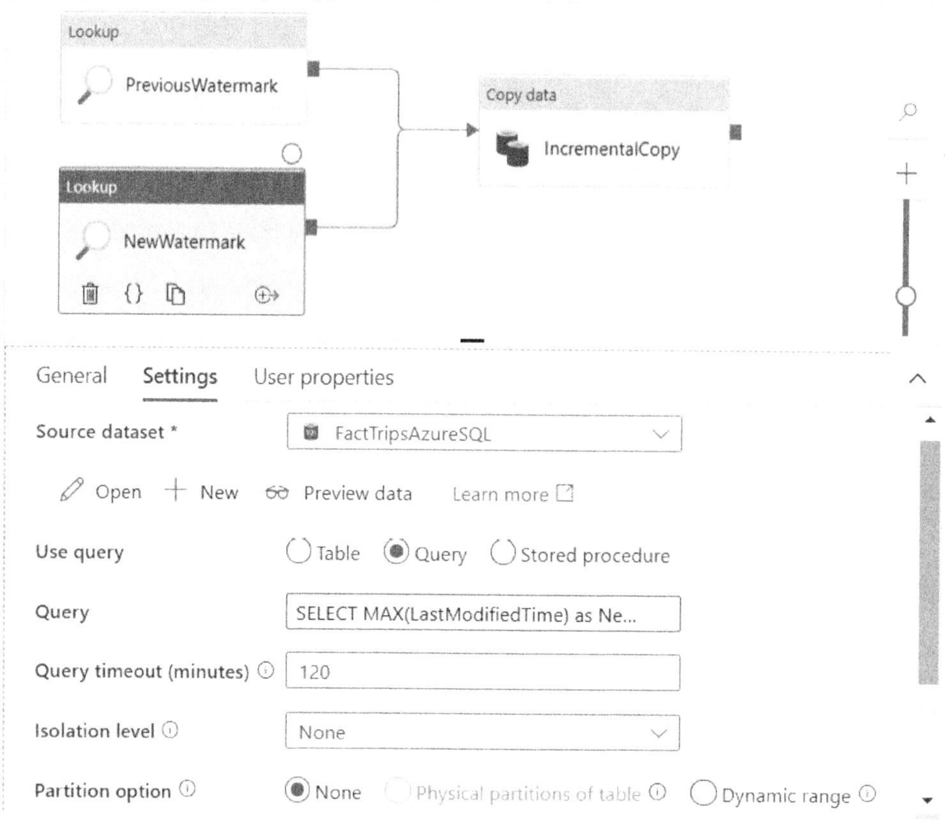

Figure 4.12 – New watermark lookup configuration using LastModifiedTime

10. Finally, add a new Copy activity (from `Activities -> Move and Transform -> Copy Data`) from the ADF authoring page, similar to the one that you saw in *Figure 4.10*.

11. In the `Query` textbox on the **Source** tab, enter the following query (*Figure 4.13*):

```
SELECT * FROM FactTrips WHERE
LastModifiedTime > '@{activity('PreviousWatermark').output.
firstRow.WatermarkValue}'
AND
LastModifiedTime <= '@{activity('NewWatermark').output.firstRow.
WatermarkValue}';
```

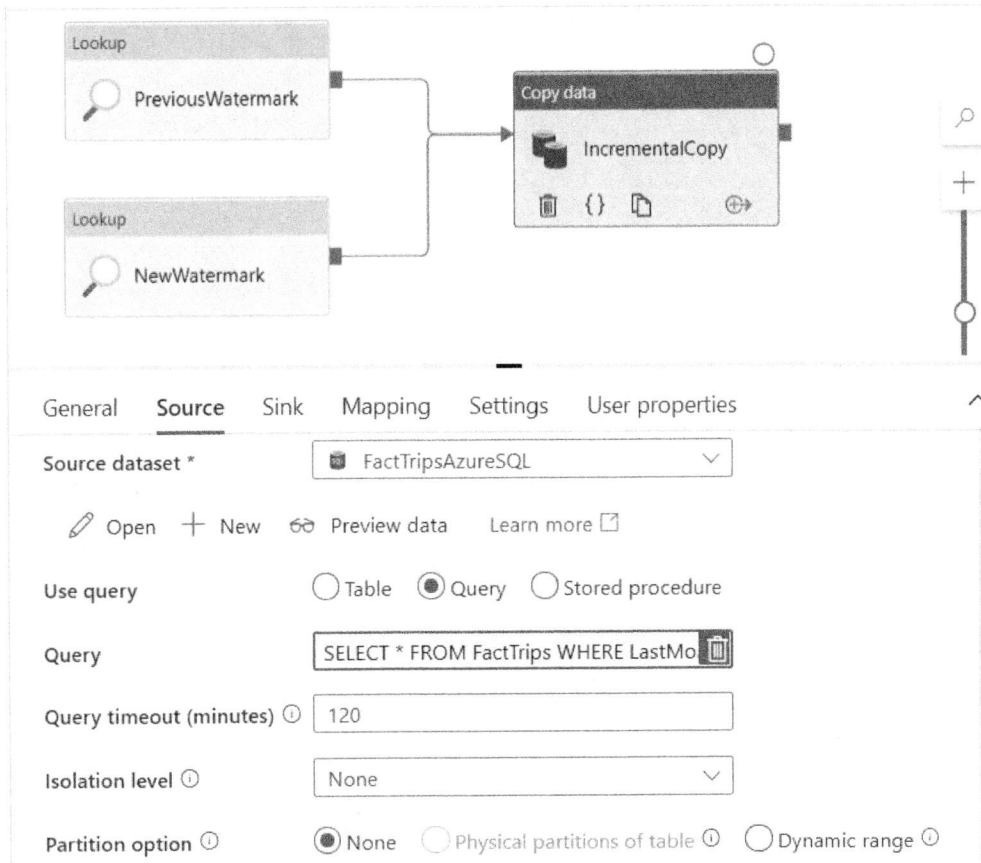

Figure 4.13 – ADF Copy activity with watermark-based delta generation

12. Click Publish all to save the preceding pipeline, which essentially deploys it to the Azure environment and enables execution.

13. Set up a Schedule trigger using the Add trigger button on the pipeline screen, as shown in *Figure 4.14*:

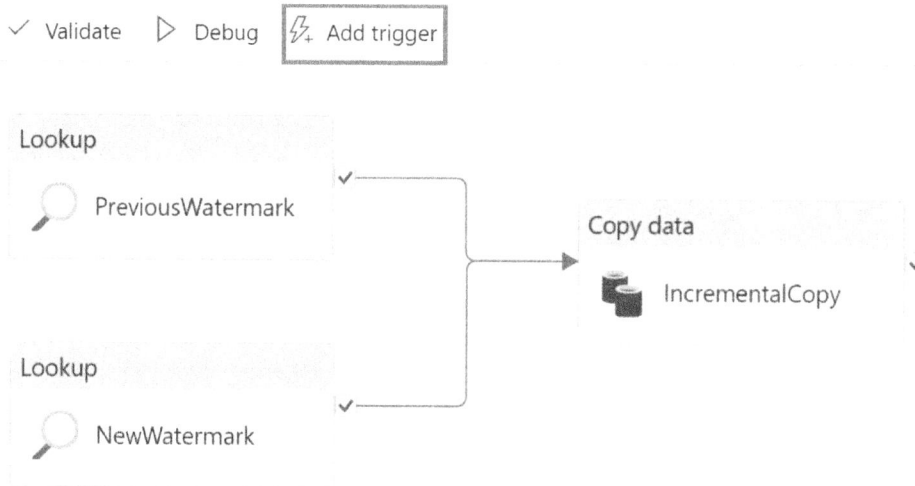

Figure 4.14 – Scheduling the ADF pipeline by clicking Add trigger

Now, every time there are changes to the FactTrips table, it will get copied into your destination table at regular intervals.

> **Note**
> You can find the complete code in the accompanying GitHub repository at https://packt.link/JQkyl.

Next, you'll learn how to do incremental copying using file timestamps.

## File Timestamps

This is another technique available through ADF's **Copy Data** functionality that allows you to incrementally load only new files from a source to a destination. This **Copy Data** tool provides an option to scan the files at the source, based on the LastModifiedDate attribute. So, all you need to do is to specify the source and destination folders and select the Incremental load: LastModifiedDate option for the **File loading behavior** field.

The following steps will help you create an incremental copy pipeline using file-modified dates:

1.  Click the plus (+) sign. Launch the Copy Data tool functionality from the **ADF** main screen, as shown in *Figure 4.15*:

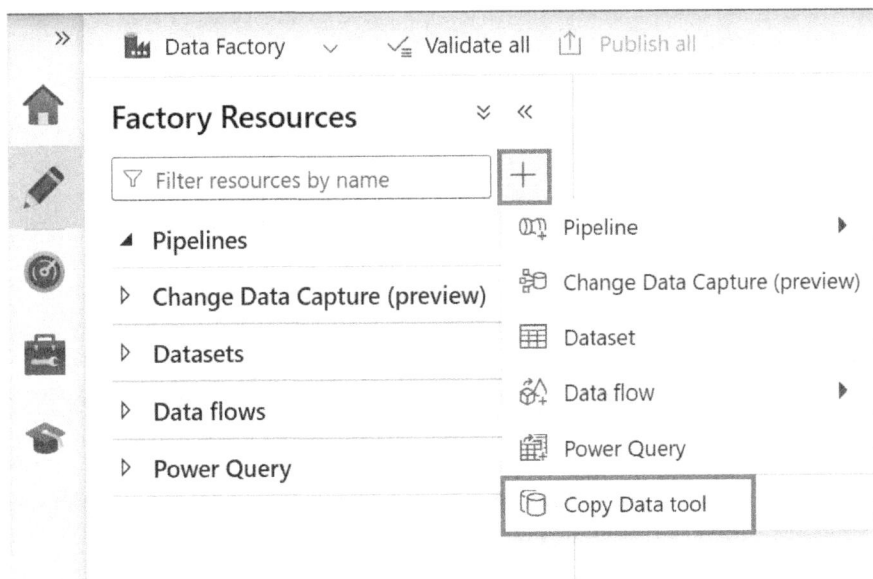

Figure 4.15 – Scanning files at the source based on the LastModifiedDate attribute

2.  Once you click Copy Data tool, a **wizard** screen is launched in which you can specify the incremental load details, as illustrated in *Figure 4.16*.

3.  In the **Properties** tab (*Figure 4.16*), select `Tumbling window` for the **Task cadence or task schedule** setting. This ensures that the incremental load option is available to you.

> **Note**
>
> If you do not select `Tumbling window`, the incremental load option won't appear.

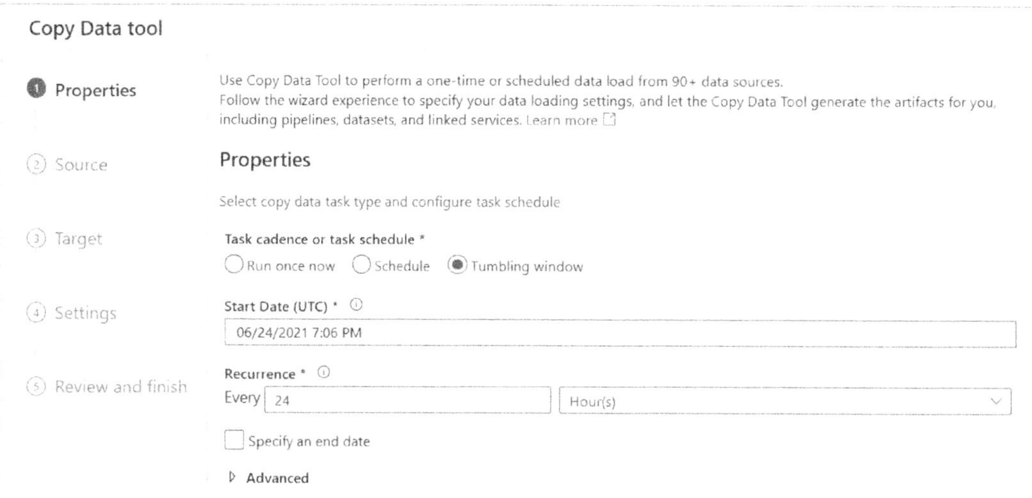

Copy Data tool

**1** Properties — Use Copy Data Tool to perform a one-time or scheduled data load from 90+ data sources. Follow the wizard experience to specify your data loading settings, and let the Copy Data Tool generate the artifacts for you, including pipelines, datasets, and linked services. Learn more ☐

(2) Source

**Properties**

Select copy data task type and configure task schedule

(3) Target

Task cadence or task schedule *
◯ Run once now   ◯ Schedule   ⦿ Tumbling window

(4) Settings

Start Date (UTC) * ⓘ
06/24/2021 7:06 PM

(5) Review and finish

Recurrence * ⓘ
Every  24                          Hour(s)              ⌄

☐ Specify an end date

▷ Advanced

Figure 4.16 – Selecting Tumbling window for an incremental load, based on the file-modified time

4.  In the **Source** tab, select the `Incremental load: LastModifiedDate` option for the **File loading behavior** field, as shown in *Figure 4.17*:

Here's a quick overview of the `File loading behavior` and `Recursively` options:

-   `Load all files`: This option will load every file from the specified source "without any filtering". It is useful when you want to import all available data without any restrictions. The `Recursively` checkbox is enabled by default, which means that the data loading process will include not just the files in the specified directory but also all files contained within any subdirectories of the directory. This ensures a comprehensive data load that includes all nested files within the folder structure, and this recursive process will be the same for the other two options, `Incremental load: LastModifiedDate` and `Incremental load: time-partitioned folder/file names`.

- `Incremental load: LastModifiedDate`: With this option, only files that have been modified since the last load operation will be imported. It is an efficient way to update your data without reprocessing files that have not changed.

- `Incremental load: time-partitioned folder/file names`: This option is similar to `LastModifiedDate` but "focuses on files by time". It will load files based on their names or the names of the folders that are available, which typically include a timestamp. This method is handy for you where files are systematically named or stored according to the time they were created or modified.

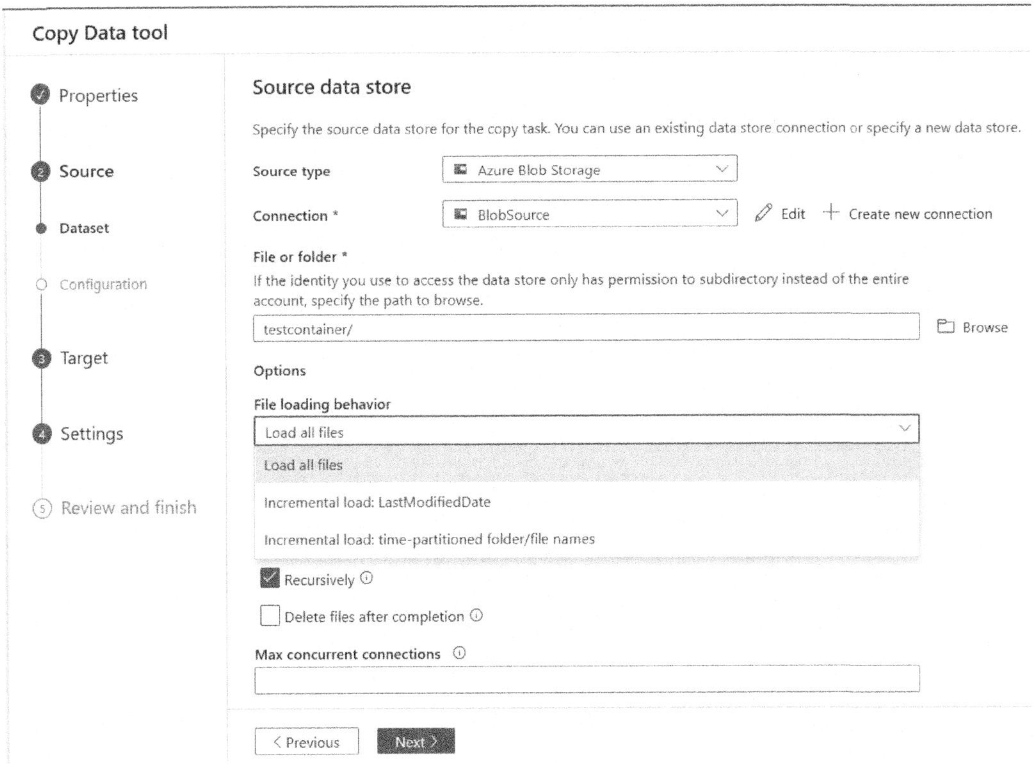

Figure 4.17 – Incremental load with LastModifiedDate timestamp behavior

5. Fill in the rest of the fields and click Next on the **Review and finish** screen to create an incremental copy pipeline using file-modified dates.

The next section covers incremental copying using file partitioning and folder structures.

## File Partitions and Folder Structures

You can use the ADF **Copy Data** tool functionality to perform incremental loading for both the options of file partitioning and data organized in date-based folder structures. Assume that your input data "lands" in a date-structured folder, as shown here:

```
New York/Trips/In/2022/01/01
```

In this context, **landing** means saving your data based on the folder path you specified, using the ADF **Copy Data** tool activity. Perform the following steps to incrementally upload this data to another location in the Blob Storage regularly:

1. Click the plus (+) sign, and then choose the Copy Data tool functionality from the **ADF** main screen to launch a **wizard** screen. Here, you can specify the incremental load details.

2. In the **Properties** tab, select Tumbling window for the **Task cadence or task schedule** setting. Then, choose the Source tab.

   Similar to how you instantiated a copy activity in the *Watermarks* section for the incremental copy based on file-modified date timestamps, you need to instantiate the **Copy Data tool** functionality with the **File Loading behavior** field set to Incremental load: time-partitioned folder/file names (*Figure 4.18*).

3. Start typing the input format using date variables such as {year}/{month}/{day} in the **File or folder** path. Then, expand the **Options** section to show the year format, month format, and day format fields (*Figure 4.18*):

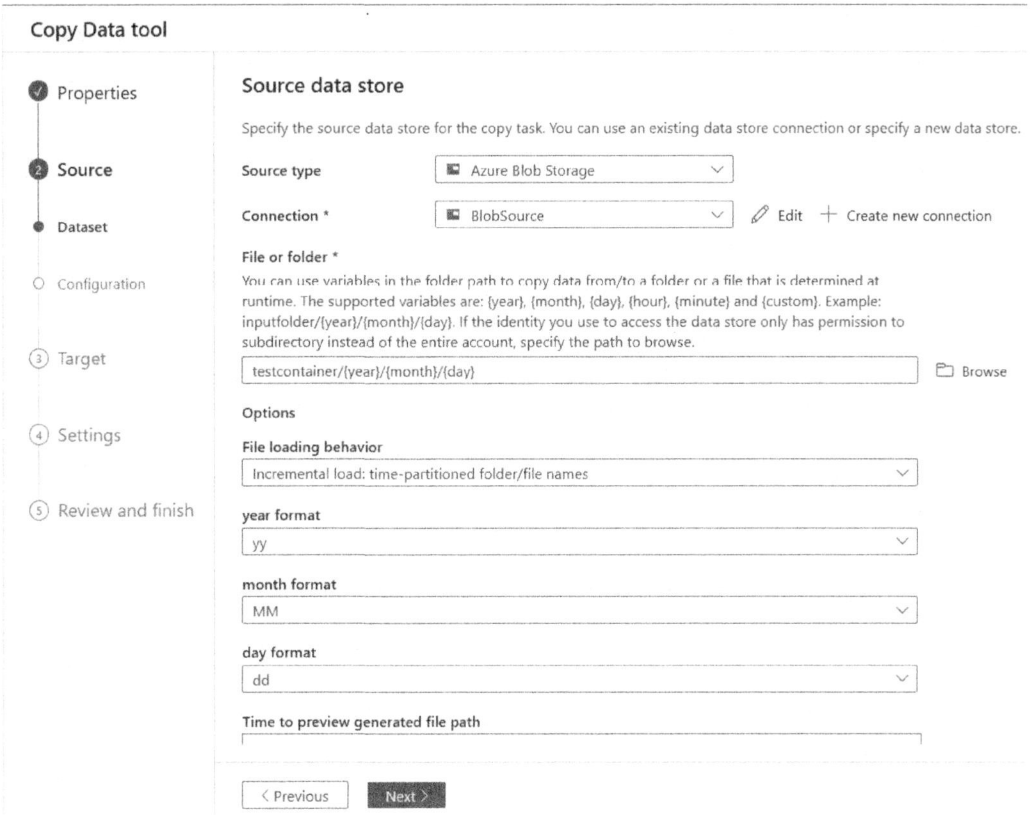

**Copy Data tool**

| | |
|---|---|
| ✓ Properties | **Source data store** |
| | Specify the source data store for the copy task. You can use an existing data store connection or specify a new data store. |
| ❷ **Source** | Source type   ▣ Azure Blob Storage  ⌄ |
| ● Dataset | Connection *   ▣ BlobSource  ⌄   ✎ Edit  + Create new connection |
| | **File or folder *** |
| ○ Configuration | You can use variables in the folder path to copy data from/to a folder or a file that is determined at runtime. The supported variables are: {year}, {month}, {day}, {hour}, {minute} and {custom}. Example: inputfolder/{year}/{month}/{day}. If the identity you use to access the data store only has permission to subdirectory instead of the entire account, specify the path to browse. |
| ③ Target | testcontainer/{year}/{month}/{day}   🗁 Browse |
| | **Options** |
| ④ Settings | **File loading behavior** |
| | Incremental load: time-partitioned folder/file names  ⌄ |
| ⑤ Review and finish | **year format** |
| | yy  ⌄ |
| | **month format** |
| | MM  ⌄ |
| | **day format** |
| | dd  ⌄ |
| | **Time to preview generated file path** |

< Previous    Next >

Figure 4.18 – ADF incremental load option with time-partitioned folders

4. Select your preferred folder structure format from the drop-down menu and complete the rest of the fields:

- `year format`: yy, yyy, or yyyy

- `month format`: M, MM, MMM, or MMMM

- `day format`: d, dd, or ddd

5. Review the details and click `Next` on the **Review and finish** screen to deploy the pipeline.

Finally, you will see that the incremental pipeline for partitioned data/folder structures has been deployed.

In this section, you learned about incremental loading for large volumes of data by processing data that has changed. You also grasped how to implement different strategies for incremental loading, such as timestamps or watermark techniques, to identify new or updated data, using Azure services such as ADF and Azure Synapse Analytics, and to automate the incremental loading process, which included setting up pipelines and activities within ADF to process only data that has changed since the last load.

## Transforming Data Using Apache Spark

This section covers the implementation and use of Apache Spark in Azure Synapse Analytics for data transformation, to handle large-scale data processing tasks efficiently. You will learn how to manage Spark pools and manipulate data with DataFrames and datasets, explore and manipulate data (including selecting, filtering, and aggregating data and optimizing Spark jobs for efficient execution plans), and review the integration of Spark with Azure services and data workload management for the scalability and reliability of data processing pipelines.

> **Note**
>
> This section primarily focuses on the **Transform data by using Apache Spark** concept of the DP-203: Data Engineering on Microsoft Azure exam.

The information in this section applies to the following flavors of Spark available on Azure:

- **Synapse Spark**: Synapse Spark is a component of Azure Synapse Analytics. It provides Apache Spark functionality within the Synapse Analytics ecosystem and enables you to run distributed data processing tasks at scale. Synapse Spark is tightly integrated with other Azure services, such as Azure Data Lake Storage and Azure SQL Data Warehouse, which enables seamless data processing and analytics workflows.

- **Azure Databricks Spark**: **Azure Databricks** (**ADB**) is a unified analytics platform provided by Microsoft Azure in collaboration with Databricks, which offers a fully managed Apache Spark environment for your data engineering, data science, and machine learning tasks. Azure Databricks Spark provides optimized performance, reliability, and scalability, along with collaborative features for you and other teams working on big data and AI projects.

- **HDInsight Spark**: HDInsight is a fully managed cloud service for open source analytics, including Apache Spark, Apache Hadoop, and Apache Hive, provided by Microsoft Azure. HDInsight Spark allows you to deploy and manage Apache Spark clusters in the cloud without the need for infrastructure provisioning or management. It offers integration with other Azure services, security features, and enterprise-grade support for Big Data Analytics workloads.

Apache Spark supports transformations with **Application Programming Interfaces (APIs)**. An **API** is a set of rules, protocols, and tools that allow different software applications to communicate with each other. It defines the methods and data structures that you can use to interact with a particular software component or a service. APIs abstract the underlying complexity of systems and provide a standardized way for applications to access functionality or data.

In the context of Apache Spark, the term **APIs** refers to the different ways you can interact with Spark to perform data processing tasks. These APIs provide a layer of abstraction over Spark's core functionalities, which makes it easier for you to work with distributed data processing frameworks such as Spark.

The three main APIs supported by Apache Spark are as follows:

- **Resilient distributed datasets**: These are the fundamental data abstraction in Spark, representing a distributed collection of objects that can be operated on in parallel. **Resilient Distributed Datasets (RDDs)** provide a low-level API to perform transformations and actions on distributed datasets, allowing you to control data partitioning and processing directly.

- **DataFrames**: These introduce a higher-level abstraction over the RDDs, providing a structured representation of data in the form of rows and columns, which are similar to a table in a relational database. DataFrames offer a more user-friendly API to perform data manipulation and analysis, with built-in optimizations for efficient processing.

- **Datasets**: These combine the benefits of RDDs and DataFrames, which offer an object-oriented API with the performance optimizations of DataFrames. Datasets allow you to work with structured data while compile-time checks and make them particularly suitable for both performance and type-safety guarantees to reduce runtime errors.

You will learn about RDDs and DataFrame transformations in this section. **Datasets** are just extensions of DataFrames, with additional features such as being type-safe (where the compiler will strictly check for data types) and providing an **Object-Oriented (OO)** interface.

## What are Resilient Distributed Datasets (RDDs)

**RDDs**, the backbone of **Spark**, is a powerful data processing framework that allows you to perform in-memory computations across large clusters in a fault-tolerant way. RDDs are like a team of data warriors at your disposal, ready to tackle even the most massive data tasks while keeping your information safe and secure. With RDDs, you can harness the power of distributed memory to conquer any challenge that comes your way. This ensures the resilience of computations even in the face of failures. RDDs support a wide variety of data formats, such as **JavaScript Object Notation (JSON)**, **Comma-Separated Values (CSVs)**, and Parquet. These data formats allow the RDDs to efficiently transform and process data by providing structured representations of it.

The following provides some details about creating RDDs and performing different transformations:

- **Creating RDDs**: There are many ways to create the RDD, but a simple one is to use the `parallelize()` function, as follows:

```
val cities = Seq(«New York», «Austin»)
val rdd=spark.sparkContext.parallelize(cities)
```

Once you have created the RDD, you can run different kinds of transformations on them.

- **RDD transformations**: The following are some of the commonly used RDD transformations in Spark:

  - `map()`: This transformation applies the function provided as a parameter to all the elements of the source and returns a new RDD. The following example can be used to do a word count:

```
val maprdd=rdd.map(word => (word,1))
maprdd.collect.foreach(println)
```

  - `flatMap()`: This is similar to `map()`, but you can apply the function to more than one element. The following example can be used to split each line of text into individual words:

```
val fmrdd = rdd.flatMap(word => word.split(" "))
fmrdd.collect.foreach(println)
```

  - `filter()`: This returns a new RDD that satisfies the filter condition. The following example can be used to remove empty strings from `rdd`:

```
val emptystrfilterrdd = rdd.filter(_.nonEmpty)
emptystrfilterrdd.collect.foreach(println)
```

  - `groupBy()`: This collects identical data into groups and can perform aggregate actions on top of it. The following example can be used to group elements of the `rdd` by the first character of each word:

```
val groupbyrdd = rdd.groupBy(word => word.charAt(0))
groupbyrdd.collect.foreach(println)
```

  - `union()`: This transformation returns a new RDD that is a union of the two datasets. The following example can be used to combine the elements of two RDDs, such as `rdd1` and `rdd2`, into a single RDD, which is `unionrdd`:

```
val rdd1 = spark.sparkContext.parallelize(List(1, 2, 3))
val rdd2 = spark.sparkContext.parallelize(List(4, 5, 6))
val unionrdd = rdd1.union(rdd2)
unionrdd.collect().foreach(println)
```

- `distinct()`: This returns a new dataset that contains only the unique elements from the input dataset. The following example can be used to remove duplicate elements from the RDD:

```
val distrinctrdd = rdd.distinct()
distrinctrdd.collect.foreach(println)
```

> **Note**
>
> You can find the complete code in the accompanying GitHub repository at `https://packt.link/xw0Dp`. In order to view the complete list of transformations supported by Spark, refer to the Apache Spark documentation at `https://packt.link/bSyiu`.

In this section, you gained knowledge about RDDs – those key building blocks that let you crunch big data in memory even across huge clusters – all while making sure your computations stay safe from any hiccups along the way. The next section will look at DataFrames.

## What Are DataFrames?

**DataFrames** are similar to tables in relational databases. Like RDDs, they are also immutable, redundant, and distributed, but they represent a higher form of data abstraction. DataFrames contain **schemas**, **columns**, and **rows**, just like relational tables, and are useful in processing large volumes of data while using relational table-like operations. DataFrames in Apache Spark provides a structured way to manipulate and transform data, much like how you would perform operations on tables in a relational database. **Data transformation** involves modifying the structure or content of data to prepare it for analysis or further processing.

The following provides details of the options to create DataFrames and their transformations:

- **Creating DataFrames**: There are a number of options that are available to create DataFrames:

  - Converting the RDD to a DataFrame using the following code:

    ```
    val df = rdd.toDF()
    ```

  - Creating a DataFrame from a CSV file:

    ```
    csvDf = spark.read.csv("/path/to/file.csv")
    ```

  - Creating a DataFrame from a JSON file:

    ```
    jsonDf = spark.read.json("/path/to/file.json")
    ```

- Creating a DataFrame with a schema:

```
data = [("Adam","Smith","Male","CA"),
        («Brenda","Jones","Female","FL")]
schema = ["firstname","lastname","gender","state"]
df = spark.createDataFrame(data = data, schema = schema)
```

- **DataFrame transformations**: For Data Analytics, DataFrame transformations are more relevant than RDD transformations, as they provide a powerful and flexible framework for Data Analytics, offering a rich set of operations tailored to the needs of modern data-driven applications. By leveraging the structured abstraction of DataFrames and the optimized execution capabilities of distributed computing platforms, you can perform complex data transformations with ease and unlock valuable insights from data.

A DataFrame transformation is eventually converted into an RDD transformation within Spark. In Spark, DataFrame transformations, such as sorting or filtering data, get converted into more efficient operations known as **RDD transformations**. This process taps into RDDs' power for distributed computing, ensuring that big data tasks run smoothly while still offering you a simple and high-level interface for data manipulation.

Some important DataFrame transformations are as follows:

> **Note**
> Here, assume that df, df1, and df2 are valid DataFrames.

- `select()`: This command selects data from a subset of columns. Its syntax is as follows:

```
df.select("firstname","lastname").show()
```

- `filter()`: This command filters rows based on a condition. Its syntax is as follows:

```
df.filter('location === "Florida").show()
```

- `distinct()`: This command selects unique rows from the input. Its syntax is as follows:

```
df.distinct().show()
```

- `orderBy()`: This command sorts rows by a particular column. Its syntax is as follows:

```
df.orderBy("location").show()
```

- `join()`: This command joins two tables based on the provided conditions. Its syntax is as follows:

```
df1.join(df2, df1("id") == df2("id"),"inner")
```

- Some more examples of `join()` are as follows:

```
#Perform inner join on "dept_id" column to join "emp_df" and
"dept_df"
emp_df.join(dept_df, emp_df("dept_id") == dept_df("dept_id),
"inner")
```

- `groupBy()` and `avg()`: These commands can be used in combination to aggregate values that are grouped together on some column values. Their syntax is as follows:

```
df.groupBy("location").avg("salary").show()
```

The preceding examples should give you a sound sense of the types of transformations available in Spark.

> **Note**
>
> You can learn more about Spark SQL, DataFrame, and dataset transformations at https://packt.link/hzsPz.

By now, you should know how to manipulate data efficiently within Spark, covering essential concepts such as creating RDDs, DataFrames, and datasets and transformations such as sorting, filtering, and aggregating, with ease, unlocking valuable insights from data.

The next section will focus on the transformations available in **Transact-SQL (T-SQL)**.

# Transforming Data Using T-SQL

T-SQL is a procedural language that is used by both dedicated and Serverless SQL ingess in Synapse. Similar to the transformations that you have seen in Spark, T-SQL also provides a rich set of transformations.

> **Note**
>
> This section primarily focuses on the **Transform data by using Transact-SQL (T-SQL) in Azure Synapse Analytics** concept of the DP-203: Data Engineering on Microsoft Azure exam.

The following are some of the most important ones:

- SELECT: This command is used to select data from a subset of columns. Its syntax is as follows:

```
SELECT[firstName], [lastName] from dbo.Driver WHERE [city] =
'New York';
```

- ORDER BY: This command is used to sort rows by a particular column. Its syntax is as follows:

```
SELECT [firstName], [lastName] from dbo.Driver ORDER BY
[firstName];
```

- DISTINCT: This command is used to select unique rows from the input. Its syntax is as follows:

```
SELECT DISTINCT [firstName], [lastName] from dbo.Driver;
```

- GROUP BY: This command is used to group rows by columns so that aggregate operations can be performed on them. Its syntax is as follows:

```
SELECT [gender], AVG([salary]) AS 'AVG salary' from dbo.Driver
GROUP BY [gender];
```

- UNION: This command is used to combine rows from two tables containing the same schema. Its syntax is as follows:

```
SELECT [firstName], [lastName] FROM
dbo.Driver
WHERE [city] = 'New York'
UNION
SELECT [firstName], [lastName] FROM
dbo.TempDriver
WHERE [city] = 'New York';
```

- JOIN: This command is used to join two tables based on the provided conditions. Its syntax is as follows:

```
SELECT driver.[firstName], driver.[lastName], feedback.[rating],
Feedback.[comment] FROM
dbo.Driver AS driver
INNER JOIN dbo.Feedback AS feedback
ON driver.[driverId] = feedback.[driverId]
WHERE driver.[city] = 'New York';
```

- VIEW: Apart from the standard transformations, T-SQL also provides a VIEW transformation, which can help in reporting and ad hoc querying. The following is a simple example of how to create and use a VIEW transformation:

```
CREATE VIEW CompleteDriverView
AS
SELECT driver.[firstName], driver.[lastName], feedback.[rating],
feedback.[comment] FROM
dbo.Driver AS driver
INNER JOIN dbo.Feedback AS feedback
ON driver.[driverId] = feedback.[driverId]
WHERE driver.[city] = 'New York';
```

The following is an example that shows how you can use a `VIEW` transformation:

```
SELECT DISTINCT * from CompleteDriverView;
```

> **Note**
>
> You can find the complete code in the accompanying GitHub repository at `https://packt.link/ppbpR`. You can find a more comprehensive list of transformations at `https://packt.link/o2IUu`.

This section covered some of the important transformations in T-SQL. T-SQL, utilized by both dedicated and Serverless SQL pools in Synapse, is a procedural language for performing data transformations akin to those seen in Spark. The next section will focus on ingestion and transforming data with ADF.

## The Transforming Options Available in ADF

**Azure Synapse Pipelines** and **ADF** ingest and transform data. While Spark and T-SQL offer code-based solutions to run ingestion and transformation tasks, ADF and Azure Synapse Pipelines offer a low-code alternative, where the ingestion and transformation process can be drawn on a canvas by dragging and dropping activities and setting their properties and conditions. The personal productivity advantage is considerable, and if you face limitations of the low-code approach unexpectedly, you can still add an activity that calls a **Spark Notebook**, a T-SQL script, or a stored procedure.

> **Note**
>
> This section primarily focuses on the **Ingest and transform data by using Azure Synapse Pipelines or Azure Data Factory** concept of the DP-203: Data Engineering on Microsoft Azure exam.

**Synapse pipelines** are simply ADF pipelines whose functionalities are ported into the Synapse workspace and can be considered, for all intents and purposes, functionally equivalent to ADF pipelines. The main difference is the easier integration with the other components of the Synapse workspace, such as SQL pools and Synapse Spark pools. You have already seen a few examples of ADF in the *Designing and Implementing Incremental Loads* section.

ADF provides convenient and code-free transformation options called **mapping data flows**. Mapping data flows provides the following three types of transformations and important options available under them:

- **Schema transformations**: Schema transformations refer to the actions that result in changing the schema of a table or DataFrames. An example of such a transformation is adding new columns. The following are some commonly used schema transformations:

  - **Aggregate**: This transformation is used to perform Min, Max, Sum, Count, and other operations on the incoming data.

  You can perform the following activities as part of the data flow shown in *Figure 4.19*:

  - **Source**: Add a source where you import data from a source file named DriverCSV2

  - **Aggregate**: Add aggregate transformation and label it to AggregateSalary, where data is grouped by Gender, and then calculate the average Salary.

  - **Sink**: Add a destination option to export the aggregated salary data to a dataset named CleanedDriverDataSet in a storage account named ADLSGen2Store2.

  - **Data Management**: The interface includes options to optimize, inspect, and preview the data.

  - For example, to find the average of the **Salary** column, perform the following steps:

  i.   Select the AggregateSalary transformation activity and then click on the Aggregate settings tab.

  ii.  Choose the Aggregates toggle.

  iii. Choose the Salary column under the Column option.

  iv.  Type the aggregate expression under the Expression option – in this case, avg(tointeger({Salary})). *Figure 4.19* shows the average of the Salary column:

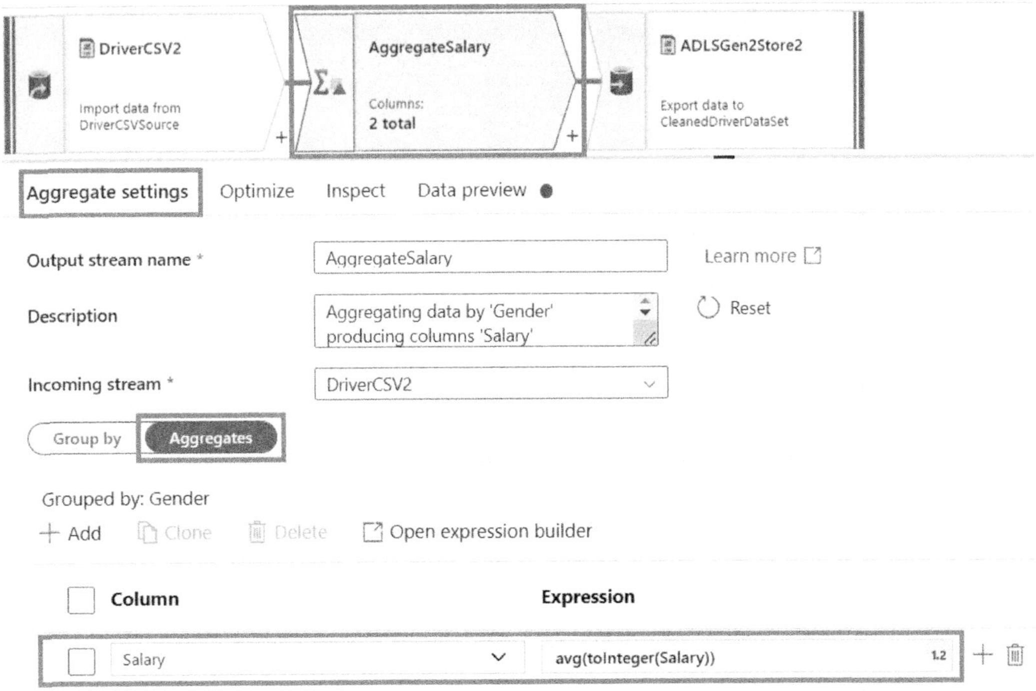

Figure 4.19 – Performing Aggregate transformation in ADF

- **Derived column**: This transformation is used to add any new columns to the existing data. *Figure 4.20* adds a simple `isActive` column to the `Driver` data extracted from a CSV file. To do so, perform the following steps:

    i.  Add `Derived Column activity`, label the output stream name as `AddNewColumn`, then click on `Derived column's settings` tab.

    ii. Click the `+Add` button.

    iii. Choose the `isActive` column under the `Column` option.

iv.  Type the aggregate expression under the `Expression` option – in this case, `true()`. *Figure 4.20* shows a column added:

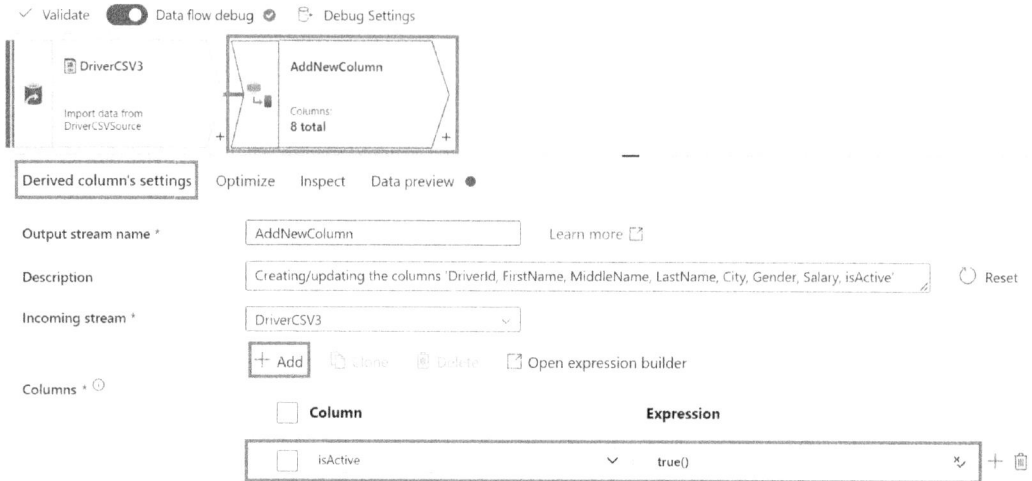

Figure 4.20 – Derived column transformation in ADF showing an added column

- **Select**: You can use this transformation to select only the required columns from the input or to change the name of the columns before storing them in a data store, as demonstrated in *Figure 4.21*:

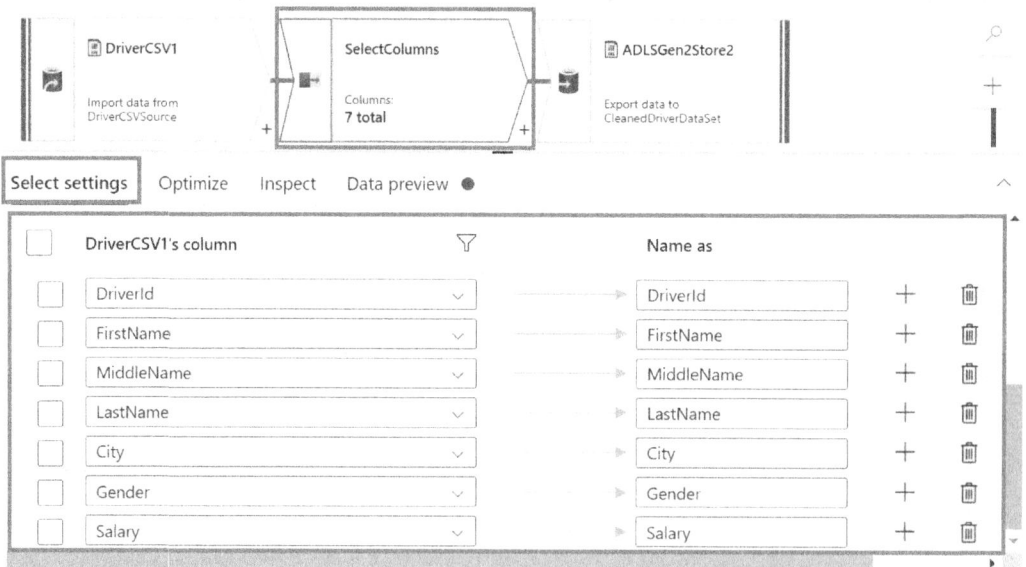

Figure 4.21 – Select transformation in ADF showing selecting required columns

You can click on the trash can icon to delete the columns that are not needed.

- **Row transformations**: Some examples of a row transformation are updating rows and creating views. The following are transformations that apply to the rows of the table:

  - **Alter row**: This transformation is used to insert, delete, update, and upsert (insert or update) rows into a database or data warehouse. For example, *Figure 4.22* shows the rows inserted into a database only if the `DriverId` value's `Null` condition is not met:

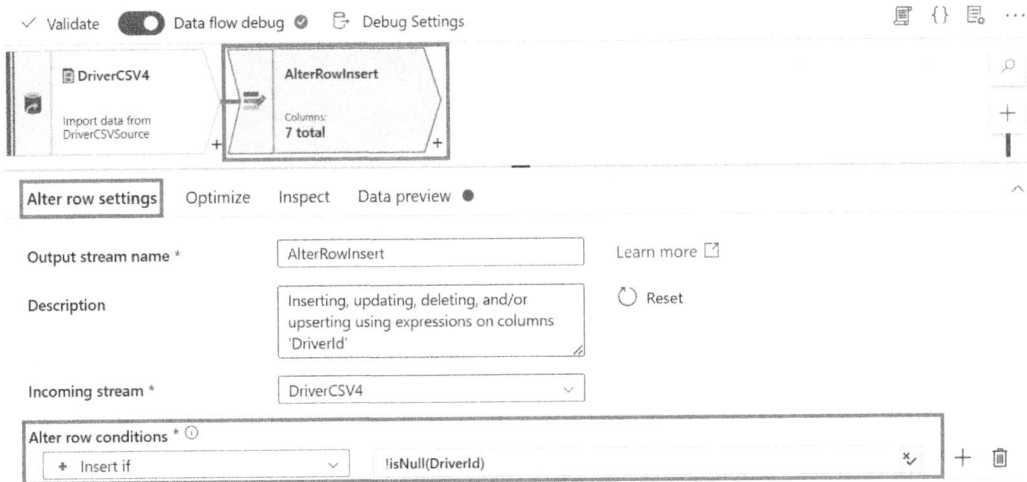

Figure 4.22 – Performing Alter row transformation as per NULL condition

Alter row works only on databases, Cosmos DB, or **REpresentational State Transfer (REST)** endpoint sinks.

- **Filter**: This is used to filter rows based on conditions. In *Figure 4.23*, rows are filtered where the City value is New York:

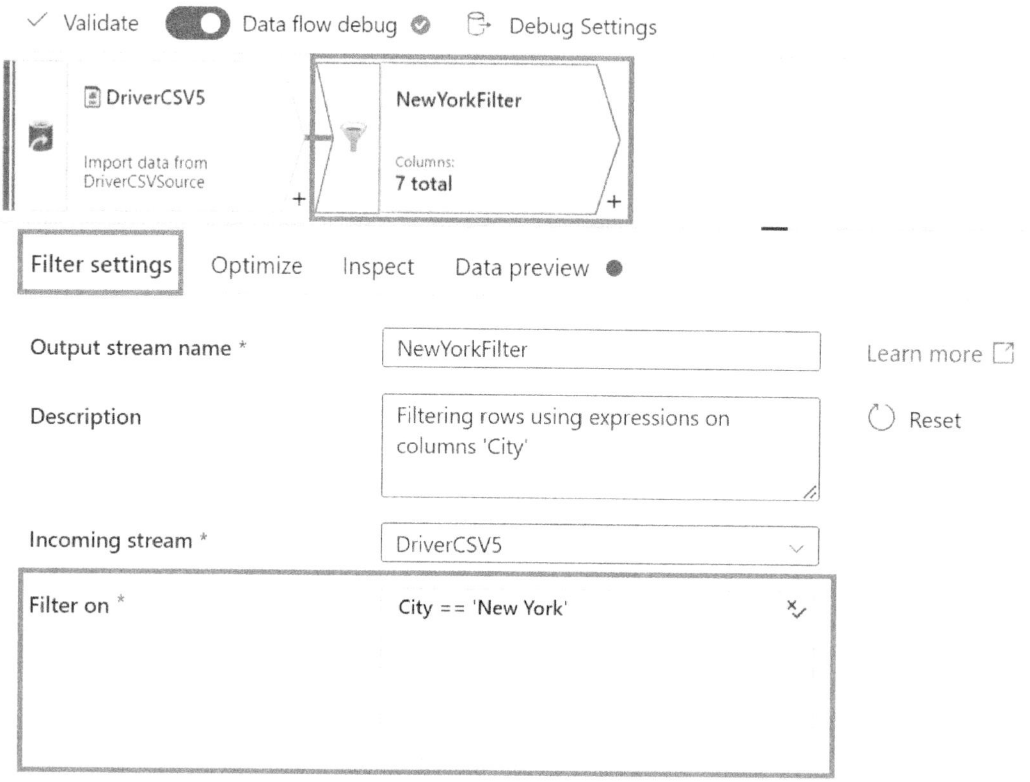

Figure 4.23 – Performing Filter transformation in ADF as per City

- **Sort**: This is used to sort rows based on any column or group of columns. *Figure 4.24* shows the **sort** conditions' Ascending order applied to the City column:

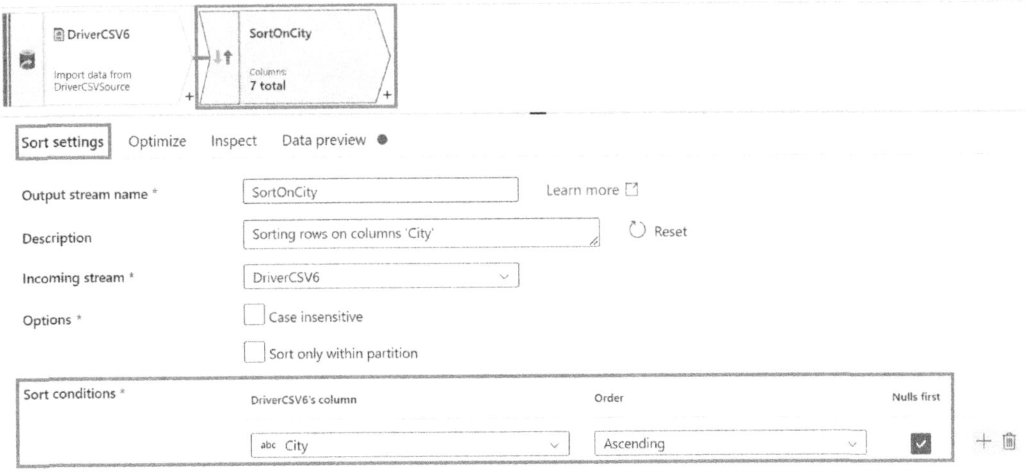

Figure 4.24 – Performing Sort transformation on specific rows

- **Multi-I/O transformations**: These are transformations that operate on more than one input or, conversely, split the input into more than one output. Some examples of such a transformation are splitting rows and merging rows, including the following:

  - **Conditional Split**: This transformation can be used to split the input into two output streams based on conditions. In *Figure 4.25*, you split the input based on Rating:

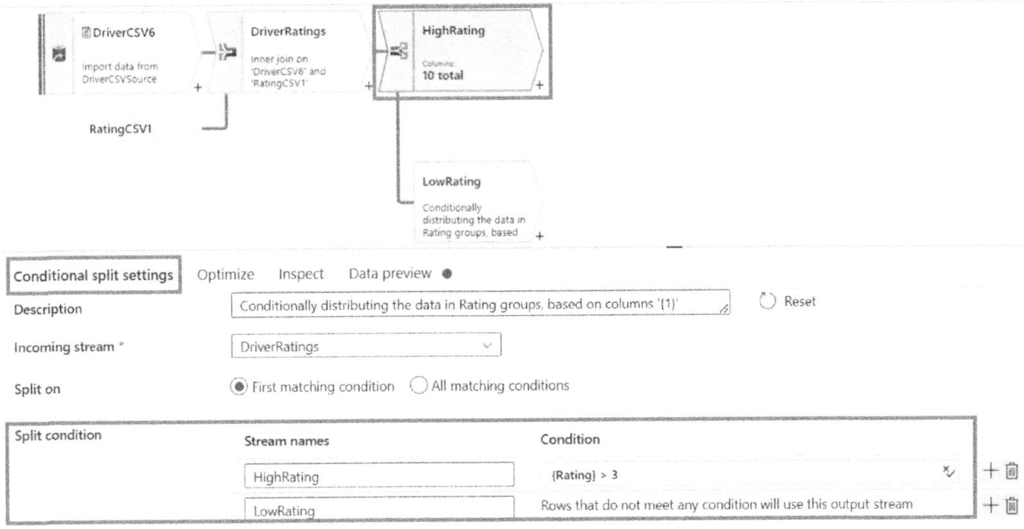

Figure 4.25 – Performing Conditional Split transformation in ADF for output or input stream

- **Join**: This transformation is used to join two streams based on one or more join conditions. *Figure 4.26* shows how to merge the `DriverCSV10` and `RatingsCSV2` datasets by using the `DriverId` value:

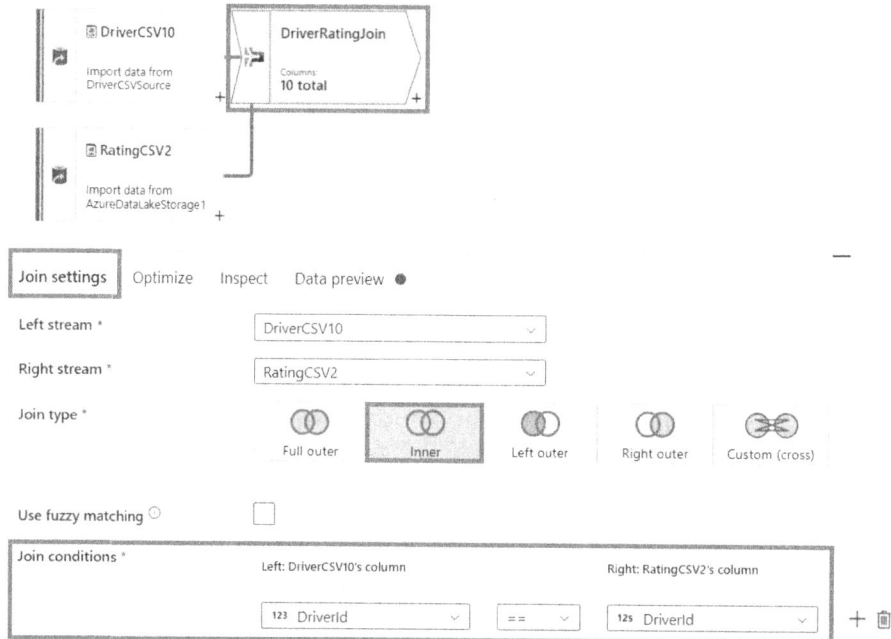

Figure 4.26 – Performing Join transformation in ADF based on join condition

- **Union**: This transformation merges two input datasets (`DriverCSV7` and `DriverCSV8`) with the same schema into one, as illustrated in *Figure 4.27*:

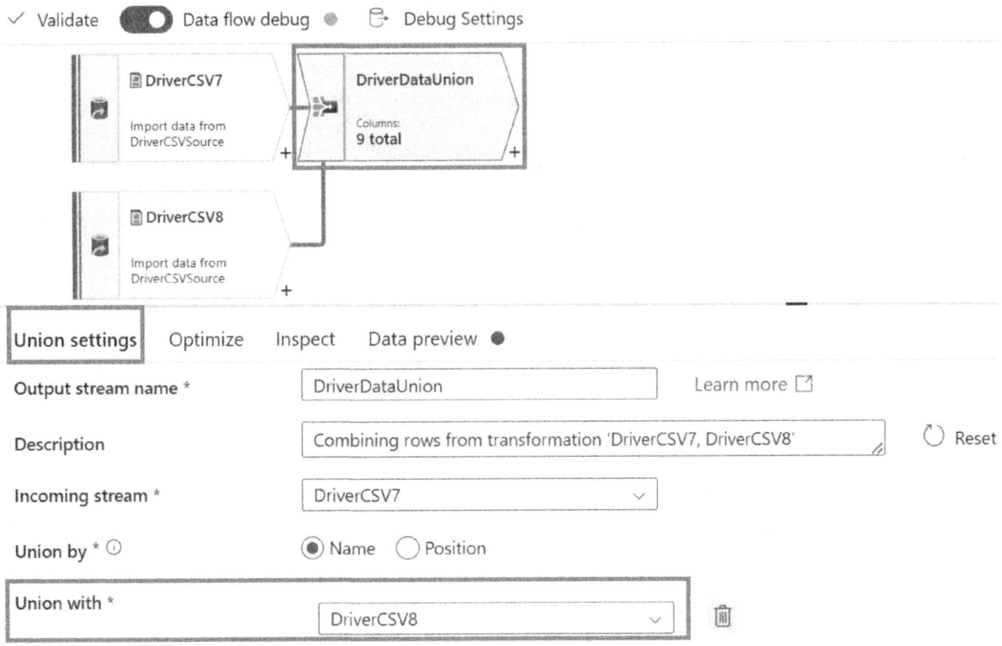

Figure 4.27 – Performing a Union example in ADF

> **Note**
>
> You can read a complete list of transformations in the Azure ADF documentation at `https://packt.link/FE1rA`.

ADF provides convenient templates that can accomplish a lot of the standard pipeline activities. The next section will throw light on that aspect.

## ADF Templates

ADF provides standard templates that you can use for various data copy and transformation activities. You can explore the templates by clicking on the pipeline `Template Gallery` link on the **ADF Studio** home page, as shown in *Figure 4.28*:

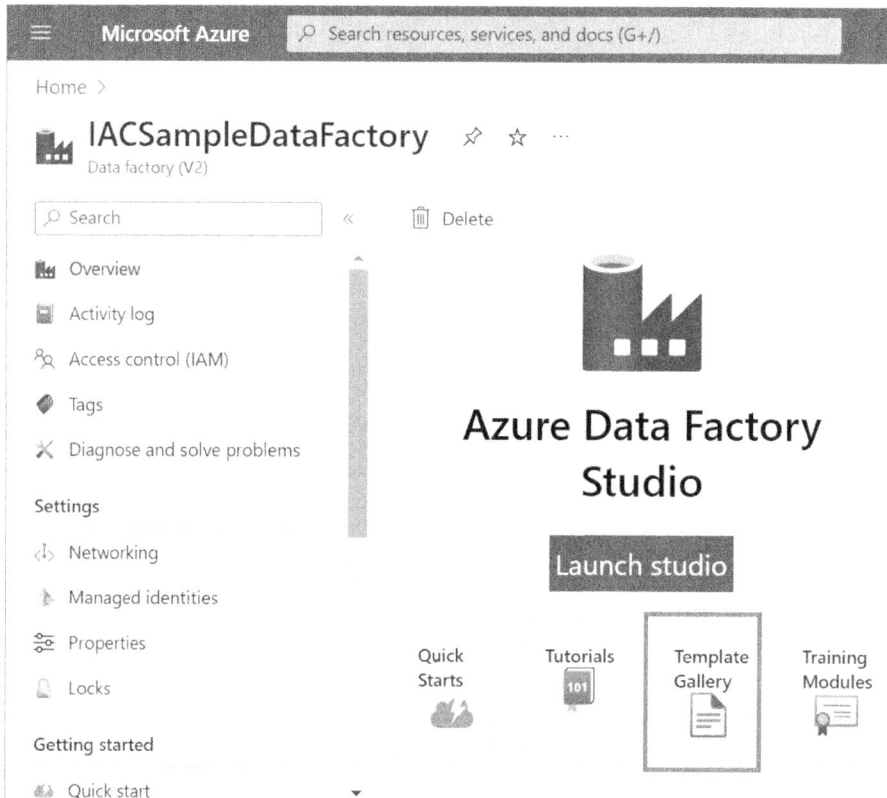

Figure 4.28 – Clicking the Template Gallery link to view the templates in ADF instance

Upon clicking the link, you will be able to view a sample of the template gallery (*Figure 4.29*):

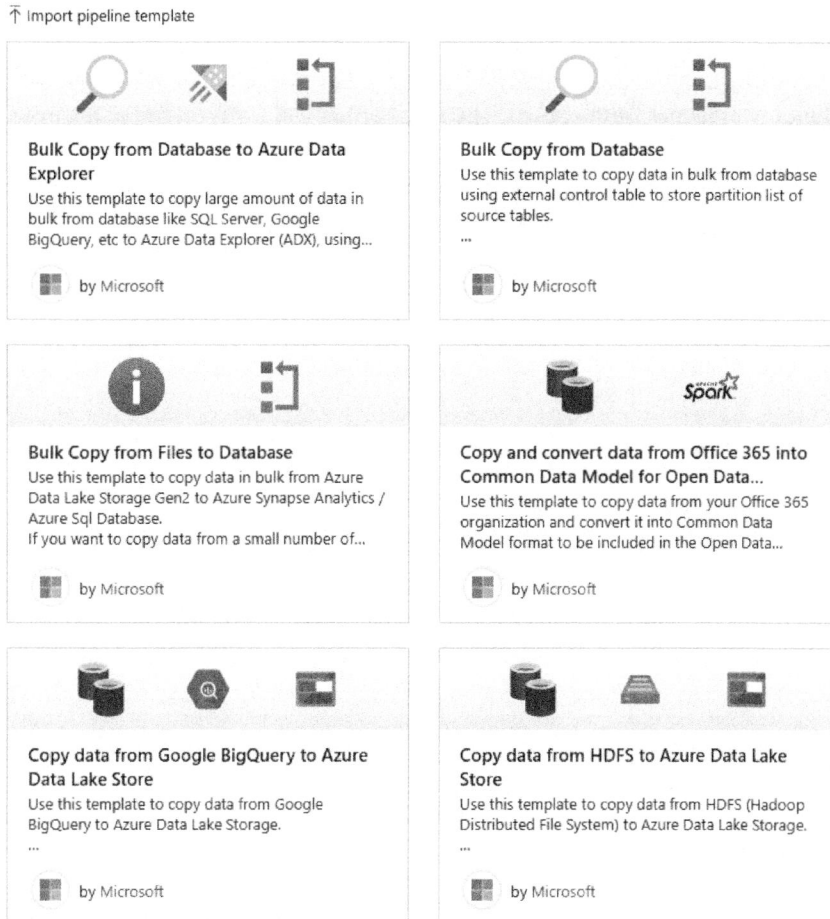

Figure 4.29 – ADF template gallery showing copy and transformation activities templates

> **Note**
>
> It may be better to use the templates wherever possible instead of reinventing the procedures, as this will save you a lot of time and prevent common pitfalls.

This section focused on Synapse pipelines that provide ADF-like capabilities within the Synapse workspace, simplifying integration with Synapse SQL and Spark pools. While both offer visual pipeline building, ADF features code-free data transformations (mapping data flows) for schema, row, and multi-I/O manipulation. You also learned how ADF provides pre-built templates for data copy and transformation under `Pipeline templates` on the ADF Studio home page, saving you time building pipelines from scratch. The next section will focus on the transformations with Synapse Pipelines.

## Transformations Using Synapse Pipelines

As mentioned earlier, Azure Synapse Pipelines are just ADF pipelines implemented inside Azure Synapse Analytics. So, the transformation examples that you saw in *The Transforming Options Available in ADF* section apply here too. The only difference is that in **Synapse Analytics**, no launch page exists, so you can directly add a pipeline activity within Synapse.

Since this is the first time you are using **Synapse Analytics** in this book, you can create an Azure Synapse Analytics workspace from the Azure portal. Perform the following steps to create a Synapse Analytics service using the Azure portal, which may come in handy in future chapters:

1.  From the **Azure portal** menu, select + `Create a resource`, as shown in *Figure 4.30*:

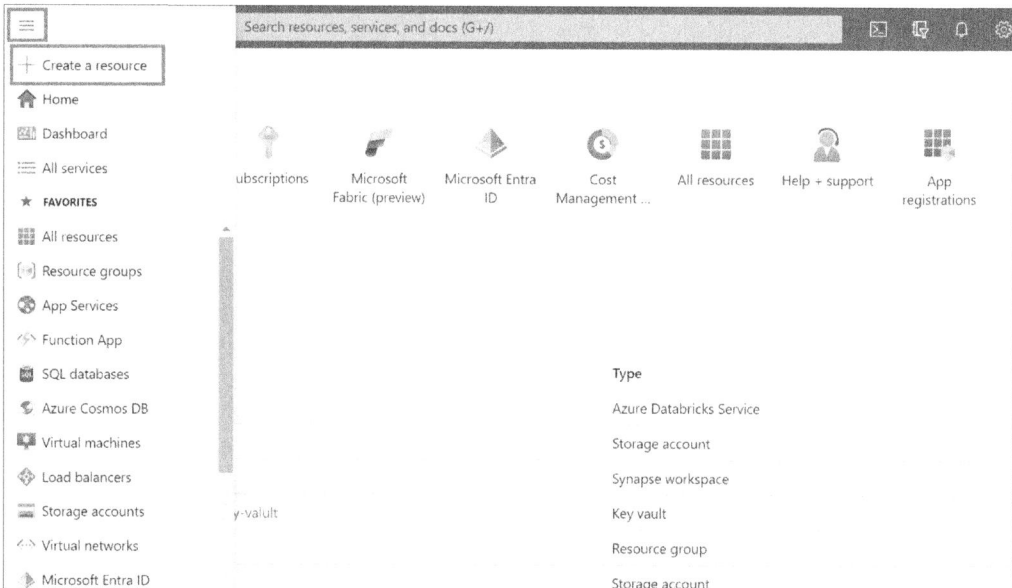

Figure 4.30 – Creating an Azure Synapse Analytics resource in the Azure portal

2.  Select Analytics, and then choose Azure Synapse Analytics, as shown in *Figure 4.31*:

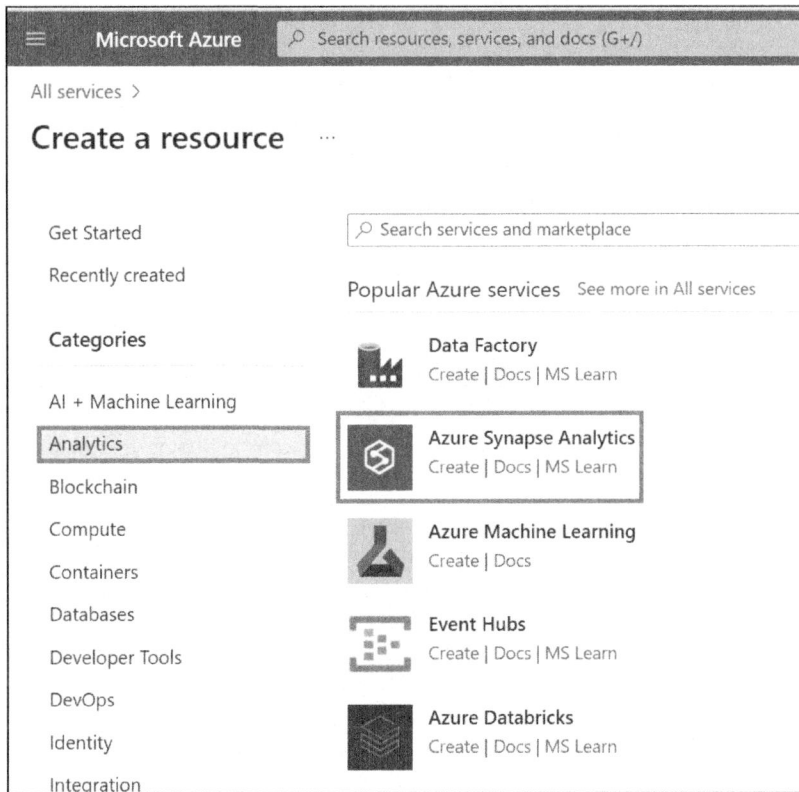

Figure 4.31 – Choosing an Azure Synapse Analytics service in the Azure portal

3. Create an Azure Synapse Analytics workspace by choosing the property. *Table 4.2* shows the description of each property:

| Property | Description |
|---|---|
| Subscription | From the dropdown, select your Azure subscription. In this case, it is Azure subscription. |
| Resource group | Specify whether you want to create a new resource group or use an existing one. For instance, here a new resource group is created, rg-dp203-synapseanalytics. |
| Workspace name | Provide a name for your Synapse Analytics workspace – for example, iacsynapsews. |
| Region | From the list of available regions in the dropdown, select the region where you want to deploy your Synapse Analytics resource. For instance, here the region chosen is UK South. |
| Data Lake Storage Gen2 | Choose the account that will be the primary storage account for your workspace, holding catalog data and metadata associated with the workspace. For instance, here, select the default option, From subscription. |
| Account name | Specify whether you want to create a new Data Lake Storage Gen2 account or use an existing one. For instance, here a new account is created, synapseazdl. |
| File system name | Specify whether you want to create a new file system (container) or use an existing one. For instance, here a new container is created, ws-container. |

Table 4.2 – Describing each property in Azure Synapse Analytics

*Figure 4.32* shows how to create an **Azure Synapse Analytics** workspace with the preceding properties entered:

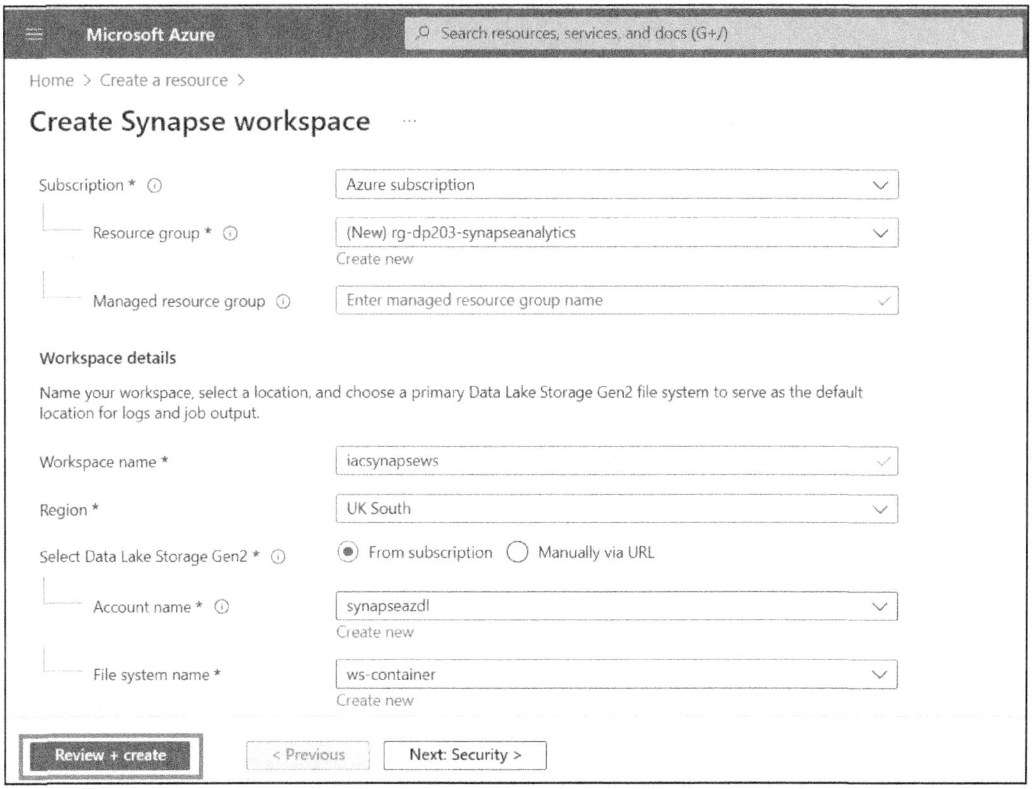

Figure 4.32 – Creating an Azure Synapse Analytics workspace

4.  Once you have provided the required property values, click `Review + create` to create the **Azure Synapse Analytics** workspace.

5.  You can launch the **Synapse Studio** to create pipelines from the `Synapse Analytics` tab, as shown in *Figure 4.33*:

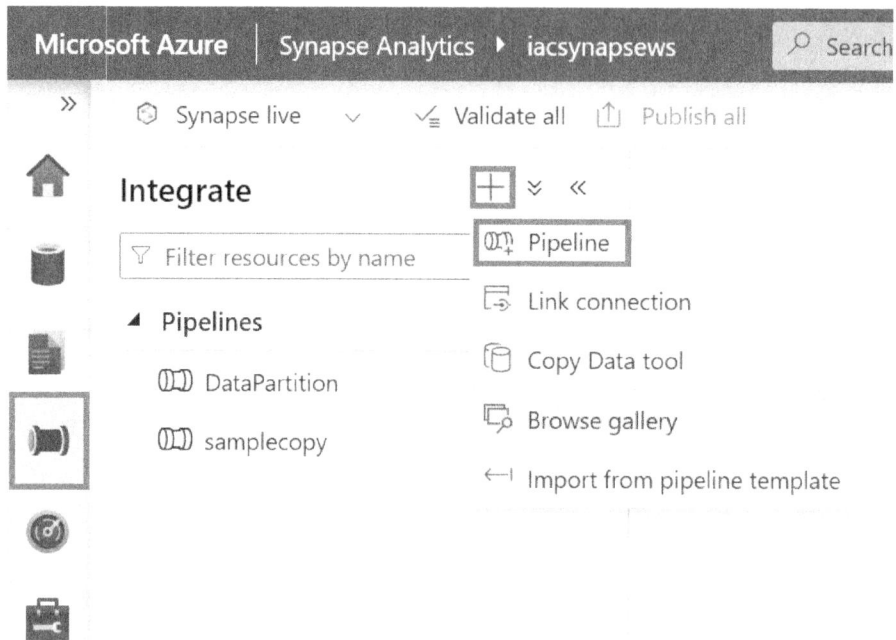

Figure 4.33 – Launching Synapse pipelines to perform transformations

By now, you should have a decent grasp of the transformations available in ADF and Synapse pipelines. The next section will take a look at the transformation options available in Stream Analytics.

> **Note**
>
> You will thoroughly explore Stream Analytics transformations, covering key concepts, best practices, and practical examples in *Chapter 6, Developing a Stream Processing Solution*. Here, the *Transforming Data Using Stream Analytics* section will provide an overview of its functionality to give you a glimpse of how it works.

# Transforming Data Using Stream Analytics

**Stream Analytics** is vital for real-time data processing, enabling transformation, filtering, and aggregation of continuous data streams from sources such as sensors, **IoT** devices, and social media. It allows you to manipulate incoming data in real time, including cleansing, calculations, enrichment, and triggering actions based on conditions.

Imagine various sensors employed throughout the city to enable effective traffic management, air quality, and energy consumption. Stream Analytics refines the raw sensor data into actionable insights by filtering out noise and aggregating information from multiple sources, creating a comprehensive picture of city traffic. It then cleanses the data of errors, calculates vehicle speeds and congestion levels, and even factors in external influences such as weather or event-related traffic jams. When congestion is detected, alerts are sent to traffic authorities, and mobile apps are updated with real-time conditions, allowing drivers to choose alternative routes.

> **Note**
>
> This section primarily focuses on the **Transform data by using Azure Stream Analytics** concept of the DP-203: Data Engineering on Microsoft Azure exam.

## Cleansing Data

**Cleansing data** is an important activity in any data pipeline. As data flows in from various sources, there are chances that the data won't adhere to the schemas, and there might be missing values, non-standard entries, duplicates, and so on. During the cleansing phase, you try to correct such anomalies.

> **Note**
>
> This section primarily focuses on the **Cleanse data** concept of the DP-203: Data Engineering on Microsoft Azure exam.

The following are a few common data-cleansing techniques:

- **Trimming inputs**: Values with trailing whitespace are a common problem. You can easily trim such values using the `trim()` method from within a **Derived column's settings** transformation. *Figure 4.34* shows an example:

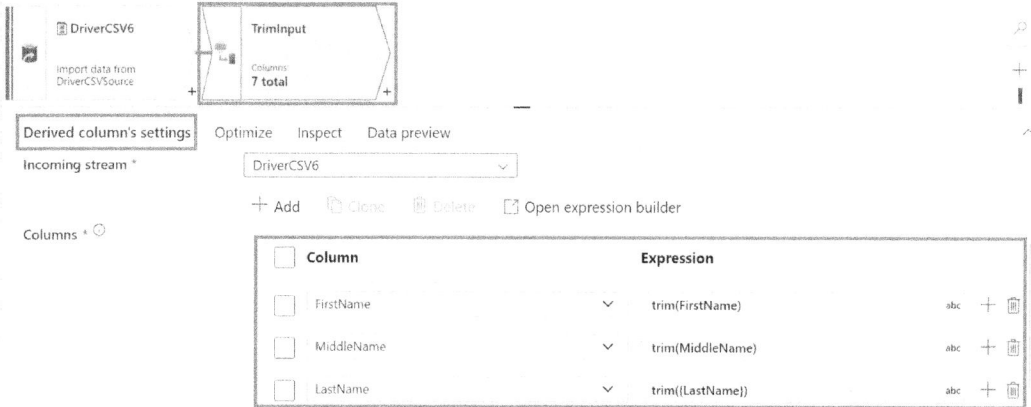

Figure 4.34 – Trimming whitespace in column values

*Figure 4.34* shows a simple operation and trims the whitespace if there is any within the specified columns. You can select the `Data preview` tab to view the output of this operation.

- **Standardizing values**: Different input sources might use different conventions for data. For example, say one of the input sources uses the $ symbol to represent the dollar value, whereas another input stream uses USD. In that case, you might want to standardize the inputs before sending them downstream for further processing.

*Figure 4.35* shows the command in the **Expression** field under the **Derived column's settings** transformation that is inserted to replace the $ symbol in the `Salary` column with USD:

```
replace({ Salary}, '$', 'USD') script:
```

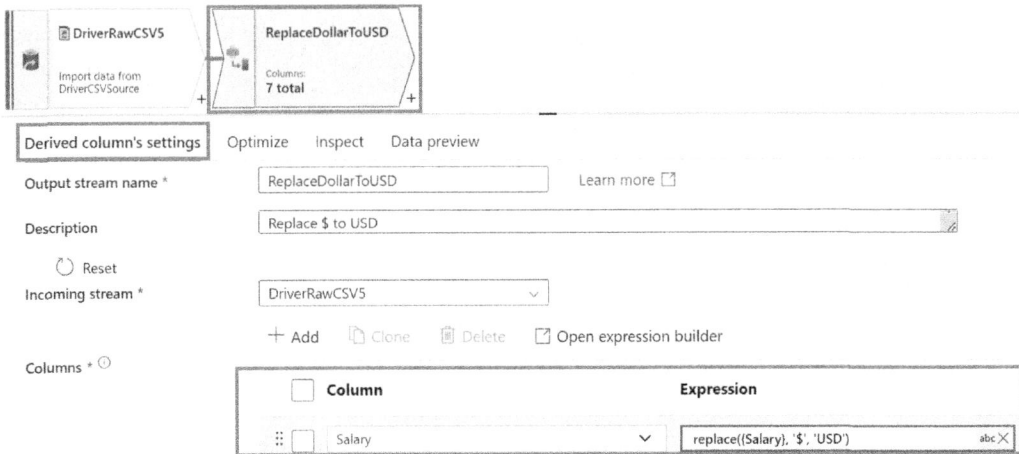

Figure 4.35 – Replacing $ values in Salary column with USD

- **Handling outliers**: If the values of some of the fields look abnormal, you could replace them with averages or median values. The example depicted in *Figure 4.36* shows the **Expression** field, substituting any value greater than 5,000 with AvgSalary in the Salary column:

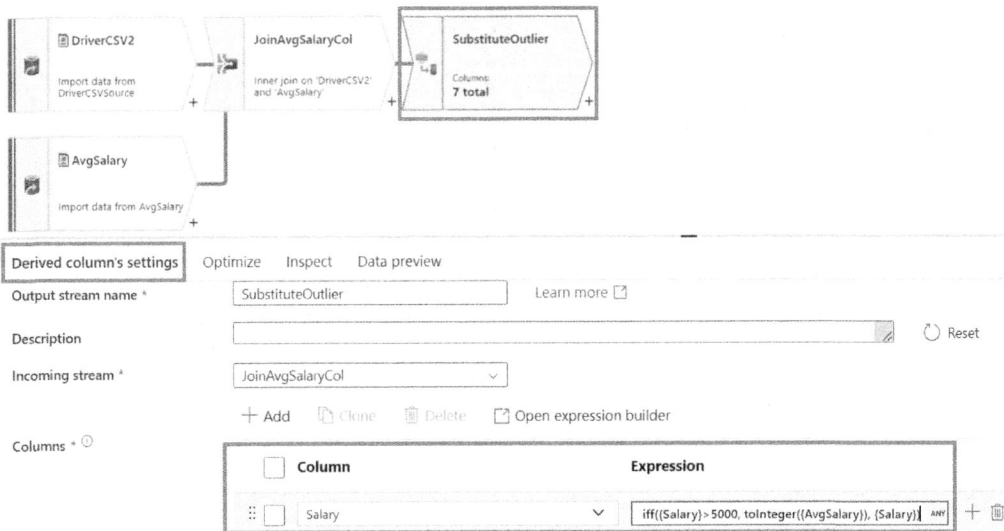

Figure 4.36 – Substituting value with AvgSalary

You can use the **Aggregate** transformation to find the average, median, min, max, and other mathematical grouping functions. You can select the `Data preview` tab to view the output of this operation.

## Handling Duplicate Data within Azure Environments

You can manage identical or similar records efficiently during data ingestion and transformation processes to maintain data integrity and accuracy. Duplicate data poses challenges, such as inconsistent analysis results and increased resource consumption.

Azure services offer solutions for handling duplicate data. ADF facilitates deduplication and cleaning during ETL processes, which involves identifying and removing duplicate records, while data cleansing corrects errors to reduce duplicates.

You can remove duplicate rows using the **Aggregate** transformation. *Figure 4.37* shows an example where the **Aggregate** transformation groups data by the `DriverId` column and calculates aggregate values to consolidate rows. This process helps to ensure that the dataset contains only unique and relevant records, which helps you with accurate analysis and reporting:

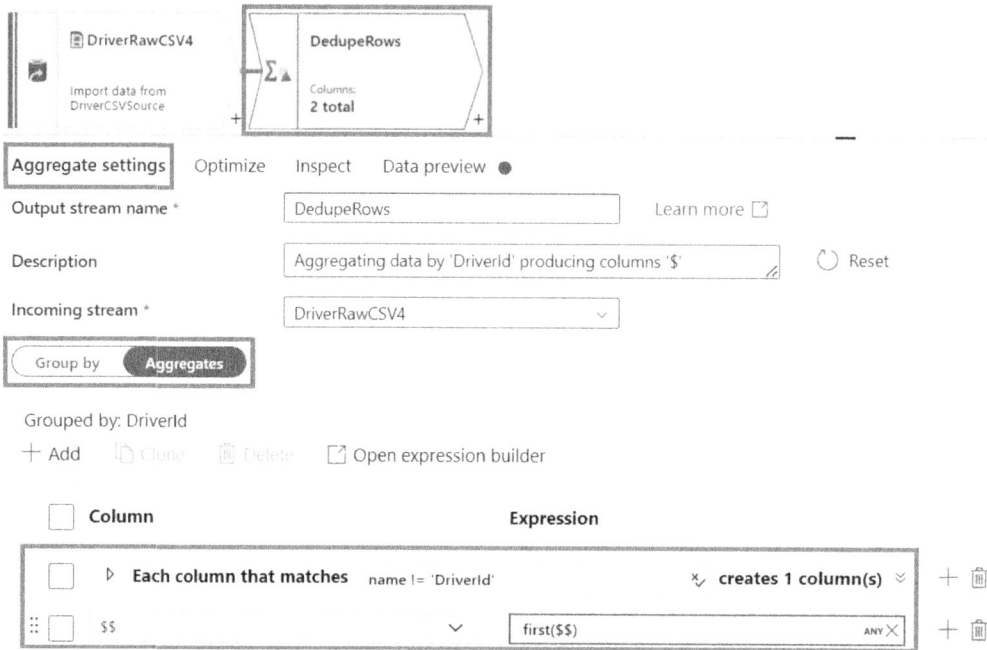

Figure 4.37 – Deduping using the Aggregate transformation

> **Note**
>
> This section primarily focuses on the **Handle duplicate data** and **Avoiding duplicate data by using Azure Stream Analytics Exactly Once Delivery data** concepts of the DP-203: Data Engineering on Microsoft Azure exam.

Aggregates by default emit only the column that is operated upon. In this case, since the aggregates are grouped on `DriverId`, they would just emit the `DriverId` column. In order to overcome this, under the **Column** field and the **Each column that matches** option, specify `name != 'DriverId'` so that all the other columns also show up in the output. You can select the `Data preview` tab to view the output of this operation.

> **Note**
>
> You can accomplish any of this cleansing and data preparation work using the Spark or SQL transformations that you read about earlier in the chapter. Those would work perfectly fine too.

By now, you are aware of the most commonly used cleansing operations. With the variety of transformations available in ADF, Spark, and SQL, you can get creative on how to accomplish your tasks efficiently. Now, you will look at how you can deal with missing data.

## Handling Missing Data

You can handle missing or Null values in multiple ways – choose to filter out such rows, substitute missing values with default values, or substitute them with some meaningful values such as mean, median, and average. The following are two of the approaches:

- **Substituting with default values**: This can be achieved using the **Derived column's settings** transformation. *Figure 4.38* shows an example where you replace missing values with a default string such as NA:

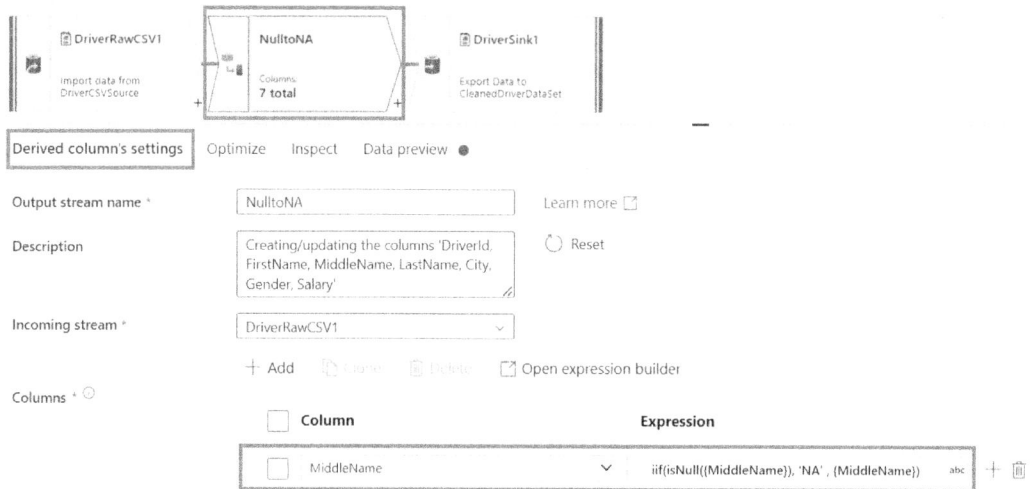

Figure 4.38 – Substituting missing values with default values

- **Filtering out Null values**: You can filter out Null values using the **Alter row** transformation, as you have already seen in *Figure 4.22*.

You can select the Data preview tab to view the output of this operation.

> **Note**
> This section primarily focuses on the **Handle missing data** concept of the DP-203: Data Engineering on Microsoft Azure exam.

# Handling Late-Arriving Data

A late-arriving data scenario can be considered at three different stages in a data pipeline – during the data ingestion, the transformation phase, and the serving phase:

- **Handling late-arriving data in the data ingestion/transformation stages**: During the ingestion and transformation scenario, the activities usually include copying data into the data lake and performing data transformations using engines such as Spark and Hive. In such scenarios, the following two methods can be used to handle data loss:

  - **Dropping the data**: This method is used if your application can handle some amount of data loss. This is the easiest option. You can keep a record of the last timestamp that was processed. And if the new data has an older timestamp, you can just ignore that message and move forward.

  - **Rerunning the pipeline**: You can rerun the pipeline from the ADF Monitoring tab if your application cannot handle data loss.

- **Handling late-arriving data in the serving phase**: In the serving phase, data handling is usually done via a star or snowflake schema for **Online Analytical Processing (OLAP)** scenarios. In such cases, there might be situations where a dimension arrives late (or a fact might arrive early). The following are a few common methods to handle such scenarios:

  - **Dropping the message**: Like in the ingestion/transformation stage, this is the easiest option, especially if the old data doesn't add much value.

  - **Storing the message and retrying after some time**: In this technique, store the early-arriving fact rows in a staging table and try inserting this fact in the next iteration, hoping that the dimension will have arrived by then. Repeat this process a pre-determined number of times before declaring failure.

  - **Inserting a dummy record in the dimension table**: In this technique, if the corresponding dimension record doesn't exist, just enter a dummy record in its place. You will have to revisit all the dummy records and update them with real values once the dimension values arrive. If you have enough details about the dimension, you can infer the dimension row and insert the newly derived dimension row with a new surrogate key.

> **Note**
> This section primarily focuses on the **Handle late-arriving data** concept of the DP-203: Data Engineering on Microsoft Azure exam.

By now, you have learned to handle late-arriving data. The ability to manage data that arrives after the expected timeframe ensures that the analytics remain accurate. Azure provides a set of tools such as Spark and Hive that offer various features to effectively handle late-arriving data. Next, you will look at how to split data in data pipelines.

## Splitting Data

ADF provides multiple ways to split data in a pipeline to enhance workflow flexibility, performance, scalability, and resource optimization. By utilizing various data splitting techniques, you can design robust data processing pipelines capable of handling diverse data processing requirements to achieve efficient data orchestration. This capability allows you to partition data into smaller subsets for parallel processing or to route data to different branches of the pipeline based on specific criteria. Within the data splitting, the important ones are **Conditional Split** and **cloning** (new branch).

> **Note**
>
> This section primarily focuses on the **Split data** concept of the DP-203: Data Engineering on Microsoft Azure exam.

While Conditional Split is used to split data based on certain conditions, the New branch option is used to just copy the entire dataset for a new execution flow. You have already seen an example of a Conditional Split in *Figure 4.25*. You will now create a new branch in the data pipeline to duplicate the entire dataset for a new execution flow. This enables parallel processing or performing different operations on the same dataset without affecting the original data flow.

Creating a new branch is useful when you need to apply additional transformations, filters, or operations to a dataset independently from the main pipeline, preserving the integrity of the original data flow. It enables you to experiment with different processing paths, conduct A/B testing, or apply alternative data processing logic while maintaining the flexibility and scalability of the overall data pipeline architecture.

To create a new branch, click on the + icon next to any data source artifact. In this case, the data source is the `DriverCSV11` block. Then, choose the `New branch` option, as shown in *Figure 4.39*. You can also see the **Conditional Split** option in the drop-down menu (*Figure 4.39*):

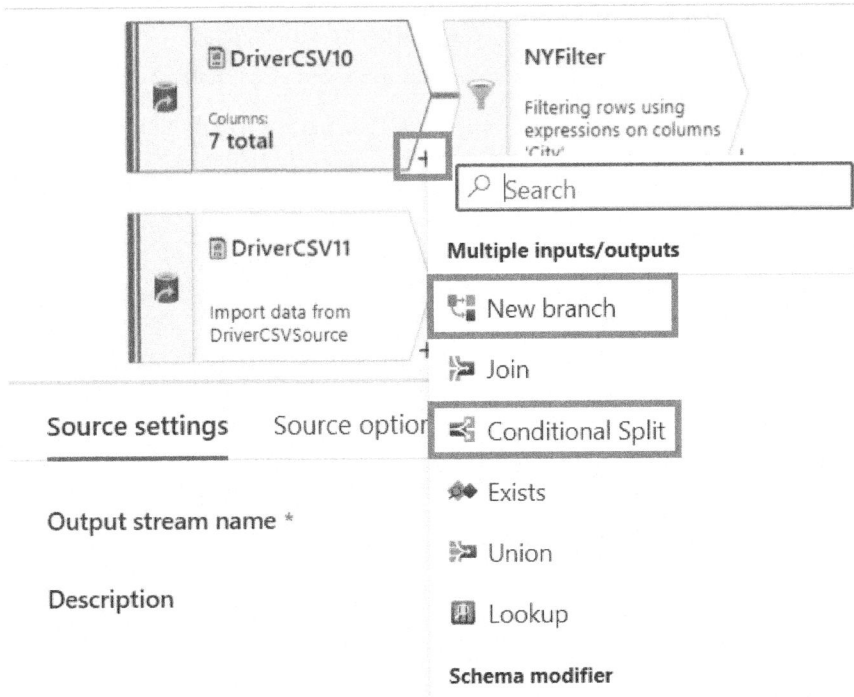

Figure 4.39 – Selecting New branch option to copy the entire dataset for a new execution flow

Apart from these two options – Conditional Split and New branch – ADF also allows you to split the input files into multiple sub-files using partitions. You can then select the Data preview tab to view the output of this operation.

## File Splits

The File splits option allows you to define how data should be divided during the dataflow process, by specifying the number of partitions. You are essentially instructing the dataflow on how to parallelize the data processing by setting a certain number of partitions, which can be processed concurrently and potentially improve performance.

To use file splits, perform the following steps:

1.  Create a new **Sink** artifact by clicking on the Sink tab.

2.  Then, choose the Optimize tab.

3.  Select Set partitioning.

4.   Select Round Robin.

5.   Specify the number of partitions required. In this case, it is 2 (*Figure 4.40*):

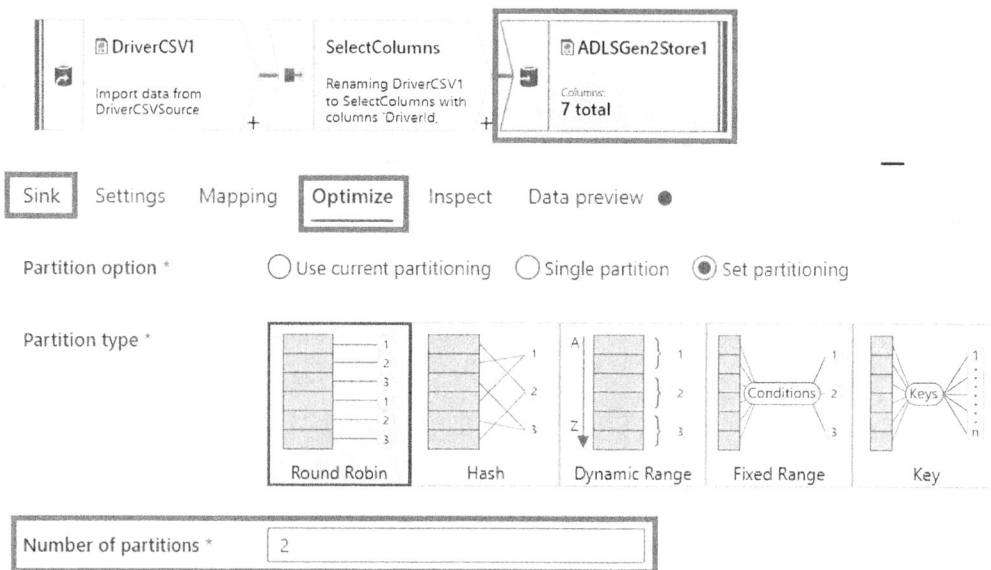

Figure 4.40 – Splitting files using ADF based on the number of partitions

You can select the Data preview tab to view the output of this operation.

You have now learned how to split the data for processing. The next section will detail how data is extracted from JSON files.

## Shredding JSON to Manage Data Elements

**Shredding JSON** is a process used in data handling where a **JSON** document is broken down into more manageable parts for easier processing and analysis. When you shred a JSON document, you are essentially decomposing it into individual components, such as key-value pairs or arrays, which can be stored in a database or used in various applications. This process is particularly useful when dealing with complex nested JSON structures, as it allows you to extract specific data elements and load them into structured storage systems, such as relational databases or data warehouses.

The following are used to shred JSON:

- **Improving data accessibility**: This makes it simpler to find and use specific pieces of information within a JSON document. This will help with tasks such as searching and analyzing data more effectively.

- **Enhancing data management**: Handling data is easier when transforming it into a format that's simpler to work with. This will save you time and effort when organizing and changing data.

- **Facilitate integration**: Combine JSON data seamlessly with other types of data and systems. This will make it easier to compare and analyze data from different sources, leading to more insightful reports and analyses.

Thus, **shredding** refers to the process of extracting data from JSON files into tables. Spark, Synapse SQL pools, and ADF provide native support to extract data from JSON.

> **Note**
> This section primarily focuses on the **Shred JSON** concept of the DP-203: Data Engineering on Microsoft Azure exam.

The following sections will provide examples of this process for each of these services:

- **Extracting values from JSON using Spark**: Spark can directly read JSON files and extract the schema from them. The following is a simple code snippet that can accomplish the JSON read:

```
val dfJSON = spark.read.json("abfss://path/to/json/*.json")
dfJSON.printSchema()
dfJSON.show(false)
```

The preceding code initializes a DataFrame by reading JSON files from a specified path. The `spark.read.json` method is used to read the JSON file and load it into the DataFrame. The `printSchema()` method is called on the DataFrame to print its schema. The schema outlines the structure of the JSON data, including the names and data types of each column. The `show(false)` method is used to display the concepts of the DataFrame in a tabular format. The `false` parameter ensures that the content is fully displayed without truncation.

On execution, the output will be displayed as shown in *Figure 4.41*:

```
root
 |-- firstname: string (nullable = true)
 |-- gender: string (nullable = true)
 |-- id: integer (nullable = true)
 |-- lastname: string (nullable = true)
 |-- location: string (nullable = true)
 |-- middlename: string (nullable = true)
 |-- salary: integer (nullable = true)


+---------+------+---+--------+----------+----------+------+
|firstname|gender| id|lastname|  location|middlename|salary|
+---------+------+---+--------+----------+----------+------+
|Catherine|Female|102|    NULL|California|   Goodwin|  4300|
|    Jenny|Female|104|  Simons|   Arizona|      Anne|  3400|
|    Bryan|  Male|101|Williams|  New York|         M|  4000|
|    Alice|Female|100|    Hood|  New York|      NULL|  4100|
|    Daryl|  Male|103|   Jones|   Florida|      NULL|  5500|
|    Daryl|  Male|103|   Jones|   Florida|      NULL|  5500|
+---------+------+---+--------+----------+----------+------+
```

Figure 4.41 – The output of JSON operation

You can also manually specify the schema, as shown in the following example:

```
import org.apache.spark.sql.types
val driverSchema = new StructType()
.add("firstname", StringType)
.add("gender", StringType)
.add("id", IntegerType)
.add("lastname", StringType)
.add("location", StringType).add("middlename", StringType)

.add("salary",IntegerType)
val dfJSON = spark.read.schema(driverSchema).json("abfss://path/
to/json/*.json")
```

Once you have the data in the DataFrame, you can use any of the transformations available in Spark on it to extract and modify data.

---

**Note**

You can find the complete code in the accompanying GitHub repository at https://packt.
link/0xOVJ.

- **Extracting values from JSON using SQL**: T-SQL provides the OPENROWSET function to query remote data stores. You can use this function to bulk-load data into dedicated or Serverless SQL instances. The following is an example of how you can load and parse JSON files from remote storage using Serverless SQL:

```
SELECT
    JSON_VALUE(doc, <$.firstname') AS firstname,
    JSON_VALUE(doc, <$.lastname') AS lastname,
    CAST(JSON_VALUE(doc, <$.id>) AS INT) as driverid,
    CAST(JSON_VALUE(doc, '$.salary') AS INT) as salary
FROM openrowset(
        BULK <abfss://path/to/json/*.json',
        FORMAT = 'csv',
        FIELDTERMINATOR ='0x0b',
        FIELDQUOTE = '0x0b'
    ) WITH (doc nvarchar(max)) AS ROWS
GO
```

You need to specify the FORMAT value as csv for JSON, as highlighted in the code snippet, which indicates that the data being processed or imported should be treated as a CSV format. This is often used in data transformation tasks where you are code-interpreting a JSON file as containing CSV data, which can be necessary when the JSON file encapsulates CSV data as a string, or when converting JSON data to a CSV format for compatibility with the system that requires CSV input.

The results for the preceding query would look something like the one shown in *Figure 4.42*:

| firstname | lastname | driverid | salary |
|-----------|----------|----------|--------|
| Alice | Hood | 100 | 4100 |
| Bryan | Williams | 101 | 4000 |
| Daryl | Jones | 103 | 5500 |
| Daryl | Jones | 103 | 5500 |
| Jenny | Simons | 104 | 3400 |
| Catherine | | 102 | 4300 |

Figure 4.42 – Sample output of parsing JSON using OPENROWSET

> **Note**
>
> You can find the complete code in the accompanying GitHub repository at `https://packt.link/Y8af0`.

- **Extracting values from JSON using ADF**: ADF provides the **Flatten** transformation functionality to convert hierarchical data structures such as JSON into flat structures, such as tables. There is another similar denormalization transformation called **Pivot**, which you will learn about in the *Normalizing and Denormalizing Values* section later in this chapter.

  Say that you have a source dataset with the following JSON:

  ```
  {
     «firstname": "Alice",
     «middlename": "",
     «lastname": "Hood",
     "id": "100",
     «locations»: [{«city»: «San Francisco","state": "CA"},
       {«city»: «San Jose","state": "CA"},
       {"city": "Miami", "state": "FL"}
     ],
     "gender": "Female"
  }
  ```

  Select the `Flatten settings` transformation from ADF and specify the `Input columns` mapping, as shown in *Figure 4.43*:

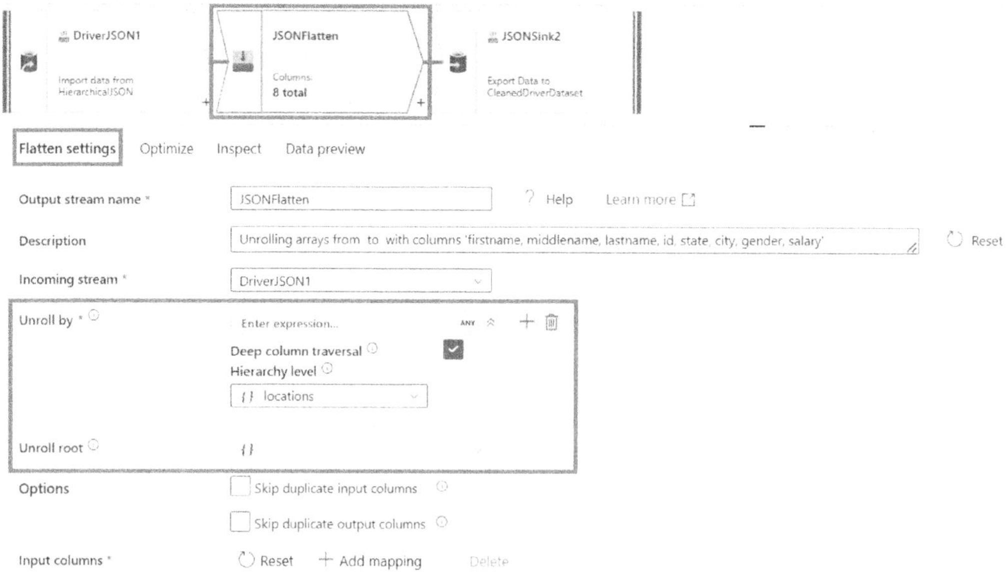

Figure 4.43 – Performing Flatten transformation in ADF

For complex structures such as arrays within JSON, you can use Unroll by to split them into multiple rows. In the example shown in *Figure 4.43*, you can see that the locations field—an array—has been denormalized into separate lines in the Input columns section, whereas the Unroll root option is blank, which typically means that the entire JSON document is considered. If you specify a root element, then only the arrays within that root element will be unrolled.

---

**Note**

You can find the complete code in the accompanying GitHub repository at `https://packt. link/fKcy4`. You can learn more about Flatten transformation at `https://packt. link/vbDmg`.

---

Now, you have extracted values using ADF. In this section, you learned the process of breaking down JSON data into a structured format that can be stored and analyzed, using services such as ADF, SQL, and Spark, which allows you to create collaborative environments to work with data and extract values. The next step is to learn how to encode and decode data.

# Encoding and Decoding Data

The **Encode** and **Decode** operations play a pivotal role in ensuring the integrity and efficiency of data ingestion and transformation processes. These operations involve converting data from one format to another and optimizing it for storage, transmission, or analysis purposes. By utilizing the following operations, you can improve data quality and streamline the data processing pipeline for enhanced efficiency and effectiveness:

- **Encoding data**: This is the process of converting data from one form to another for efficient transmission or storage. In data ingestion, encoding can involve compressing data, encrypting it for security, or transforming it into a format suitable for the target system.

- **Decoding data**: This is a reverse process of encoding, where decoding involves converting encoded data back to its original form. This is essential for data analysis and reporting, and decoding also ensures that data remains accurate and usable after it has been stored.

In this section, you will see how to take care of encoding and decoding values such as **American Standard Code for Information Interchange** (**ASCII**), **Unicode Transformation Format-8** (**UTF-8**), and UTF-16 while reading or writing data from different sources.

---

**Note**

This section primarily focuses on the **Encode and decode data** concept of the DP-203: Data Engineering on Microsoft Azure exam.

---

You will see examples using Spark, SQL, and ADF as follows:

- **Encoding and decoding using SQL**: In Synapse SQL, **collation** defines the encoding type, sorting type, and so on in SQL strings. Collation can be set at both the **database** and **table** levels. At the database level, you can set the collation, as follows:

```
CREATE DATABASE TripsDB COLLATE Latin1_General_100_BIN2_UTF8;
```

At the table level, you can set it as follows:

```
CREATE EXTERNAL TABLE FactTrips (
    [tripId] VARCHAR (40) COLLATE Latin1_General_100_BIN2_UTF8,
    . . .
)
```

Once you define the right collation, Synapse SQL takes care of storing the data in the right format and using the right set of encoding for further operations on that dataset.

- **Encoding and decoding using Spark**: Spark supports methods called `encode` and `decode`, which can be used to accomplish conversion. The following Spark SQL example shows a simple `encode` and `decode` operation:

```
>SELECT hex(encode('Azure', 'UTF-16'));
FEFF0041007A007500720065
>SELECT decode(X'FEFF0041007A007500720065', 'UTF-16')
Azure
```

In the code, note that you convert the data to hexadecimal (`hex`) format to display the results in a compact and readable format. However, you can directly use the `encode` and `decode` methods without the `hex()` function. The `encode` and `decode` methods are also available in the Python and Scala versions of Spark.

- **Encoding and decoding using ADF**: ADF allows you to specify the "right" encoding in the dataset artifacts. So, click on the `Connection` tab to see the **Encoding** field, as shown in *Figure 4.44*:

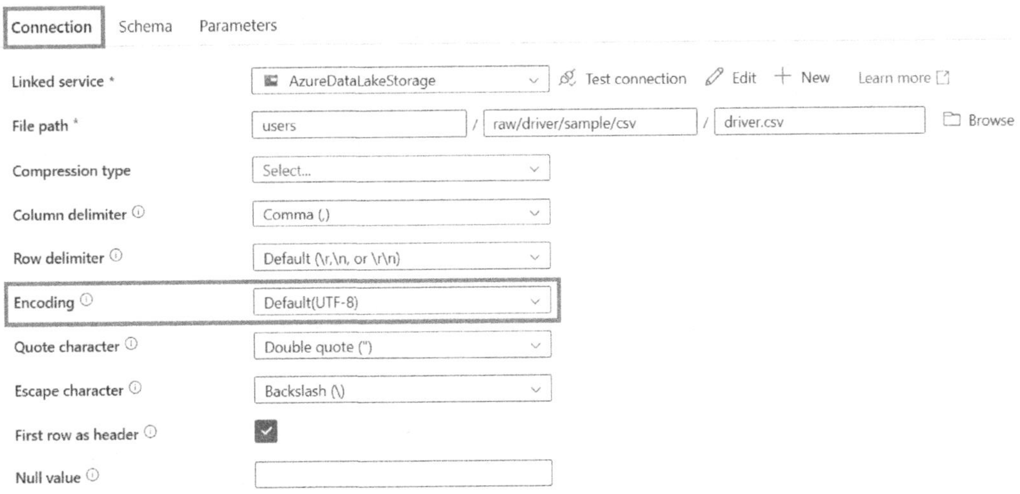

Figure 4.44 – Using the Encoding function in ADF source datasets

Apart from the dataset encoding option, ADF also provides functions to encode and decode **Uniform Resource Identifiers (URIs)**, Base64, and so on using its conversion commands. A few conversion commands from the ADF documentation are displayed in *Table 4.3*:

| Commands | Description |
| --- | --- |
| base64 ToBinary ( ) | This returns the binary version for a Base64-encoded string |
| base64ToString ( ) | This returns the string version for a Base64-encoded string |
| decodeBase64 ( ) | This returns the string version for a Base64-encoded string |
| dataUriToBinary ( ) | This returns the binary version for a data URI |
| dataUriToString ( ) | This returns the string version for a data URI |
| decodeDataUri ( ) | This returns the binary version for a data URI |

Table 4.3 – The encoding/decoding functions available in ADF

> **Note**
> You can find the complete code in the accompanying GitHub repository at https://packt. link/VTTF1. You can find a detailed list of conversion functions in ADF at https:// packt.link/7rgWz.

Now that you have grasped the encoding and decoding values such as ASCII, UTF-8, and UTF-16, you'll learn to configure error handling in ADF transformations in the following section.

## Configuring Error Handling for the Transformation

In all the examples of ADF pipelines you used in this chapter, you have only seen success cases. However, ADF also provides a separate flow to handle errors and failures.

> **Note**
>
> This section primarily focuses on the **Configure error handling for a transformation data** concept of the DP-203: Data Engineering on Microsoft Azure exam.

In fact, ADF supports four different flows—Success, Failure, Completion, and Skipped—as shown in *Figure 4.45*:

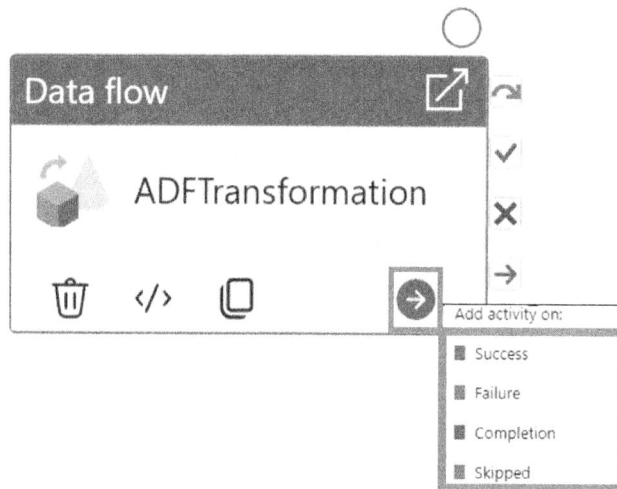

Figure 4.45 – ADF supporting four activity flows

If any errors are encountered at any step of the pipeline, you can build an error-handling branch that can be used to either fix the errors or store them for future actions. *Figure 4.46* shows one such pipeline. You will have to connect the indicated line to the error-handling activity:

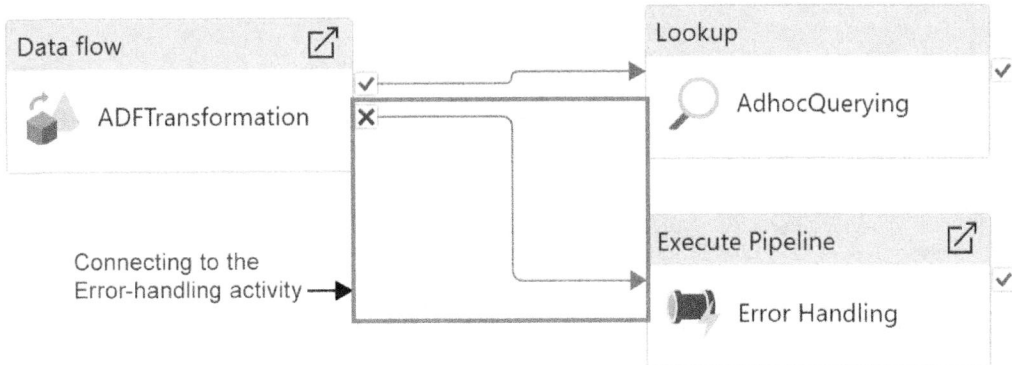

Figure 4.46 – Creating an error-handling pipeline

Select the Execute Pipeline activity and link the failure flow (Error Handling) activity from the other activities to it. This new **Execute Pipeline** activity could be a full-fledged pipeline in itself (as with the transformation pipelines that you saw earlier in the chapter in the *Transforming Options Available in ADF* section), or it could be a simple standalone activity to just record the error logs. It can also be configured to insert the error details into a database so that you can analyze the errors later using the familiar SQL scripts.

ADF Sink also provides options to automatically write error lines to an external data store such as a **Blob Storage**. This is another convenient option that helps analyze errors asynchronously. It can be configured using the `Error row handling settings` option on the `Settings` tab of the `Sink` activity, as shown in *Figure 4.47*:

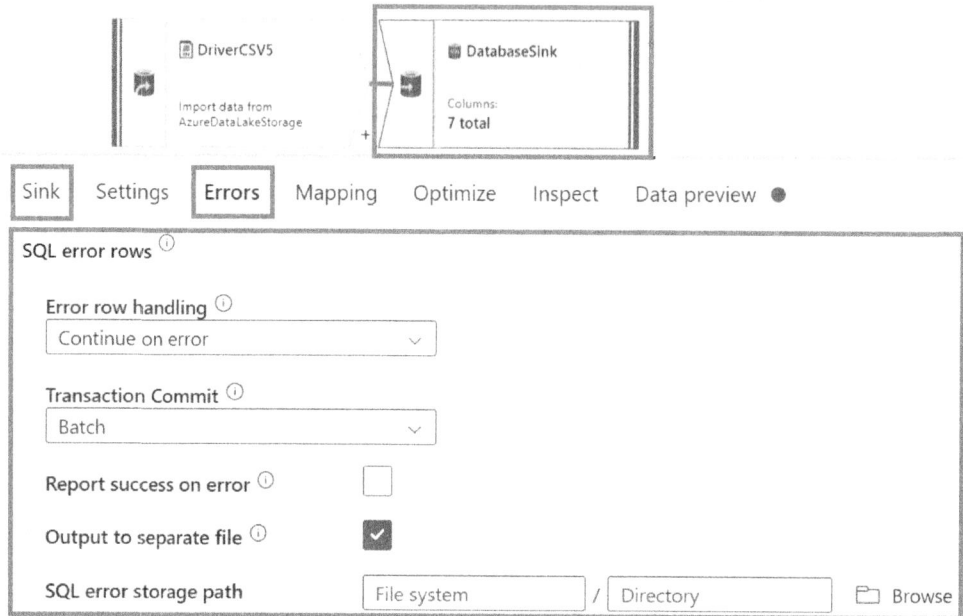

Figure 4.47 – Redirecting error lines to Blob Storage

You can find the output of the operation by clicking the `Data preview` tab. Now, you have learned to manage the errors that occur during the data transformation process to implement an error-handling mechanism, using ADF, to redirect errors to different activities for further analysis. Next, you'll look at the Pivot and Unpivot features, which are used to normalize and denormalize tables.

## Normalizing and Denormalizing Values

You already know about the ADF Flatten activity from the *Shredding JSON to Manage Data Elements* section, which helps to denormalize data. There are two more such transformations to help normalize and denormalize datasets – **Pivot** and **Unpivot**.

Normalization and denormalization are two fundamental processes in data management. **Normalization** is like getting your data's house in order. It ensures everything has its proper place, reducing clutter to enhance data integrity. It is all about breaking down a dataset into multiple tables and establishing clear relationships between them, thus making it simpler to find what you need without duplicates or confusion. It is like organizing a messy bookshelf into neat sections.

Conversely, **denormalization** is the process of combining multiple table data into a single table. This is done to improve the performance of the database by reducing the complexity of queries that join multiple tables, which can be slow and resource-intensive.

Normalization can be seen as a way of organizing data in a structured manner, similar to how pivoting can restructure data for better analysis. Denormalization, on the other hand, can be viewed as a form of optimization, which may involve reverting pivoted data to a more denormalized state for better performance.

The **Pivot** operation transforms rows into columns, allowing for a more compact data representation that is often used in reporting and visualization. You can transform unique values from one column into multiple columns and summarize data in the process.

Conversely, **Unpivot** is the reverse operation, where you can transform columns into rows. This is useful for normalizing data and making it more suitable for analysis, as it converts a wide format to a long format, effectively increasing the number of rows and decreasing the number of columns.

> **Note**
>
> This section primarily focuses on the **Normalize and denormalize data** concept of the DP-203: Data Engineering on Microsoft Azure exam.

The following sections will delve into the detailed processes of denormalization values using Pivot, and normalization values using Unpivot.

## Denormalizing Values Using Pivot

Assume that you have a table with a normalized column to store `City` values. For reporting purposes, you want to have one column per city in your tables. In such a case, you can use the **Pivot** function to denormalize the table. The Pivot function takes the unique row values and converts them into table columns.

Using this example, you would perform the following steps to pivot the tables:

1.  Review the following sample (*Table 4.4*):

| Driverld 123 | FirstName abc | MiddleName abc | LastName abc | City abc | Gender abc | Salary 123 |
|---|---|---|---|---|---|---|
| 200 | A | NULL | J | New York | Female | 4100 |
| 201 | B | G | K | New York | Male | 4000 |
| 202 | C | H | Null | California | Female | 4300 |
| 203 | D | Null | L | Florida | Male | 5500 |
| 204 | E | I | M | Arizona | Female | 3400 |
| 203 | F | Null | N | Florida | Male | 5500 |

Table 4.4 – Sample table before pivoting

2.  Select the `Pivot settings` activity from the **ADF Data Flow activity**.
3.  In the `Group by` tab, **Name as** the column as `Gender`, as shown in *Figure 4.48*:

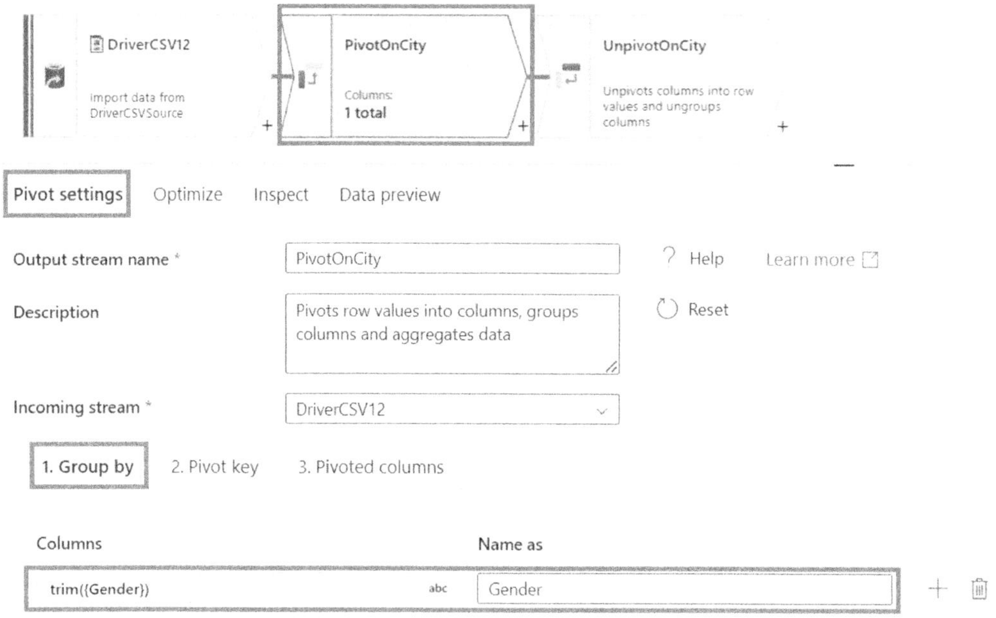

Figure 4.48 – Using Group by settings on Gender for the Pivot operation

4.  Select the `Pivot key` tab and specify `City` as the pivot key (*Figure 4.49*):

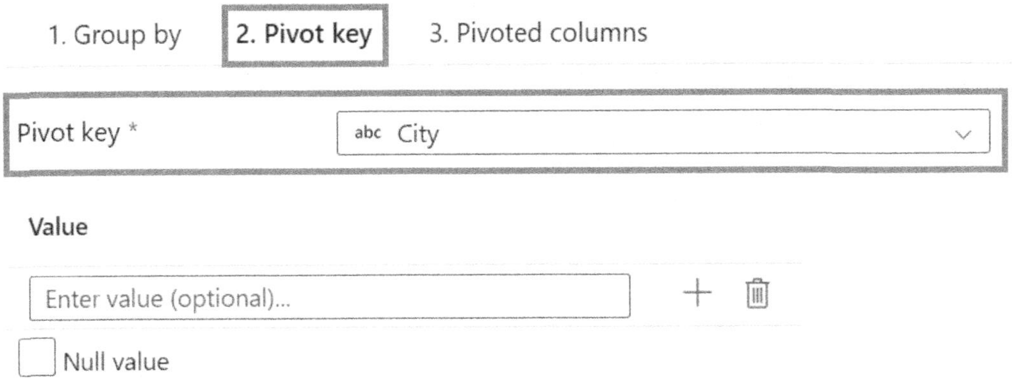

| 1. Group by | **2. Pivot key** | 3. Pivoted columns |

**Pivot key ***    abc  City

**Value**

Enter value (optional)...    +  🗑

☐ Null value

Figure 4.49 – Using City for the Pivot operation

5.  Click the `Pivoted columns` tab. Then, specify any aggregation that you need, along with the prefix to be used for the column names. In this case, the `Salary` column is used as the aggregate and `Avg` is used as the prefix (*Figure 4.50*):

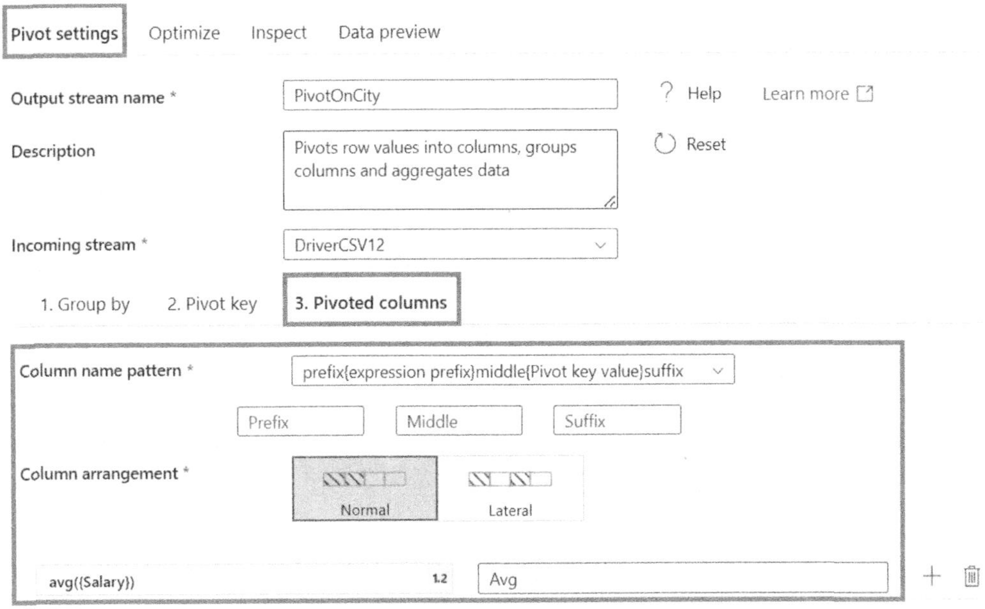

**Pivot settings**    Optimize    Inspect    Data preview

| Output stream name * | PivotOnCity | ?  Help    Learn more 🔗 |

Description    Pivots row values into columns, groups columns and aggregates data    🔄 Reset

Incoming stream *    DriverCSV12

| 1. Group by | 2. Pivot key | **3. Pivoted columns** |

Column name pattern *    prefix{expression prefix}middle{Pivot key value}suffix

    Prefix    Middle    Suffix

Column arrangement *    〔Normal〕    〔Lateral〕

avg({Salary})    1.2    Avg    +  🗑

Figure 4.50 – Specifying the column name pattern and aggregation for the Pivot function

After the Pivot operation, select the `Data preview` tab and the table should look like the one shown in *Figure 4.51*:

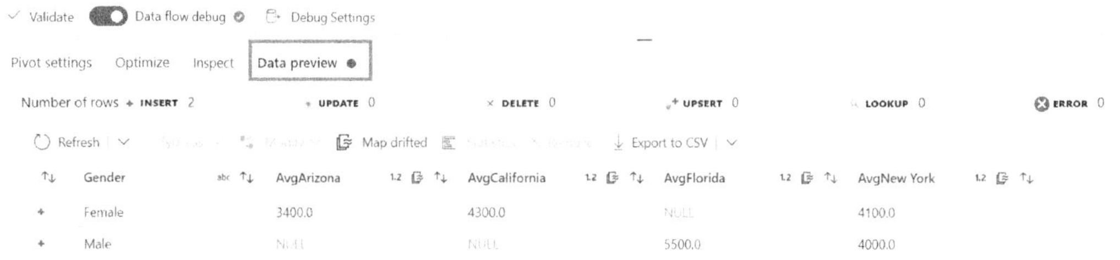

| ↑↓ | Gender | abc ↑↓ | AvgArizona | 1.2 ↑↓ | AvgCalifornia | 1.2 ↑↓ | AvgFlorida | 1.2 ↑↓ | AvgNew York | 1.2 ↑↓ |
|----|--------|--------|------------|--------|---------------|--------|------------|--------|-------------|--------|
| + | Female | | 3400.0 | | 4300.0 | | NULL | | 4100.0 | |
| + | Male | | NULL | | NULL | | 5500.0 | | 4000.0 | |

Figure 4.51 – The post-Pivot table showing values

You can see that the rows of *Table 4.4* have been converted to columns, where each distinct `City` becomes a separate column prefixed with `Avg`, and the data is grouped by the `Gender` column. Next, you'll look at the Unpivot operation.

## Normalizing Values Using Unpivot

**Unpivot** is the reverse of **Pivot** and can be used to normalize data. For example, if you have a column each for multiple cities, then you can unpivot them into a single column called `City`. Perform the following steps to do so:

1. Open the `Unpivot settings` activity.

2. Select the `1. Ungroup by`.

3. Under `Columns`, specify the column. In this case, `Gender` is specified (*Figure 4.52*):

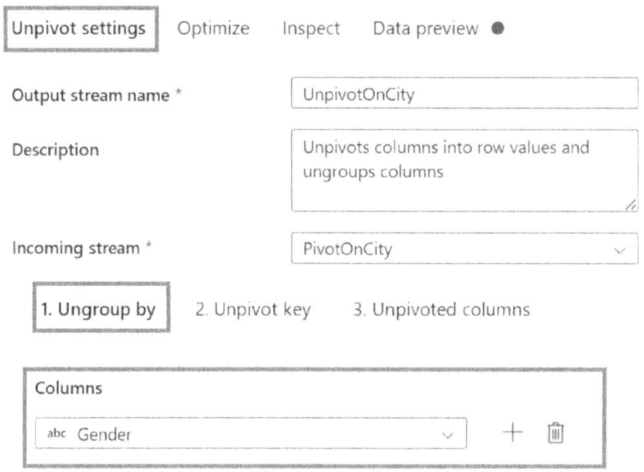

Figure 4.52 – Using the Ungroup by tab for Unpivoting on a single column Gender

4. Click the `Unpivot key` tab. Add a new name, `Cities`, inside the **Unpivot column name** field, and select `double` from the **Unpivot column type** dropdown (*Figure 4.53*):

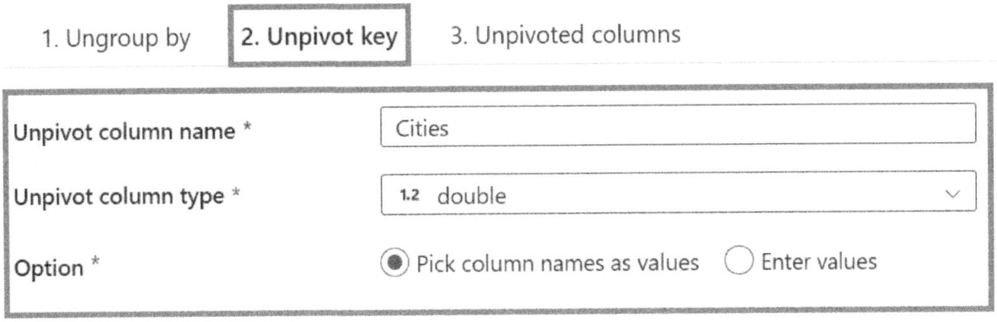

Figure 4.53 – Specifying Unpivot key for the Unpivot operation

5. Click the `Unpivoted columns` tab. Specify the aggregate operations (in this case, `AvgSalary` and `double`), as illustrated in *Figure 4.54*:

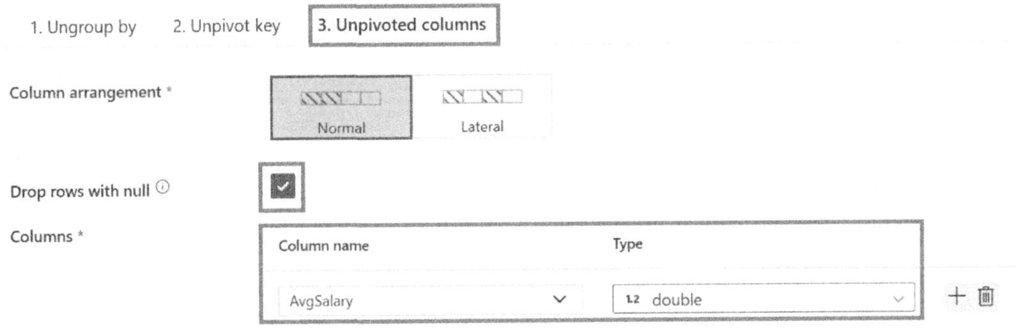

Figure 4.54 – Using the Unpivoted columns tab to calculate AvgSalary by Gender and Cities

After the Unpivot operation, the output table displayed will be similar to that shown in *Figure 4.55*:

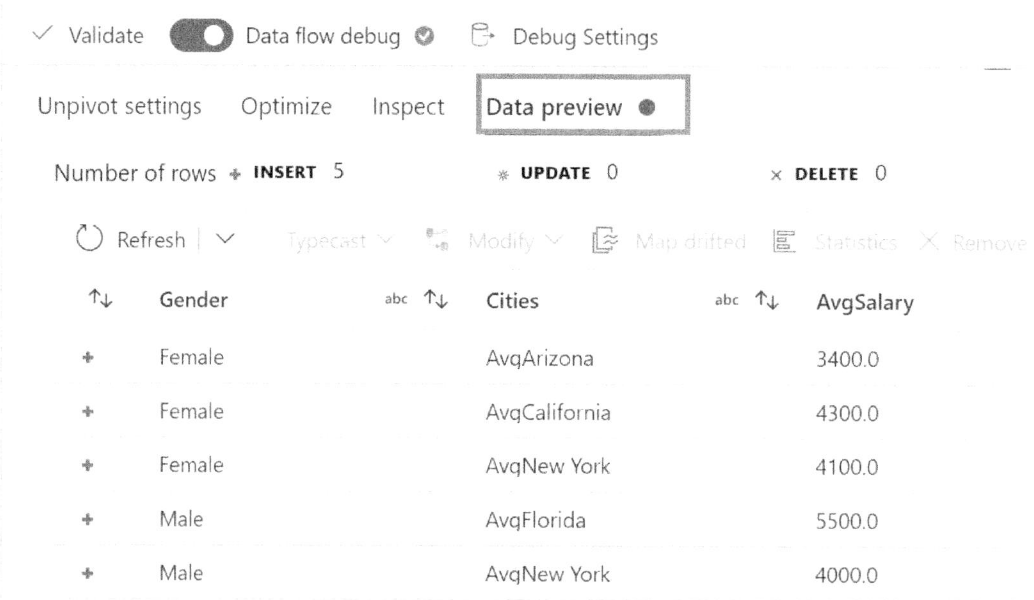

| ✓ Validate | 🔘 Data flow debug ✅ | 🗗 Debug Settings |
| --- | --- | --- |

| Unpivot settings | Optimize | Inspect | **Data preview** ● |
| --- | --- | --- | --- |

Number of rows  **+ INSERT**  5          ✳ **UPDATE**  0          ✕ **DELETE**  0

🔄 Refresh | ⌄     Typecast ⌄     Modify ⌄     Map drifted     Statistics     ✕ Remove

| ↑↓ | Gender | abc ↑↓ | Cities | abc ↑↓ | AvgSalary |
| --- | --- | --- | --- | --- | --- |
| + | Female | | AvgArizona | | 3400.0 |
| + | Female | | AvgCalifornia | | 4300.0 |
| + | Female | | AvgNew York | | 4100.0 |
| + | Male | | AvgFlorida | | 5500.0 |
| + | Male | | AvgNew York | | 4000.0 |

Figure 4.55 – Displaying an unpivoted table as output

You have now learned how to denormalize and normalize using the Pivot and Unpivot operations. You gained knowledge on when to normalize and denormalize data, and this is critical in the data transformation process. This knowledge will also help you to balance the efficiency of data storage and the performance of data retrieval, which is essential for effective data management and analysis. The next section will focus on performing data exploratory analysis using Spark, SQL, and ADF.

# Performing Data Exploratory Analysis

Data exploration is much easier from inside Synapse Studio, as it provides easy one-click options to examine various formats of data. You can learn about some of the options available for data exploration using Spark, SQL, and ADF/Synapse pipelines.

> **Note**
> This section primarily focuses on the **Perform data exploratory analysis** concept of the DP-203: Data Engineering on Microsoft Azure exam.

## Data Exploration Using Spark

**Data exploration** is a crucial step in the data analysis process, allowing you to analyze the patterns and correlations within data. Apache Spark, an open source distributed processing system in Azure for data exploration, offers a powerful and scalable approach for handling large datasets efficiently.

Perform the following steps to do so:

1.  From within the **Synapse Studio**, right-click on the data file and select the Load to DataFrame option, as shown in *Figure 4.56*:

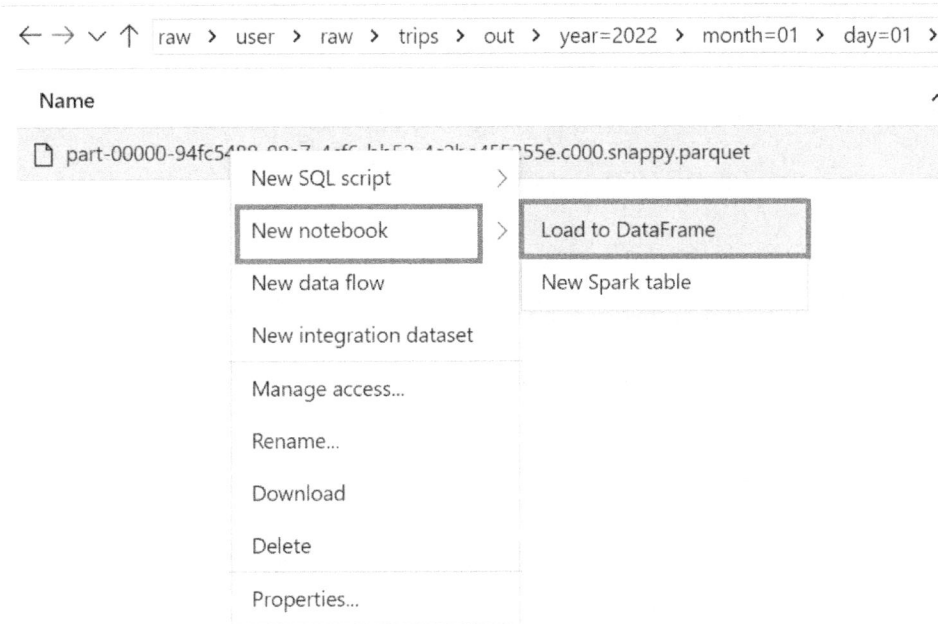

Figure 4.56 – Launching a DataFrame from the Synapse data file

Once you click on the Load to DataFrame option, Synapse creates a new notebook, as shown in *Figure 4.57*.

2.  Click on the Run icon (the little triangle symbol on the left pane) to see the contents of the file. *Figure 4.57* shows the content displayed:

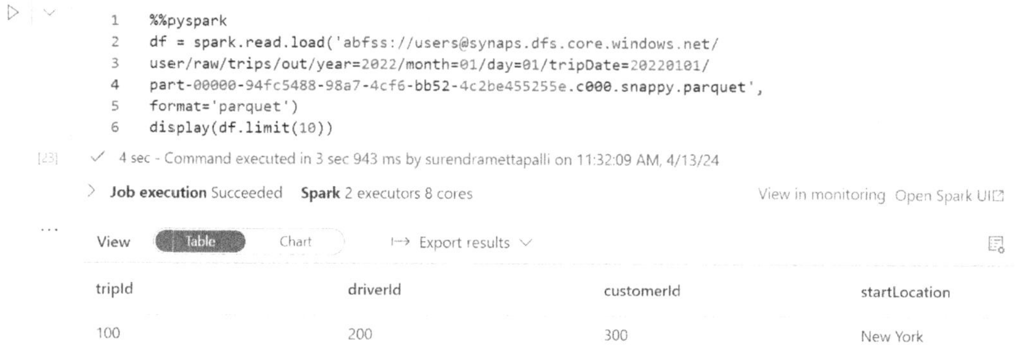

```
1   %%pyspark
2   df = spark.read.load('abfss://users@synaps.dfs.core.windows.net/
3   user/raw/trips/out/year=2022/month=01/day=01/tripDate=20220101/
4   part-00000-94fc5488-98a7-4cf6-bb52-4c2be455255e.c000.snappy.parquet',
5   format='parquet')
6   display(df.limit(10))
```

[23]    ✓  4 sec - Command executed in 3 sec 943 ms by surendramettapalli on 11:32:09 AM, 4/13/24

> **Job execution** Succeeded   **Spark** 2 executors 8 cores                            View in monitoring  Open Spark UI

···   View   ( Table )    Chart        ↦ Export results ∨

| tripId | driverId | customerId | startLocation |
|--------|----------|------------|---------------|
| 100    | 200      | 300        | New York      |

Figure 4.57 – Loading data to a DataFrame to explore using Spark

This is one easy way to explore the contents of a file.

## Data Exploration Using SQL

Data exploration analysis using SQL is a powerful approach to gaining insights into structured datasets. By leveraging SQL for exploratory analysis, you can efficiently query and manipulate data to uncover hidden trends and correlations. You can benefit from this by writing a simple SQL query to explore data, without the need for complex programming skills optimized to handle large datasets, providing data manipulation, and integrating Azure services such as **Azure Synapse Analytics** and **Azure Data Lake Storage** within an Azure environment.

Synapse SQL also provides similar options to explore data. Perform the following steps to explore data:

1.  Select the file, in this case, `part-00000-5a233c41-`.

2.  Click on `New SQL script`, and then choose the `Select TOP 100 rows` option, as shown in *Figure 4.58*:

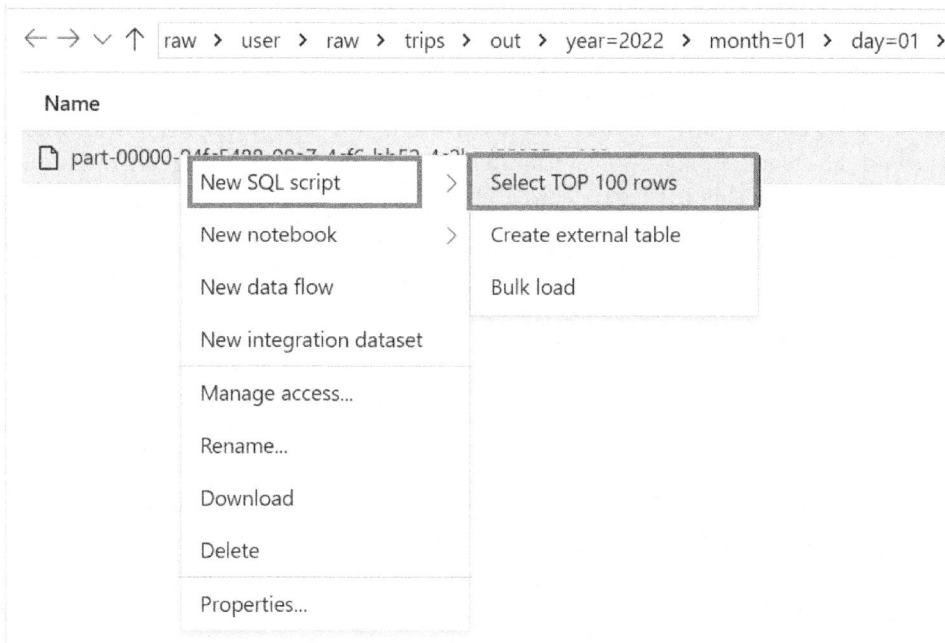

Figure 4.58 – Launching a SQL script to explore data from the Synapse data file

3. Click the Run button to open a new SQL script of the top 100 rows (*Figure 4.59*):

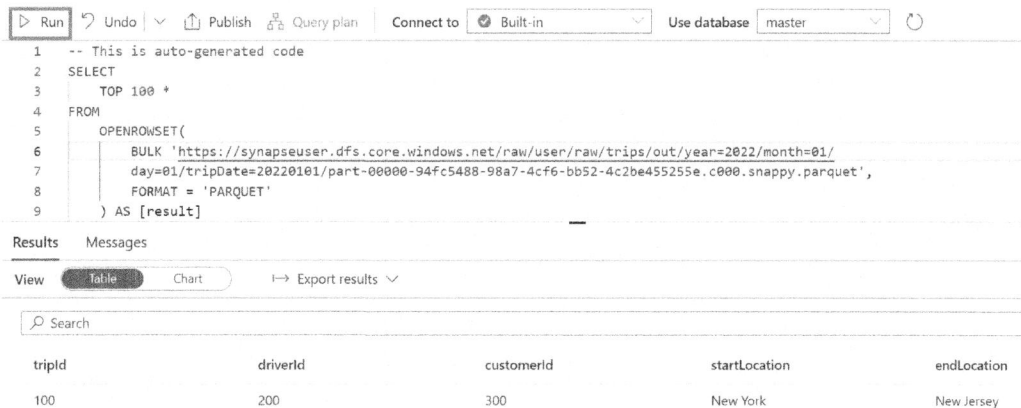

Figure 4.59 – SQL script auto-launched by Synapse to help explore data

The final section covers how to accomplish this in ADF.

## Data Exploration Using ADF

ADF provides a `Data preview` tab that works when you have the `Data flow debug` setting turned on. With this setting, a small **ADB cluster** (called the **ADF Integration Runtime (IR)**) runs behind the scenes and fetches real data so that you can quickly explore and fine-tune your transformations and pipelines. An example of exploring data using ADF can be seen by selecting the `Data preview` tab, as shown in *Figure 4.60*:

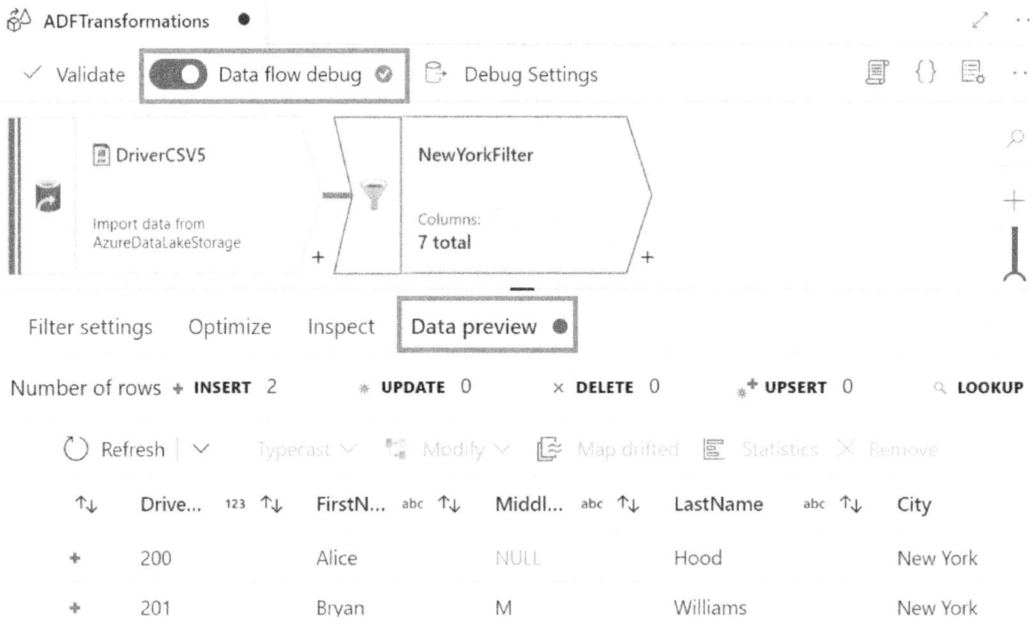

Figure 4.60 – ADF Data preview tab showing fine-tuned transformations and pipelines

This section simplified data exploration by selecting the debugging option that is available with ADF. You are now familiar with Synapse and ADF and how they make it very easy to explore data without having to leave the studio.

Now, you know that data exploration on Azure, which provides comprehensive knowledge of the tools and methodologies, such as Spark, SQL, and ADF, is used to clean, enrich, and transform raw data into a usable format by loading data and running simple queries to explore it.

# Summary

With that, you have come to the end of this interesting chapter. There were lots of examples and screenshots to help you learn the concepts. It might be overwhelming at times, but the easiest way to follow is to open a live Spark, SQL, or ADF session and try to execute the examples in parallel.

You covered a lot of details in this chapter, such as performing transformations in Spark, SQL, and ADF, data cleansing techniques, reading, and parsing JSON data, encoding and decoding, error handling during transformations, normalizing and denormalizing datasets, and finally, a bunch of data exploration techniques. This is one of the important chapters in the syllabus. You should now be able to comfortably build data pipelines with transformations involving Spark, SQL, and ADF.

In the upcoming chapter, you will create resilient batch-processing solutions leveraging Azure's analytics services including Data Lake Storage, Databricks, Synapse Analytics, and Data Factory.

# Exam Readiness Drill – Chapter Review Questions

Apart from a solid understanding of key concepts, being able to think quickly under time pressure is a skill that will help you ace your certification exam. That is why working on these skills early on in your learning journey is key.

Chapter review questions are designed to improve your test-taking skills progressively with each chapter you learn and review your understanding of key concepts in the chapter at the same time. You'll find these at the end of each chapter.

> **How to Access These Materials**
>
> To learn how to access these resources, head over to the chapter titled *Chapter 11, Accessing the Online Resources*.

To open the Chapter Review Questions for this chapter, perform the following steps:

1.  Click the link – `https://packt.link/DP203E2_CH04`.

    Alternatively, you can scan the following **QR code** (*Figure 4.61*):

Figure 4.61 – QR code that opens Chapter Review Questions for logged-in users

2. Once you log in, you'll see a page similar to the one shown in *Figure 4.62*:

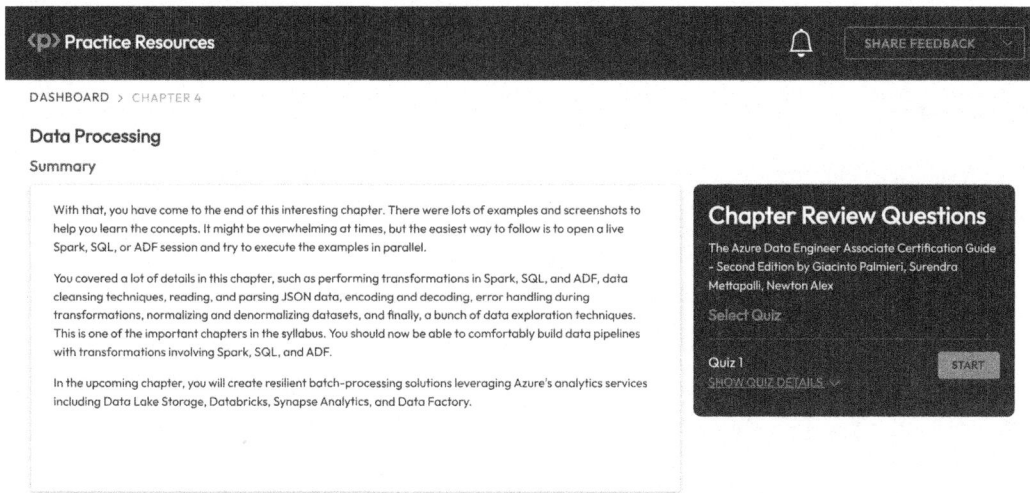

Figure 4.62 – Chapter Review Questions for Chapter 4

3. Once ready, start the following practice drills, re-attempting the quiz multiple times.

## Exam Readiness Drill

For the first three attempts, don't worry about the time limit.

### *ATTEMPT 1*

The first time, aim for at least **40%**. Look at the answers you got wrong and read the relevant sections in the chapter again to fix your learning gaps.

## *ATTEMPT 2*

The second time, aim for at least **60%**. Look at the answers you got wrong and read the relevant sections in the chapter again to fix any remaining learning gaps.

## *ATTEMPT 3*

The third time, aim for at least **75%**. Once you score 75% or more, you start working on your timing.

> **Tip**
> You may take more than **three** attempts to reach 75%. That's okay. Just review the relevant sections in the chapter till you get there.

# Working On Timing

**Target**: Your aim is to keep the score the same while trying to answer these questions as quickly as possible. Here's an example of how your next attempts should look like:

| Attempt | Score | Time Taken |
| --- | --- | --- |
| Attempt 5 | 77% | 21 mins 30 seconds |
| Attempt 6 | 78% | 18 mins 34 seconds |
| Attempt 7 | 76% | 14 mins 44 seconds |

Table 4.5 – Sample timing practice drills on the online platform

> **Note**
> The time limits shown in the above table are just examples. Set your own time limits with each attempt based on the time limit of the quiz on the website.

With each new attempt, your score should stay above **75%** while your "time taken" to complete should "decrease". Repeat as many attempts as you want till you feel confident dealing with the time pressure.

# 5

# Developing a Batch Processing Solution

In *Chapter 4*, *Ingesting and Transforming Data*, you learned about services such as Spark, **Azure Data Factory** (**ADF**), and Synapse SQL. You will continue doing so here and learn about a few more batch-processing-related technologies.

In this chapter, you will develop robust batch-processing solutions using Azure's analytics services such as Data Lake Storage, Databricks, Synapse Analytics, and Data Factory. Focus areas include optimizing SQL pool data loading with PolyBase and implementing Azure Synapse Link for seamless data querying. You'll create scalable data pipelines, optimize batch sizes, and ensure pipeline integrity through rigorous testing. Integration of notebooks will enhance analytical capabilities.

You will also master data manipulation techniques such as upserting, reverting data states, configuring advanced exception handling, and managing batch retention policies for effective data life cycle management. Interacting with Delta Lakes for versioned data repository maintenance will be covered, preparing you to manage large-scale data-processing tasks efficiently.

By the end of this chapter, you will be proficient in building comprehensive batch pipelines, integrating Spark notebooks, leveraging PolyBase for efficient data transfer, managing late-arriving data, scaling clusters, debugging pipeline issues, and ensuring security and compliance using Synapse SQL, **Azure Databricks** (**ADB**) Spark, PolyBase, and ADF.

This chapter will prepare you to answer questions on the following confidently:

- Batch-processing solutions using Azure Data Lake Storage, ADB, Azure Synapse Analytics, and ADF
- PolyBase and Azure Synapse Link
- Data pipelines and scaling resources
- Batch size and Jupyter/Python notebooks

- Upserting data

- Exception handling

- Batch retention

- Delta lake

As everywhere else in this book, the order of the syllabus topics will be followed, although it may not always correspond to the natural or logical order of topics. Those transitions will be made smoother by offering the required logical links.

> **Note**
>
> This chapter primarily focuses on the **Develop a batch processing solution** topic of the DP-203: Data Engineering on Microsoft Azure exam.

The best way to grasp the concept of batch processing is to consider it alongside stream processing, which will be the subject of the next chapter, *Chapter 6, Developing a Stream Processing Solution*.

## Technical Requirements

For this chapter, you will need an Azure account (free or paid), an active Synapse workspace, and an active Azure Data Factory workspace.

## Batch-Processing Technologies

Consider, for instance, the case of credit card processing. First and most obviously, it will involve the processing of the credit card transaction in real time, as the buyer and the seller will need to know as quickly as possible whether the transaction was approved. This is an example of stream processing. On the other hand, if the credit card company sends a statement at the end of the month with all the transactions made by the cardholder, that is an example of batch processing.

So, batch processing is characterized by the larger quantity of data processed (in the example, a month's worth of transactions as opposed to a single transaction) and at longer intervals of time (in the example, every month as opposed to as soon as possible) than is customary in stream processing. Another example can be offered by the data ingestions and transformations required as part of an **Extract, Transform, Load** (**ETL**) or **Extract, Load, Transform** (**ELT**) process, described in *Chapter 4, Ingesting and Transforming Data*. Refreshing your data warehouse is indeed something that requires injecting and processing a potentially large quantity of data and is typically executed at scheduled intervals.

In terms of the Azure offering of data services, notebooks running on Spark and pipelines running on ADF or Synapse represent the obvious choice to implement this type of process. The main difference is that the first required writing code, typically in Python, while the second represents a low-code alternative. The choice, however, is not exclusive: you can start with a pipeline and then call a notebook from it whenever you need to use code.

In this section, you will try to build an end-to-end batch pipeline using the following technologies:

- Azure Data Lake Storage

- Azure Databricks

- Azure Synapse Analytics

- Azure Data Factory

> **Note**
>
> This section primarily focuses on the **Develop batch processing solutions by using Azure Data Lake Storage, Azure Databricks, Azure Synapse Analytics, and Azure Data Factory** concept of the DP-203: Data Engineering on Microsoft Azure exam.

You can use the **Imaginary Airport Cab** (**IAC**) example from *Chapter 1*, *Introducing Azure Basics*, and *Chapter 2*, *Implementing a Partition Strategy*, to create a sample requirement for your batch-processing pipeline.

Assume you are continuously getting trip data from different regions (zip codes) that are stored in Azure Blob Storage, and the trip fares that are stored in Azure SQL Server. You need to merge these two datasets and generate daily revenue reports for each region.

In order to take care of this requirement, you can build a pipeline as shown in *Figure 5.1*:

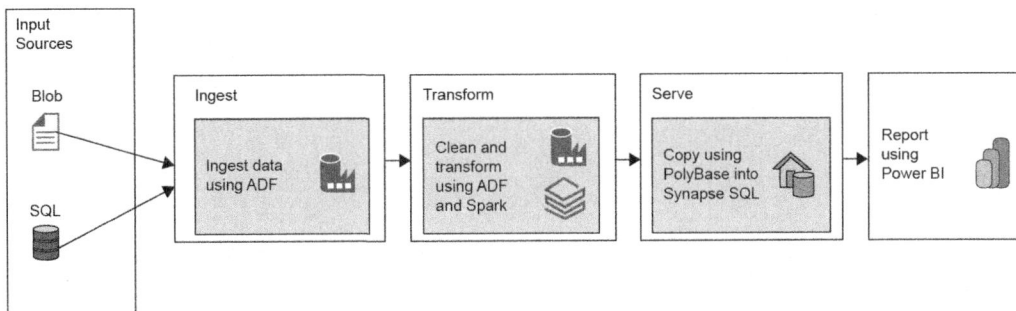

Figure 5.1 – High-level architecture of the batch use case

The pipeline, shown in *Figure 5.1*, when translated into an ADF pipeline would look like the one shown in *Figure 5.2*:

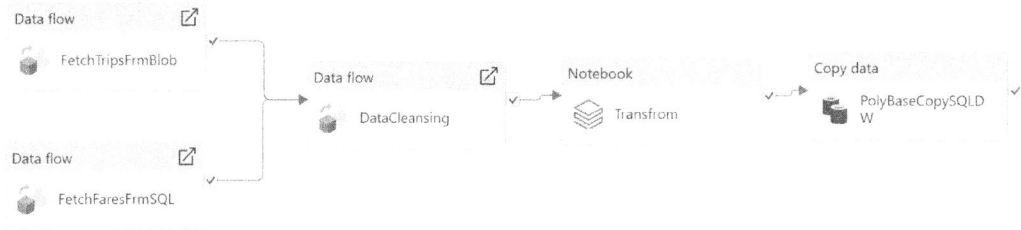

Figure 5.2 – Sample data pipeline in ADF

In *Figure 5.2*, you can see that the pipeline has four stages. These are as follows:

- **Data ingestion**: The first two stages—FetchTripsFrmBlob and FetchFaresFrmSQL—get the data into the data lake. The first-stage FetchTripsFrmBlob activity is responsible for retrieving trip-related data from Azure Blob Storage, whereas FetchFaresFrmSQL involves extracting trip fare information from a SQL database. Together, these stages form the initial steps using which you can construct a comprehensive dataset that will undergo data cleansing.

- **Data cleansing**: The DataCleansing stage cleans up the data and you can perform a series of operations such as validation to remove nulls, incorrect, or irrelevant parts of the data; deduplication to remove duplicate records to prevent redundancy; sorting data in a specific order for further analysis; and error logging to record any errors encountered during the cleansing process for review and correction.

- **Transformation**: The Spark notebook Transform stage transforms the data. This is a critical phase in your data pipeline where the cleansed data undergoes various modifications, such as filtering, aggregating, normalizing, and joining with other datasets to prepare for analysis or operational use.

- **Loading into an analytical database**: The PolyBaseCopySQLDW stage copies the data into a Synapse SQL pool using PolyBase technology for high-performance data ingestion and integration into Azure Synapse Analytics.

> **Note**
> The last stage would be **BI tools reading** from the analytical database and generating reports. This is not shown in *Figure 5.2* as that is not an ADF activity.

Before you start looking into each of these stages, you must first define the nature of your storage.

# Storage

In today's data-driven world, storing and managing vast amounts of information is crucial. Consider ADLS Gen2 as your data lake storage. **Azure Data Lake Storage Gen2** (**ADLS Gen2**) offers a secure and scalable solution specifically designed for Big Data Analytics.

You can create the following folder structure to handle your batch pipeline:

- The raw trip data can be stored here: `iac/raw/trips/2024/01/01`.

- The cleaned-up data can be copied over to the `transform/in` folder: `iac/transform/in/2024/01/01`.

- The output of the transformed data can be moved into the `transform/out` folder: `iac/transform/out/2024/01/01`.

- Finally, you can import the data from `transform/out` into a Synapse SQL dedicated pool using PolyBase.

Note that tools such as ADF and PolyBase also provide the ability to directly move data between Spark and Synapse SQL dedicated pools. You can choose this direct approach instead of storing the intermediate data in the data lake if that works better for you in terms of performance and cost. But in most data lakes, more than one tool might access the intermediate data from the data lake, and it will be useful to keep historical datasets for future analysis. Hence, it might make sense to keep a copy in the data lake also.

You can now look into each of the batch pipeline stages in detail.

# Data Ingestion

**Data ingestion** is the process of getting all the raw data into the data lake. Data from various sources lands in the raw zone of the data lake. Based on where the data is coming from (such as on-premises systems, other cloud systems, and so on), you could use different ingestion tools. The following are some of the options available in Azure to ingest data:

- **Azure Data Factory**: You are already familiar with the ADF technology, which provides data ingestion support from hundreds of data sources, and even from other clouds such as **Amazon Web Services** (**AWS**), **Google Cloud Platform** (**GCP**), and Oracle. You will be using this again to build your pipeline as recommended in the syllabus.

- **Azure Copy**: As a command-line tool, **Azure Copy** (**AzCopy**) can be used to copy data over the internet and is ideally suited for smaller data sizes (preferably in the 10–15 TB range).

> **Note**
> You can learn more about AzCopy at `https://packt.link/zAACw`.

- **Azure ExpressRoute**: If you need a secure way to transfer data into Azure, then use **ExpressRoute**. It routes your data through dedicated private connections to Azure instead of the public internet. This is also the preferred option if you want to have a dedicated pipeline with a faster data transfer speed.

> **Note**
>
> You can learn more about Azure ExpressRoute at `https://packt.link/5bA41`.

Now consider an ingestion example using ADF to read from the Blob Storage. First, to connect to the Blob Storagee, you will have to create a linked service in ADF. Perform the following steps to do so:

1. Click the `Manage` tab of ADF, as shown in *Figure 5.3*:

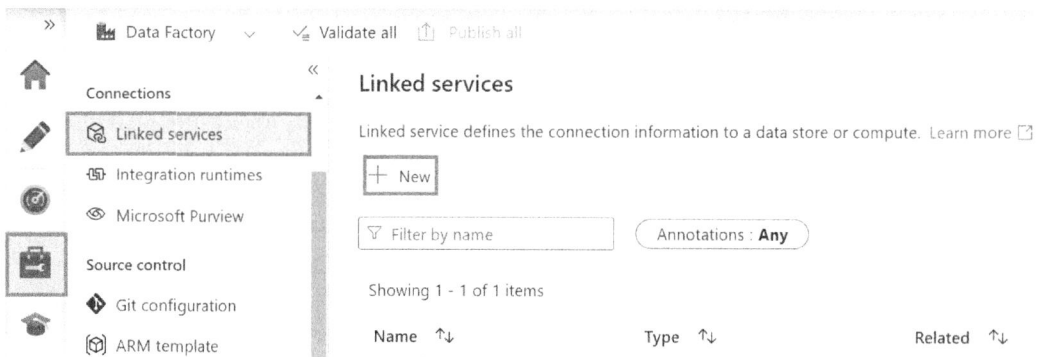

Figure 5.3 – Configuring a linked service in ADF

Now you have to fill in the details to create the linked service so that you will be able to access the data in your Blob Storage directly from ADF.

2. Select the `Linked services` option and click on the `+ New` option.

3. Choose `Azure Blob Storage` from the list. You will get a screen like the one shown in *Figure 5.4*:

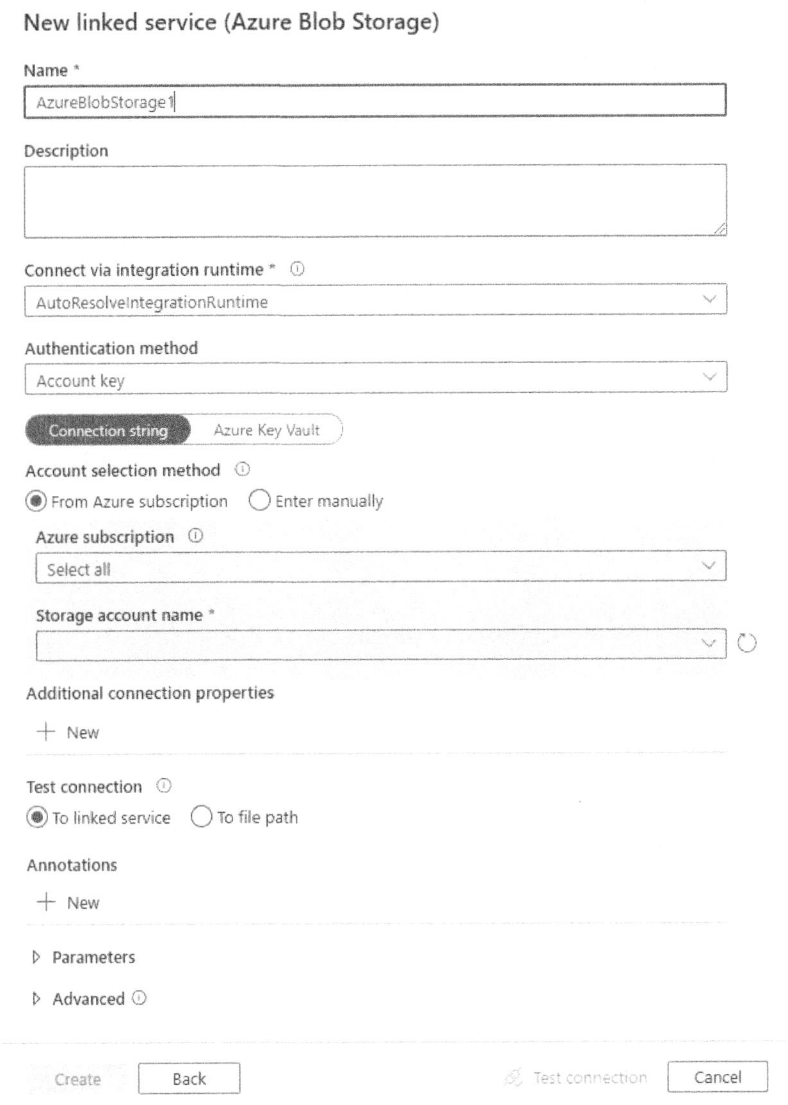

New linked service (Azure Blob Storage)

Name *

AzureBlobStorage1

Description

Connect via integration runtime * ⓘ

AutoResolveIntegrationRuntime

Authentication method

Account key

( **Connection string**     Azure Key Vault )

Account selection method  ⓘ

⦿ From Azure subscription   ◯ Enter manually

Azure subscription  ⓘ

Select all

Storage account name *

Additional connection properties

+ New

Test connection  ⓘ

⦿ To linked service   ◯ To file path

Annotations

+ New

▷ Parameters

▷ Advanced ⓘ

Create   │ Back │       ◎ Test connection   │ Cancel │

Figure 5.4 – Creating an Azure Blob Storage linked service

4.   Enter the name. In this case, it is Azure Blob Storage1.

5.   Fill in the integration runtimes under the **Connect via integration runtime** option. In this case, it is AutoResolveIntegrationRuntime.

6.   Select an option from the **Authentication method** dropdown—for example, Account key.

7.   Select the From Azure subscription radio button under **Account selection method**.

8.  Choose `Select all` for the **Azure subscription** option.

9.  Choose the `To linked service` radio button under the **Test connection** option (visible in *Figure 5.4*) and finally, click on the `Create` button.

    Next you will proceed to create a data flow in ADF.

10. To create a data flow in ADF, first click on the `Data flows` option and then choose the `New data flow` option (*Figure 5.5*):

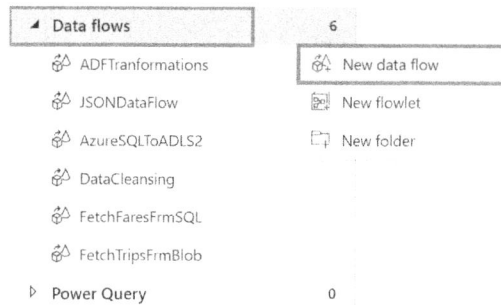

Figure 5.5 – Creating a new data flow in ADF

In the data flow, you now have to specify the source and destination.

11. Type a name beside the **Output stream name** option. In this case, it is `SourceTripsDataBlob`.

12. For the **Source** type, under the **Source settings** tab, select the `Dataset` option (*Figure 5.6*).

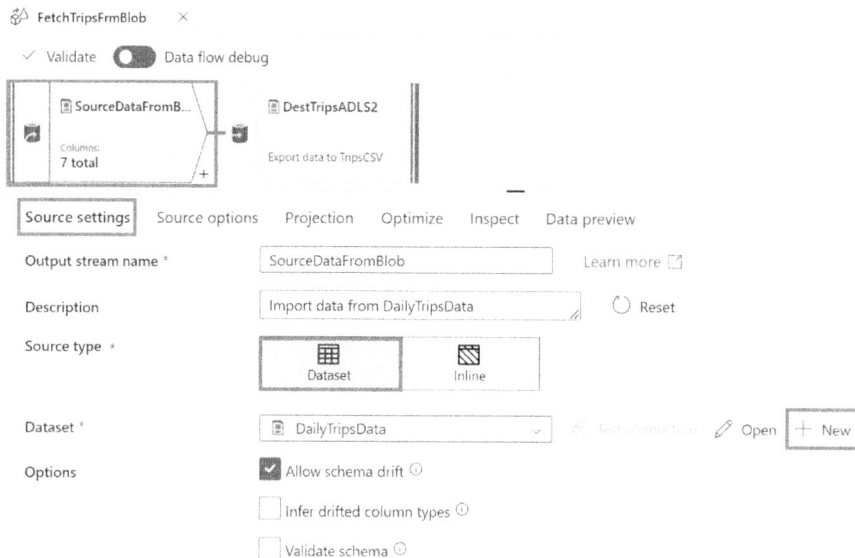

Figure 5.6 – Creating source and destination datasets in a data flow

Now you need to define a new dataset using the Blob Storage linked service that you created from *Step 1* to *Step 10* of this section, i.e., the *Data Ingestion* section.

13. Click the + New button to create a dataset. The following screenshot shows the dataset creation screen that will appear (*Figure 5.7*):

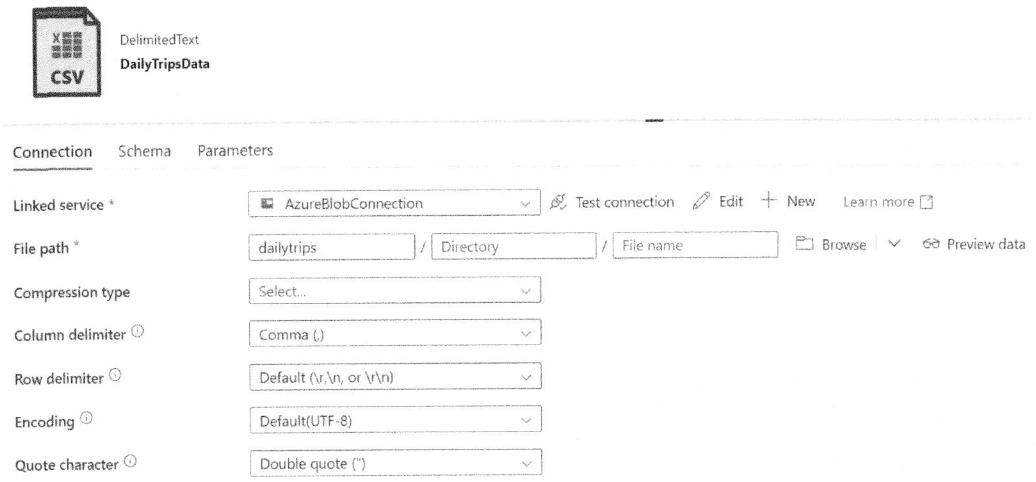

Figure 5.7 – Sample dataset screen to create a dataset named DailyTripData

With the data flow created, you now have the data ingestion part taken care of. Currently, the step is still not complete as you still have to add this copy data step to your pipeline and run it to see the results. But before that, you need to learn about all the remaining batch-processing components. So next, you will look at data transformation.

> **Data Preparation/Data Cleansing**
>
> In *Chapter 4, Ingesting and Transforming Data*, you explored multiple data cleansing transformations, such as handling missing data, deduplicating, and removing outlier data in the *Transforming Data Using Stream Analytics* section. You can use the same transformations for this stage. As you have already explored the details in the previous chapter, they will not be repeated here. So, for now, jump to the *Transformation* section.

# Transformation

Once your data is in a clean format and prepared for further activities such as transformations, you can run the transformation logic using services such as **Spark**, **SQL**, and **Hive**. In this example, as per the certification syllabus, you will use ADB Spark. But first, you need to create an ADB workspace, followed by the ADB cluster that will run the transformations, and then write the Spark code within the **Cmd** blocks. Perform the following steps to do so:

1.  Select `Azure Databricks` from the **Azure portal** and click `+Create` to create a new workspace. *Figure 5.8* shows the **Create an Azure Databricks workspace** screen.

2.  Enter the name for the workspace beside the **Workspace name** option. In this case, it is `DP-203-databricks-workspace`. Then select an option from the **Region** dropdown. In this case, it is `UK South`.

3.  Next, select an option from the **Pricing Tier** dropdown. In this case, it is `Standard (Apache Spark, Secure with Microsoft Entra ID)` (*Figure 5.8*):

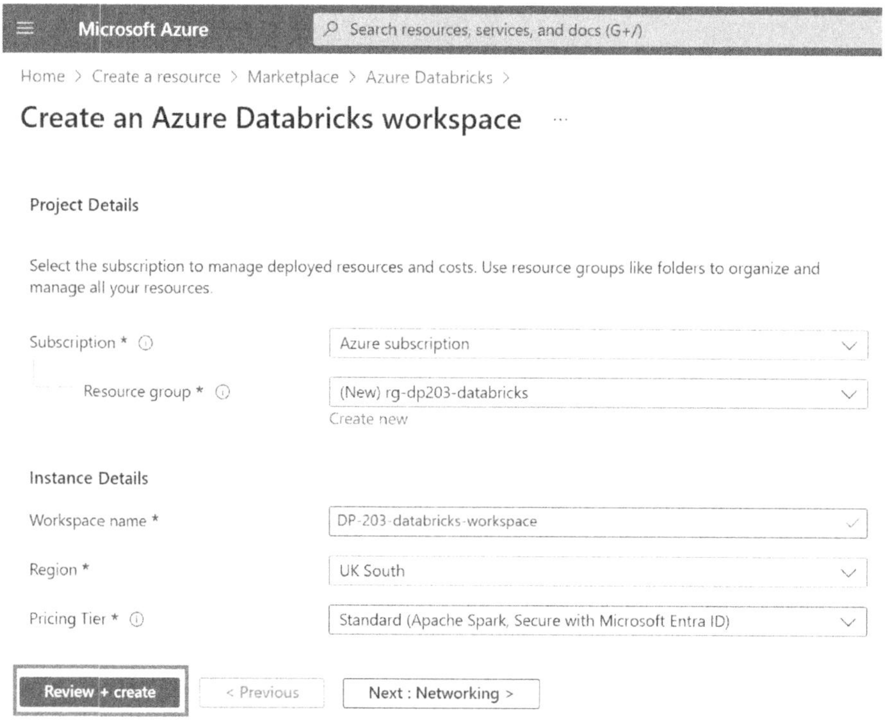

Figure 5.8 – Sample Azure Databricks workspace creation screen

4.  Click the `Review + create` button to create the workspace. Here it will take a few seconds to deploy your Databricks resource, and upon completion, you can click on `Go to resource`.

5.  Click on the Launch Workspace button to launch the workspace. This will take you to the
    **Azure Databricks** portal, as shown in *Figure 5.9*:

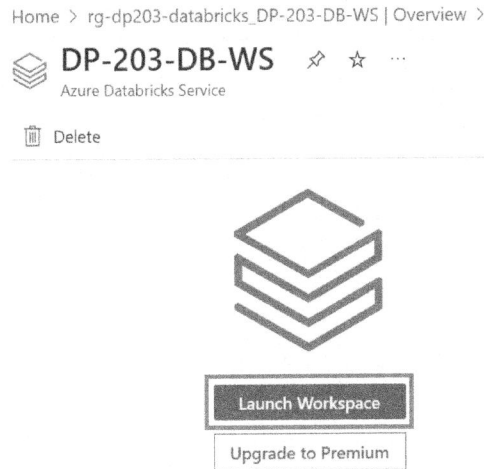

Figure 5.9 – Launching the Azure Databricks workspace

From this screen, you can create clusters, notebooks, and more. That brings us to the next step
of creating an ADB cluster (*Figure 5.10*):

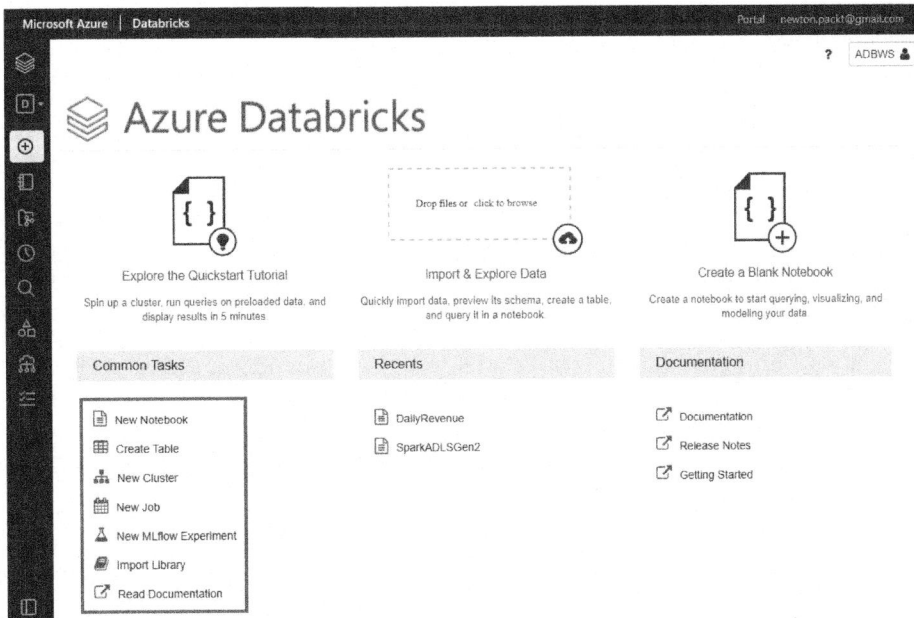

Figure 5.10 – Azure Databricks portal

6.  Click the New Cluster link in the Databricks portal. This will open the **New Cluster** screen, as shown in *Figure 5.11*:

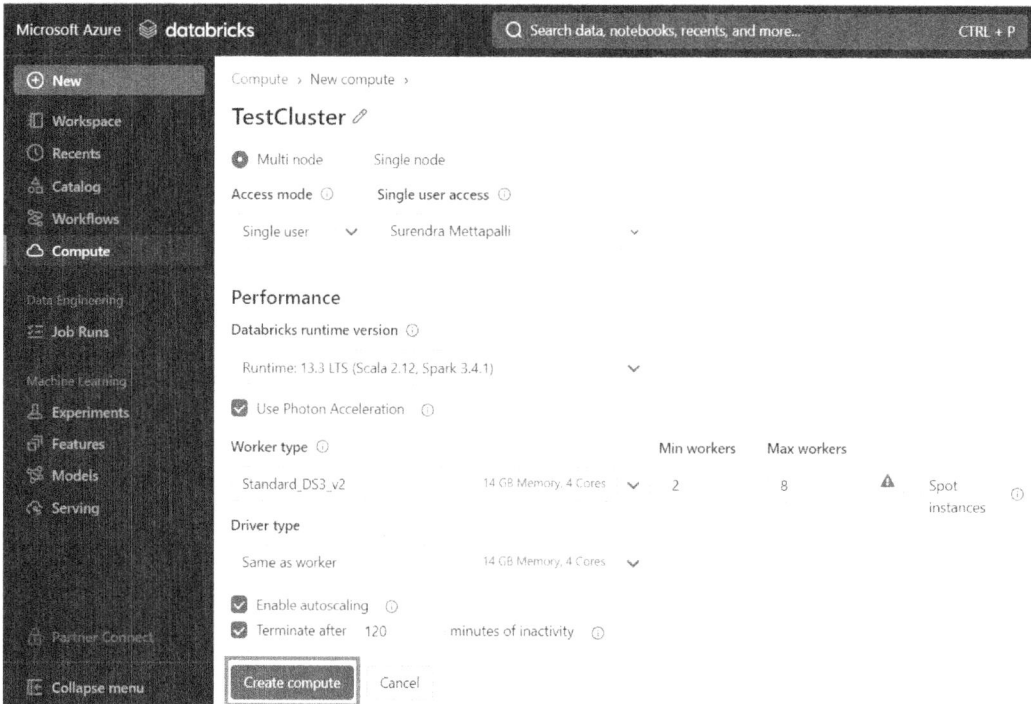

Figure 5.11 – Azure Databricks cluster creation screen

7.  Fill in the **Cluster Name** field. For this example, TestCluster is used. Then select an option for **Cluster Mode**—in this case, Standard.

8.  Next, choose an option from the **Databricks Runtime Version** dropdown, for example, Runtime: 8.3 (Scale 2.12 Spark 3.1.1).

9.  Tick Enable autoscaling. When you enable autoscaling, Databricks automatically adjusts the number of worker nodes in your cluster based on the current workload. This means that as the demand for computational resources increases, more worker nodes are added to handle the load efficiently. On the other hand, as demand declines, the excess nodes are removed to conserve resources. Check the **Terminate after minutes of inactivity** checkbox and enter the time in minutes (120, in this example).

10. Set **Work Type** to Standard_DS3_v2 and fill in the **Min Workers** and **Max Workers** fields. In this case, these will be 2 and 8, respectively.

11. Set the **Driver Type** option, for example, `Same as worker`.

    This will create a cluster required to run the transformations for the batch pipeline. You must now create a notebook to build your transformation logic.

> **Note**
>
> The `DBU / hour: 2.25 - 6.75` refers to the range of **Databricks Units** (**DBUs**) that can be consumed per hour by the cluster. This range is determined by the number of workers utilized in the cluster. Each worker is allocated 0.75 DBU/h. So, it is 1.5 DBU/h for one worker, 2.25 DBU/h for two workers, and so on.

12. From the **Azure Databricks** portal, click the `+ Create` button from the sidebar. Choose the `Notebook` option, as shown in *Figure 5.12*:

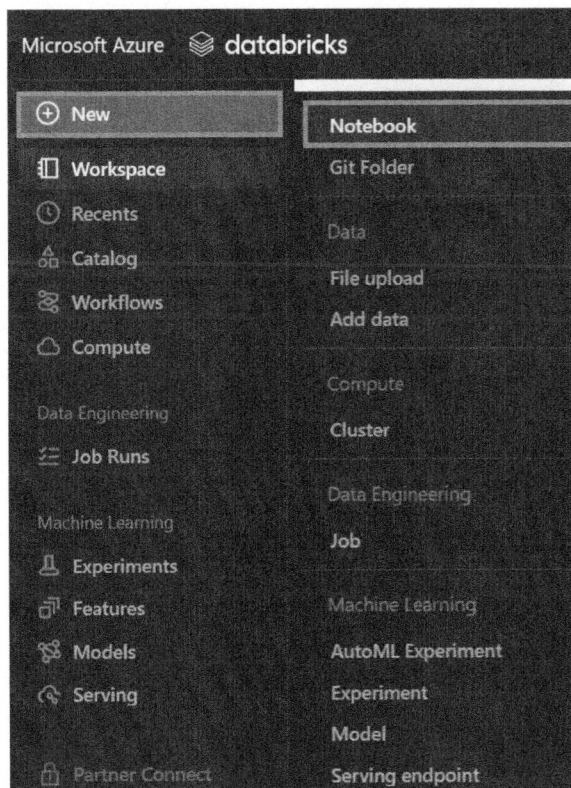

Figure 5.12 – Azure Databricks new notebook creation

Once you create the new notebook, you will get an editor as shown in *Figure 5.13*. You can write the Spark code within the Cmd blocks. ADB supports the Scala, Python, SQL, and R languages.

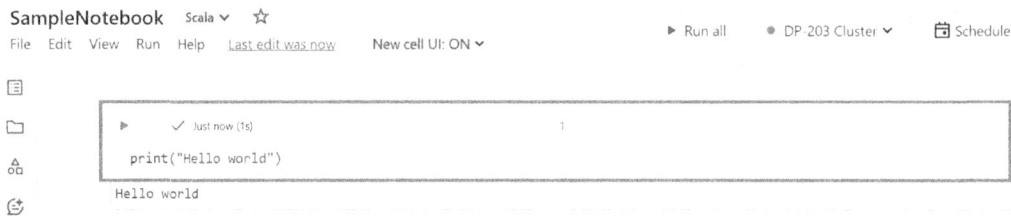

Figure 5.13 – Azure Databricks notebook with Spark code inserted within the Cmd block

13. To generate a daily trip report, write the following simple Scala transformation script (into the Cmd sections):

I.   First, set up the initial configs for **ADB Spark** to talk to **ADLS Gen2**, as follows:

```
spark.conf.set("fs.azure.account.auth.type." +
storageAccountName + ".dfs.core.windows.net", "Oauth")
spark.conf.set("fs.azure.account.oauth.provider.type." +
storageAccountName + ".dfs.core.windows.net", "org.apache.
hadoop.fs.azurebfs.oauth2.ClientCredsTokenProvider")
spark.conf.set("fs.azure.account.oauth2.client.id." +
storageAccountName + ".dfs.core.windows.net", "" + appID + "")
spark.conf.set("fs.azure.account.oauth2.client.secret." +
storageAccountName + ".dfs.core.windows.net", "" + secret + "")
spark.conf.set("fs.azure.account.oauth2.client.endpoint." +
storageAccountName + ".dfs.core.windows.net", "https://login.
microsoftonline.com/" + tenantID +
"/oauth2/token")
spark.conf.set("fs.azure.createRemoteFileSystemDuring
Initialization", "true")
spark.conf.set("fs.azure.createRemoteFileSystemDuring
Initialization", "false")
```

In the preceding code, note the following:

- `storageAccountName.dfs.core.windows.net`: This line sets the authentication type for accessing the ADLS Gen2 storage account to OAuth.

- `ClientCredsTokenProvider`: This provider handles obtaining OAuth tokens for accessing Azure services.

- `appID`: This command authenticates with Azure AD to access the specified storage account.

- `secret`: Here, the OAuth client secret associated with the client ID is configured for authentication.

- `"https://login.microsoftonline.com/" + tenantID + "/oauth2/token"`: The token endpoint URL obtains access tokens required to authenticate requests to the storage account.

- `"fs.azure.createRemoteFileSystemDuringInitialization", "true"`: This setting is crucial for establishing connectivity with ADLS Gen2.

- `"fs.azure.createRemoteFileSystemDuringInitialization", "false"`: This command line sets the option back to `false`, soon after initialization, indicating that the remote filesystem initialization is complete and should not be triggered again unnecessarily.

II. Now read the trip data (stored as a **Comma Separated Values (CSV)** file) using Apache Spark:

```scala
%scala
        .add("tripId",IntegerType)
        .add("driverId",IntegerType)
        .add("customerId",IntegerType)
        .add("cabId",IntegerType)
        .add("tripDate",IntegerType)
        .add("startLocation",StringType)
        .add("endLocation",StringType)
    val tripsCSV = spark.read.format("csv")
        .option("header", "true")
        .schema(tripsSchema)
        .load("abfss:/path/to/csv")
```

In the code, the `StructType` schema named `tripsSchema` is defined for the trip data. Each field of the schema corresponds to a column in the CSV file with its name (`"tripId"`, `"driverId"`, `"customerId"`, `"cabId"`, `"tripDate"`, `"startLocation"`, and `"endLocation"`) and the corresponding data type.

Here, `tripsCSV` is a DataFrame containing the data from the CSV file and `spark.read.format("csv")` specifies the data source to be read (in this instance, in CSV format). The command `.option("header", "true")` specifies that the first row of the CSV file contains the column names. The command `.schema(tripsSchema)` indicates `tripsSchema` is used to interpret the CSV file's structure. `.load("abfss:/path/to/csv")` loads the CSV file located at the specified path.

III. Now read the `fare` data (stored as **Parquet** files) using Apache Spark:

```scala
%scala
val faresSchema = new StructType()
        .add("tripId",IntegerType)
        .add("fare",IntegerType)
        .add("currency",StringType)
    val faresParquet = spark.read.format("parquet")
```

```
.schema(faresSchema)
.load("abfss:/path/to/parquet")
```

Here, a `StructType` named `faresSchema` consists of three fields: `tripId`, `fare`, and currency. The `spark.read.format("parquet")` specifies that Parquet files are to be read, `.schema(faresSchema)` specifies the schema (`faresSchema`) that is used when reading the Parquet files, and `.load("abfss:/path/to/parquet")` loads the Parquet files located at the specified path.

IV.    Perform data-processing tasks by joining the `tripsCSV` and `faresParquet` datasets with `tripId` and group by `startLocation`:

```
val joinDF = tripsCSV.join(
faresParquet,tripsCSV("tripId") ===
      faresParquet("tripId"),"inner")
.groupBy("startLocation")
.sum("fare");
```

In the preceding code, the `tripsCSV("tripId") === faresParquet("tripId")` join condition specifies that the `tripId` column from the `tripsCSV` DataFrame must match the `tripId` column from the `faresParquet` DataFrame. `"inner"` specifies the type of join that returns only the rows where `tripId` values match in both DataFrames. `.groupBy("startLocation")` groups the joined DataFrame (`joinDF`) by the `startLocation` column, and `.sum("fare")` calculates the sum of the `fare` column.

V.    Print the output table with the `City` and `Fare` columns:

```
import org.apache.spark.sql.functions.col;
val outputDF = joinDF.select(col("startLocation").
alias("City"),col("sum(fare)").alias("Fare"));
```

The `col` function is used to create a column object and is imported from the `org.apache.spark.sql.functions` package. The `select` method is used to select specific columns from the `joinDF` DataFrame to create a new DataFrame (`outputDF`). `col("startLocation")` represents the column named `"startLocation"` from `joinDF`.

VI.    Next, write the output back to ADLS Gen2 under the `transform/fares/out` folder:

```
outputDF.write.mode("overwrite").parquet("abfss:/path/to/
output")
```

In the preceding code, `outputDF` contains the data you want to write to storage. `.mode("overwrite")` specifies the mode of writing, in this case, `"overwrite"`. This means that if the data already exists at the specified location (`abfss:/path/to/output`), it will be overwritten with the new data. `.parquet("abfss:/path/to/output")` indicates the output path and `abfss` is used to access the **Azure Blob File System** (**ABFS**). You may need to replace `path/to/output` with the actual path you want to use.

14. Finally, run the code and debug any issues within ADB before you hook it up to the ADF pipeline.

ADB provides a library called `dbutils` that can be used for filesystem operations such as listing files and managing secrets, along with data operations such as summarizing datasets. Here is an example of copying the file from one location to another location in the **Databricks File System (DBFS)**:

```
dbutils.fs.cp("/path/to/source.txt", "/path/to/destination.txt")
```

> **Note**
>
> You can learn more about `dbutils` at `https://packt.link/uRT6k`. You can find the complete code in the accompanying GitHub repository at `https://packt.link/LVRZD`.

Next, you'll configure ADF to call the Spark notebook that you have just created.

## Configuring an ADB Notebook Activity in ADF

Setting up an **Azure Databricks Notebook** activity within ADF is like crafting a personalized pathway for your data journey. It is about creating a seamless flow that guides your data through the complicated landscapes of Databricks. This approach becomes invaluable when you find that the standard **Data Factory** tools don't quite capture the essence of your data needs, especially when it comes to fine-tuning and transforming the data.

In this section, you will dive into the process of setting up your ADB notebook activity within ADF. The following are the steps to add an ADB notebook to an ADF pipeline:

1. From the ADF **Activities** tab, select `Databricks` and then choose the `Notebook` option under **Databricks**.

2. Add it to the pipeline by dragging the icon into the worksheet area, as shown in *Figure 5.14*:

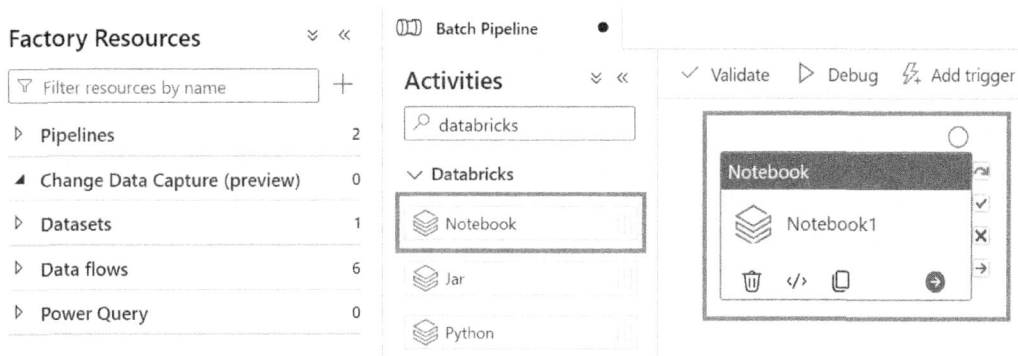

Figure 5.14 – Choosing an Azure Databricks activity in ADF

You now have to link this notebook activity to the notebook that you created in the previous exercise shown in *Figure 5.13*. In order to link the notebook, you will have to first get the access token from ADB.

3.  To generate the access token from the Azure Databricks portal, click on the User Settings option.

4.  Finally, click the Generate New Token button to create a new access token (*Figure 5.15*):

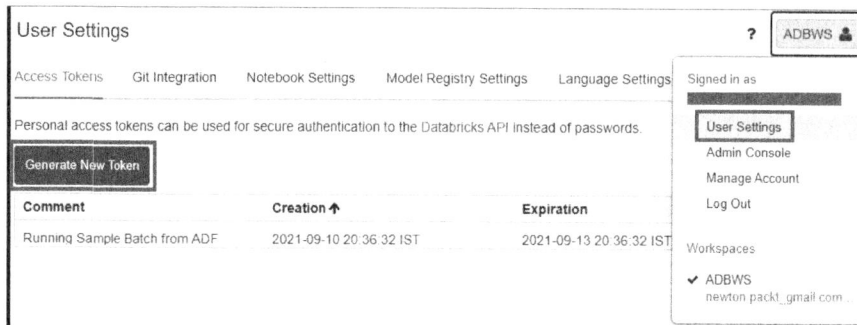

Figure 5.15 – Selecting the access token from the Azure Databricks portal

5.  Now you need to link the previously created ADB notebook using a linked service. Similar to how you created a linked service to Azure Blob Storage in the *Data Ingestion* section in this chapter, you need to create one for ADB Spark too. *Figure 5.16* shows the linked service configuration for ADB:

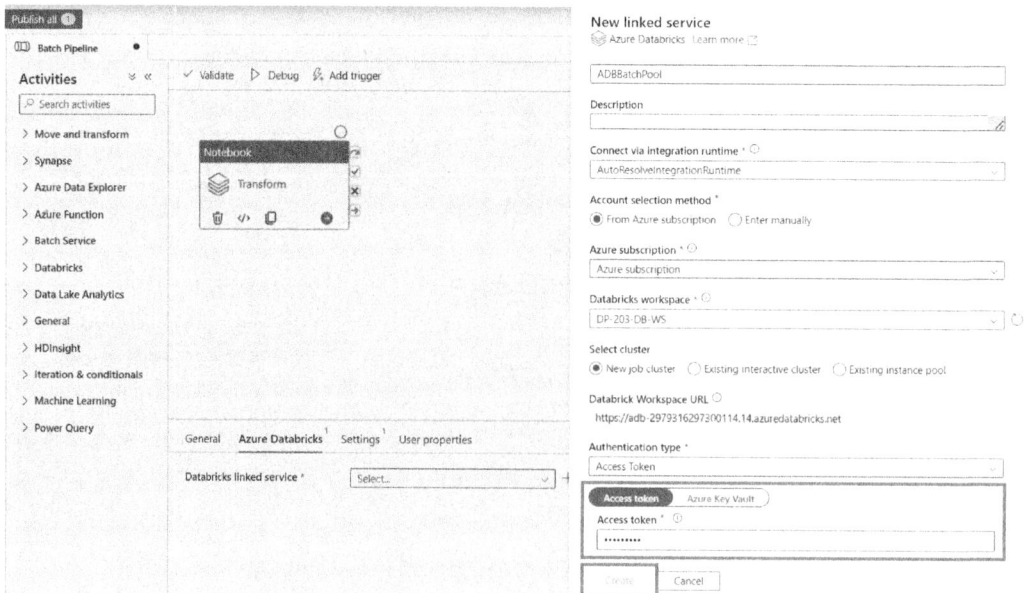

Figure 5.16 – Creating an Azure Databricks linked service

You will have to fill in the Databricks workspace URL and the **Access token** field with the access token that you generated in the previous step, select whether you want to spin up a new job cluster or point to an existing interactive cluster, and so on.

Once you have created the linked service and entered the details into the ADF notebook activity, your sample transformation stage will be complete. The final step that is pending is to import the data from this transformation stage into a dedicated SQL pool and to serve the data from there to Power BI.

> **Note**
> You can learn more about configuring ADB notebook activities in Azure Data Factory at `https://packt.link/txoHs`.

But before you go there, you must look at the options available for batch processing in Azure.

## Batch-Processing Technology Choices

**Batch processing** is a method of executing a series of jobs all at once without manual intervention in the Azure platform. The batch-processing technologies, specifically **Azure Data Lake Analytics**, **Azure Synapse**, **HDInsight with Spark**, **HDInsight with Hive**, **HDInsight with Hive LLAP**, and **Azure Databricks**, are compared based on different capabilities, such as autoscaling, in-memory caching of data, and authentication.

The choice of technology would depend on the specific requirements of the task. For example, if autoscaling is a priority, ADB might be an excellent choice. If in-memory caching of data is important, HDInsight with Hive LLAP could be considered. It is important to evaluate each technology based on the specific needs of your project. *Table 5.1* helps you decide on the technologies to use for your batch scenarios:

| Capability | Azure Data Lake Databricks | Azure Synapse | HDInsight with Spark | HDInsight with Hive | HDInsight with LLAP | Azure Databricks |
|---|---|---|---|---|---|---|
| Autoscaling | No | No | Yes | Yes | Yes | Yes |
| Scale-out granularity | Per job | Per cluster | Per cluster | Per cluster | Per cluster | Per cluster |
| In-memory caching of data | No | Yes | Yes | No | Yes | Yes |
| Query from external relational stores | Yes | No | Yes | No | No | Yes |
| Authentication | Microsoft Entra ID | SQL/Microsoft Entra ID | No | Microsoft Entra ID; required when using an HDInsight cluster | Microsoft Entra ID ; required when using an HDInsight cluster | Microsoft Entra ID |

| Capability | Azure Data Lake Databricks | Azure Synapse | HDInsight with Spark | HDInsight with Hive | HDInsight with LLAP | Azure Databricks |
|---|---|---|---|---|---|---|
| Auditing | Yes | Yes | No | Yes; required when using an HDInsight cluster | Yes; Required when using an HDInsight cluster | Yes |
| Row-level security | No | Yes; Filters only when Row-level Security applies | No | Yes; Required when using an HDInsight cluster | Yes; required when using an HDInsight cluster | Yes |
| Supports firewalls | Yes | Yes | Yes | Yes; supported when using a **Virtual Network (VNet)** | Yes; supported when using a VNet | Yes |
| Dynamic Data Masking | No | Yes | No | Yes; required when using an HDInsight cluster | Yes; required when using an HDInsight cluster | Yes |

Table 5.1 – Comparison of batch-processing technologies in Azure

> **Note**
> You can learn more about the batch-processing choices at `https://packt.link/boFQL`.

In this section, you explored how to develop efficient batch-processing solutions using a range of Azure services tailored to handling large volumes of data. These services, including Azure Data Lake Storage, ADB, Azure Synapse Analytics, and ADF, offer a comprehensive toolkit for you to deal with diverse data-processing needs.

By leveraging these Azure offerings together, you can tackle the challenges of batch processing effectively. Whether it's ingesting data from diverse sources, performing complex transformations, or running analytics at scale, these services provide the flexibility, scalability, and performance required to meet the demands of your modern data-processing workflows.

The next section will focus on how you can copy the data generated from the transformation stage into Synapse SQL using PolyBase.

## Using PolyBase to Load Data to a SQL Pool

**PolyBase** is a tool that enables services such as SQL Server and Synapse dedicated SQL pools to copy and query data directly from external locations, including sources such as Azure Storage, Oracle, Teradata, Hadoop, and MongoDB. PolyBase is integrated into T-SQL, so every time you use a `COPY INTO <table> FROM` command to read data from an external storage location, PolyBase kicks in. It is one of the fastest and most scalable ways to copy data.

> **Note**
>
> This section primarily focuses on the **Use PolyBase to load data to a SQL pool** concept of the DP-203: Data Engineering on Microsoft Azure exam.

For the data lake scenario, you are going to use PolyBase to copy the transformed data from ADB into a Synapse-dedicated SQL pool using a staging ADLS or Blob Storage. Perform the following steps to do so:

1. Prepare the source data in text files in ADLS or the Blob Storage.

2. Define an external table with the right schema in the dedicated SQL pool instance.

> **Note**
>
> The format of the incoming data should match the external table schema accurately. If not, rows might get dropped.

   If the data is coming from a non-relational source, you will have to transform it into a rows and columns format that matches the external table schema correctly.

3. Run the COPY INTO command to load the data into dedicated SQL pool external tables using PolyBase. From here, you can either serve the data directly for reporting purposes or do more processing using a dedicated SQL pool before serving it to BI tools such as **Power BI**.

4. The following example code shows how to create EXTERNAL FILE FORMAT as follows:

```
CREATE EXTERNAL FILE FORMAT [Dp203ParquetFormat]
WITH (FORMAT_TYPE = PARQUET)
CREATE EXTERNAL DATA SOURCE [Dp203DataSource]
WITH (
LOCATION = 'abfss://path/to/storage/location'
)
```

5. With the CREATE EXTERNAL TABLE <table name> AS SELECT (CETAS) statement shown in the following code, PolyBase copies the data into a Synapse dedicated SQL pool:

```
CREATE EXTERNAL TABLE TripExtTable
WITH (
LOCATION = '/path/to/data/*.parquet',
DATA_SOURCE = [Dp203DataSource],
FILE_FORMAT = [Dp203ParquetFormat]
) AS
SELECT
[tripId] INT,
[driverId] INT,
```

```
.  .  .
[endLocation] VARCHAR(50)
FROM
    OPENROWSET(BULK '/path/to/data/*.parquet', FORMAT='PARQUET')
```

6.  Now copy the data from the external table (`TripsExtTable`) into an actual SQL table (`TripsProdTable`):

```
CREATE TABLE TripsProdTable
WITH
(
    CLUSTERED COLUMNSTORE INDEX,
    DISTRIBUTION = ROUND_ROBIN
)
AS
SELECT * FROM TripsExtTable
```

In the preceding code, a new table, `TripsProdTable`, is created. The `WITH` keyword is used to specify optional properties. `CLUSTERED COLUMNSTORE INDEX` specifies that the new table, `TripsProdTable`, will use a clustered `COLUMNSTORE` index. `DISTRIBUTION = ROUND_ROBIN` specifies the distribution method for data across nodes in a distributed database environment (such as Azure SQL Data Warehouse). The line `AS SELECT * FROM TripsExtTable` indicates that the new table, `TripsProdTable`, will be populated with the data from the external table, `TripsExtTable`.

PolyBase does not support extended ASCII, fixed-width format, and nested formats such as JSON, XML, and WinZip as of the time of writing this book. For JSON files, you could try to flatten the data first using the techniques you saw in *Chapter 4, Ingesting and Transforming Data*, in the *Shred JSON* section.

---

> **Note**
>
> You can learn more about PolyBase at `https://packt.link/PiqEG`. You can find the complete code in the accompanying GitHub repository at `https://packt.link/BCdwr`.

---

## Options for Loading with PolyBase

**PolyBase** is a powerful tool for loading data into Azure Synapse Analytics. It enables querying and analyzing data stored in ADSL or Azure Blob Storage directly using T-SQL statements within the Synapse Analytics environment.

It is available as part of the following services:

- **ADF**: This version of PolyBase can be used as an activity within ADF. The **Copy Data activity** can be defined as a pipeline that can be scheduled regularly.

> **Note**
> You can read more about it at `https://packt.link/7n1Ac`.

- **ADB**: This version of PolyBase can be used to transfer data between Azure Databricks and Synapse SQL pools.

> **Note**
> You can learn more about it at `https://packt.link/25X3p`.

- **SQL Server**: This version can be used if the source is SQL Server. The **SQL Server Integration Services (SSIS)** platform can be used to define the source and destination mappings and do the orchestration while using the SSIS version of PolyBase.

> **Note**
> You can learn more about it at `https://packt.link/R4VxA`.

In this section, you gained knowledge about the PolyBase feature in Azure Synapse Analytics, which allows you to query and import external data from various sources, such as **Azure Blob Storage** or **Azure Data Lake Storage**, into a SQL pool, including considerations for optimizing performance and handling large volumes of data efficiently. The next section will cover how you can synchronize Synapse SQL pools with instances of Azure SQL or on-premises SQL Server by means of Azure Synapse Link.

# Implementing Azure Synapse Link and Querying Replicated Data

Before diving into the implementation of **Azure Synapse Link** and querying replicated data, it is essential to know the rationale behind integrating these two different products. This learning is crucial because SQL pools on Synapse offer most of the features provided by **Transact-SQL** on SQL Server or Azure SQL. Consequently, it is natural to feel some confusion about when and why to use one product over the other. The easiest approach to clarifying this confusion is to consider the distinction between **transactional** workloads and **analytical** workloads.

> **Note**
>
> This section primarily focuses on the **Implement Azure Synapse Link and query the replicated data** concept of the DP-203: Data Engineering on Microsoft Azure exam.

**Transactional workloads** consist of the insertion, update, or deletion of production data, and the main concern here is "data quality" and "consistency." **Analytical workloads** consist of the analysis of data after their production and are typically created or updated only as a result of an import or a refresh, with the main concern represented in this case by the "performance" of the queries and the reports.

With this distinction in mind, it becomes easier to grasp how these products relate to each other: **SQL Server** and its cloud porting **Azure SQL** are optimized for transactional workloads, while **Synapse SQL** pools are optimized for analytical workloads. One way in which this optimization is achieved is by the difference in the following default settings:

- SQL Server uses **rowstore indexes** (optimized for the retrieval of all the columns for a single row, as in the case of a row update) by default.

- Synapse uses **columnstore indexes** (optimized to the values of a single column on multiple rows, as in the case of an aggregation).

- In SQL Server, transactions typically operate under the default isolation level of **Read Committed**, where only committed transactions are visible. This setting ensures data consistency but may impact performance.

- For Synapse, the default setting is **Read Uncommited** (where performance is vital and you are not expecting many transactions to hit a data warehouse anyway).

In an analytics setup where you deal with complex queries and need top-notch performance, the ability to run multiple tasks in parallel becomes crucial. This is where **Azure Synapse** stands out from SQL Server in terms of T-SQL support. It lets you decide how your data should be spread across different nodes in your pools when creating a table. This distribution strategy is key because it ensures that tasks can be executed in parallel, boosting overall efficiency.

On the other hand, when creating a table in Synapse, it is not possible to specify **foreign key constraints**, which are important for transactional workloads. With all this in mind, it is hopefully clear why you may want to use both **Synapse** on one side and **SQL Server** or **Azure SQL** on the other and, consequently, why you might feel the need for a seamless integration between your production system and your data warehouse.

This seamless integration is offered by **Synapse Link**, which can be accessed via the **Integrate** hub. Before you can link an instance of Azure SQL or SQL Server, you need to first create a linked service to it using the Manage hub in the left-side panel, as shown in *Figure 5.17*:

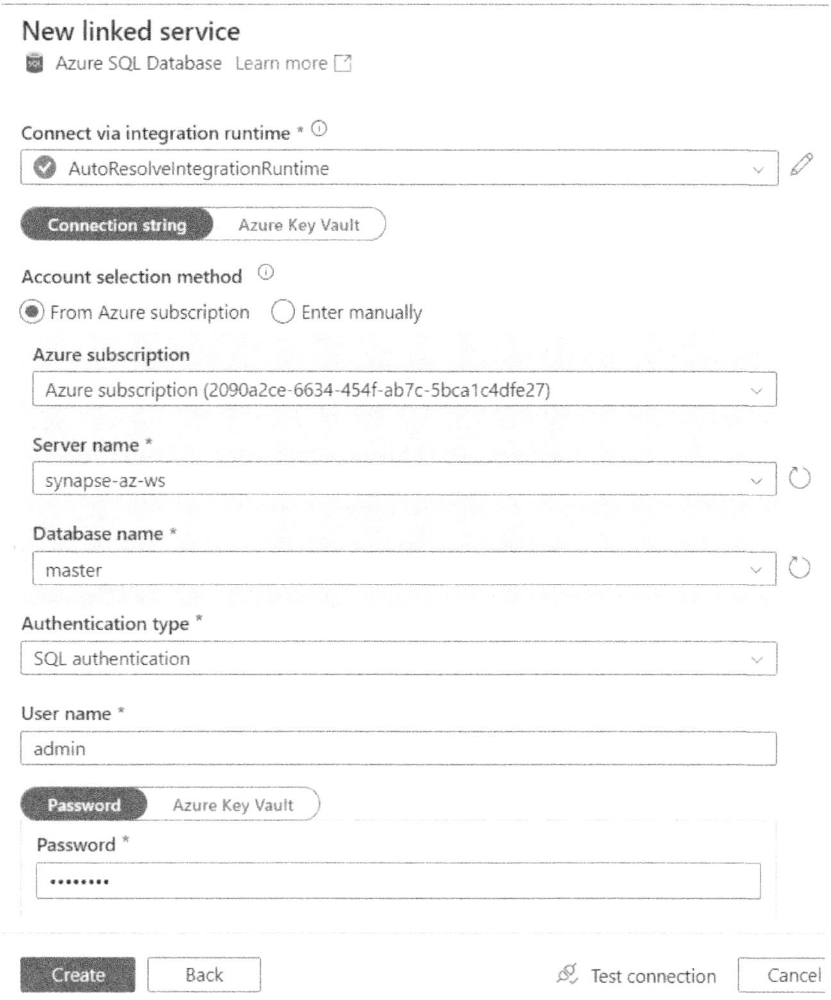

Figure 5.17 – Creating a linked service for Synapse Link

Whenever you create a link service of any type, the best practice is to always click **Test connection** to be sure that the service is accessible. A common cause for a failure is that, by default, Azure SQL instances do not allow for public network access, which needs to be explicitly allowed for this integration to work unless the two services that you are trying to integrate are endpoints on the same VNet.

Once the linked service is created and tested successfully, you can create a **Synapse Link** by selecting one or more tables from the `Source linked service` dropdown. In this case, it is `SampleData` that you wish to be automatically replicated to your **Synapse pool**, as shown in *Figure 5.18*:

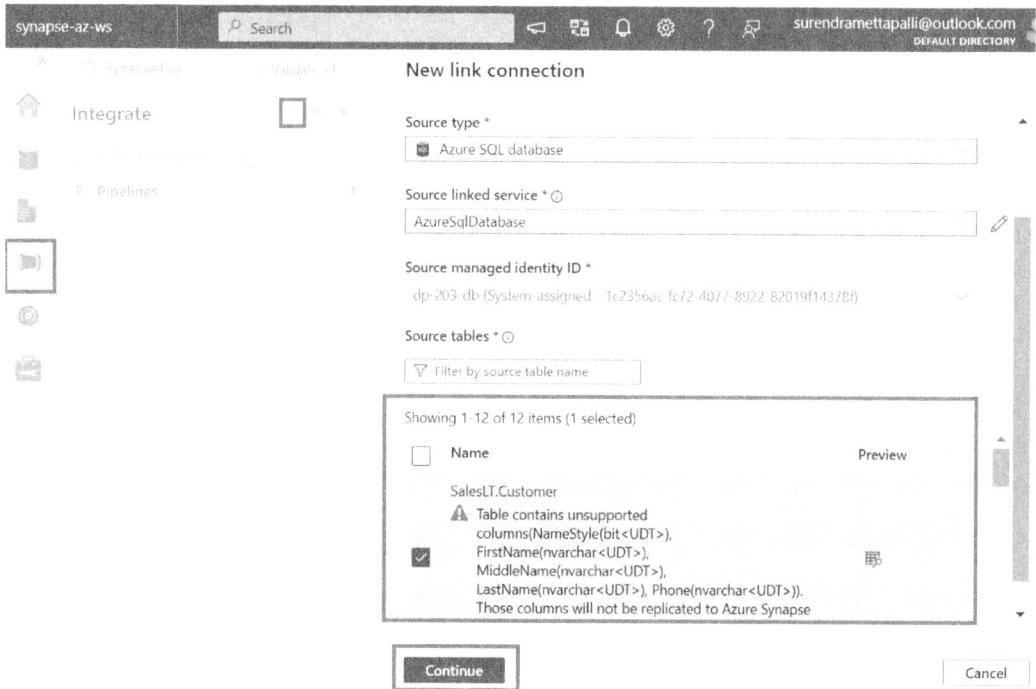

Figure 5.18 – Data replication with Synapse Link

Note that in *Figure 5.18*, not all column types are supported for replication. For instance, replication is not supported for the column of the **User-Defined Type** (**UDT**). You can still select the table, but those columns will be ignored by the replication.

**UDTs** are custom data types that you can define to their specific needs within a database management system. While most database systems come with predefined data types, such as integers, strings, and dates, UDTs offer the flexibility to define new data types that can represent more complex or specialized information. You can identify the UTDs in the table in *Figure 5.18*, where you can see the `SalesLT.Product` and `SalesLT.ProductCategory` columns are unsupported as these columns are UDTs and will not be replicated to Azure Synapse Analytics.

The next steps consist of selecting the target pool and whether the integration should run continuously or by means of scheduled updates. Once created, the linked connection can be monitored and managed as shown in *Figure 5.19*:

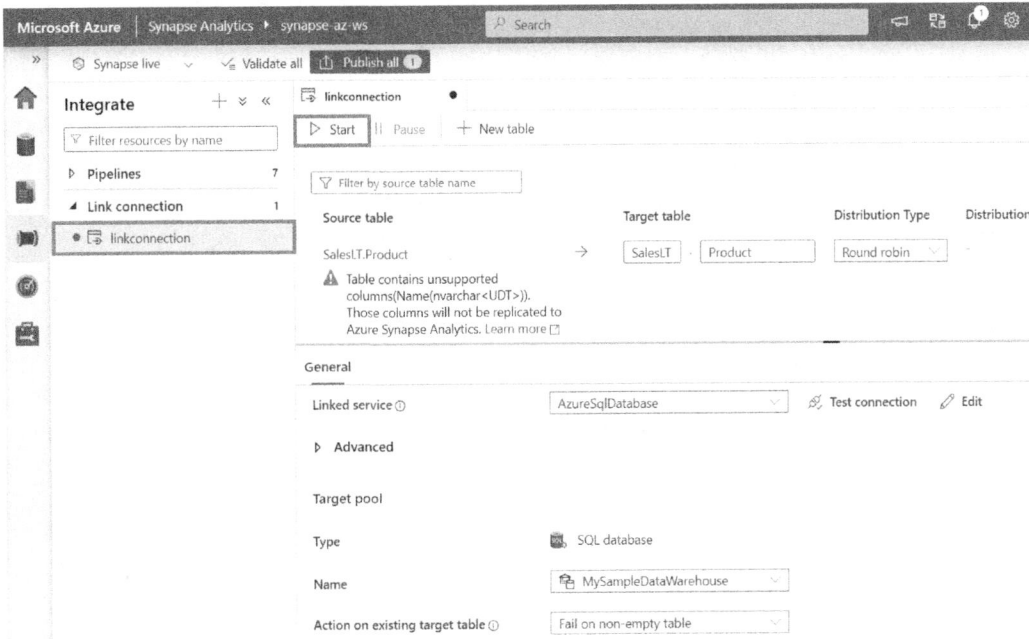

Figure 5.19 – Monitoring replication with Synapse Link

Once the integration is up and running, querying data becomes trivial, as the replicated data will be available as part of the target SQL pools exactly like any other table.

This section dealt with the implementation process for Azure Synapse Link and querying replicated data. You also learned the foundation behind integrating these two products, which revolves around distinguishing between transactional and analytical workloads. This distinction helps you know when and why to use Azure Synapse SQL pools over other similar products, including SQL Server or Azure SQL, ensuring a more informed decision-making process for data-processing tasks. In the next section, you will learn how to create data pipelines to copy and transform data with ADF and Synapse.

# Creating Data Pipelines

**Data pipelines** are a collection of various data-processing activities arranged in a particular sequence to produce the desired insights from raw data. You have already seen many examples in Azure Data Factory in various sections, such as *Designing and Implementing Incremental Loads*, *Transform Options Available in ADF*, and *ADF Templates* (*Chapter 4, Ingesting and Transforming Data*), where you chain the activities together to produce a final desirable outcome. ADF is not the only technology available in Azure; Azure also supports **Synapse pipelines**—an implementation of ADF within Synapse—and open source technologies such as **Oozie** (available via Azure HDInsight), which can help orchestrate pipelines.

> **Note**
>
> This section primarily focuses on the **Create data pipelines** concept of the DP-203: Data Engineering on Microsoft Azure exam.

If your workload only uses open-source software, then Oozie will be an alternative solution. However, if the pipeline uses other Azure or external third-party services, then **ADF** might be a better fit as ADF provides readily available source and **sink plugins** for a huge list of technologies. Perform the following steps to create an end-to-end batch pipeline:

1. Click the `Pipeline` tab of Azure Data Factory and choose the `New pipeline` option.

2. Select the activities for your pipeline from the **Activities** tab. Then click and drag it into the canvas.

3. Link the activities using the square box (on the right side of each activity) and chain the blocks together either sequentially or parallelly to derive the required output. *Figure 5.20* shows an example:

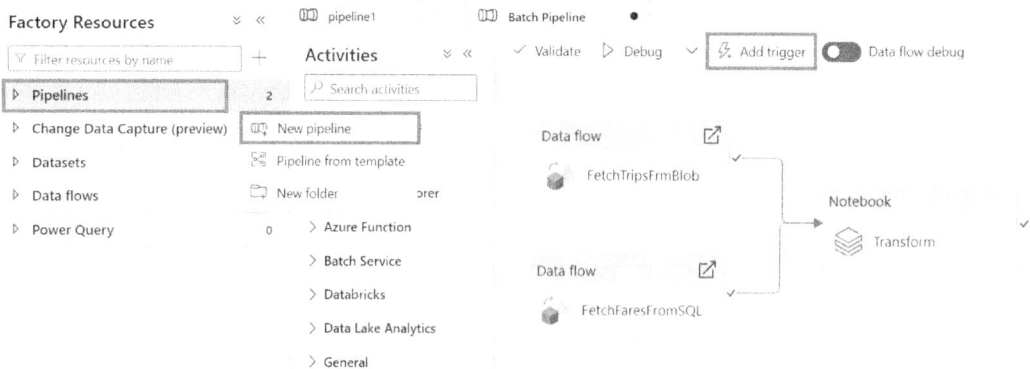

Figure 5.20 – Creating new pipelines in ADF

4.   Once you have the pipeline stitched together, you can trigger it using the **Add trigger** button. The trigger could be one-time, event-based, or recurring.

You now know what data pipelines are and have learned how to create and publish an end-to-end batch pipeline. The next section, *Scaling Resources*, is dedicated to data pipelines.

# Scaling Resources

Recall the example of credit card processing described at the beginning of the chapter involving the processing of credit card transactions in real time. The buyer and the seller will need to know as quickly as possible whether the transaction was approved. This was an example of stream processing.

> **Note**
> This section primarily focuses on the **Scale resources** concept of the DP-203: Data Engineering on Microsoft Azure exam.

In contrast to stream processing, batch processing involves processing a great quantity of data and executing at longer intervals of time, so it involves a steep spike in the resources required for its execution. Therefore, the need for scaling arises to efficiently manage and adapt the allocation of resources to accommodate these fluctuations in demand. Fortunately, cloud technology makes scaling much easier, and that applies to all the services covered in this chapter.

## ADF and Synapse Pipelines

As a pipeline is just a sequence of activities, you will need to scale resources at the activity level, probably starting with the **Copy Data activity**. As with many other data services, the resources allocated are not specified directly in terms of CPU cores, memory, and so on, but by describing the level of performance required while letting Azure find the best way to provision them.

In this specific Copy activity case, that level of performance is expressed by means of **Data Integration Units** (**DIUs**), specified in *Figure 5.21*:

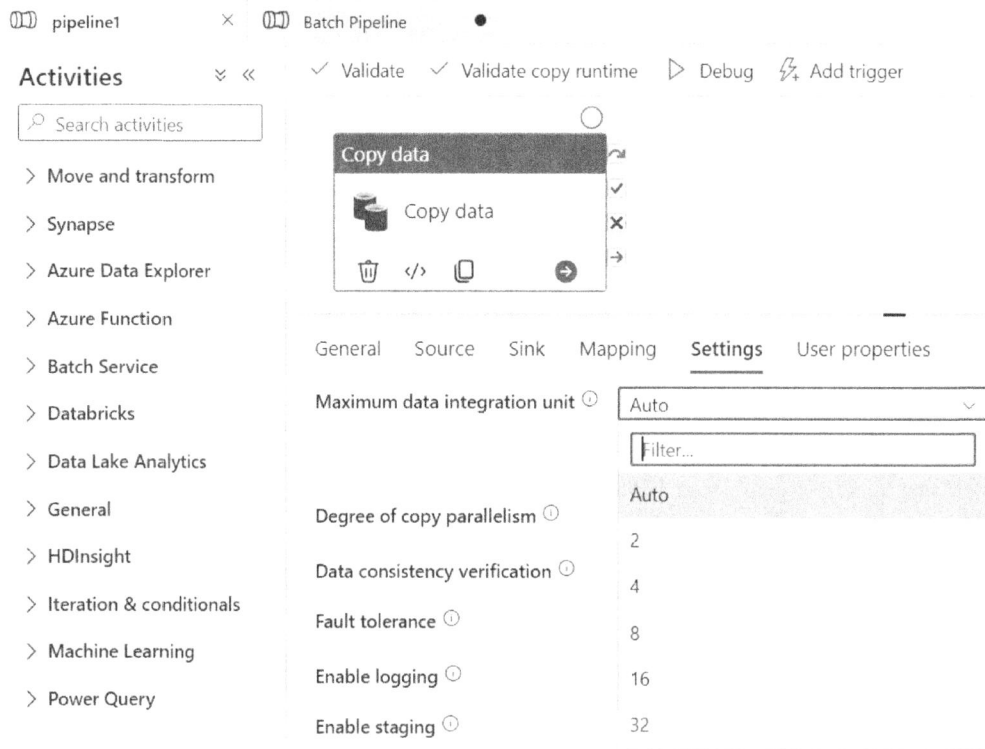

Figure 5.21 – Specifying data integration units for the Copy activity

Under the **Settings** tab, beside the **Maximum data integration unit** option, choose Auto. **Auto** allows you to enable autoscaling, which is, of course, the automatic allocation of resources according to the requirements. Alternatively, you can specify a number of DIUs, either by choosing between 2, 4, 8, 16, and 32 or by clicking on the Edit link and specifying your own value.

While the idea of allowing users to specify the level of performance without having to specify how it is delivered is excellent in theory, one of the consequences of hiding the implementation details is it sometimes becomes difficult for you to know what these units are. The problem is not limited to the following **DIUs**:

- Azure SQL has **Database Transaction Units** (**DTUs**)
- Synapse Analytics has **Data Warehouse Units** (**DWUs**)
- Cosmos DB has **Request Units** (**Rus**)

Probably the best approach is to start with a small number of units, monitor the performance, and then adjust the allocation accordingly.

One more setting you can specify is the **Degree of parallelism**—the higher the number, the better the performance whenever data can be copied by multiple executors running in parallel, for instance, when copying from multiple files. If you are using this option in combination with the **Auto** setting for the number of DIUs, however, the higher level of parallelism will also result in a higher number of DIUs allocated and hence in higher costs.

## Azure Databricks

In ADB, while creating the cluster, you can select `Enable Autoscaling` and specify the `Min Workers` and `Max Workers` numbers (see *Figure 5.22*). The cluster will automatically scale up and down between these two numbers based on the load. Unlike Azure Batch ADF and Synapse pipeline scaling, you don't have the flexibility to provide your scaling formula here.

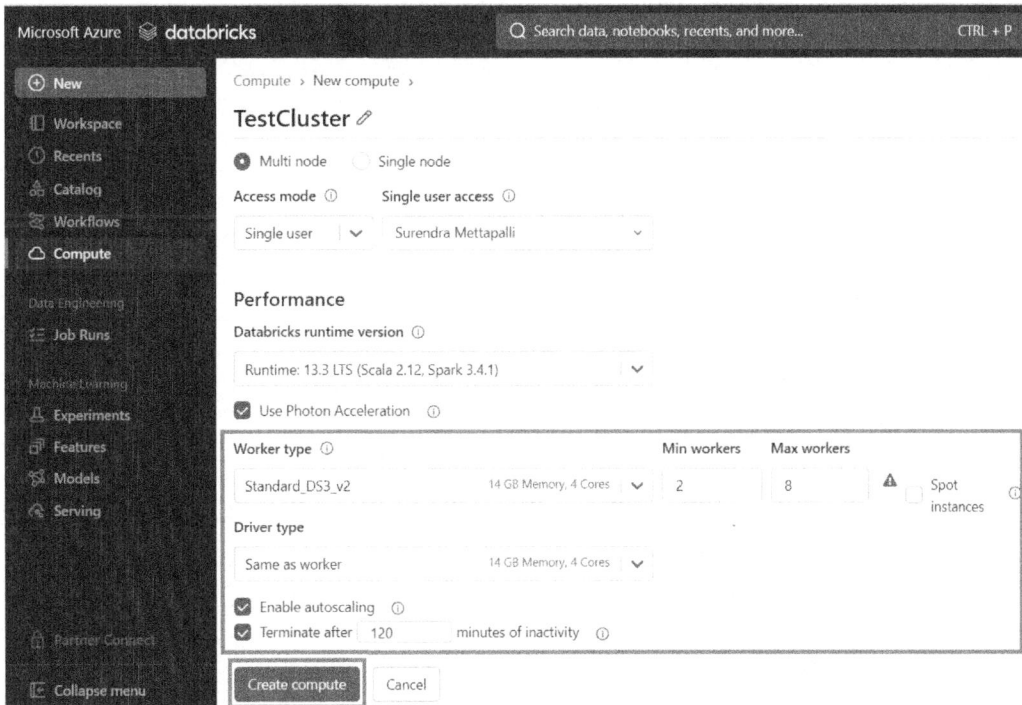

Figure 5.22 – Enabling the Azure Databricks cluster autoscale option

With a fixed-size cluster, the cluster is unable to automatically adjust its size based on workload demands. Instead, to do so, you have to uncheck the `Enable autoscaling` option and provide the exact worker count.

You can save on the cost of your clusters by using Spot instances. **Spot instances** are unused Azure **Virtual Machines (VMs)** that are offered by Azure at a cheaper cost but with no availability guarantees. If Azure needs the capacity back, it can pull back the Spot VMs with "30 seconds' notice." You can use this option if your jobs can handle interruptions, such as exceptionally large batch jobs and dev/test jobs.

The next section will deal with Synapse Spark.

## Synapse Spark

Synapse Spark is the integration of Apache Spark, a robust big data-processing engine, within Microsoft's Azure Synapse Analytics. This powerhouse combination lets you analyze massive datasets residing in Azure using Spark's advanced functionalities—from in-depth data analysis to building complex machine learning models.

Similar to ADB, **Synapse Spark** also provides the option to autoscale on the cluster creation screen. *Figure 5.23* shows the screen with the autoscale options:

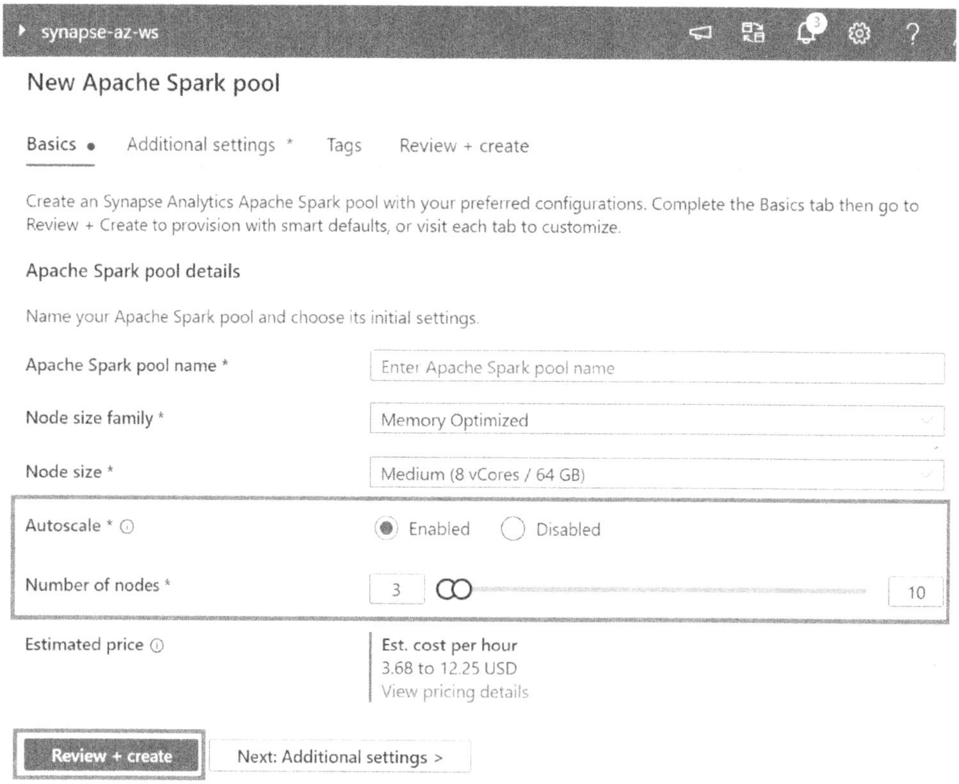

Figure 5.23 – Selecting the Synapse Spark Autoscale option for autoscaling

The **Number of nodes** option in Microsoft Azure Synapse Analytics refers to a setting for configuring an Apache Spark pool. The Spark pool in Azure Synapse Analytics serves the purpose of allocating computing nodes based on data volume and complexity, with each node contributing processing power and memory for data operations. Contrasting with Databricks, Synapse Analytics offers deeper integration with various Azure services and provides additional management and security features. The choice between the two platforms depends on specific use cases and preferences. Spark is favored for its enhanced security features, tight integration with Azure services, and granular control over resource allocation and scaling within the Synapse environment.

Spark on Azure Synapse Analytics is preferred when you need tighter Azure integration and granular control, while Databricks excels in user-friendliness and built-in features.

Next, look at the options available for Synapse SQL dedicated pools.

## Synapse SQL

**Synapse SQL** doesn't provide the option to autoscale, but it provides the option to scale out compute for performance and scale back compute to save costs, as shown in *Figure 5.24*. The higher the number, the better the performance.

A dedicated SQL pool represents a collection of analytical resources, including a combination of CPU, memory, and IO; they are bundled into units called **Data Warehouse Units** (**DWUs**). DWUs impact how quickly a standard query scans the data rows and performs complex aggregations and also influence the speed at which data is ingested from **Azure Blob Storage** or **Azure Data Lake**.

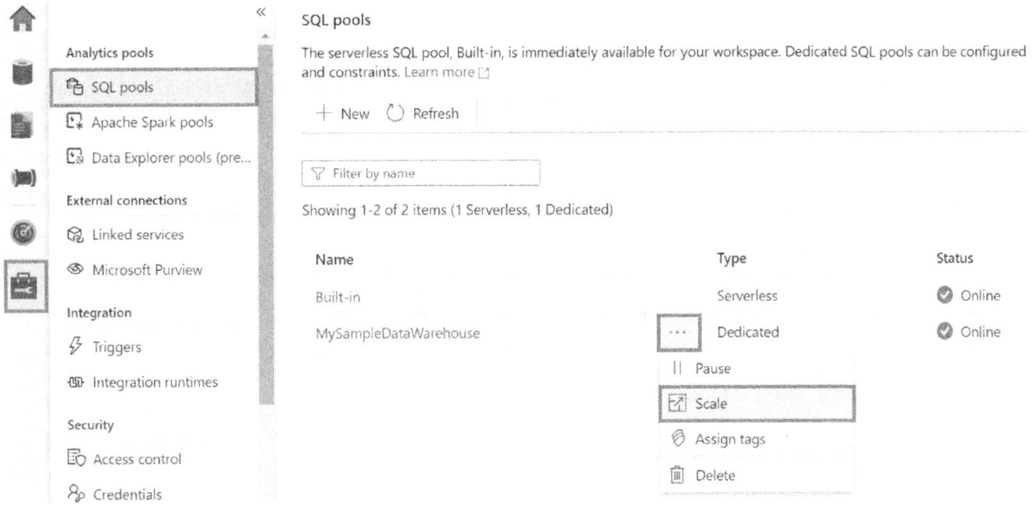

Figure 5.24 – Selecting the Synapse SQL Scale option

In the **Scale** panel, move the **Performance level** slider left or right to change the DWU setting to scale your Synapse dedicated SQL pool, as shown in *Figure 5.25*:

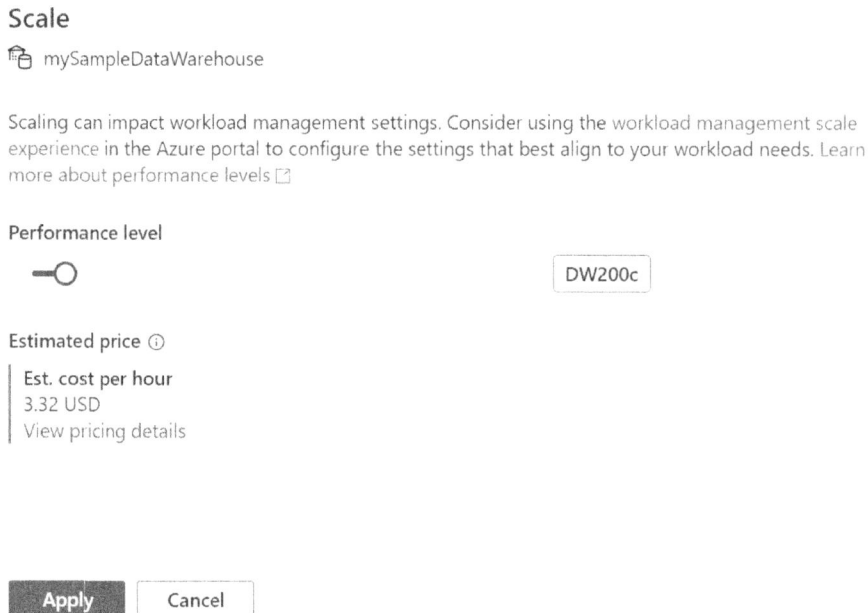

## Scale

🗄 mySampleDataWarehouse

Scaling can impact workload management settings. Consider using the workload management scale experience in the Azure portal to configure the settings that best align to your workload needs. Learn more about performance levels ⧉

Performance level

━⃝                                                    DW200c

Estimated price ⓘ

Est. cost per hour
3.32 USD
View pricing details

[ **Apply** ] [ Cancel ]

Figure 5.25 – Synapse SQL Scale option to scale out for performance and scale in to save costs

You have now learned about various scale resources available in Azure, including **Azure Data Lake Storage**, **Azure SQL Data Warehouse**, **ADB**, and **Azure Synapse Analytics**. Each resource serves a distinct purpose in the data pipeline and their capabilities are used for optimal resource allocation. You also got to learn about each scaling option; for example, **Synapse SQL** is best suitable for structured data analysis and SQL-driven workloads, whereas **Synapse Spark** suits big data processing and provides autoscaling and Databricks excels in real-time analytics and cost efficiency.

The next section will deal with configuring batch size, which allows you to specify how many rows should be inserted into the database for each batch.

## Configuring Batch Size

Batch size refers to the number of data records processed together during a task, influencing the speed of task completion significantly. Using a larger batch size can enhance efficiency by minimizing data transfer and processing overhead. However, if the batch size is excessively large, it may strain system resources and impede performance. The optimal batch size is contingent upon the characteristics of the specific data being processed, including volume, complexity, and variability. For instance, a Copy activity is used to copy data between a Source and a **sink**, where the sink represents the destination.

> **Note**
>
> This section primarily focuses on the **Configure the batch size** concept of the DP-203: Data Engineering on Microsoft Azure exam.

When the sink is represented by a relational database, one option that can be specified is `Write batch size`, as shown in *Figure 5.26*, taken from an ADF pipeline:

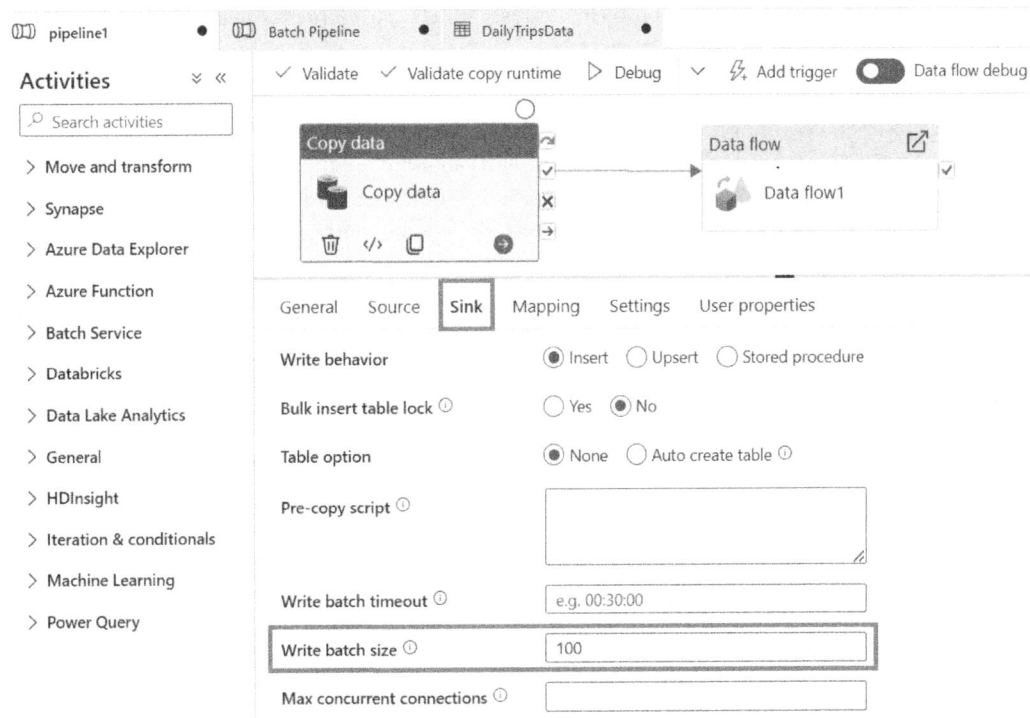

Figure 5.26 – Specifying the batch size for the Copy activity

That batch size setting allows you to specify how many rows should be inserted in the database for each batch. If you specify `100`, for instance, the Copy activity will produce the equivalent of `100` `INSERT` statements before sending them as a batch to the destination database. A higher number will result in fewer write connections to the destination database, but you should keep in mind the size of each row. If the rows are too big and you are sending too many of them at the same time, a copy failure might result from overloading the database.

The next section will focus on ensuring the reliability and correctness of your data pipelines, so you can create robust data pipelines that undergo thorough testing and ensure accuracy in handling your batch-processing tasks.

## Creating Tests for Data Pipelines

You have now created your ADF or Synapse pipeline. You have seen many examples in ADF, which were explained in the *Creating Data Pipelines* section of this chapter. Now you need to run the pipeline by assigning a trigger to it.

> **Note**
>
> This section primarily focuses on the **Create tests for data pipelines** concept of the DP-203: Data Engineering on Microsoft Azure exam.

If you want to test its execution, you can choose the `Trigger now` option, which will result in an immediate execution of the pipeline. At that point, you can switch to the **Monitor hub**, where you can see the status of your pipeline and check whether it is running or completed and, in the latter case, how long it took and whether it completed successfully or failed with an error.

> **Note**
>
> You will find a reference to the testing process for data pipelines in *Chapter 6, Developing a Stream Processing Solution*, within the section titled *Developing Testing Processes for Data Pipelines*.

After a successful run, you can verify whether the pipeline has produced the expected result, for instance, by checking that the destination table contains the expected data.

> **Note**
>
> For a more repeatable and automated approach, you can use **Test plans** in **Azure DevOps**, a service that is outside the scope of the DP-203 exam as it is the subject of an entirely separate exam, namely **AZ-400**. For the purposes of DP-203, you will only need to be aware of this possibility.

Now you will learn how to call a Spark notebook from a pipeline, in all those cases where a low-code solution needs to be integrated with the execution of code.

## Integrating Jupyter/Python Notebooks into a Data Pipeline

Integrating **Jupyter/Python** notebooks into a data pipeline provides flexibility, transparency, and efficiency throughout the data-processing life cycle. It bridges the gap between your exploration, development, and production, making it an essential practice in your data-engineering workflows. Integrating Jupyter/Python notebooks into your ADF data pipeline can be done using the Spark activity in ADF. You will need an Azure HDInsight Spark cluster for this example.

> **Note**
>
> This section primarily focuses on the **Integrate Jupyter or Python notebooks into a data pipeline** concept of the DP-203: Data Engineering on Microsoft Azure exam.

The prerequisites for integrating Jupyter notebooks are as follows:

- Create linked services to Azure Storage
- Create HDInsight from ADF
- Have an HDInsight Spark cluster running

> **Note**
>
> You have already learned how linked services are created in the *Data Ingestion* section, the *Configuring an ADB Notebook Activity in ADF* section, the *Implementing Azure Synapse Link and Querying Replicated Data* section, and the *Batch-Processing Technology Choices* section, which covered batch-processing solutions by using Data Factory, Data Lake, Spark, Azure Synapse pipelines, PolyBase, and ADB, earlier in this chapter. Therefore, they will not be repeated here.

You will now learn how to run Jupyter notebooks from data pipelines. Perform the following steps to do so:

1. Select the Spark activity from ADF.

2. Specify the HDInsight linked service that you created in the **HDInsight linked service** field under the **HDI Cluster** tab. In this case, it is HDInsight LS, as shown in *Figure 5.27*:

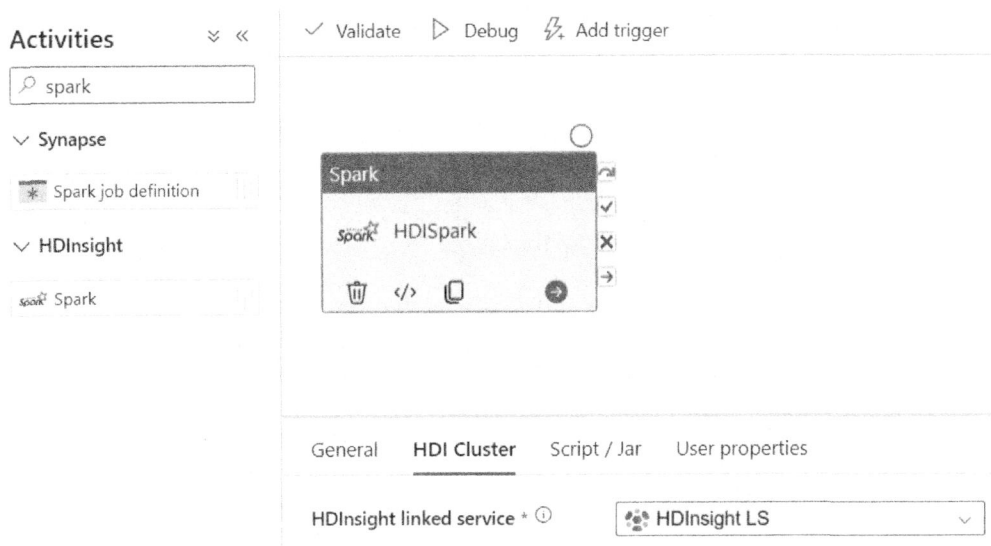

Figure 5.27 – Configuring a Spark activity in ADF

3.  Start the **Jupyter notebook** by going to `https://<YOURHDICLUSTER>.azurehdinsight.net/jupyter` or from the HDInsight dashboard, as shown in *Figure 5.28*:

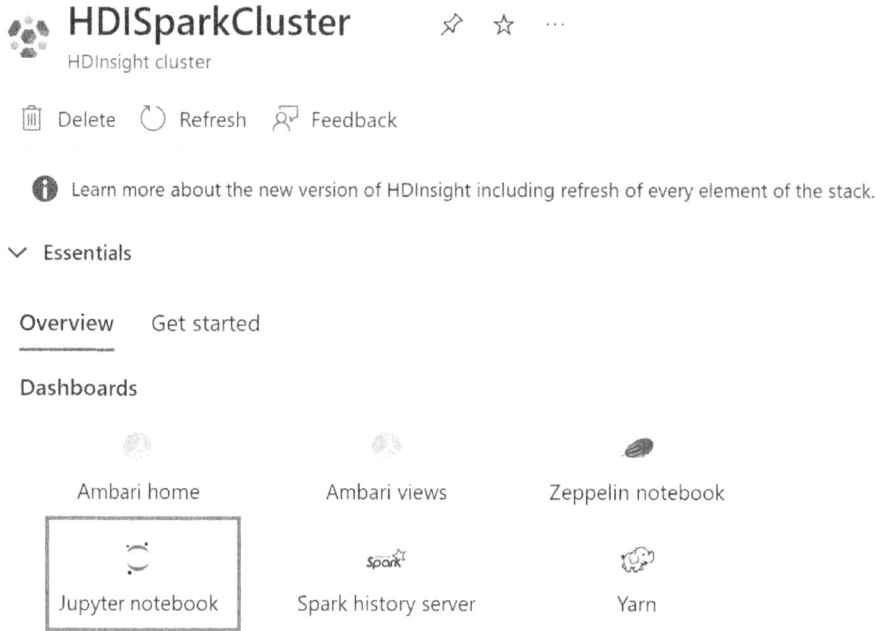

Figure 5.28 – Launching the Jupyter notebook from HDInsight

4.  From the **Jupyter** launch screen, select `PySpark` or `PySpark3` to start a **Python notebook**. For this example, `PySpark` is selected (*Figure 5.29*):

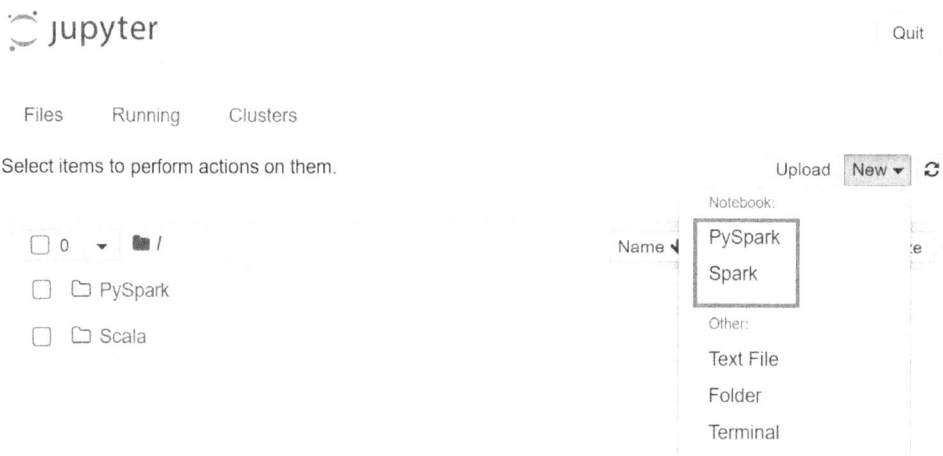

Figure 5.29 – Launching a PySpark Jupyter notebook from HDInsight

5.  Write your transformations in the Jupyter notebook.

6.  Run it using the ADF pipelines like any other ADF activity.

    Now you know how to run **Jupyter** notebooks from data pipelines.

> **Note**
> You can learn more about running Spark notebooks from ADF at `https://packt.link/azprS`.

The next few sections will focus on a few advanced techniques for loading data and data preparation. Some of these topics, such as Azure Synapse Analytics database templates, transforming data using Apache Spark, and the transformation options available in ADF, were covered in *Chapter 3, Designing and Implementing the Data Exploration Layer*, and *Chapter 4, Ingesting and Transforming Data*, so they will be skipped over with references to the previous chapters provided, so you can focus on the new topics that have not already been covered.

## Upserting Data

**Upserting** refers to UPDATE or INSERT transactions in data stores to streamline data management. This technique automatically updates existing records or inserts new ones into a database, depending on whether a matching record already exists. The data stores could be relational, key-value, or any other store that supports the concept of updating rows or blobs.

> **Note**
> This section primarily focuses on the **Upsert data** concept of the DP-203: Data Engineering on Microsoft Azure exam.

ADF supports upsert operations if the sink is an SQL-based store. The only additional requirement is that the sink activity must be preceded by an `Alter Row` operation. *Figure 5.30* is an example screenshot of an ADF sink with `Allow upsert` enabled:

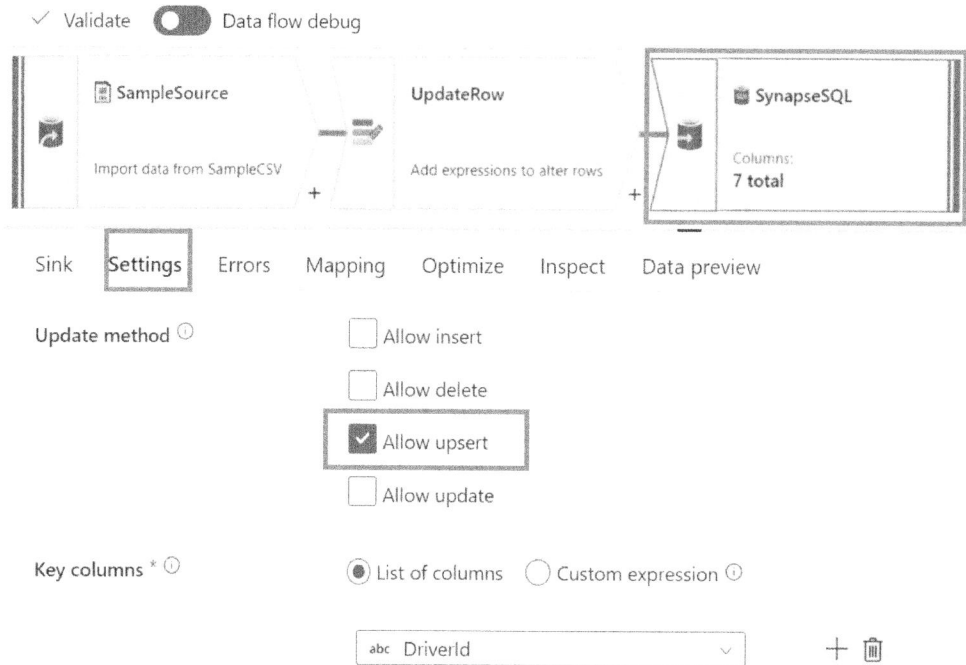

Figure 5.30 – Upsert operation in ADF used for updating and inserting data

Once you have saved the preceding setup, ADF will automatically do an upsert if a row already exists in the configured sink.

Now you will dive into a simple example of **Upsert**, which combines `INSERT` and `UPDATE` operations. When data is copied from a source (`SampleSource`) to a sink (`SynpaseSQL`), if a row already exists in the sink, it updates the existing row, or else a new row is inserted into a sink. Imagine you have a source CSV file in `SampleSource` with the following data:

- `id, name`
- `1, A`
- `2, C`
- `3, T`
- `4, J`
- `6, M`

Your sink table already contains some data:

- `id, name`
- `1, A`
- `2, C`
- `3, T`
- `4, J`

Now, insert completely new rows into the source:

- `id, name`
- `8, S`
- `9, F`

When you perform an upsert operation, rows with IDs 8 and 9 are inserted into the sink as they are new records. Rows with IDs 1, 2, 3, and 4 are updated in the sink as they already exist.

In the next section, you'll learn how to revert data to a previous state, which is essential for you to maintain data accuracy and is an effective state in case of errors or issues with the data by using the fault tolerance and data consistency verification settings.

## Reverting Data to a Previous State

Reverting data to a previous state or rolling back to a stable state is a very commonly used technique in databases and **Online Transaction Processing (OLTP)** scenarios. In OLTP scenarios, the transformation instructions are grouped together into a transaction, and if any of the instructions fail or reach an inconsistent state, then the entire transaction rolls back.

Although databases provide such functionality, you don't have such ready-made support in ADF or Oozie (HDInsight) today. You will have to build your own rollback stages depending on the activity.

> **Note**
> This section primarily focuses on the **Revert data to a previous state** concept of the DP-203: Data Engineering on Microsoft Azure exam.

ADF provides options for checking consistency and setting limits for fault tolerance. Now look at an example to learn how the rollback of a **Copy Data activity** is done in ADF. You can enable **Data consistency verification** and **Fault tolerance** in the Settings tab of a Copy activity, as shown in *Figure 5.31*:

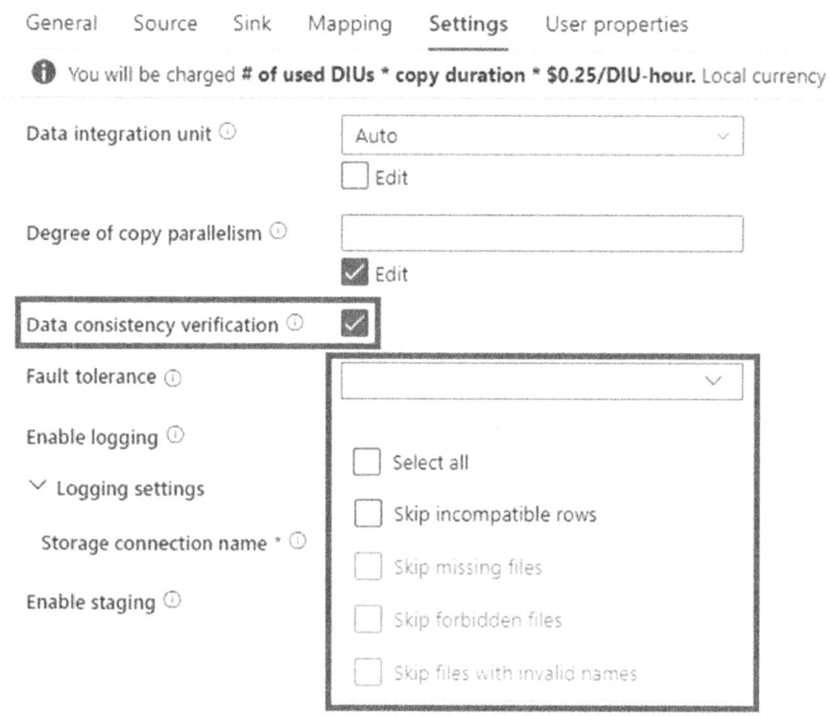

Figure 5.31 – Enabling consistency verification and fault tolerance in an ADF Copy activity

**Data consistency verification** ensures your data transferred between the source and sink remains consistent and compares the data before and after transfer to detect any discrepancies. On the other hand, **fault tolerance** ensures pipeline reliability even if you face any failures during the pipeline run and performs various operations, as follows:

- **Skip incompatible rows**: This indicates to proceed to other rows if an incompatible one is encountered.

- **Skip missing files**: This indicates continued processing if certain files are missing.

- **Skip forbidden files**: This ignores files with restricted access.

- **Skip files with invalid names**: This bypasses files with invalid naming conventions.

If the activity fails due to consistency checks or fault tolerance reaching or going beyond a particular level, you can define a follow-up Delete activity on the failure path (the down arrow pointing to the **Delete** activity) to completely clean up the directory, as shown in *Figure 5.32*:

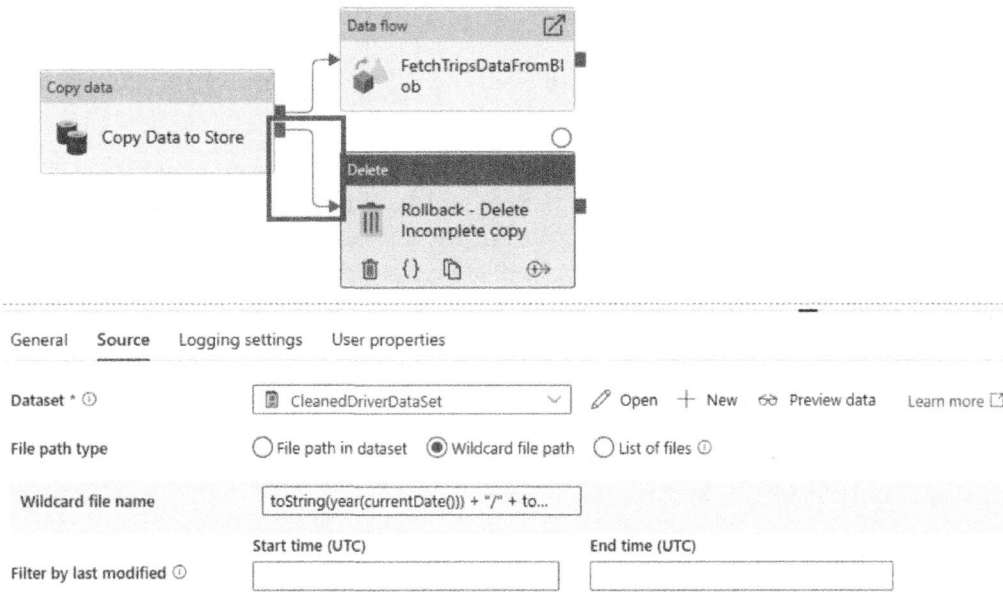

Figure 5.32 – Deleting an incomplete Copy activity

You can select the `Recursively` checkbox to process all files in the input folder and its subfolders iteratively.

Note that the **Delete** activity technique can be extended to other scenarios, such as data insertion into tables and retrying transformations. The corresponding rollback techniques in such cases will also be different, such as deleting files and deleting rows in a table.

> **Note**
>
> You will learn about implementing data rollback to previous states and configuring exception handling in the *Handling Failed Batch Loads* section of *Chapter 7, Managing Batches and Pipelines.*

With this, you have now grasped how a rollback to a previous stage occurs using ADF. Next, you will focus on exception handling to prevent failures from disrupting the data flow, identify exceptions during data transfer, and implement mechanisms to handle errors to maintain data integrity.

## Configuring Exception Handling

In the *Creating Tests for Data Pipelines* section, you learned that a pipeline run can terminate with a failure due to an unhandled error. Just like, when developing code, you tend to attempt to prevent exception errors such as `expected file missing` from happening, and handle them before they result in a failure, in pipelines, you connect one activity to the next using one of the four available dependency conditions: `On Success` (green arrow), `On Fail` (red arrow), `On Completion` (blue arrow), and `On Skip` (gray arrow).

In particular, you can use `On Fail` to connect your action with another action that can provide a workaround or a limitation strategy for that possible failure. If no workaround is possible, your exception-handling action can just be to log the problem and maybe send an alert. In any case, the exception will be considered handled, and the pipeline will not appear as a failure, provided, of course, that the handling action is in turn executed successfully.

You can also concatenate multiple `On Fail` conditions if you want to try multiple handling strategies. For instance, if you want the next activity to be executed regardless of whether the previous activity ended with a success or failure, you can use the `On Completion` condition. Conversely, `On Skipped` can be employed to execute an activity if the previous one was not executed, such as when an activity's dependency condition is not satisfied.

> **Note**
>
> This section primarily focuses on the **Configure exception handling** concept of the DP-203: Data Engineering on Microsoft Azure exam.

It is also possible to configure some forms of exception handling within a specific activity. For instance, the **Copy** activity has **Retry** and **Retry interval** settings, which you can use to specify how many times a failed connection attempt to the source, or the sink should be retried and after how many seconds the next connection should be attempted, respectively.

However, despite all your best efforts to catch exceptions, pipelines might still encounter unrecoverable conditions and thus fail. The **Alerts & metrics** section of the **Monitor** hub can be used to specify alerts according to thresholds based on a wide range of metrics, including metrics related to failed pipelines, as shown in *Figure 5.33*:

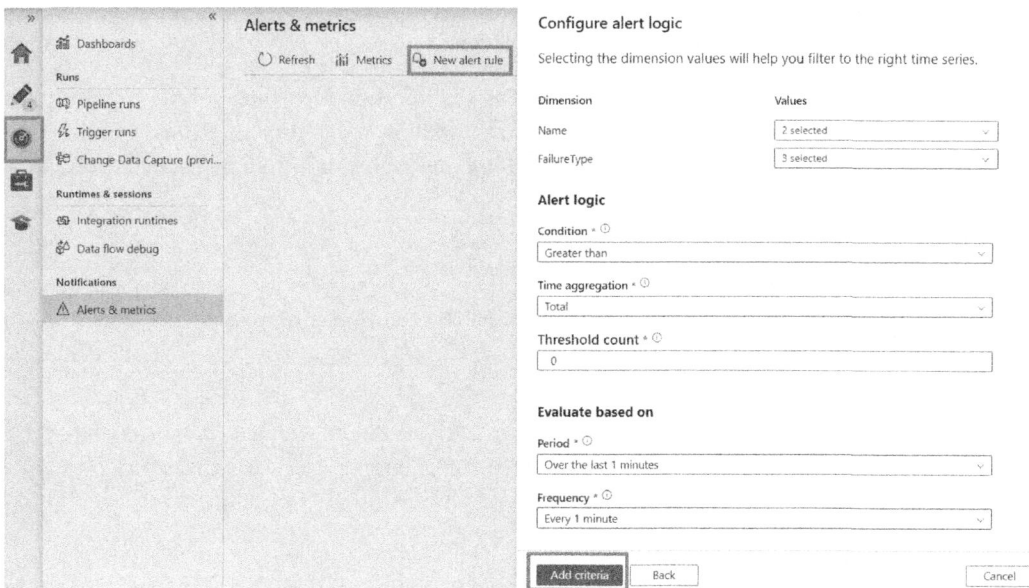

Figure 5.33 – Configuring an alert for pipeline failure

> **Note**
>
> You will learn about implementing data rollback to previous states and configuring exception handling in the *Handling Failed Batch Loads* section of *Chapter 7, Managing Batches and Pipelines*.

With this, you have learned about exception handling using the **Retry** and **Retry interval** settings and monitoring the specific alerts based on a wider range of metrics within pipelines using alerts and metrics.

The next section will deal with configuring batch retention to define how long data should be retained before it is archived, deleted, or transformed by using the storage tiers mechanism for efficient data management, compliance, and cost-effectiveness in batch-processing solutions.

# Configuring Batch Retention

**Configuring batch retention** involves determining the duration for which you want to keep the information related to batch runs, such as when they ran, how much time they took, whether they completed successfully or with a failure, and how long the staging data used by the batch is kept on the disk.

> **Note**
>
> This section primarily focuses on the **Configure batch retention** concept of the DP-203: Data Engineering on Microsoft Azure exam.

A service that allows you to control batch retention is **Azure Batch**, which is an Azure service that can be used to perform large-scale parallel batch processing. It is typically used for high-performance computing applications such as image analysis, 3D rendering, genome sequencing, and optical character recognition.

However, you can create an **Azure Batch activity** in a pipeline and use it to run some part of the process for better control of the executing environment, including the possibility to specify the retention period (see *Figure 5.34*):

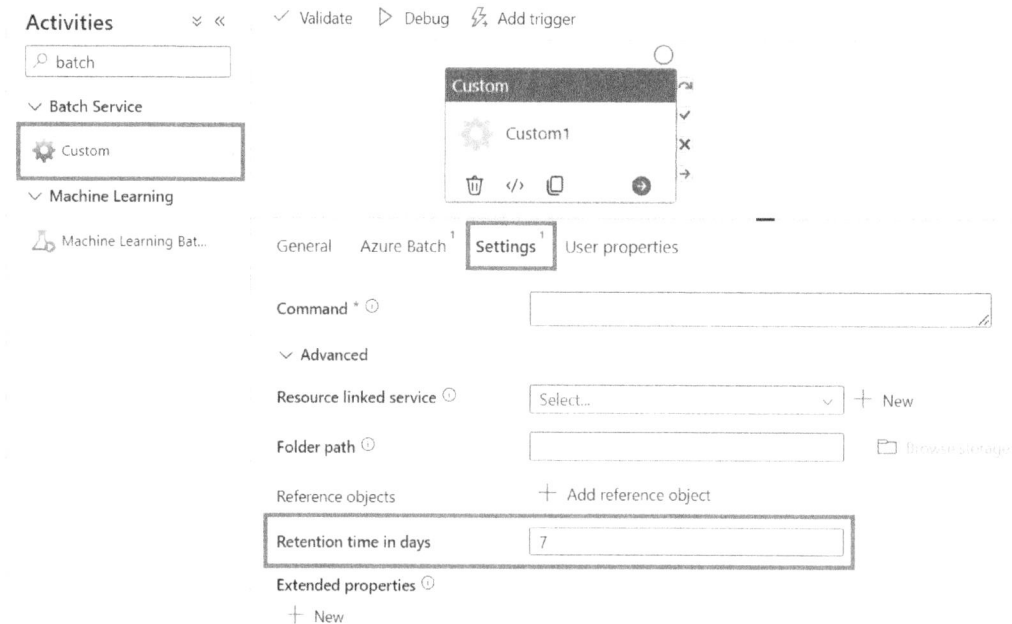

Figure 5.34 – Configuring batch retention for an Azure Batch activity in a pipeline

The next section will deal with reading from and writing to a Delta Lake, which allows efficient reads of the data using various files and allows you to query data at different points in time.

# Reading from and Writing to a Delta Lake

In *Chapter 3, Designing and Implementing the Data Exploration Layer*, you first encountered the concept of a **Delta Lake**. This is a layer of relational tables, called **delta tables**, on top of the files stored in a data lake. While the ability to see data in a tabular format and use SQL to query is also offered by creating an external table over CSV or Parquet files, creating a delta table adds extra benefits, such as versioning and transaction support.

> **Note**
> This section primarily focuses on the **Read from and write to a delta lake** concept of the DP-203: Data Engineering on Microsoft Azure exam.

In Synapse, aside from creating delta tables from templates, as shown in *Chapter 3, Designing and Implementing the Data Exploration Layer*, you can also create custom tables, as shown in *Figure 5.35*:

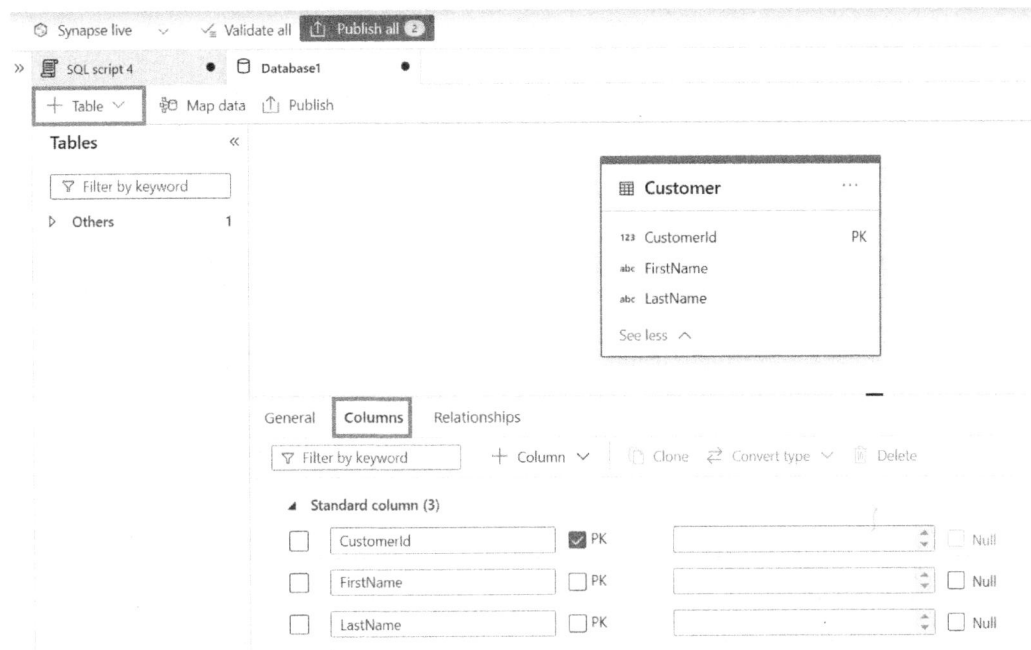

Figure 5.35 – Creating a custom delta table in Synapse

Alternatively, you can create a delta table from an existing file after uploading the file to a folder in your data lake and choosing the From data lake option at the moment of adding the new table. Once the delta table is created, it can be queried as any other table and the query will run against the built-in serverless SQL pool, as shown in *Figure 5.36*:

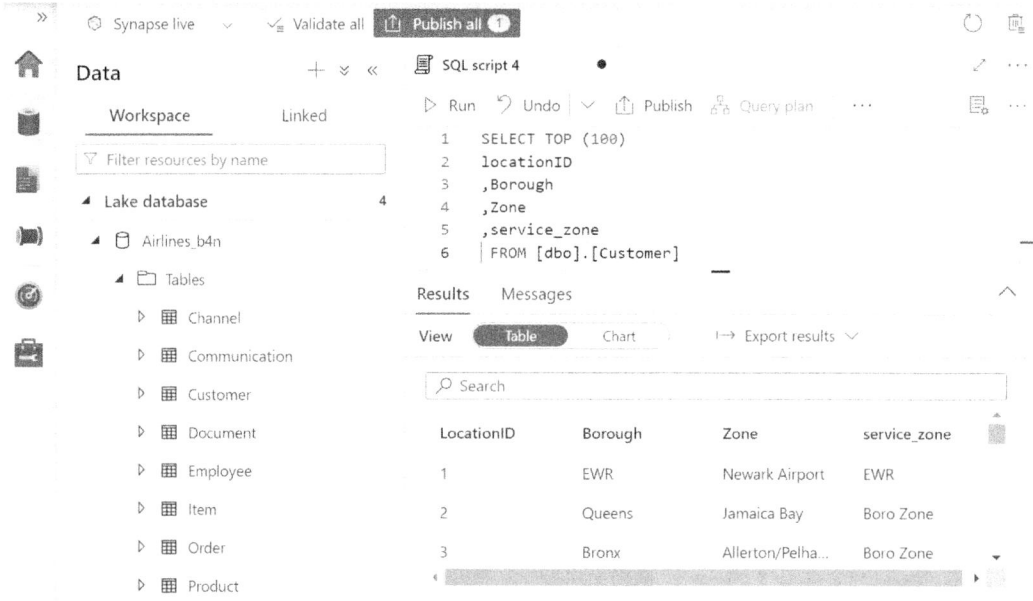

Figure 5.36 – Querying a delta table in Synapse

What Synapse does is create an external table over the files contained in the folder. What makes this table a **delta table**, however, is that the folder contains a subfolder of metadata (in JSON format) called the **delta log**, which allows for time traveling (i.e., reverting to a specific version in time) and adds support for **Atomicity, Consistency, Isolation, and Durability** (**ACID**) transactions.

While data insertion or update will create a new Parquet file, given that Parquet files are immutable, the metadata will allow this data to appear as part of a single table. This allows you, for instance, to **roll back** the transaction, as the delta log will contain the necessary information for the table to be re-directed to the previous Parquet file. So, a folder of immutable Parquet files is displayed and consumed as a single table with a version history. This is particularly useful if the **delta table** is the destination of a pipeline that periodically inserts or updates the data.

By now, you've learned that Delta Lakes provide robust tools to manage that data securely and reliably. It scales with your needs and ensures data consistency through ACID transactions, making it a valuable asset for organizations with growing data volumes and strict compliance requirements.

## Summary

With this chapter, you have gained a profound knowledge of crafting batch-processing solutions within Azure's ecosystem. You've mastered data integration with PolyBase, queried replicated data using Synapse Link, and orchestrated tasks through data pipelines. Now, you can seamlessly scale resources, optimize batch sizes, and ensure pipeline reliability with testing. Additionally, Python notebooks empower you with advanced data processing, upserting, and data reversion for agile data management. Finally, your expertise in exception handling, retention policies, and Delta Lakes ensures efficient handling of big data.

The next chapter will focus on how you can design and develop a stream-processing solution. You will explore the utilization of Spark structured streaming to efficiently handle data streams. Furthermore, you will gain insights into processing time-series data, managing data across partitions, and optimizing processing within a single partition. Scalability is another focus, where you will learn to scale resources.

# Exam Readiness Drill – Chapter Review Questions

Apart from a solid understanding of key concepts, being able to think quickly under time pressure is a skill that will help you ace your certification exam. That is why working on these skills early on in your learning journey is key.

Chapter review questions are designed to improve your test-taking skills progressively with each chapter you learn and review your understanding of key concepts in the chapter at the same time. You'll find these at the end of each chapter.

> **How to Access These Materials**
>
> To learn how to access these resources, head over to the chapter titled *Chapter 11, Accessing the Online Resources*.

To open the Chapter Review Questions for this chapter, perform the following steps:

1. Click the link – `https://packt.link/DP203E2_CH05`.

   Alternatively, you can scan the following **QR code** (*Figure 5.37*):

Figure 5.37 – QR code that opens Chapter Review Questions for logged-in users

2.   Once you log in, you'll see a page similar to the one shown in *Figure 5.38*:

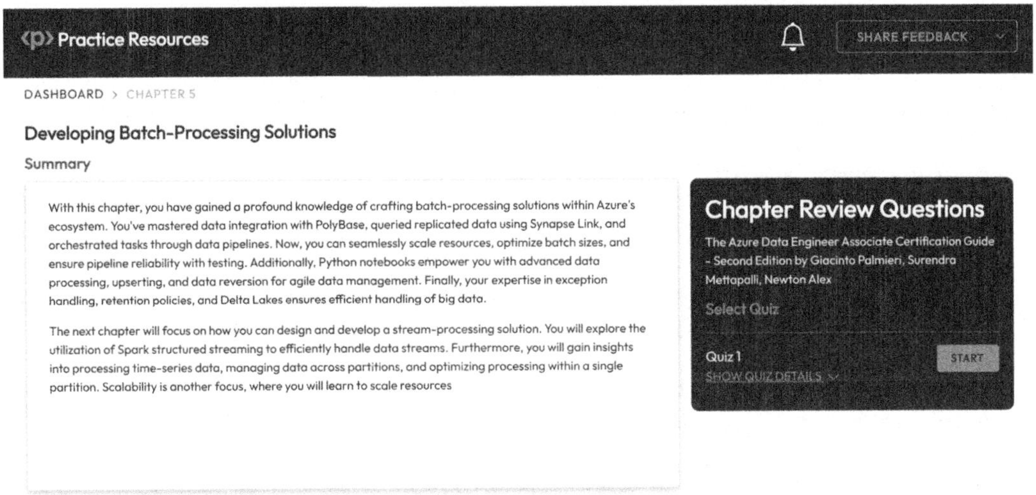

Figure 5.38 – Chapter Review Questions for Chapter 5

3.   Once ready, start the following practice drills, re-attempting the quiz multiple times.

## Exam Readiness Drill

For the first three attempts, don't worry about the time limit.

### *ATTEMPT 1*

The first time, aim for at least **40%**. Look at the answers you got wrong and read the relevant sections in the chapter again to fix your learning gaps.

## *ATTEMPT 2*

The second time, aim for at least **60%**. Look at the answers you got wrong and read the relevant sections in the chapter again to fix any remaining learning gaps.

## *ATTEMPT 3*

The third time, aim for at least **75%**. Once you score 75% or more, you start working on your timing.

> Tip
>
> You may take more than **three** attempts to reach 75%. That's okay. Just review the relevant sections in the chapter till you get there.

# Working On Timing

**Target**: Your aim is to keep the score the same while trying to answer these questions as quickly as possible. Here's an example of how your next attempts should look like:

| Attempt | Score | Time Taken |
|---------|-------|------------|
| Attempt 5 | 77% | 21 mins 30 seconds |
| Attempt 6 | 78% | 18 mins 34 seconds |
| Attempt 7 | 76% | 14 mins 44 seconds |

Table 5.2 – Sample timing practice drills on the online platform

> Note
>
> The time limits shown in the above table are just examples. Set your own time limits with each attempt based on the time limit of the quiz on the website.

With each new attempt, your score should stay above **75%** while your "time taken" to complete should "decrease". Repeat as many attempts as you want till you feel confident dealing with the time pressure.

# 6

# Developing a Stream Processing Solution

Building on the foundation of Spark, **Azure Data Factory** (**ADF**), and Synapse pipelines, *Chapter 5, Developing a Batch Processing Solution*, equipped you to effectively process large amounts of data.

In this chapter, you will cover another data method, **stream processing** solutions, also known as **real-time processing systems**. Similar to batch processing, stream processing is another important segment of data pipelines. This chapter will focus on introducing the concepts and technologies involved in building a **stream processing system**. You will be learning about technologies such as **Azure Stream Analytics** (**ASA**), Azure Event Hubs, and Spark (from a streaming perspective).

You will learn how to build end-to-end streaming solutions using these technologies and explore important streaming concepts such as checkpointing, windowed aggregates, replaying older stream data, handling drift, and stream management concepts such as distributing streams across partitions, scaling resources, handling errors, and upserting data.

> **Note**
>
> This chapter primarily focuses on the **Develop a stream processing solution** topic of the DP-203: Data Engineering on Microsoft Azure exam.

Once you have completed this topic, you should be confident enough to build an end-to-end streaming pipeline using the technologies that are available in Azure. As with the other chapters, the topics from the exam syllabus are rearranged by grouping the related ones together. This helps create an effective flow for the chapter.

By the end of this chapter, you will be able to answer questions on the following confidently:

- Stream processing solutions

- Windowed aggregates

- Schema drifts

- Time series data, data across partitions, and within one partition

- Scale resources

- Tests for data pipelines and optimized pipelines

- Interruptions

- Exception handling

- Upsert data

- Archived stream data

## Technical Requirements

For this chapter, you will need an Azure account (this could be either free or paid) and the ability to read basic Python code (don't worry, it is very easy).

## Implementing a Streaming Use Case with Azure

**Stream processing systems**, or **real-time processing systems**, are systems that perform data processing in near real time. Think of stock market updates, real-time traffic updates, and real-time credit card fraud detection. Incoming data is processed as and when it arrives with very minimal latency, usually in the range of milliseconds to seconds. This section primarily focuses on the **Create a stream processing solution by using Stream Analytics and Azure Event Hubs** concept of the DP-203: Data Engineering on Microsoft Azure exam.

The streaming pipeline, as depicted by the gray boxes in *Figure 6.1*, involves several key stages:

- **Real-time ingestion**: This is where data is captured and imported into the system.

- **Stream processing**: This involves the real-time analysis and manipulation of the ingested data.

- **Analytical data store**: This is where processed data is stored for further analysis.

- **Analytics and reporting**: This is the final stage where data is visualized and interpreted to provide actionable insights.

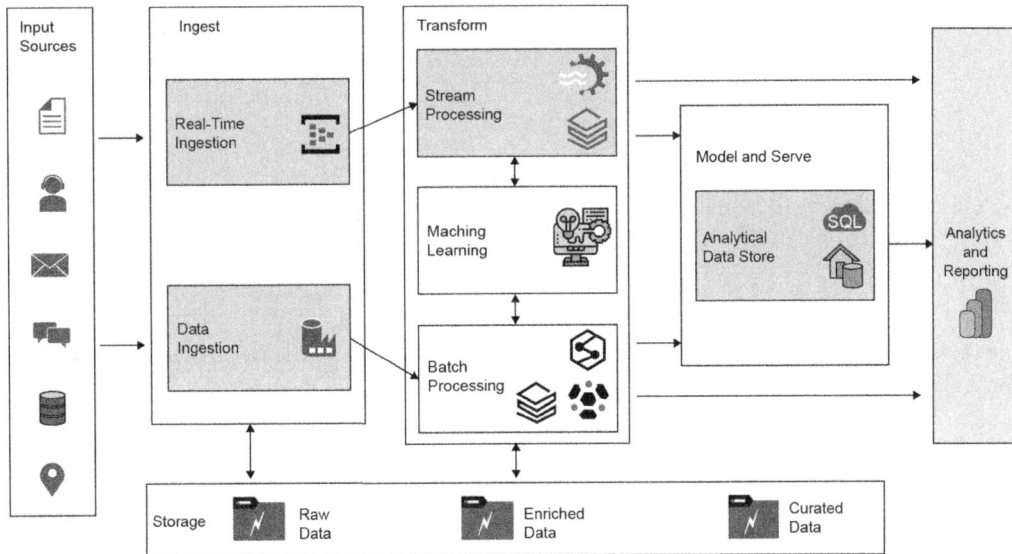

Figure 6.1 – Stream processing architecture with several key stages

Stream processing systems consist of four main components:

- **Event ingestion**: An event ingestion service, such as Azure Event Hubs, Azure **Internet of Things (IoT)** Hub, and Apache Kafka, captures, stores, and transmits events from multiple input sources to the stream processing services. It acts as a buffer between the input sources and the data processing services. Sometimes, the event ingress rate might be too much for the stream processing systems to handle, and other times too little. If the event ingress rate is high, then the ingestion service would store the events until the downstream services can process them. If the event ingress rate is low, the ingestion service can batch them up for efficiency and send them downstream.

- **Stream processing**: Stream processing systems, such as ASA, Spark Streaming, Apache Storm, and Apache Flink, provide the ability to quickly filter, join, and aggregate incoming events to derive insights. They are very similar to batch transformations but process the data with greater frequency and in smaller batches. This reduces latency meaning they are more suitable for scenarios that require real-time processing.

- **Analytical data stores**: Examples of these include Synapse's dedicated SQL pool, Cosmos DB, and HBase, which store the processed data from the stream processing systems for **Business Intelligence (BI)** reporting and other ad hoc queries. Some systems, such as ASA, can directly send data to reporting systems such as Power BI without an analytical data store.

- **Reporting systems such as Power BI**: This is the final piece of the pipeline, where you present the processed data in the form of reports for business consumption and decision-making.

> **Note**
>
> ASA works on the principle of "exactly once" processing and "at least once" delivery of events. You can find more information about event delivery guarantees at `learn.microsoft.com/en-us/stream-analytics-query/event-delivery-guarantees-azure-stream-analytics`.

The next section will look at the services that are available in Azure to build stream processing systems. You will start with Azure Event Hubs.

## Introducing Azure Event Hubs

**Azure Event Hubs** is a distributed ingestion service that can ingest, store, and transfer millions of events from various input sources to multiple consumers. It acts as a **buffer** between the **event producers** and the **event consumers** and "decouples" the event producers from the event consumers. This helps the downstream stream components, such as ASA or Spark Streaming, to asynchronously process the data. Azure Event Hubs is a fully managed **Platform-as-a-Service** (**PaaS**) service, so you don't have to worry about the upkeep of the service. Event Hubs can auto-inflate to meet the increasing requirements of the streaming system.

*Figure 6.2* shows a simplified architectural diagram of Azure Event Hubs:

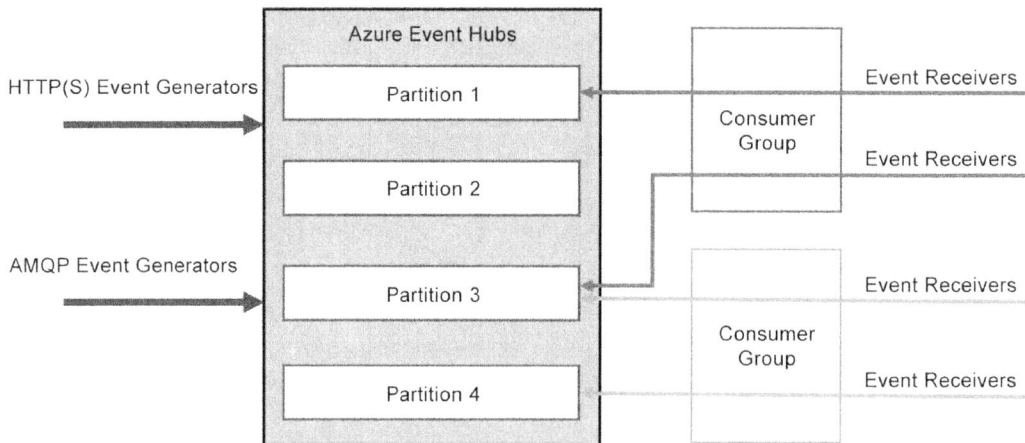

Figure 6.2 – Azure Event Hubs architecture

As you can see from the preceding diagram, Event Hubs can take inputs via two protocols: the **Hypertext Transfer Protocol** (**HTTP**) or the **Advanced Message Queuing Protocol** (**AMQP**). It then distributes the data into partitions. The event receivers, which are part of consumer groups, can subscribe to the partitions and read the events from there, with their own view of the Event Hub.

Now, you can learn what these terms, including partitions and consumer groups, mean:

- **Event Hubs partitions**: Event Hubs distribute the incoming data into one or more partitions, as shown in *Figure 6.2*. Partitions help with horizontal scaling as they allow multiple consumers to read data in parallel.

- **Event Hubs consumer groups**: A consumer group is a view of the Event Hub. There could be many consumer groups for each Event Hub, and each consumer group can have its own view of the Event Hub. In other words, they have access to different sets of streams or partitions. The consumers (typically, downstream applications) access the partitions via their own consumer group. The consumer group maintains state-like offsets in the stream, checkpointing information, and more. The applications within a consumer group can independently process the data without worrying about other clients.

> **Note**
> You can learn more about Event Hubs at `https://packt.link/A9zIq`.

This section highlighted a simplified architectural diagram of Azure Event Hubs. You learned about Event Hubs partitions and Event Hubs consumer groups. Next, you will look at ASA.

## Introducing Azure Stream Analytics (ASA)

ASA is Azure's primary stream processing engine. It can process large volumes of data with minimal latency and can be used to perform analytical functions, such as filter, aggregate, and join, to derive quick results from the incoming stream of data. ASA can also be utilized in scenarios such as retail point-of-sale analysis, credit card fraud detection, IoT sensing and failure detection, click-stream analysis, and so on. Typically, an ASA job has the following three stages:

1. It reads from an ingestion service such as Event Hubs, IoT Hub, or Kafka.

2. It processes the data and generates insights.

3. Finally, it writes the data into an analytical store, such as Azure Synapse Analytics or Cosmos DB, or it sends the results directly to a BI reporting service. ASA can directly send the results to Power BI.

Similar to Event Hubs, ASA is also a fully managed PaaS service. So, customers are relieved from the need to carry out any maintenance, complex patching, or upgrade operations.

> **Note**
>
> You can learn more about ASA at `https://packt.link/FSSSo`.

## Introducing Spark Streaming

In the previous chapter, *Chapter 5, Developing a Batch Processing Solution*, you looked at Spark from a batch processing perspective, but what you might not be aware of is that you can use the same Apache Spark core APIs to build a streaming solution. Similar to ASA, Spark can also read from data ingestion services (such as Azure Event Hubs, and Kafka), implement the data transformations, and write the output to analytical databases—or any other store, for that matter. Spark Streaming internally splits the incoming stream into micro-batches and processes them, so the output will be a stream of micro-batches.

> **Note**
>
> You can learn more about Spark Streaming at `https://packt.link/jiK1X`.

Next, you will look at building a stream processing solution using all the technologies that you have learned about so far. In the following sections, you will look at two examples: one with ASA as the streaming engine and another with Spark as the streaming engine. You will use a dummy **event generator** to continuously generate trip events and configure both ASA and **Azure Databricks Spark** to perform real-time processing and publish the results.

First, you will start with ASA.

## Streaming Solution Using Event Hubs and ASA

In this example, you will be creating a streaming pipeline by creating Event Hubs and ASA instances and linking them together. The pipeline will then read a sample stream of events, process the data, and display the result in Power BI. Perform the following steps to do so:

1. First, create an Event Hub instance. From the **Azure portal**, search for **Event Hubs** and click on the `Create` button, as shown in *Figure 6.3*:

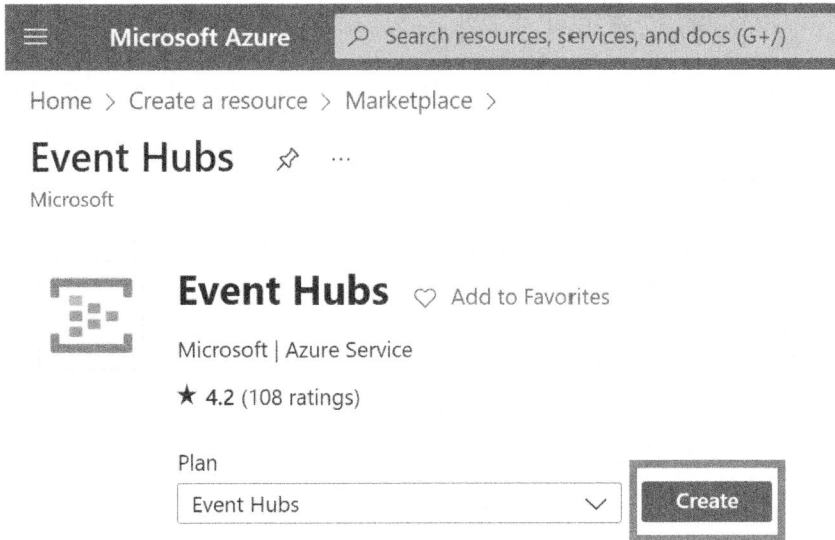

Figure 6.3 – The Event Hubs creation screen

This will bring up the Event Hubs **Create Namespace** screen, as shown in *Figure 6.4*:

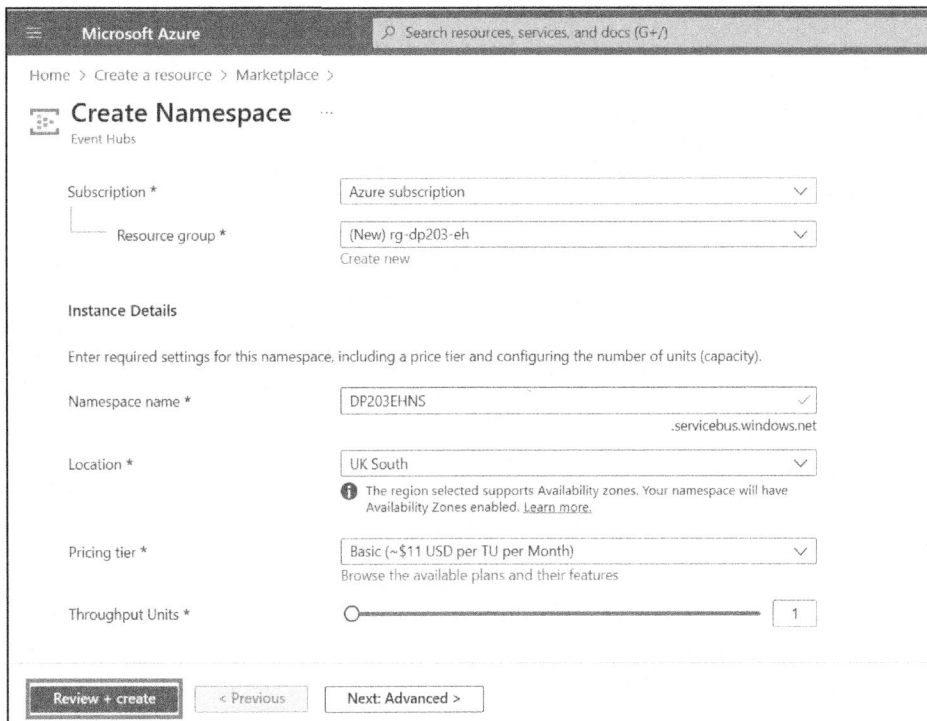

Figure 6.4 – Creating the Event Hubs namespace

2.  Enter the **Subscription** name. In this case, that will be `Azure subscription`.

3.  Specify whether you want to create a new **Resource group** or use an existing one. In this case, create `rg-dp203-eh`.

4.  Type a name in the **Namespace name** box; for example, `DP203EHNS`.

5.  Choose the location from the **Location** dropdown (in this case, `UK South`).

6.  Select the Pricing Tier from the **Pricing tier** dropdown; for example, `Basic (~$11 USD per TU per Month)`.

7.  Stretch the **Throughput units** slider to a value (`1`, in this example).

8.  Click on the `Review + create` button to create the Event Hubs workspace.

9.  On the **Event Hubs** screen, click on the `+ Event Hub` link, as shown in *Figure 6.5*, to create a new Event Hub within the workspace:

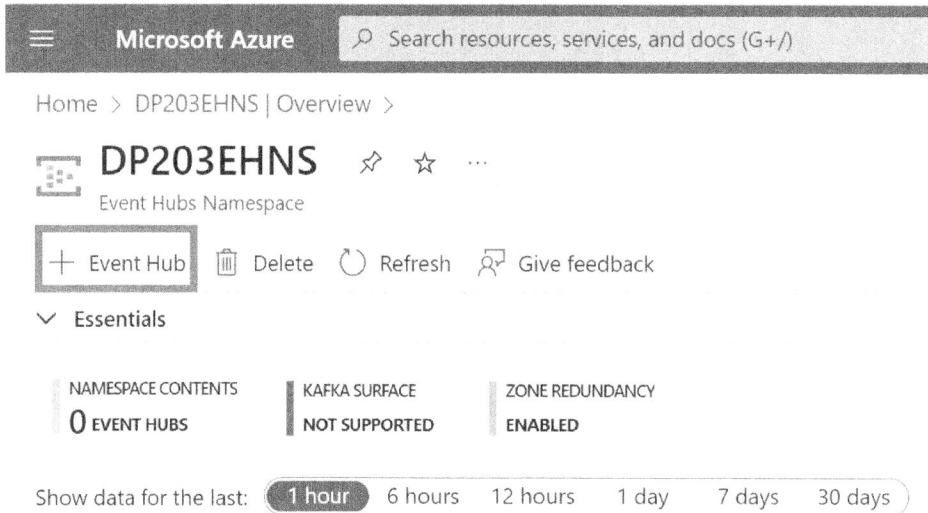

Figure 6.5 – Creating an Event Hub from within the Event Hubs workspace

10. In the Create Event Hub screen, as shown in *Figure 6.6*, enter a name in the **Name** field. In this case, it is `Asaeh`.

11. Select the **Partition count** value; in this case, it is `1`.

> **Note**
>
> You will learn more about partitions in the *Processing Data across Partitions* section later in this chapter.

12. Select a cleanup policy from the **Cleanup policy** dropdown in the **Retention** configuration settings; for example, the Delete policy is chosen here.

13. Specify the **Retention time (hrs)** value; in this case, the retention time is taken as 1 (*Figure 6.6*):

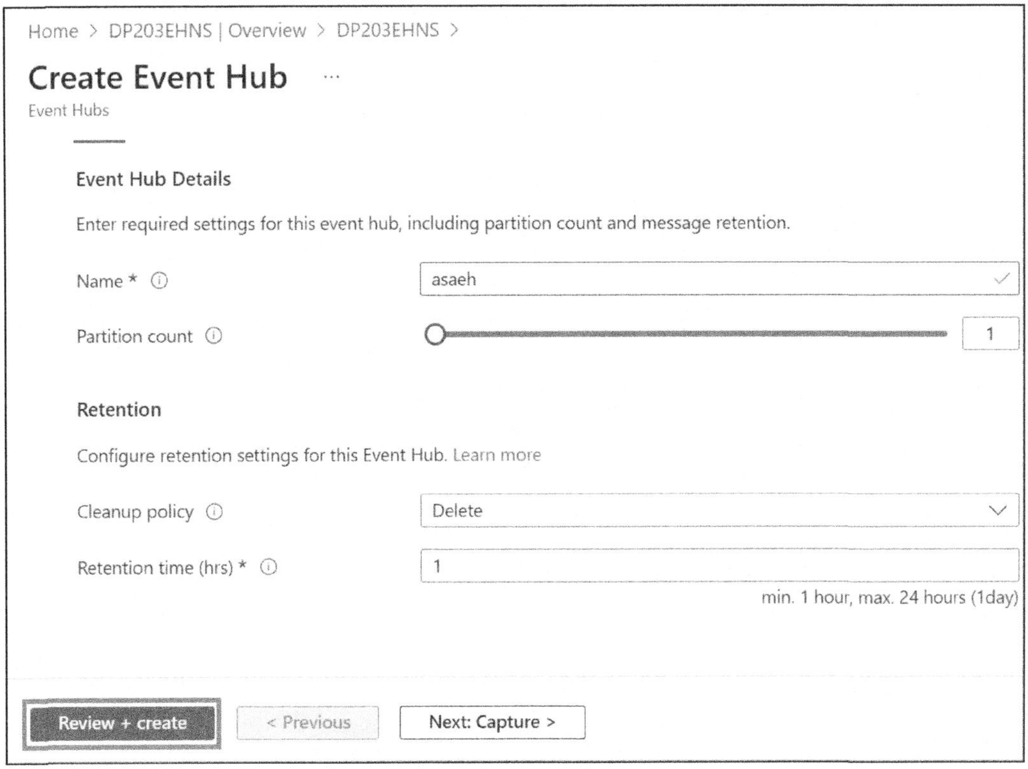

Home > DP203EHNS | Overview > DP203EHNS >

## Create Event Hub  ...
Event Hubs

___

### Event Hub Details

Enter required settings for this event hub, including partition count and message retention.

| Name * ⓘ | asaeh | ✓ |

Partition count ⓘ                                                      | 1 |

### Retention

Configure retention settings for this Event Hub. Learn more

| Cleanup policy ⓘ | Delete | ⌄ |

| Retention time (hrs) * ⓘ | 1 |

min. 1 hour, max. 24 hours (1day)

Review + create    < Previous    Next: Capture >

Figure 6.6 – The Create Event Hub screen

14. Finally, click on the Review + create button.

You now have an Event Hub. Next, you will create an ASA instance.

15. Search for `Stream Analytics jobs` in the **Azure portal** and select the `Stream Analytics job` service(*Figure 6.7*):

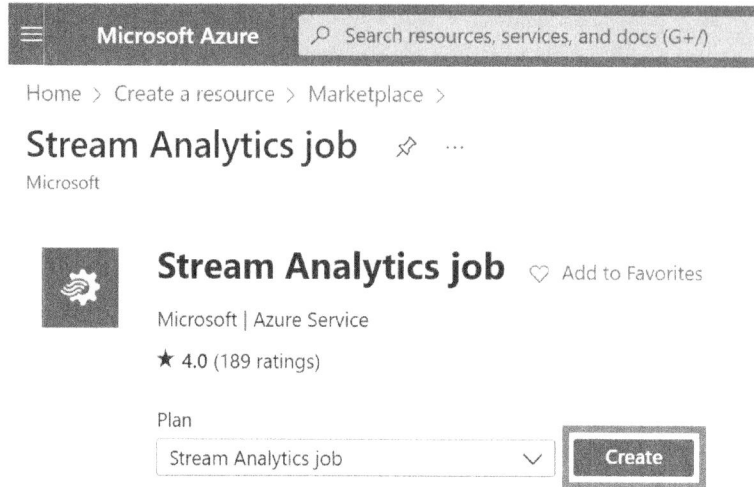

Figure 6.7 – Creating an ASA job

16. On the **Stream Analytics jobs** screen, click on the `Create` link to call the **New Stream Analytics job** screen:

17. Now, fill in the details in the New Stream Analytics job screen (*Figure 6.8*). Type a name for your **Stream Analytics job** instance; in this case, `SampleASAJob`.

18. Enter `Azure Subscription`, which manages the costs, in the **Subscription** field.

19. Enter the name of the container holding the resources for your job in the **Container** field; in this case, `rg-dp203-eh`.

20. Enter the region that indicates the location of the resources in the **Region** field. In this case, it is `(Europe) UKSouth`.

21. Click `Cloud` as the **Hosting environment** option.

22. Next, specify the number of **Streaming Units (SUs)** you need; in this case, it is 1.

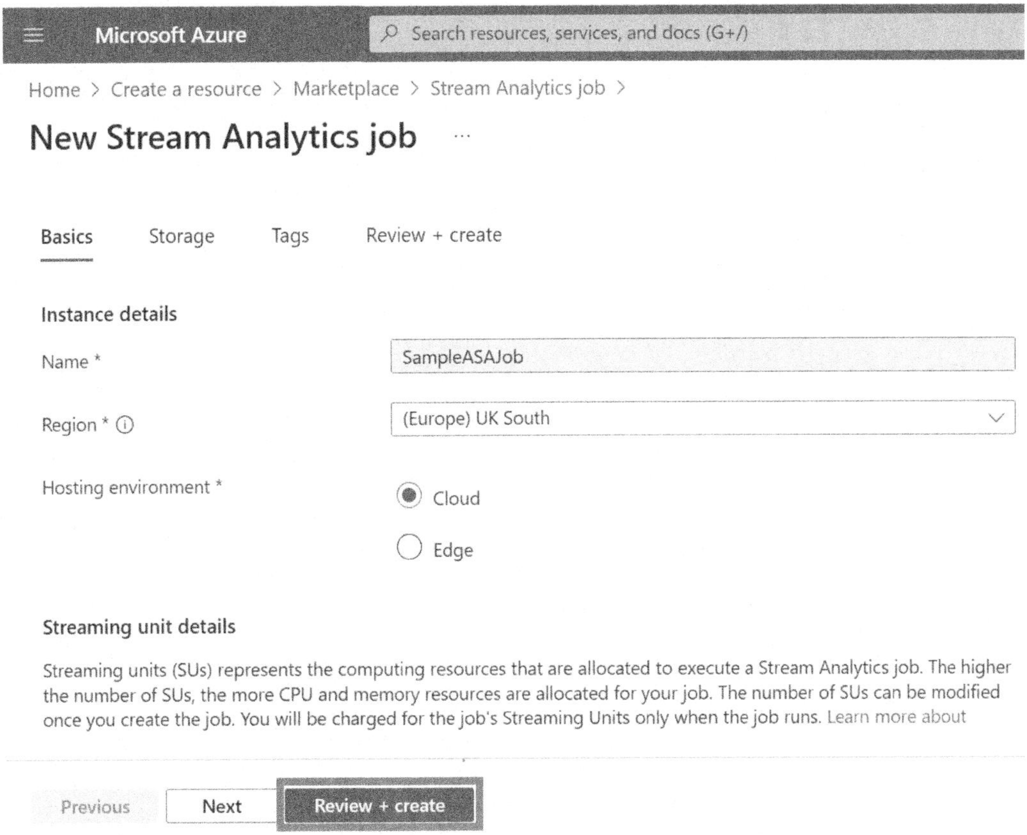

Figure 6.8 – The ASA job creation screen

23. Finally, click on the Review + Create button to create a new ASA job.

    The next step is to link the input to Event Hubs. Before this step, you will need to get the connection string from Event Hubs. To do so, continue following these steps:

24. Go to the **Event Hubs** screen and click on Shared access policies.

25. Click on the + Add button.

26.  On the **Add SAS policy** screen, add a **Policy name**. In this case, the policy name is entered as EH-ASA-Access (*Figure 6.9*):

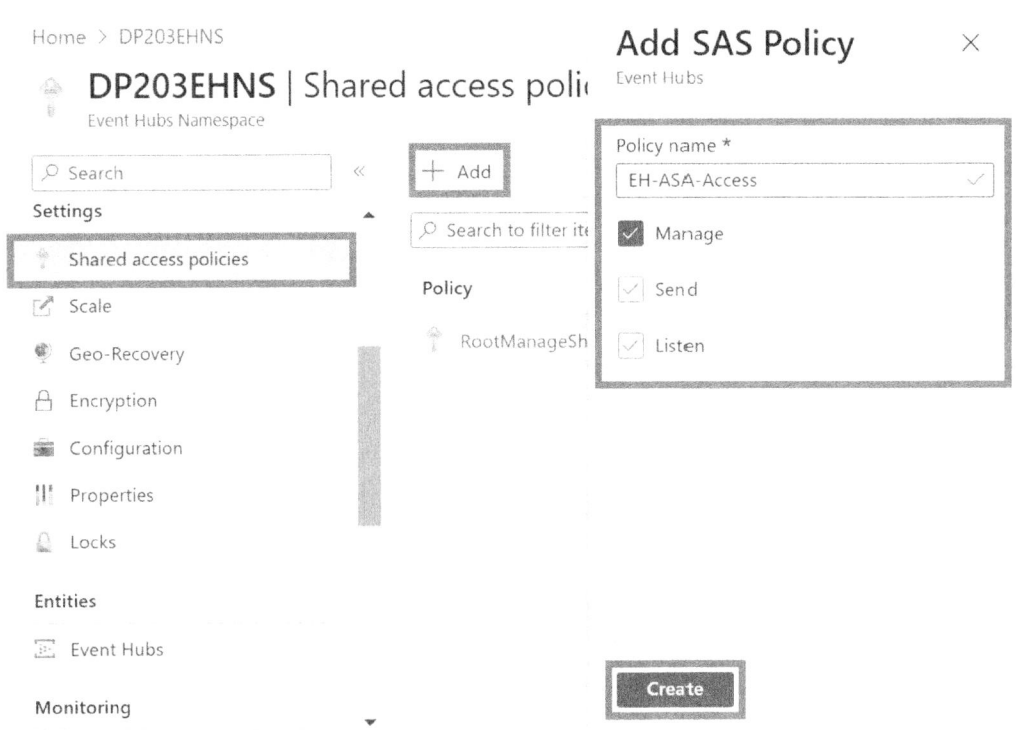

Figure 6.9 – Creating shared access policies in Event Hubs

27. Once the policy has been created, click on the EH-ASA-Access policy to copy the Connection string-primary key link, as shown in *Figure 6.10*:

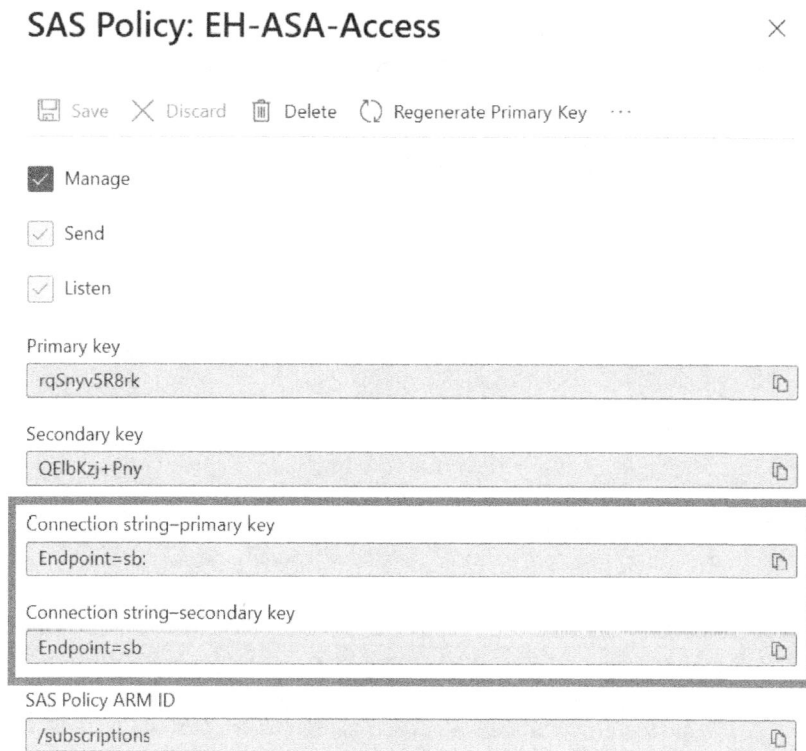

## SAS Policy: EH-ASA-Access                                    ✕

🖫 Save    ✕ Discard    🗑 Delete    ◌ Regenerate Primary Key    ⋯

☑ Manage

☑ Send

☑ Listen

Primary key

| rqSnyv5R8rk | 🗇 |

Secondary key

| QEIbKzj+Pny | 🗇 |

Connection string–primary key

| Endpoint=sb: | 🗇 |

Connection string–secondary key

| Endpoint=sb | 🗇 |

SAS Policy ARM ID

| /subscriptions | 🗇 |

Figure 6.10 – Accessing the connection string for Event Hubs

The Connection string-primary key and Connection string-secondary key are retrieved because they provide the necessary credentials for applications to connect to the Event Hub. These connection strings include the **primary key** and **secondary key**, which are part of the shared access policy and are used for authentication. Also, these keys are crucial for maintaining security and ensuring that only authorized users and applications can access the Event Hubs services. Here is a brief explanation of them:

- **Primary key**: This is the main key that you can use to connect to the Event Hub. It's part of the connection string and is used for authentication.

- **Secondary key**: This key serves as a backup and can be used in case the primary key is compromised or needs to be regenerated.

28. Now, you need to go back to the ASA portal and link the input (Event Hubs) and output (Power BI) to the ASA instance. So, go to the **Inputs** tab.

29. Select Event Hub from the + **Add stream input** drop-down list (*Figure 6.11*):

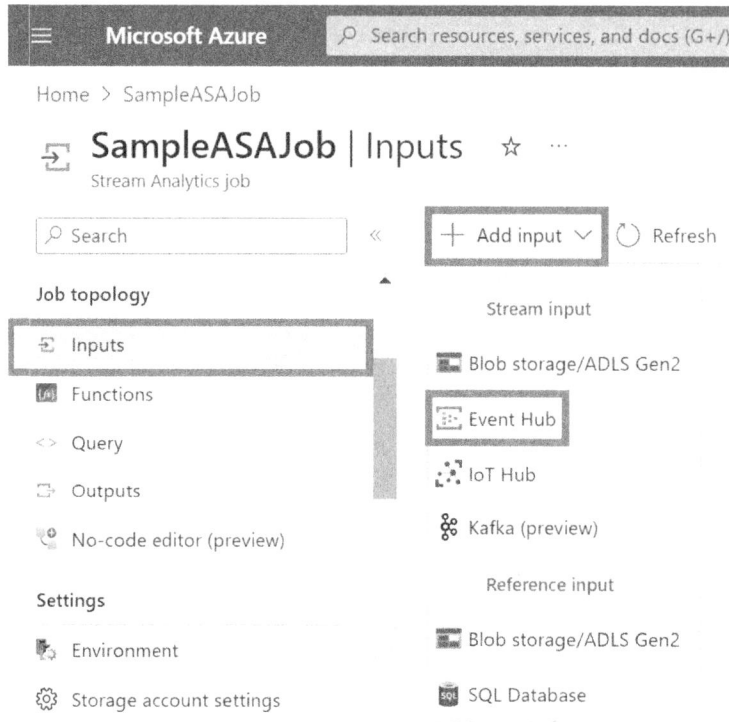

Figure 6.11 – Selecting an Event Hub as input for the ASA job

A screen will then pop up where you can select the Event Hub instance that you created earlier.

30. On the **Event Hub New input** screen, specify the new **Input alias** or proceed with the default alias. In this case, it is a new alias named EH-ASA-Stream.

31. Choose the Select Event Hub from your subscriptions radio button.

32. Click the **Subscription** to manage the resource cost; in this case, it is Azure subscription.

33. Select the **Event Hub namespace** from the **Event Hub namespace** drop-down list, which was created as part of *Step 4*. In this case, it is DP203EHNS.

34. Select the Use existing radio button beside the **Event Hub name** and choose asaeh.

35. Under **Event Hub consumer group**, click the Use existing radio button and then select the consumer's name. In this case, it's $Default.

36. Select the authentication mode from the **Authentication mode** drop-down list. Here, it is `Connection string`.

37. Next in the **Event Hub policy name** section, click the `Use existing` policy radio button and choose a policy name, as shown in *Figure 6.12*. In this case, it is `EH-ASA-Access`, which you created in *Figure 6.9*.

    By default, the connection string will be saved, and you do not need to copy the connection string from *Step 27* (shown in *Figure 6.10*). In case, you want to programmatically create a connection to the Event Hub using Azure CLI, then copy the connection string-primary key value to authenticate and interact with the Event Hub.

38. On selecting an existing key (`EH-ASA-Access`) from your subscriptions (under **Event Hub policy name**), saving this endpoint will store and retrieve the current value of the selected key, displaying it under **Event Hub policy key**.

    If your input is partitioned by a key, it's recommended to specify that key under the **Partition key** option to optimize performance.

39. In this case, the input is not partitioned with any key, so you can leave that `blank`.

40. Next, the **Event serialization format** drop-down list makes sure that your queries work the way you expect. Stream Analytics needs to know which serialization format you are using for incoming data streams. In this case, choose `JSON`.

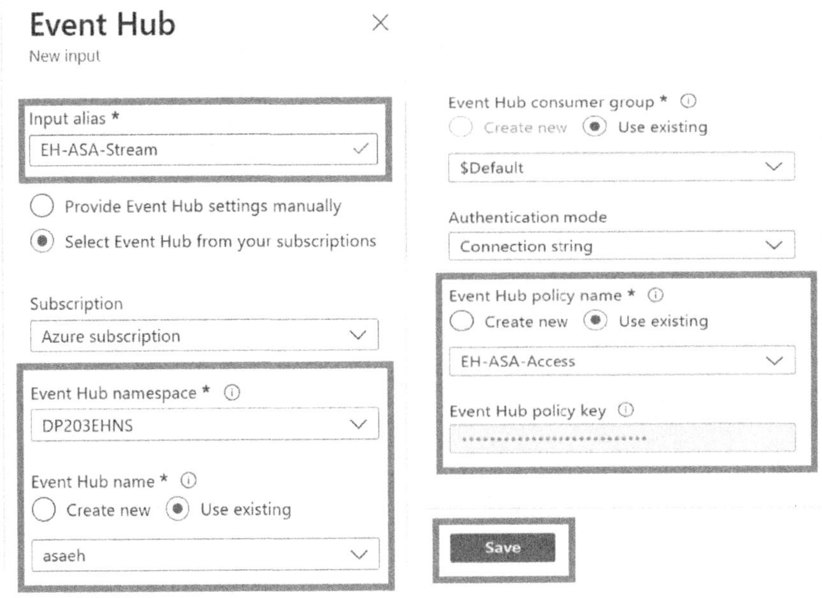

Figure 6.12 – Linking the Event Hub as an input in ASA

41. Select Save to create a connection to an Event Hub input.

42. Go to the **Outputs** tab and select Power BI for the ASA output from the +**Add output** drop-down list (*Figure 6.13*):

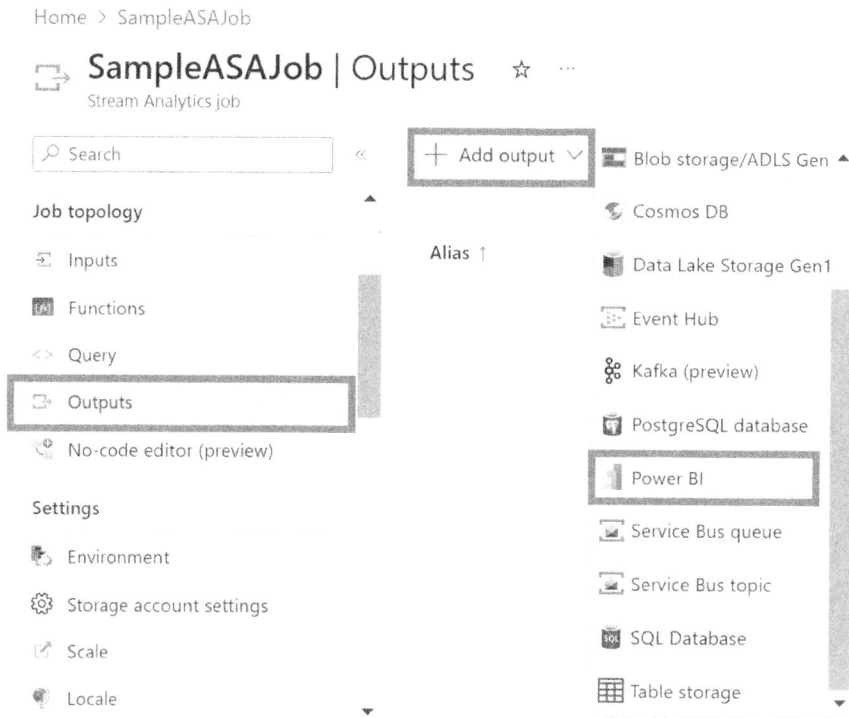

Figure 6.13 – Selecting Power BI as the output for the ASA job

This will pop up a **Power BI New output** screen, as shown in *Figure 6.14*. Continue to perform the following steps to fill in your Power BI details:

43. Specify **New Output alias**. In this case, it is ASA-PowerBI.

44. Select the Provide Group workspace settings manually radio button.

45. Input the group workspace in the **Group workspace** field in your Power BI URL for the workspace. This is the ID for the workspace, which can be found in your Power BI URL for the workspace (e.g., groups/{Worksapce Id}/).

46. Choose the authentication mode from the **Authentication mode** drop-down list. In this case, it is User token.

47. Specify **Dataset name**. In this case, it is `ASADataset`.

   Stream Analytics will create a streaming dataset using the name in your Power BI workspace. The job must be running and have processed at least one event for the dataset to be created.

48. Input the table name in the **Table name** field, where the streaming data will be saved into the table. In this case, it is `ASATable` (*Figure 6.14*):

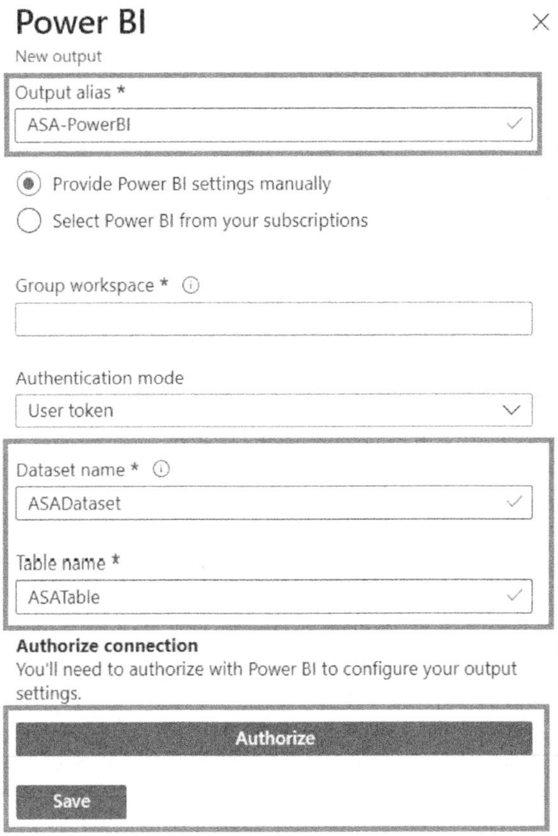

Figure 6.14 – Configuring the Power BI sink details for the ASA job

49. Click the `Authorize` button under **Authorize connection** to sign in to your Power BI account.

50. Finally, select **Save** to create a connection to a Power BI output.

Now that you have the input and output set up and ready, you will run a sample event generator to generate test events using tools such as Visual Studio Code.

> **Note**
>
> All the entries within the angular brackets, < >, are user-provided values. You can learn more about sending events to or receiving events from Event Hubs by using Python with Visual Studio Code at `https://packt.link/N3y01`.

The following are the simple Python event generator modules:

A.  Import the required Event Hub libraries:

```python
from azure.eventhub.aio import EventHubProducerClient
from azure.eventhub import EventData
```

In the preceding code, `EventHubProducerClient` is a class from the `Azure-eventhub` library that provides a high-level interface for sending events to your Azure Event Hub.

B.  Instantiate a producer client:

```python
producer = EventHubProducerClient.from_connection_string(
        conn_str=<SAS Access Connection String>,
        eventhub_name=<Event Hub Name>)
```

In the preceding code, note the following:

- `From_connection_string`: This is a method of the `EventHubProducerClient` class that creates a new instance of the client using a connection string. The connection string is a special string that contains information needed to connect to the Event Hub, including the fully qualified domain name and credentials.

- `Conn_str`: This parameter is where you pass the **Shared Access Signature** (**SAS**) connection string. The SAS connection string is a type of credential that grants limited access to resources in your Azure account. It includes the endpoint, the shared access key name, and the shared access key value. In this case, it is `Connection string-primary key`.

- `<Eventhub_name>`: This parameter specifies the name of the Event Hub within the namespace that you want to send events to. You replace `<Event Hub Name>` with the actual name of your Event Hub. In this case, it is `asaeh`.

C.  Create an event batch instance:

```python
eventDataBatch = await producer.create_batch()
```

D.  Create a JSON event:

```
cityList = ["San Franciso", "San Jose", "Los Angeles",…]
tripDetail = {'tripId': str(uuid.uuid4()),
    <timestamp>: str(datetime.datetime.utcnow()),
    <startLocation>: random.choice(cityList),
    <endLocation>: random.choice(cityList),
    <distance>: random.randint(10, 1000),
    <fare>: random.randint(100, 1000) }
```

E.  Add events to the batch:

```
eventDataBatch.add(
    EventData(json.dumps(tripDetail)))
```

F.  Send the batch of events to the Event Hub:

```
producer.send_batch(eventDataBatch)
```

You can repeat steps *D*, *E*, and *F* in a `for` loop if you need to send a large number of events.

> **Note**
>
> You can find the complete code used in the accompanying GitHub repository at `https://packt.link/WAKhQ`.

When you run the preceding code from the command line, you will be able to view the events arriving at the Event Hub on the **Event Hubs overview** screen (*Figure 6.15*):

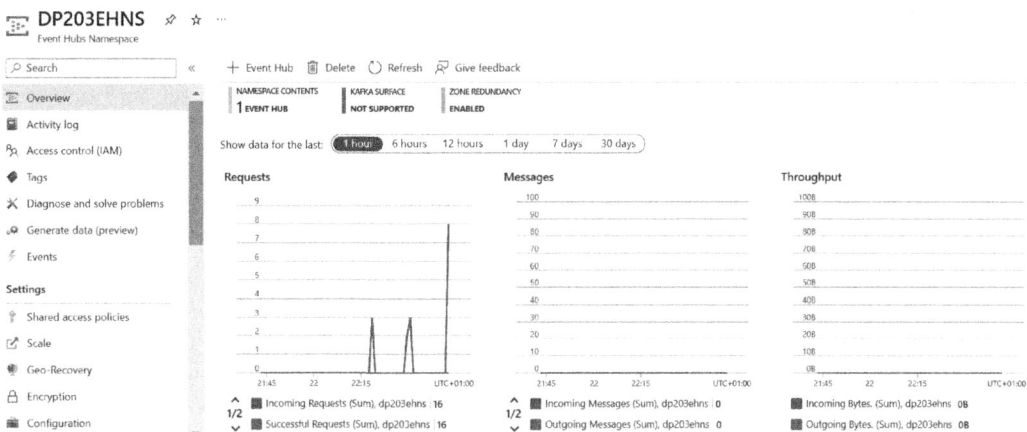

Figure 6.15 – The Event Hubs overview screen showing the event metrics

Now, you will read this data and publish the number of trips per location. So, go back to the **ASA Overview** screen, **SampleASAJob**, to run the query to read the input stream and process it to Power BI. Before you proceed to run the query, you must learn the basic configurations, such as the **Inputs**, **Query**, and **Outputs** settings that are needed in ASA. These settings collectively define how data flows through the ASA job—from ingestion to processing and ultimately to the output destination.

The following are the details about these basic configurations:

- **Inputs**: This configuration determines the data source, serialization format, timestamp field, and event time policy, and optionally links static lookup tables for enriching data. The following are the various configuration settings related to **Inputs** for an ASA job:

  - **Source**: This defines where the ASA job will obtain its data from (e.g., Azure Event Hub, IoT Hub, Blob Storage, etc.)

  - **Serialization format**: You can specify how the incoming data is structured (e.g., JSON, Avro, CSV, etc.)

  - **Timestamp field**: It helps you identify the field containing timestamps in the data

  - **Event time policy**: This determines how ASA should extract event timestamps (from the data or system time)

  - **Reference data**: It optionally links static lookup tables (reference data) to enrich the streaming data

- **Query**: You can compose SQL-like queries for processing incoming data, including windowing functions for time-based or count-based aggregations and updating reference data based on query results. The following are the various configuration settings related to Query for an ASA job:

  - **SQL query**: The ASA query is written in SQL-like syntax, which processes incoming data and performs transformations, filters, and joins.

  - **Windowing functions**: It defines time-based or count-based windows for aggregations (e.g., tumbling, sliding, and hopping windows).

  - **Output to reference data**: It updates the reference data based on the query results.

- **Outputs**: You can specify the destination for processed data, serialization format, and the partitioning method, and assign an output alias for referencing in the query. The following are the various configuration settings related to **Outputs** for an ASA job:

  - **Destination**: You can specify where you want the processed data to be sent (e.g., Azure SQL Database, Power BI, Blob Storage, etc.)

  - **Serialization format**: You can set the format for the output data (e.g., JSON, Avro, CSV, etc.)

- **Partitioning**: You can choose how you want to partition the output data (e.g., by device ID, timestamp, etc.)

- **Output alias**: It assigns a name to the output for referencing in the query

51. On the **ASA Overview** screen, enter the following query:

```
SELECT System.Timestamp as WindowEnd,
startLocation as Location,
COUNT(*) as TripCount
INTO [ASA-PowerBI]
FROM [EH-ASA-Stream]
GROUP BY TUMBLINGWINDOW(s, 5), startLocation
```

In the preceding code, `System.Timestamp as WindowEnd` retrieves the current timestamp (`System.Timestamp`) and renames it as `WindowEnd`. The `startLocation as Location` command selects the `startLocation` column from the input stream and renames it as `Location`. `COUNT(*) as TripCount` calculates the count of records (`trips`), names the result as `TripCount`, with the results directed into an output named `[ASA-PowerBI]`. The `[EH-ASA-Stream]` is the source of the data input for the query, which could be an Event Hub (EH) connected to Azure Stream Analytics (ASA), from which streaming data is ingested and processed. The `GROUP BY TUMBLINGWINDOW(s, 5), startLocation` groups the data within each `TUMBLINGWINDOW` (specifies a Tumbling Window of 5 seconds) based on the `startLocation` column:

52. Next, click on `Start`, as shown in *Figure 6.16*:

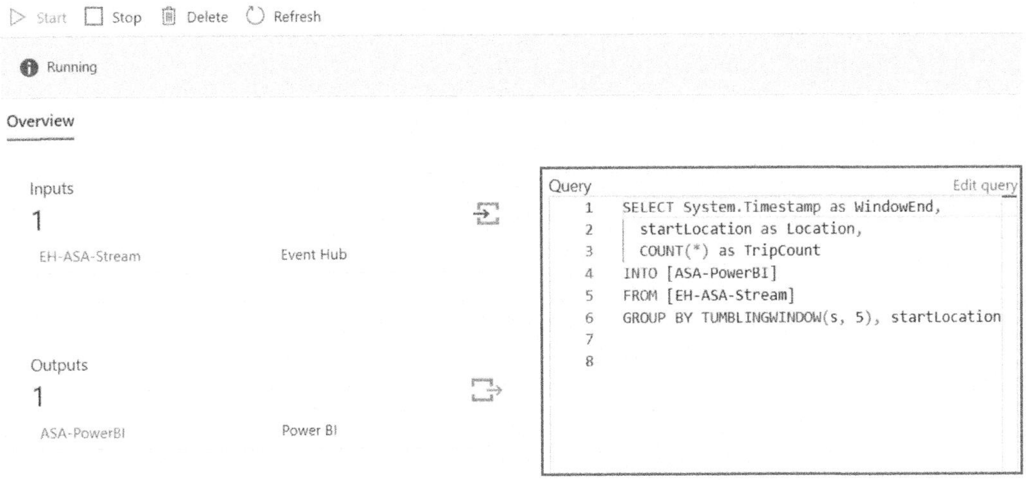

Figure 6.16 – ASA sample code reading input event from Event Hub and outputs to Power BI

Now, the ASA job will continuously read the input Event Hub stream, process the data, and publish it to Power BI.

> **Note**
>
> You can find the complete code in the accompanying GitHub repository at `https://packt.link/TcxRU`.

53. Navigate to **My workspace** in your **Power BI** portal to see the ASA dataset (*Figure 6.17*) that was configured earlier on the Power BI output configuration screen (*Figure 6.14*):

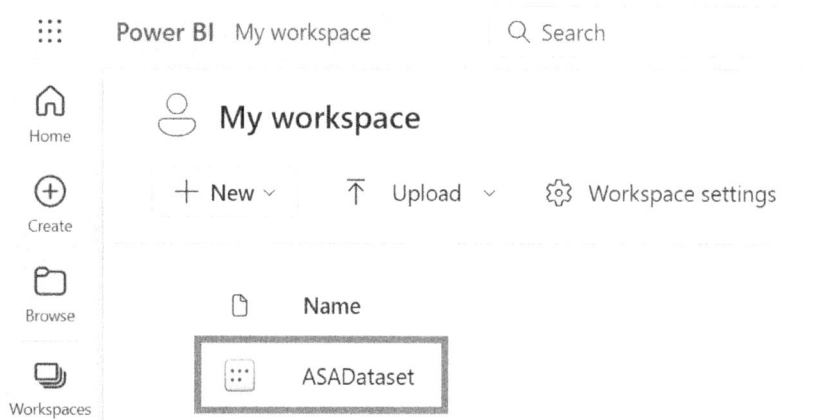

Figure 6.17 – My workspace showing the configured ASA dataset in the Power BI dataset

54. Right-click on the dataset and create a report out of it.

The report, shown in *Figure 6.18*, shows a bounding outline at the bottom center of the image highlighting the **Axis** section. In this case, the x axis shows the location, and the y axis shows the number of trips taken. The bounding outline located top right shows the fields. Here are `TripCount` and `Location` from `ASATestTable`.

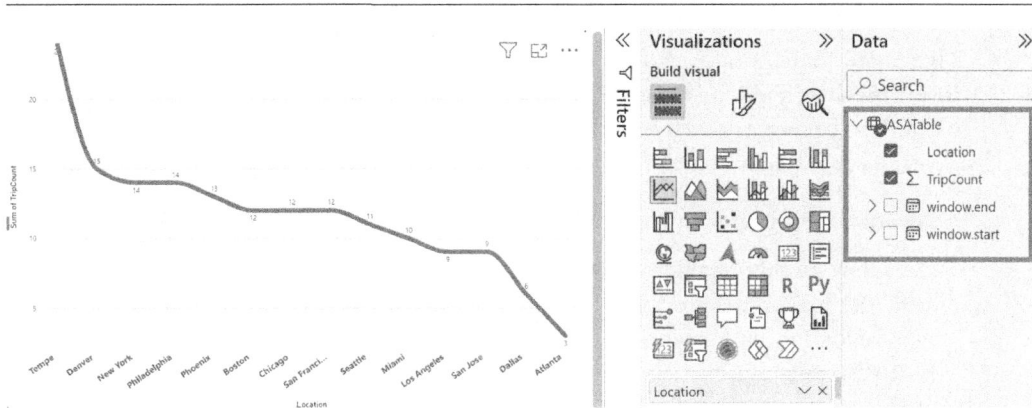

Figure 6.18 – Creating the Power BI dashboard from the ASA streaming output

Now, you know how to build a streaming pipeline using Event Hubs, ASA, and Power BI.

ASA can also work with IoT Hub as the ingestion service. With IoT Hub, ASA can be deployed in two different modes. They are as follows:

- **Cloud mode**: In this mode, the IoT devices send the events to an ASA job on the Azure Cloud, which is very similar to the Event Hubs model. ASA operates in the Azure Cloud and processes the incoming events centrally. Some of the key points to consider within Cloud mode are as follows:

  - **Location**: The ASA job resides in the Azure Cloud.

  - **Data flow**: The data comes from IoT devices (sensors, cameras, etc.) that generate events to telemetry data and Azure IoT Hub acts as the central hub for receiving data from IoT devices. ASA jobs process the incoming data, perform real-time analytics, transform, filter, and aggregate the data, and then send it to various destinations (e.g., Azure Storage, Azure SQL Database, Power BI, etc.).

  - **Use cases**: For scenarios where you deal with large data volumes to filter or aggregate data before sending it to the cloud, operational data requires ultra-low latency responses such as manufacturing safety systems and missing-critical systems that need to analyze data even during intermittent cloud connectivity.

- **Edge mode**: In this mode, ASA can run directly on the IoT devices themselves, perform real-time processing, and send the events to the IoT Hub. In this mode, ASA runs directly on the IoT devices themselves, performs real-time processing at the edge, and then sends the processed events to the IoT Hub. Some of the key points to consider within Edge mode are as follows:

  - **Location**: ASA runs within the Azure IoT Edge framework on the IoT devices.

  - **Data flow**: In this data flow, IoT devices equipped with Azure IoT Edge runtime locally host ASA logic. ASA processes data in near real time to perform tasks such as filtering, aggregation, and custom analytics. Processed data is then sent from ASA to Azure IoT Hub, which acts as a transmission intermediary to the cloud. In the cloud, the data can undergo further analysis or be stored.

  - **Use cases**: Some of the scenarios are as follows:

    - Leveraging near real-time analytics at the edge for immediate actions based on sensor data analysis (e.g., stopping a machine or triggering alerts)

    - ASA operates independently in scenarios with intermittent cloud connectivity, enabling selective data transmission to the cloud

    - Optimizing bandwidth usage by filtering or pre-processing data locally before sending it to the cloud, ensuring efficient data transmission

> **Note**
>
> You can find more details about ASA's Edge mode at `https://packt.link/nu9pk`.

Next, you'll look at how to build a streaming solution using Azure Databricks Spark.

## Streaming Solution Using Event Hubs and Spark Streaming

In this example, you will use the same Event Hub (from *Figure 6.12*) and data generator that's been used for the ASA option. The only change is that you will use **Azure Databricks Spark** instead of ASA.

> **Note**
>
> Event generator to generate test events using tools such as Visual Studio Code, discussed in *Steps 50* and *51*.

The next step is to read data from **Event Hubs** using Databricks Spark, but before you can do this, you will have to create a Spark cluster. Perform the following steps to do so:

1. You learned how to create a **Databricks Spark cluster** in the *Batch Processing Technologies* section of *Chapter 5, Developing a Batch Processing Solution*. Please use the same instructions to create a new Spark cluster.

2. Once the Spark cluster is up and running, open a **Spark Notebook** and enter the following sample code to process the stream data into the notebook:

```
EHConnectionString = "<EVENT HUB CONNECTION STRING>"
EHConfig = {}
EHConfig['eventhubs.connectionString'] = sc._jvm.org.apache.
spark.eventhubs.EventHubsUtils .encrypt( EHConnectionString )
```

3. Set the connection to the **Event Hubs** instance, DP203EHNS, in the same way that you generated it in *Figure 6.12*.

---

**Note**

All the entries within the angular brackets, < >, are user-provided values.

---

In the preceding code, an Event Hub connection string is initialized and encrypted for secure communication. The variable is named EHConnectionString and assigns the value of <EVENT HUB CONNECTION STRING>. This connection string typically includes necessary authentication details and other parameters for connecting to the Event Hub. An empty dictionary named EHConfig is created, and this dictionary will be used to store configuration options required for connecting to the Event Hub. The encrypted connection string is then stored in the EHConfig dictionary under the eventhubs.connectionString key.

4. Connect to the Event Hub by running the following command:

```
EHStreamDF = spark.readStream.format("eventhubs")
.options(**EHConfig).load()
```

In the preceding code, you are creating a streaming DataFrame called EHStreamDF using Spark's readStream method, specifying the data source format as eventhubs, which indicates that the DataFrame will read data from an Event Hub. EHConfig unpacks the dictionary, passes its key-value pairs as keyword arguments to the options method, and loads the streaming DataFrame with data from the Event Hub using the specified configuration options.

5.   Next, define the schema of the streaming input:

```
JsonSchema = StructType() \
.add("tripId", StringType()) \
.add("createdAt", TimestampType()) \
.add("startLocation", StringType()) \
.add("endLocation", StringType()) \
.add("distance", IntegerType()) \
.add("fare", IntegerType())
```

In the preceding code, JsonSchema is defined using Apache Spark's StructType to specify the structure of the data expected to be read or processed. Field names such as tripId, startLocation, and endLocation are added to the schema with the data type specified as StringType(), createdAt is added to the schema with the data type as TimestampType() and distance, and fare fields are added to the schema as IntegerType().

6.   Now, define the stream-handling DataFrame (EHStreamJsonDF) to extract the key values from the incoming JSON events:

```
stringDF = EHStreamDF.selectExpr("CAST(body AS STRING)")
jsonDF= stringDF.withColumn('tripjson', from_
json(col('body'),schema=JsonSchema))
EHStreamJsonDF= jsonDF.select("tripjson.*")
```

In the preceding code, the resulting stringDF DataFrame contains the body of each message in STRING format from the Event Hub streaming DataFrame called EHStreamDF. You can use the from_json function on each row of the stringDF DataFrame to parse the JSON content of the body column according to JsonSchema. The parsed JSON data is stored in a new column named tripjson within the jsonDF DataFrame. The resulting EHStreamJsonDF DataFrame selects all columns from the jsonDF DataFrame that are nested in the tripjson struct column and extracts the parsed JSON data into separate columns.

7.   Up to this point, you have ensured that the events from the Event Hub can be processed and acted upon directly using DataFrames. Now, define the transformation to be applied and actually start the streaming:

```
EHStreamJsonDF.groupBy(window('createdAt',"1
minutes"),'startLocation').count().orderBy('window')\
.writeStream.format("memory") \
.outputMode("complete") \
.option("truncate", "false") \
.option("checkpointLocation", "dbfs:/tripsCheckpointLocation/")
\
.queryName("TripsTumblingQuery").start()
```

In the preceding code, `EHStreamJsonDF` groups the data by `startLocation` and you can count the occurrences within each window of the Tumbling Windows for every 1 minute. The result will order the window start time and `writeStream` to an in-memory table for query processing. The entire updated result table will be written by specifying the mode as complete and the complete results will be displayed without truncation. You can input `checkpointLocation` to ensure that fault tolerance and checkpoint information can be stored to start the execution of the defined operations on the streaming data.

Once you run *Step 6*, the streaming starts and continuously looks for events from the Event Hub, processes them, and sends the output to a table named `TripsTumblingQuery`.

8.  Type `SELECT *` from the table to view the trip counts, as shown in *Figure 6.19*:

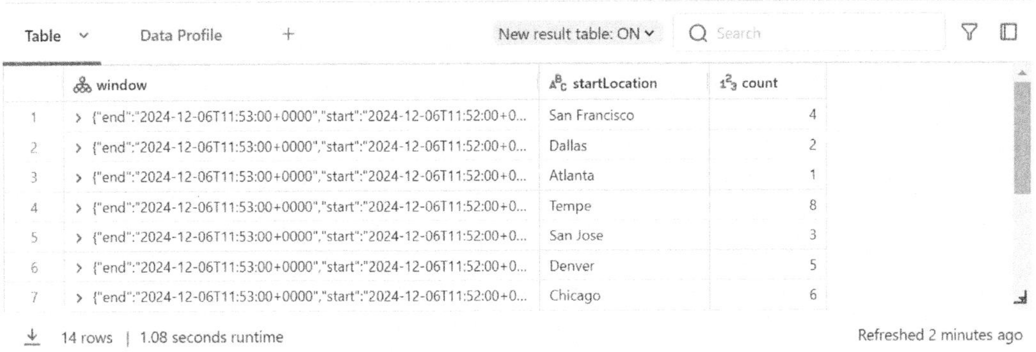

| Table ⌄    Data Profile    +  | New result table: ON ⌄ | Q Search | ▽ ▢ |
| --- | --- | --- | --- |

| | ⧎ window | ᴬᵦᴄ startLocation | ₁²₃ count | |
| --- | --- | --- | --- | --- |
| 1 | › {"end":"2024-12-06T11:53:00+0000","start":"2024-12-06T11:52:00+0... | San Francisco | 4 | |
| 2 | › {"end":"2024-12-06T11:53:00+0000","start":"2024-12-06T11:52:00+0... | Dallas | 2 | |
| 3 | › {"end":"2024-12-06T11:53:00+0000","start":"2024-12-06T11:52:00+0... | Atlanta | 1 | |
| 4 | › {"end":"2024-12-06T11:53:00+0000","start":"2024-12-06T11:52:00+0... | Tempe | 8 | |
| 5 | › {"end":"2024-12-06T11:53:00+0000","start":"2024-12-06T11:52:00+0... | San Jose | 3 | |
| 6 | › {"end":"2024-12-06T11:53:00+0000","start":"2024-12-06T11:52:00+0... | Denver | 5 | |
| 7 | › {"end":"2024-12-06T11:53:00+0000","start":"2024-12-06T11:52:00+0... | Chicago | 6 | |

⤓  14 rows  |  1.08 seconds runtime                                        Refreshed 2 minutes ago

Figure 6.19 – Viewing the results of the streaming query

9.  Stop the streaming with the following code block:

```
for s in spark.streams.active:
    s.stop()
```

In the preceding code, the `for` loop iterates the overall active streaming queries in the Spark session. Then, `spark.streams.active` returns a list of currently active streaming queries. Within each iteration of the loop, a `stop` method is called on the streaming query, and it stops the execution of the streaming query and releases any associated resources.

Now, you can connect Azure Databricks to Event Hubs and process real-time data.

> **Note**
>
> You can learn more about Azure Databricks and Event Hubs at `https://packt.link/IqDQe`. You can find the complete code in the accompanying GitHub repository at `https://packt.link/K8emb`.

In this section, you have seen how you can use Azure Databricks and Event Hubs in basic streaming solutions. In the upcoming sections, you will learn about windowing, the different output modes, and checkpointing for the monitoring of your stream, but first, you will look at how **Spark Structured Streaming** can be used to handle complex event processing in real time by applying models to streaming data.

## Processing Data Using Spark Structured Streaming

**Structured Streaming** is a feature in Apache Spark where the incoming stream is treated as an unbounded table. The incoming streaming data is continuously appended to the table. This feature makes it easy to write streaming queries, as you can now write streaming transformations in the same way you handle table-based transformations. Hence, the same Spark batch-processing syntax can be applied here, too.

> **Note**
>
> This section primarily focuses on the **Process data by using Spark structured streaming** concept of the DP-203: Data Engineering on Microsoft Azure exam.

Spark treats the Structured Streaming queries as incremental queries on an unbounded table and runs them at frequent intervals to continuously process the data. Spark supports three writing modes for the output of Structured Streaming:

- **Complete mode**: In this mode, the entire output (also known as the **result table**) is written to the sink. The sink could be a Blob Storage, a data warehouse, or a **BI tool**.

- **Append mode**: In this mode, only the new rows from the last time are written to the sink.

- **Update mode**: In this mode, only the rows that have changed are updated; the other rows will not be updated.

In the *Implementing a Streaming Use Case with Azure* section, when you used Azure Databricks Spark to process the stream, you applied the concept of Spark Structured Streaming. Every time you use the `writestream` or `readstream` methods, Spark uses Structured Streaming. Now, you'll look at another example in which you will continuously write the streaming trip data and query it like a regular table:

```
EHStreamJsonDF.selectExpr(
                «tripId»\
                ,"timestamp"\
                ,»startLocation»\
                ,»endLocation»\
                ,"distance"\
                ,»fare»)\
```

```
.writeStream.format("delta")\
.outputMode("append")\
.option("checkpointLocation", "dbfs:/TripsCheckpointLocation/")\
.start("dbfs:/TripsEventHubDelta")
```

In the preceding code, you are specifying the column names to be extracted as part of `selectExpr`, the format to be written as `delta`, the output mode as `append`, the checkpoint location as `dbfs:/TripsCheckpointLocation`, and finally, the sink location to be written as `dbfs:/TripsEventHubDelta` within the `start()` method.

**Delta** is an open-source storage layer that can be run on top of data lakes. It enhances the data lake to support features such as **Atomicity, Consistency, Isolation, and Durability** (**ACID**) transactions, updates, deletes, unified batches, and interactive streaming systems via Spark. You will learn more about Delta in the *Managing Small Files* section of *Chapter 10, Optimizing and Troubleshooting Data Storage and Data Processing*.

Now, you can query the data like a regular table, as follows:

```
%sql
CREATE TABLE IF NOT EXISTS TripsAggTumbling
    USING DELTA LOCATION «dbfs:/TripsEventHubDelta/»
SELECT * FROM TripsAggTumbling
```

This is how you can use Spark Structured Streaming to handle streaming data.

In the preceding code, you create a Delta Lake table named `TripsAggTumbling` and specify its storage location as `dbfs:/TripsEventHubDelta/`. Then, you execute a SELECT query to retrieve all data from this table for further processing or analysis.

> **Note**
>
> You can learn more about Structured Streaming at `https://packt.link/Cr1du`. You can find the complete code used in the accompanying GitHub repository at `https://packt.link/Ry8id`.

Now that you have seen how structured streaming can be used to enable scalable and fault-tolerant processing of streaming data, it is time to consider how you can monitor the streaming performance.

## Creating Windowed Aggregates

**Windowed aggregates** are essential for processing time series data, which is simply data recorded continuously over time. Examples of time series data could include stock prices recorded over time and IoT sensor values, which show the health of machinery over time.

> **Note**
>
> This section primarily focuses on the **Create windowed aggregates** concept of the DP-203: Data Engineering on Microsoft Azure exam.

In the subsequent sections, you'll explore the different windowed aggregates that are available in ASA. ASA supports the following five types of windows:

- **Tumbling Windows**: These are fixed-size, non-overlapping windows where each window covers a specific time duration, and data is aggregated separately for each window.

- **Hopping windows**: Similar to Tumbling Windows, hopping windows also have a fixed size, but they can overlap with each other. This allows more flexibility in capturing data and analyzing trends over time.

- **Sliding windows**: Sliding windows slide or move over the data stream by a specified interval. They may overlap with each other, enabling continuous processing of data over time with a new window created at each interval.

- **Session windows**: Session windows group data into sessions based on certain criteria, such as a gap in activity. They are useful for analyzing sequences of events or activities within a session.

- **Snapshot windows**: Snapshot windows capture the current state of the data stream at specific points in time. They are useful for taking periodic snapshots of data for analysis or reporting purposes.

You will now look at each of them in detail. The following sample event schema will be used in the examples:

- `eventSchema = StructType()`
- `.add("tripId", StringType())`
- `.add("createdAt", TimestampType())`
- `.add("startLocation", StringType())`
- `.add("endLocation", StringType())`
- `.add("distance", IntegerType())`
- `.add("fare", IntegerType())`

You'll start with Tumbling Windows.

## Tumbling Windows

**Tumbling Windows** are fixed-size and non-overlapping windows used for grouping streaming data into discrete chunks based on time intervals. All the windows are of the same size. *Figure 6.20* depicts a Tumbling Window dividing a stream into discrete, non-overlapping segments of 10 seconds each. Each event (labeled 1, 2, 3, etc.) is in one, and only one, of the 10-second windows:

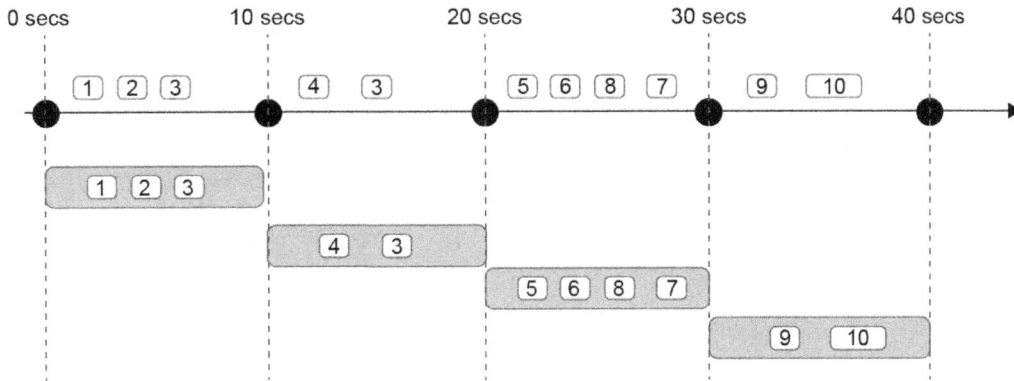

Figure 6.20 – A Tumbling Window showing a stream segmented into 10-second time windows

The following is the syntax of using a Tumbling Window:

```
{TUMBLINGWINDOW | TUMBLING} ( timeunit  , windowsize, [offsetsize] )
{TUMBLINGWINDOW | TUMBLING} ( Duration( timeunit  , windowsize ),
[Offset(timeunit  , offsetsize)] )
```

The preceding code allows you to define `TumblingWindow` in structured streaming applications, providing options for specifying `WindowSize`.

The following is the sample code for using a Tumbling Window in ASA:

```
SELECT System.Timestamp() AS WindowEnd, tripLocation, COUNT(*)
INTO [Output]
FROM [Input] TIMESTAMP BY createdAt
GROUP BY tripLocation, TumblingWindow(Duration(second, 10),
Offset(millisecond, -1))
```

In the preceding code, you process the streaming data from `Input`, then aggregate it within a `TumblingWindow` of 10 seconds with a -1 millisecond offset and write the result into the `Output` sink.

> **Note**
>
> You can find the complete code used in the accompanying GitHub repository at https:// packt.link/ubDg6.

## Hopping Windows

**Hopping windows** are just overlapping Tumbling Windows, meaning that each window will have a fixed-size overlap with the previous window. *Figure 6.21* depicts a hopping window:

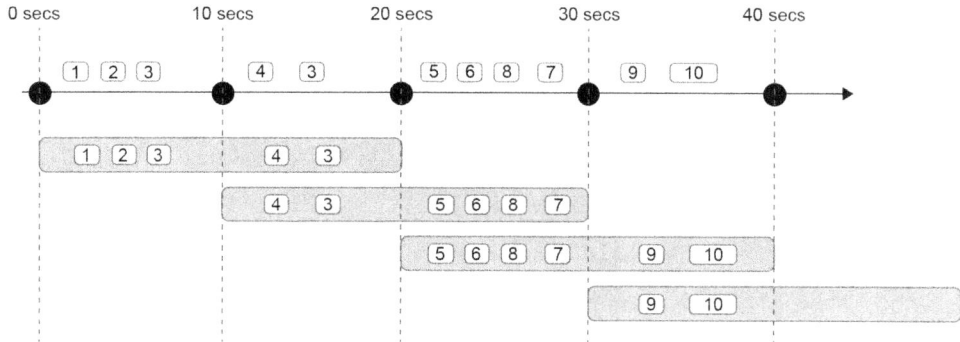

Figure 6.21 – A hopping window showing a fixed-size overlap with the previous window

The following is the syntax for a hopping window:

```
{HOPPINGWINDOW | HOPPING} ( timeunit  , windowsize , hopsize,
[offsetsize] )
{HOPPINGWINDOW | HOPPING} ( Duration( timeunit  , windowsize ) , Hop
(timeunit  , windowsize ), [Offset(timeunit  , offsetsize)])
```

In the preceding code, you define HOPPINGWINDOW in structured streaming applications, providing options for specifying the windowsize, hopsize, and optional window with the specified timeunit. As defined earlier, hopping windows are sliding windows that move forward by a fixed interval (hopsize) and may overlap with each other.

The following is an example of a hopping window:

```
SELECT System.Timestamp() AS WindowEnd, tripLocation, COUNT(*)
INTO [Output]
FROM [Input]  TIMESTAMP BY createdAt
GROUP BY tripLocation, HoppingWindow(Duration(second, 20), Hop(second,
10), Offset(millisecond, -1))
```

In the preceding code, you can process streaming data from Input, timestamp it, aggregate it within the hoppingwindow, and write the results into the Output sink. Every 10 seconds, the code fetches the trip count per tripLocation for the last 20 seconds. Here, the hopping window size is 20 seconds and the hop size is 10 seconds.

> **Note**
>
> You can find the complete code used in the accompanying GitHub repository at `https://packt.link/M802h`.

## Sliding Windows

Similar to tumbling and hopping windows, sliding windows have a fixed size and continuously move forward based on a predefined time interval. However, instead of emitting results at fixed time intervals, they are evaluated continuously, and results are reported only when there is a change (i.e., an event is added to or removed from the window). This approach ensures that the output windows are always of a fixed length, but the frequency of receiving results is determined by changes in the events, not by set time intervals.

Reporting on the window's contents may occur when events are added or removed but it can also be scheduled at regular intervals regardless of event activity. *Figure 6.22* shows a sliding window:

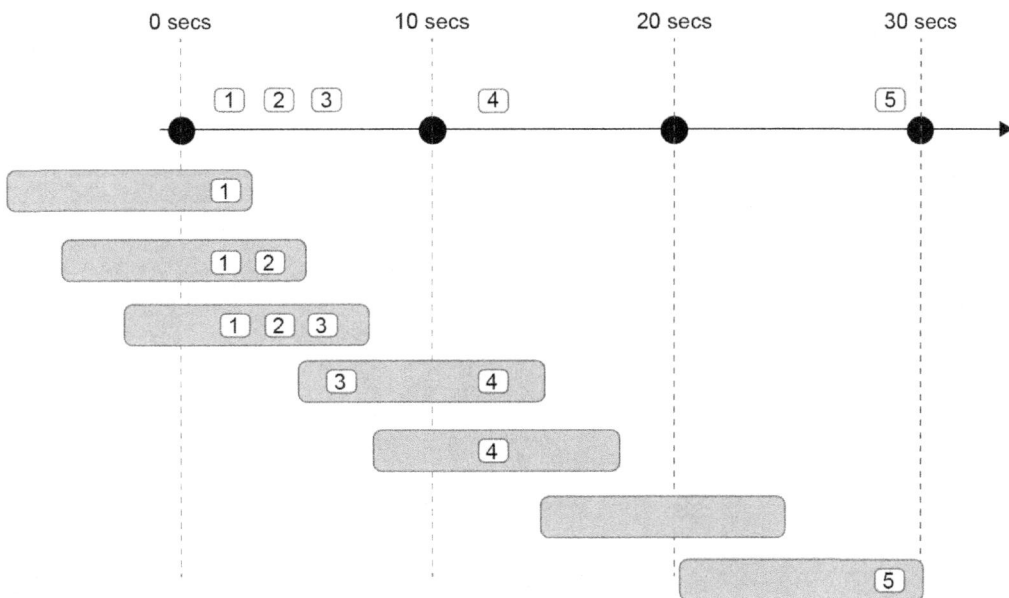

Figure 6.22 – A sliding window reporting when an event is added or removed

The following is the syntax for a sliding window:

```
{SLIDINGWINDOW | SLIDING} ( timeunit, windowsize )
{SLIDINGWINDOW | SLIDING} ( Duration( timeunit, windowsize ) )
```

In the preceding code, you can define a sliding window using either the SLIDINGWINDOW or SLIDING notation, with parameters specifying timeunit and windowsize. The parameters can be directly specified or passed through a Duration function for processing.

The following is an example of a sliding window:

```
SELECT System.Timestamp() AS WindowEnd, tripLocation, COUNT(*)
INTO [Output]
FROM [Input] TIMESTAMP BY createdAt
GROUP BY tripLocation, SlidingWindow(second, 10)
HAVING COUNT(*) > 5
```

In the preceding code, the data coming from an Input input source is grouped by tripLocation within SlidingWindows for 10 seconds. It then calculates the count of records in each window and outputs the results into an output table or data stream named Output. Additionally, you can filter out windows where the count of records is not greater than 5.

> **Note**
>
> You can find the complete code used in the accompanying GitHub repository at https://packt.link/fQu8u.

## Session Windows

**Session windows** don't have fixed sizes. You need to specify a maximum window size and timeout duration for session windows. The session window tries to grab as many events as possible within the maximum window size. On the other hand, if there are no events, the window closes after the timeout duration. *Figure 6.23* shows what a session window looks like:

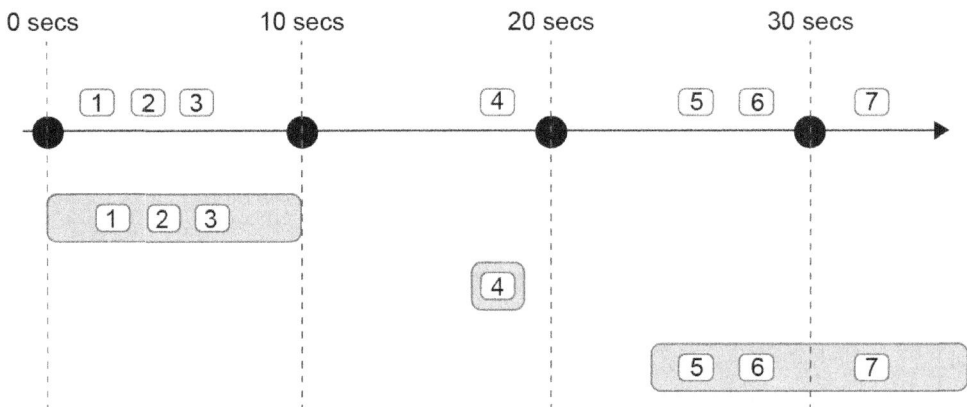

Figure 6.23 – An example of a session window with no fixed sizes

The following is the syntax for a session window:

```
{SESSIONWINDOW | SESSION} (timeunit, timeoutSize, maxDurationSize)
[OVER (PARTITION BY partitionKey)]
{SESSIONWINDOW | SESSION} (Timeout(timeunit , timeoutSize),
MaxDuration(timeunit, maxDurationSize)) [OVER (PARTITION BY
partitionKey)]
```

The following is an example of a session window that finds the number of trips that occur within 5 seconds of each other:

```
SELECT System.Timestamp() AS WindowEnd, tripId, COUNT(*)
INTO [Output]
FROM [Input] TIMESTAMP BY createdAt
GROUP BY tripId, SessionWindow(second, 5, 10)
```

In the preceding code, your query processes data from `Input`, timestamps it by `createdAt`, groups it by `tripId`, and defines sessions using a `sessionwindow` timeout of 5 seconds and a maximum duration of `10` seconds. It then calculates the count of records within each session and stores the results in an output table or data stream named `Output`.

> **Note**
>
> You can find the complete code used in the accompanying GitHub repository at `https://packt.link/ZIXj5`.

## Snapshot Windows

A **snapshot window** is not really a windowing technique. It gives an overview of events at a specific time:

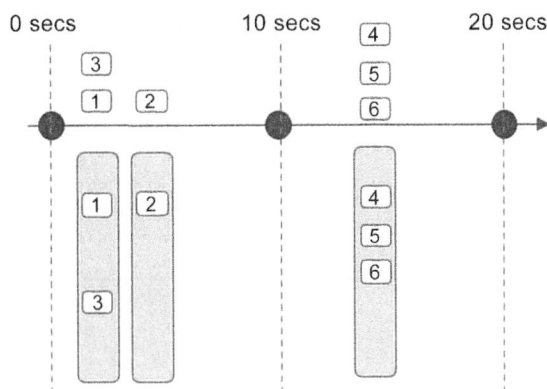

Figure 6.24 – A snapshot window showing an overview of an event at a particular time

The following is the syntax for a snapshot window:

```
{SNAPSHOTWINDOW | SNAPSHOT} (timeunit, snapshotSize) [OVER (PARTITION
BY partitionKey)]
{SNAPSHOTWINDOW | SNAPSHOT} (Snapshot(timeunit, snapshotSize)) [OVER
(PARTITION BY partitionKey)]
```

The following syntax shows how you can use a snapshot window:

```
SELECT tripId, COUNT(*)
INTO [Output]
FROM [Input] TIMESTAMP BY createdAt
GROUP BY tripId, System.Timestamp()
```

In the preceding code, you are counting the number of records per `tripId` with each count associated with the `TIMESTAMP` at which the query is executed. The `System.Timestamp` in the `GROUP BY` clause is used to achieve the aggregate result.

> **Note**
>
> You can find the complete code used in the accompanying GitHub repository at `https://packt.link/1DiE3`.

This concludes all the windowing options in ASA.

> **Note**
>
> You can learn more about the ASA windowing functions at `https://packt.link/b5ZP9`.

When dealing with time series data, it is important to consider checkpointing, watermarking, and schema drift because these elements collectively ensure data integrity, manage late-arriving data, and adapt to changes in data structure over time, which is critical for maintaining accurate and reliable analytics. The *Configuring Checkpoints and Watermarking* section is important for dealing with the fault tolerance and latency inherent in data streaming, and these topics will be discussed later.

First, you will look at maintaining consistent processing logic in evolving data streams, commonly known as **schema drift**.

# Handling Schema Drifts

A **schema drift** refers to the changes in schema over time due to changes happening in the event sources. This could be due to newer columns or fields getting older, columns getting deleted, and more. For example, a large online US marketplace might measure real-time purchasing data in order to analyze shopping habits over a holiday period. The company then starts to expand internationally and wants to add fields for customer location, currency, and shipping costs. The company wants to be able to make this change without compromising the integrity of the data stream.

> **Note**
>
> This section primarily focuses on the **Handle schema drift** concept of the DP-203: Data Engineering on Microsoft Azure exam.

## Handling Schema Drifts Using Event Hubs

One way of ensuring data integrity is for the schema details to always be shared with data. However, if an event publisher needs to share schema details with the consumer, they must serialize the schema along with the data, using formats such as **Apache Avro**, and send it across **Event Hubs**. In Event Hubs, the schema must be sent with every event, which is inefficient. To address the issue of inefficiency, there is a static schema on the consumer side, removing the need to serialize schema with the data. However, this introduces the potential for issues if the schema changes, since the consumer's static schema may no longer align with the data, leading to processing errors or data loss.

**Apache Avro** is a data serialization system that provides rich data structures in a compact, fast, binary data format. It is used for serializing structured data and is particularly well-suited for Big Data processing frameworks such as **Apache Hadoop**, **Apache Spark**, and **Apache Flink**.

> **Note**
>
> You can explore more about Avro files in Azure Event Hubs at `https://packt.link/zvnw5`.

Event Hubs provides a feature called **Azure Schema Registry** to handle Schema Evolution and schema drift. It provides a central repository to share the schemas between event publishers and consumers. You'll examine how to create and use Azure Schema Registry in the next section.

## Registering a Schema with Schema Registry

Registering a schema with **Schema Registry** is a fundamental step in modern data engineering, especially in distributed systems and streaming architectures such as **Event Hubs**. Schema Registry acts as a central repository where you can store and manage the schemas of your data in a structured and organized manner.

In event streaming and messaging scenarios, each event or message often includes specific data. To effectively manage this information, schema-driven formats like Apache Avro are commonly used for serializing and deserializing the data. Avro provides a common language between event producers and consumers, ensuring smooth communication. When an event is produced, it is formatted according to a predefined schema, making it easy for consumers to know and process. This schema-driven approach ensures consistency and compatibility throughout the entire event stream from production to consumption.

While an event producer uses a schema to serialize the event payload and publish it to an event broker, such as Azure Event Hubs, an event consumer reads the event payload from the broker and deserializes it by using the same schema. This ensures that both producers and consumers validate the integrity of the data consistently.

The subsequent example shows how the schema is registered. You can run the following code in various **Python** environments including your local machine, **Visual Studio Code** (**VS Code**), and a **Databricks** notebook:

1. Import the necessary libraries:

    ```
    from azure.schemaregistry import SchemaRegistryClient
    from azure.identity import DefaultAzureCredential
    ```

    In the preceding code, you are importing the modules that are necessary for interacting with Azure Schema Registry's `SchemaRegistryClient` and for managing your authentication using `DefaultAzureCredential`. It sets up the environment for working with Azure services in a Python script or application.

2. Define your schema:

    ```
    sampleSchema = """
    {"namespace": "com.azure.sampleschema.avro",
    "type": "record",
    "name": "Trip",
    "fields": [
        {«name»: «tripId», «type»: «string»},
        {«name»: «startLocation», «type»: «string»},
        {«name»: «endLocation», «type»: «string»}
    ]
    }"""
    ```

In the preceding code, the schema definition outlines the structure and data types for a `Trip` record in the `Avro` format. It is ready to be used for serializing and deserializing data conforming to this schema, which is `sampleschema`.

3.  Create the Schema Registry client:

```
azureCredential = DefaultAzureCredential()
schema_registry_client = SchemaRegistryClient(
fully_qualified_namespace=<SCHEMA-NAMESPACE>.servicebus.windows.
net,
credential=azureCredential)
```

> **Note**
>
> All the entries within the angular brackets, < >, are user-provided values.

The preceding code initializes `Azure Credential` using the default authentication method and then creates a `client` object for interacting with the Azure Schema Registry service, providing the necessary authentication credentials and the fully qualified namespace of the Schema Registry service. This `client` object can be used to perform operations such as registering schemas, retrieving schemas, and managing schema versions within the Azure Schema Registry.

4.  Register the schema with `schema_registry_client`:

```
schema_properties = schema_registry_client.register_schema(
   <SCHEMA_GROUPNAME>,
   <SCHEMA_NAME>,
   sampleSchema,
   "Avro")
```

In the preceding code, you register a schema with the Azure Schema Registry service, providing the necessary parameters such as the schema group name, schema name, schema content, and serialization type. After successful registration, the properties of the registered schema are stored in the `schema_properties` variable for further use, such as retrieving schema information or managing schema versions.

5.  Get the schema ID from `schema_properties`:

```
schema_id = schema_properties.id
```

In the preceding code, the `schema_id` variable is assigned `schema_properties`, which contains properties or information about a schema. `.id` is a property or attribute of the `schema_properties` object that represents the ID associated with a schema.

> **Note**
>
> You can find the complete code used in the accompanying GitHub repository at `https://packt.link/SHOiI`.

## Retrieving a Schema from Schema Registry

The following example shows the high-level steps for retrieving the schema:

1. Import the necessary libraries:

   ```
   from azure.identity import DefaultAzureCredential
   from azure.schemaregistry import SchemaRegistryClient
   ```

   The preceding code imports the `DefaultAzureCredential` class from the `azure.identity` package and the `SchemaRegistryClient` class from the `azure.schemaregistry` package.

2. Create the Schema Registry client:

   ```
   azureCredential = DefaultAzureCredential()
   schema_registry_client = SchemaRegistryClient(
   fully_qualified_namespace=<SCHEMA-NAMESPACE>.servicebus.windows.
   net,
   credential=azureCredential)
   ```

> **Note**
>
> All the entries within the angular brackets, <   >, are user-provided values.

The preceding code initializes your `AzureCredential` object using the default authentication method and then creates a `client` object for interacting with the Azure Schema Registry service, providing the necessary authentication credentials and the fully qualified namespace of the Schema Registry service. This `client` object can be used to perform operations such as registering schemas, retrieving schemas, and managing schema versions within the Azure Schema Registry.

3. Retrieve the schema with `schema_registry_client`:

```
schema = schema_registry_client.get_schema(schema_id)
definition = schema.definition
properties = schema.properties
```

In the preceding code, you can retrieve a schema from the Azure Schema Registry service using `schema_id`. Then extracts the schema definition and associated properties from the retrieved schema object for further use in the application.

> **Note**
>
> You can find the complete code used in the accompanying GitHub repository at `https://packt.link/amAub`.

Once you have the schema, you can define your events and start reading the data in the correct format.

> **Note**
>
> You can learn more about Event Hubs Schema Registry at `https://packt.link/z4Olj`.

Next, you'll learn to handle schema drifts in Spark.

## Handling Schema Drifts in Spark

**Azure Databricks Delta Lake** provides a feature called **Schema Evolution** to take care of schema changes over time. It automatically adapts to the new schema when new columns are added. Schema Evolution can be enabled by adding the `.option('mergeSchema', 'true')` option to the `writeStream` streaming command. The following is a simple example to enable Schema Evolution:

```
StreamDF.writeStream.format("delta")\
.option("mergeSchema", "true") \
.outputMode("append")\
.option("checkpointLocation", "dbfs:/CheckpointLocation/")\
.start("dbfs:/StreamData")
```

In the preceding code, you set up a streaming write operation using **Delta Lake format** in Apache Spark Structured Streaming. It enables Schema Evolution, specifies the output mode as append, sets a `checkpointLocation`, and starts the streaming query to write data to a Delta Lake table. Once the `mergeSchema` option has been specified, Spark handles new columns in the stream automatically.

Now that you have seen how to mitigate against the issues that changes in schema can cause, it is time to dive back into the methods of processing time series data.

# Processing Time Series Data

In the earlier section dedicated to windowed aggregates, you were taught that time series data is defined as a series of data over time, such as the measurements from sensors or the prices of a share. Indeed, time series data is mostly used to analyze historical trends and identify any abnormalities in data such as credit card fraud, real-time alerting, and forecasting. Time series data will always be appended heavily with very rare updates.

> **Note**
>
> This section primarily focuses on the **Process time series data** concept of the DP-203: Data Engineering on Microsoft Azure exam.

Time series data, or data processed over consistent intervals of time, often requires real-time processing applications such as financial market analysis. The stream processing solutions that you learned earlier in this chapter, in the *Implementing a Streaming Use Case with Azure* section, would perfectly work for time series data.

Now, you can look at some of the important concepts of time series data.

## Types of Timestamps

The central aspect of any time series data is the **time attribute**. There are two types of time in time series data:

- **Event time**: This indicates the actual time when the event occurred
- **Processing time**: The time when the event is processed by a data processing system

It is important to consider the event time while processing events rather than the processing time, as the latter might be delayed due to processing speed, network delays, and other issues in the stream processing pipeline.

## Windowed Aggregates

Since time series events are unbounded events, or in other words, since they don't have a well-defined end time, it is necessary to process the events in small batches (that is, windows of time).

> **Note**
>
> This section primarily focuses on the **Create windowed aggregates** concept of the DP-203: Data Engineering on Microsoft Azure exam.

There are different windowing mechanisms available, such as Tumbling Windows, hopping windows, and sliding windows, and these were covered earlier in the chapter in the *Creating Windowed Aggregates* section.

## Checkpointing or Watermarking

**Checkpointing** (also called **watermarking**) refers to the process of keeping track of the last event or timestamp that was processed by the stream processing engine. This helps ensure that you start from the previously stopped event and don't miss out on processing any events after outages, system upgrades, processing delays, and more. You will learn to achieve this in the *Configuring Checkpoints and Watermarking* section of this chapter.

## Replaying Data from a Previous Timestamp

You might be required to reprocess older events in the case of machine failures or errors in processing logic. If the machine hosting the stream processing system fails unexpectedly, it could result in a loss of data processing capability. This could be due to hardware failures, network issues, or other technical issues.

When such failures occur, events that were in the middle of being processed at the time of failure might not have been fully processed. Even if the system is functioning normally, errors in the processing logic itself can occur. These errors might lead to incorrect or incomplete processing of events. In such cases, reprocessing is required to correct the errors and ensure accurate processing of data using tools such as **Event Hubs**, which provide features that allow you to replay the events again from a previous offset location.

> **Note**
> You can learn more about time series data at `https://packt.link/ZtTqb`.

Next, you'll look at how partitions impact stream data processing.

# Processing Data across Partitions

In streaming data scenarios, processing data across partitions is vital for ensuring efficient and scalable data pipelines. Partitions serve as segmented slices into which streaming data is divided, enabling parallel processing, and facilitating the handling of large volumes of data in real time. Efficient partitioning strategies involve evenly distributing data across partitions and dynamically adjusting partitioning strategies based on workload characteristics to optimize resource utilization and scalability.

When you design streaming solutions, it is crucial to consider how data is distributed across partitions and how processing operations can be efficiently applied across them. Various techniques facilitate processing across partitions, including aggregations, windowed operations, join operations, and stateful processing, each serving different analytical needs. An uneven distribution of data across partitions can lead to imbalanced workload distribution and performance issues, highlighting the importance of selecting an appropriate partition key and continuously monitoring partition behavior.

By effectively addressing these aspects, you can build robust and scalable streaming data pipelines that efficiently handle real-time data processing requirements while maintaining accuracy and relevance in analysis results.

Before you look at how to process data across partitions, first learn about partitions.

> **Note**
>
> This section primarily focuses on the **Process data across partitions** concept of the DP-203: Data Engineering on Microsoft Azure exam.

## What Are Partitions?

Event Hubs can distribute incoming events into multiple streams so that they can be accessed, in parallel, by the consumers. These parallel streams are called **partitions**. Each partition stores the actual event data and **metadata** of the event, such as its offset in the partition, its server-side timestamp when the event was accepted, and its number in the stream sequence. Partitioning helps in scaling real-time processing, as it increases **parallelism** by providing multiple input streams for **downstream processing** engines. Additionally, it improves availability by redirecting the events to other healthy partitions if some of the partitions fail.

> **Note**
> You can learn more about Event Hubs partitions at `https://packt.link/oUFfZ`.

Now, look at how you can send data across partitions and process data across partitions. In order to access Event Hubs, client libraries are available in different languages, such as C#, Python, and Java. In the examples in this section, you will use the Python library.

Event Hubs provides the `EventHubConsumerClient` class as part of the Python client libraries to consume the data from the Event Hub. `EventHubConsumerClient` is a fundamental component in Azure's event streaming ecosystem and it offers a powerful tool for consuming real-time data from **Azure Event Hubs**. As a high-level client library provided by Azure **Software Development Kits (SDKs)**, `EventHubConsumerClient` simplifies the process of building applications that need to ingest and process streaming data.

With its intuitive interface and robust functionality, you can easily connect to Event Hubs, efficiently retrieve events, and handle them in near real time. Whether it is processing telemetry data, monitoring IoT devices, or implementing real-time analytics, `EventHubConsumerClient` provides a seamless solution for you to harness the full potential of Azure Event Hubs.

This class can be used to read events from all the partitions with load balancing and checkpointing. You will use this class in the checkpointing example provided in the *Checkpointing in Event Hubs* section. The same example will work for reading across partitions. Here, you will provide the important steps again for convenience.

The following is example code that performs checkpointing in Event Hubs to read events from all the partitions with load balancing and checkpointing:

1.  Instantiate the checkpoint store:

```
storeChkPoint = BlobCheckpointStore.from_connection_string(
        <STORE_CONN_STRING>,
        <STORE_CONTAINER_NAME>
    )
```

> **Note**
>
> All the entries within the angular brackets, < >, are user-provided values.

In the preceding code, you can create an instance of `BlobCheckpointStore` using a connection string (`<STORE_CONN_STRING>`) and a container name (`<STORE_CONTAINER_NAME>`), presumably to manage checkpoints in some distributed processing scenario, likely using Azure Blob Storage for persistence.

2.  Instantiate the `EventHubConsumerClient` class:

```
ehClient = EventHubConsumerClient.from_connection_string(
        <EVENTHUB_CONN_STRING>,
        <CONSUMER_GROUP_NAME>,
        eventhub_name=<EVENTHUB_NAME>,
        checkpoint_store= storeChkPoint # This enables load
balancing across partitions
    )
```

In the preceding code, `EventHubConsumerClient` consumes events from a specific Event Hub using a provided connection string (`<EVENTHUB_CONN_STRING>`) and consumer group name (`<CONSUMER_GROUP_NAME>`). It also specifies a `checkpoint_store` to enable load balancing across partitions.

3.  Define an on_event method to process the event when it arrives:

```
def on_event(partition_context, event):
    # Process the event
    partition_context.update_checkpoint(event)
```

In the preceding code, `partition_context.update_checkpoint(event)` depends on the specific event processing framework or library being used. The `partition_context` object provides methods and attributes related to managing the state and progress of event processing for a specific partition or shard in the event stream. Similarly, the `event` parameter represents the event that is being processed, but its structure and properties are determined by the event source and processing system.

4.  Call the on_event method when an event arrives:

```
with ehClient:
    ehClient.receive(
        on_event=on_event,
        starting_position=»-1»,   # To start from the beginning
of the partition.
    )
```

In the preceding code, you set up an event processing loop that continuously receives events from an Azure Event Hub using the `ehClient` object. Each received event triggers the `on_event` callback function and the consumption starts from the beginning of the partition. The `with` statement ensures proper resource management for the `ehClient` object. When you don't specify a specific partition while instantiating the `EventHubConsumerClient` class, it will automatically read from across all the partitions in the specified consumer group.

> **Note**
>
> You can learn more about the Event Hubs Python libraries at `https://packt.link/TpV0O`.

Now that you have learned how to send data across partitions and process data across partitions, it is time to look at the details of how to process the data within a partition.

## Processing within One Partition

Similar to the previous example, where you learned how to process across partitions, you can use the `EventHubConsumerClient` class to process data within single partitions, too.

Processing data within single partitions using the `EventHubConsumerClient` class allows you to specifically target and handle data from individual partitions within an Azure Event Hub. Each partition in an Event Hub operates independently and this functionality enables you to gain more granular control over the data processing pipeline.

Here are some scenarios where processing data within single partitions will be useful:

- **Load balancing**: Distributing the workload across multiple consumer instances, each handling data from a specific partition, can achieve better load balancing. This can help in evenly distributing the processing load and preventing bottlenecks.

- **Parallel processing**: You can process data from different partitions in parallel, leveraging the scalability of the processing infrastructure. This can significantly improve the throughput and reduce processing latency.

- **Order guarantees**: While Event Hubs guarantee ordered delivery within a partition, there might be scenarios where maintaining order across partitions is not necessary. Processing data within single partitions allows you to maintain order within each partition while still benefiting from parallel processing across partitions.

- **Fault isolation**: Handling data within single partitions allows better fault isolation. If there's an issue with processing data from one partition, it doesn't affect the processing of data from other partitions, thus enhancing the overall resilience of the system.

- **Custom processing logic**: You might have different processing requirements for data from different partitions. Processing data within single partitions enables the implementation of custom processing logic tailored to the specific characteristics of each partition.

> **Note**
>
> This section primarily focuses on the **Process within one partition** concept of the DP-203: Data Engineering on Microsoft Azure exam.

All you have to do is specify the partition ID in the `client.receive` call, as demonstrated in the following code snippet (the rest of the code will remain the same as the previous example):

```
with client:
    client.receive(
        on_event=on_event,
        partition_id=>0>, # To read only partition 0
    )
```

This is how you can programmatically process the data from specific Event Hubs partitions. Next, look at how you can apply checkpoints and watermarking to the analysis of data streams.

# Configuring Checkpoints and Watermarking

ASA, Event Hubs, and Spark offer checkpointing and watermarking options to ensure fault tolerance and manage event time handling. The different platforms are explained as follows:

- Checkpoints track the progress of data processing, allowing you to resume from the point of failure or interruption. Azure Event Hubs uses checkpoints to save the state of activities in your pipeline. By defining a storage account for checkpoint data, you ensure recovery after failures and minimize downtime.

- Watermarking marks progress within a specific column (e.g., timestamp). It is useful for incremental data updates, where you process only newly added or modified records. By configuring a watermark column, you identify the latest processed record during subsequent runs.

## Checkpointing in ASA

ASA does internal checkpointing periodically and users do not need to do explicit checkpointing. The checkpointing process is used for job recoveries during system upgrades, job retries, node failures, and more. The following describes the importance and benefits of checkpointing in a computing environment:

- **System upgrades**: During system upgrades, such as upgrading the underlying infrastructure or software components, job recoveries are essential to ensure that any ongoing processes are not lost. Checkpointing allows the system to resume processing from the point where it was interrupted before the upgrade.

- **Job retries**: In scenarios where your job encounters errors or failures, it may need to be retried to ensure successful completion. Checkpointing helps in storing the state of the job, including the progress made and the data processed, so that the job can be retried from the last checkpoint instead of starting from scratch.

- **Node failures**: If a node in a distributed computing environment fails while executing a job, checkpointing ensures that the progress made by the job on that node is not lost. The job can be recovered on another available node, starting from the last checkpoint to minimize data loss and processing overhead.

- **Service upgrades**: When a service undergoes upgrades or maintenance activities, it may result in interruptions to ongoing jobs or processes. Checkpointing helps you preserve the state of these jobs so that they can be recovered and resumed once the upgrade is completed.

- **Network failures**: Network failures can disrupt the communication between nodes or services, leading to job failures or interruptions. Checkpointing allows the system to recover from such failures by resuming the processing from the last checkpoint thereby reducing the impact of network disruptions on job execution.

- **Resource constraints**: If there are resource constraints, such as memory limitations or CPU overload that cause a job to fail or be interrupted, checkpointing enables the job to be recovered and resumed once the resources become available again.

During node failures or OS upgrades, ASA automatically restores the failed node state on a new node and continues processing. During ASA service upgrades (not OS upgrades), the checkpoints are not maintained, and the stream corresponding to the downtime needs to be replayed.

> **Note**
>
> This section primarily focuses on the **Configure checkpoints and watermarking during processing** concept of the DP-203: Data Engineering on Microsoft Azure exam.

## Checkpointing in Event Hubs

**Checkpointing** (also known as **watermarking**) in Event Hubs refers to the process of marking the **offset** within a stream or partition to indicate the point up to where the processing is complete and is the responsibility of the event consumer process. Since checkpointing is a relatively expensive operation, it is usually better to checkpoint after a batch of event processing. The main idea of checkpointing is to have a restart point if the Event Hub fails or undergoes service upgrades.

The following code shows how you can perform checkpointing in Event Hubs using the `BlobCheckpoint` store:

```
Import asyncio
from azure.eventhub.aio import EventHubConsumerClient
from azure.eventhub.extensions.checkpointstoreblobaio import
BlobCheckpointStore
async def on_event(partition_context, event):
    # Process the event
    # Checkpoint after processing
    await partition_context.update_checkpoint(event)
async def main():
    storeChkPoint = BlobCheckpointStore.from_connection_string(
        <STORE_CONN_STRING>,
        <STORE_CONTAINER_NAME>
    )
    ehClient = EventHubConsumerClient.from_connection_string(
        <EVENTHUB_CONN_STRING>,
        <CONSUMER_GROUP_NAME>,
        eventhub_name=<EVENTHUB_NAME>,
        checkpoint_store= storeChkPoint
    )
    async with ehClient:
```

```
            await ehClient.receive(on_event)
    if __name__ == '__main__':
        loop = asyncio.get_event_loop()
        loop.run_until_complete(main())
```

The preceding code demonstrates the asynchronous consumption of events from an Azure Event Hub using the `azure-eventhub` library with the `asyncio` support. It sets up an Event Hub consumer client, defines an asynchronous `on_event` event processing function, and uses a Blob Storage-based `checkpoint_store` to track the progress of event consumption. The main function orchestrates the event consumption process, ensuring proper cleanup. To use the code, replace the placeholders with your actual connection strings, container names, and Event Hub details.

The following steps will ensure that your code or application can securely connect to Blob Storage using the specified connection string and store checkpoints or data within the specified Blob container:

- `STORE_CONN_STRING`:

    I.    In the **Azure portal**, locate your storage account.

    II.   Go to the **Access keys** section under **Settings**.

    III.  Copy either of the connection strings (either primary or secondary). This connection string contains all the information you need to connect to your storage account, including the account name, account key, and endpoint.

    IV.   Replace `<STORE_CONN_STRING>` in the code with your connection string.

- `STORE_CONTAINER_NAME`:

    I.    After obtaining the connection string, specify the name of the **Blob container** to store the checkpoints.

    II.   If the container does not exist, create it in your storage account.

    III.  Replace `<STORE_CONTAINER_NAME>` in the code with the name of your Blob container.

The next section will look at checkpointing in Spark.

## Checkpointing in Spark

The Structured Streaming feature of Spark delivers end-to-end exactly-once semantics. In other words, it ensures that an event is delivered exactly once. Spark uses checkpointing and write-ahead logs to accomplish this.

In your Structured Streaming example earlier in the *Processing Data Using Structured Streaming* section, you learned how to configure the checkpointing location in the Spark queries. The following is another simple example:

```
EHStreamJsonDF.writeStream.format("delta")\
 .outputMode("append")\
 .option("checkpointLocation", "dbfs:/TripsCheckpointLocation/")\
 .start("dbfs:/TripsEventHubDelta")
```

Spark Structured Streaming takes care of checkpointing internally. This is so that the user does not need to worry about manually checkpointing the input stream.

You will go through the topic of checkpointing again in the *Replaying Archived Stream Data* section at the end of this chapter. First, though, you will learn how to scale resources when processing data streams.

# Scaling Resources

**Scaling resources** is pivotal for optimizing stream processing and involves strategies to efficiently allocate and utilize resources, ensuring scalability and performance services such as Event Hubs, ASA, and Azure Databricks. The key aspects include the following:

- **Balancing load**: It distributes workloads across resources to prevent bottlenecks.

- **Resource optimization**: It efficiently uses CPU, memory, and storage.

- **Scalability**: It designs systems to handle varying data volumes.

- **Partition processing**: It manages data within partitions effectively.

> **Note**
> This section primarily focuses on the **Scale resources** concept of the DP-203: Data Engineering on Microsoft Azure exam.

In the ensuing sections, you will look at how you can scale resources in Event Hubs, ASA, and Azure Databricks Spark.

## Scaling in Event Hubs

There are two ways in which Event Hubs support scaling:

- **Partitioning**: You have already learned how partitioning can help scale your Event Hubs instance by increasing the **parallelism** with which the event consumers can process data. For scaling, partitioning helps reduce **contention** if there are too many producers and consumers, which, in turn, makes it more efficient.

- **Auto-inflate**: This is an automatic scale-up feature of Event Hubs. As the usage increases, `eventhub` adds more **Throughput Units** (**TUs**) to your Event Hub instance, thereby increasing its capacity. You can enable this feature if you have already saturated your quota using the partitioning technique that you explored earlier, in the *Processing Data across Partitions* section.

You'll next explore the concept of throughput units.

### What Are TUs?

When scaling resources, it's important to know how throughput impacts system performance. **TUs** directly relate to the system's capacity to handle incoming events. These units allow you to allocate capacity based on your workload and you can make informed decisions about how many TUs to provision as the system grows. Also, when optimizing for performance, TUs play a crucial role in adjusting your resources dynamically.

TUs are units of capacity that can be purchased in Event Hubs. A single TU allows the following:

- An ingress of up to 1 MB per second or 1,000 events per second
- An egress of up to 2 MB per second or 4,096 events per second

> **Note**
>
> In the Event Hubs Premium Tier, TUs are called **processing units**.

### Auto-Inflate Scaling

The **auto-inflate scaling** in Azure Event Hubs is a dynamic mechanism that automatically adjusts the throughput capacity of **Event Hubs** based on workload demands. This ensures that your Event Hubs can handle varying workloads efficiently. Initially, you choose the minimum required TUs to start with. Once your traffic increases, the auto-inflate feature dynamically scales up the TUs to meet your usage needs. It automatically increases the number of TUs without any manual requests.

You have seen the Event Hubs namespace creation already, shown in *Figure 6.4*. The only difference here is you are selecting the Pricing Tier as Standard to enable the **Auto-inflate** option. The following steps will help you enable the auto-inflate feature in Event Hubs:

1. In the **Azure portal**, search for **Event Hubs** and create the Event Hubs namespace, as shown in *Figure 6.25*.

2. Choose the subscription details in the **Subscription** field. In this case, it is `Azure subscription`.

3. Choose the existing **Resource** group or "create" a new one. In this case, it is the existing resource group called `rg-dp203-eh`.

4. Under the **Instance Details** section, type the name of the namespace. For example, here, it is asaeh.

5. Select the location, for instance, East US.

6. Choose the Pricing Tier from the **Pricing tier** dropdown—for example, Standard (20 Consumer groups, 1000 Brokered connections).

7. Configure the **Throughput Units** toggle, which starts from 1. In this case, it is kept at 5 units.

8. Select the Enable Auto-inflate option.

9. Arrange the **Auto-Inflate Maximum Throughput Units** toggle. Here, it is kept as 5 units (*Figure 6.25*):

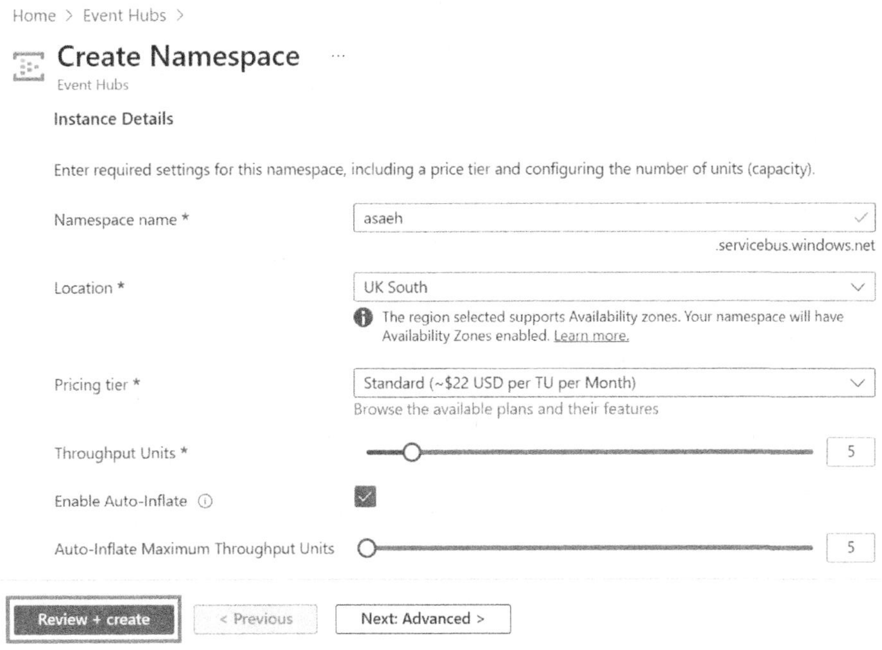

Figure 6.25 – Enabling auto-inflate feature in Event Hubs

10. Finally, click the Review + create button.

Now, you have enabled an auto-inflate feature in Event Hubs.

---

**Note**

You can learn more about Event Hubs' scalability at https://packt.link/Gb7s0.

## Scaling in ASA

You can scale your ASA clusters directly from the Azure portal. To find the ASA jobs you created already, shown in *Figure 6.8*, navigate to the Azure home screen, search for `Stream Analytics jobs`, and select your ASA job. In this case, it is `SampleASAJob`.

Just click on the `Scale` tab on the **ASA** home page, which you created previously, shown in *Figure 6.8*, and configure the **Streaming units** toggle to 1, as shown in *Figure 6.26*:

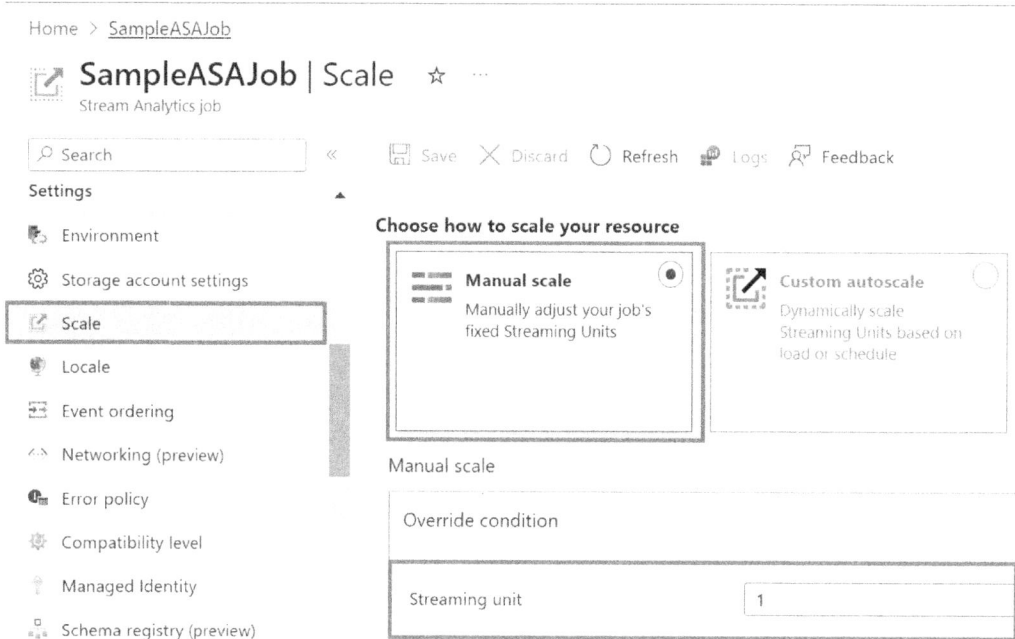

Figure 6.26 – Scaling an ASA job

> **Tip**
>
> For ASA queries that are not using the `PARTITION BY` transformation, the recommendation is to start with "six" SUs and then modify the numbers iteratively by running your jobs and monitoring the SU percentage utilization metric.

SUs are a measure of the streaming capacity. Scaling units don't have an absolute capacity configuration like in the case of Event Hubs TUs. In general, the higher the number of SUs, the higher the capacity. You will have to do some trial-and-error runs to identify the sweet spot. Here, "sweet spot" refers to conducting trial-and-error runs or performance testing with different configurations of SUs to determine the most suitable setup for the specific workload and requirements.

> **Note**
>
> You can learn about SU optimization at `https://packt.link/sHEXK`. You can learn more about scaling ASA at `https://packt.link/K7xdp`.

ASA doesn't have an internal auto-scale mechanism. However, you can simulate one using services such as **Azure Automation**. This is an external service that can be used to monitor the ASA metrics and can trigger a scale-up or scale-down externally.

> **Note**
>
> If you are interested in learning more about autoscale, you can refer to `https://packt.link/OM2D1`.

### Scaling in Azure Databricks Spark Streaming

You learned how to configure autoscaling for Azure Databricks in *Chapter 5*, *Developing a Batch Processing Solution*, in the *Scaling Resources* section. Please refer to that section to refresh your memory regarding how to configure autoscaling for Spark.

To summarize, the **scaling** options in **Azure Databricks** emphasize the flexibility of autoscaling based on your workload demands. When creating a cluster, you can enable autoscaling and set the minimum and maximum number of workers, allowing the cluster to dynamically adjust its size. Alternatively, you can opt for a fixed-size cluster by disabling autoscaling and specifying the exact worker count. Additionally, the concept of **Spot Instances** is introduced, offering cost savings by utilizing unused Azure **Virtual Machines** (**VMs**) at a cheaper rate, although with the caution of potential interruptions with short notice. These options cater to different workload scenarios, from fluctuating demands to cost optimization strategies.

The next section was covered in *Chapter 5*, *Developing a Batch Processing Solution*, in the *Creating Tests for Data Pipelines* section. You will touch upon this topic before learning about efficient optimization.

## Developing Testing Processes for Data Pipelines

This section was covered in To summarize, you explored the process of creating data pipelines using **ADF** or **Synapse**. You also learned how to design and construct these pipelines to orchestrate data movement and transformations effectively. Additionally, you delved into triggering these pipelines and monitoring their executions to ensure they run as expected.

You also integrated low-code solutions with code execution by learning how to call a **Spark Notebook** from within a pipeline. This capability will allow you to seamlessly blend the simplicity of low-code approaches with the power and flexibility of code execution, enabling more versatile and efficient data workflows. By learning how to incorporate Spark Notebooks into your pipelines, you can enhance your data processing capabilities and streamline your data engineering tasks.

> **Note**
>
> This section primarily focuses on the **Create tests for data pipelines** concept of the DP-203: Data Engineering on Microsoft Azure exam.

# Optimizing Pipelines for Analytical or Transactional Purposes

In this section, you will learn about efficient optimization, which involves applying best practices and advanced techniques tailored for analytical and transactional workloads. The following are some key points to consider:

- **Resource scaling**: You can allocate resources based on the specific workload. For analytical tasks consider using services, such as **Azure Databricks**, for efficient data processing.

- **Incremental loading**: Implement incremental loading strategies to minimize data transfer and improve pipeline efficiency. This approach ensures that only changed or new data is processed, reducing the overall processing time.

- **Exception handling**: Configure robust exception-handling mechanisms to manage errors during pipeline execution. This includes handling connectivity issues, data format mismatches, and other unexpected scenarios.

- **Monitoring and optimization**: Continuously monitor pipeline performance using tools such as **Azure Monitor**. Optimize resource utilization, identify bottlenecks, and fine-tune configurations for optimal results.

As in previous chapters, you will follow the sequence of the Study Guide.

> **Note**
>
> The order and arrangement of topics are designed to facilitate learning based on the prescribed curriculum. This approach helps learners navigate through the material in a structured manner, with inclusive coverage of the subject matter as it pertains to the exam or study requirements.

Keep in mind that the type of optimization for data pipelines (discussed in this section) is based on the distinction between **analytical** and **transactional** processes, which is completely independent of the distinction between batch and stream processes.

> **Note**
>
> Before the 6 February 2023 update, the topic of optimizing pipelines for analytical or transactional purposes appeared twice in the DP-203 Study Guide—once as part of the section dedicated to stream processing and once, more sensibly, as part of the section dedicated to performance optimization. With the February 2023 update, however, the duplication was removed and in the former direction, meaning that this would appear only in the stream processing section. A further update, dated 4 May 2023, confirmed this decision.

You may have heard the terms **Online Analytical Processing (OLAP)** and **Online Transaction Processing (OLTP)** if you have been working in the data domain. To reiterate, **Cloud data systems** can be broadly classified as either OLTP or OLAP systems. You will now go through each of these at a high level as follows:

- **OLTP Systems**: OLTP systems, as the name suggests, are built to efficiently process, store, and query transactions. They usually have transaction data flowing into a central ACID-compliant database. The databases contain normalized data that adhere to strict schemas. Data here are usually smaller, in the range of gigabytes or terabytes. Predominantly **Relational Database Management System (RDBMS)**-based systems, such as Azure SQL and MySQL, are used for the main database.

- **OLAP systems**: On the other hand, OLAP systems are usually Big Data systems that typically have a warehouse or key value-based store as the central technology to perform analytical processing. The tasks could be data exploration, generating insights from historical data, predicting outcomes, and so on. The data in an OLAP system arrives from various sources that don't usually adhere to any schemas or formats. They usually contain large amounts of data in the range of terabytes, petabytes, and above. The storage technology used is usually **column-based storage** such as **Azure Synapse SQL pool**, **HBase**, and **Cosmos DB analytical storage**, which have a better read performance.

> **Note**
>
> This section primarily focuses on the **Optimize pipelines for analytical or transactional purposes** concept of the DP-203: Data Engineering on Microsoft Azure exam.

You can optimize the pipelines for either OLAP or OLTP, but how do you optimize for both? Enter **Hybrid Transactional/Analytical Processing (HTAP)** systems.

**HTAP** systems are a new breed of data systems that can handle both transactional and analytical processing. They combine row- and column-based storage to provide hybrid functionality. These systems remove the requirement for maintaining two sets of pipelines—one for transactional processing and the other for analytical processing. Having the flexibility to perform both transactional and analytical systems simultaneously opens up a new realm of opportunities, such as real-time recommendations during transactions, real-time leaderboards, and the ability to perform ad hoc queries without impacting the transaction systems.

Now, look at building an HTAP system using Azure technologies.

## Implementing HTAP Using Synapse Link and Cosmos DB

HTAP is accomplished in Azure using Azure Synapse and Azure Cosmos DB via Azure Synapse Link. You have already learned about Azure Synapse in *Chapter 4, Ingesting and Transforming Data*. So, you will look into Cosmos DB and Synapse Link here.

## Introducing Cosmos DB

**Cosmos DB** is a fully managed globally distributed No-SQL database that supports various API formats, including SQL, **MongoDB**, **Cassandra**, **Gremlin**, and **Key-Value**. It is extremely fast and seamlessly scales across geographies and allows you to enable multi-region writes across the globe with just a few simple clicks. Cosmos DB is suitable for use cases such as retail platforms for order processing, cataloging, and gaming applications that need low latency with the ability to handle spurts in traffic, telemetry, and logging applications to generate quick insights.

Cosmos DB internally stores the operational data in a row-based transactional store, which is efficient for OLTP workloads. However, it also provides support to enable a secondary column-based analytical store that is persisted separately from the transaction store, which is efficient for analytical workloads. So, it provides the best of both the OLTP and OLAP environments. Cosmos DB is therefore perfectly suited for the HTAP workloads. Since the row store and column store are separate from each other, there is no performance impact on running transactional workloads and analytical workloads simultaneously. The data from the transactional store is automatically synced to the columnar store in almost real time.

## Introducing Azure Synapse Link

**Synapse Link**, as the name suggests, links Synapse and Cosmos DB to provide **cloud-native HTAP capability**. You can use any of the Synapse compute engines, be it the Synapse serverless SQL pool or the Spark pool, to access the Cosmos DB operational data and run analytics without impacting the transactional processing on Cosmos DB. This is significant because it completely eliminates the need for **Extract**, **Transform**, and **Load** (ETL) jobs, which were required earlier. Prior to the availability of Synapse Link, you had to run ETL pipelines to get the transactional data into an analytical store such as a data warehouse before you could run any analysis or BI on the data. Now, you can directly query the data from the Cosmos DB analytical store for BI.

*Figure 6.27* shows the Synapse Link architecture reproduced from the Azure documentation:

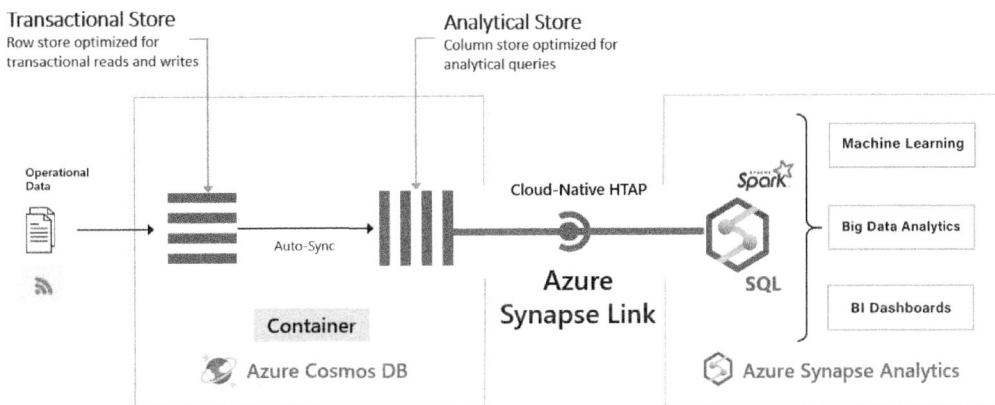

Figure 6.27 – Azure Synapse Link for Cosmos DB architecture

> **Note**
>
> At the time of writing this book, accessing the **Azure Cosmos DB** analytics store using the **Azure Synapse Dedicated SQL pool** was not supported. Only the **serverless SQL pool** was supported for this purpose.

Perform the following steps to create a **Synapse Link** and set up an HTAP system:

1. In order to first create a Cosmos DB instance, select `Cosmos DB` in the **Azure portal**.

2. In the **Cosmos DB** portal, select the `+ Create` button to create a new **Cosmos DB** instance, as shown in *Figure 6.28*:

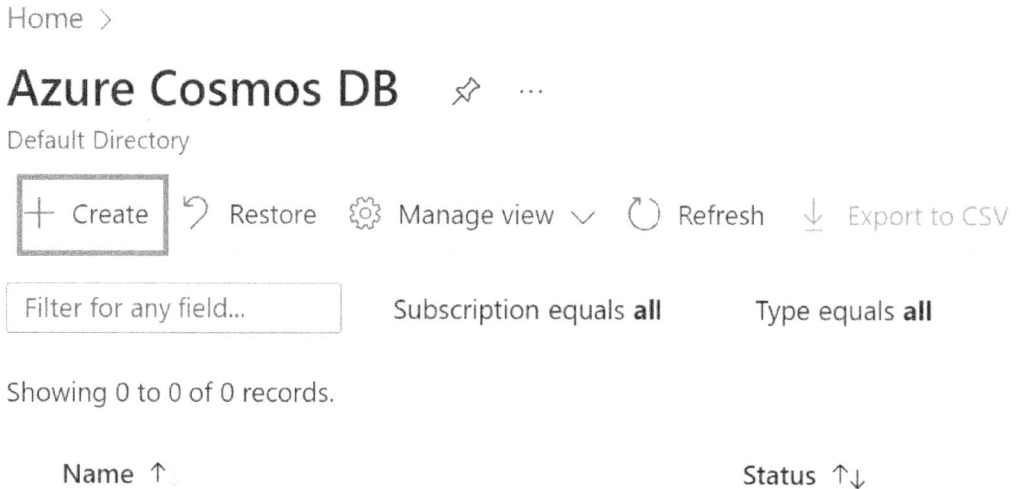

Home >

# Azure Cosmos DB  ✗  ...
Default Directory

| + Create |   ᕲ Restore   ⚙ Manage view ⌄   ↻ Refresh   ↓ Export to CSV

Filter for any field...              Subscription equals **all**        Type equals **all**

Showing 0 to 0 of 0 records.

Name ↑                                                     Status ↑↓

Figure 6.28 – Creating a new Cosmos DB instance

You will see the different API options available in Cosmos DB.

3. Select `Azure Cosmos DB` for **NoSQL**.

   Once this is selected, you will see the **Create Azure Cosmos DB Account for NoSQL** screen, as shown in *Figure 6.29*:

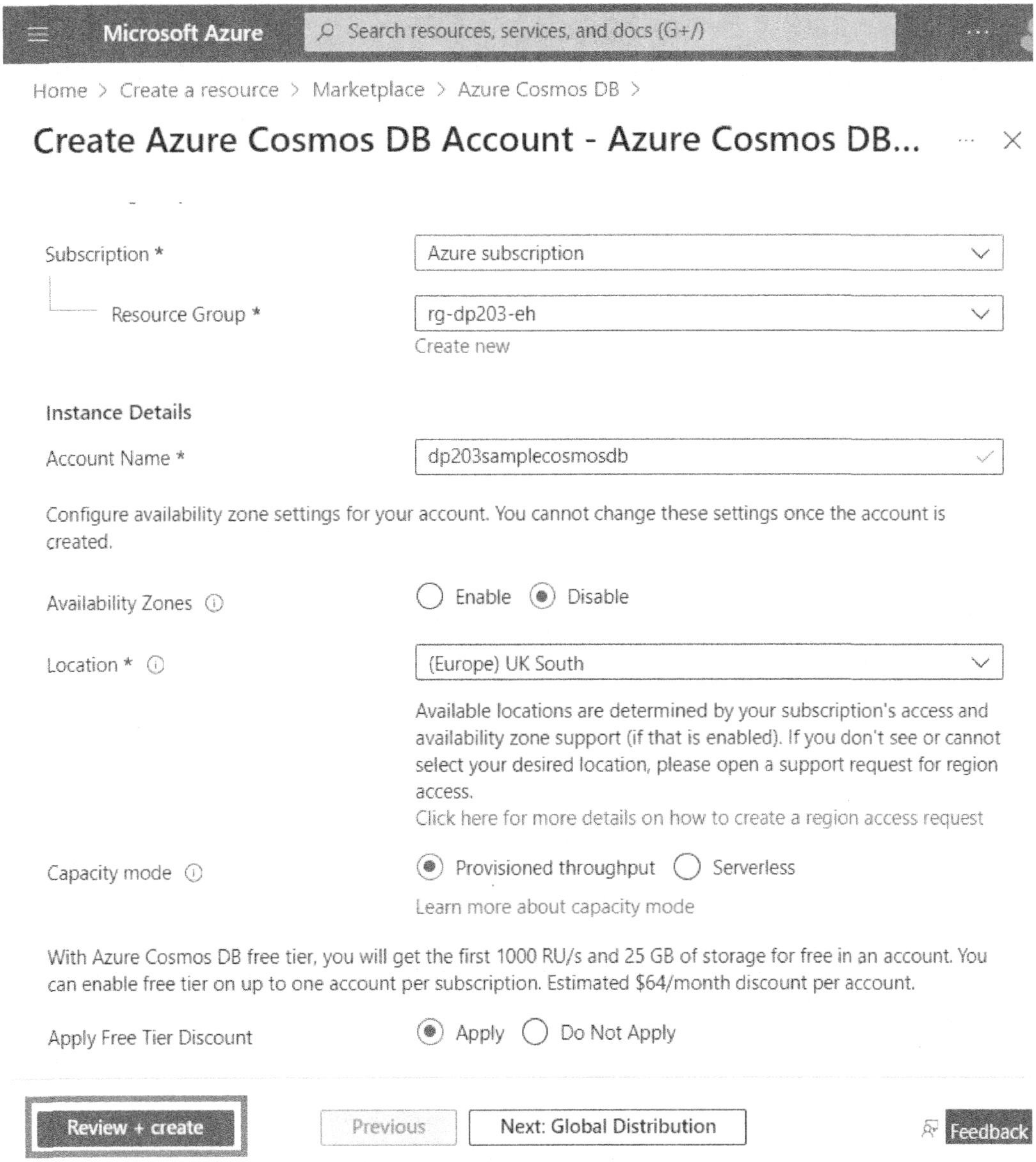

Figure 6.29 – Cosmos DB creation screen for building a NoSQL account

4.  Enter the **Subscription** name. In this case, it is Azure subscription.

5.  Enter the resource group in the **Resource Group** field. In this case, it is rg-dp2023-eh.

6.  Under the **Instance Details** section, type the account name in the **Account Name** field, for example, dp203samplecosmosdb.

7. Choose to enable or disable availability zones; in this case, `Disable` is selected.

8. Choose the location, in this case, `(Europe) UK South`.

9. Choose one of the **Capacity mode** options. Here, `Provisioned throughput` is selected. *Table 6.1* shows the various capacity modes under **Provisioned Throughput**:

| Feature | Provisioned Throughput | Serverless |
|---|---|---|
| **Functionality** | This configures a fixed amount of RUs/s. | This has no provisioned capacity; RUs consumed per operation. |
| **Best Suited For** | Sustained traffic, predictable performance. | Intermittent or unpredictable traffic. |
| **Geo-Distribution** | Available across multiple Azure regions. | Limited to a single Azure region. |
| **Max Storage/Container** | Unlimited storage capacity. | Up to 1 TB (GA); RU/sec depends on stored data. |
| **Performance** | Low-latency (<10 ms for reads and writes), SLA covered. | Low-latency (<10 ms for reads, <30 ms for writes), SLO. |
| **Billing Model** | Billed per hour for provisioned RUs, regardless of consumption. | Billed per hour for RUs consumed by operations. |

Table 6.1 – Cosmos DB Account creation screen showing capacity modes

10. Select the `Apply` radio button for the **Apply Free Tier Discount** option.

11. Finally, click on the `Review + create` button to create the new Cosmos DB instance.

    Once you have created the Cosmos DB instance, it will prompt you to create a container and a sample dataset.

12. Add a container and a sample dataset, in this case, these are `SampleContainer` and `SampleDB`.

13. Now, go to the **Azure Synapse Link** tab under **Integrations**.

14. Click on the `Enable` button to enable an Azure Synapse Link for this account, as shown in *Figure 6.30*:

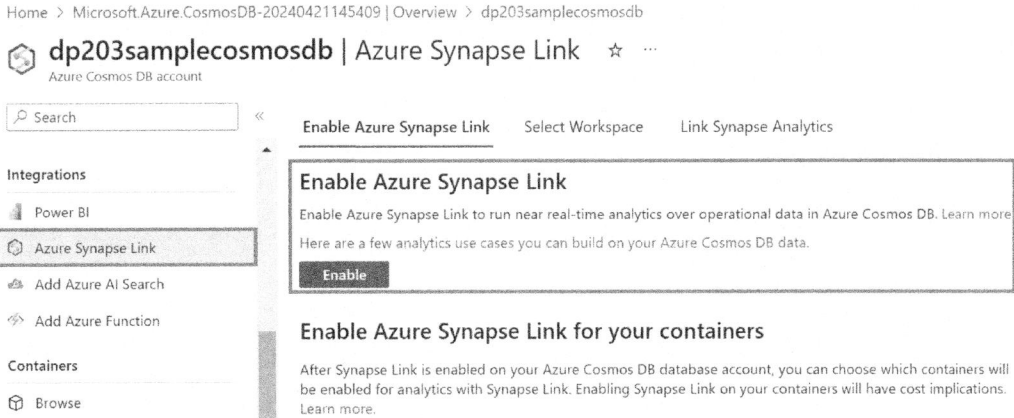

Figure 6.30 – Enabling Synapse Link in Cosmos DB

The **Register** button is for enabling a **Synapse Link** on any existing container individually instead of an entire account.

15. Next, go to the **Data Explorer** tab and click on New  Container. A **New Container** screen is displayed, as shown in *Figure 6.31*:

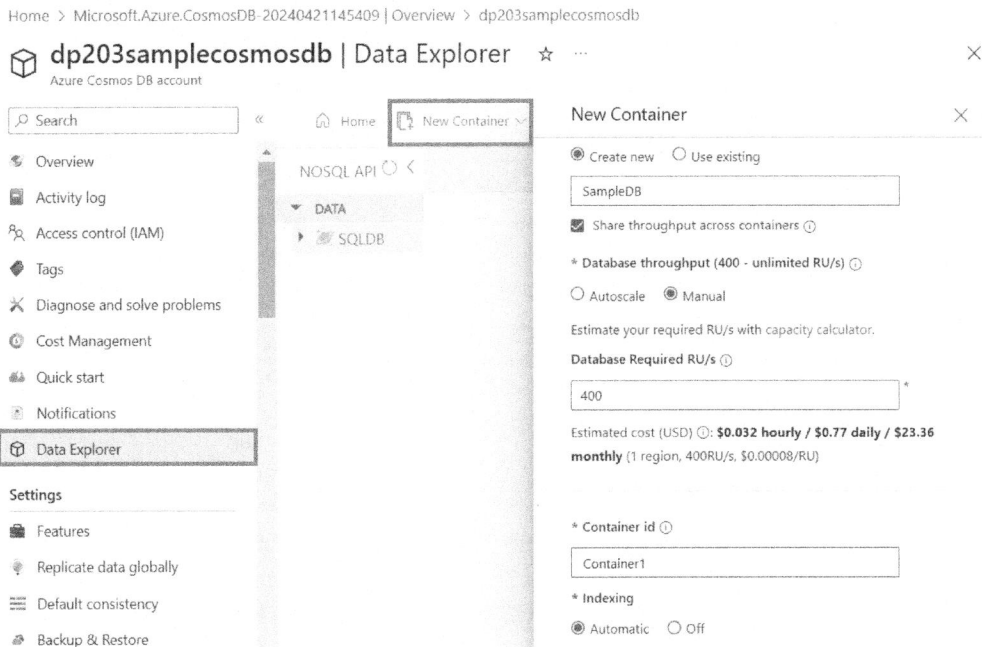

Figure 6.31 – Configuring a new container by selecting Analytical store

16. In the **New Container** screen, select the existing database ID or create a new one. In this case, the `Create new` option is chosen.

17. Enter the container ID in the **Container id** box (in this case, `Container1`).

18. Enter the partition key in the **Partition key** box. For example, the `/address/zip` partition key is entered.

19. Enter the RU estimation in the **Estimate your required RU/s with capacity calculator** box; for example, `400`.

    The + **Add unique key** refers to a field or combination of fields that ensures the uniqueness of documents within the container. In this case, you can leave this as it is optional.

20. For **Container throughput**, choose either **Autoscale** or **Manual**. In this case, `Manual` is chosen.

21. Select `On` for the **Analytical store** option.

    The **Advanced** tab can be selected to enable or disable analytical capabilities for your container and you can specify the duration after which documents expire and are automatically removed. In this case, it can be skipped.

    This should set up the Cosmos DB for a Synapse Link. Now, you have to set up Synapse to talk to Cosmos DB. To do so, you have to first set up a linked service to Cosmos DB from the Synapse workspace. Continue to follow these steps:

22. From the **Synapse** portal, go to the **Manage** tab and then select `Linked Services`.

23. Click on the + New button. A **New linked service** screen is displayed.

24. Select `Azure Cosmos DB (SQL API)`, as shown in *Figure 6.32*:

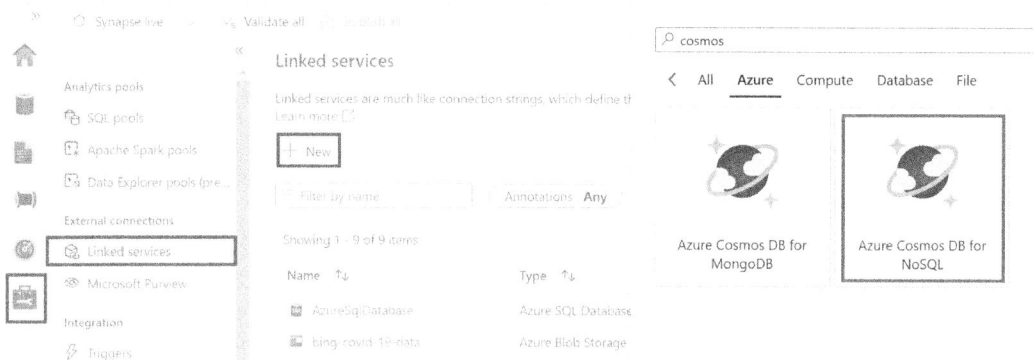

Figure 6.32 – Creating a linked service to Cosmos DB

25. Click on the newly created linked service, that is, `Azure Cosmos DB (SQL API)`, to show the details of the Cosmos DB linked service along with the connection string details, as shown in *Figure 6.33*:

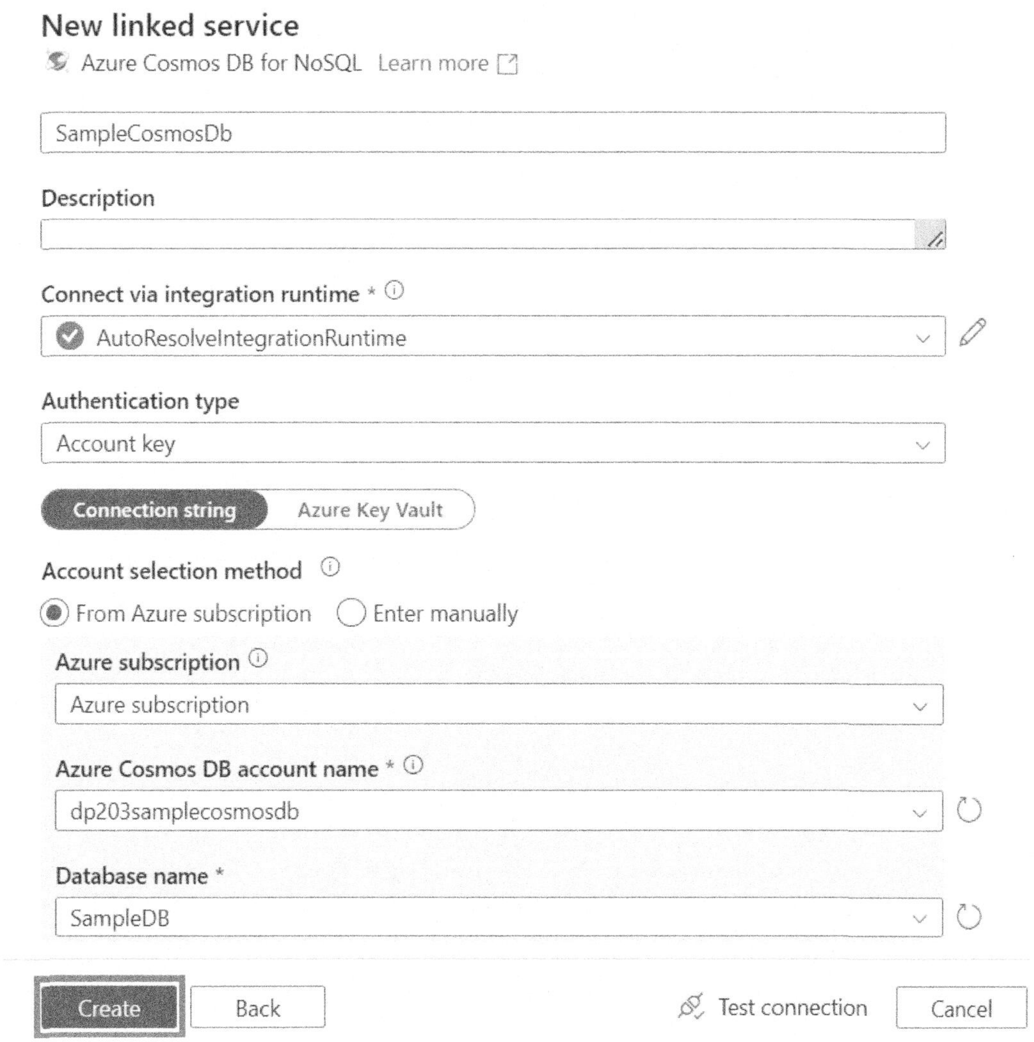

# New linked service

Azure Cosmos DB for NoSQL   Learn more 

SampleCosmosDb

**Description**

**Connect via integration runtime** * 

AutoResolveIntegrationRuntime

**Authentication type**

Account key

**Connection string**    Azure Key Vault

**Account selection method** 

◉ From Azure subscription    ◯ Enter manually

**Azure subscription** 

Azure subscription

**Azure Cosmos DB account name** * 

dp203samplecosmosdb

**Database name** *

SampleDB

Create    Back                                    Test connection    Cancel

Figure 6.33 – Cosmos DB linked service showing Cosmos DB for Synapse Link

You have now completed the Synapse Link setup.

26. Now, go to **Synapse workspace** and select the `Data` tab.

    You should now be able to see an Azure Cosmos DB entry. You can explore the data in Cosmos DB by clicking on the container names under the Azure Cosmos DB entry.

27. Click a container name under Azure Cosmos DB, in this case, it is `SampleContainer`.

28. Select the `Load to DataFrame` option under **New notebook**, as shown in *Figure 6.34*:

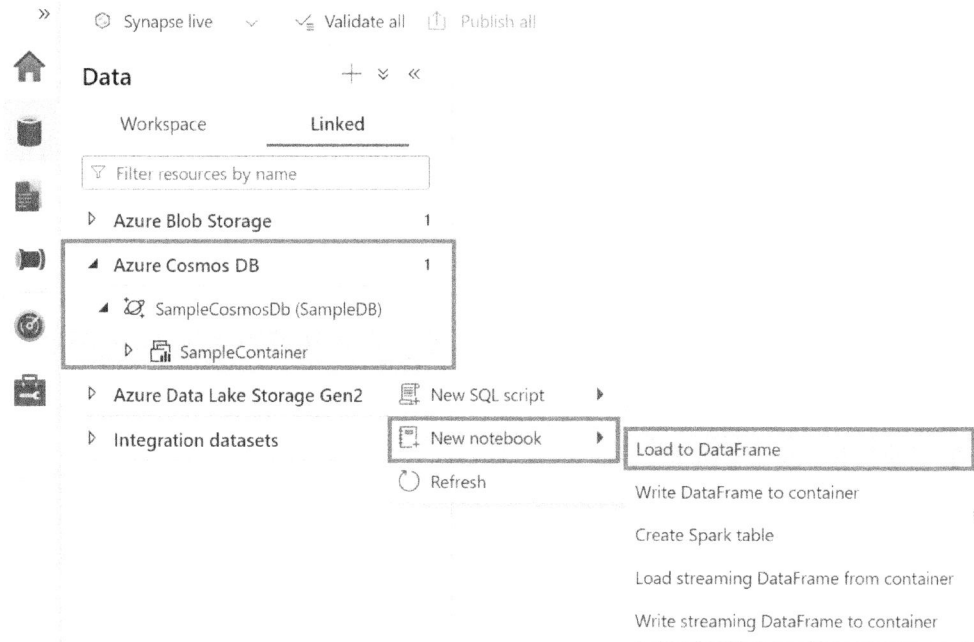

Figure 6.34 – Loading Cosmos DB data using the Synapse Link

29. You can query the Cosmos DB data from the Spark Notebook using OLAP (`cosmos.olap`), as follows:

```
df = spark.read.format("cosmos.olap")\
    .option(«spark.synapse.linkedService», «<Linked Service Name>»)\
    .option(«spark.cosmos.container», «<CosmosDB Container Name>»)\
    .load()
```

In the preceding code, you set up Spark to read data from a Cosmos DB container using **Synapse Link**, utilizing the provided connection details and container name. The loaded data will be accessible through the `df` DataFrame for further processing and analysis using Spark's capabilities. For OLTP queries, change the format to `cosmos.oltp` instead of `cosmos.olap`.

You now know how to implement an HTAP system and query from it.

> **Note**
>
> You can learn more about HTAP and the Azure Synapse Link at `https://packt.link/JLzSf`.

In this segment, you have learned about optimizing pipelines for analytical and transactional purposes. Additionally, you have been introduced to implementing HTAP using **Azure Synapse** and **Azure Cosmos DB** via **Azure Synapse Link** and learned how Cosmos DB supports both row-based transactional stores and secondary column-based analytical stores, making it suitable for HTAP workloads. You grasped how Synapse Link connects Synapse and Cosmos DB to provide cloud-native HTAP capability without the need for ETL jobs, enabling direct querying of data from Cosmos DB's analytical store for BI purposes.

Now that you have addressed the detour prompted by the Study Guide's requirements, you can refocus on stream processing and specifically discuss strategies for managing interruptions.

## Handling Interruptions

Interruptions to stream processing might occur due to various reasons such as network connectivity issues, background service upgrades, or intermittent bugs. Event Hubs and ASA provide options to handle such interruptions natively using the concept of **Azure availability zones**. **Availability zones** are physically isolated locations in Azure that help applications become resilient to local failures and outages. Azure lists the regions that are paired together to form availability zones.

> **Note**
>
> This section primarily focuses on the **Handle interruptions** concept of the DP-203: Data Engineering on Microsoft Azure exam.

Services that support availability zones deploy their applications to all the locations within the availability zone to improve fault tolerance. Additionally, they ensure that service upgrades are always done one after the other for the availability zone locations. Therefore, they ensure that at no point will all the locations suffer an outage due to service upgrade bugs. Both Event Hubs and ASA support availability zones.

The subsequent section will explain how you can enable this feature for both Event Hubs and ASA.

## Handling Interruptions in Event Hubs

When Event Hubs is deployed to regions that are part of the availability zones, both the metadata and events are replicated to all the locations in that availability zone. In order to use availability zones, all you need to do is select a region that supports the availability zone for the **Location** field, as shown in *Figure 6.35*:

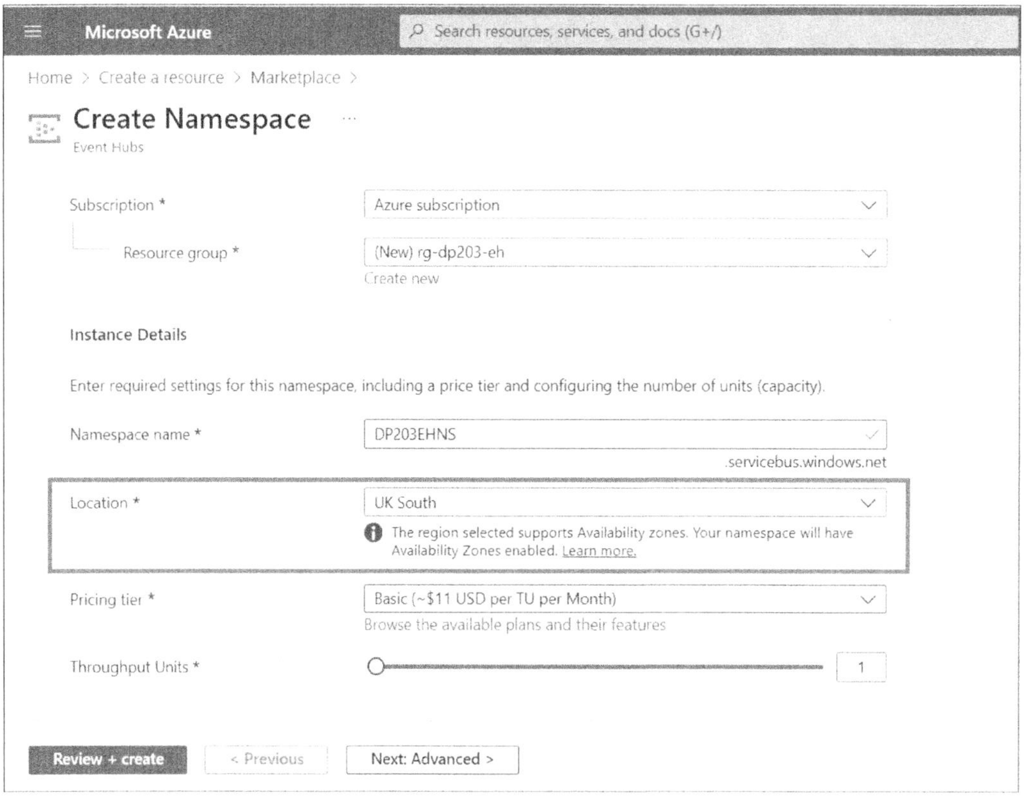

Figure 6.35 – Choosing locations with availability zones in Event Hubs

Once you have chosen the availability-zone-supported region, in this case, UK South, click on the Review + create button.

The Event Hubs instance is created in all the locations of the availability zone. The following are a few other points to make the Event Hubs instance more resilient:

- Try to build back off and retry logic into your applications. This is done so that transient errors can be caught, and the stream processing can be retried. If your application is built using the **Event Hubs SDKs**, then the retry logic is already built in.

- If the application doesn't need strictly ordered messages, you can send the events without specifying a partition. This will ensure that the Event Hubs load balances the events across all partitions. If a partition fails, the Event Hubs instance will distribute the event to other partitions, thereby improving availability.

> **Note**
>
> You can learn more about Event Hubs availability zones at `https://packt.link/F6kiD`.

## Handling Interruptions in ASA

Similar to Event Hubs, ASA also deploys to availability zones (or Azure-paired regions) by default. Additionally, ASA ensures that service updates always happen in separate batches between the locations of the availability zones. There is no configuration required from the users.

> **Note**
>
> At the time of writing, the Central India region does not have a paired region for ASA. The availability zones provide zonal resiliency within a region, ensuring high availability. For disaster recovery, you need to set up regional resiliency by deploying resources across multiple regions. Combining both approaches ensures both local and global resilience for your service. You can learn more about availability zones and interruption handling in ASA at `https://packt.link/EV6Ow`.

By now, you have a sound knowledge of handling interruptions, which has highlighted the importance of addressing potential interruptions to stream processing, such as network connectivity issues or service upgrades. Azure availability zones are introduced as a solution, providing physically isolated locations within Azure regions to enhance fault tolerance. Both Event Hubs and ASA support availability zones, automatically replicating metadata and events across all locations within the zone.

Additionally, the section emphasized building retry logic into applications to handle transient errors, particularly with **Event Hubs SDKs** already integrating this functionality. Finally, it suggested optimizing availability by sending events without specifying a partition, allowing Event Hubs to distribute events across partitions for improved fault tolerance.

Next, look at how you can design and configure exception handling.

# Configure Exception Handling

Event Hubs' exceptions provide very clear information regarding the reason for errors. All Event Hub issues throw an `EventHubsException` exception object. The `EventHubsException` exception object, `IsTransient`, indicates the actual reason for the exception and whether the exceptions can be retried.

> **Note**
>
> This section primarily focuses on the **Configure exception handling** concept of the DP-203: Data Engineering on Microsoft Azure exam.

Some examples include timeouts, exceeding quota limits, exceeding message sizes, and client connection disconnects. The following is a simple example of how you can catch exceptions in .NET:

```
try
{
    // Process Events
}
catch (EventHubsException ex) where
(ex.Reason == EventHubsException.FailureReason.MessageSizeExceeded)
{
    // Take action for the oversize messages
}
```

The preceding code demonstrates how to catch and handle a specific type of exception (`EventHubsException` with the reason of `messagesizeexceeded`) that may occur during event processing in an **Azure Event Hubs** application.

> **Note**
>
> You can learn more about exception handling at `https://packt.link/H4XMc`.

The next section deals with upserting data using Synapse Analytics.

# Upserting Data

Upserting refers to the INSERT or UPDATE activity in a database or any analytical data store that supports it. You have already learned about UPSERT as part of the batch activity, in the *Upserting Data* section of *Chapter 5, Developing a Batch Processing Solution*.

> **Note**
>
> This section primarily focuses on the **Upsert data** concept of the DP-203: Data Engineering on Microsoft Azure exam.

ASA supports UPSERT with Cosmos DB, which is a fully managed, globally distributed No-SQL database. ASA has two different behaviors based on the compatibility level that is set. ASA supports three different compatibility levels. You can think of compatibility levels as API versions. As and when the ASA evolved, the compatibility levels increased—1.0 is the first compatibility version, and 1.2 is the latest compatibility version. The main change in version 1.2 is the support for the **AMQP**. You can set the compatibility level, as shown in *Figure 6.36*.

To find the ASA jobs you created in *Figure 6.8*, navigate to the Azure home page, search for **Stream Analytics jobs**, and select your ASA job. In this case, it is SampleASAJob (*Figure 6.36*):

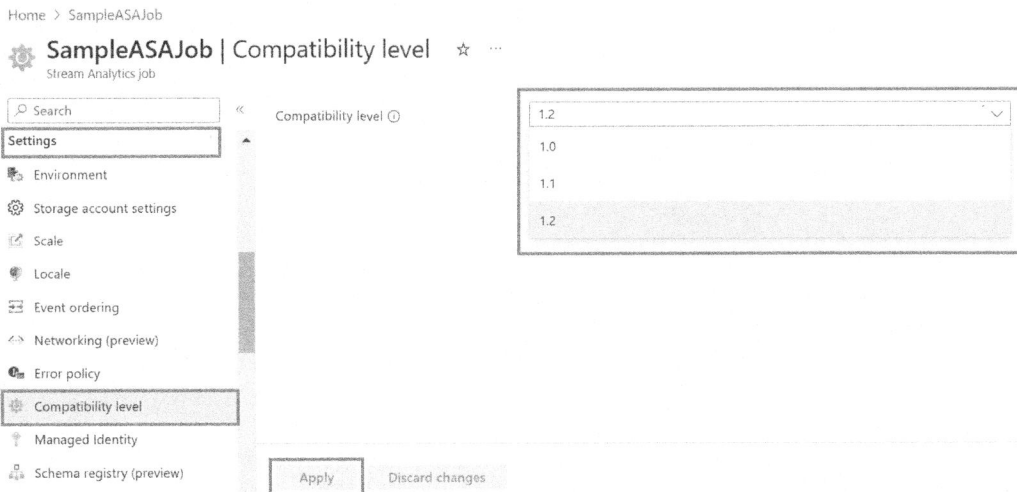

Figure 6.36 – Updating the compatibility level in ASA to insert or update within a document

With the compatibility levels of 1.0 and 1.1, ASA does a property level INSERT or UPDATE operation within the document. It enables partial updates to the document as a PATCH operation.

With a compatibility level of 1.2 onward, ASA does an INSERT or UPDATE document operation. First, ASA does an INSERT operation. If that operation fails due to a document ID conflict, then it does an UPDATE operation. Upserts work in Cosmos DB when the document ID is set. If it has not been set, the update scenarios will throw an error.

> **Note**
>
> You can learn more about ASA and Cosmos DB upserts at https://packt.link/wAsZy.

The next section will talk about replay archived stream data. When you receive new data streams, you often need to compare them with historical data to determine whether an event is an insert or an update. Read on to learn more about it.

## Replaying Archived Stream Data

Replaying archived stream data complements the upsert process. When you replay historical data, you're essentially processing events that occurred in the past. By analyzing archived data, you can identify changes, updates, and new records that need to be upserted into your system. This historical context helps maintain data integrity and consistency. Event Hubs stores up to seven days of data, which can be replayed using the Event Hub consumer client libraries.

The following is a simple Python example:

```
Consumer_client = EventHubConsumerClient.from_connection_string(
    conn_str=CONNECTION_STR,
    consumer_group=>$Default>,
    eventhub_name=EVENTHUB_NAME,
)
consumer_client.receive(
    on_event=on_event,
    partition_id=»0»,
    starting_position=»-1» # «-1» is the start of the partition.
)
```

The preceding code sets up a consumer_client to receive events from the 0 partition of the specified **Event Hub** (starting from the beginning of the partition) and specifies a callback function, on_event, to handle each received event. You can specify offsets or timestamps for the starting_position value.

> **Note**
>
> This section primarily focuses on the **Replay archived stream data** concept of the DP-203: Data Engineering on Microsoft Azure exam. You can learn more about the Python Event Hub APIs at https://packt.link/rKd10.

# Summary

That brings us to the end of this chapter. This is one of the most important chapters, both from a syllabus perspective and a data engineering perspective. Batch and streaming solutions are fundamental to building an effective Big Data processing system.

To summarize what you learned in this chapter, you started with designs for streaming systems using Event Hubs, ASA, and Spark Streaming and moved on to grasp time series data and the important concepts such as windowed aggregates, checkpointing, replaying archived data, handling schema drifts, scaling using partitions, and adding processing units. You then followed the exam Study Guide into a detour dedicated to the distinction between analytical processes and transactional processes and how you can optimize pipelines for each type of access, using Cosmos DB as a notable example. Finally, you returned to the topic of stream data and explored the upsert feature, and towards the end, learned about error handling and interruption handling.

You should now be comfortable with creating streaming solutions in Azure. As always, go through the follow-up links that have been provided to learn more and try the examples yourself to grasp the nitty-gritty details of these technologies. All example codes are provided on GitHub.

In the next chapter, you will learn how to manage batches and data pipelines in ADF or Azure Synapse and implement version control for pipeline artifacts.

# Exam Readiness Drill – Chapter Review Questions

Apart from a solid understanding of key concepts, being able to think quickly under time pressure is a skill that will help you ace your certification exam. That is why working on these skills early on in your learning journey is key.

Chapter review questions are designed to improve your test-taking skills progressively with each chapter you learn and review your understanding of key concepts in the chapter at the same time. You'll find these at the end of each chapter.

> **How to Access These Materials**
>
> To learn how to access these resources, head over to the chapter titled *Chapter 11, Accessing the Online Resources*.

To open the Chapter Review Questions for this chapter, perform the following steps:

1.  Click the link – `https://packt.link/DP203E2_CH06`.

    Alternatively, you can scan the following **QR code** (*Figure 6.37*):

Figure 6.37 – QR code that opens Chapter Review Questions for logged-in users

2.  Once you log in, you'll see a page similar to the one shown in *Figure 6.38*:

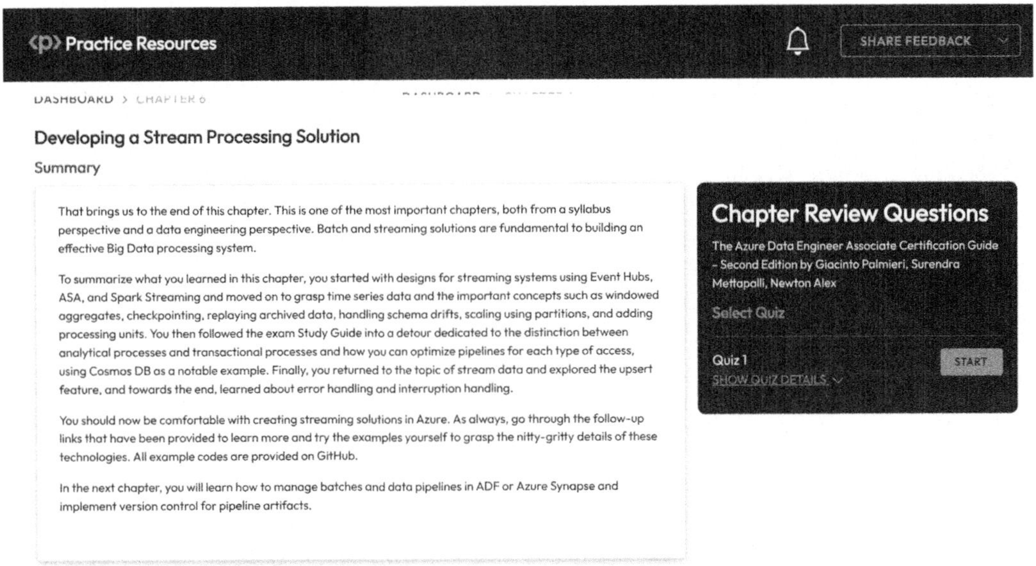

Figure 6.38 – Chapter Review Questions for Chapter 6

3.  Once ready, start the following practice drills, re-attempting the quiz multiple times.

## Exam Readiness Drill

For the first three attempts, don't worry about the time limit.

### *ATTEMPT 1*

The first time, aim for at least **40%**. Look at the answers you got wrong and read the relevant sections in the chapter again to fix your learning gaps.

### *ATTEMPT 2*

The second time, aim for at least **60%**. Look at the answers you got wrong and read the relevant sections in the chapter again to fix any remaining learning gaps.

*ATTEMPT 3*

The third time, aim for at least **75%**. Once you score 75% or more, you start working on your timing.

> Tip
>
> You may take more than **three** attempts to reach 75%. That's okay. Just review the relevant sections in the chapter till you get there.

## Working On Timing

**Target**: Your aim is to keep the score the same while trying to answer these questions as quickly as possible. Here's an example of how your next attempts should look like:

| Attempt | Score | Time Taken |
|---------|-------|-----------------------|
| Attempt 5 | 77% | 21 mins 30 seconds |
| Attempt 6 | 78% | 18 mins 34 seconds |
| Attempt 7 | 76% | 14 mins 44 seconds |

Table 6.2 – Sample timing practice drills on the online platform

> Note
>
> The time limits shown in the above table are just examples. Set your own time limits with each attempt based on the time limit of the quiz on the website.

With each new attempt, your score should stay above **75%** while your "time taken" to complete should "decrease". Repeat as many attempts as you want till you feel confident dealing with the time pressure.

# 7

# Managing Batches and Pipelines

In *Chapter 6, Developing a Stream Processing Solution*, you grasped the foundational elements of building effective Big Data processing systems with an emphasis on the importance of both batch and streaming solutions in the realm of data engineering. You explored the design principles of streaming systems, utilizing Azure services such as Event Hubs, **Azure Stream Analytics** (**ASA**), and Spark Streaming, and handled time series data, including concepts such as windowed aggregates, checkpointing, and schema drifts.

In this chapter, you will be focusing on four broad categories: triggering batch jobs, handling failures in batch jobs, managing pipelines, and configuring version control for pipelines. Once you complete this chapter, you should be able to comfortably set up and manage batch pipelines using **Azure Data Factory** (**ADF**) or Synapse pipelines.

> **Note**
>
> This chapter primarily focuses on the **Manage batches and pipelines** topic of the DP-203: Data Engineering on Microsoft Azure exam.

By the end of this chapter, you will be able to answer questions on the following confidently:

- Trigger batches
- Batch loads
- Data pipelines in Data Factory or Synapse pipelines
- Version control for pipeline artifacts
- Spark jobs in a pipeline

# Technical Requirements

For this chapter, you will need an Azure account (free or paid), an active Synapse workspace, and an active ADF workspace.

# Trigger Batches

By their nature, **batch processes** run when specific conditions occur; they do not run continuously. Specifying these conditions can also be described as defining a **trigger** for these processes. There are two types of triggers and they are as follows:

- **Schedule triggers**: Here, the conditions are the occurrence of a specific date or time.

- **Event trigger**: Here, the condition is the occurrence of something specific, such as the creation of a new Blob on a storage account.

> **Note**
>
> It is also common to use the term "triggers" to refer to event triggers, while "schedules" refers to schedule triggers.

You will explore schedule triggers in the *Scheduling Data Pipelines in ADF or Synapse Pipelines* section later. You will simply focus on event triggers for now.

> **Note**
>
> This section primarily focuses on the **Trigger batches** concept of the DP-203: Data Engineering on Microsoft Azure exam.

Many services in Azure allow the specification of event triggers for the execution of batch activities, including **Azure Functions** and **Logic Apps**. Batch data processes, however, are usually run as part of an **ADF** or a **Synapse pipeline**. ADF and Synapse pipeline services support three types of event triggers, the first of which is the **Tumbling Window**.

With a trigger of this type, a pipeline will be executed at periodic intervals while maintaining its state; that is, the trigger recognizes which window of data was processed last and restarts from there. You will now create a "new trigger" with the essential options for configuring triggers within ADF or Synapse Analytics pipelines. Perform the following steps to do so:

1. Type a descriptive name for the trigger in the **Name** field. In this case, it is `tr_tumbling_window`.

2. Add additional context or notes about the trigger in the **Description** field. In this case, you can type `Trigger scheduled is set to run every 15 minutes`.

3. Choose the **Type** of trigger from the drop-down list. In this example, `Tumbling window` is selected.

4. Set the initial activation point for your trigger in the **Start Date (UTC)** field. In this case, it is `4/1/2024, 12:00:00 AM`. This field indicates the date and time when the trigger begins operating.

5. With the **Recurrence** option, specify how often the trigger occurs. In this case, it is set to `Every 15 Minute(s)`.

6. Choose the **Specify an end date** option to define a specific date and time in the **End On (UTC)** field when the trigger should stop operating. In this case, it is `12/31/2024, 11:59:59 PM`. *Figure 7.1* shows the options that can be specified for this type of trigger:

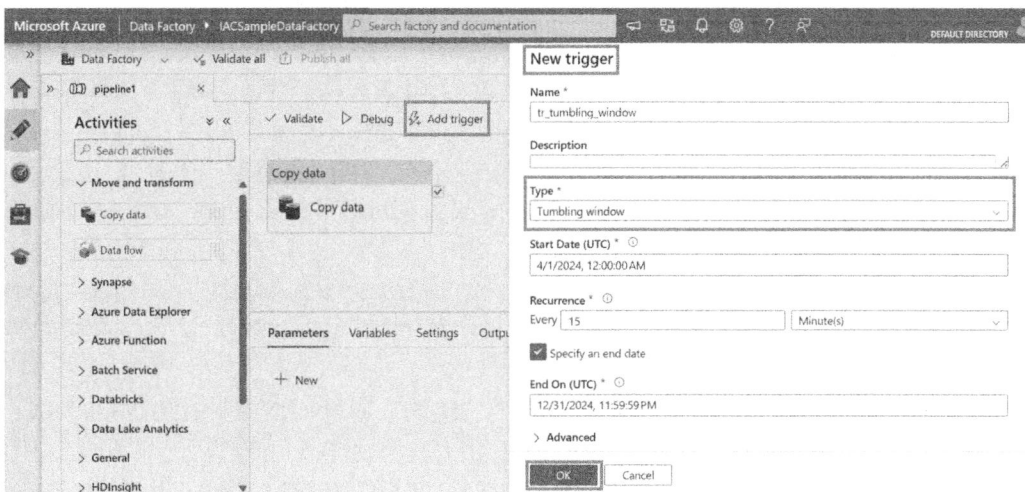

Figure 7.1 – Defining a Tumbling Window trigger for a pipeline

7.  In the **Advanced** options, set the **Delay** option to `00:00:00`.

    The **Delay** option allows you to introduce a delay before the trigger executes.

8.  Specify the maximum number of concurrent trigger executions allowed with the **Max Concurrency** option. In this case, it is `50`.

9.  Set the **Retry Policy Count** option for how many times the trigger will retry if it fails. In this case, it is `0`.

10. Set the time interval between retry attempts in the **Retry Policy Interval (in seconds)** option. In this case, it is `30`.

11. Finally, select the **Start trigger** checkbox and select `OK` to start the trigger after its creation.

    With these steps, you created a new trigger in ADF or Synapse Analytics pipelines.

A second type of Event trigger is based on Storage Events. In this case, the pipeline will be executed when a Blob is created or deleted in a storage account, including instances within **Data Lake Gen2**. The options specify the container name and apply filters to the path contents. Additionally, you can choose between triggering the pipeline upon creation or deletion actions. You will now create a new trigger with the essential options for configuring **Storage Event** triggers within ADF or Synapse. Perform the following steps to do so:

1.  Type a descriptive name for the trigger in the **Name** option. In this case, it is `tr_storage_events`.

2.  Add additional context or notes about the trigger in the **Description** box for documentation. In this case, you can type `Trigger executed when a blob created or deleted`.

3.  Choose the **Type** of trigger from the drop-down list. In this case, choose `Storage events`. This means the trigger will respond to events related to Azure Storage.

4.  Choose the **Account selection method** from two options. In this case, it is `From Azure subscription`.

5.  On selecting an Azure subscription, a dropdown displays the available subscriptions for you to select your specific subscription to filter the storage accounts. Select the name of the subscription. In this example, it is `Azure subscription`.

6.  Select the storage account associated with this trigger in the **Storage account name** option. In this case, it is `synapseazdl`.

7.  Type the **Container name** within your storage where events are monitored. In this case, it is set as `raw`.

8.  The **Blob path begins with** and **Blob path ends with** options are used to define prefixes and suffixes for blobs to filter which ones activate this trigger. In this case, blobs starting with `2024` and ending in `.csv` would trigger this event.

9.  Choose the "type" of **Event** as `Blob created` (*Figure 7.2*):

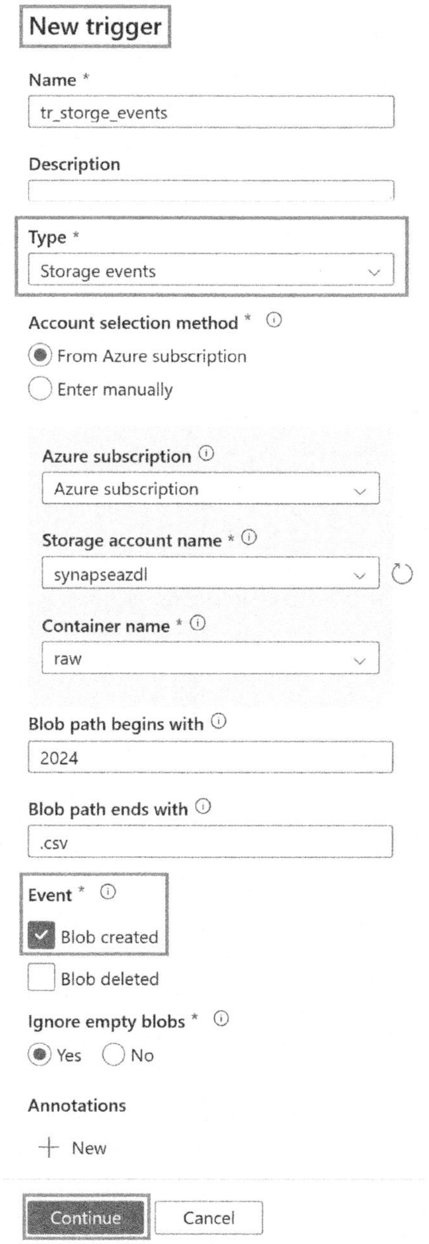

Figure 7.2 – Defining a Storage Event trigger for a pipeline

While the **Blob created** trigger activates when a new Blob that matches the specified criteria is created, the **Blob deleted** trigger activates upon deletion of a Blob matching specified criteria.

10. Finally, select the **Start trigger** checkbox and select Continue to start the trigger after its creation.

A further type is triggers based on custom events. In this case, the pipeline is triggered by events received via **Azure Event Grid**, which is a service that allows the distribution of events defined by users by means of topics and potentially sent by a wide variety of services.

This capability allows the integration of services in a way that is both "agnostic" (in the sense that producers of events do not need to know that services will consume them) and "asynchronous," in that the producers will not need to wait for consumers to finish, nor the other way round.

This makes this type of service ideal for implementing a type of architecture often described as **microservices architecture**. Rather than building a single, all-encompassing monolithic system, the microservices architecture advocates for the integration of several smaller services, each dedicated to fulfilling specific purposes.

To discriminate between events within the same topic, the schema of **Event Grid events** specifies a subject, which can be included in the definition of a trigger.

Now, create a new trigger with the essential options for configuring **custom event** triggers within ADF or Synapse. Perform the following steps to do so:

1. Type a descriptive name for the trigger under the **Name** field. In this case, it is tr_custom_ event.

2. Add additional context or notes about the trigger in the **Description** field for documentation. In this case, it is Custom Event Trigger.

3. Choose the **Type** of trigger from the drop-down list. In this example, it is Custom events. This means the trigger responds dynamically to changes or events happening in your data source or external systems.

4. Choose the **Account selection method** from the two options. In this case, choose From Azure subscription.

5. From the drop-down menu, select the **Azure subscription**—in this case, Azure subscription.

6. The dropdown displays the available subscriptions so you can select your specific subscription to filter the Azure Event Grid topic names. Select the event grid topic name associated with this trigger under the **Event grid topic name** option. In this case, it is customEventDemo.

7. **Subject filters** allow you to filter based on **Subject begins with** or **Subject ends with** specific characters or words. Type factories under the **Subject begins with** option.

8. Click New to add new **event types**.

9. Choose one event type to activate this trigger. In this case, you can add CopyCompleted and CopySucceeded (*Figure 7.3*):

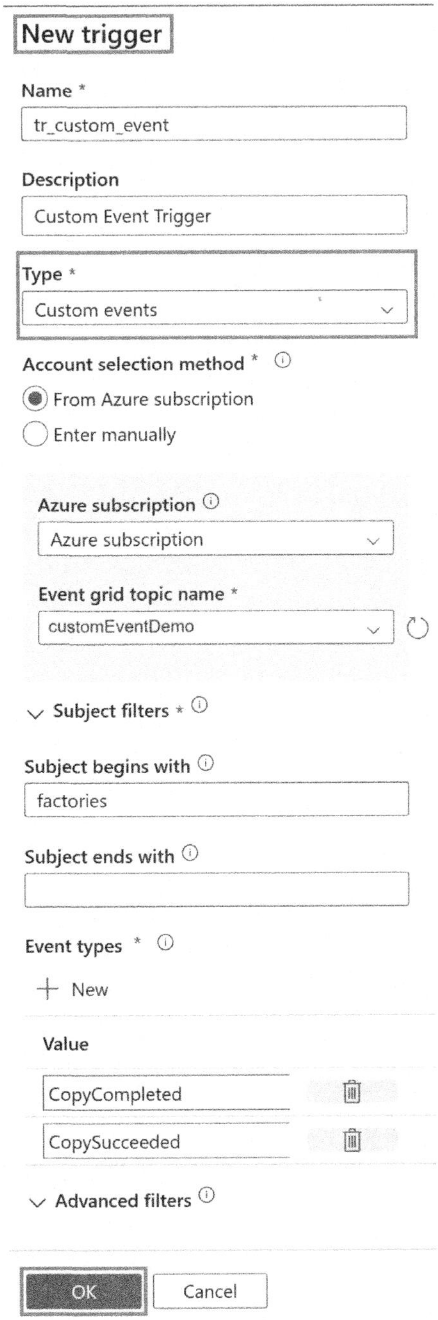

Figure 7.3 – Defining a custom Event trigger for a pipeline

10. Finally, select the **Start trigger** checkbox and select OK to start the trigger after its creation.

This section highlighted trigger batches, which are pivotal mechanisms that operate on an event-driven basis, automating various data processing tasks. They come into play in response to specific events such as file uploads or database alterations, serving as initiators for data pipelines or workflows. What's fascinating is the level of customization they offer, allowing you to tailor trigger conditions to exact specifications, thereby optimizing efficiency and reliability within data processing workflows. Next, you will learn how to handle failed batch process executions.

## Handling Failed Batch Loads

In data process management, two key strategies emerge: **Reverting data to previous state** and **Configuring exception handling**. While databases offer roll-back features for stability, ADF does not have built-in support for this. Instead, ADF focuses on consistency checks and fault tolerance settings to ensure data integrity.

For exception handling, connecting activities based on "success," "failure," "completion," or "skip" outcomes provides control. Failed actions trigger fallback plans or alerts, ensuring pipeline continuity. Knowing about these mechanisms empowers smoother data workflows in both development and operational scenarios.

> **Note**
>
> This section primarily focuses on the **Handle failed batch loads** concept of the DP-203: Data Engineering on Microsoft Azure exam. The topic of what to do when batch data workloads fail has already been covered in *Chapter 5, Developing a Batch Processing Solution*, specifically in the *Reverting Data to a Previous State* and *Configuring Exception Handling* sections. As the topic has already been addressed previously, it is summarized here briefly. The next section will delve into batch loads.

## Validating Batch Loads

**Validating batch loads** is essential for maintaining data integrity and accuracy throughout the loading process. You are responsible for loading batches of data into your system to ensure data integrity and accuracy. Validating these batches is key and means checking that the data meets expected formats, follows standards, and aligns with business rules. But it doesn't stop there—you also need to handle any errors, anomalies, or missing values that crop up.

Techniques such as data profiling and cleansing come into play, alongside defining validation rules. It is also crucial to keep a close eye on everything through logging and monitoring. Validating your batches thoroughly ensures smooth operations for reliable analytics and reporting downstream.

> **Note**
>
> This section primarily focuses on the **Validate batch loads** concept of the DP-203: Data Engineering on Microsoft Azure exam.

ADF provides functionalities for validating the outcome of jobs. Think of a scenario where you are handling daily sales data for a retail company and validating incoming data before loading it into data warehouses for further processing. In that case, you would dive into data profiling to find data characteristics, utilize data cleansing to address anomalies, define validation rules tailored to sales data, and set up logging and monitoring for auditing and troubleshooting.

Perform the following steps to use the **Validation activity** in ADF to check the correctness of batch loads:

1.  Use the `Validation activity` of ADF to check for a file's existence before proceeding with the rest of the activities in the pipeline.

    The validation pipeline will look similar to *Figure 7.4*:

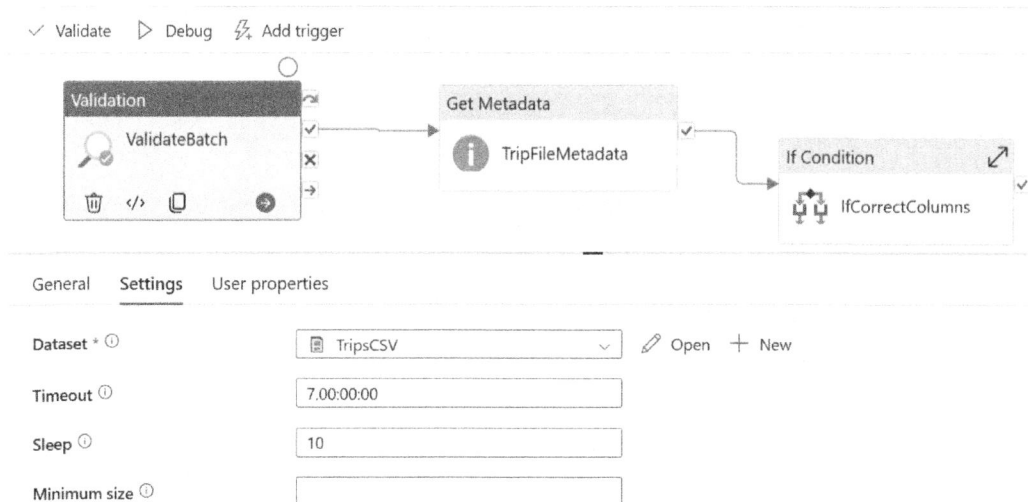

Figure 7.4 – Using the ADF Validation activity to check for a file's existence

2.  Once you have verified that the file exists, use the `Get Metadata` activity to get more information about the output file (*Figure 7.5*).

    This collects metadata such as file properties (whether it exists, column count, size, last modified timestamp, etc.), column names and data types, and schema details (field delimiter and encoding).

    The output displayed in the **Column count** and **Exists** fields helps to decide whether the number of columns matches the expected count of columns and checks the existence of files.

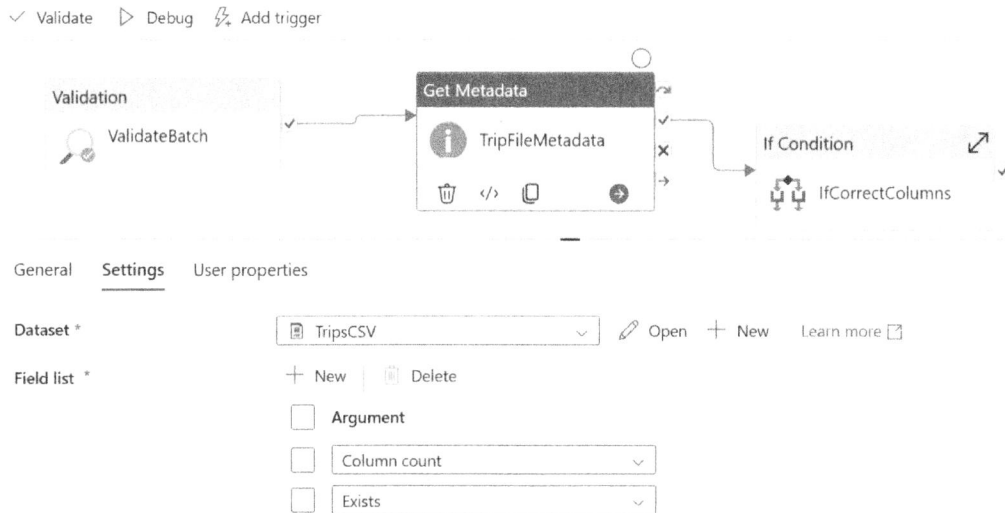

Figure 7.5 – Configuring the Get Metadata activity to publish the column count

3.  Use the `If Condition` activity to decide whether you want to continue processing the pipeline based on the metadata from the previous stage.

    For example, you can use the `If Condition` activity to check whether certain conditions are met before proceeding with further processing in the pipeline. If the condition evaluates to `true`, the pipeline continues with one set of activities; if it evaluates to `false`, it can proceed with another set of activities or take alternative actions.

    Overall, the `If Condition` activity adds flexibility and control to your data workflows in ADF by allowing conditional branching based on metadata or other criteria.

4.  Use the following condition beside the **Expression** field to check whether the number of columns is equal to the expected column count. In this example, 5 columns are expected (*Figure 7.6*):

    ```
    @equals(activity('TripFileMetadata').output.columnCount, 5)
    ```

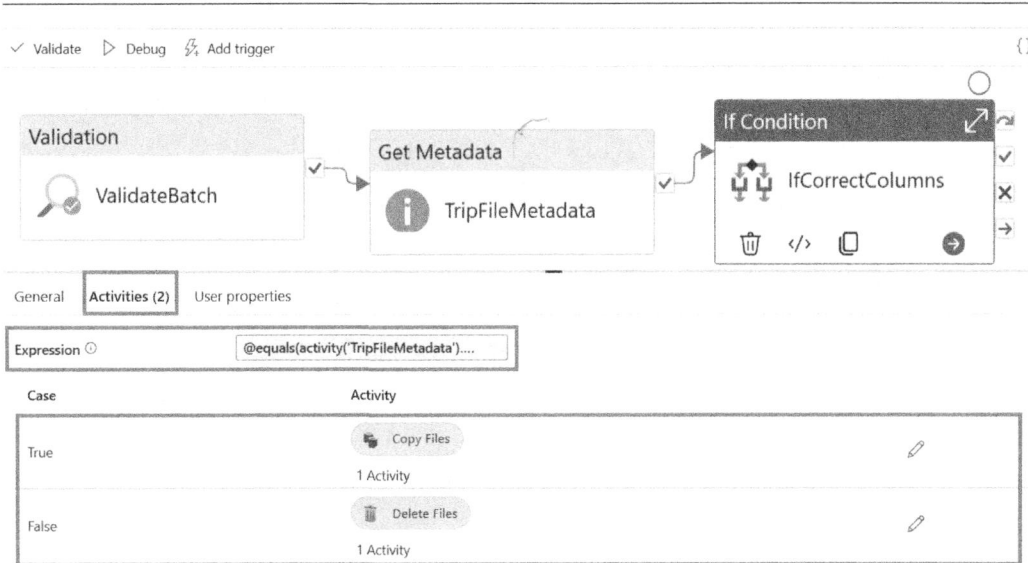

Figure 7.6 – Using the metadata from the Get Metadata activity to make a decision

You can perform similar validation checks using a combination of **ADF activities** for batch and other technologies.

You have now learned how ADF offers data validation for batch loads through its **Validation** activity. The next section will demonstrate how to manage data pipelines in ADF or Synapse.

# Managing Data Pipelines in ADF or Synapse

Effective management of data pipelines is integral to streamlined data processing in the dynamic field of data engineering, whether utilizing ADF or Azure Synapse pipelines. This encompasses various facets, including pipeline orchestration to design, create, and orchestrate pipelines efficiently, data movement techniques for seamless transfer across diverse sources and destinations, and transformation logic for handling activities such as cleaning, aggregating, enriching, and shaping data. While robust monitoring, logging, and error-handling practices are crucial for effective monitoring and troubleshooting, adherence to stringent security standards and compliance requirements ensures data integrity and regulatory compliance, whether navigating Big Data challenges, managing real-time event streams, or orchestrating batch processing.

ADF and Synapse pipelines provide two tabs or hubs called **Manage** and **Monitor** that can help you manage and monitor pipelines, respectively.

> **Note**
>
> This section primarily focuses on the **Manage data pipelines in Azure Data Factory or Azure Synapse Pipelines** concept of the DP-203: Data Engineering on Microsoft Azure exam.

In the **Manage** tab (of the **Settings** menu), you can add, edit, and delete `Linked services`, `Integration runtimes`, `Triggers`, `Git configuration`, and more, as shown in *Figure 7.7*:

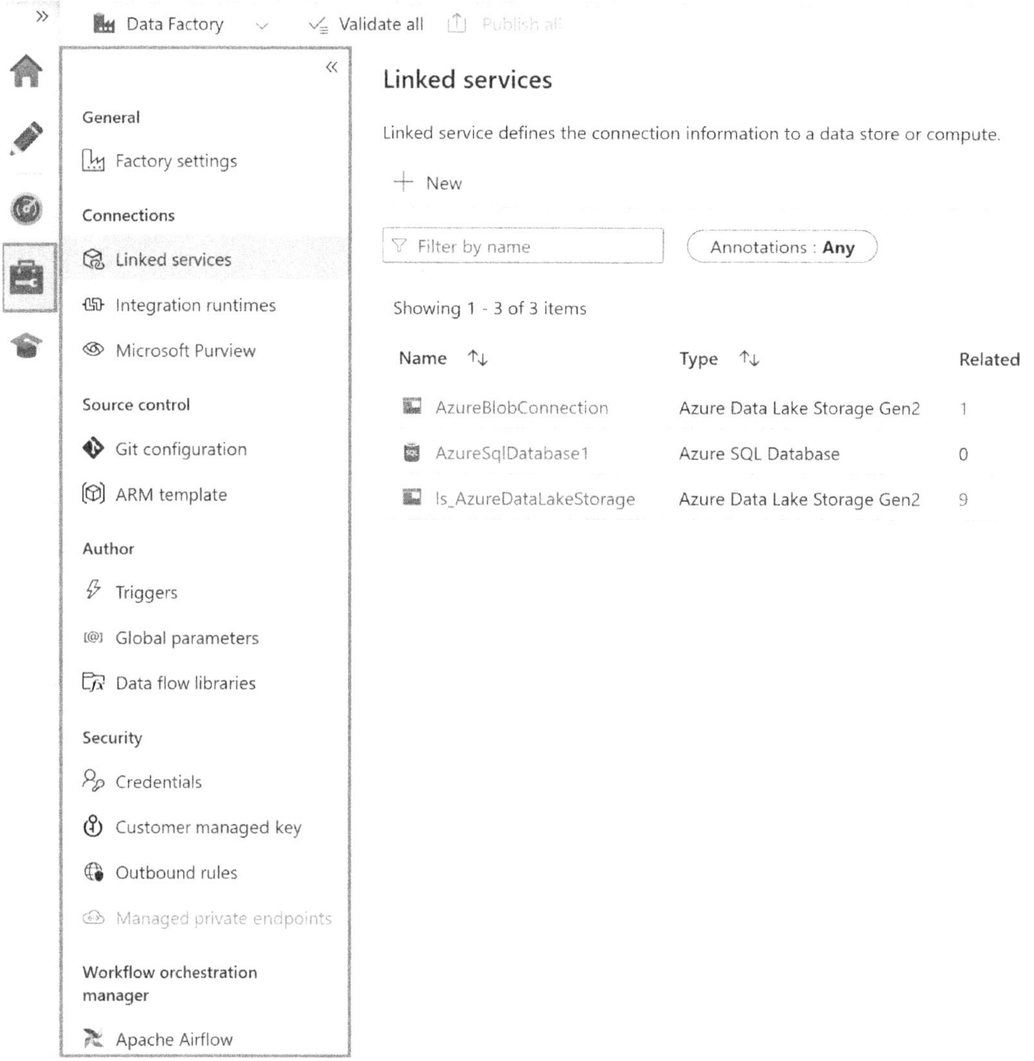

Figure 7.7 – The Manage screen of ADF showing the settings
menu options to manage various components

Now, you will learn how to add and delete a **Linked service** in ADF:

- **Adding a linked service**: This involves accessing the `Settings` menu, selecting the desired connector, configuring the service details, such as connection strings and authentication, and finally testing and creating the new linked service.

- **Deleting a linked service**: This is a straightforward process of accessing the `Linked services` section, locating the service to be removed, and confirming its deletion. These actions streamline data connectivity and maintenance within your Data Factory environment.

You have already learned about linked services, throughout this book. So, in the next section, you'll explore the topic of **Integration Runtimes (IRs)** in ADF and Synapse pipelines and the monitoring options. Synapse pipelines also provide similar **Manage** and **Monitor** screens.

## Integration Runtimes (IRs)

An IR refers to the compute infrastructure that is used by ADF and Synapse pipelines to run data pipelines and data flows. These are the actual machines or **Virtual Machines (VMs)** that run the job behind the scenes.

The IR takes care of running data flows, copying data across public and private networks, dispatching activities to services such as Azure HDInsight and **Azure Databricks (ADB)**, and executing **SQL Server Integration Services (SSIS)**.

You can create IRs from the **Manage** tab (the toolkit icon) of ADF and Synapse pipelines by clicking on the + New button, as shown in *Figure 7.8*:

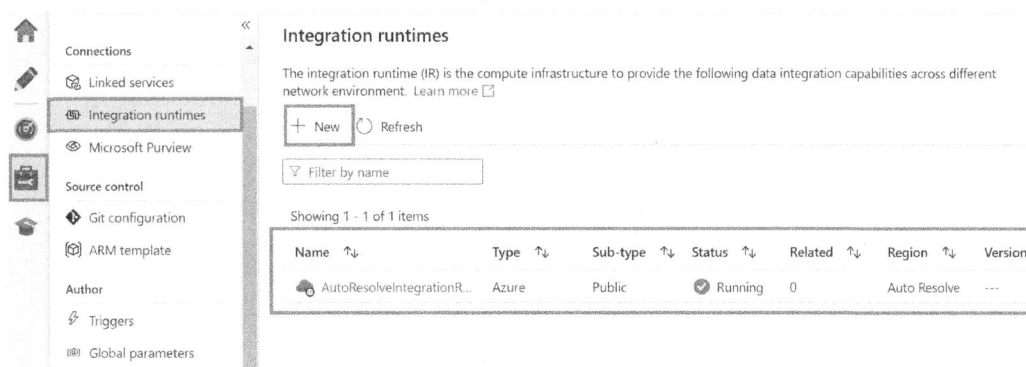

Figure 7.8 – Creating a new IR to run data pipelines and data flows

ADF and Synapse Analytics provide support for three types of IRs:

- **Azure IR**: This is the default option and allows for the connection of data stores and compute services across public endpoints. Use this option to copy data between Azure-hosted services. **Azure IR** also supports connecting data stores using private links.

- **Self-Hosted IR**: Use this option when you need to copy data between on-premises clusters and Azure services. You will need machines or VMs on the on-premises private network to install a self-hosted IR.

- **Azure—SSIS IR**: The SSIS IRs are used for SSIS lift and shift use cases.

> **Note**
>
> You can learn more about IRs at `https://packt.link/x9lKu`.

Next, you'll look at the monitoring options in ADF.

## Monitoring in ADF and Synapse Analytics

Pipelines can be triggered manually or automatically (using triggers). Once they're triggered, you can monitor the pipelines for their execution status, progress, and any errors or warnings that may occur during their execution from the **Monitor** tab within ADF and Synapse workspace, as shown in *Figure 7.9*:

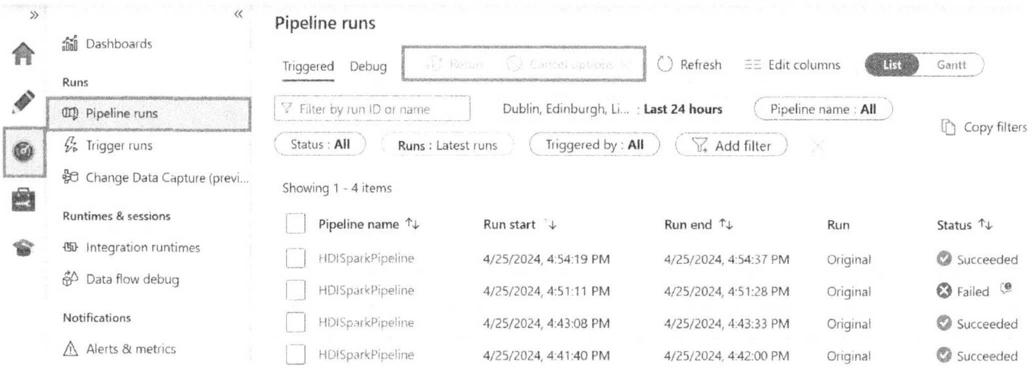

Figure 7.9 – Monitoring ADF pipelines

You can stop any in-progress runs by clicking `Cancel` and rerun any failed pipelines by clicking `Rerun` from the **Monitor** tab. Additionally, you can click on each of those runs to look at the details of each flow, as shown in *Figure 7.10*:

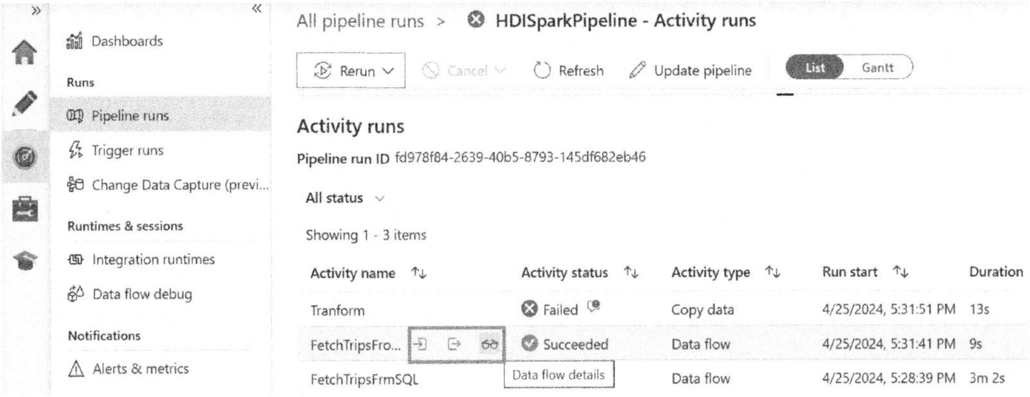

Figure 7.10 – Activity runs tab showing the Data flow details

Click on the spectacles icon for statistics about the run, such as how many stages there were, how many lines were processed, and how long each stage took.

In the previous section, you learned that effective management of data pipelines in data engineering, using tools such as ADF and Azure Synapse pipelines, is key to data engineering efficiency, as it encompasses designing pipelines (orchestration), transferring data seamlessly, and cleaning, shaping, and enriching the data (transformations). You also learned that robust monitoring, logging, and error-handling practices are essential for effective troubleshooting, while adherence to security standards and compliance ensures data integrity and regulatory adherence amid Big Data challenges, real-time event streams, or batch processing. IR serves as the compute infrastructure supporting data flow execution, data copying, and service dispatching across Azure services and on-premises clusters.

The next section will focus on how you can schedule an ADF and Synapse pipeline.

# Scheduling Data Pipelines in ADF or Synapse

**Scheduling pipelines** refers to the process of defining when and how a pipeline needs to be started. The process is the same for ADF and Synapse pipelines. ADF and Azure Synapse pipelines offer robust scheduling capabilities, crucial for automating and orchestrating data workflows. By defining schedules, pipelines execute at specific intervals or times, guaranteeing timely data processing and seamless integration tasks.

> **Note**
>
> This section primarily focuses on the **Schedule data pipelines in Data Factory or Azure Synapse pipelines** concept of the DP-203: Data Engineering on Microsoft Azure exam.

In order to schedule pipelines, ADF and Synapse pipelines have a button named **Add trigger** in the **Pipelines** (*Figure 7.11*):

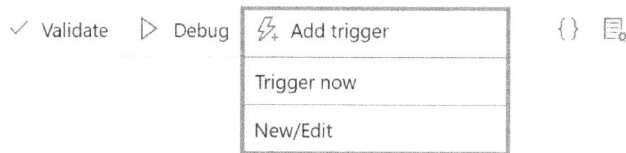

Figure 7.11 – Adding a trigger from ADF/Synapse pipelines

On clicking the `Add Trigger` button, a screen like the one shown in *Figure 7.12* shows the details that are required to configure a schedule trigger. Now, you can create a "new trigger" with the essential options, shown in *Figure 7.12*, for configuring schedule triggers within ADF or Synapse.

Perform the following steps to do so:

1. Provide a descriptive name for the trigger in the **Name** field. In this case, it is `trigger1`.

2. Add additional context or notes about the trigger in the **Description** field. In this case, it is not mandatory, so it has been left blank.

3. Choose the **Type** of trigger from the drop-down list. In this example, it is `Schedule`.

   This means the trigger will execute based on a predefined schedule.

4. Select the **Start date** to set the date and time when the trigger should start. The trigger will begin executing based on this specified start date.

5. Specify the **Time zone** for the trigger. Some time zones observe daylight saving, so select `Coordinated Universal Time (UTC)` to disregard auto adjustment.

6.  Select the **Recurrence** type, which determines how often the trigger occurs. In this example, it is set to execute `Every 15 Minute(s)`.

    The **Specify an end date** checkbox enables you to set an end date for the trigger. If checked, the trigger will stop executing after the specified end date. In this case, it is not selected.

7.  You can add **Annotations** by clicking the `+ New` button for additional notes or tags related to the trigger.

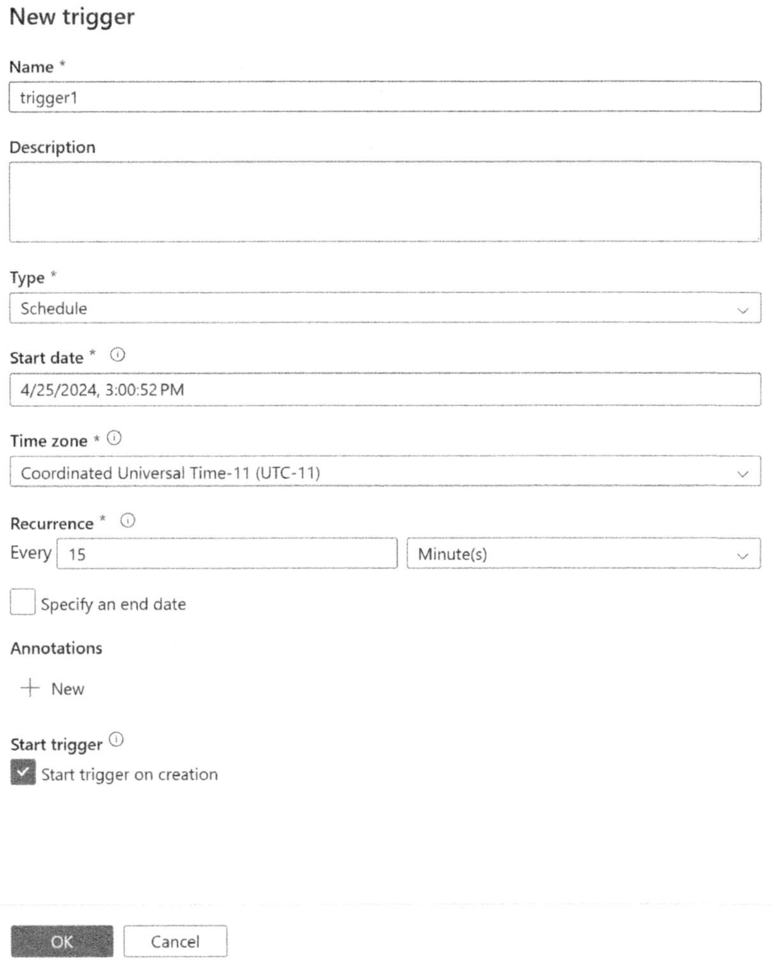

New trigger

Name *

| trigger1 |

Description

| |

Type *

| Schedule ⌄ |

Start date * ⓘ

| 4/25/2024, 3:00:52 PM |

Time zone * ⓘ

| Coordinated Universal Time-11 (UTC-11) ⌄ |

Recurrence * ⓘ

Every | 15 | | Minute(s) ⌄ |

☐ Specify an end date

Annotations

+ New

Start trigger ⓘ

☑ Start trigger on creation

OK    Cancel

Figure 7.12 – Defining the trigger in ADF or Synapse pipelines

8.  Finally, select the `Start trigger` checkbox and select `OK` to start the trigger as soon as it is created.

Once the **Schedule trigger** has been set, you can see the pipelines being triggered automatically from the **Monitor** tab of ADF or Synapse pipelines.

> **Note**
>
> You can learn more about triggers and scheduling pipelines at `https://packt.link/ GwzZU`.

In this section, you have learned how to manage and monitor data pipelines in ADF and Synapse pipelines. In the next section, you will review version control for ADF and Synapse pipeline artifacts using Azure DevOps to monitor the history of changes, enabling collaboration to ensure reproducibility.

# Implementing Version Control for Pipeline Artifacts

By default, ADF and Synapse pipelines save pipeline details in their **internal stores**. These internal stores don't provide options for collaboration, version control, or any other benefits provided by source control systems. Every time you click on the **Publish All** button, your latest changes are saved within the service.

To overcome this shortcoming, both ADF and Synapse pipelines provide options to integrate with source control systems such as **Global Information Tracker (Git)**. The following sections will walk you through this and other methods to configure this version control for your pipeline artifacts.

> **Note**
>
> This section primarily focuses on the **Implement version control for pipeline artifacts** concept of the DP-203: Data Engineering on Microsoft Azure exam.

## Configuring Source Control in ADF

Before diving into the specifics of configuring source control in ADF, it's essential to know the critical role it plays in the development life cycle. **Source control** allows you and your teams to collaboratively manage and track changes to Data Factory artifacts, ensuring version control, traceability, and seamless collaboration across multiple developers. By integrating source control into ADF, teams can effectively manage code changes, track history, roll back to previous versions if needed, and maintain a standardized development process. Now, explore how to set up source control in ADF using **Set up code repository**.

ADF provides a **Set up code repository** button at the top of the home screen, as shown in *Figure 7.13*, to start the Git configuration process:

Figure 7.13 – Configuring the Git repository using the Set up code repository button

Alternatively, you can click the `Git configuration` option from the **Manage** tab, and then click the `Configure` option, as shown in *Figure 7.14*:

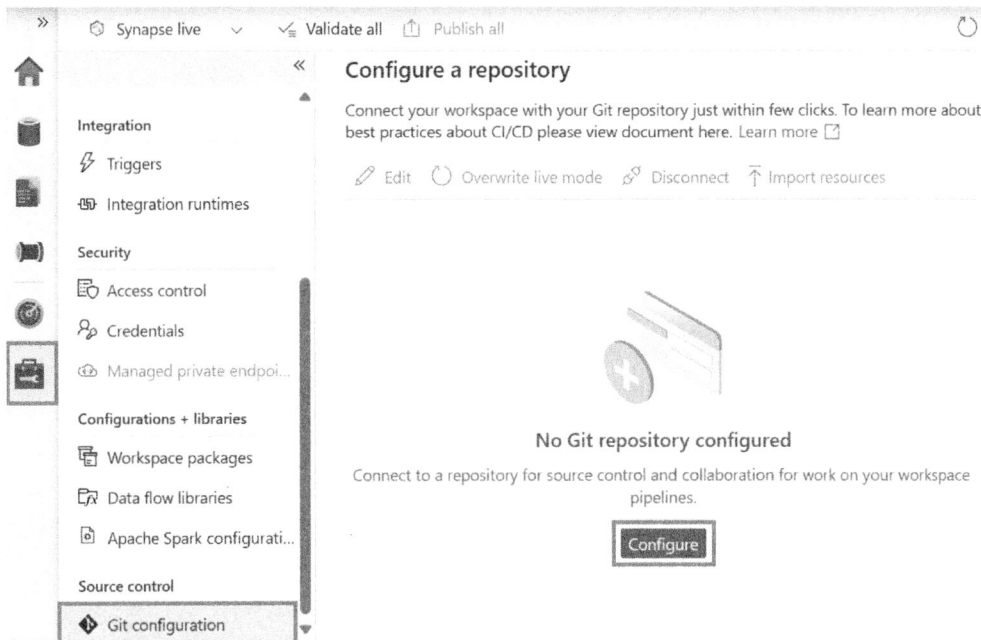

Figure 7.14 – Launching Git configuration from Synapse's Manage tab (the same in ADF)

This screenshot shows Synapse pipelines, but ADF also has a similar screen. Both ADF and Synapse pipelines support the **Azure DevOps** version of Git and external GitHub accounts. Read on to learn how to integrate both these source control systems into ADF and Synapse.

## Integrating with Azure DevOps

Azure DevOps is a full set of tools and services. It aims to help make your software development lifecycle simpler—from starting planning and coding to deep testing and smooth deployment. Azure DevOps gives all you require to manage projects effectively and efficiently. It offers robust version control with Git repositories, agile project management features, continuous integration and delivery pipelines, and extensive collaboration capabilities. With Azure DevOps, you can effectively plan, build, and deliver high-quality software products while fostering collaboration and innovation across the development life cycle. Now, it is time to learn how to configure **Azure DevOps** for seamless integration with your project.

Look at the configuration for Azure DevOps. To configure **Azure DevOps**, you need to first have an existing Azure DevOps account.

Perform the following steps to first create an Azure DevOps account and then save the changes to the Git repository:

1. Search for `Azure DevOps Organizations` from the **Azure portal**.

2. Click on the `My Azure DevOps Organizations` button on the **Azure DevOps** screen, as shown in *Figure 7.15*, to create an account:

Figure 7.15 – Creating a new DevOps organization for managing and organizing projects

> **Note**
> Alternatively, you could directly get started with Azure DevOps from `https://packt.link/bMNDv`.

Once you have created a new Azure DevOps organization, you can create new Git repositories under it.

3.   Go back to the **Azure Synapse Analytics Git Configuration** screen and click on the `Configure` button (*Figure 7.14*).

4.   Here, you will be able to choose between Azure DevOps and GitHub. For this example, choose `Azure DevOps Git`, shown in *Figure 7.16*:

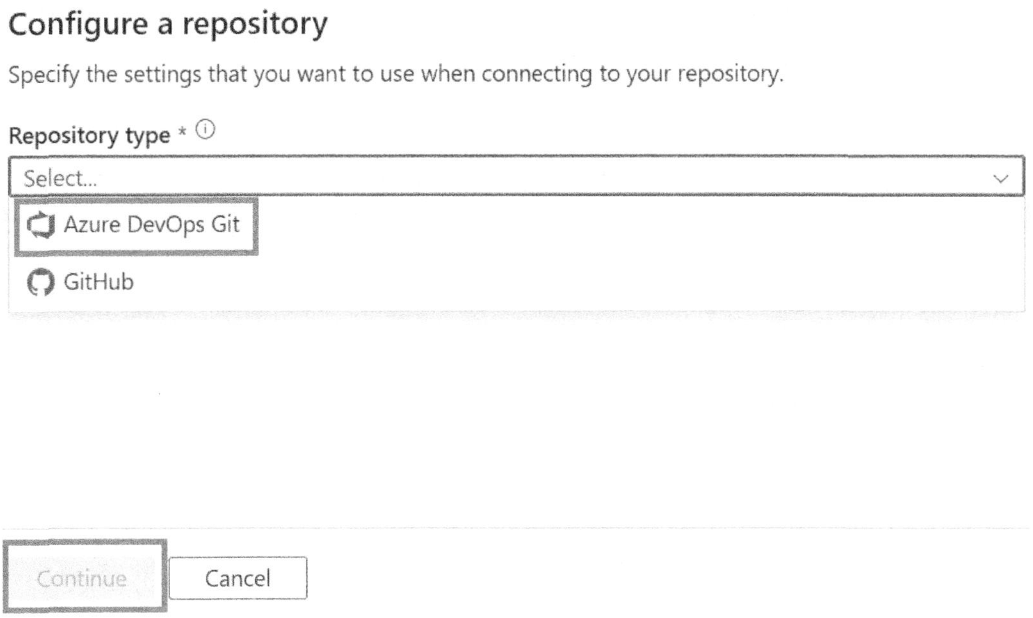

## Configure a repository

Specify the settings that you want to use when connecting to your repository.

**Repository type** * ⓘ

| Select... | ⌄ |
|---|---|

| 🗋 Azure DevOps Git |
|---|

| ⚪ GitHub |
|---|

| Continue | Cancel |
|---|---|

Figure 7.16 – Configuring a repository to select the Azure DevOps Git repository type

Once you select `Azure DevOps Git`, as shown in *Figure 7.16*, the **Configure a repository** screen (shown in *Figure 7.17*) gets displayed.

5.  Click the radio button beside `Select repository`.

    It allows you to choose a repository if you have an existing repository. Alternatively, you can select `Use repository link` and provide a repository link (e.g., a `GET URL`). Now, fill in the details beside the respective fields.

6.  Enter the **Azure DevOps organization name** to specify the organization where the repository resides, in this case, `DevOps`.

7.  From the **Project name** drop-down list, select the project associated with the repository—in this case, `ADF`.

8.  Select the type of **Repository name**, for example, `DEV`.

9.  Select the branch from the **Collaboration branch** dropdown. In this case, it is `main`.

    The collaboration branch determines the branch where your team members collaborate on code changes.

10. From the **Publish branch** dropdown, select the branch where you intend to publish your code changes, merge, or deploy. In this case, that will be `adf_publish`.

11. Input the root folder within the repository in the **Root folder** box. In this case, it is `/`, as shown in *Figure 7.17*:

    The root folder is the starting point for organizing files and folders. This forward slash (`/`) is a universal convention used to represent the root directory in filesystems and signifies the highest level of the directory hierarchy.

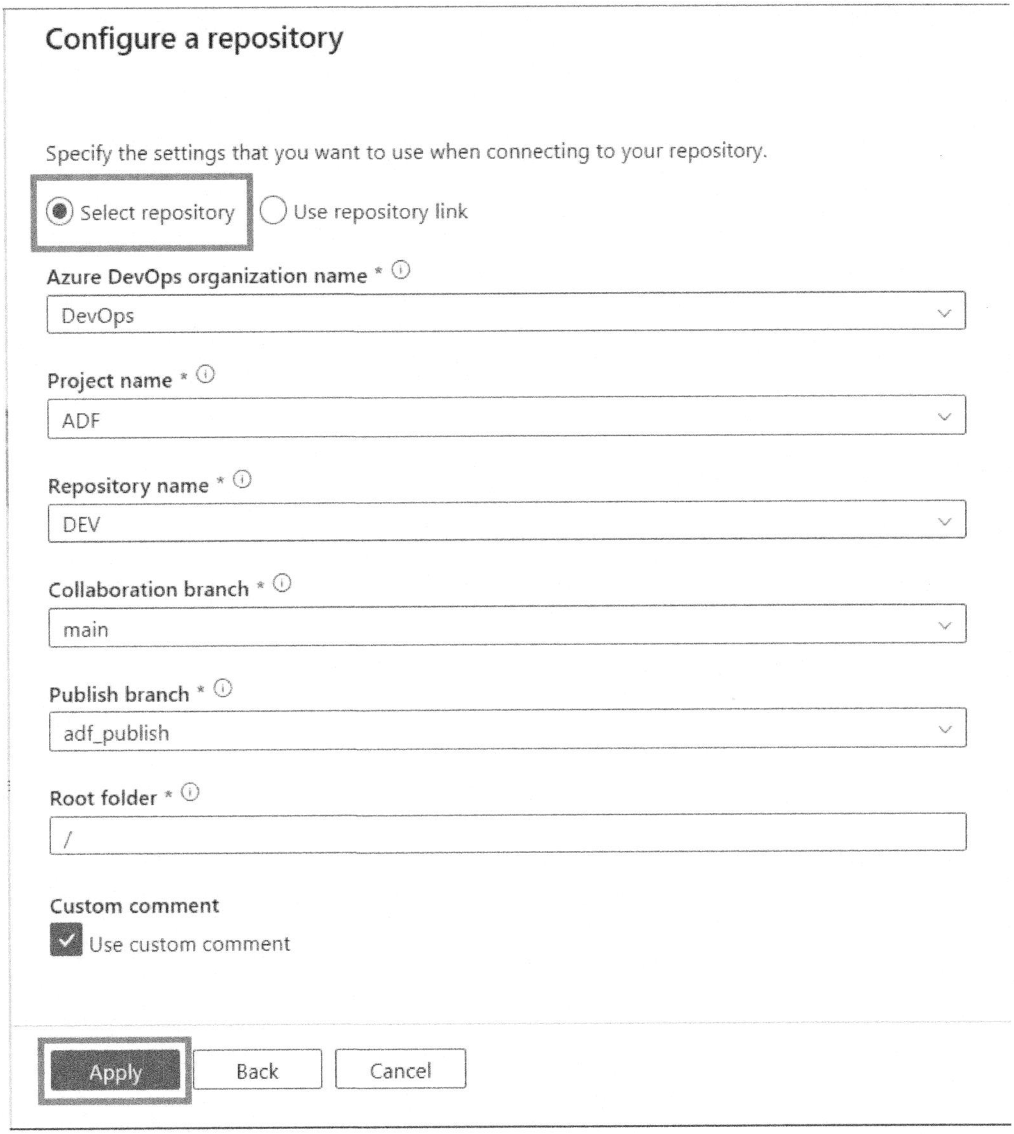

## Configure a repository

Specify the settings that you want to use when connecting to your repository.

( ● ) Select repository      ( ○ ) Use repository link

**Azure DevOps organization name** * ⓘ

| DevOps | ⌄ |

**Project name** * ⓘ

| ADF | ⌄ |

**Repository name** * ⓘ

| DEV | ⌄ |

**Collaboration branch** * ⓘ

| main | ⌄ |

**Publish branch** * ⓘ

| adf_publish | ⌄ |

**Root folder** * ⓘ

| / |

**Custom comment**

☑ Use custom comment

[ Apply ]      [ Back ]      [ Cancel ]

Figure 7.17 – Configuring Azure DevOps Git as the source control for ADF

12. Click the `Apply` button to configure the **Azure DevOps Git** repository.

   From now on, every time you click `Publish`, the changes made in your ADF instance will be committed and pushed to the configured Git repository in Azure DevOps.

Now, you have created an Azure DevOps account and saved the changes to the Git repository.

## Integrating with External GitHub

Integrating with external GitHub in ADF allows seamless collaboration and version control for your data engineering projects. By connecting your ADF instance to an external GitHub repository, you can leverage Git's robust version control features, streamline collaboration among team members, and maintain a centralized repository for managing ADF artifacts.

The configuration screen for GitHub is also very similar to DevOps configuration. On the **Configure a repository** screen (*Figure 7.18*), you can specify attributes. Perform the following steps to do so:

1. Select the repository name from the **Repository name** dropdown; in this case, it is adf.

2. Choose the branch from the **Collaboration branch** dropdown. In this case, it is main.

3. Select the branch where you want to publish from the **Publish branch** dropdown. In this case, it is adf_publish.

4. Enter the root folder. In this case, it is /.

5. Select the Import existing resources to repository option to import your existing project resources to this repository (*Figure 7.18*):

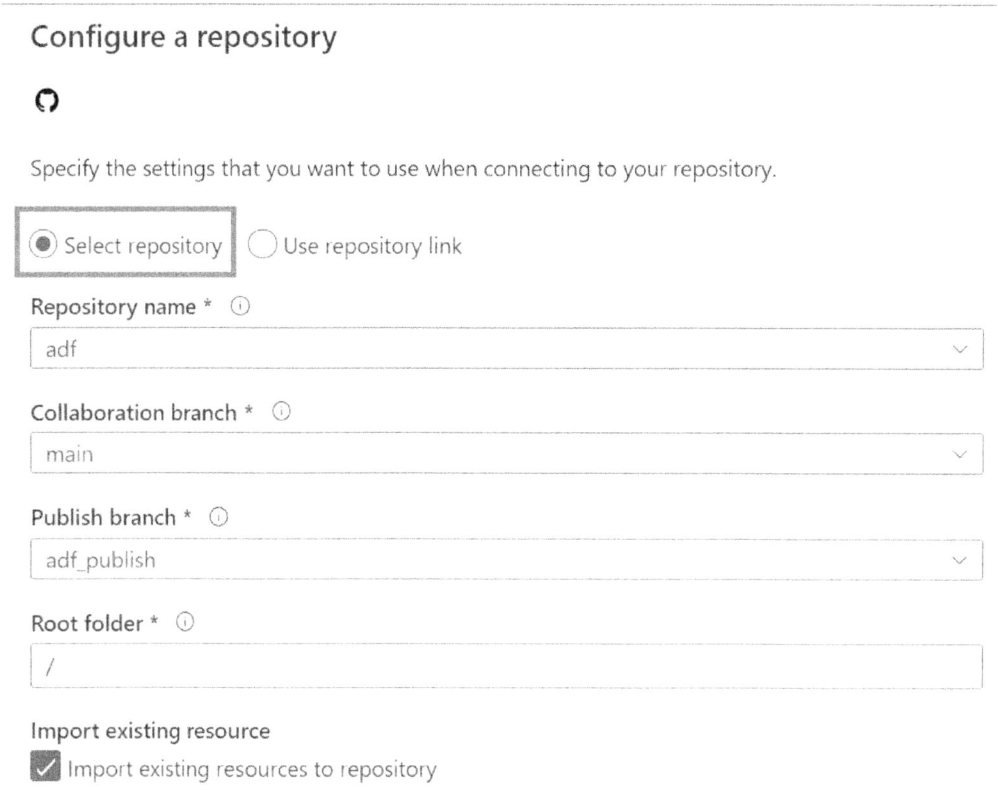

## Configure a repository

Specify the settings that you want to use when connecting to your repository.

⦿ Select repository    ◯ Use repository link

Repository name * ⓘ

| adf | ⌄ |

Collaboration branch * ⓘ

| main | ⌄ |

Publish branch * ⓘ

| adf_publish | ⌄ |

Root folder * ⓘ

| / |

Import existing resource

☑ Import existing resources to repository

Figure 7.18 – Configuring GitHub as the source control for ADF or Synapse

In the **Import resource into this branch** dropdown, select the specific branch to import resources into or leave it blank. In this case, it is blank.

6.  Click the `Apply` button to configure the **Azure DevOps Git** repository.

    You have now configured the Azure DevOps or GitHub version of Git. So, every time you click on `Publish`, the pipeline artifacts will be stored in the Git repository.

In both these cases, ADF creates a new branch called `adf_publish`, which it will use as the source to publish to the ADF service. You will not be able to make changes to this branch directly, but you can merge your changes via pull requests.

Now that you know how to configure version control for pipeline artifacts, you'll look at managing Spark jobs in a pipeline.

## Managing Spark Jobs in a Pipeline

Before delving into the details of managing Spark jobs within ADF or Azure Synapse pipelines, it is essential to know the significance of leveraging Spark for Big Data processing tasks. **Apache Spark** is a powerful open-source distributed computing framework that provides high-performance processing capabilities for large-scale Data Analytics and machine learning workloads. By incorporating Spark into ADF or Synapse pipelines, you can use its parallel processing capabilities to efficiently process vast amounts of data.

Managing Spark jobs in a pipeline involves the following two aspects:

*   **Managing the attributes of the pipeline's runtime that launches the Spark activity**: Managing the Spark activity pipeline attributes is no different than managing any other activities in a pipeline. The managing and monitoring screens you saw in *Figure 7.7*, *Figure 7.8*, *Figure 7.9*, *Figure 7.10*, *Figure 7.11*, and *Figure 7.12* are the same for any Spark activity. You can use the options provided on these screens to manage your Spark activity.

*   **Managing Spark jobs and configurations**: This involves knowledge of how Spark works, being able to tune jobs, and so on. *Chapter 10*, *Optimizing and Troubleshooting Data Storage and Data Processing*, is completely dedicated to optimizing resource management and troubleshooting Spark jobs, in addition to managing and tuning Spark jobs.

> **Note**
>
> This section primarily focuses on the **Manage Spark jobs in a pipeline** concept of the DP-203: Data Engineering on Microsoft Azure exam.

In this section, you will learn how to add an Apache Spark job (via HDInsight) to your pipeline so that you get an idea of the parameters that can be configured while setting up a Spark job using ADF and HDInsight. This is slightly different from adding Databricks notebooks to the ADF pipeline.

Perform the following steps to do so:

1. First create a Linked service for an `HDInsight` cluster from the **Manage** tab of ADF. Specify the name of the **New linked service**. For this example, it is `HDInsight LS`.

2. Choose the type from the two **Type** options—in this case, `Bring your own HDInsight`.

   This connects to an existing HDInsight cluster. On the other hand, **On-demand HDInsight** would allow you to create a new HDInsight cluster on demand.

3. In the **Connect via integration runtime** field, type your HDInsight cluster since they are also hosted on Azure. In this case, this will be `AutoResolveIntegrationRuntime`.

4. Specify the **Account selection method** as `From Azure subscription`.

5. Now, select the existing **Hdi Cluster** name. For this example, this is `DP203HDISpark`.

6. Storage accounts associated with the cluster will be displayed automatically based on the selection of `Hdi Cluster`.

7. Choose from the two **Azure Storage linked service** options. In this case, select `Blob Storage`.

8. Next, enter the **Azure Storage linked service** name associated with the storage account for that HDI cluster to create the **Linked service**. Here, that will be `HDIBlobStorageLS` (*Figure 7.19*):

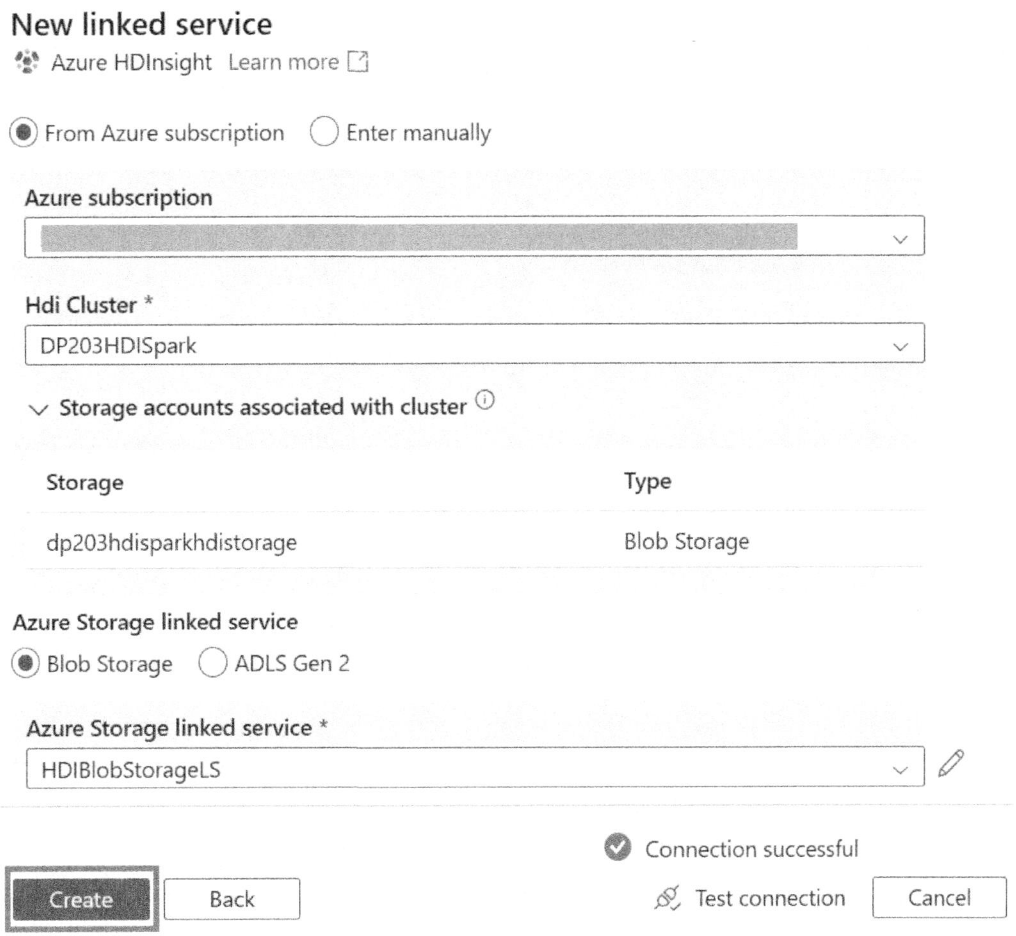

# New linked service

Azure HDInsight   Learn more ⬏

◉ From Azure subscription   ◯ Enter manually

**Azure subscription**

|                                                          ⌄ |

**Hdi Cluster** *

| DP203HDISpark                                            ⌄ |

⌄ Storage accounts associated with cluster ⓘ

| Storage | Type |
| --- | --- |
| dp203hdisparkhdistorage | Blob Storage |

**Azure Storage linked service**

◉ Blob Storage   ◯ ADLS Gen 2

**Azure Storage linked service** *

| HDIBlobStorageLS                                      ⌄ | 🖉 |

✅ Connection successful

| Create | Back |         🖉 Test connection   | Cancel |

Figure 7.19 – Creating an HDInsight linked service

9.  Next, select Spark activity from the **ADF activity** tab.

10. In the **HDI Cluster** tab, select the `HDInsight linked service` that you created in *Step 1* in the **HDInsight linked service** field (*Figure 7.20*):

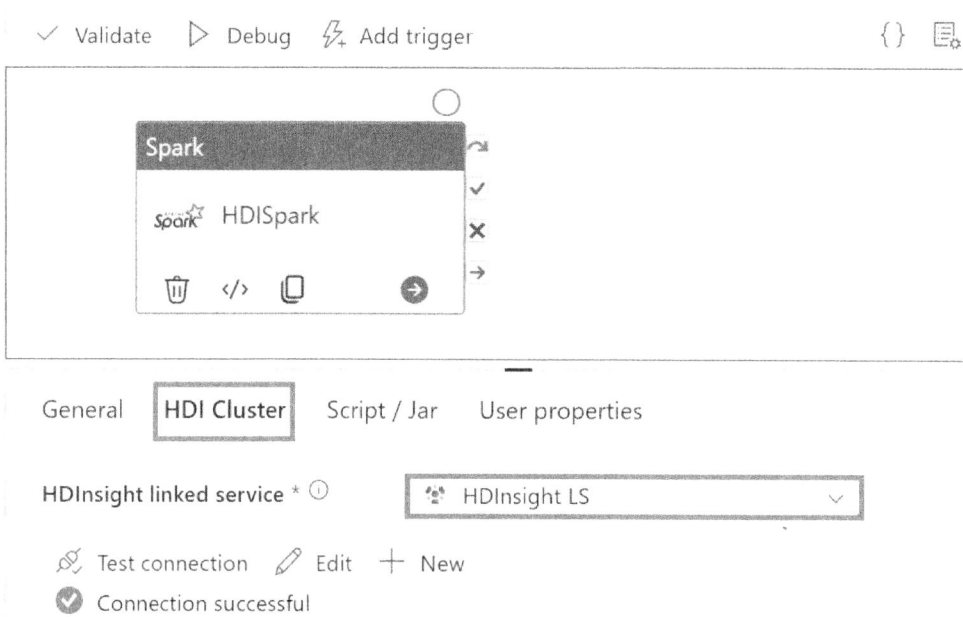

Figure 7.20 – Configuring the HDInsight Spark cluster in the ADF pipeline

11. In the **Script / Jar** tab, provide the link to the actual Spark driver job file. In this case, you are pointing it to a wordcount script (`wordcount.py`), which was uploaded into the **Blob Storage** (*Figure 7.21*):

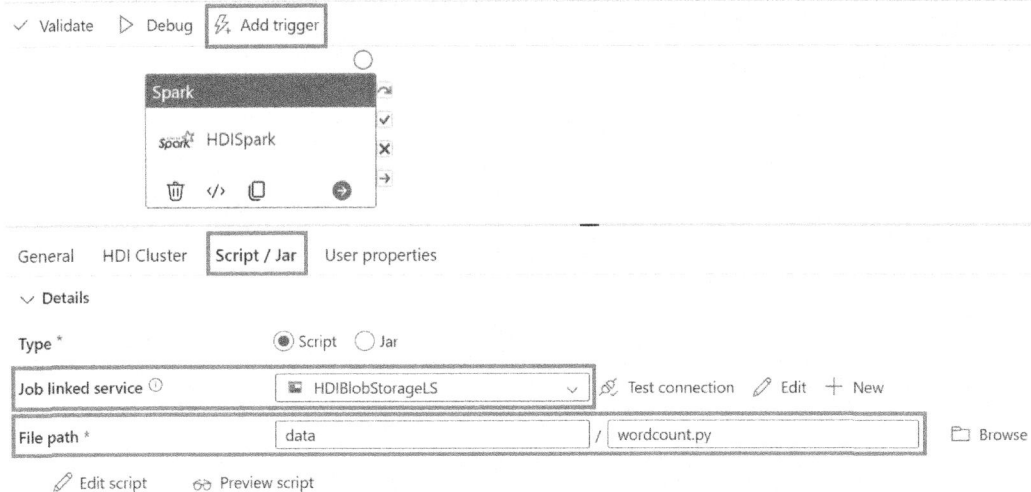

Figure 7.21 – Creating a pipeline with Spark

12. Now, click the Add trigger button to trigger this pipeline. The entire Spark pipeline will run.

That should have given you sufficient knowledge of how to manage Spark in pipelines. By now, you have learned that the management of Spark jobs within ADF or Azure Synapse pipelines is crucial for unlocking the full potential of Big Data processing capabilities. By leveraging Apache Spark's parallel processing capabilities, you can efficiently handle large-scale Data Analytics and machine learning tasks. Effective orchestration, monitoring, and optimization of Spark jobs ensure the smooth execution of data workflows, maximizing performance and resource utilization. With these strategies in place, you can drive impactful insights and innovation to make informed decisions and derive value from data assets.

## Summary

With that, you have come to the end of this chapter. In the preceding sections, you learned how to define event triggers with ADF and Synapse pipelines, set managing and monitoring pipelines, run Spark pipelines, and configure version control in ADF and Synapse pipelines. With all this knowledge, you should now be confident in creating and managing data batch workloads and pipelines.

This chapter marks the end of the **Develop Data Processing** domain, which accounts for about 40-45% of the certification goals.

From the next chapter onward, you will move on to the **Secure, Monitor, and Optimize Data Storage and Processing** domain, where you will be focusing on the security aspects of data processing—that is, implementing data security, monitoring data storage, and optimizing resource management.

# Exam Readiness Drill – Chapter Review Questions

Apart from a solid understanding of key concepts, being able to think quickly under time pressure is a skill that will help you ace your certification exam. That is why working on these skills early on in your learning journey is key.

Chapter review questions are designed to improve your test-taking skills progressively with each chapter you learn and review your understanding of key concepts in the chapter at the same time. You'll find these at the end of each chapter.

> **How to Access These Materials**
>
> To learn how to access these resources, head over to the chapter titled *Chapter 11, Accessing the Online Resources.*

To open the Chapter Review Questions for this chapter, perform the following steps:

1.  Click the link – `https://packt.link/DP203E2_CH07`.

    Alternatively, you can scan the following **QR code** (*Figure 7.22*):

Figure 7.22 – QR code that opens Chapter Review Questions for logged-in users

2.    Once you log in, you'll see a page similar to the one shown in *Figure 7.23*:

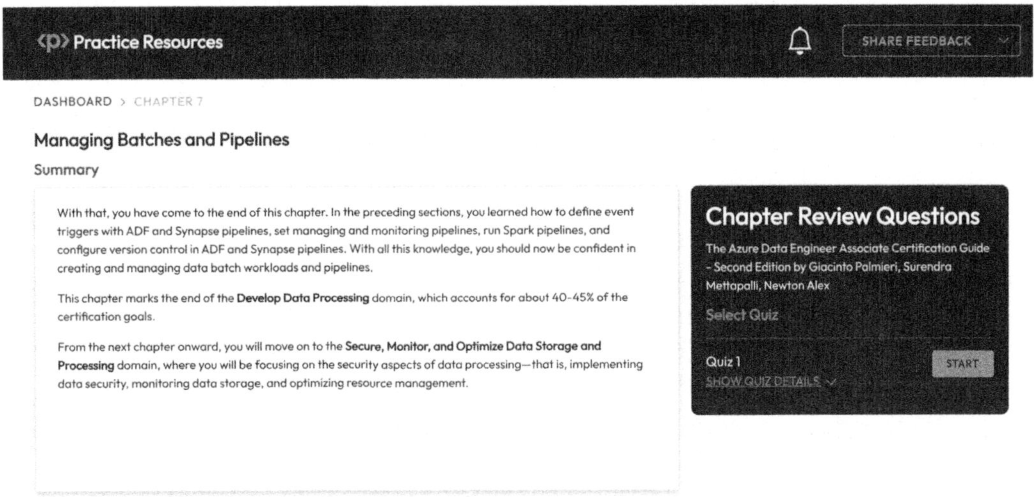

Figure 7.23 – Chapter Review Questions for Chapter 7

3.    Once ready, start the following practice drills, re-attempting the quiz multiple times.

## Exam Readiness Drill

For the first three attempts, don't worry about the time limit.

### *ATTEMPT 1*

The first time, aim for at least **40%**. Look at the answers you got wrong and read the relevant sections in the chapter again to fix your learning gaps.

### *ATTEMPT 2*

The second time, aim for at least **60%**. Look at the answers you got wrong and read the relevant sections in the chapter again to fix any remaining learning gaps.

## *ATTEMPT 3*

The third time, aim for at least **75%**. Once you score 75% or more, you start working on your timing.

> **Tip**
>
> You may take more than **three** attempts to reach 75%. That's okay. Just review the relevant sections in the chapter till you get there.

# Working On Timing

**Target**: Your aim is to keep the score the same while trying to answer these questions as quickly as possible. Here's an example of how your next attempts should look like:

| Attempt | Score | Time Taken |
| --- | --- | --- |
| Attempt 5 | 77% | 21 mins 30 seconds |
| Attempt 6 | 78% | 18 mins 34 seconds |
| Attempt 7 | 76% | 14 mins 44 seconds |

Table 7.1 – Sample timing practice drills on the online platform

> **Note**
>
> The time limits shown in the above table are just examples. Set your own time limits with each attempt based on the time limit of the quiz on the website.

With each new attempt, your score should stay above **75%** while your "time taken" to complete should "decrease". Repeat as many attempts as you want till you feel confident dealing with the time pressure.

# Part 4:
# Secure, Monitor, and Optimize Data Storage and Processing

The **Secure, Monitor,** and **Optimize Data Storage and Data Processing** domain in the DP-203: Data Engineering on Microsoft Azure exam focuses on the crucial aspects of data management and performance in Azure environments.

This domain will cover the implementation of data security capabilities for data storage and processing services. This includes exploring data protection techniques such as encryption in transit and at rest, managing keys and secrets, and implementing data masking. You will also review access control mechanisms to manage permissions and secure data access using **Role-Based Access Control (RBAC)**.

Additionally, you will delve into monitoring data storage and processing with tools such as **Azure Monitor** and **Azure Log Analytics**. These tools help track performance metrics and logs, enabling you to interpret monitoring data to know the health and performance of data systems. You will then set up alerts for potential issues and establish steps for troubleshooting common problems. Furthermore, you will investigate performance tuning techniques for optimizing data storage and processing performance, such as indexing and partitioning. Finally, you will explore strategies and approaches to manage and reduce costs, as well as troubleshooting issues related to data storage and processing.

This segment of the book comprises the following chapters:

- *Chapter 8, Implementing Data Security*
- *Chapter 9, Monitoring Data Storage and Data Processing*
- *Chapter 10, Optimizing and Troubleshooting Data Storage and Data Processing*

# 8
# Implementing Data Security

In this chapter, you will learn how to recognize sensitive information and implement various sensitive information-handling techniques, such as data masking, row- and column-level security, role-based access and access-controlled lists, encryption, and more. These skills will enable you to design and maintain the security of your data lake and ensure customer privacy.

> **Note**
>
> This chapter primarily focuses on the **Implementing data security** topic of the DP-203: Data Engineering on Microsoft Azure exam.

By the end of this chapter, you will be able to answer questions on the following confidently:

- Data masking and data encryption for data at rest and in motion
- Row-level and column-level security
- Azure **Role-Based Access Control** (RBAC)
- POSIX-like **Access Control Lists** (ACLs) for ADLS Gen2
- Data retention policy and secure endpoints (private and public)
- Resource tokens in Azure Databricks
- DataFrames and sensitive information
- Encrypted data in tables or Parquet files

## Technical Requirements

For this chapter, you will need an Azure account (free or paid).

# Implementing Data Masking

**Data masking** is a technique used in SQL technologies to hide sensitive data in SQL query results from non-privileged users. In a Synapse SQL customer table, for example, credit card info might be masked as XXXX-XXXX-XXXX-1234 rather than displaying the complete number. The data itself is not changed in the tables, but the queries and views modify the data dynamically to mask sensitive information.

> **Note**
>
> This section primarily focuses on the **Implement data masking** concept of the DP-203: Data Engineering on Microsoft Azure exam.

The data masking feature helps enforce the following two requirements of **Imaginary Airport Cabs (IAC)**:

- Not everyone should have access to all the data; it should be on a need-to-know basis.

- Customer privacy must be maintained at all costs.

- Older data should be safely deleted after a period of time, that is, from the time the data is created or becomes obsolete.

You can easily create a data mask in **Azure Synapse SQL** (dedicated SQL pool and in Azure SQL) using a feature called **Dynamic Data Masking (DDM)**. DDM does not encrypt the column. It only masks the values during queries. *Figure 8.1* shows you how this can be done in Azure Synapse SQL. Perform the following steps to do so:

1.  Access your Synapse workspace through the Azure portal and choose the Dedicated SQL Pool option to perform DDM. A screen similar to *Figure 8.1* is displayed.

2.  Click on the + Add mask link to add a masking rule for a desired field, as shown in *Figure 8.1*:

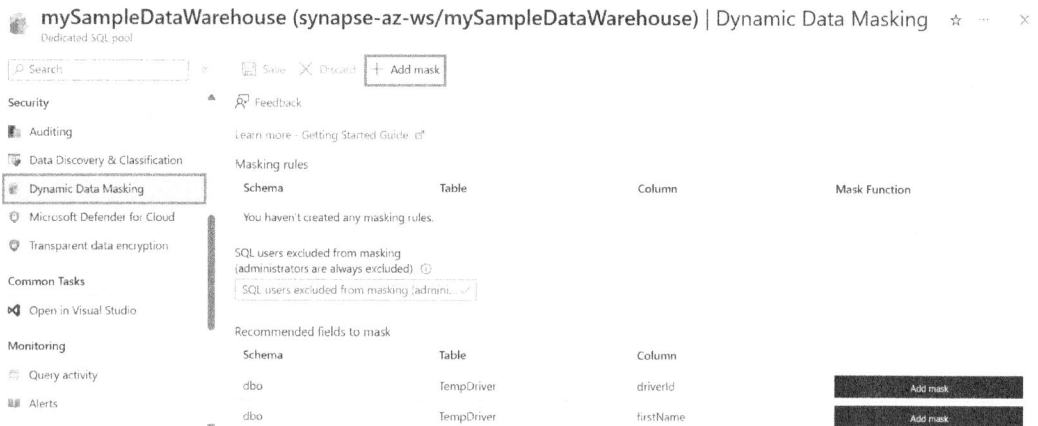

Figure 8.1 – Setting up DDM from the Azure portal

3. Choose as many fields as you want to mask.

   This will create a rule for the specific field that you are trying to mask dynamically. A mask name is auto-generated, with a mask function associated with it depending on the type of data detected in the field. The masking function may not be an exact match, but the closest available masking function is associated.

4. Choose the **Schema**, in this case, dbo.

5. Next choose the **Table** with the data, in this case, CustomerContact.

6. Now select the **Column** that holds the data, in this case, Email (varchar).

7. Now apply a **Masking field rule** to a specific field. To hide email addresses, for example, select the Email option from the drop-down list.

8. Choose how to mask the Email field, with the **Select how to mask** dropdown. This dropdown has several masking formats you can use.

9. Choose a format—in this case, the entire email address except for the first letter, a, and the domain .com has been replaced with x (*Figure 8.2*):

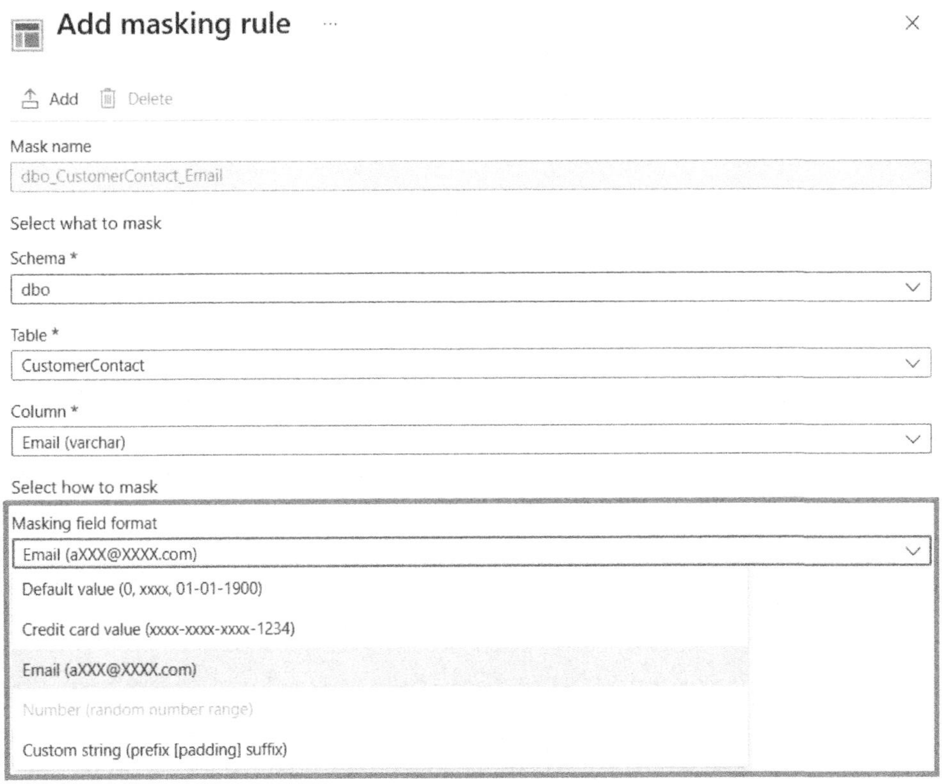

Figure 8.2 – Creating an email mask

10. Once you've made your selection, click on the Save button.

This will result in the rules being applied to the database objects and the DDM settings being saved.

*Figure 8.2* shows other options that you can use, such as Credit card value, Number, and Custom string. You can run the code by connecting to the SQL pool with **SQL Server Management Studio (SSMS)** or additionally setting up DDM using T-SQL in Azure Synapse SQL by connecting to the dedicated SQL pool database, as shown in the following code snippet:

```
ALTER TABLE dbo.DimCustomer
ALTER COLUMN emailId ADD MASKED WITH (FUNCTION = 'email()');
```

The preceding code alters the table named DimCustomer in the dbo schema and specifically modifies the column named emailId. The alteration involves adding data masking functionality to the emailId column. The data masking function used is email(), which suggests that the data stored in this column will be masked to appear as email addresses, providing privacy protection by obscuring the original data.

> **Note**
>
> You can find the complete code in the accompanying GitHub repository at https://packt.link/UZ2gr. You can learn more about DDM at https://packt.link/F0CDv.

Having learned how to mask data, you will now learn how to encrypt it, both in transit and in motion.

## Encrypting Data at Rest and in Motion

Encrypting data at rest and in motion refers to keeping your data safe when it is stored and when it is being transferred. Data at rest is information that's not actively being used, stored digitally. Data in motion, on the other hand, is data moving from one place to another, either over the internet or through a private network. By using strong encryption methods, you ensure that sensitive information is protected and can't be accessed by unauthorized parties. This helps prevent data breaches and ensures that you meet regulatory standards. The usual questions from anyone who wants to store data on a public cloud are as follows:

- How safe is my data?
- Can the employees of the cloud company access my data?
- Can any outsiders access my data?

Such concerns are usually addressed by cloud companies, such as Azure, using **encryption at rest and in transit**. This also happens to be the first of the example requirements for IAC. First, you will look at encryption at rest in detail.

> **Note**
> This section primarily focuses on the **Encrypt data at rest and in motion** concept of the DP-203: Data Engineering on Microsoft Azure exam.

## Encryption at Rest

**Encryption at rest** is the process of **encrypting** data before writing it to disks and **decrypting** the data when requested by applications. Encryption at rest protects data from physical disk theft, retrieval of data from lost disks, unauthorized data access by malicious cloud company employees, and so on. Unless someone has the **decryption key** or possesses insanely powerful supercomputing resources (the kind that governments might have, though even then, it is extremely difficult if the encryption key is strong and big enough), the data cannot be retrieved. It will just appear as gibberish if anyone tries to directly copy the data from the disks.

This form of security has become a fundamental requirement for any data stored on the cloud, and Azure does an effective job of providing encryption-at-rest options for most of its storage solutions. In the next section, you will look at the encryption-at-rest options available in Azure Storage and Azure Synapse SQL.

Note that encryption at rest and in transit is usually required for compliance with various regulations. So, it is not just about customer concerns; it might be required by law too.

> **Note**
> You can learn about the various regulations and the levels of compliance provided by the various Microsoft services at `https://packt.link/jyHsv`.

Now you'll learn how Azure Storage and Synapse SQL pools provide encryption at rest.

### Encryption at Rest in Azure Storage

Azure Storage provides encryption at rest by default. It secures your data without you even requesting it. In fact, you cannot disable Azure Storage encryption. Azure Storage uses its own keys to encrypt data and also provides the option for customers to use their own encryption keys. This provides additional control to the user. Such user-provided keys are called **Customer-Managed Keys** (**CMKs**).

You can select the ADLS Gen2 account that you created earlier or create a new storage account from the Azure portal if you don't have one. You can enable CMKs from the Azure Storage screen, as in *Figure 8.3*:

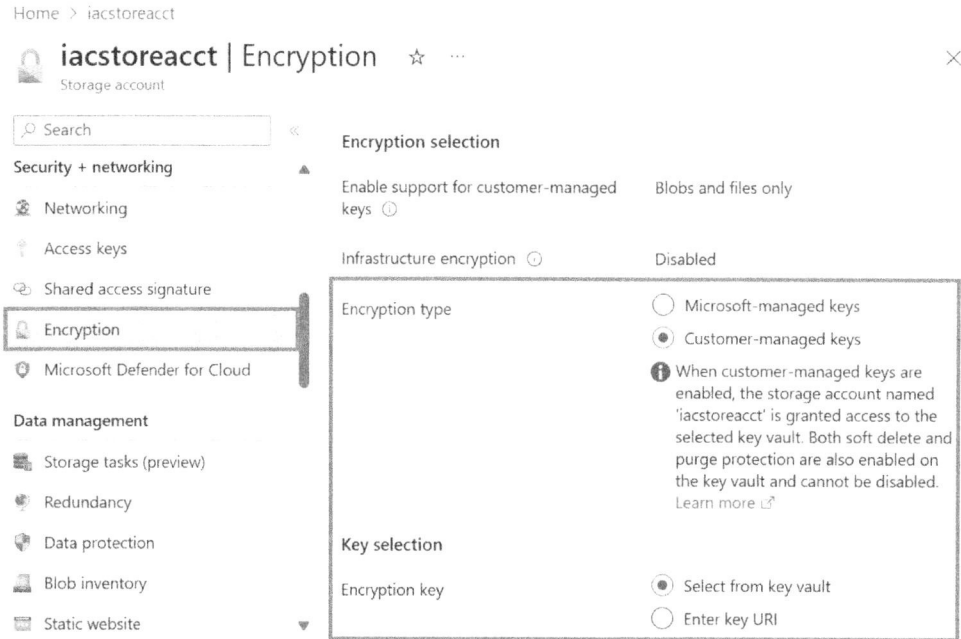

Figure 8.3 – Enabling CMKs in Azure Storage

Encryption using CMKs will address IAC's security requirement of ensuring that access to data is on a need-to-know basis because, by default, anyone trying to access the data must have a key. One of the requirements of the CMK is that the customer's key needs to be safely stored in Azure Key Vault. Think of Azure Key Vault as an online version of a physical vault. You can store all your passwords, secret keys, access keys, and so on in Key Vault and applications can access these keys securely during runtime. This method ensures that secrets and passwords need not be stored as part of the code base. You will learn more about Key Vault in *The Always Encrypted Feature of Azure SQL* section later in this chapter.

> **Note**
> You can learn more about CMKs at `https://packt.link/RInRU`.

### Encryption at Rest in Azure Synapse SQL

This section applies to Azure SQL technologies in general. In **Azure Synapse SQL**, encryption at rest is accomplished using a feature called **Transparent Data Encryption** (**TDE**). In TDE, the encryption happens in real time at the page level, meaning that pages are encrypted before writing to disk and decrypted before reading back into memory. Unlike Azure Storage, TDE must be "manually enabled" for Azure Synapse SQL. But for other SQL technologies, such as **Azure SQL**, it is enabled by default.

You can enable `Data encryption` (TDE) in Azure Synapse SQL from the **SQL pool** screen under the **Transparent data encryption** option (*Figure 8.4*):

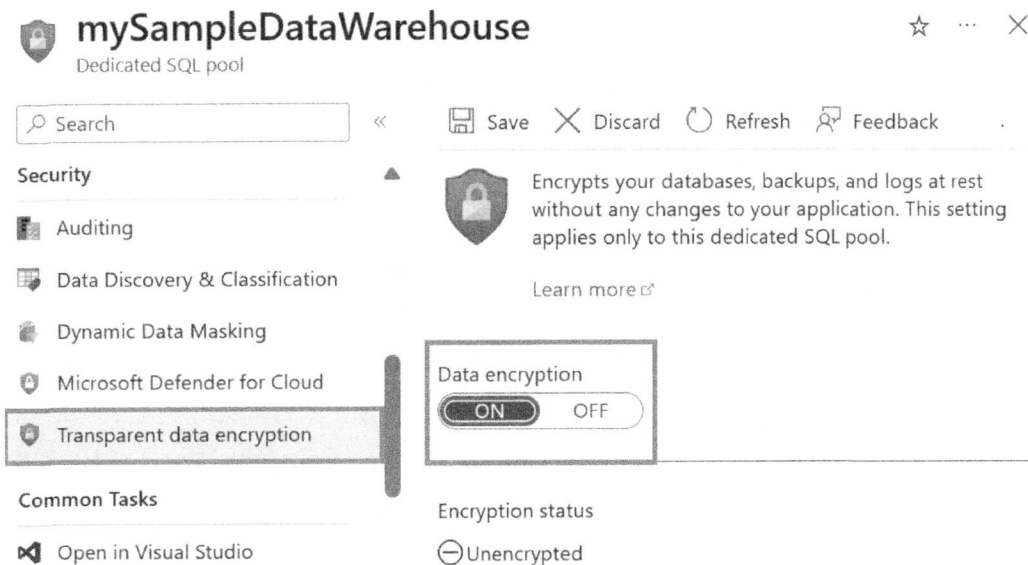

Figure 8.4 – Enabling TDE using Azure Synapse SQL

You can also enable TDE by executing the following statement as an admin user on the Azure Synapse SQL terminal:

```
ALTER DATABASE <TABLENAME> SET ENCRYPTION ON;
```

TDE encrypts the database and secures it against data theft by encrypting the backup and snapshot files too.

> **Note**
> You can learn more about TDE at `https://packt.link/Znre4`.

Azure Synapse SQL also provides the option for customers to bring in their encryption keys. If you need to configure a **CMK**, you should enable double encryption using a CMK during the creation of the **Synapse workspace** itself. *Figure 8.5* shows the **Double encryption using a customer-managed key** option enabled:

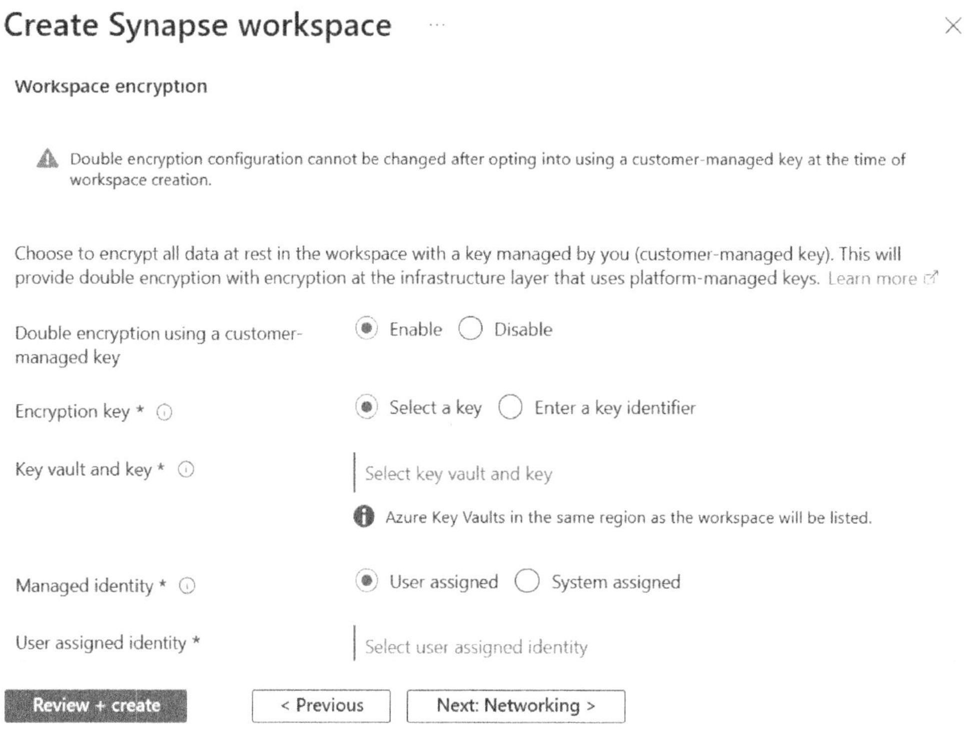

## Create Synapse workspace  ···                                        ✕

**Workspace encryption**

⚠ Double encryption configuration cannot be changed after opting into using a customer-managed key at the time of workspace creation.

Choose to encrypt all data at rest in the workspace with a key managed by you (customer-managed key). This will provide double encryption with encryption at the infrastructure layer that uses platform-managed keys. Learn more ⌕

| | |
|---|---|
| Double encryption using a customer-managed key | ⦿ Enable  ◯ Disable |
| Encryption key * ⓘ | ⦿ Select a key  ◯ Enter a key identifier |
| Key vault and key * ⓘ | Select key vault and key |
| | ⓘ Azure Key Vaults in the same region as the workspace will be listed. |
| Managed identity * ⓘ | ⦿ User assigned  ◯ System assigned |
| User assigned identity * | Select user assigned identity |

| Review + create | | < Previous | Next: Networking > |
|---|---|---|---|

Figure 8.5 – Configuring a CMK in Azure Synapse SQL

In this case, it is enabled for infrastructure-level encryption using the platform-managed keys. You can enable Select a key next to **Encryption key** and will see the Azure Key Vaults in the same region as the workspace will be listed message. Choose User assigned next to **Managed identity** to secure data at rest within the workspace and ensure compliance and protection against unauthorized access.

> **Note**
> You can learn more about CMKs with TDE at https://packt.link/h8JB6.

## The Always Encrypted Feature of Azure SQL

**Always Encrypted** is a feature provided by Azure SQL and SQL Server databases to encrypt selected database columns using client drivers. The Always Encrypted client driver fetches the **encryption key** from a secure location such as **Azure Key Vault** to encrypt or decrypt the specified column data. Since the encryption key is never available to the database engine, the database administrators cannot access the data; only the data owners who have access to the encryption keys will be able to access the data.

The following are the two types of keys used for Always Encrypted:

- **Column encryption key**: The key that is used to encrypt/decrypt a column
- **Column master key**: The protection key to encrypt column encryption keys

Here is sample code to encrypt the `Email` and **Social Security Number** (**SSN**) columns of a **Customer** table:

```
CREATE COLUMN MASTER KEY CMK
WITH (
     KEY_STORE_PROVIDER_NAME = 'AZURE_KEY_VAULT',
     KEY_PATH = <KeyVault/key/path'
   );
-----------------------------------------------
CREATE COLUMN ENCRYPTION KEY CEK
WITH VALUES (
    COLUMN_MASTER_KEY = CMK,
    ALGORITHM = 'RSA_OAEP',
    ENCRYPTED_VALUE = 0x020002134......
);
-----------------------------------------------
CREATE TABLE Customer (
    [name] VARCHAR(30),
    [email] VARCHAR(10)
        COLLATE  Latin1_General_BIN2 ENCRYPTED WITH (COLUMN_
ENCRYPTION_KEY = CEK,
        ENCRYPTION_TYPE = RANDOMIZED,
        ALGORITHM = 'AEAD_AES_256_CBC_HMAC_SHA_256'),
    [phone] VARCHAR (12),
    [SSN] VARCHAR (11)
        COLLATE  Latin1_General_BIN2 ENCRYPTED WITH (COLUMN_
ENCRYPTION_KEY = CEK,
        ENCRYPTION_TYPE = DETERMINISTIC ,
        ALGORITHM = 'AEAD_AES_256_CBC_HMAC_SHA_256'),
);
```

In the preceding SQL code, you create a column master key named CMK, which specifies that the key store provider is Azure Key Vault and provides the key path within the vault. Next, you create a **Column Encryption Key** named CEK associated with CMK using the RSA_OAEP encryption algorithm to encrypt values 0x020002134.... Next, a table called Customer is created to store sensitive data. The email and SSN columns are encrypted using COLUMN_ENCRYPTION_KEY = CEK. The email column uses RANDOMIZED encryption, ensuring unique encryption for each value. The SSN uses DETERMINISTIC encryption, ensuring consistent encryption for the same input. Both columns employ the AEAD_AES_256_CBC_HMAC_SHA_256 algorithm for encryption and authentication to ensure data integrity and confidentiality.

> **Note**
>
> You can find the complete code in the accompanying GitHub repository at https://packt.link/LIjph.

The DETERMINISTIC property specified for email ensures the client driver always generates the same encrypted value for the given plain text. The RANDOMIZED property, on the other hand, generates a different encrypted value each time.

> **Tip**
>
> If you plan to use the encrypted column in JOIN, INDEXES, AGGREGATES, and so on, use the DETERMINISTIC type and not a random type.

The following are the four database permissions needed for Always Encrypted:

- ALTER ANY COLUMN MASTER KEY: This permission is used to create and delete column master keys.

- ALTER ANY COLUMN ENCRYPTION KEY: This permission creates and deletes column encryption keys.

- VIEW ANY COLUMN MASTER KEY DEFINITION: This permission reads column master keys to query encrypted columns.

- VIEW ANY COLUMN ENCRYPTION KEY DEFINITION: This permission reads column master keys to query encrypted columns.

Since the encryption and decryption are done using a client driver, server-side operations such as `SELECT INTO`, `UPDATE`, and `BULK INSERT` will not work with Always Encrypted columns.

> **Note**
>
> You can learn more about Always Encrypted at `https://packt.link/sEP1V`.

By now, you have gained insights into encryption practices within Azure SQL technologies and learned about TDE, a feature used in **Azure Synapse SQL** to encrypt data at rest, operating at the page level in real time. Additionally, you discovered **Always Encrypted**, a feature available in Azure SQL and SQL Server databases, enabling encryption of specific database columns using client drivers. You learned how encryption keys are fetched from secure locations such as **Azure Key Vault**, ensuring data privacy, and how these encryption methods contribute significantly to safeguarding data integrity and confidentiality within **Azure SQL environments**.

The next section will look at encryption in transit for Azure Storage and Synapse SQL.

## Encryption in Transit

Another important security concept is **encryption in transit**, which refers to encrypting the data that is sent over the wire or, in other words, any data that is moved from one place to another. Examples of data movement could be data being read by an application, data getting replicated to a different zone, or data being downloaded from the cloud. Safeguarding the data during transfer is as important as keeping it safe during storage.

Encryption in transit is usually accomplished via one of two protocols: **Secure Sockets Layer** (**SSL**) or **Transport Layer Security** (**TLS**). SSL support is being discontinued for some Azure services, so **TLS** is the preferred network protocol to encrypt data during transit.

The following sections will cover how Azure Storage and Synapse SQL pools provide encryption in transit.

### Enabling Encryption in Transit for Azure Storage

TLS is used to secure the data transmitted between your applications and Azure Storage services, ensuring that data is encrypted in transit. This protects sensitive information from eavesdropping, tampering, and forgery attacks.

In this section, you will enable TLS in Azure Storage. Perform the following steps to do so:

1. Go to the Blob or `ADLS Gen2 storage` home page and select the `Configuration` tab under **Settings**.

2. On the **Configuration** screen, configure **Minimum TLS version**. The recommendation is to go with TLS `Version 1.2` (see *Figure 8.6*).

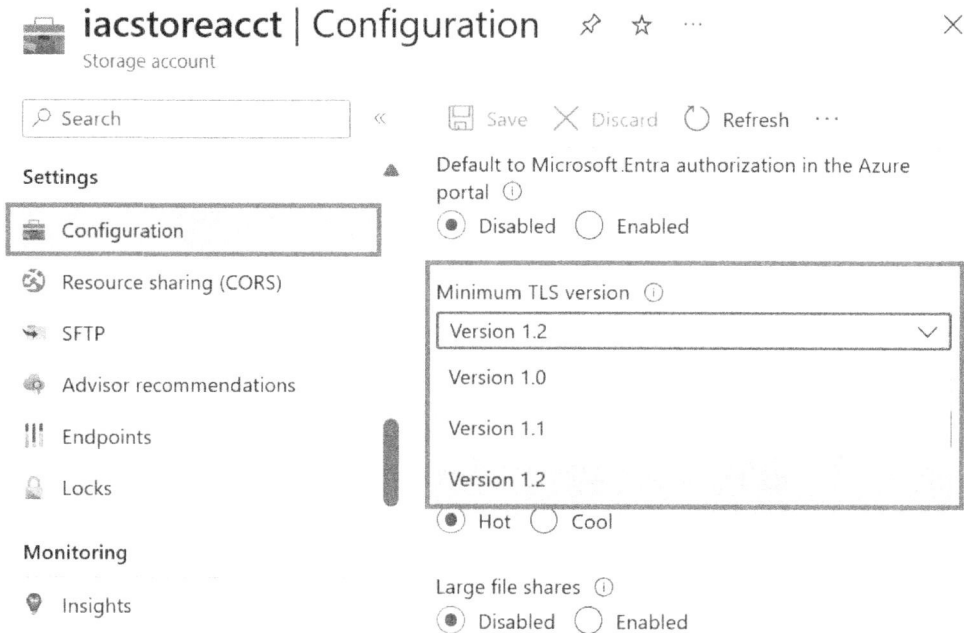

Figure 8.6 – Enabling TLS in Azure Storage

You have now enabled TLS for Azure Storage. Next, you will look at configuring TLS in a Synapse SQL pool.

### Enabling Encryption in Transit for Azure Synapse SQL

Azure Synapse SQL automatically secures data in transit using TLS protocols. In fact, Synapse SQL enforces encryption of all connections irrespective of the setting of `Encrypt` or `trustServerCertificate` in the connection string. So, you don't need to do any additional configurations from your side.

> **Note**
>
> In Storage, the user needs to enable TLS to encrypt the data in transit, whereas in Synapse there is a default option that automatically encrypts data in transit using TLS protocols. Also, if the user creates a database, newly created databases are encrypted by default, and the database encryption key is protected by built-in TLS.

The `trustServerCertificate` parameter is used in SQL Server connection strings, including Azure Synapse SQL. When this is set to `true`, it directs the TLS to utilize SSL encryption without validating the entire certificate chain, essentially skipping the trust validation process. Even if encryption is enabled and `Encrypt` is set to `false`, the server encryption level will be applied. This prioritizes encryption over certificate validation. `trustServerCertificate = true` can be convenient for you during the development or testing phase, ensuring a secure connection without certificate validation concerns to mitigate security risks.

The following is an example of `Encrypt` and `trustServerCertificate` within the connection string to connect your Synapse SQL:

```
jdbc:sqlserver://synapse-az-ws.sql.azuresynapse.net:1433;
database=mySampleDataWarehouse;user=synapseadmin@synapse-az-
ws;password={your_password_here};
encrypt=true;
trustServerCertificate=false;
hostNameInCertificate=*.sql.azuresynapse.net;
loginTimeout=30;
```

The preceding code uses the `sqlserver` JDBC driver to connect to an Azure Synapse Analytics instance named `synapse-az-ws` on port `1433`. It authenticates with the username `synapseadmin@synapse-az-ws` and the password against the `mySampleDataWarehouse` database. Encryption is enforced (`encrypt=true`), and the server's SSL certificate is validated against `*.sql.azuresynapse.net` (`trustServerCertificate=false`). A `30`-second connection timeout (`loginTimeout=30`) is set to prevent indefinite waiting.

> **Note**
>
> You can learn more about information protection in Azure Synapse SQL and other Azure SQL variants at `https://packt.link/GpZq5`.

Apart from encryption, the other ways to secure data while in transit are to set up dedicated **Virtual Private Networks** (**VPNs**) or to use Azure ExpressRoute.

### *Enabling Encryption in Transit for VPNs*

Securing data exchanges is crucial. SSL/TLS protocols help accomplish this, especially with continuous data movement. Isolating communication through a **VPN** between on-premises and cloud systems enhances security. For data transfers between on-premises and Azure, safeguards like **HTTPS** or VPN are advisable. Specifically, when transmitting encrypted traffic between **Azure Virtual Networks** (**VNets**) and on-premises locations over the public internet, utilizing **Azure VPN Gateway** ensures secure transmission. These measures collectively strengthen data protection strategies and mitigate the risk of unauthorized access during data transit.

The following are a few best practices to utilize VPN Gateway, SSL/TLS, and HTTPS:

- **Securing access from multiple workstations**: In this approach, you utilize a site-to-site VPN. It creates a safe link between your company network and Azure VNet, which allows all computers at work to access Azure resources safely.

- **Securing access from individual workstations**: For safe access from individual work on computers, use a point-to-site VPN. The secure connection allows remote employees or specific devices to securely access resources in Azure VNet.

- **Moving large data sets**: To transfer large data sets securely, use a high-speed **Wide Area Network** (**WAN**) link like **ExpressRoute**. If using ExpressRoute, think about encrypting data with SSL/TLS protocols. That keeps data secure while moving between on-premises and Azure.

- **Interacting with Azure Storage**: Use HTTPS, when connecting to Azure Storage via the portal to encrypt data transfers, ensuring data security. Alternatively, use the Storage REST API through HTTPS for secure storage interactions. This ensures data is encrypted between apps and Storage, preventing unauthorized access and tampering.

> **Note**
>
> You can find more information about VPNs at `https://packt.link/NIRaH`.

**ExpressRoute** provides a private connection from your on-premises network to the **Azure Cloud**. It uses connectivity providers for the connection and doesn't use the public internet. As such, the connections are fast, reliable, and secure.

> **Note**
>
> You can find out more about Azure ExpressRoute at `https://packt.link/6GrO7`.

In this section, you have explored the options for encryption and the ways to enable them. Encryption, however, does not allow you to show or hide specific data for specific users or groups of users. This can be done by applying row-level and column-level security, which is the topic of the next section.

# Implementing Row-Level and Column-Level Security

Azure Synapse SQL (and Azure SQL) provides some very useful fine-grained security at the level of rows and columns in a table. **Row-Level Security** (**RLS**) and column-level security are mechanisms for safeguarding sensitive data within Azure Synapse SQL (and Azure SQL). With RLS, you can implement security policies that control access to specific rows within a table, ensuring that only authorized users can view or manipulate the data.

Similarly, with column-level security you restrict access to specific columns within a table. This method goes beyond merely masking sensitive information to completely blocking unauthorized users from accessing selected columns.

Both row and column restriction features are important when dealing with sensitive information that must not be separated into separate storage locations. Both techniques help with data visibility at a granular level.

> **Note**
>
> This section primarily focuses on the **Implement row-level and column-level security** concept of the DP-203: Data Engineering on Microsoft Azure exam.

## Designing Row-Level Security (RLS)

**RLS** restricts access to unauthorized users to certain table rows. At a high level, this is similar to the use of WHERE conditions in a SELECT statement. When you apply a WHERE condition in a SELECT statement, you are essentially filtering the rows returned by the query based on specific criteria. Similarly, RLS sets up rules or conditions within a database that determine which rows of a table are accessible to different users or roles. These rules act as filters, allowing only authorized users to access specific rows of data while restricting access to unauthorized users.

In essence, just like a WHERE condition limits the rows returned by a SELECT statement, RLS controls which rows users can view or interact with in a database. RLS is achieved by creating security policies. You will look at an example of how to create such a rule next. These rules reside in the database itself, meaning that no matter whether the data is accessed via queries, views, or any other methods, the data access restriction will be enforced.

Look at an example using the **IAC** scenario again. Imagine that the IAC company is trying to launch its service in some new locations, but they want to keep the details concealed. So, they define two sets of users—one called HiPriv_User that has access to all the rows, and the other called LowPriv_Users that doesn't have access to all the rows. Now perform the following steps to see how this **RLS** example is implemented in Azure Synapse SQL:

1. Start a Synapse dedicated pool and open an editor from the Synapse workspace.

2. Create a new schema to store your row access policy:

   ```
   CREATE SCHEMA Security;
   ```

3.  Create a T-SQL function (Security.tvf_securitypredicate) that has the logic to decide who has access to the pre-launch data.

    In this case, assume that all the tripId >= 900 trips are the pre-launch locations:

    ```
    CREATE FUNCTION Security.tvf_securitypredicate(@tripId AS int)
        RETURNS TABLE
    WITH SCHEMABINDING
    AS  RETURN SELECT 1 AS tvf_securitypredicate_result
    WHERE  @tripId >= 900 OR USER_NAME() = 'HiPriv_User';
    ```

    In the preceding code, the Security.tvf_securitypredicate function returns a single-row table with a tvf_securitypredicate_result column containing the value 1 if either @tripId is less than 900 or USER is HiPriv_User. Otherwise, it returns an empty result set.

4.  Create a security policy using the previously defined function (Security.tvf_securitypredicate):

    ```
    CREATE SECURITY POLICY PrivFilter
    ADD FILTER PREDICATE Security.tvf_securitypredicate(tripId)
    ON dbo.TripTable WITH (STATE = ON);
    ```

    The preceding code creates a security policy named PrivFilter that applies a filter predicate defined in Security.tvf_securitypredicate to dbo.TripTable. This filter predicate is used to restrict access to rows in dbo.TripTable.

5.  Now, test the records in dbo.TripTable with HiPriv_User:

    ```
    EXECUTE AS USER = 'HiPriv_User';
    SELECT * from dbo.TripTable
    ```

When executed as `HiPriv_User`, all the rows, including the pre-launch rows show up on the screen (see *Figure 8.7*):

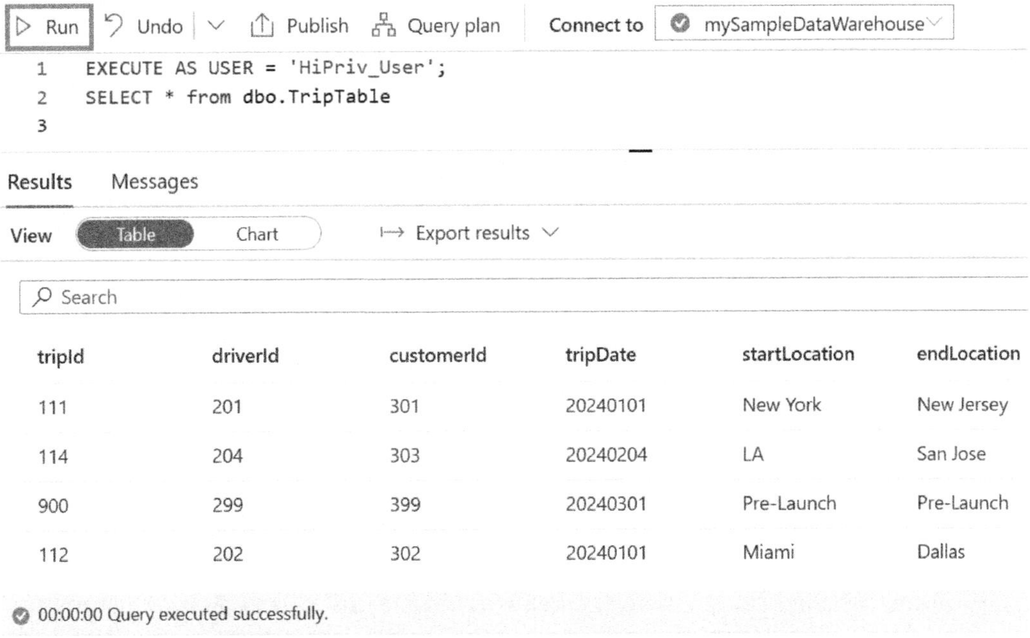

| ▷ Run | ↻ Undo ∨ | ⬆ Publish | 🔗 Query plan | **Connect to** | ✅ mySampleDataWarehouse ∨ |
|-------|----------|-----------|---------------|----------------|---------------------------|

```
1   EXECUTE AS USER = 'HiPriv_User';
2   SELECT * from dbo.TripTable
3
```

**Results**   Messages

View ( **Table** ) ( Chart )    ↦ Export results ∨

🔍 Search

| tripId | driverId | customerId | tripDate | startLocation | endLocation |
|--------|----------|------------|----------|---------------|-------------|
| 111 | 201 | 301 | 20240101 | New York | New Jersey |
| 114 | 204 | 303 | 20240204 | LA | San Jose |
| 900 | 299 | 399 | 20240301 | Pre-Launch | Pre-Launch |
| 112 | 202 | 302 | 20240101 | Miami | Dallas |

✅ 00:00:00 Query executed successfully.

Figure 8.7 – Displaying all rows including pre-launch for user HiPriv_User

6. Now test `dbo.TripTable` with `LowPriv_User`, as shown in the following code:

```
EXECUTE AS USER = <LowPriv_User>;
SELECT * from dbo.TripTable
```

When executed as `LowPriv_User`, the pre-launch lines are hidden, as shown in *Figure 8.8*:

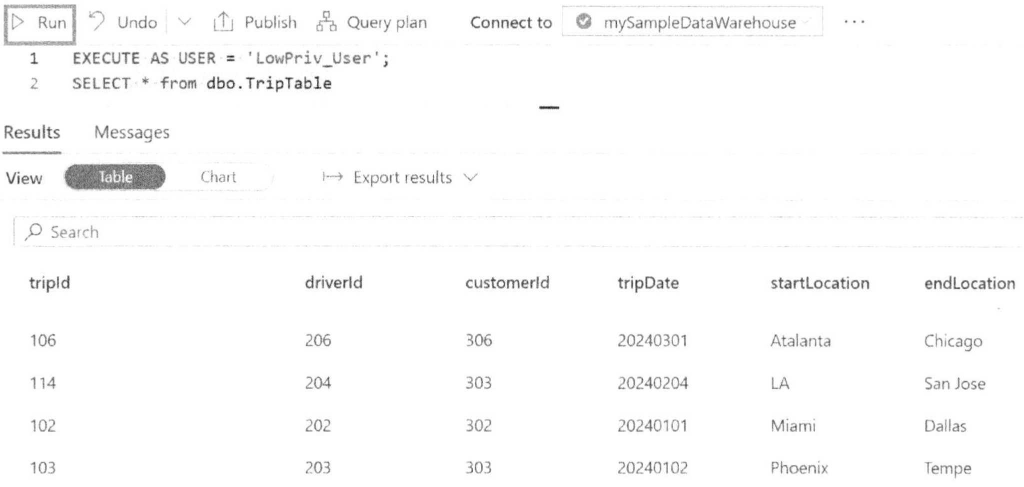

Figure 8.8 – Row-Level Security (RLS) blocking the pre-launch location rows

With this, you have learned about the RLS concept and gained knowledge about how RLS functions within a database system. You also learned that RLS operates similarly to the `WHERE` condition in a `SELECT` statement, filtering data based on specific criteria. Just as a `WHERE` condition limits the rows returned by a query, RLS controls which rows users can access in a database. Additionally, through the IAC example, you grasped how RLS can be practically applied to restrict access to certain rows based on user roles or privileges, thereby maintaining data confidentiality.

> **Note**
>
> You can find the complete code in the accompanying GitHub repository at `https://packt.link/3bbgv`.

Now look next at column-level security.

## Designing Column-Level Security

**Column-level security** is similar to the data masking feature that you saw earlier in this chapter, in the *Implementing Data Masking* section. But instead of just masking the values of the column, here, you restrict the column access completely from unauthorized users. And, as with RLS, column-level rules also reside within the database such that here too, data access—that is, via queries, views, or any other method—is enforced irrespective of the access method.

The following example will demonstrate how to implement column restrictions. Consider the IAC example, the DimCustomer dimension table. Perform the following steps to implement column-level security:

1.  Define the table as follows:

    ```
    CREATE TABLE dbo.DimCustomer
    (
        [customerId] INT NOT NULL,
        [name] VARCHAR(40) NOT NULL,
        [emailId] VARCHAR(40),
        [phoneNum] VARCHAR(40),
        [city] VARCHAR(40)
    )
    ```

2.  In order to restrict access, use the GRANT command, as shown here:

    ```
    GRANT SELECT ON dbo.DimCustomer (customerId, name, city) TO
    LowPriv_User;
    ```

    Here, you just give LowPriv_User access to the customerId, name, and city columns. LowPriv_User will not have access to the emailId or phoneNum column.

3.  Now run the query given in the following code:

    ```
    SELECT * FROM dbo.DimCustomer;
    ```

    When you run the query as LowPriv_User, you will get the following error:

    ```
    -- The SELECT permission was denied on the column 'emailId'
    of the object 'DimCustomer', database 'DedicatedSmall', schema
    'dbo'. The SELECT permission was denied on the column 'phoneNum'
    of the object 'DimCustomer', database 'DedicatedSmall', schema
    'dbo'.
    ```

    The row and column restriction features are particularly useful when only a very small subset of the data in the table is sensitive. This avoids the need to split the table and store the sensitive data separately. When the subset of sensitive data is larger, relying solely on row and column restrictions may become less practical. This is because managing a large number of individual access rules can become cumbersome and may not scale efficiently as the data volume grows. Additionally, enforcing fine-grained access controls on a large dataset might impact performance.

---

**Note**

You can learn more about column-level security at https://packt.link/iTBrI. You can find the complete code in the accompanying GitHub repository at https://packt.link/EhzAj.

In this section, you have seen how to specify rules at the level of rows or columns to control who can see specific data. This technique, however, only applies to Azure SQL and Synapse. Next, you will instead focus on RBAC, which is a technique that can be applied to all Azure data services.

## Implementing Azure Role-Based Access Control

RBAC guarantees that you have appropriate permissions to perform specific actions on Azure resources. By assigning roles to users, administrators can enforce fine-grained access control, ensuring security, compliance, and efficient data management.

This section deals with restricting data access to unauthorized users and satisfies the requirement of the sample IAC requirements established in the *Implementing Data Masking* section:

> *Not everyone should have access to all the data. It should be on a need-to-know basis.*

Azure uses and recommends the principle of least privilege, which means assigning the least possible privilege required to accomplish a task. You will see how RBAC helps to achieve this goal.

> **Note**
>
> This section primarily focuses on the **Implement Azure role-based access control (RBAC)** concept of the DP-203: Data Engineering on Microsoft Azure exam.

**Azure RBAC** is an authorization system that controls who can access what resources in Azure. It works hand in hand with Microsoft Entra ID. RBAC has the following three components:

- **Security principal**: This could be any user, group, or managed identity (service accounts whose life cycle is completely managed by Azure) created within Microsoft Entra ID. You can think of the service principal as the "who" part of the authorization. It is the entity that you are requesting permission for. Security principals may be real people or service accounts that are used to run services automatically without human intervention.

- **Role**: Think of the examples of admin roles or read-only guest roles that you have used to log in to any system. An **admin** role would have had complete access to create, read, write, delete, and so on, while a **guest** account might have just had read-only access. A **role** defines what actions can be performed by a user. Azure has a huge list of predefined roles, such as **Owner**, **Contributor**, and **Reader**, with the right list of permissions already assigned. So, you can just choose to use one of them instead of creating a new role.

- **Scope**: Scope refers to all the resources where the role needs to be applied. Do you want the rules to apply only to a resource group? Only to a container in storage? Multiple containers? And so on.

In order to define an RBAC rule, you need to define all three of the preceding and assign a role and scope to the **security principal**. Now, look at how you can accomplish this for a data lake. Perform the following steps to do so:

1. From the **Azure Storage** home page (see *Figure 8.6*), select Access Control (IAM) in order to **Add role assignment**, as shown in *Figure 8.9*:

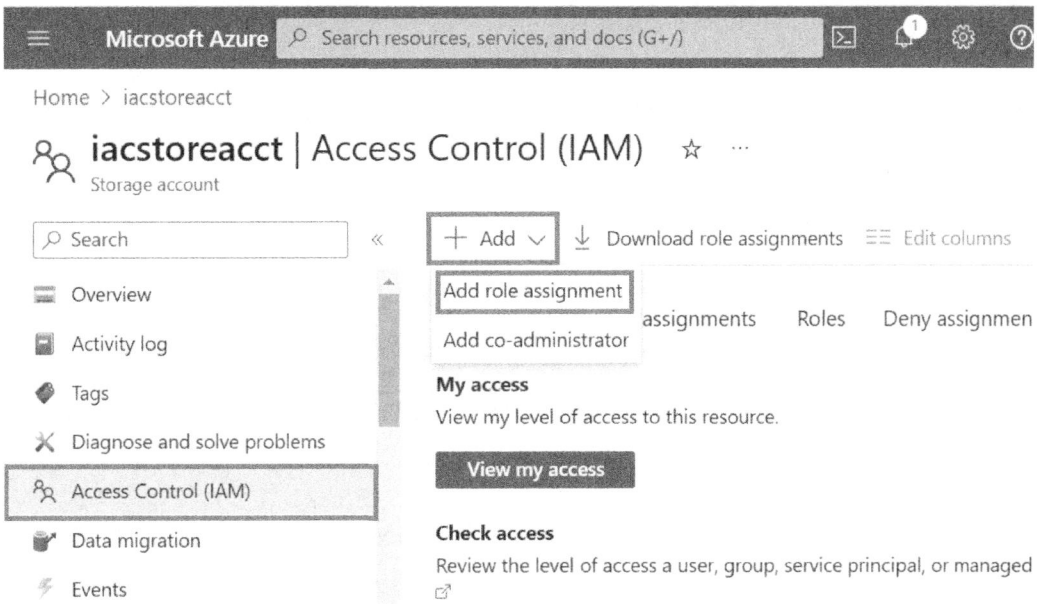

Figure 8.9 – Adding role assignment in storage account through Access Control IAM

2. Select the role from the **Role** field, in this case, it is Storage Blob Data Owner.

3. Choose an option from the **Assign access to** field, for example, User, group, or service principal.

4.  Use + `Select members` to add one or more members you want to assign to the role for this storage account, as shown in *Figure 8.10*.

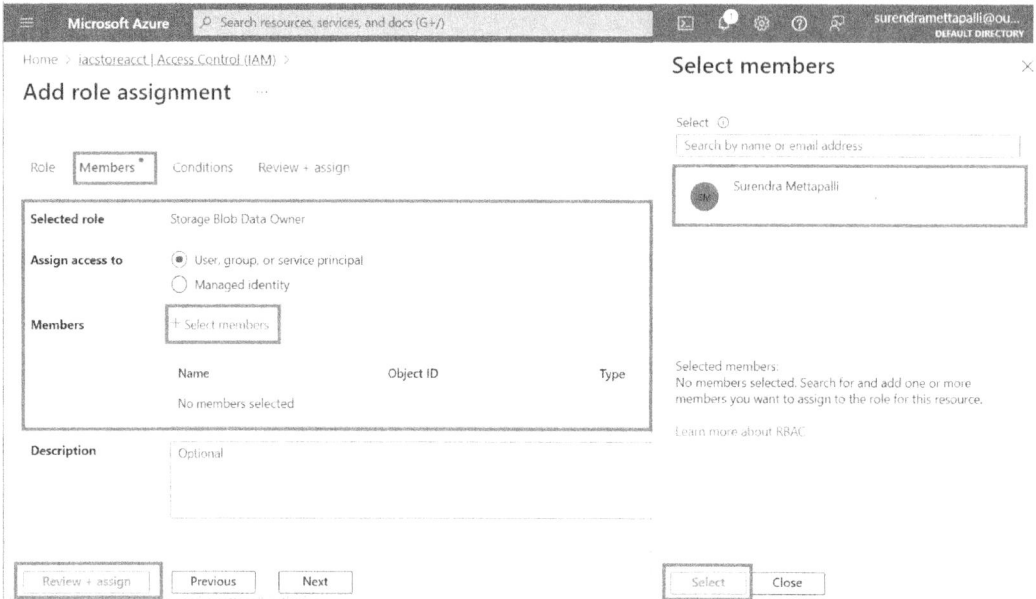

Figure 8.10 – Configuring the RBAC role assignment in ADLS Gen2

---

**Note**

You can learn more about Azure RBAC at `https://packt.link/rKXKW`.

---

The limit of RBAC is that it only allows you to set the same set of permissions on the entire resource. If you need to assign different access rules on different directories or files of the same data lake, you will need **ACLs**, which is the topic of the next section.

# Implementing POSIX-Like ACLs for ADLS Gen2

While Azure RBAC provides coarse-grained access such as who can read/write data in an account, ACLs provide more fine-grained access such as who can read data from a specific directory or a file. In this way, RBAC and ACL complement each other to provide a wide spectrum of access control.

> **Note**
>
> This section primarily focuses on the **Implement POSIX-like access control lists (ACLs) for Data Lake Storage Gen2** concept of the DP-203: Data Engineering on Microsoft Azure exam.

Each directory and file in Azure Storage has an ACL. You can assign any (or all) of the read, write, and execute permissions to individual security principals (users) or groups to provide them with the required access to the file or directory. ACLs are enabled by default for ADLS Gen2.

Here is how you can assign ACLs in **ADLS Gen2**. Just right-click on the file or folder name within your storage account (in this case, `customers`) and select `Manage ACL` (see *Figure 8.11*):

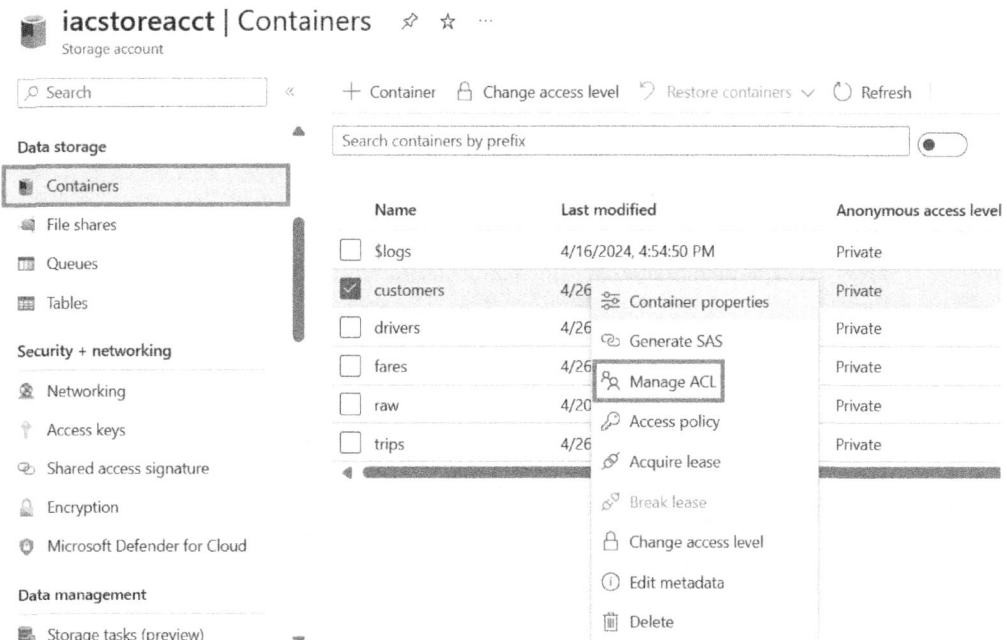

Figure 8.11 – Selecting Manage ACL to provide required access permissions

On the **Manage ACL** screen, as shown in *Figure 8.12*, you can assign Read, Write, and Execute access to the users or groups under **Security principal**:

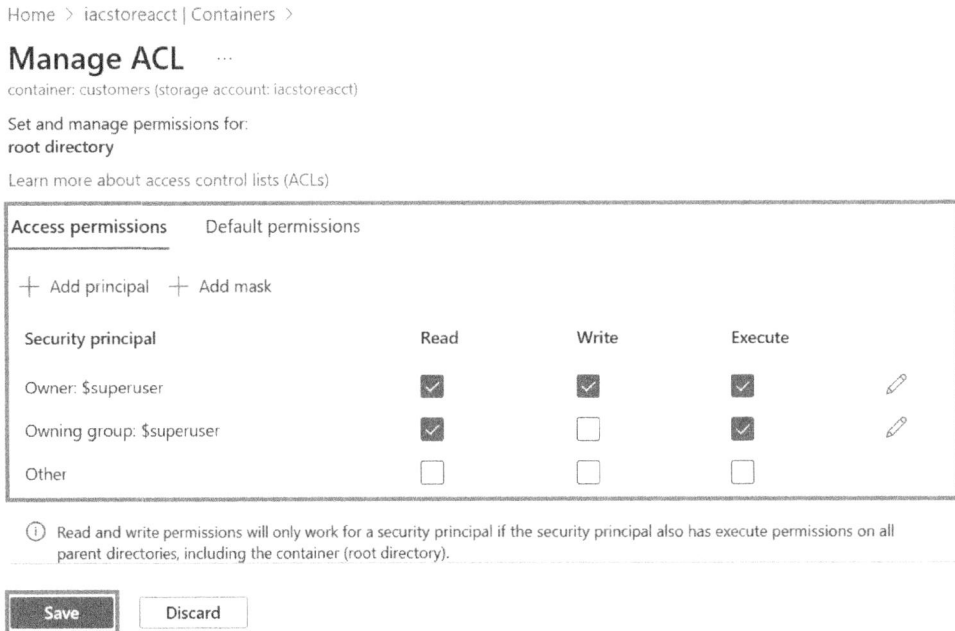

Figure 8.12 – Configuring the ACL in ADLS Gen2 to provide the required access to users

*Figure 8.12* shows **Security principal** under the **Access permissions** tab. The following are the details about the principles—Owner, Owning Group, and Other users:

- **Owner ($superuser)**: The $superuser is the designated owner—in this case, with full control over the resource. As the owner, $superuser has all permissions (Read, Write, and Execute) for managing ACLs.

- **Owning Group ($superuser)**: In this case, $superuser owns the group, which consists of users who share certain permissions. However, the owning group has limited permissions:

    - Read permission (can view ACLs)

    - Execute permission (can execute ACL-related actions)

    - No write (cannot modify ACLs)

- **Other**: This refers to users who are neither the owner nor part of the owning group and have no permissions to read, write, or execute ACL-related actions.

You can configure the right access level for users according to your requirements. Next, see the order in which Azure evaluates RBAC and ACLs.

## Resolving Conflicting Rules: RBAC and ACLs

**Azure RBAC** and **ACLs** are two key mechanisms for managing access control in Azure. RBAC focuses on defining roles and permissions for users, groups, and service principals, granting specific permissions at different levels, such as subscription, resource group, or resource. It's particularly useful for high-level access control across Azure resources. ACLs, on the other hand, operate at a finer granularity, allowing the association of security principals with specific access levels for files and directories within a storage account. Each file and directory has its own ACL, making it essential for controlling access to individual resources within the storage account.

*Figure 8.13* shows a flow chart reproduced from Azure that shows how the authorization decision is made between RBAC and ACL:

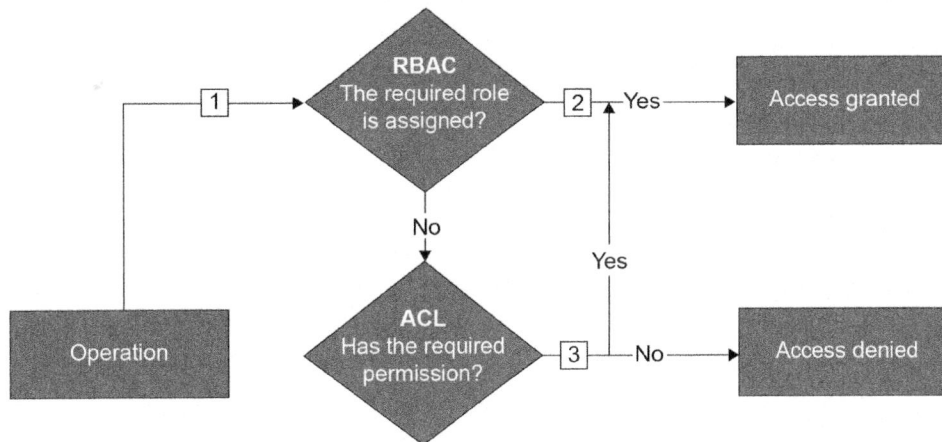

Figure 8.13 – RBAC and ACL evaluation sequence

Imagine a situation where a user has both RBAC permissions and ACLs set on a specific file—conflict can occur. For instance, if the RBAC permission grants read access and the ACL denies read access, a conflict will arise. In such conflicts, Azure recommends a specific order of evaluation:

- RBAC takes precedence over ACLs.

- If a user has a role assignment (RBAC), then that role's permission applies.

- If no role assignment exists, then ACLs come into play.

In this scenario, the RBAC permission prevails, allowing the users to read the file despite the conflicting ACLs in your storage.

## Limitations of RBAC and ACLs

The following are some other restrictions of RBAC and ACL that you should be aware of while designing for security and privacy requirements:

- Azure RBAC allows **2,000 role assignments** per subscription.
- ACL allows up to **32 ACL entries** per file and directory. This number is a bit restricting, so ensure that you don't end up adding too many individual users; instead, create groups and "add only groups to ACLs."

> **Note**
> You can learn more about ACLs at `https://packt.link/hRJ5G`.

Azure also supports two other authentication methods called **Shared Key authorization** and **Shared Access Signature (SAS)** authorization. Shared Key authorization involves sharing an **access key**, which basically gives admin-like access to the resource to anyone possessing the key. SASs are slightly better because you can define what actions are allowed with the SAS key.

If you use the shared key or SAS authorization methods, they will override both RBAC and ACLs. The recommendation is to use **Microsoft Entra ID RBAC** and ACLs wherever possible.

## Access Keys and Shared Access Keys in Azure Storage

When you set up an Azure Storage Account, it automatically creates two access keys. These keys can be used to access the data in the storage accounts. Each access key is 512 bits in length. When these keys are used to authenticate access, it is called the **Shared access key authentication** method. You can view the access keys from your storage account by selecting the **Security + networking** tab and choosing the `Access Keys` option.

Access keys are like root passwords. They give complete access to all the resources in a storage account. If you need to give restricted access to someone or some application, you can either use the Azure RBAC option that was discussed earlier, in the *Implementing Azure Role-Based Access Control* section, or use a SAS. A SAS is a URI that grants restricted access for a specific period, to specific IP addresses, with specific permissions. Unlike access keys, SAS keys will not have permission to modify or delete accounts.

The following are three types of SAS keys:

- **Service SAS**: This type of SAS key provides access to just one of the storage services, such as **Blob**, **Table**, **Files**, or **Queue**. Service SAS keys are signed using storage access keys.

- **Account SAS**: This type of SAS key provides access to multiple storage services such as **Blob**, **Table**, **Files**, and **Queue**. Account SAS keys provide access to read, write, and delete operations on multiple services such as blob containers, tables, queues, and files. **Account SAS keys** are signed using storage access keys.

- **User delegation SAS**: When a SAS key is signed by Entra ID, the SAS is called a **user delegation SAS**. This is the SAS approach recommended by Azure. But this option works only for **Blob Storage** and no other storage options, such as the Table, Queue, or Files services.

> **Note**
>
> You can learn more about SAS keys and how to generate them at `https://packt.link/iBcGZ`.

So far in this chapter, you have explored different options to control access to your data. Another important aspect of security, however, concerns what data you should keep and for how long. So, in the next section, you will focus on data retention policies.

## Implementing a Data Retention Policy

Implementing a data retention policy in Azure is like organizing and managing your digital files securely and efficiently. This policy does a couple of important things: it decides how long different kinds of data should stick around and whether it should be stored away for safekeeping or discarded permanently.

Azure gives you the tools to do this precisely, such as Azure Blob Storage, Azure SQL database, and ADLS. In addition, there are handy features such as soft delete and time-based rules to help manage things automatically. You can follow the best practices, including collaboration with compliance teams, clear documentation, communication of the policy to stakeholders, and regular reviews and adjustments of the policy, as needed to ensure its effectiveness.

The last requirement for IAC (see the *Implementing Data Masking* section) was to securely delete the data so that it doesn't get into the hands of any malicious users. Older data should be safely deleted after a period of time, which refers to data life cycle management.

> **Note**
>
> This section primarily focuses on the **Implement a data retention policy** concept of the DP-203: Data Engineering on Microsoft Azure exam.

One tool that can be very useful for this purpose is the **data life cycle management** rules provided by **Azure Storage** and **ADLS Gen2** accounts. As this life cycle also involves access tiers on top of data deletion, you will briefly be introduced to this notion first.

**Access tiers** are ways to specify (for a Blob stored in a container) whether you expect frequent access to it to minimize access costs or less frequent access but higher volume to minimize costs associated with volume. Azure provides the following three tiers of storage:

- The **Hot Access Tier** is ideal for data that is "accessed frequently." It has the lowest access costs but at a higher storage cost. Think of it like new products on an e-commerce website; there's not much data since it's just for the current month, but you expect people to look at it often, so you want to keep access costs down.

- The **Cold Access Tier** is ideal for data that is accessed "occasionally," such as slightly older data that is probably used for backups or monthly reports. For example, in the e-commerce example, products put on sale more than a month ago, but not longer than one year ago, will require occasional access. The Cold Access Tier has lower storage costs but higher access costs. Azure expects the Cold Access Tier data to be stored for at least 30 days. Early deletion or a tier change might result in extra charges.

- The **Archive Access Tier** is ideal for storing data for "long durations" for compliance reasons, long-term backups, data archival, and so on. The archive Access Tier is an offline storage solution, which means you will not be able to access the data unless you rehydrate that data from the archive to an Online Tier. This is the cheapest storage option among all the tiers. Azure expects Archive Tier data to be stored for at least 180 days. Early deletion or a tier change might result in extra charges. In the e-commerce example, this might apply to the data related to products put on sale more than one but less than five years ago that you do not want to be displayed as on sale anymore but cannot delete yet, as fiscal rules in your country require data to be kept for five years.

# Data Life Cycle Management

**Azure Blob Storage** provides features for data life cycle management. Using these features, you can define policies such as how long particular data needs to be in the **Hot Access Tier** when to move the data between the different access tiers, when to delete blobs, and so on. Azure runs these policies daily. In the e-commerce website example described, you can specify that every blob is created with the Hot Tier associated, then after one month is moved to cold, then after one year is moved to an archive, then after five years is deleted (after being briefly moved to hot or cold, as archive blobs cannot be accessed while in the archive, not even to be deleted; this part of the process is called rehydration). The possibility of adding automatic deletion to your data life cycle is the reason why this feature can be so useful in implementing a retention policy.

You will now go through an example showing how to apply a deletion rule as part of a data life cycle. Perform the following steps to explore how to first create a data life cycle policy using the Azure portal:

1. In the Azure portal, select your storage account. In this case, it is `iacstoreacct`.

2. Go to the **Data Management** tab and select `Life Cycle Management`.

3. Click on `+ Add a rule` to add a new rule.

4. On the **Details** screen, add a name for your rule, for example, `delete-blobs-after-365-days`.

5. Select the scope of blobs this rule needs to apply to. In this case, `Apply rule to all blobs in your storage account` is selected.

6. Choose **Blob type** as `Block blobs` and **Blob subtype** as `Base blobs`.

7. Click `Next` to add a rule on the **Base blobs** screen.

8. Choose the rule – go to the **Base blobs were** option under **If** section and select the `Last modified` radio button.

9. Enter `365` under **More than (days ago)**.

10. Select the `Delete the blob` action under **Then** for the life cycle management of storage, as shown in *Figure 8.14*:

You can use the `+ Add conditions` option to add multiple rules to implement in this condition. In this case, this is not required.

# Add a rule     ···                                                        ×

⊘ Details    ❷ Base blobs

Lifecycle management uses your rules to automatically move blobs to cooler tiers or to delete them. If you create multiple rules, the associated actions must be implemented in tier order (from hot to cool storage, then archive, then deletion).

If                                                                            🗑

Base blobs were *

🔘 Last modified

◯ Created

More than (days ago) *

365

↓

Then

Delete the blob                                                              ⌄

↓

+ Add conditions

Previous     **Add**

Figure 8.14 – Configuring data life cycle management

11. Once done, click on the `Add` button.

This way, based on the requirements, you can configure entire batches of data to be deleted after a specified time.

> **Note**
>
> You can learn more about data life cycle management on ADLS at `https://packt.link/h4GE4`.

Now that you have learned how to specify the duration to retain your data, explore the networking features of Azure to implement an extra layer of control.

## Implementing Secure Endpoints: Public and Private

Securing your data storage and processing in Azure involves the implementation of **secure endpoints**. These endpoints serve to safeguard sensitive data and control access, whether they're public or private. **Public endpoints** enable external access to Azure services such as APIs and web apps, requiring robust authentication, authorization, and encryption measures to ensure security over the internet. On the other hand, private endpoints facilitate secure communication within a VNet or Azure service, shielding resources from exposure to the public internet. Use cases for private endpoints include connecting securely to services such as Azure Storage, Azure SQL database, or Azure Cosmos DB within a protected environment.

A **public endpoint** refers to the default way of creating Azure services (such as **Azure Storage**, **Azure Synapse**, and **Azure SQL**), where the service can be accessed from a public IP address. So, any service that you create in Azure without configuring a VNet would fall under the public endpoint category.

On the other hand, **private endpoints** are more secure setups involving private IP addresses. A private endpoint is part of a bigger service called the **Private Link service**. Using the Private Link service makes your Azure service available to only certain private IP addresses within your VNets. No one from outside your VNets will even be aware of the existence of such a service.

Private endpoint technically refers to the network interface that uses the private IP from your VNet, and Private Link service refers to the overall service that comprises the private endpoints and the private network (that is, the link) over which the traffic traverses. When you establish a private link to your Azure service, all the data to that service traverses through Microsoft's backbone network without being exposed to the public internet.

> **Note**
>
> This section primarily focuses on the **Implement secure endpoints (private and public)** concept of the DP-203: Data Engineering on Microsoft Azure exam.

Perform the following steps to create a private link to one of the existing Synapse workspaces:

1. First, you will create a VNet. From the Azure portal, select `Virtual networks` and click on the `Create virtual network` option. A **Create virtual network** screen, like the one shown in *Figure 8.15*, will be displayed:

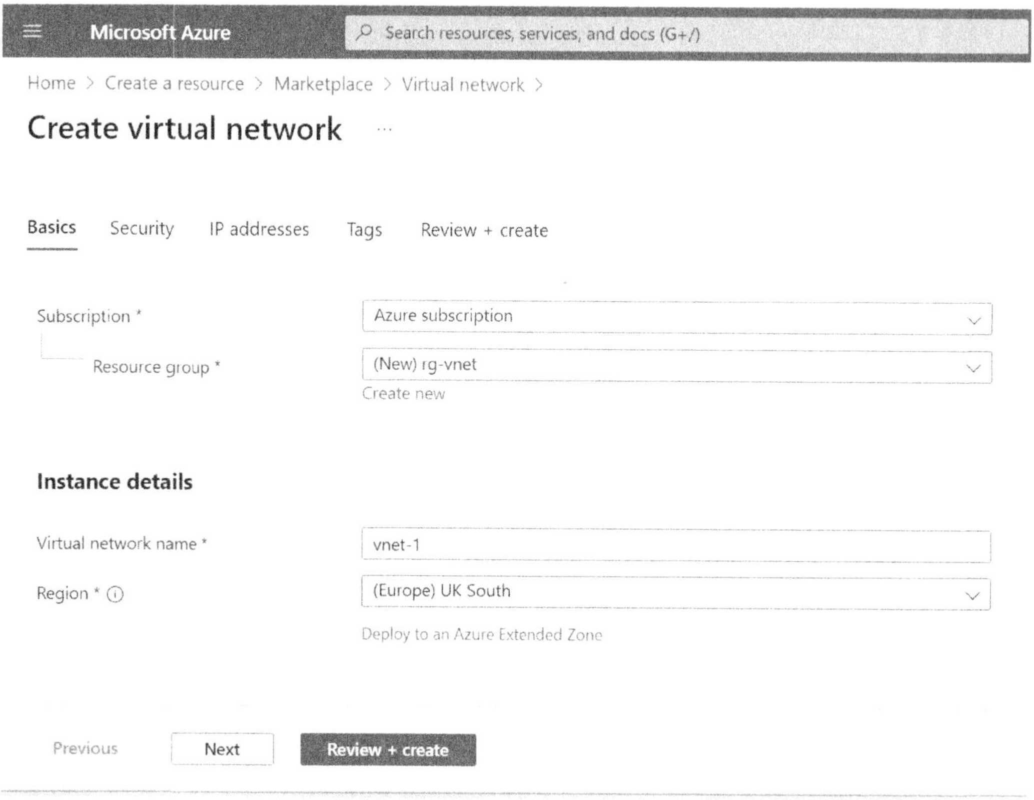

Figure 8.15 – Creating a new VNet

2. Select your subscription from the dropdown. In this case, it is `Azure subscription`.

3. Under **Resource group**, select the existing resource group if you want to deploy this VNet resource or create a new one, for example, `rg-vnet`.

4. Input the name of the instance. In this case, it is `vnet-1`.

5. Select the region, for example, `(Europe) UK South`.

6. On the **IP addresses** tab, specify your IP address range in the IPv4 address space. In this case, it is 10.0.0.0/16, as shown in *Figure 8.16*.

7. Click + Add subnet to add a subnet or choose the default subnet. In this case, it is 10.0.0.0/24.

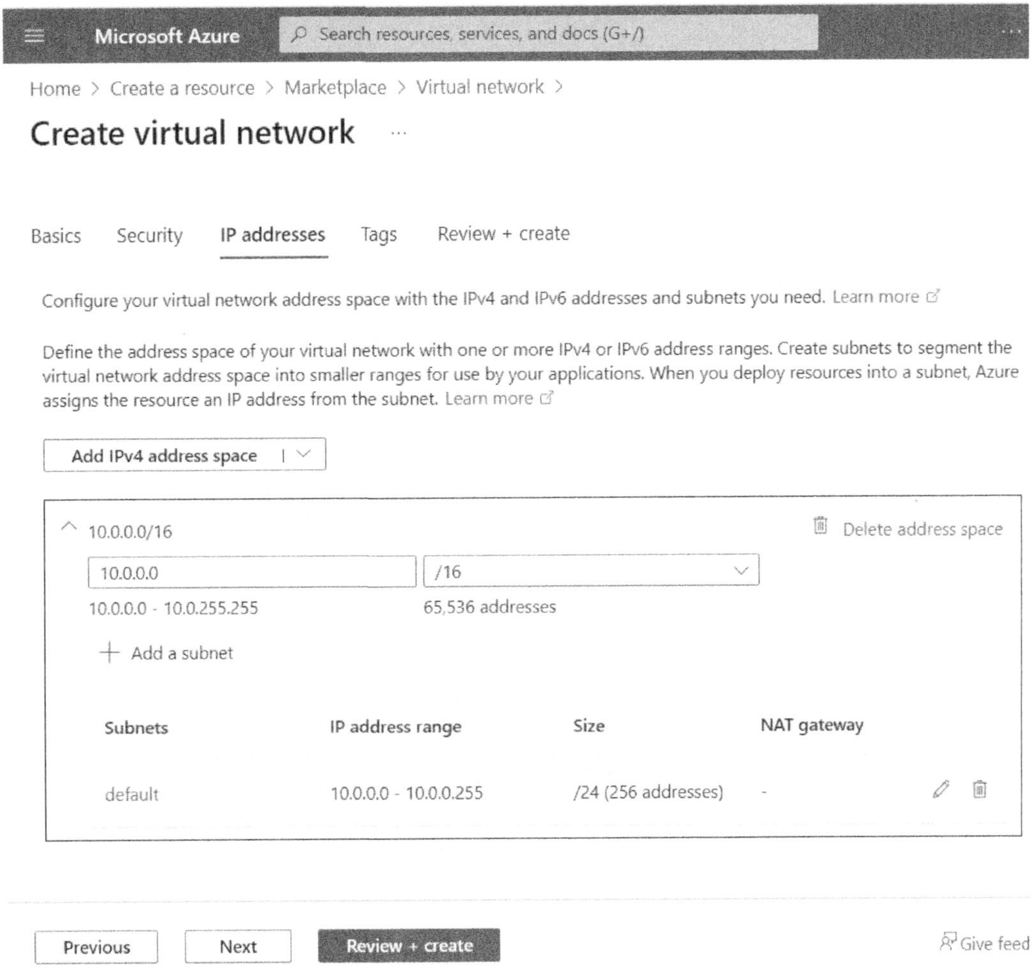

Figure 8.16 – Configuring IP details for the new VNet

8. Finally, click on Review + create to create the new VNet.

9. From the Azure portal, search for **private link** and select Private Link service.

10. On the **Private Link Center** screen, select the Private endpoints option.

11. Click on the + Create tab, shown in *Figure 8.17*, to display the **Create a private endpoint** screen:

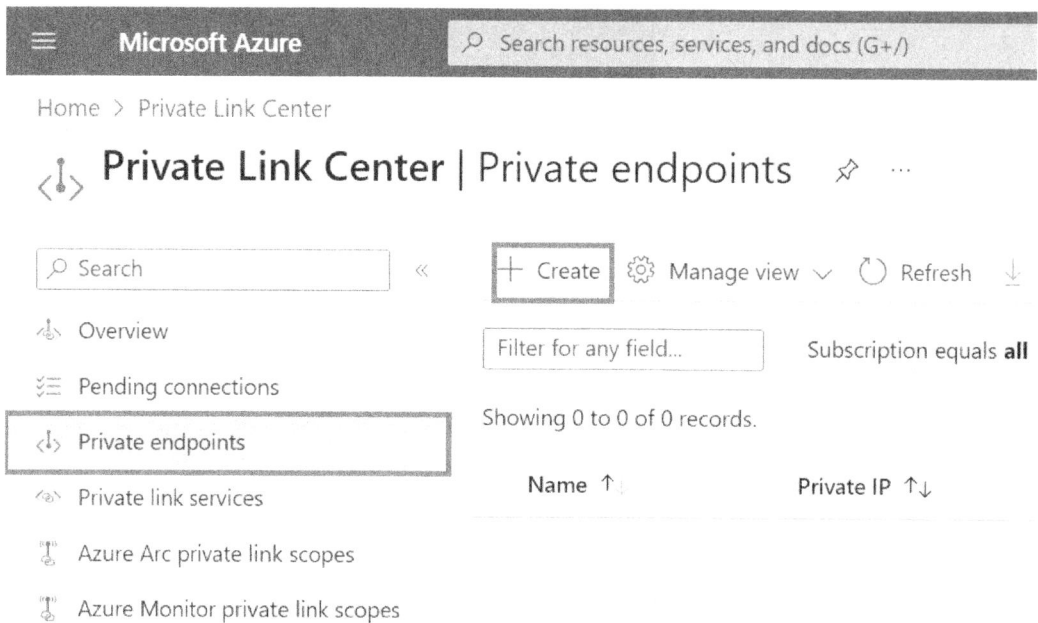

Figure 8.17 – Creating a private endpoint from Private Link Center

12. On the **Create a private endpoint** screen, select the resource you want the endpoint to be created in.

13. On the **Basics** tab, select the general project details, such as your subscription and resource group, and provide the name of the private endpoint and the region where you want to deploy this resource.

14. On the **Resource** tab, choose the **Resource** name. In this case, it is `synapse-az-ws` (see *Figure 8.18*):

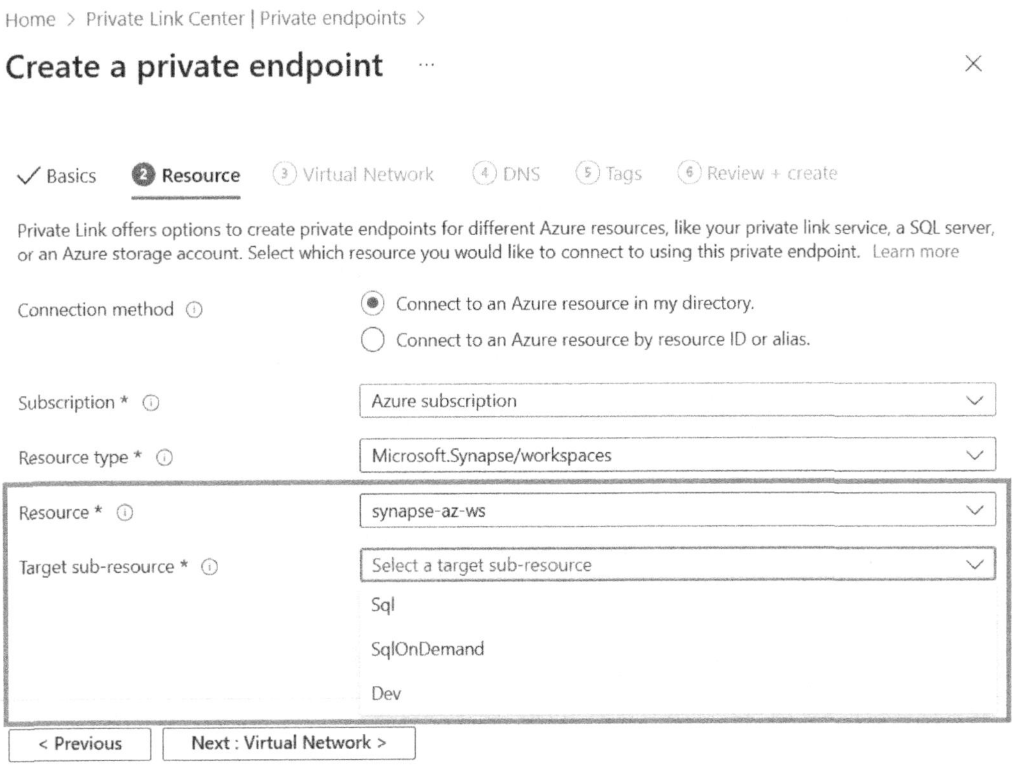

Home > Private Link Center | Private endpoints >

# Create a private endpoint   ⋯                                                                ✕

✓ Basics    **② Resource**    ③ Virtual Network    ④ DNS    ⑤ Tags    ⑥ Review + create

Private Link offers options to create private endpoints for different Azure resources, like your private link service, a SQL server, or an Azure storage account. Select which resource you would like to connect to using this private endpoint.  Learn more

| Connection method ⓘ | ◉ Connect to an Azure resource in my directory. |
| | ○ Connect to an Azure resource by resource ID or alias. |

| Subscription * ⓘ | Azure subscription ⌄ |
| Resource type * ⓘ | Microsoft.Synapse/workspaces ⌄ |

| Resource * ⓘ | synapse-az-ws ⌄ |
| Target sub-resource * ⓘ | Select a target sub-resource ⌄ |
| | Sql |
| | SqlOnDemand |
| | Dev |

< Previous      Next : Virtual Network >

Figure 8.18 – Configuring a service for creating the private endpoint

15. Select **Target sub-resource** from the list displayed, as shown in *Figure 8.18*, and click the `Next : Virtual Network >` button.

16. On the **Virtual Network** tab, provide the **Virtual network** name. In this case, it is `vnet-1` (`rg-vnet`).

17. Keep the subnet as default, as shown in *Figure 8.19*:

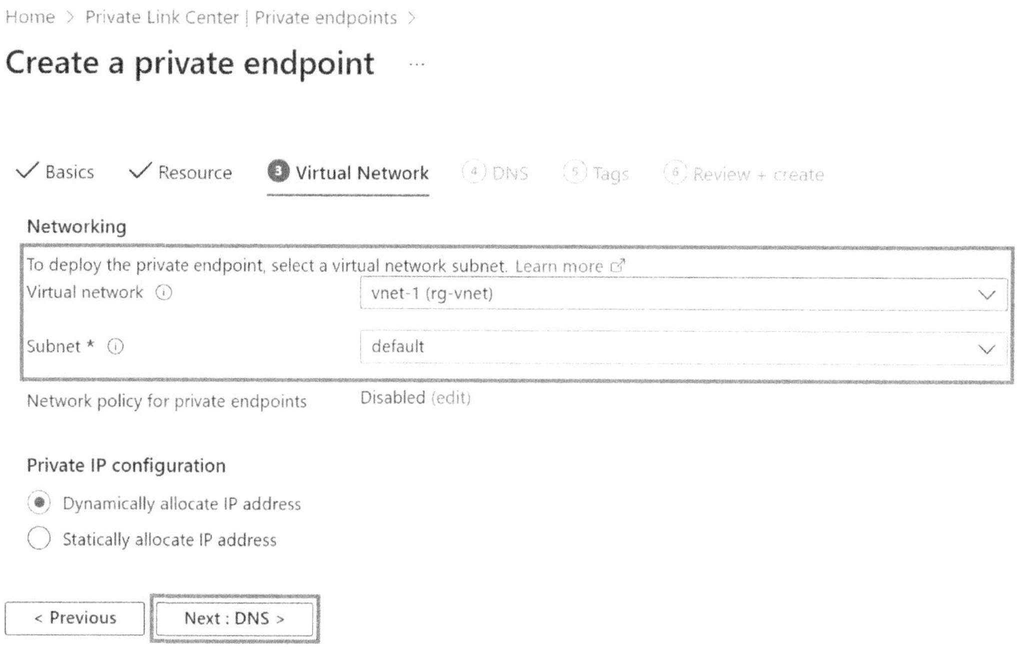

Home > Private Link Center | Private endpoints >

## Create a private endpoint  ...

✓ Basics      ✓ Resource      **③ Virtual Network**    ④ DNS    ⑤ Tags    ⑥ Review + create

### Networking

| To deploy the private endpoint, select a virtual network subnet. Learn more ⬈ | |
|---|---|
| Virtual network  ⓘ | vnet-1 (rg-vnet) ⌄ |
| Subnet *  ⓘ | default ⌄ |

Network policy for private endpoints        Disabled (edit)

### Private IP configuration

◉ Dynamically allocate IP address

○ Statically allocate IP address

[ < Previous ]   [ Next : DNS > ]

Figure 8.19 – Configuring VNet for private endpoint

18. Click Next: DNS> to move to the **DNS** tab.

19. On the **DNS** tab, select Yes for the **Integrate with private DNS Zone** option.

20. Once the preceding details are entered, click the Review + create button on the final screen to create the private endpoint.

From now on, the Synapse workspace can be accessed only within vnet1 specified in the example (see *Figure 8.19*).

> **Note**
>
> You can learn more about private endpoints at https://packt.link/jolk4.

Now that you know how to create a private endpoint, there is an alternative, easier way to do so using a managed VNet and managed endpoints. To do so, perform the following steps:

1. Create a Synapse workspace.

2. Select the **Networking** tab.

3. Enable the `Managed virtual network` radio button.

   When you enable `Managed virtual network`, Synapse takes care of creating the VNet, the private endpoints, the right firewall rules, the right subnets, and so on. This is a very convenient and less error-prone way to create private endpoints. A managed private VNet and endpoints are no different than manually created ones. It is just that the life cycle of managed VNets and endpoints is taken care of by the host service, which in your case is Synapse.

4. Enable the `Create managed private endpoint to primary storage account` radio button, as shown in *Figure 8.20* (this is not a mandatory option, so you can select No):

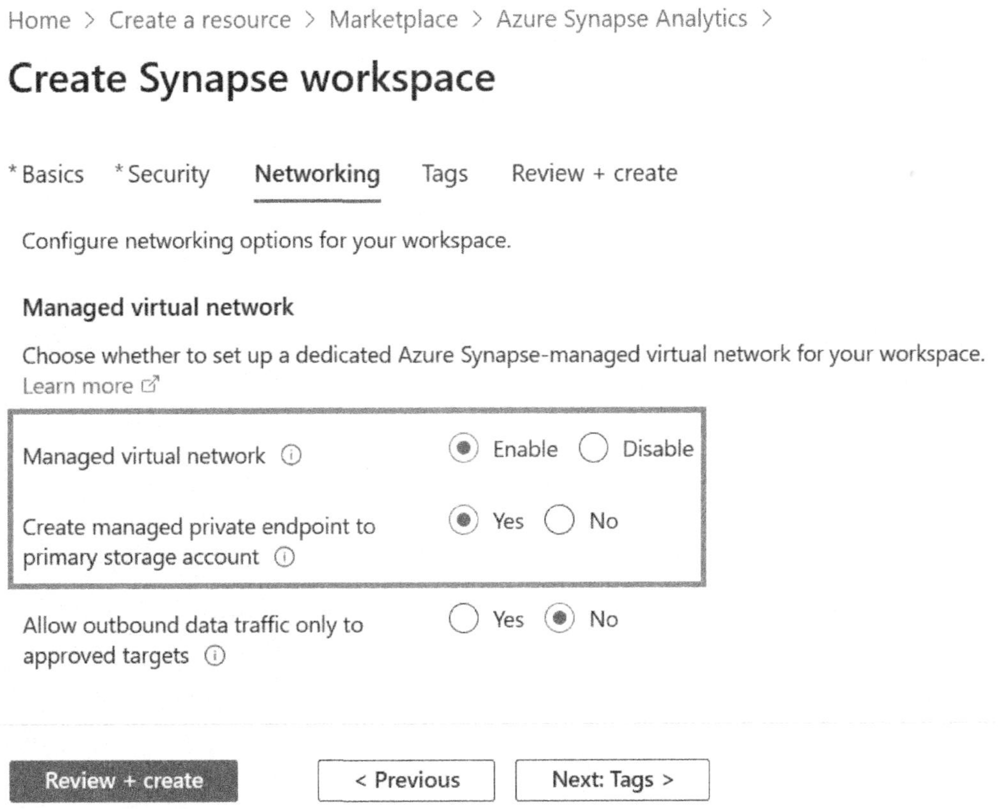

Home > Create a resource > Marketplace > Azure Synapse Analytics >

# Create Synapse workspace

\* Basics    \* Security    **Networking**    Tags    Review + create

Configure networking options for your workspace.

## Managed virtual network

Choose whether to set up a dedicated Azure Synapse-managed virtual network for your workspace.
Learn more ⬏

| | |
|---|---|
| Managed virtual network ⓘ | ⦿ Enable ◯ Disable |
| Create managed private endpoint to primary storage account ⓘ | ⦿ Yes ◯ No |

Allow outbound data traffic only to approved targets ⓘ      ◯ Yes  ⦿ No

| Review + create | | < Previous | Next: Tags > |
|---|---|---|---|

Figure 8.20 – Enabling a Synapse-managed VNet to create a private endpoint

You have now learned how to take advantage of the networking features of Azure to control who can access your data at the network level. Next, following the exam syllabus, you will learn how to use access tokens in Azure Databricks.

# Implementing Resource Tokens in Azure Databricks

Resource tokens offer a convenient way to manage access to your Azure Databricks workspace resources and play a crucial role in securing your Databricks environment, ensuring that only authorized users can access sensitive data and resources. By managing resource tokens effectively, you can enhance data protection and maintain control over your workspace.

> **Note**
>
> This section primarily focuses on the **Implement resource tokens in Azure Databricks** concept of the DP-203: Data Engineering on Microsoft Azure exam.

Azure Databricks provides access tokens called **Personal Access Tokens** (**PATs**) that can be used to authenticate Azure Databricks APIs. Perform the following steps to create a new Azure Databricks PAT:

1. Go to the **Azure portal**, then search for and select the `Azure Databricks` service that you created. If you have not created one, follow the next steps.

2. Select the `User Settings` option under **Settings** (*Figure 8.21*):

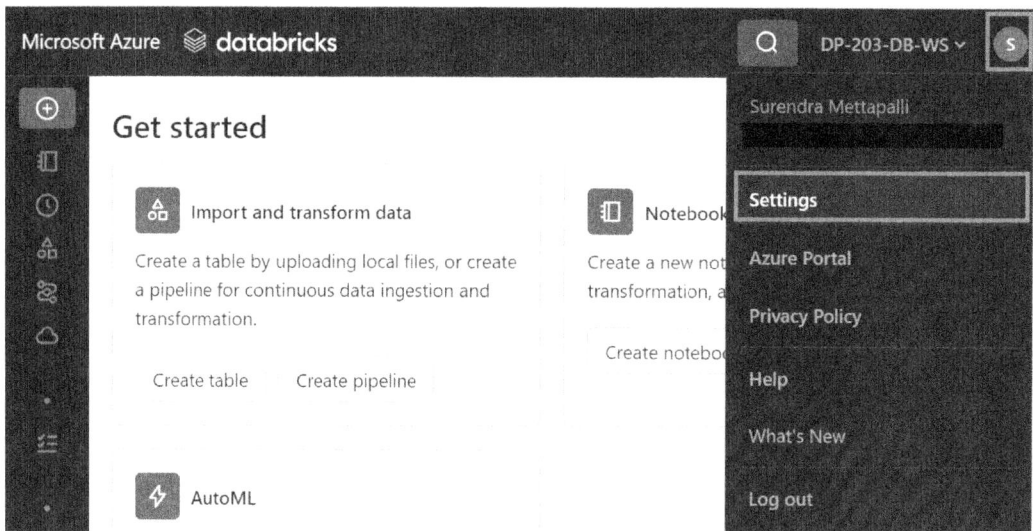

Figure 8.21 – Accessing User Settings in Azure Databricks for developer settings

3.  Select the `Developer` tab under **User Settings** to view the **Access tokens | Manage** option (see *Figure 8.22*):

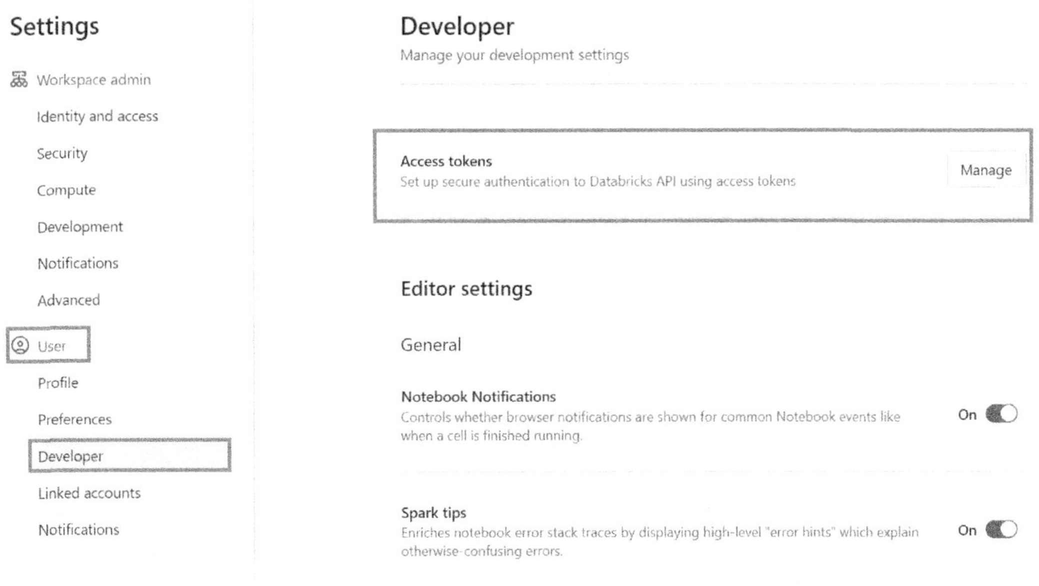

## Settings

- Workspace admin
    - Identity and access
    - Security
    - Compute
    - Development
    - Notifications
    - Advanced
- User
    - Profile
    - Preferences
    - Developer
    - Linked accounts
    - Notifications

## Developer

Manage your development settings

---

**Access tokens**                                                        Manage
Set up secure authentication to Databricks API using access tokens

## Editor settings

General

**Notebook Notifications**                                               On
Controls whether browser notifications are shown for common Notebook events like
when a cell is finished running.

**Spark tips**                                                           On
Enriches notebook error stack traces by displaying high-level "error hints" which explain
otherwise-confusing errors.

Figure 8.22 – Accessing Developer settings to manage access tokens

4.  Under the **Access Tokens** tab, click on `Manage`. Then click the `Generate New Token` button (*Figure 8.23*):

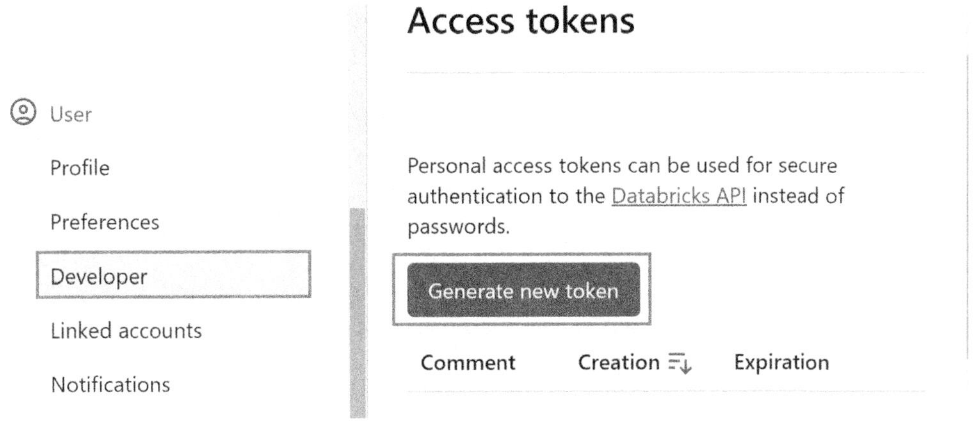

## Access tokens

- User
    - Profile
    - Preferences
    - Developer
    - Linked accounts
    - Notifications

Personal access tokens can be used for secure authentication to the Databricks API instead of passwords.

**Generate new token**

Comment        Creation        Expiration

Figure 8.23 – Generating New Token in Azure Databricks

5.  Fill in the **Comment** field, for example, you can use `databrick-access-token`.

6.  Fill in the **Lifetime (days)** field for the token. In this case, make this `90` (see *Figure 8.24*):

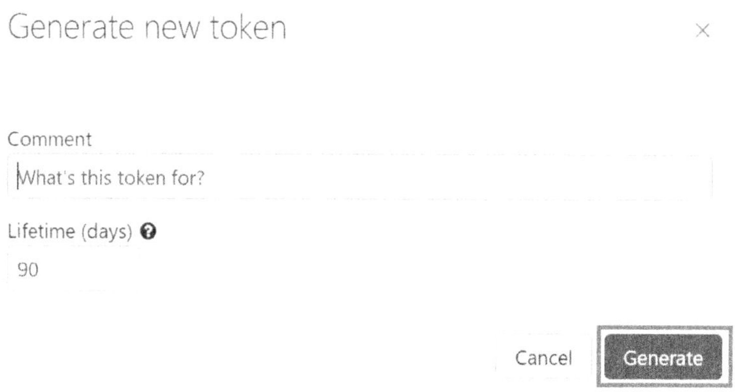

Figure 8.24 – Creating a new Azure Databricks PAT

7.  Click the `Generate` button to bring up a screen with the token (see *Figure 8.25*). Copy and store the token safely:

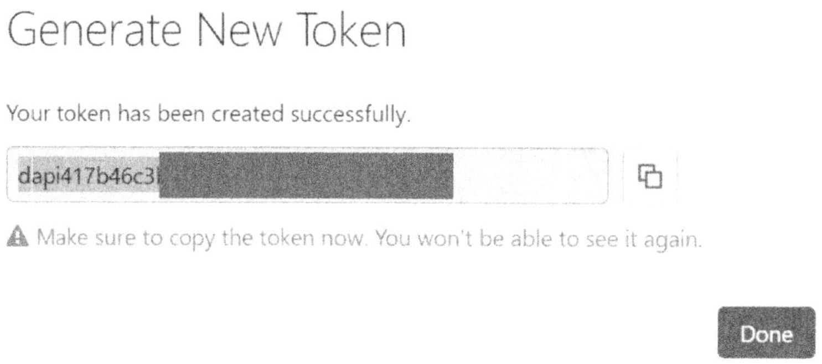

Figure 8.25 – Copying the successfully generated token

You will not be able to copy that token again once that screen is closed. If you lose the token, you will have to delete it and generate a new one.

8.  You can also create a PAT using APIs. The following code shows a request for a token that will be valid for 1 day (86400 seconds):

```
curl --netrc --request POST \
https://<databricks-instance>/api/2.0/token/create \
--data '{ "comment": "ADB PAT token", "lifetime_seconds": 86400
}'
```

In the preceding code, the command line uses `curl` to send an HTTP POST request to a Databricks instance, specifically to the `/api/2.0/token/create` endpoint. It includes authentication details from the `.netrc` file. The request body is in JSON format, containing a comment describing the token and the token's lifetime as 86400 seconds (24 hours, in this case). This process generates an access token for Azure Databricks with the specified properties.

9.  Once you have a PAT, you can use it in the APIs, as shown in the following code block:

```
export DATABRICKS_TOKEN=<INSERT YOUR TOKEN>
curl -X GET --header "Authorization: Bearer $DATABRICKS_TOKEN"
https://<ADB-INSTANCE>.azuredatabricks.net/api/2.0/clusters/list
```

In the preceding code, the script sets an environment variable, `DATABRICKS_TOKEN`, to hold an access token for Azure Databricks. Then, it uses `curl` to make an HTTP GET request to a specific endpoint (`/api/2.0/clusters/list`) on the Azure Databricks instance (`<ADB-INSTANCE>.azuredatabricks.net`). The request includes an authorization header with the access token retrieved from the environment variable. This script essentially fetches a list of clusters from the Azure Databricks instance using the provided access token for authentication. The maximum number of PATs per Azure Databricks workspace is 600.

> **Note**
> All the entries within angular brackets, < >, are user-provided values. You can learn more about PATs at `https://packt.link/yxxq8`.

Similar to the PATs of **Azure Databricks**, regular **Microsoft Entra ID** tokens can also be used for authorization.

> **Note**
> You can read about Microsoft Entra ID tokens at `https://packt.link/0xiF6`.

By now, you have learned how to use access tokens to manage access to a Databricks instance. In the next section, you will focus on handling sensitive information within Spark DataFrames.

## Loading DataFrames with Sensitive Information

When working with data, especially sensitive data, it is crucial to handle and load information securely. In this context, you will focus on loading a DataFrame containing sensitive information. You will get to know the best practices for ensuring data security while using tools such as **Azure Databricks**. By following secure loading practices, you can protect sensitive data and maintain compliance with privacy regulations.

Earlier in this chapter, you learned about techniques such as data masking and row- and column-level security for Azure Synapse SQL.

> **Note**
>
> This section primarily focuses on the **Load a DataFrame with sensitive information** concept of the DP-203: Data Engineering on Microsoft Azure exam.

Spark, at the time of writing this book, didn't have techniques, other than **Personally Identifiable Information** (**PII**), for handling sensitive information. If handling sensitive data goes beyond PII, you can utilize it by applying encryption, access controls, and secure practices, and safeguard all types of sensitive information within your **Databricks** environment. Right now, PII is the best option for the most common, critical types of sensitive information.

Now look at an example showing the best way to emulate handling sensitive information such as **PII** using encryption and decryption. Perform the following steps to do so:

1. Create a simple table that contains PII such as SSNs using PySpark:

```
from pyspark.sql.types import StructType,StructField,
StringType, IntegerType
cols = StructType([ \
    StructField("Name",StringType(),True), \
    StructField("SSN",StringType(),True), \
    StructField("email",StringType(),True)
  ])
data = [("Adam Smith","111-11-1111","james@james.com"),
    («Brenda Harman»,»222-22-2222»,»brenda@brenda.com»),
    («Carmen Pinto»,»333-33-3333», «carmen@carmen.com»)
  ]
piidf = spark.createDataFrame(data=data,schema=cols)
display(piidf)
```

In the preceding code, you use `pyspark` to create a DataFrame, `piidf`, from a list of tuples data with a specified schema—`cols`. The schema defines the structure of the DataFrame with three columns: `Name`, `SSN`, and `email`, each of type `StringType()`. The `spark.`

`createDataFrame()` function creates the DataFrame, passing `data` and `schema` as arguments. Finally, the `display(piidf)` function visualizes the DataFrame.

The output will be something like that shown in *Figure 8.26*:

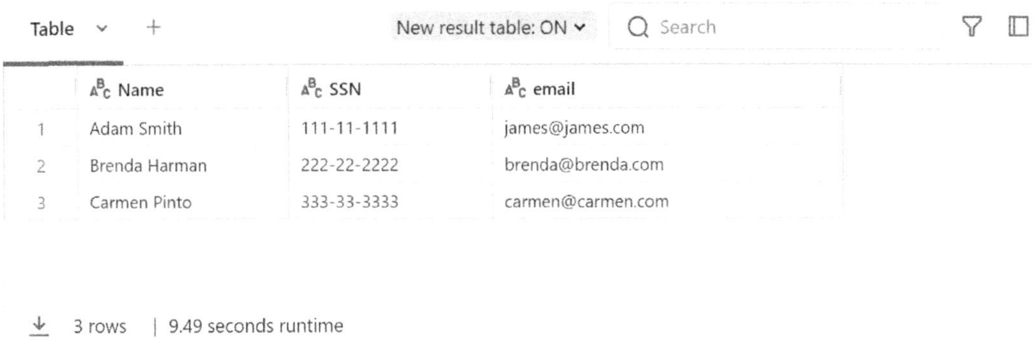

| | A<sup>B</sup><sub>C</sub> Name | A<sup>B</sup><sub>C</sub> SSN | A<sup>B</sup><sub>C</sub> email |
|---|---|---|---|
| 1 | Adam Smith | 111-11-1111 | james@james.com |
| 2 | Brenda Harman | 222-22-2222 | brenda@brenda.com |
| 3 | Carmen Pinto | 333-33-3333 | carmen@carmen.com |

Table ∨  +                            New result table: ON ∨    Q Search

↓  3 rows  |  9.49 seconds runtime

Figure 8.26 – Output displaying PII, such as SSN

2.  Import the `Fernet` encryption library, which provides the ability to encrypt and decrypt text in the following ways:

```
from cryptography.fernet import Fernet
encryptionKey = Fernet.generate_key()
```

In the preceding code, Python utilizes the cryptography library to generate an `encryptionKey` using the `Fernet` symmetric encryption scheme. The `Fernet.generate_key()` function generates a random 32-byte key that is suitable for symmetric encryption and decryption operations. This generated key can then be used with the `Fernet` algorithm to encrypt and decrypt data securely.

> **Note**
> You can download the Fernet library from `https://packt.link/USKrM`.

3.  Define the `encrypt` **User-Defined Function (UDF)**:

```
def encryptUdf(plaintext, KEY):
    from cryptography.fernet import Fernet
    f = Fernet(KEY)
    encryptedtext = f.encrypt(bytes(plaintext, 'utf-8'))
    return str(encryptedtext.decode('ascii'))
encrypt = udf(encryptUdf, StringType())
```

4.  Define the `decrypt` UDF:

    ```
    def decryptUdf(encryptedtext, KEY):
        from cryptography.fernet import Fernet
        f = Fernet(KEY)
        plaintext=f.decrypt( encryptedtext.encode()).decode()
        return plaintext
    decrypt = udf(decryptUdf, StringType())
    ```

5.  Encrypt the SSN column DataFrame:

    ```
    df = piidf.withColumn("SSN", encrypt("SSN", lit(encryptionKey)))
    display(encrypteddf)
    ```

    The output will now be shown encrypted (*Figure 8.27*):

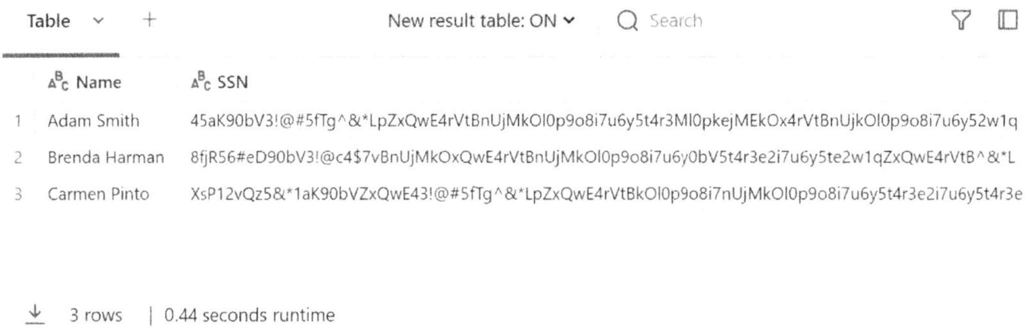

| Table ∨ + | New result table: ON ∨   Q Search |
|---|---|
| Aᴮc Name | Aᴮc SSN |
| 1  Adam Smith | 45aK90bV3!@#5fTg^&*LpZxQwE4rVtBnUjMkOl0p9o8i7u6y5t4r3Ml0pkejMEkOx4rVtBnUjkOl0p9o8i7u6y52w1q |
| 2  Brenda Harman | 8fjR56#eD90bV3!@c4$7vBnUjMkOxQwE4rVtBnUjMkOl0p9o8i7u6y0bV5t4r3e2i7u6y5te2w1qZxQwE4rVtB^&*L |
| 3  Carmen Pinto | XsP12vQz5&*1aK90bVZxQwE43!@#5fTg^&*LpZxQwE4rVtBkOl0p9o8i7nUjMkOl0p9o8i7u6y5t4r3e2i7u6y5t4r3e |

↓  3 rows   |  0.44 seconds runtime

Figure 8.27 – Displaying output with encrypted PII

6.  Now, save the DataFrame as a table:

    ```
    df.write.format("delta").mode("overwrite").
    option("overwriteSchema", "true").
    saveAsTable("PIIEncryptedTable")
    ```

    Alternatively, you can also write the encrypted file to Parquet, as shown here:

    ```
    encrypted.write.mode("overwrite").parquet("abfss://path/to/
    store")
    ```

    From now on, only individuals holding the encryption key will be able to decrypt and see the PII.

7.  If you have the encryption key, decrypt the column as follows:

    ```
    decrypted = encrypteddf.withColumn("SSN",
    decrypt("SSN",lit(encryptionKey)))
    display(decrypted)
    ```

The output will now be shown decrypted (see *Figure 8.28*):

▶ 🖼 decrypted: pyspark.sql.dataframe.DataFrame = [Name: string, SSN: string

| | Name ▲ | SSN ▲ | email ▲ |
|---|---|---|---|
| 1 | Adam Smith | 111-11-1111 | james@james.com |
| 2 | Brenda Harman | 222-22-2222 | brenda@brenda.com |
| 3 | Carmen Pinto | 333-33-3333 | carmen@carmen.com |

Figure 8.28 – Displaying output with decrypted PII

You have now learned how to perform column-level encryption and decryption using DataFrames. This technique would work fine with both Synapse Spark and Databricks Spark.

> **Note**
>
> You can find the complete code in the accompanying GitHub repository at https://packt. link/qSiVz.

Next, you will see how to write encrypted data into tables and files.

## Writing Encrypted Data into Tables or Parquet Files

Protecting sensitive data is crucial, especially when storing it in **Azure Databricks**. Encrypting data at rest is a key step in ensuring its security and compliance with regulations. By encrypting data, you safeguard it from unauthorized access, maintaining its confidentiality even if breaches occur. Consider implementing column-level encryption for specific sensitive columns, balancing security with performance. Proper key management is essential to utilize services such as **Azure Key Vault** to securely handle encryption keys. Additionally, verify data integrity during read and write operations, and implement authentication mechanisms to ensure encrypted data remains intact. These best practices help maintain the security and integrity of your data in Azure Databricks, offering peace of mind while handling sensitive information.

> **Note**
>
> This section primarily focuses on the **Write encrypted data to tables or Parquet files** concept of the DP-203: Data Engineering on Microsoft Azure exam.

You learned to how write encrypted data into tables and Parquet files in the example provided in the *Loading DataFrames with Sensitive Information* section. In the following code, the DataFrame is again written to tables:

```
df.write.format("delta").mode("overwrite").option("overwriteSchema",
"true").saveAsTable("PIIEncryptedTable")
```

The following shows the encrypted data written to Parquet files:

```
encrypted.write.mode("overwrite").parquet("abfss://path/to/store")
```

By now, you have gained insight into the importance of securely handling and loading data, particularly sensitive data, using tools such as **Azure Databricks**. You have also learned about best practices for ensuring data security during the loading process to protect sensitive information while adhering to privacy regulations effectively. You gained knowledge on the significance of encrypting data at rest to prevent unauthorized access and maintain confidentiality in the event of breaches, in addition to the benefits of implementing column-level encryption for specific sensitive columns while managing performance considerations. You grasped the importance of ensuring the integrity of encrypted data and maintaining data integrity during read-and-write operations through authentication mechanisms. By following these best practices, you can confidently manage sensitive information within Azure Databricks, thus ensuring security and compliance.

The next section will look at some guidelines for managing sensitive information.

> **Note**
>
> You can find the complete code in the accompanying GitHub repository at `https://packt.link/7lzcz`.

## Managing Sensitive Information

Any organization that handles sensitive information is usually bound by its country or state laws and other compliance regulations to keep the data secure and confidential. Aside from legal obligations, keeping sensitive data protected is very important for the reputation of an organization and helps to reduce the risk of identity theft for its customers.

> **Note**
>
> This section primarily focuses on the **Manage sensitive information** concept of the DP-203: Data Engineering on Microsoft Azure exam.

Azure security standards recommend the following techniques to keep sensitive data safe:

- **Identifying and classifying sensitive data**: The very first step is to analyze and identify all the sensitive data in your data stores. Some might be straightforward, such as SQL tables or structured files, and some might be not so straightforward, such as PII data being logged in log files.

Azure also provides tools that can help with the identification and classification of data. For example, the **Synapse SQL portal** provides a feature for **Data Discovery & Classification**, which automatically suggests sensitive columns. *Figure 8.29* shows the **Data Discovery & Classification** screen:

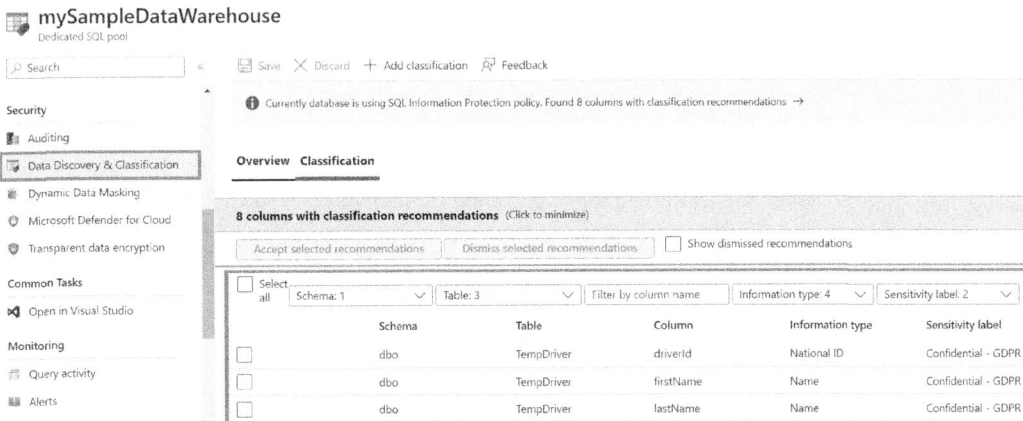

Figure 8.29 – Displaying Data Discovery & Classification in Synapse SQL

- **Protecting the sensitive data**: Once you have cataloged all the sensitive data in the data stores, the next step is to take the necessary steps to protect it. This includes all the techniques that have been discussed in this chapter, in the *Implementing Data Masking* and *Encrypting Data at Rest and in Motion* sections, such as separating the sensitive data into different accounts, partitions, or folders, restricting access using RBAC and ACLs, encrypting data at rest, encrypting data in transit, data masking, and row- and column-level security.

- **Monitoring and auditing the consumption of sensitive data**: The best security policy is to not trust anyone, not even the folks who officially have access to the sensitive data. So, adding strong monitoring capabilities and enabling audit trails helps in actively and passively tracking down any malicious data access.

You will also briefly look at other services available in Azure to help with security and threat management. They are as follows:

- **Microsoft Defender**: In order to further strengthen your Azure application's security and threat management ability, Azure provides a service called **Microsoft Defender**. It provides the tools and services required to continuously monitor, alert, and mitigate threats to Azure services. Microsoft Defender is natively integrated into most Azure services, so it can be enabled easily without requiring major changes to your applications.

- **Microsoft Defender for Storage**: Microsoft Defender for Storage can help identify threats such as anonymous access, malicious content, compromised credentials, privilege abuse, and so on.

> **Note**
>
> You can learn more about Microsoft Defender for Storage at `https://packt.link/y04zo`.

- **Microsoft Defender for SQL**: Microsoft Defender for SQL can help identify threats such as SQL injection, brute-force attacks, and privilege abuse. A critical component of an organization's defense-in-depth strategy is providing robust protection against a wide range of threats targeting SQL Server databases. Its proactive threat detection capabilities coupled with seamless integration with the broader security ecosystem make it an essential tool for safeguarding critical data assets in today's dynamic threat landscape.

> **Note**
>
> You can learn more about Microsoft Defender for SQL at `https://packt.link/MwiMe`.

In this final section, you have gained insight into Azure's recommendations to protect your data. This is done for legal compliance, to protect sensitive information, and to prevent data leakages that could harm a company's reputation. Encryption, data masking, and row- and column-level security are all powerful techniques for data protection, but it is also important to follow tasks and rituals such as identifying, monitoring, and auditing the consumption of sensitive data. Azure services, such as Microsoft Defender, both for storage and SQL, can help you achieve optimum levels of security.

> **Note**
>
> You can find more information about handling sensitive information and data protection guidelines at `https://packt.link/3aXEo` and `https://packt.link/QwBgS`.

## Summary

In this chapter, you learned about encryption at rest and in transit, enabling auditing for ADLS and Synapse SQL, implementing data masking, RBAC and ACL rules, row- and column-level security, and data retention and purging. You also gained knowledge about secure endpoints and details about tokens and encryption in Spark.

By now, you have covered all the important topics relating to handling security and privacy. You should now be able to design and implement a complete security and privacy solution on top of ADLS.

You will be exploring monitoring for data storage and data processing in the next chapter.

# Exam Readiness Drill – Chapter Review Questions

Apart from a solid understanding of key concepts, being able to think quickly under time pressure is a skill that will help you ace your certification exam. That is why working on these skills early on in your learning journey is key.

Chapter review questions are designed to improve your test-taking skills progressively with each chapter you learn and review your understanding of key concepts in the chapter at the same time. You'll find these at the end of each chapter.

> **How to Access These Materials**
>
> To learn how to access these resources, head over to the chapter titled *Chapter 11, Accessing the Online Resources*.

To open the Chapter Review Questions for this chapter, perform the following steps:

1.  Click the link – `https://packt.link/DP203E2_CH08`.

    Alternatively, you can scan the following **QR code** (*Figure 8.30*):

Figure 8.30 – QR code that opens Chapter Review Questions for logged-in users

2.    Once you log in, you'll see a page similar to the one shown in *Figure 8.31*:

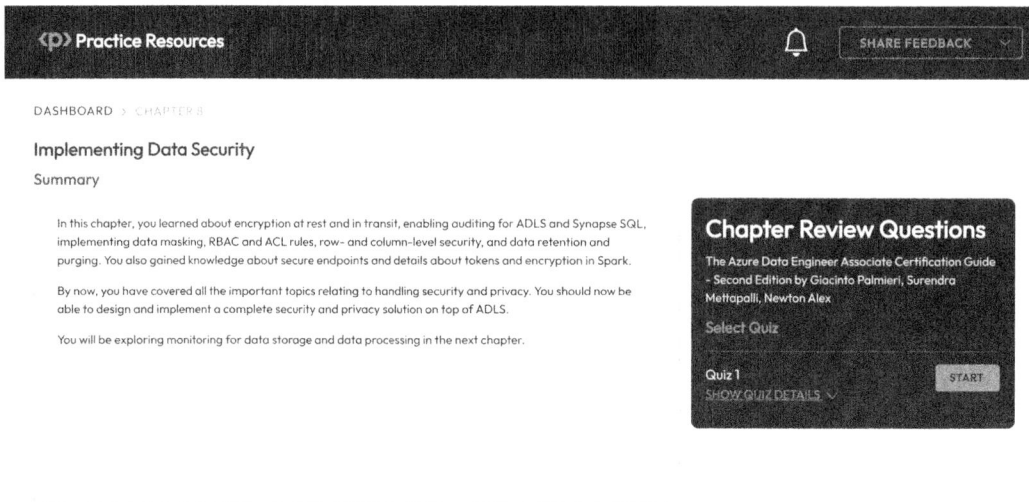

Figure 8.31 – Chapter Review Questions for Chapter 8

3.    Once ready, start the following practice drills, re-attempting the quiz multiple times.

## Exam Readiness Drill

For the first three attempts, don't worry about the time limit.

### ATTEMPT 1

The first time, aim for at least **40%**. Look at the answers you got wrong and read the relevant sections in the chapter again to fix your learning gaps.

### ATTEMPT 2

The second time, aim for at least **60%**. Look at the answers you got wrong and read the relevant sections in the chapter again to fix any remaining learning gaps.

## *ATTEMPT 3*

The third time, aim for at least **75%**. Once you score 75% or more, you start working on your timing.

> **Tip**
>
> You may take more than **three** attempts to reach 75%. That's okay. Just review the relevant sections in the chapter till you get there.

# Working On Timing

**Target**: Your aim is to keep the score the same while trying to answer these questions as quickly as possible. Here's an example of how your next attempts should look like:

| Attempt | Score | Time Taken |
|---------|-------|------------|
| Attempt 5 | 77% | 21 mins 30 seconds |
| Attempt 6 | 78% | 18 mins 34 seconds |
| Attempt 7 | 76% | 14 mins 44 seconds |

Table 8.1 – Sample timing practice drills on the online platform

> **Note**
>
> The time limits shown in the above table are just examples. Set your own time limits with each attempt based on the time limit of the quiz on the website.

With each new attempt, your score should stay above **75%** while your "time taken" to complete should "decrease". Repeat as many attempts as you want till you feel confident dealing with the time pressure.

# 9

# Monitoring Data Storage and Data Processing

In *Chapter 8, Implementing Data Security*, you learned to protect the most valuable asset: data. With clear policies on data retention and meticulous care in handling sensitive information, you learned how data remains secure and inviolable against the ever-present threats of the modern digital environment.

In this chapter, you will learn about the monitoring aspect of data storage and pipelines. By the end of this chapter, you should be able to set up monitoring for any of your Azure Data Services, custom logs, and process logs, using tools such as Azure Log Analytics, monitor stream processing, and schedule monitor pipeline tests. As with the previous chapters, the topic sequence will strictly follow that of the syllabus.

This chapter primarily focuses on the **Monitor data storage and data processing** topic of the DP-203: Data Engineering on Microsoft Azure exam.

This chapter will equip you with the confidence to effectively answer questions on the following:

- Logging used by Azure Monitor
- Monitoring services and stream processing
- Data movement and monitoring statistics about data across a system
- Data pipelines and query performance
- Scheduling and monitoring pipeline tests
- Azure Monitor metrics and logs
- Pipeline alert strategies

## Technical Requirements

For this chapter, you will need an Azure account (free or paid) and an active **Azure Data Factory** (**ADF**) workspace.

## Implementing Logging by Azure Monitor

**Azure Monitor's logging** feature offers a robust solution for aggregating, analyzing, and leveraging telemetry data across your cloud and on-premises environments. It consolidates data from diverse sources such as applications, infrastructure, and services, enabling real-time analysis of vast datasets. Additionally, Azure Monitor distinguishes itself by contextualizing data and learning the intricate relationships between applications and infrastructure for more precise analysis. Moreover, it offers advanced analytics capabilities, including customizable dashboards, sophisticated queries, and intelligent alerting mechanisms for prompt issue detection. Furthermore, Azure Monitor seamlessly integrates with other Azure services, supporting its functionality and enabling monitoring across various resources such as **Virtual Machines** (**VMs**), containers, and databases.

Monitoring with Azure Monitor is essential for performance optimization, identifying resource bottlenecks, and enhancing efficient resource utilization. It contributes to security by detecting anomalies, unauthorized access attempts, and potential threats. Monitoring facilitates cost management by tracking expenses, identifying inefficiencies, and optimizing spending. It not only ensures compliance with industry standards and regulations, safeguarding against potential penalties and reputational damage, but also supports reliability by proactively addressing issues, thereby maintaining service availability, and enhancing overall operational resilience.

**Azure Monitor** is the service you use to monitor infrastructure, services, and applications. It records two types of data—metrics and logs. **Metrics** are numerical values that describe an entity or an aspect of a system at different instances of time—for example, the number of **Gigabytes** (**GBs**) of data stored in a storage account at any point in time, the current number of active pipelines in ADF, and so on. Metrics are stored in time-series databases and can be easily aggregated for alerting, reporting, and auditing purposes.

**Logs**, on the other hand, are usually text details of what is happening in a system. Unlike metrics, which are recorded at regular intervals, logs are usually event-driven. For example, a user logging into a system, a web app receiving a **REpresentational State Transfer** (**REST**) request and triggering a pipeline in ADF could all generate logs.

> **Note**
>
> This section primarily focuses on the **Implement logging used by Azure Monitor** concept of the DP-203: Data Engineering on Microsoft Azure exam.

Since Azure Monitor is an independent service, it can aggregate logs from multiple services and instances of the same service in Azure to give a global perspective of what is happening with all your Azure services.

*Figure 9.1* is an architecture diagram reproduced from the Azure documentation that shows the core components of Azure Monitor and the sources and destinations for the metrics and logs data:

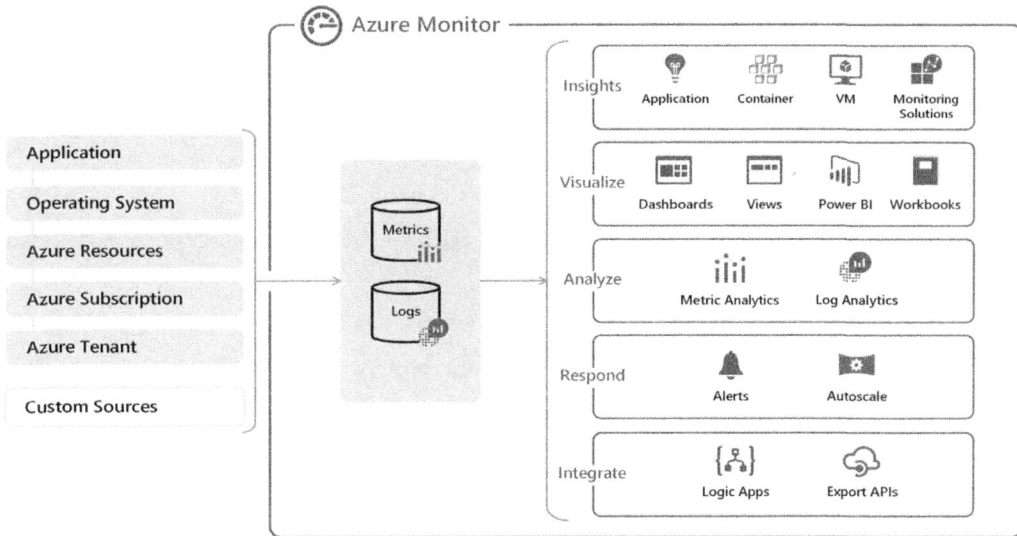

Figure 9.1 – Azure Monitor architecture showing the core components of Azure Monitor, Metrics, and Logs

You will first focus on adding Activity logs to **Azure Monitor**, which requires an introduction to what Azure Monitor calls Log Analytics workspaces. A **Log Analytics** workspace is a component of Azure Monitor that specializes in processing and exploring log messages. You can access **Log Analytics** from the **Logs** tab of any **Azure service** or the Logs tab of Azure Monitor's menu. Log Analytics supports a powerful query language called **Kusto Query Language** (**KQL**) that can be used to perform analysis on log data. You will be seeing some examples of KQL in the *Interpreting Azure Monitor Logs* section in this chapter.

Log Analytics is one of the options to store logs, and it might incur additional charges based on the storage cost and the number of Kusto queries run. Log Analytics is recommended when organizations prioritize real-time log processing, advanced querying capabilities, centralized log management, and seamless integration with Azure services. You can also choose to store logs on regular Azure Storage options such as **Blob** and a **data lake** or use services such as **Event Hubs** to do real-time processing of logs.

Log Analytics stands out as a preferable option for storing logs. While other options such as Blob Storage, data lake storage, or Event Hubs offer storage capabilities, Log Analytics excels in its ability to efficiently manage and analyze log data. It provides advanced querying capabilities through its KQL, enabling you to perform complex queries and gain valuable insights from the logs. Additionally, it offers built-in integration with Azure services and tools, streamlining the monitoring and troubleshooting processes. Furthermore, its centralized log management approach simplifies log aggregation from various sources, facilitating comprehensive analysis and reporting.

Perform the following steps to log data to a Log Analytics workspace:

1. Search for **Log Analytics** workspaces in the **Azure portal** and click on the result to create a new Log Analytics workspace.

2. Click the + `Create` button on the **Log Analytics** home page.

3. On the displayed **Create Log Analytics workspace** screen, select the subscription name beside the **Subscription** field. In this case, it is `Azure subscription`.

4. Choose the **Resource group**. In this case, it is `rg-dp203-log-analytics`.

5. Enter a name beside the **Name** field for the Log Analytics instance, for example, `dp203-loganalytics`.

6. Pick a region beside the **Region** field under the **Instance details** section, for example, `UK South`, as shown in *Figure 9.2*:

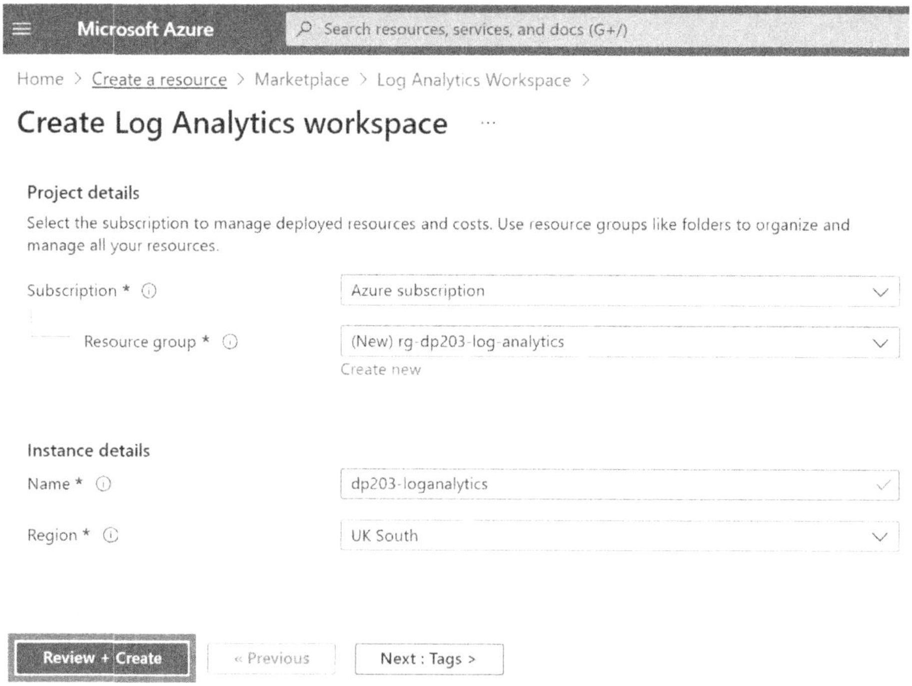

Figure 9.2 – Choosing a subscription to deploy resources during Log Analytics workspace creation

7.   Click on the Review + Create button to create a new Log Analytics workspace.

8.   Next, select the Azure Monitor service from the **Azure portal**, as shown in *Figure 9.3*:

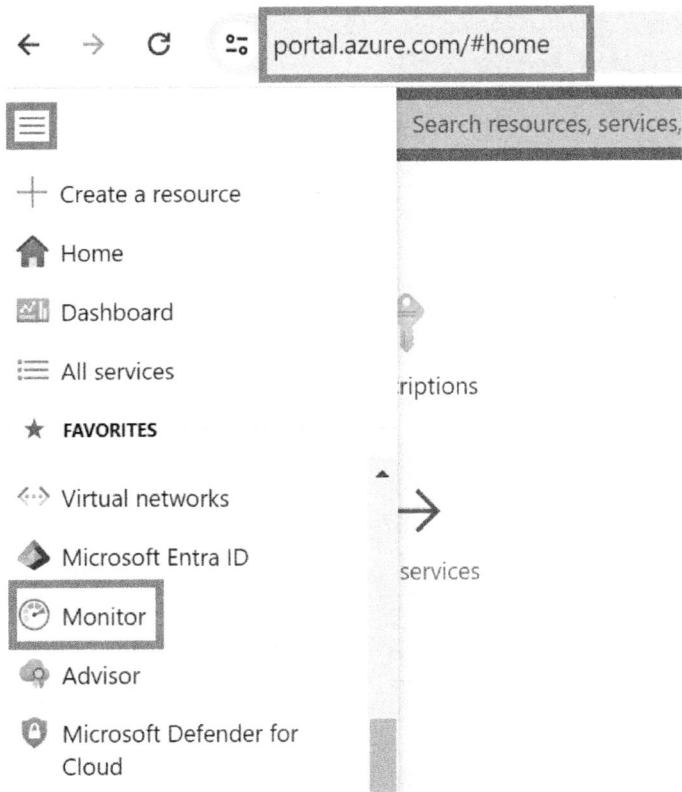

← → C ⚏ portal.azure.com/#home

≡                                          Search resources, services,

+ Create a resource

🏠 Home

📊 Dashboard

≣ All services                        riptions

★ **FAVORITES**

⟨⋯⟩ Virtual networks                  →

◆ Microsoft Entra ID                  services

⊙ Monitor

🔍 Advisor

🛡 Microsoft Defender for
   Cloud

Figure 9.3 – Selecting the Monitor service from the Azure portal

9.  Click on the `Activity log` tab on **Monitor** service to display the **Activity log** screen, as illustrated in *Figure 9.4*:

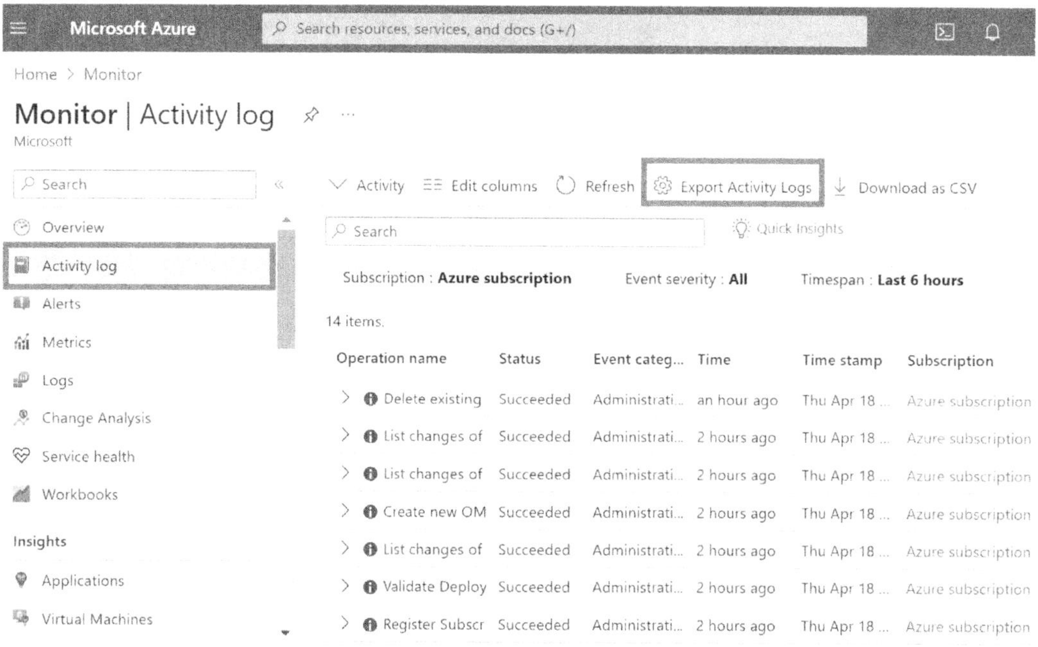

Figure 9.4 – Azure Monitor Activity log screen showing all the activity logs

10. Click on the `Export Activity Logs` tab to open the **Diagnostic setting** screen, as shown in *Figure 9.5*:

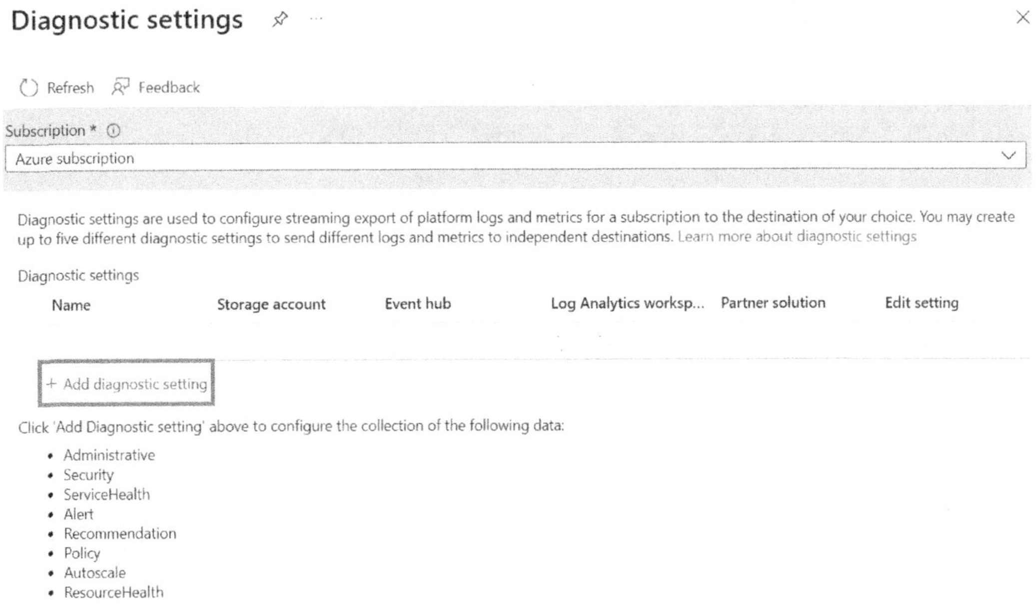

## Diagnostic settings ⚲ ⋯

◯ Refresh  ⃗ Feedback

Subscription * ⓘ

Azure subscription

Diagnostic settings are used to configure streaming export of platform logs and metrics for a subscription to the destination of your choice. You may create up to five different diagnostic settings to send different logs and metrics to independent destinations. Learn more about diagnostic settings

Diagnostic settings

| Name | Storage account | Event hub | Log Analytics worksp... | Partner solution | Edit setting |
| --- | --- | --- | --- | --- | --- |

+ Add diagnostic setting

Click 'Add Diagnostic setting' above to configure the collection of the following data:

- Administrative
- Security
- ServiceHealth
- Alert
- Recommendation
- Policy
- Autoscale
- ResourceHealth

Figure 9.5 – Configuring logs in the Diagnostic settings screen

11. Click on `+ Add diagnostic setting` to specify the **diagnostic setting** name as `LogManagement`.

12. Select all the logs that you want to send to the **Log Analytics workspace**. In this example (*Figure 9.6*), all the checkboxes for `Administrative`, `Security`, `ServiceHealth`, `Alert`, `Recommendation`, `Policy`, `Autoscale`, and `ResourceHealth` are selected (for the workspace name you created in *Step 4*, which is `dp203-loganalytics`).

13. Under the **Destination details** option, click the `Send to Log Analytics workspace` checkbox to select the subscription (`Azure subscription`) and Log Analytics workspace (`dp203-loganalytics`), as illustrated in *Figure 9.6*:

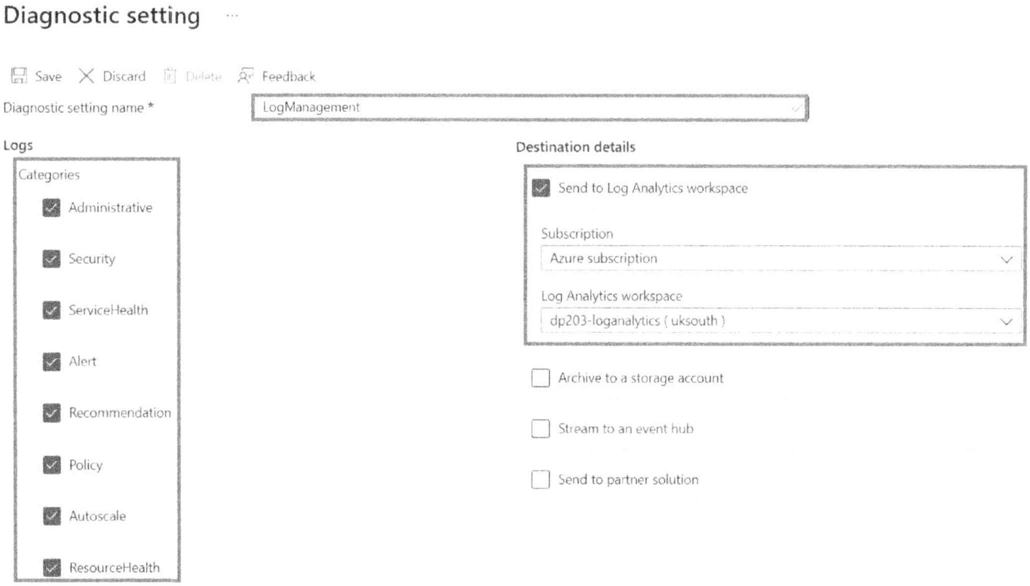

Figure 9.6 – Selecting a list of categories for the Log Analytics workspace in Diagnostic setting

14. Select the `Save` options to configure the diagnostic settings.

15. Navigate to the `Logs` tab to view the tables and run the queries for log results, shown in *Figure 9.7*.

    After a few minutes, you will notice a list of tables created in the Log Analytics workspace.

16. Simply select the `AzureActivity` table and click the `Run` button to view the resulting logs data, as shown in *Figure 9.7*:

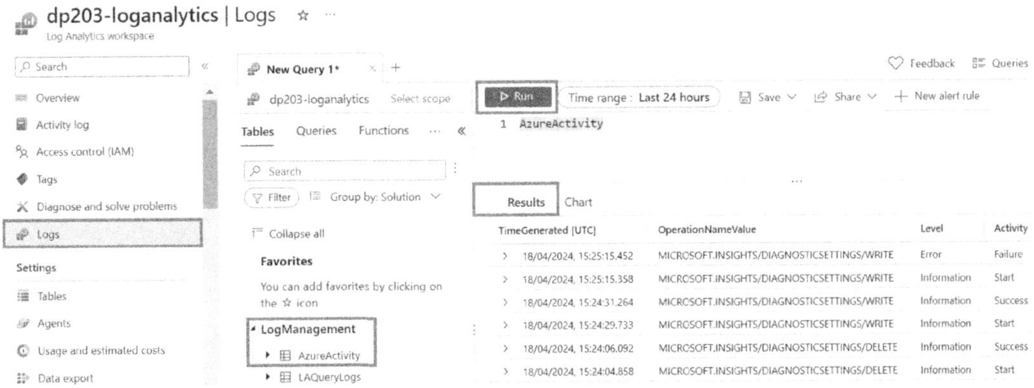

Figure 9.7 – The AzureActivity table displaying various log results in the Log Analytics workspace

From now on, all the Activity logs will be populated in the **AzureActivity** table, as shown in *Figure 9.7*. You can query the table using KQL to gain insights into the log.

> **Note**
> You can learn more about sending logs to a Log Analytics workspace at `https://packt.link/dU4Ct`.

So far, you have learned how to set up robust logging mechanisms to capture activity log data from various resources and send that to the Log Analytics workspace to analyze and run the analytics. By configuring Azure Monitor's logging feature, you gained insights into system behavior, performance, and security. With this knowledge, you will move on to the next section, which will delve into the specifics of configuring monitoring solutions to ensure comprehensive visibility and proactive management.

# Configuring Monitoring Services

**Azure Monitor** is enabled as soon as you create an Azure resource. By default, the basic metrics and logs are recorded without requiring any configuration changes from the user side, but you can perform additional configurations such as sending the logs to Log Analytics, as you saw in the previous section.

> **Note**
> This section primarily focuses on the **Configure monitoring services** concept of the DP-203: Data Engineering on Microsoft Azure exam.

You can configure monitoring at multiple levels, as outlined in *Table 9.1*:

| Monitoring levels | Configurations performed |
|---|---|
| Application monitoring | Metrics and logs for the applications that you have written on top of Azure services. |
| Operating System (OS) monitoring | OS-level metrics and logs, such as CPU usage, memory usage, and disk usage. |
| Azure resource monitoring | Metrics and logs from Azure services such as Azure Storage, Synapse Analytics, and Event Hubs. |
| Subscription-level monitoring | Metrics and logs of Azure subscriptions, such as how many people are using a particular account and what the account usage is. |
| Tenant-level monitoring | Metrics and logs of tenant-level services such as Microsoft Entra ID. |

Table 9.1 – Configuration at multiple levels

For resource, subscription-level, and tenant-level monitoring, most of the data is already generated; you just need to enable the diagnostic setting (as shown in *Figure 9.6*) to move that data into the Log Analytics workspace, Event Hubs, and storage account.

But for applications and guest OS monitoring, you will have to install the **Azure Monitor Agent** (**AMA**) or the Log Analytics agent to start collecting metrics and logs. The AMA can be installed in multiple ways, but one of the easiest is via **VM** extensions on a Linux server.

> **Note**
> All the entries within the angular brackets, < >, are user-provided values.

You can log in to the Azure **Command-Line Interface** (**CLI**) and run the following command:

```
az vm extension set \
  --resource-group <YOUR_RESOURCE_GROUP> \
  --vm-name <VM_NAME> \
  --name OmsAgentForLinux \
  --publisher Microsoft.EnterpriseCloud.Monitoring \
  --protected-settings <{«workspaceKey":"<YOUR_WORKSPACE_KEY>"}' \
  --settings <{«workspaceId":"<YOUR_WORKSPACE_ID>"}'
```

In the preceding code, the Azure CLI command sets up the AMA extension on a Linux VM within a specified Azure resource group. It configures the extension with the necessary settings to connect to a Log Analytics workspace for monitoring.

> **Note**
>
> You can find other ways to install monitoring clients at `https://packt.link/sL7cu`.

The rest of this section will focus on the options available to monitor Azure resources, as this is important from a certification perspective. Take the example of Azure Storage.

Metrics such as **Ingress**, **Egress**, and **Blob Capacity** indicate the status of operations within Azure Storage and are directly available in the **Metrics** tab of **Azure Storage**. You can "filter, create new graphs, and create new alerts" using all the metrics available on this page, as shown in *Figure 9.8*.

You can access your previously created storage account within the Azure portal. If you haven't created one yet, you can do so now. In this example, it is a previously created storage account, `iacstoreacct` (*Figure 9.8*):

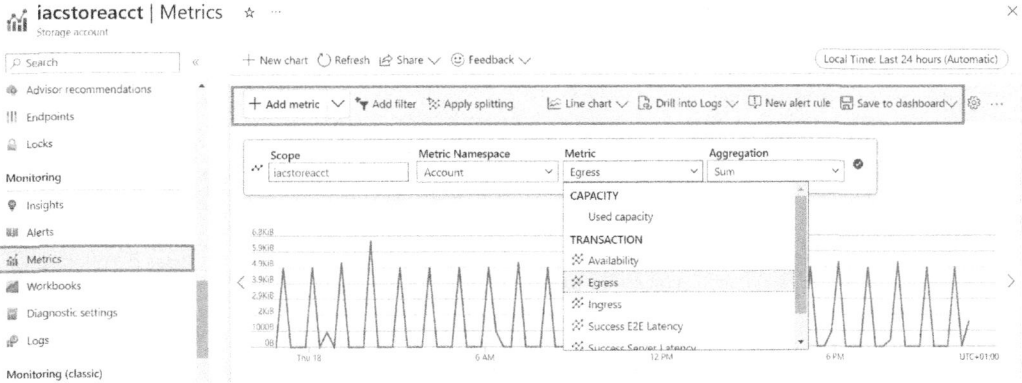

Figure 9.8 – Configuring metrics for Azure Storage

If you need to find the status of the storage service itself, such as the availability of the Blob Storage account, then you will have to look at Azure Monitor. From **Azure Monitor**, select `Storage accounts`. You should be able to see the details, such as **Transactions**, **Transactions Timeline**, and **E2E Latency**, as shown in *Figure 9.9*:

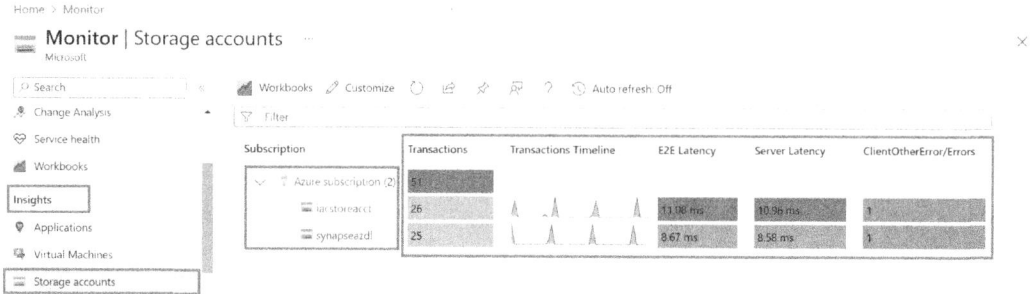

Figure 9.9 – The Monitor Storage account showing storage service metrics from the Azure Monitor service

If you click on any of the storage account links under the **Subscription** section (say, `iacstoreacct`) and select the **Insights** tab to show the details for **Failures**, **Performance**, **Availability**, and **Capacity**, as shown in *Figure 9.10*:

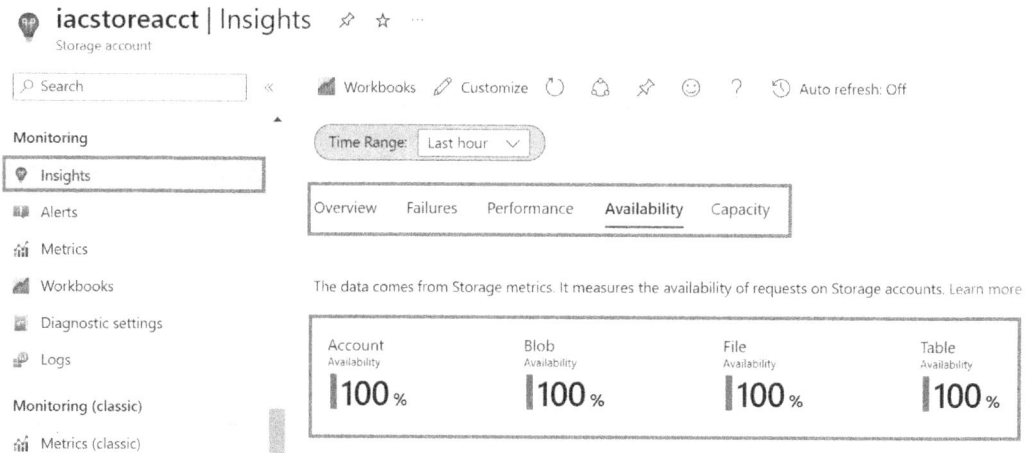

Figure 9.10 – Checking storage availability and status with Azure Monitor

This is how you can use the monitoring features available within the service and with Azure Monitor to check the availability and status of operations within Azure Storage, gaining a complete picture of the health of your service.

This section emphasized that Azure Monitor is automatically enabled upon creating an Azure resource, capturing basic metrics and logs without your intervention. However, you have the flexibility to further configure monitoring by directing logs to Log Analytics or other storage solutions. This customization allows for enhanced visibility and management of resources within Azure, facilitating effective monitoring and troubleshooting. Next, you will learn how to monitor stream processing.

## Monitoring Stream Processing

As you learned in *Chapter 6, Developing a Stream Processing Solution*, the two services that are most typically used in Azure for stream processing are **Event Hubs** (the service dedicated to providing a data stream) and **Stream Analytics** (the service dedicated to analyzing this data stream and providing some data points as a result). **Monitoring stream processing** will then consist of the collection and visualization of logs and metrics from these services.

> **Note**
>
> This section primarily focuses on the **Monitor stream processing** concept of the DP-203: Data Engineering on Microsoft Azure exam.

Start with Event Hubs to access your previously created **Event Hubs namespace** within the Azure portal. In this example, you will work with the previously created Event Hubs namespace, DP203EHNS.

> **Note**
>
> To create an Event Hubs namespace, DP203EHNS, refer to the steps in the *Streaming Solution Using Event Hubs and ASA* section of *Chapter 6, Developing a Stream Processing Solution* in *Part 3*.

You can set the metrics and logs you want to collect, as well as the destination where you want to send them, by accessing the `Diagnostic settings` tab for a specific **Event Hubs namespace**, as shown in *Figure 9.11*:

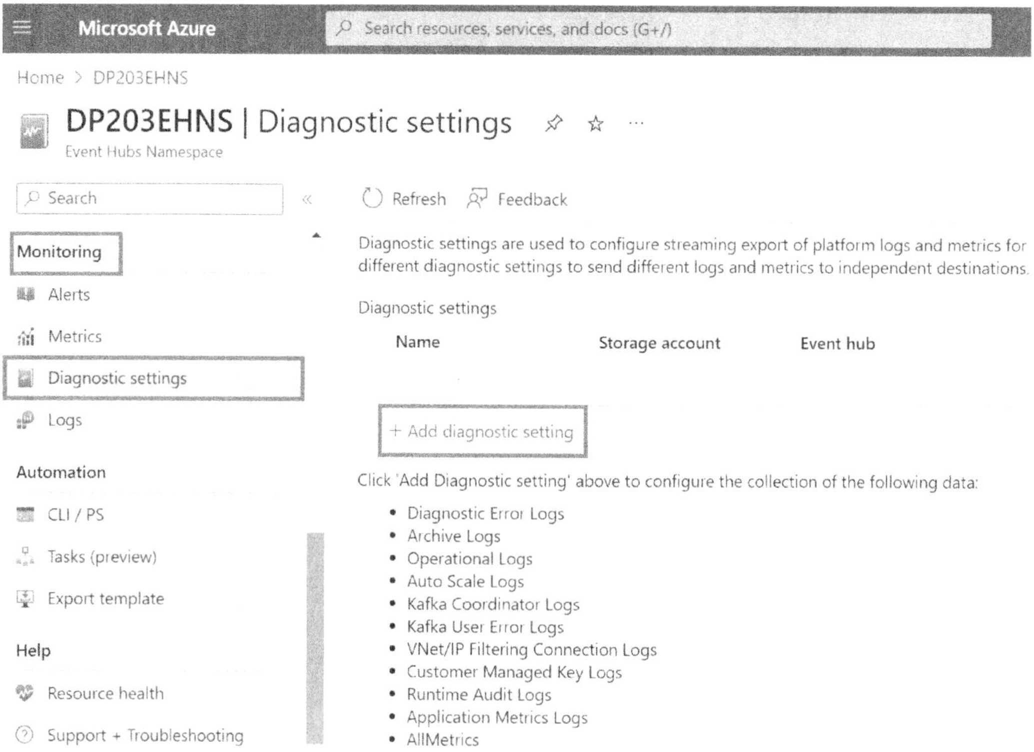

Figure 9.11 – Configuring new diagnostics for Event Hub

You will then see the **Diagnostic settings** screen. Click on the Add diagnostic setting to display the form shown in *Figure 9.12*:

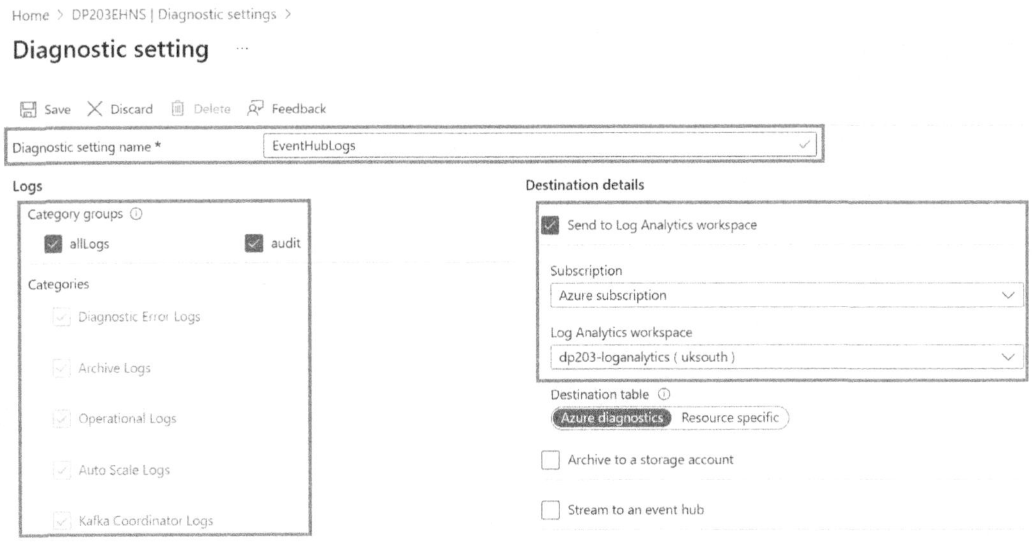

Figure 9.12 – Adding diagnostic settings for Event Hubs

*Figure 9.12* shows that logs can be sent to a **Log Analytics** workspace, which is accessible not only via Azure Monitor but also through a storage account, or even another instance of Event Hubs. It is also possible to specify whether all logs need to be sent to the destination or just a subset based on type and origin.

For metrics, the options are limited to capturing them all and sending them to **Azure Monitor** or capturing none. This means that when it comes to metrics (quantitative data points used for monitoring), you have two choices – either you collect and send all available metrics to Azure Monitor for analysis, or you choose not to capture any metrics at all. There's no in-between option to selectively capture certain metrics. If the collection is enabled, the collected metrics will include request metrics, such as the number of requests sent to a service in a specific period, and message metrics, such as the number and the size of the incoming messages in a specific period. These metrics can be useful to verify the correct allocation of resources.

Logs can be useful to identify errors, such as the timing out of requests or authentication failures. Unlike metrics, which have limited options for capturing, logs offer valuable insights into system behavior and issues.

Regarding **Stream Analytics** (similar to Event Hubs), you can access diagnostic settings by clicking on the **Diagnostic settings** option and then selecting the Add diagnostic settings link, for a specific **Azure Analytics** job. The possible destinations are the same as for Event Hubs, with the only difference being in the list of the different event categories available for collection. As in the case of metrics, the only options are collecting all or none.

Now, you have learned how **Azure Monitor** is automatically enabled upon the creation of an Azure resource. It starts recording basic metrics and logs without needing any configuration. However, you can make additional configurations, such as directing logs to **Log Analytics**, as demonstrated in the *Configuring Monitoring Services* section.

Monitoring stream processing is closely related to measuring the performance of data movement because it provides insights into how efficiently data is being processed and moved through a system in real-time. **Stream processing** involves continuously processing data as it is generated or ingested, making it crucial to monitor various metrics such as **throughput**, **latency**, and **error rates** to ensure optimal performance. By monitoring stream processing, you can identify bottlenecks, detect anomalies, and optimize the data movement pipeline to achieve better overall performance. Therefore, monitoring stream processing is an essential aspect of measuring the performance of data movement in real-time systems.

In the next section, you will focus on monitoring data movement along with the tools and techniques to assess how data flows within the pipelines.

## Measuring the Performance of Data Movement

This section equips you with the tools and techniques to assess how data flows within pipelines. By monitoring and analyzing data movement metrics, you can identify bottlenecks, ensure timely delivery, and maintain data integrity. In this section, you will explore the key concepts, best practices, and practical approaches to measuring and enhancing data movement efficiency.

> **Note**
>
> This section primarily focuses on the **Measure performance of data movement** concept of the DP-203: Data Engineering on Microsoft Azure exam.

ADF provides a rich set of performance metrics under its **Monitoring** tab. Say you have a sample **Copy Data** activity as part of a pipeline called `FetchDataFromBlob`, which copies data from **Blob Storage** into **Azure Data Lake Storage Gen2** (**ADLS Gen2**). In order to see the details of each of the pipelines, click on the `Pipeline runs` option under the **Monitoring** tab, as shown in *Figure 9.13*. To check the diagnostic settings in ADF, perform the following steps:

1. Navigate to **ADF**. In this case, it is `IACSampleDataFactory`.

2. Run any of your created **pipelines**. In this example, it is `CopyfromBlobToADLSGen2`.

3. In the **Monitor** hub of ADF, locate the `Pipeline runs`.

4. Now, select a specific pipeline to run. In this case, your pipeline is `CopyfromBlobToADLSGen2`.

5. Click on the `Spectacle` option to view the status of the pipeline, and select the `Sink` to view the `diagnostic details` for that pipeline run (*Figure 9.13*):

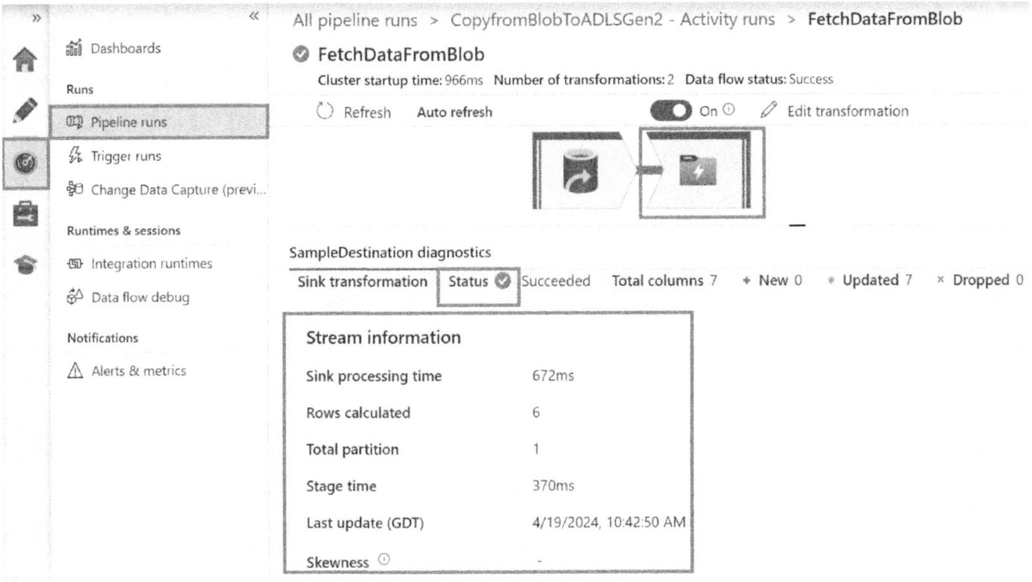

Figure 9.13 – Displaying data movement performance details

6. Click the `Status` tab under the **SampleDestination diagnostics** tab to explore the **Stream information** section for comprehensive performance monitoring:

   - **Sink processing time**: Pay attention to how long data takes to reach its final destination (sink). Longer processing times may indicate inefficiencies. Here, it is set at 672 minutes.

   - **Rows calculated**: This option allows you to know the volume of data being processed. High row counts might impact performance. In this case, it is set at 6.

- **Stage time**: This option allows you to analyze the time spent at different stages of data movement and optimize slow stages. Here, it is set at 370 minutes.

- **Last update (GDT)**: Here, you must note the timestamp (set at 4/19/2024 10:42:50 AM) for context.

This way, you can monitor the performance of data movement.

> **Note**
>
> You can learn more about Copy Data monitoring at https://packt.link/IqEC3.

Now, you will look at how you can collect statistics about your data.

# Monitoring and Updating Statistics

Statistics is an important concept in query optimization. Generating statistics is the process of collecting metadata about your data—such as the number of rows and the size of tables—which can be used as additional inputs by the **Structured Query Language** (**SQL**) engine to optimize query plans.

> **Note**
>
> This section primarily focuses on the **Monitor and update statistics about data across a system** concept of the DP-203: Data Engineering on Microsoft Azure exam.

For example, if two tables have to be joined and one table is exceedingly small, the SQL engine can use this statistical information to pick a query plan that works best for such highly skewed tables. The Synapse SQL pool engine uses something known as **Cost-Based Optimizers** (**CBOs**). These optimizers choose the least expensive query plan from a set of query plans that can be generated for a given SQL script.

Now, look at how you can create statistics for both Synapse dedicated and serverless pools.

## Creating Statistics for Synapse Dedicated Pools

By default, in an **Azure Synapse SQL** dedicated pool, the automatic creation of statistics is turned on. If your Data Warehouse doesn't have auto statistics enabled, you can enable statistics in a Synapse SQL dedicated pools using the following command:

```
ALTER DATABASE [DW_NAME] SET AUTO_CREATE_STATISTICS ON;
```

The following is an example of how you enable statistics in a Synapse SQL dedicated SQL pool:

```
ALTER DATABASE mySampleDataWarehouse SET AUTO_CREATE_STATISTICS ON;
```

In the preceding code, once the AUTO_CREATE_STATISTICS is ON, any SELECT, INSERT-SELECT, CTAS, UPDATE, DELETE, and EXPLAIN statements will automatically trigger the creation of statistics for the columns involved in the query, if not already present. Automatic creation of statistics is not available for temporary or external tables.

You can create statistics on demand using the following command in a dedicated SQL pool to generate statistics on specified tables and columns:

```
CREATE STATISTICS [statistics_name]
    ON [schema_name].[table_name]([column_name])
    WITH SAMPLE 40 PERCENT;
```

The following example uses the preceding command to show how you can create statistics on a table and specific column within a Synapse SQL dedicated SQL pool:

```
CREATE STATISTICS TripStats
    ON dbo.FactTrips (tripId)
    WITH SAMPLE 40 PERCENT;
```

In the preceding example, you use a 40 PERCENT sample. If you do not provide a sample value, the default value is 20 PERCENT. As a recommendation, while creating statistics for SQL tables, the default sampling rate for testing should be 20 PERCENT of the total rows. In the case of large datasets (where the dataset is greater than 1M rows), the output data sampling rate can be from 2 PERCENT to 10 PERCENT max.

You can also do a full scan instead of sampling by using the following command:

```
CREATE STATISTICS [statistics_name]
    ON [schema_name].[table_name]([column_name])
    WITH FULLSCAN;
```

The following example uses the preceding command to show how you can perform a full scan instead of sampling:

```
CREATE STATISTICS TripStats
    ON dbo.FactTrips (tripId)
    WITH FULLSCAN;
```

You now know that enabling statistics in Azure Synapse SQL dedicated pools is a vital step toward optimizing query performance and ensuring efficient data analysis within your data warehouse.

By default, the automatic creation of statistics is enabled, but if disabled, you can easily enable it using the provided command. You learned about creating statics for tables with sampling and a full scan. This ensures that the Query Optimizer has accurate information about the data distribution, leading to better query plans and overall system performance. Now, you can update the statistics directly in Synapse dedicated SQL pools, as the statistics are created and available to perform updates on tables and specific columns.

You will now look at updating statistics for Synapse dedicated pools.

## Updating Statistics for Synapse Dedicated Pools

Similar to creating statistics, you can periodically update statistics. Periodically updating statistics in **Azure Synapse SQL**-dedicated pools serves the crucial purpose of ensuring that the Query Optimizer continues to make informed decisions based on the most accurate data distribution and cardinality estimates. As data within your warehouse evolves due to inserts, updates, and deletes, statistics can become outdated, potentially leading to suboptimal query plans and performance degradation.

You can use the following command to refresh the statistics associated with specific tables and columns:

```
UPDATE STATISTICS [schema_name].[table_name]([stat_name]);
```

The following example uses the preceding command to show how you can perform an update statistic operation on Synapse SQL pools:

```
UPDATE STATISTICS dbo.FactTrips(TripStats);
```

The preceding code recalculates the distribution and density of data values, providing the Query Optimizer with up-to-date information to make better decisions when generating query execution plans.

Regularly updating statistics is particularly beneficial in scenarios where data distribution changes significantly, such as when large data loads occur or when there are substantial modifications to existing data. This practice helps maintain query performance and to deliver accurate and timely insights.

It is a sound practice to update statistics after every fresh data load. Updating statistics after every fresh data load is considered a best practice in database management. By refreshing statistics after each data load, you help maintain query performance and deliver accurate insights. This proactive approach to updating statistics enhances the overall efficiency and effectiveness of data analysis within a data warehouse environment.

> **Note**
>
> You can find more information on statistics in Synapse SQL pools at https://packt.link/wd22W. You can find the complete code in the accompanying GitHub repository at https://packt.link/2Lt70.

Next, you will learn how to create statistics for Synapse Serverless pools.

## Creating Statistics for Synapse Serverless Pools

The concept of statistics is the same for dedicated and serverless pools. In the case of serverless pools, the **auto-creation** of statistics is turned on by default for **Parquet** files but not for **Comma-Separated Values** (**CSV**) files with PARSER_VERSION 1.0. Sampling is not supported, and the automatic creation of statistics will not happen with sampling less than 100%.

The following is an example showing how you read the data from an external CSV file within serverless SQL pool:

```
SELECT *
FROM OPENROWSET(
    BULK 'https://<storage_account>.dfs.core.windows.net/container/
tripdata.csv',
    FORMAT = 'CSV',
    PARSER_VERSION = '1.0'
) AS [TripData];
```

In the preceding code, when you read a CSV file with PARSER_VERSION 1.0, sampling is not supported. So, the automatic statistics creation does not happen with the sampling percentage less than 100%.

You can also create an external table using a CSV file with PARSER_VERSION 2.0 in a serverless SQL pool. Since you deal with external tables in serverless pools, you will have to create statistics for external tables. The command for external tables is as follows:

```
CREATE STATISTICS [statistics_name]
ON { external_table } ( column )
    WITH
        { FULLSCAN
          | [ SAMPLE number PERCENT ] }
        , { NORECOMPUTE }
```

The following example uses the preceding command to show how you can create statistics on an external table and specific column within the Synapse Serverless SQL pool:

```
CREATE STATISTICS TripStats
ON dbo.TripsExtTable ( tripsId )
WITH
SAMPLE 10 PERCENT,
NORECOMPUTE;
```

Here, you create statistics on an external table as you are dealing with a CSV file. The auto-creation of statistics is not supported with the CSV PARSER_VERSION 1.0. So, you should create an external table first to create statistics on that.

Next, you will learn how to update statistics for Synapse Serverless pools.

## Updating Statistics for Synapse Serverless Pools

In **Azure Synapse Analytics Serverless SQL** pools, maintaining optimal performance requires periodic updates to statistics. This ensures improved query execution plans and enhances overall query performance. As data evolves, outdated statistics can impact query optimization, underscoring the importance of regular updates to reflect changes in data distribution.

You can update the statistics manually on external tables using the following command:

```
UPDATE STATISTICS [statistics_name]
ON external_table (column1);
```

In the preceding command, the UPDATE STATISTICS SQL command is used to update the statistics object, [statistics_name], for a specific column1 of external_table in a database.

The following example uses the preceding command to show how you can perform an update statistic on the Synapse Serverless SQL pool:

```
UPDATE STATISTICS TripStats
ON dbo.TripsExtTable ( tripsId );
```

In the preceding command, UPDATE STATISTICS updates the statistics object, TripStats, for the tripsId column in the TripsExtTable table within the dbo schema. Statistics collection might cause a slight performance degradation if statistics are missing for the columns in a query. However, once statistics are generated, future queries will be much faster.

> **Note**
>
> You can learn more about generating statistics at https://packt.link/ta4Zv. You can find the complete code in the accompanying GitHub repository at https://packt.link/ZAhts.

# Monitoring Synapse SQL Pool Performance

The **Synapse SQL Metrics** screen itself has quite a lot of metrics that can be easily used to identify any performance regressions. *Figure 9.14* shows a sample screenshot of the Synapse SQL **Metrics** option:

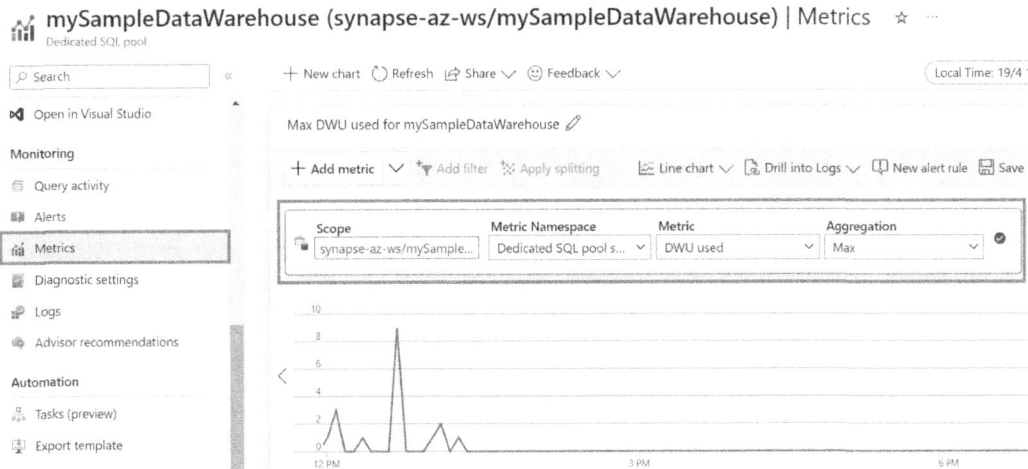

Figure 9.14 – Displaying metrics identifying performance regression in Synapse SQL pool

The **Metrics** option in a Synapse SQL provides metrics for **Data Warehouse Unit** (**DWU**) usage, memory usage, and so on, but it doesn't provide details about query performance or query wait times. You will have to use one of the following two approaches to get such query performance details:

- **System tables**: System tables in Azure Synapse SQL provide detailed insights into query performance metrics and execution statistics. These tables store information about query execution plans, resource consumption, and historical query performance. Analyzing data from system tables allows you to identify performance bottlenecks, optimize queries, and troubleshoot issues effectively.

- **Query Store**: The Query Store feature in Azure Synapse SQL provides a centralized repository for storing query execution statistics and performance metrics. It captures query plans, execution statistics and wait statistics over time, allowing you to track query performance trends and identify regressions. With Query Store, you can easily monitor query performance, analyze historical execution plans, and troubleshoot performance issues.

### Querying System Tables

Synapse SQL pool provides the following **system tables** that can be used to monitor query performance:

- `sys.dm_pdw_exec_requests`: This contains all the current and recently active requests in Azure Synapse Analytics. It contains details such as `total_elapsed_time`, `submit_time`, `start_time`, `end_time`, `command`, and `result_cache_hit`.

- `sys.dm_pdw_waits`: This contains details of the wait states in a query, including locks and waits on transmission queues.

> **Note**
>
> You can find details on all such system tables with monitoring and management information at `https://packt.link/IyrN3`.

Next, we'll look at how you can get performance details using a feature called Query Store.

### Using Query Store

Azure SQL and Synapse SQL support a feature called **Query Store** that can be used for both query performance monitoring and performance tuning. It is supported in a Synapse SQL pool and other flavors of SQL in Azure. Query Store is used to store the history of queries, plans, and runtime statistics. This historical data can then be used to aid in query optimization by identifying query regressions, monitoring trends in resource utilization such as CPU and memory for queries, identifying wait time patterns in query plans, and so on.

Query Store is not enabled by default for Synapse SQL pool. You can enable Query Store using the following **Transact-SQL** (**T-SQL**) command:

```
ALTER DATABASE <database_name> SET QUERY_STORE = ON;
```

The preceding code enables the Query Store feature for a specified database in **Azure Synapse SQL**. Enabling Query Store allows the database to capture and store historical information about query execution, aiding in monitoring and analyzing performance trends and optimizing queries over time.

Query Store in a Synapse SQL stores the following three main components:

- **Query details**: This includes details such as query parameters, compilation times, and compilation counts. The following are the specific tables that contain Query Store query details:

  - `sys.query_store_query`: The following command is used to run this table:

    ```
    SELECT * FROM sys.query_store_query;
    ```

  - `sys.query_store_query_text`: The following command is used to run the table:

    ```
    SELECT * FROM sys.query_store_query_text;
    ```

- **Plan details**: This includes query plan details such as the **Query Identifier** (**QID**), query hash, and query text. The following is the specific table that contains Query Store plan details:

  - `sys.query_store_plan`: The following command is used to run the table:

    ```
    SELECT * FROM sys.query_store_plan;
    ```

- **Runtime statistics**: This includes the runtime details of queries such as the time taken, CPU time, average duration, and row counts. The following are the specific tables that contain runtime statistics:

  - `sys.query_store_runtime_stats`: The following command is used to run the table:

    ```
    SELECT * FROM sys.query_store_runtime_stats;
    ```

  - `sys.query_store_runtime_stats_interval`: The following command will retrieve information about the runtime statistics:

    ```
    SELECT * FROM sys.query_store_runtime_stats_interval;
    ```

*Figure 9.15* shows a sample of the `sys.query_store_runtime_stats` table that is executed in a dedicated SQL pool:

Figure 9.15 – Displaying a sample Query Store runtime statistics

> **Note**
>
> Wait statistics are not yet available for Azure Synapse SQL at the time of writing. However, they are available in other Azure SQL flavors, such as Azure SQL Database. You can learn more about Query Store at `https://packt.link/zoRis`.

Now, you have learned how to monitor and update statics across systems that play well in query optimization within **Azure Synapse SQL** dedicated and serverless pools. You also know now that generating statistics involves collecting metadata about the data, such as row counts and table sizes, which aids the SQL engine in optimizing query plans. Additionally, you also learned that periodic updates to statistics are necessary to ensure that the Query Optimizer continues to make informed decisions based on accurate data distribution and cardinality estimates. Similarly, in Azure Synapse Analytics Serverless SQL pools, the auto-creation of statistics is enabled by default for Parquet files but not for CSV files with certain configurations. Overall, you gained knowledge about the significance of maintaining up-to-date statistics in both dedicated and serverless environments to ensure optimal query performance as data evolves.

> **Note**
>
> You can find the complete code in the accompanying GitHub repository at `https://packt.link/uA6Hm`.

The next section will focus on how you can monitor the performance of data pipelines.

## Monitoring Data Pipeline Performance

Data pipelines facilitate the seamless flow of data from various sources to destinations, enabling critical processes such as data transformation, enrichment, and loading. However, ensuring the efficiency and health of data pipelines is essential for maintaining optimal performance. In this context, monitoring plays a pivotal role.

Monitoring allows you to identify bottlenecks, inefficiencies, and resource-intensive stages within your data pipelines. By analyzing performance metrics, you can fine-tune pipeline components, optimize query execution, and reduce latency.

Similar to the data movement metrics you saw in the *Measuring Performance of Data Movement* section, ADF provides metrics for overall pipelines too.

> **Note**
>
> This section primarily focuses on the **Monitor data pipeline performance** concept of the DP-203: Data Engineering on Microsoft Azure exam.

You can select the `Pipeline runs` option under the **Monitoring** tab to display the **Pipeline runs** screen. On the screen, when you hover over the pipeline runs, a small **Consumption** icon appears, as shown in *Figure 9.16*:

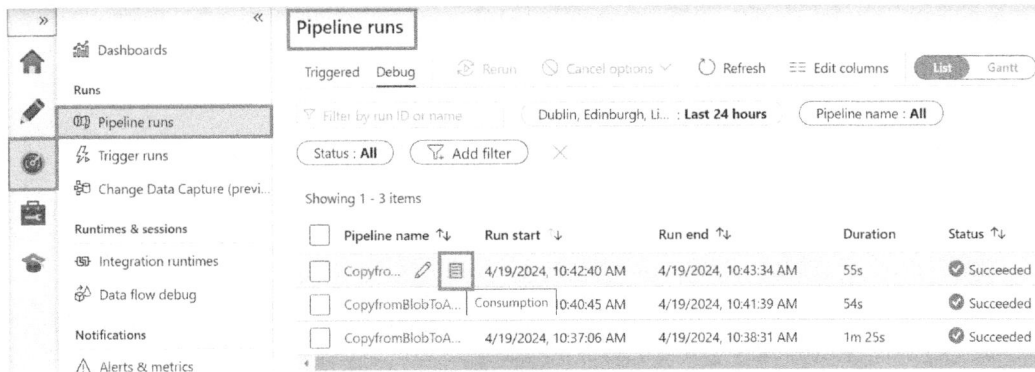

Figure 9.16 – The pipeiline name showing a Consumption icon to display the details

If you click on the `Consumption` icon, ADF shows the pipeline consumption details (*Figure 9.17*):

**Pipeline run consumption**

**Name**
HDISparkPipeline

**Status**
✔ Succeeded

**Run ID**
dd73e5a7-e7f4-405a-9eab-4519950abf05

|  | Quantity | Unit |
|---|---|---|
| **Pipeline orchestration** | | |
| Activity runs | 3 | Activity runs |
| **Pipeline execution** | | |
| **Azure integration runtime** | | |
| Data movement activities | 0.0667 | DIU-hour |
| **Data flow** | | |
| Data Flow | 0.4330 | vCore-hour |

Close

Figure 9.17 – Resource consumption details screen showing the status of the resources

You can also get additional metrics about each of the runs from the **Gantt** chart section on the **Pipeline runs** screen. You can change the view from **List** to **Gantt** by switching to the **Gantt** option in the top right-hand corner (*Figure 9.16*). The Gantt chart will appear, as shown in *Figure 9.18*:

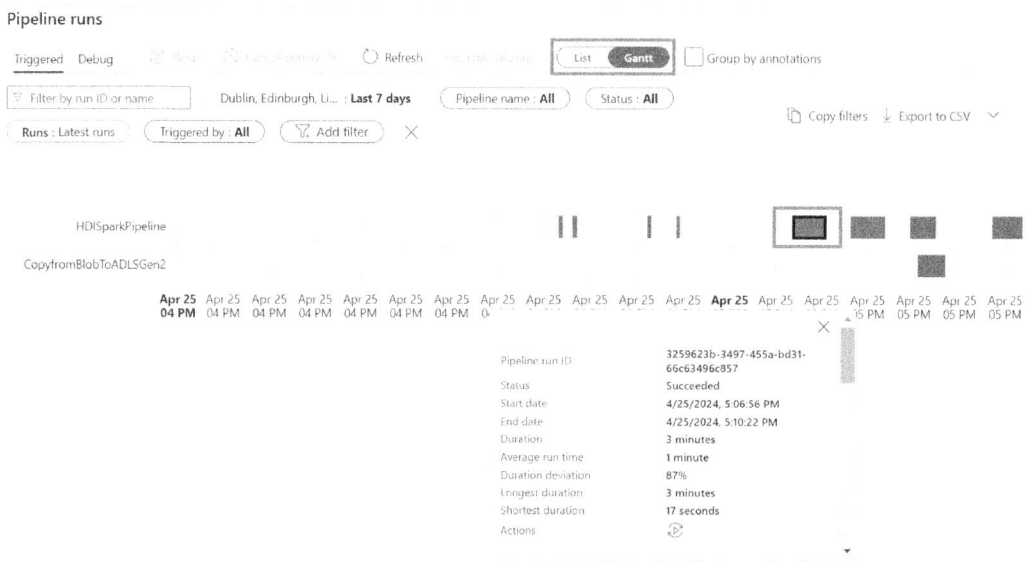

Figure 9.18 – Displaying additional pipeline details in the Gantt chart screen

ADF only maintains **pipeline execution** details and metrics for 45 days. If you need to analyze the pipeline data for more than 45 days, you will have to send the data to **Log Analytics** and then use **Kusto** queries to get the performance details.

This is how you can keep track of pipeline performance. Next, you will learn how to measure the performance of your queries.

## Measuring Query Performance

The efficient queries not only facilitate swift data retrieval and processing but also pinpoint areas for improvement and resource optimization. Key metrics such as execution time, resource consumption, and data movement efficiency play pivotal roles in this process. Leveraging tools such as **Azure Monitor**, query profiling, and indexing strategies helps to track and fine-tune query performance. Ultimately, by comprehending the impact of query design, resource allocation, and data movement, you can construct robust and efficient data solutions on the Azure platform.

Query performance is a remarkably interesting topic in databases and analytical engines such as **Spark** and **Hive**. In this section, you will get an overview of how to monitor query performance in **Synapse dedicated SQL pools** and Spark.

> **Note**
>
> This section primarily focuses on the **Measure query performance** concept of the DP-203: Data Engineering on Microsoft Azure exam.

Additional links for further reading are provided in each section so that you can learn more about the techniques. *Chapter 10, Optimizing and Troubleshooting Data Storage and Data Processing*, will focus on how to actually optimize the queries.

To measure the performance of any SQL-based queries, it is recommended to set up the **Transaction Processing Performance Council H** (**TPC-H**) or **Transaction Processing Performance Council DS** (**TPC-DS**) benchmarking suite and run it regularly to identify any regressions in the platform. TPC-H and TPC-DS are industry-standard benchmarking test suites.

> **Note**
>
> You can learn more about TPC-H and TPC-DS at `https://packt.link/ICk1E` and `https://packt.link/EsmGw`, respectively.

In the next section, you will learn how to monitor pipeline tests.

## Scheduling and Monitoring Pipeline Tests

In *Chapter 7, Managing Batches and Pipelines*, you were briefly introduced to **Azure DevOps** for version control. Azure DevOps provides another feature called **Azure Pipelines**, which can be used to create **Continuous Integration** (**CI**)/**Continuous Deployment** (**CD**) pipelines to deploy ADF. **CI/CD** is an automated method of continuously testing and deploying applications to a production environment.

> **Note**
>
> This section primarily focuses on the **Schedule and monitor pipeline tests** concept of the DP-203: Data Engineering on Microsoft Azure exam.

In this section, you will learn how to create, schedule, and monitor a CI/CD pipeline.

> **Note**
>
> You can learn more about CI/CD for Azure Synapse Analytics at `https://packt.link/LN9rJ`.

Perform the following high-level steps to create a CI/CD pipeline using Azure pipelines:

1.  Sign in to your `Azure DevOps` account.

2.  On the **Azure DevOps** screen, select `Releases` under **Pipelines** and click the `New Pipeline` button. The **New release pipeline** screen will appear.

3.  Choose the `Empty job` option, as shown in *Figure 9.19*:

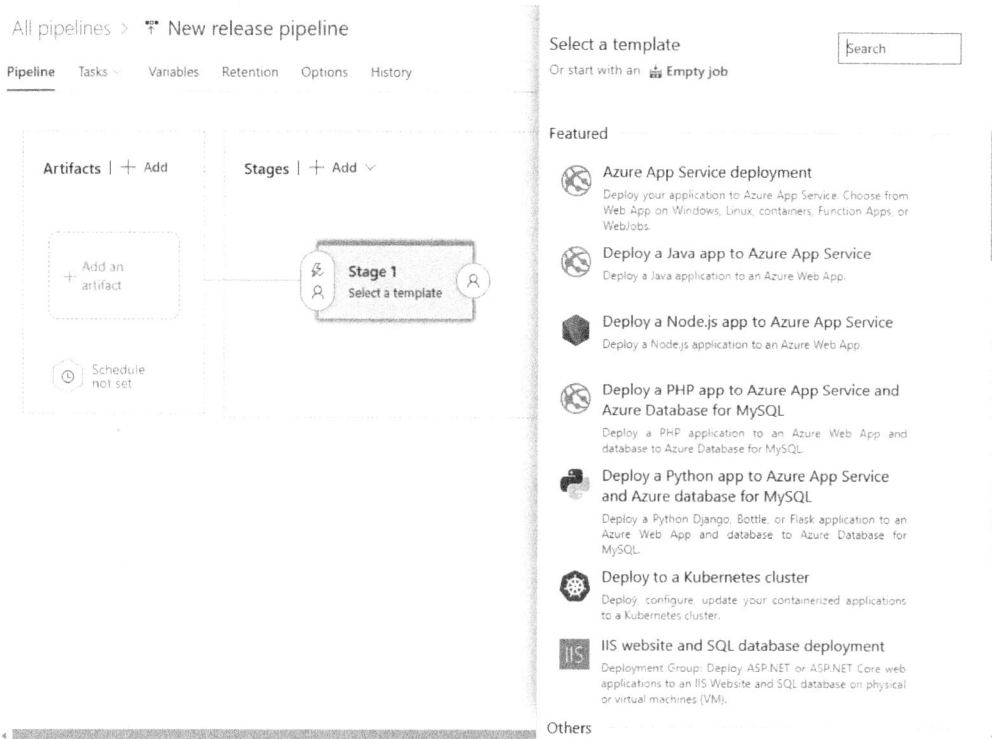

Figure 9.19 – The Azure release pipeline creation wizard creating an empty job

4.  Next, click on the `Add an artifact` option. The **Add an artifact** screen will appear.

5.  Update your ADF source repository details by first entering the **Project** name. In this case, it is `DP-203`.

6.  Next, choose the **Source (repository)** option, for example, `adf-dev`.

7.  Select the **Default-branch** option, for example, `main`.

8.  Pick the **Default version** option, in this case, it is `Latest from the default branch`.

9.  You can leave the `Checkout submodules` checkbox unselected.

10. You can leave the `Checkout files from LFS` checkbox unselected.

11. You can enter the values in the **Shallow fetch depth** field. In this case, it is left as blank.

12. Type in the **Source alias** name. In this case, it is `_adf-dev`. The updated **Add an artifact** screen is shown in *Figure 9.20*:

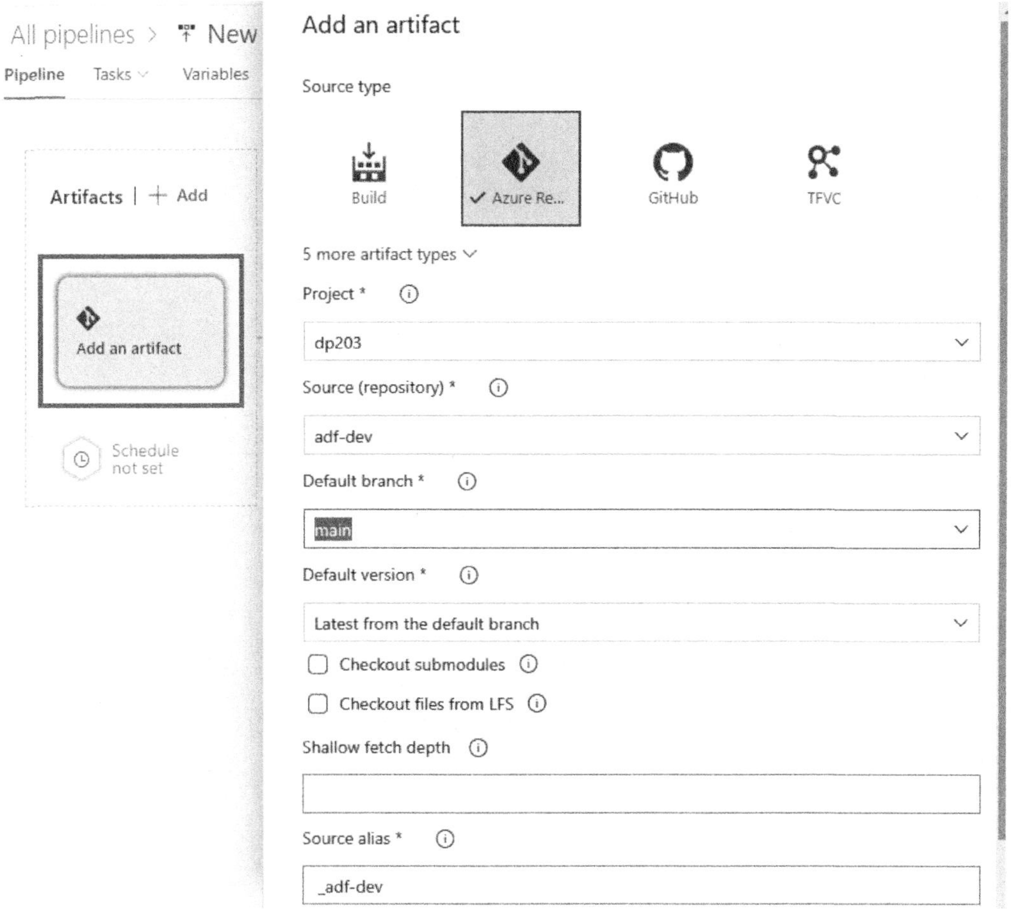

Figure 9.20 – Updating artifact information in Azure Pipelines

13. Once the fields are complete, click on the Add button to complete the artifact settings.

14. Click on **Tasks** on the release pipeline screen, shown in *Figure 9.19*, to view the Agent job, and then click on the + symbol. The **Add tasks** screen will appear.

15. From the task list, choose the ARM template deployment task, as illustrated in *Figure 9.21*:

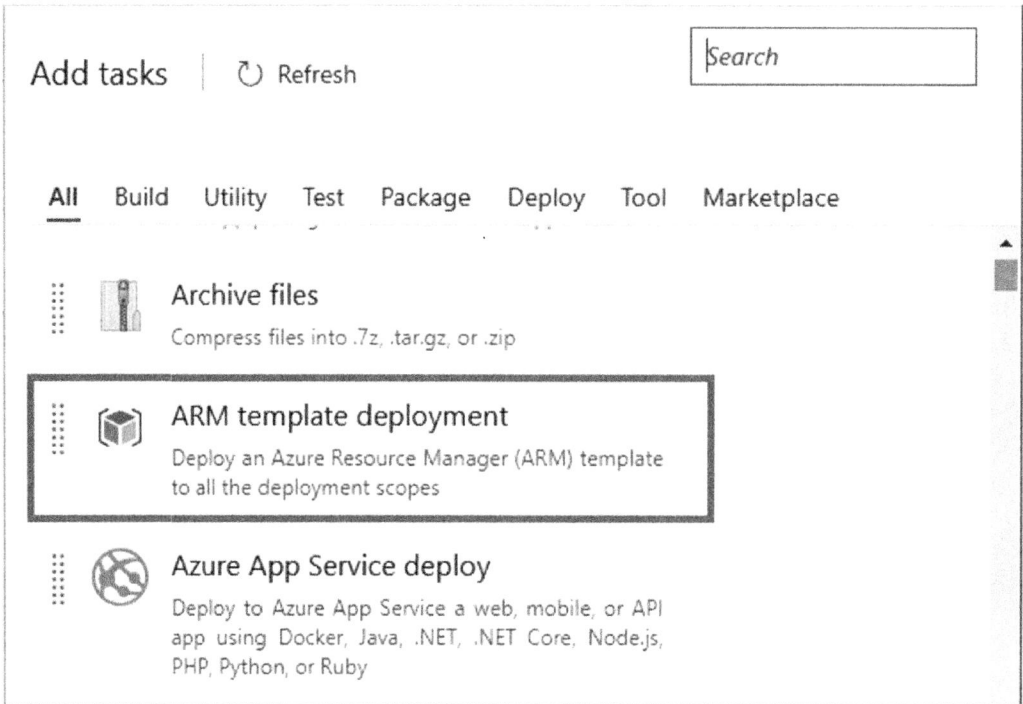

Figure 9.21 – Choosing ARM template deployment from the Add tasks screen

This will bring up the **Azure Resource Manager (ARM)** template configuration screen, as shown in *Figure 9.22*:

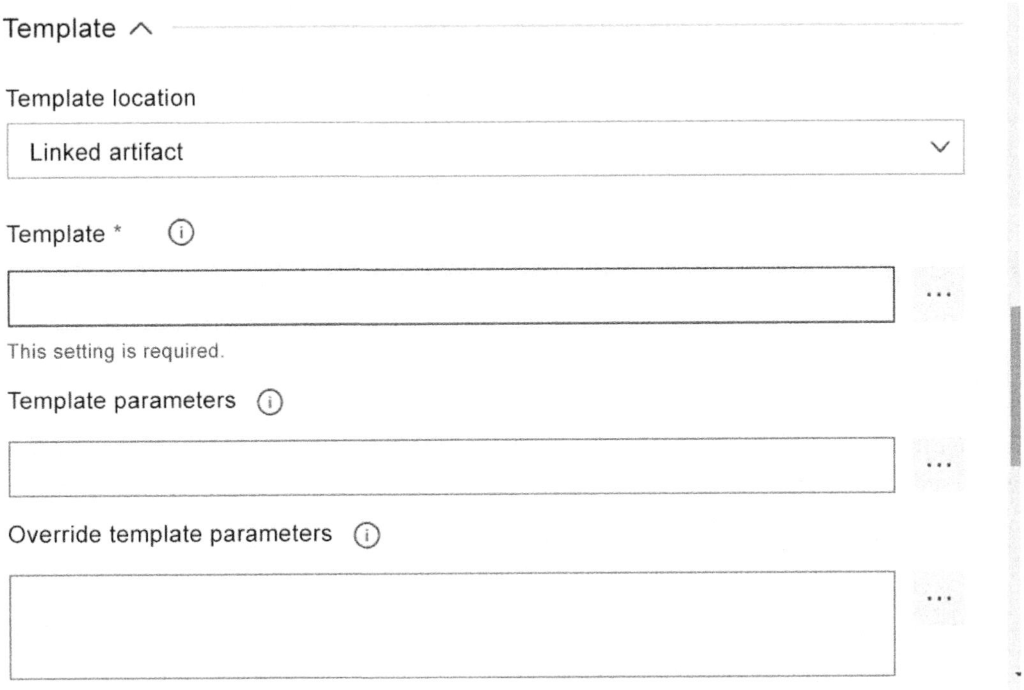

Template ∧

Template location

| Linked artifact | ∨ |

Template *   ⓘ

|  | ... |

This setting is required.

Template parameters   ⓘ

|  | ... |

Override template parameters   ⓘ

|  | ... |

Figure 9.22 – Specifying the ARM template and template parameters

16. In the **Template** textbox, browse to the file named ARMTemplateForFactory.json in the ADF folder of the **adf_publish** branch.

17. In the **Template parameters** textbox, choose the ARMTemplateParametersForFactory.json file in the ADF folder of the **adf_publish** branch.

18. In the **Override template parameters** textbox, choose whether you want to override the existing parameters settings (*Figure 9.22*).

19. After filling in all the details, click the Save button to save the page.

20. Finally, click on the Create Release button positioned at the top to create a CI/CD pipeline.

Now that you have a pipeline to deploy CI/CD, it can be scheduled in multiple ways. The following are some of the ways to schedule it:

- **A CI trigger**: This triggers a pipeline when a user pushes a change to the git branch

- **A Pull request trigger**: This is triggered when a **Pull Request (PR)** is raised, or changes are submitted to the PR.

- **A Scheduled trigger**: This is time-based scheduling.

- **A pipeline Completion trigger**: This is a trigger based on the completion of previous pipelines.

> **Note**
>
> You can learn more about implementing triggers at `https://packt.link/erjxy`.

Once you have the triggers set up, the pipelines will continue to get tested and deployed. You can monitor the progress from the `Releases` tab of Azure DevOps. *Figure 9.23* shows the **Pipelines** screen with a summary of the pipelines that were run:

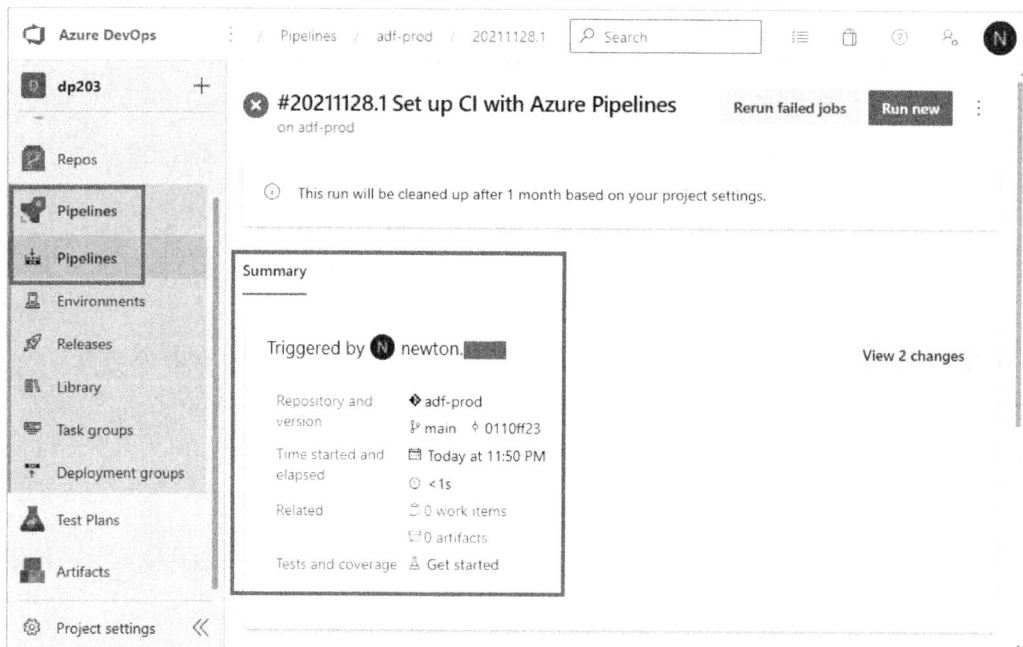

Figure 9.23 – The pipelines CI/CD monitoring screen showing the monitoring process

> **Note**
>
> **Azure DevOps** and pipelines are a huge topic of their own, and the small section here will not do them justice. This topic is not part of the DP-203 exam, so the details provided in this section are all you need to know about DevOps in terms of monitoring release pipelines. You can find more about ADF CI/CD at `https://packt.link/qj6Fw`.

In this section, you gained knowledge about the importance of automating and scheduling tests within their software development pipelines, as well as how to set up triggers to initiate testing processes in response to specific events, such as code changes or PRs. Additionally, you were introduced to the concept of monitoring pipeline progress, particularly through the **Releases** tab of Azure DevOps, which allows developers and teams to track the status of automated testing and deployment processes, ensuring that changes to the code base are systematically validated and deployed according to predefined schedules and criteria. Overall, the topic equips you with the tools necessary to streamline the testing and deployment workflow within **Azure DevOps**, ultimately contributing to improved efficiency and reliability in software development practices.

Next, you will learn how to analyze the metrics and logs you learned to collect in the previous sections.

# Interpreting Azure Monitor Metrics and Logs

This section provides a sound knowledge of Azure Monitor's capabilities in gathering and analyzing data from monitored resources. Metrics offer a snapshot of system health, categorized into **Native**, **Platform**, **Custom**, and **Prometheus** metrics, aiding in monitoring and alerting. Meanwhile, Azure Monitor Logs offer detailed context and historical information, enabling deeper analysis and troubleshooting. By leveraging both metrics and logs, you can make informed decisions to uphold a robust Azure infrastructure, optimizing performance and reliability effectively.

> **Note**
>
> This section primarily focuses on the **Interpret Azure Monitor metrics and logs** concept of the DP-203: Data Engineering on Microsoft Azure exam.

As you have seen in the *Configuring Monitoring Services* section, metrics and logs form the two main sources of data for monitoring. The next subsections will explore how to view, interpret, and experiment with these two types of monitoring data.

## Interpreting Azure Monitor Metrics

Azure Monitor Metrics provides analysis of the performance and health of resources deployed in Azure. It provides insights into resource utilization, pinpoints performance bottlenecks, and allows for trend monitoring. This proactive approach empowers organizations to optimize their Azure deployments for both reliability and efficiency.

The metrics data collected from Azure resources is usually displayed on the **Overview** screen of the resource itself, with more details under the **Metrics** tab. *Figure 9.24* shows a storage account:

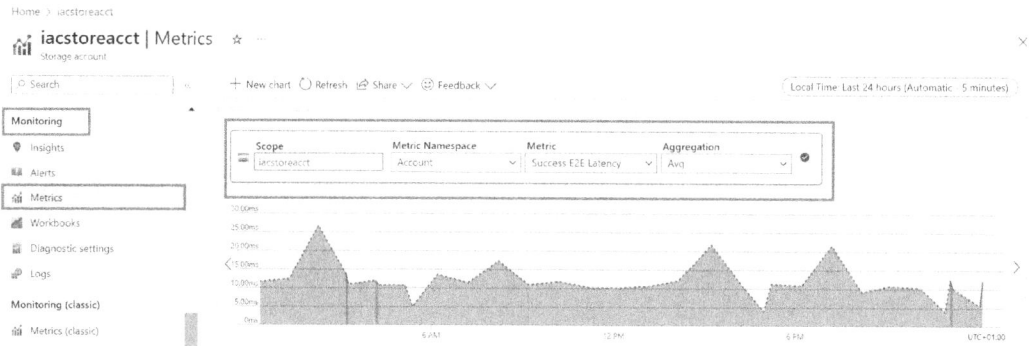

Figure 9.24 – Displaying Metrics data for a storage account collected from Azure resources

For each of the metrics, you can aggregate based on Sum, Avg, Min, and Max under the **Aggregation** dropdown. The tool also provides the flexibility to overlay with additional metrics using the **Add metric** option, filter out unwanted data using the **Add filter** option, and so on. You can access the data for up to "30 days" using this metrics explorer.

## Interpreting Azure Monitor Logs

You already learned how to send logs to **Log Analytics**, so in this section, you will explore how to read and experiment with logs in Log Analytics. Once you start sending logs to Log Analytics, you will be able to see the tables for the Azure resource you configured. In *Figure 9.25*, you will use the AzureActivity, AzureDiagnostics, AzureMetrics, and LAQueryLogs tables and populate them with logs continuously:

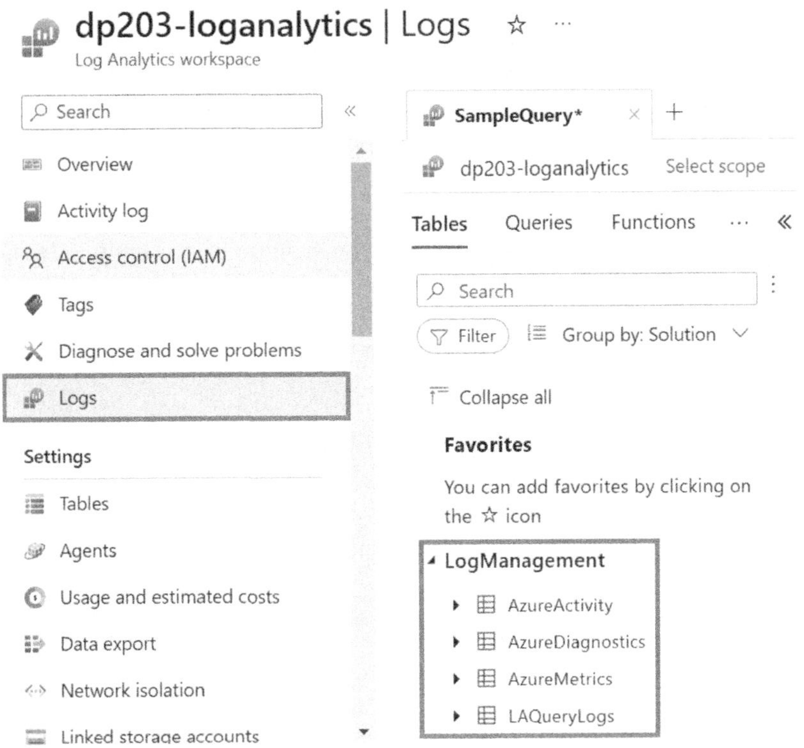

Figure 9.25 – Running the Log Analytics tables to view the different logs from each one

Once you have the log data in the tables, you can use the **KQL query language** provided by Azure Monitor to query the tables, as you do in SQL. KQL queries can be directly typed into the query block, as shown in *Figure 9.26*:

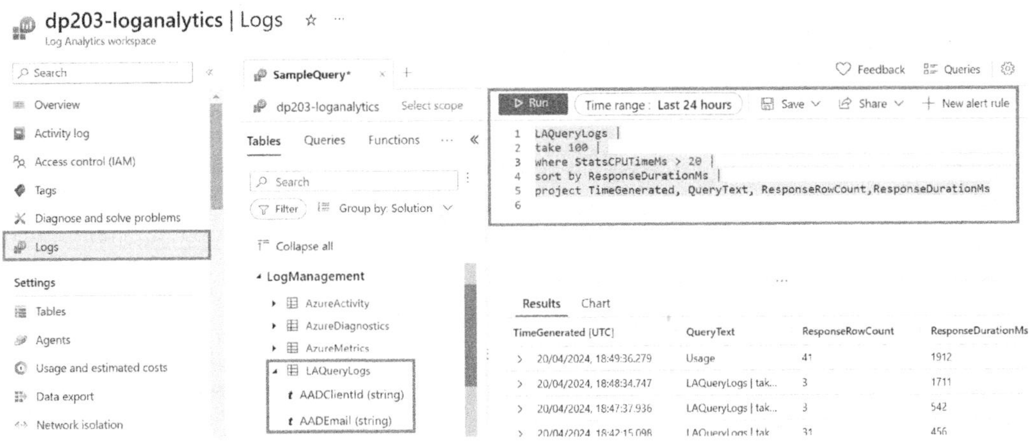

Figure 9.26 – Kusto query statements displaying the table contents

A **Kusto query** consists of a sequence of statements that can be delimited by semicolons. You start with a source of data, such as a table, and then use pipes ( | ) to transform the data from one step to another.

For example, in *Figure 9.26*, you start with the LAQueryLogs table and just specifying the name of the table will list the contents of the table. You then pipe that data to take 100 rows. The 100 entries are then piped through the next statement, where StatsCPUTimeMs > 20, which filters the rows whose CPUTime is higher than 20 milliseconds. You then sort it in descending order on the ResponseDurationMs column and print out a table containing three columns—TimeGenerated, QueryText, ResponseRowCount, and ResponseDurationMs. The table will show how long the particular operation took to return a response.

> **Note**
> By default, ascending is the default order for sorting.

As you can see, KQL—a mix of SQL and Linux pipes (|)—is a very intuitive language. Once you grasp how the language behaves, you can generate powerful insights by using log data in Log Analytics.

> **Note**
> You can learn more about KQL at https://packt.link/Ks2UB.

Now that you have learned about configuring and interpreting metrics and logs for Azure services, you will explore the ways to measure the performance of data movements within such services while using ADF.

## Implementing a Pipeline Alert Strategy

Implementing a pipeline alert strategy in Azure is a proactive approach to detect and address issues, ensuring seamless data flow and minimizing disruptions. Key considerations include knowing the challenges pipelines may face, such as data skew or resource bottlenecks, and implementing alerts to notify specific conditions such as data spillage, excessive resource utilization, or pipeline failures. You can achieve this by leveraging Azure services such as **Azure Monitor**, **ADF**, or **Azure Synapse Pipelines** to set up alerts based on predefined thresholds or custom conditions. Alert types encompass pipeline failures due to connectivity issues or incorrect configurations, monitoring resource consumption to prevent exceedance, identifying data spillage or skew, and tracking pipeline execution time or data delivery delays.

> **Note**
>
> This section primarily focuses on the **Implement a pipeline alert strategy** concept of the DP-203: Data Engineering on Microsoft Azure exam.

Both ADF and Synapse pipelines allow you to state alert rules by specifying conditions for alerts to be sent, based on signals such as reaching a metric threshold or the occurrence of an event.

In the case of Synapse, you can define alerts on the **Alerts** blade of the **Synapse workspace** (not on the Monitor hub of Synapse Studio) in the Azure portal after clicking on `Create an alert rule`. *Figure 9.27* shows the resulting screen, with the "list of available signals" expanded after clicking on the `See all signals` link on the **Create an alert rule** screen:

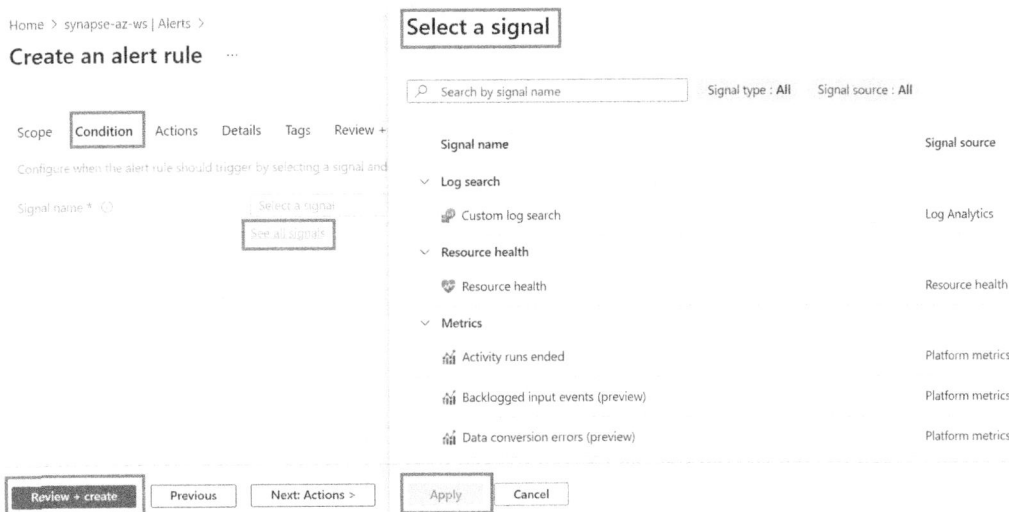

Figure 9.27 – Creating an alert rule for Synapse pipelines

After choosing the signal, you can specify the threshold condition (even if the signal is based on a metric), the frequency between successive evaluations of the conditions, and the action to be performed. Then, go to the **Actions** section of the rule settings, and select the **Subscription**, **Resource group**, and **Region** settings. For this example, you have chosen `Azure subscription`, `rg-az-synapse`, and `Global`, respectively, as shown in *Figure 9.28*. In the **Instance details** section, you can choose `Alert-Action` for **Action group name** and `login alert` for **Display name** (*Figure 9.28*):

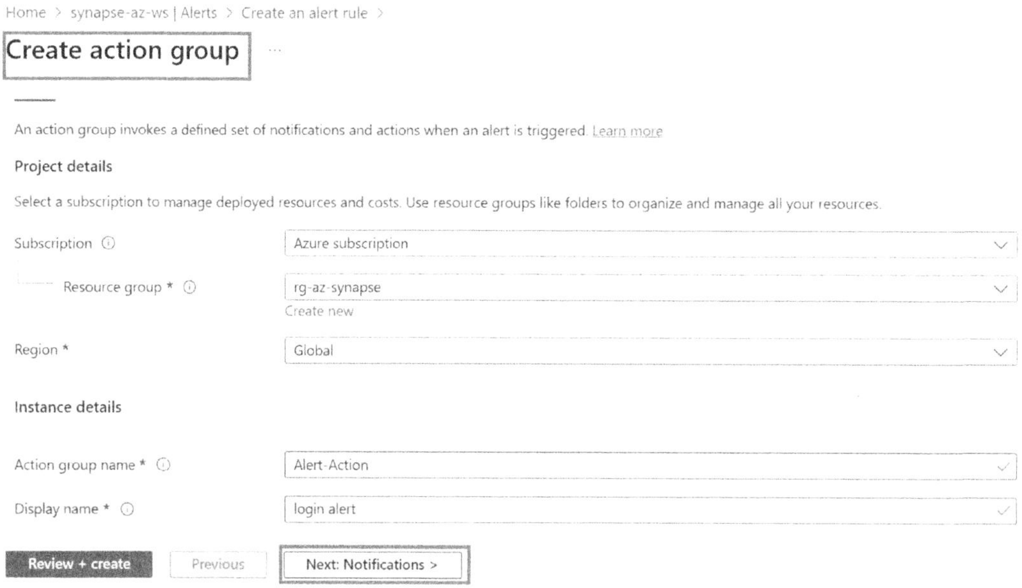

Figure 9.28 – Creating an action group for an alert rule in the Synapse workspace

Then, click the `Next: Notifications >` button to move to the next screen. For notifications, you can choose to send an email, an SMS, or a voice message. For actions, you can execute an `Automation Runbook` (an automation script) to trigger an Azure Function to send an event to an Event Hub, create a ticket on an **IT Service Management** (**ITSM**) system, or call a Webhook. This will allow you to implement, when possible, corrective actions in response to the alert condition, such as increasing the allocation of resources.

You are now aware of the importance of implementing a pipeline alert strategy in Azure to proactively detect and address issues, ensuring smooth data flow and minimizing disruptions. Furthermore, you learned about the process of defining alert rules in both ADF and Synapse Pipelines, along with the actions to be taken in response to alert conditions.

# Summary

In this chapter, you were introduced to Azure Monitor and Log Analytics. You then learned to send log data to Log Analytics, define custom logging options, and interpret metric and log data. Later sections focused on measuring the performance of data movements, pipelines, data streams, and SQL queries and setting up alerts for pipelines.

Applying these concepts, you should now be able to set up a monitoring solution for your data pipelines and be able to tell whether your data movement, pipeline setups, and query runs are performing optimally.

In the next chapter, you will focus on query optimization and troubleshooting techniques.

# Exam Readiness Drill – Chapter Review Questions

Apart from a solid understanding of key concepts, being able to think quickly under time pressure is a skill that will help you ace your certification exam. That is why working on these skills early on in your learning journey is key.

Chapter review questions are designed to improve your test-taking skills progressively with each chapter you learn and review your understanding of key concepts in the chapter at the same time. You'll find these at the end of each chapter.

> **How to Access These Materials**
>
> To learn how to access these resources, head over to the chapter titled *Chapter 11, Accessing the Online Resources*.

To open the Chapter Review Questions for this chapter, perform the following steps:

1. Click the link – `https://packt.link/DP203E2_CH09`.

    Alternatively, you can scan the following **QR code** (*Figure 9.29*):

Figure 9.29 – QR code that opens Chapter Review Questions for logged-in users

2.  Once you log in, you'll see a page similar to the one shown in *Figure 9.30*:

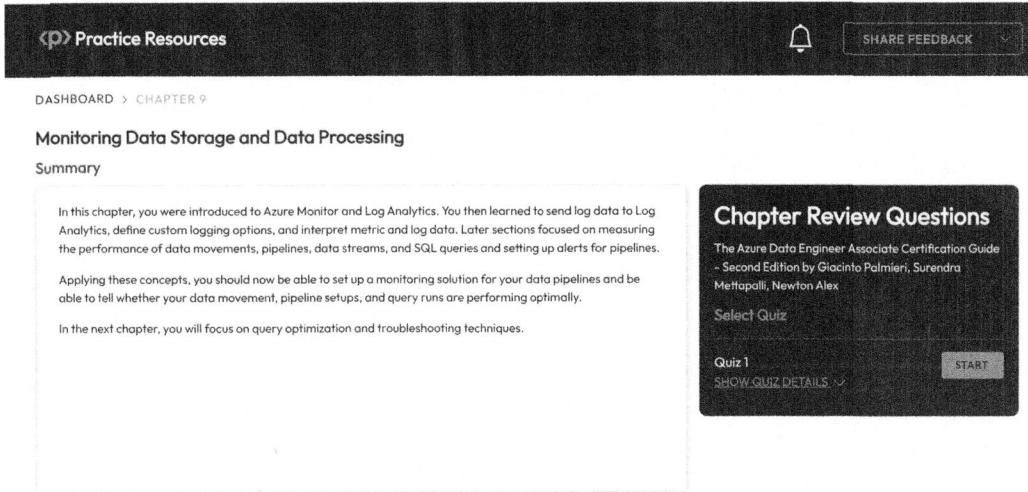

Figure 9.30 – Chapter Review Questions for Chapter 9

3.  Once ready, start the following practice drills, re-attempting the quiz multiple times.

## Exam Readiness Drill

For the first three attempts, don't worry about the time limit.

### ATTEMPT 1

The first time, aim for at least **40%**. Look at the answers you got wrong and read the relevant sections in the chapter again to fix your learning gaps.

### ATTEMPT 2

The second time, aim for at least **60%**. Look at the answers you got wrong and read the relevant sections in the chapter again to fix any remaining learning gaps.

## ATTEMPT 3

The third time, aim for at least **75%**. Once you score 75% or more, you start working on your timing.

> Tip
>
> You may take more than **three** attempts to reach 75%. That's okay. Just review the relevant sections in the chapter till you get there.

# Working On Timing

**Target**: Your aim is to keep the score the same while trying to answer these questions as quickly as possible. Here's an example of how your next attempts should look like:

| Attempt | Score | Time Taken |
| --- | --- | --- |
| Attempt 5 | 77% | 21 mins 30 seconds |
| Attempt 6 | 78% | 18 mins 34 seconds |
| Attempt 7 | 76% | 14 mins 44 seconds |

Table 9.2 – Sample timing practice drills on the online platform

> Note
>
> The time limits shown in the above table are just examples. Set your own time limits with each attempt based on the time limit of the quiz on the website.

With each new attempt, your score should stay above **75%** while your "time taken" to complete should "decrease". Repeat as many attempts as you want till you feel confident dealing with the time pressure.

# 10

# Optimizing and Troubleshooting Data Storage and Data Processing

This is the final chapter of *Part 4* of the syllabus. In *Chapter 8, Implementing Data Security*, you focused on identifying sensitive information and applying various techniques to handle it securely. This includes techniques such as data masking, which hides sensitive data from unauthorized users, and implementing row- and column-level security to control access to specific data rows or columns. You also learned about **Role-Based Access Control** (**RBAC**), which assigns permissions based on user roles, and **Access Control Lists** (**ACLs**) for managing access to data in **Azure Data Lake Storage** (**ADLS**) Gen2. Moreover, you focused on encryption methods for securing data at rest and in motion. These skills will enable you to design and maintain a secure data lake environment, safeguarding customer privacy effectively.

In *Chapter 9, Monitoring Data Storage and Data Processing*, you learned about Azure Monitor and Log Analytics and how to send log data to Log Analytics, customize logging options, and interpret metrics and log data. You delved into measuring the performance of data movements, pipelines, data streams, and SQL queries, as well as setting up alerts for pipelines. By applying these concepts, you can track the performance of your data movement, pipeline setups, and query runs, ensuring everything is running smoothly and optimally.

In this chapter, you will master optimizations and troubleshooting tricks for data storage and data processing technologies. First, you will tackle Spark and Synapse SQL queries and then move on to compacting small files and handling data skew, shuffles, indexing, cache management, and other nifty techniques that will empower you to optimize like a pro in no time. Finally, you will also learn about troubleshooting. You will also walk through Spark and Synapse pipelines with step-by-step guidance to help you identify and fix any hiccups along the way, in addition to receiving some general tips for optimizing any analytical pipeline you come across.

> **Note**
>
> This section primarily focuses on **Optimizing and troubleshooting data storage and data processing** topic of the DP-203: Data Engineering on Microsoft Azure exam.

By the end of this chapter, you will be a **Subject Matter Expert** (**SME**) in optimizing and troubleshooting data processing workflows.

This chapter will prepare you to answer questions on the following confidently:

- Processing small files

- Skew in data and data spill

- Resource management

- Tune queries by using indexers and cache

- A failed Spark job, and a failed pipeline run

# Technical Requirements

To follow along with this chapter, you will need an Azure account (free or paid), **Azure Data Factory** (**ADF**) or a Synapse workspace, and an Azure Databricks workspace.

# Managing Small Files

Processing small files can be a headache for big data systems. Both engines such as **Spark**, **Synapse SQL**, and **Google BigQuery**, and cloud storage platforms such as Blob and **ADLS** Gen2, thrive on large files. So, how do you optimize your data pipelines? The answer lies in consolidating those pesky small files into more manageable ones.

> **Note**
>
> This section primarily focuses on the **Compact small files** concept of the DP-203: Data Engineering on Microsoft Azure exam.

In the Azure ecosystem, you can achieve this efficiency boost using **ADF** and Synapse pipelines. Imagine you have a directory filled with tiny **Comma Separated Values** (**CSV**) files, and your goal is to merge them into a single, cohesive large file to pave the way for smoother data processing. The steps for Synapse pipelines will closely mirror those in ADF.

Perform the following steps to streamline your pipelines:

1. Head over to the **ADF** portal and select the `Copy Data` activity, as shown in *Figure 10.1*:

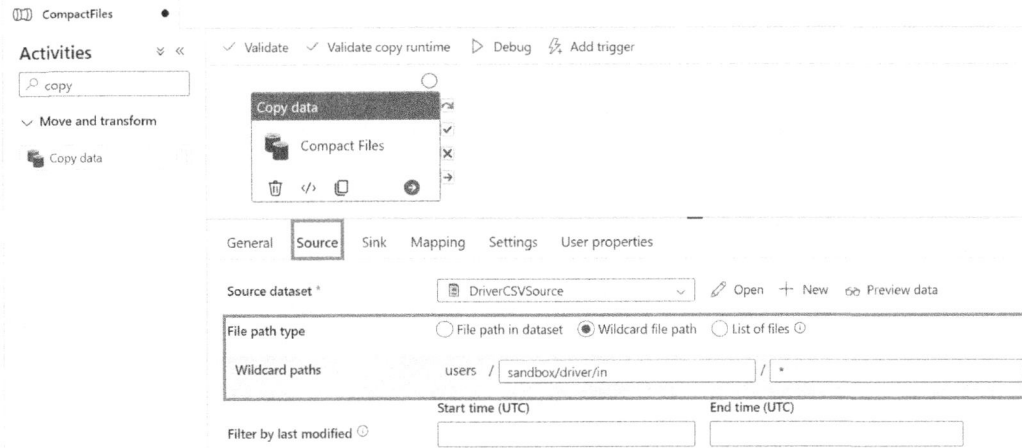

Figure 10.1 – Using wildcards to specify the source folder in Copy activity

2. Select the `Source` tab. This gives you two options: either pick an existing source dataset or create a brand-new one. Make sure to point it to the data storage where those pesky small files are hanging out. For this exercise, **Source dataset** is set as `DriverCSVSource`.

3. In the **File path type** section, choose the `Wildcard file path` option.

4. In the **Wildcard paths** field, type in the folder path (in this case, `sandbox/drive/in`), and end it with an asterisk (`*`).

> **Note**
>
> The **File path type** options allow you to specify how files are selected. `File path in dataset` allows you to use the file path that is defined in the dataset. The `List of files` option lets you specify a list of individual file paths to include in the operation. `Start time (UTC)` and `End time (UTC)` within the **Filter by last modified** option allows you to filter files based on the last modified date and time, which means only the files that were last modified within the specified date and time range will be included.

That asterisk tells the **Copy Data activity** to scoop up all the files in that folder. *Figure 10.2* shows all the small files are present in the folder named `sandbox/driver/in`:

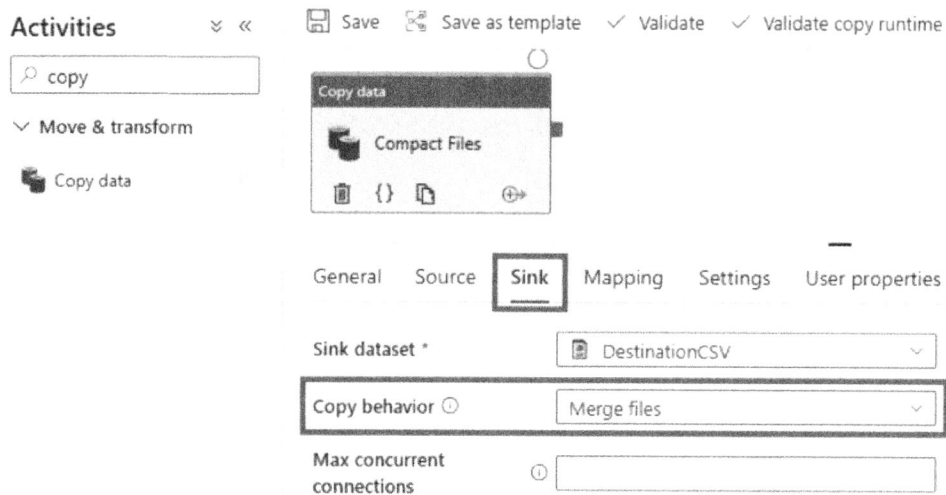

Figure 10.2 – The copying behavior of merging files in the Copy activity of ADF

5.  Switch to the **Sink** tab to choose your destination dataset. Set **Sink dataset** to `DestinationCSV`.

    You can pick an existing sink dataset or create a brand-new one. You next need to decide how you want those files to behave when they reach their destination.

6.  Choose the `Merge files` option beside the **Copy behavior** field, as shown in *Figure 10.2*.

7.  Specify **Max concurrent connections** to determine the maximum number of simultaneous connections that can be established between the source and sink during data transfer. In this case, it is kept blank.

8.  Select `Validate` and then `Debug` to execute this pipeline.

The files in the source folder, in this case `DriverCSVSource`, will get merged into a single file in the destination folder (sink dataset); in this case, it is the DestinationCSV dataset.

> **Note**
>
> You can learn more about the merge option of Copy activity in ADF at `https://packt.link/pdPLc`.

An additional approach to compacting small files involves using the **incremental copy** method, which you previously explored in *Chapter 4, Ingesting and Transforming Data*, specifically within the *Designing and Implementing Incremental Loads* section. In this method, you incrementally update tables with small incoming changes. Notably, this process qualifies as a compaction option because it incrementally merges those small files into a single, larger file using different options such as using watermarks, file timestamps, partition data, and folder structure.

Another approach to compacting small files involves **Azure Databricks** and **Synapse**. Spark introduces a feature known as **bin packing**, which is facilitated by its specialized storage layer called Delta Lake. **Delta Lake** enhances the capabilities of **data lakes**, providing essential features such as **Atomicity, Consistency, Isolation, and Durability (ACID)** transactions, unified batch, interactive streaming, and support for updates and deletes. It's a powerful tool for managing and optimizing data within your ecosystem.

**Delta Lake** is a reliable and open method of storing data that ensures the data is consistent and accurate. It does this by keeping track of the changes made to the data and allows you to undo or correct if needed. The data is stored in online services that offer large and cheap storage spaces, such as **Microsoft Azure Storage**.

Delta Lake provides the following features:

- **ACID transactions**: Delta Lake enables ACID transactions on top of data lakes. As with databases and data warehouses, ACID transactions ensure data consistency and reliability. They allow you to perform complex operations while maintaining data integrity.

- **Unified batch, interactive, and streaming system**: Tables defined in Delta Lake serve as a unified source for various processing systems:

  - **Batch processing**: You can use Delta Lake tables as the foundation for batch jobs, allowing you to process large volumes of data efficiently.

  - **Interactive systems** (e.g., notebooks): Delta Lake seamlessly integrates with interactive systems and makes it easy to explore and analyze data.

  - **Streaming systems**: Delta Lake supports both batch and streaming data, providing a consistent experience across different workloads.

- **Updates and deletes**: Delta Lake goes beyond mere data storage. You can modify existing records in Delta Lake tables. It allows you to remove unwanted records from your dataset. Delta Lake merges data from different sources, supporting operations such as **Slowly Changing Dimensions (SCDs)** and streaming upserts.

- **Time Travel**: Delta Lake provides a powerful feature called **Time Travel** that allows you to access and revert to earlier versions of data. This is useful for audits, roll backs, or reproducing specific states.

- **Schema Evolution and enforcement**: Delta Lake ensures that your data adheres to a consistent schema, and it prevents inferior data from causing corruption by enforcing schema rules.

- **Audit history**: Every change made to a Delta Lake table is logged, creating a comprehensive audit trail, and you can trace back who modified the data, when, and why.

- **Platform agnostic**: Use Delta Lake with any query engine on any cloud (AWS, Azure, or GCP), on-premises or locally. It is designed to be versatile and adaptable.

- **Open source and community-driven**: Delta Lake is an exciting open source project, adopted by a diverse community of developers. This collaborative spirit certifies its ongoing evolution and widespread adoption, free from the constraints of a single entity.

- **Lakehouse foundation**: Delta Lake is the foundation of a cost-effective, highly scalable lakehouse. It combines the best of data lakes (scalability and flexibility) and data warehouses (reliability and performance). Delta Lake simplifies data management by replacing data silos with a single home for structured, semi-structured, and unstructured data.

The Delta Lake engine comes pre-enabled in **Azure Databricks** and **Synapse Spark**. Simply connect your Spark notebook to any Databricks or Synapse Spark cluster to execute the Delta commands. The subsequent subsections will take you through a few example commands demonstrating how to read, write, and create tables in Delta Lake.

## Creating a Table

You can create a Delta Lake table as shown in the following code snippet:

```
# Load the data from its source.
df=spark.read.load("/databricks/DP203/learning/books/book.delta")
# Write the data and save the table name as book.
table_name = "book"
df.write.saveAsTable(table_name)
```

## Upserting to a Table

When you want to combine new updates and additions with an already existing Delta table, you can use the MERGE INTO statement. For example, say you have a source table and you want to integrate its data into a target Delta table. Here's how it works:

- Delta Lake compares the rows in both tables.

- If a row matches in both tables, Delta Lake updates the specified data column according to the provided expression.

- However, if there is no matching row, Delta Lake simply adds a new row. This process is commonly referred to as an **upsert**.

The following code shows an upsert:

```
CREATE OR REPLACE TEMP VIEW book_updates (
  id, title, author, genre, price, rating
) AS VALUES
  (998, 'Into the World', 'John', 'Science Fiction',9.99, 4.5),
  (999, 'First Step', 'Adams', 'Romance',7.99, 4.2),
  (1000, 'Great War', 'Stephen', 'History',19.99, 4.8),
  (2001, 'Dream World', 'Saliken', 'Fantasy',8.99, 4.4),
  (2002, 'little boy in town', 'Suren', 'Science Fiction',9.99, 4.9),
  (2003, 'Hope you can', 'David', 'New-age',14.99, 4.6);


MERGE INTO book
USING book_updates
ON book.id = book_updates.id
WHEN MATCHED THEN UPDATE SET *
WHEN NOT MATCHED THEN INSERT *;
```

When you use the * symbol, it updates or adds all columns in the target table called book. However, this only works if the source table book_updates has the same columns. If they're different, the query will throw an error.

## Reading a Table

You can access data in Delta tables with table_name or table_path, as shown in the following code snippet:

```
book_df = spark.read.table(table_name)
display(book_df)
## or
Book_df = spark.read.load(table_path)
display(book_df)
```

## Writing to a Table

Delta Lake uses the standard syntax for writing data to tables. To add new data to an existing Delta table, use the append mode; to replace all data in a table, use the overwrite mode. The following code shows an example:

```
## To append
df.write.mode("append").saveAsTable("book")
## To overwrite
df.write.mode("overwrite").saveAsTable("book")
```

> **Note**
>
> You can learn more about Delta Lake at `https://packt.link/MkoSX`.

Diving into another approach to performance enhancement, this time you will optimize small files in Delta Lake. You will especially focus on **bin packing**, which consolidates smaller files into large ones. This process significantly improves the efficiency of read queries. To achieve this, you can utilize the `optimize` command to merge the small files in the folder into optimal large files, as shown in the following example:

```
from delta. tables import *
# Enable bin packing (compaction) for a Delta Lake table
deltaTable = DeltaTable.forPath(spark, "/path-to-delta-table")
deltaTable.optimize().executeCompaction()
```

You can also enable the `optimize` feature by default when creating a table using the following properties:

- `delta.autoOptimize.optimizeWrite = true`: This enables automatic optimization during write operations, ensuring efficient data organization and compaction.

- `delta.autoOptimize.autoCompact = true`: This instructs Delta Lake to automatically run the `optimize` command (bin packing) on the specified folder, coalescing small files into larger ones.

The following example demonstrates how you can set the table properties:

```
from delta. tables import *
# Create a Delta Lake table with auto-optimization properties
spark.sql ("""
  CREATE TABLE Customer (
    id INT,
    name STRING,
    location STRING
  )
  USING DELTA
  TBLPROPERTIES (
    'delta.autoOptimize.optimizeWrite' = 'true',
    'delta.autoOptimize.autoCompact' = 'true'
  )
""")
```

The preceding code creates a **Delta Lake** table named `Customer` with three columns: `id`, `name`, and `location`. It sets two Delta Lake properties for automatic optimization and compaction for enhancing both the write and read performance of the Delta Lake table; `delta.autoOptimize.optimizeWrite` is set to `true`, enabling optimization of write operations, and `delta.autoOptimize.autoCompact` is set to `true`, enabling automatic compaction of small files.

```
# Load data into the table (replace '/path/to/data' with your actual
data location)
spark.sql ("""
  INSERT INTO Customer
  SELECT * FROM delta. `/path/to/data`
""")
```

In the preceding code, `spark sql` executes an `INSERT INTO` statement, which inserts data into the `Customer` table. The data is selected from a **Delta Lake** path and the `INSERT INTO` statement copies all data from the specified Delta Lake path into the `Customer` table.

> **Note**
>
> You can learn more about compact data files with optimize on Delta Lake at `https://packt.link/1ALKv`. You can find the complete code in the accompanying GitHub repository at `https://packt.link/YWdfG`.

## Handling Skew in Data

**Data skew** refers to the asymmetry or lack of balance in the distribution of data within a dataset. When data is skewed, it tends to cluster more heavily toward one end of the scale, creating what is often referred to as a **long tail** on one side of the distribution curve, that is, the values are not evenly distributed across the range.

Imagine a histogram or a bell curve representing the distribution of data points. In a skewed distribution, instead of a symmetrical bell shape, you can see that the curve is stretched out to one side with relatively fewer data points on the other side. This long tail indicates that outliers or extreme values are pulling the distribution away from the center.

In a positively skewed distribution, the tail extends toward the higher end of the scale, indicating that some very high values are relatively rare compared to the majority of the data. Conversely, in a negatively skewed distribution, the tail extends toward the lower end of the scale, indicating that some very low values are relatively rare.

Data skew is a dominant problem that can affect the efficiency of your Spark tasks. This issue arises when data is split into several parts, known as **partitions**, and one partition is significantly larger than the rest. This "uneven distribution" can cause a slowdown in the overall execution process.

> **Note**
>
> This section primarily focuses on the **Handle skew in data** concept of the DP-203: Data Engineering on Microsoft Azure exam.

Take, for instance, the number of trips per month of the **Imaginary Airport Cab** (**IAC**) example. Assume the data distribution in the graph shown in *Figure 10.3*:

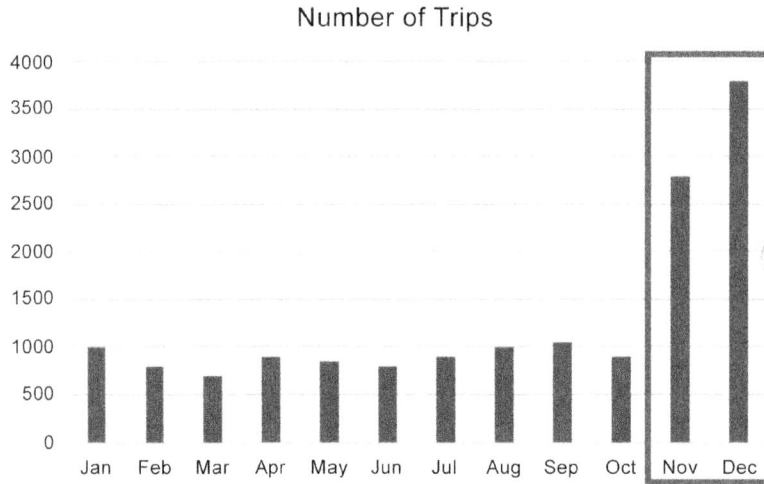

Figure 10.3 – Skewed data example showing the uneven distribution of trips per month

From the graph, it is evident that the number of trips in the months Nov and Dec is significantly higher than the rest of the months. This disproportionate distribution of data is known as **data skew**. If you distribute this monthly data across individual computing nodes, the nodes processing November and December data will take considerably longer than those processing data from other months. If you are compiling an annual report, all other stages would have to pause until the November and December stages finish.

These delays are detrimental to job performance, and so, to enhance efficiency, you need to devise a strategy to allocate roughly equal amounts of processing data to each computing node. You will look into several Azure-recommended methods for managing such data skews. Skew can be addressed at either the storage or compute level.

## Handling Skew at the Storage Level

Data skew is a common challenge in distributed data systems, where the uneven distribution of data can lead to inefficient resource utilization and processing delays. Skewness occurs when certain values are overrepresented in a dataset, causing an imbalance that can affect performance. To address this, Azure provides tools for partitioning and scaling resources to distribute data more evenly. Effective monitoring is also crucial, allowing you to identify skewness and take corrective actions promptly. By implementing these strategies, you can ensure a balanced load across storage and compute resources, leading to more efficient operations and cost savings in Azure data solutions.

This section discusses a few strategies to address skew at the storage level. The following are the strategies:

- **Rethink your distribution strategy**: If the compute time is not balanced, it might be worth considering a different partition strategy. For instance, in the monthly trip count scenario, you can break down the data into smaller segments at the weekly level or even try partitioning along a different dimension, such as ZIP codes.

- **Introduce a secondary partition key**: If the primary key is not distributing the data evenly, then switching to a new distribution key may not be the best option. Instead, you can introduce a secondary partition key. For example, once the data is divided into months, you can further divide it by states within each month. If you are looking at data from the USA, this would result in 50 additional splits and potentially lead to a more balanced distribution.

- **Employ the round-robin technique**: If finding an optimal distribution key proves challenging, you can try round-robin distribution. By randomizing the data and evenly distributing it into partitions, this method ensures a balanced distribution.

Note that it might not always be possible to recreate tables or distributions. So, some pre-planning is important when you first decide on the partition strategy. However, if you end up in a situation where the partitioning strategies are not helping, you might still have one more option left to improve your skew handling. This option is to trust your compute engine to produce an intelligent query plan that is aware of the data skew.

> **Note**
>
> You already encountered distribution strategies in the *Designing Partition Strategy for Analytical Workloads* section in *Chapter 2, Implementing a Partition Strategy*.

## Handling Skew at the Compute Level

Handling skew at the compute level refers to the uneven distribution of computational workloads across different nodes in a distributed system, which can lead to certain nodes being overburdened while others remain underutilized. This imbalance can cause significant delays in data processing and may lead to increased costs due to inefficient resource usage.

To mitigate compute skew, Azure offers a suite of tools and services that enable you to balance the load effectively. Techniques such as dynamic resource allocation, workload partitioning, and performance tuning are essential to ensure that compute resources are optimally utilized. Additionally, Azure's monitoring capabilities allow for the real-time tracking of compute operations, enabling quick identification and resolution of any skew-related issues.

Using these techniques, you can build robust, scalable, and efficient data processing pipelines in Azure, ensuring that compute resources are harmoniously aligned with the demands of the data workload.

The following are a few techniques for fixing skew at the compute level:

- **Enhance the query plan through statistics**: As discussed in *Chapter 9, Monitoring Data Storage and Data Processing*, enhancing query plans through statistics involves collecting and utilizing statistical information about the data in a database. The **Query Optimizer** in SQL Server uses these statistics to estimate the cardinality or the number of rows that will be returned by a query, which in turn helps it to decide the most efficient way to execute the query. For instance, statistics can help the Query Optimizer choose between a full table scan or an index seek operation. Regularly updating statistics ensures that the Query Optimizer has the most current information, leading to more accurate estimations and efficient query execution plans. This is particularly important in dynamic databases where data distributions can change frequently, affecting the Query Optimizer's ability to generate optimal plans.

- **Improving query performance with statistics**: Enabling statistics can significantly improve your query plan. Once statistics are enabled, the query engines, such as the **Synapse SQL engine**, which employs a cost-based optimizer, will leverage these statistics to formulate the most efficient plan based on the associated costs of each plan. The optimizer can detect data skew and automatically implement suitable optimizations to manage the skew.

- **Disregard insignificant outlier data**: This is the most straightforward option, although it may not be applicable in all scenarios. If the skewed data is not particularly crucial, it can be safely ignored.

> **Note**
>
> You already saw how to enable statistics in the *Monitoring and Updating Statistics* section in *Chapter 9, Monitoring Data Storage and Data Processing*.

As you are handling skew at the compute level, you can check Synapse Spark, which has a cool feature that lets you see data skew at each stage of your Spark job. Go to the **Monitoring** section of your Synapse workspace and click on the `Apache Spark applications` tab. Then click on any of the jobs; in this case, `Job 0`. You will then find the skew details, as shown in *Figure 10.4*:

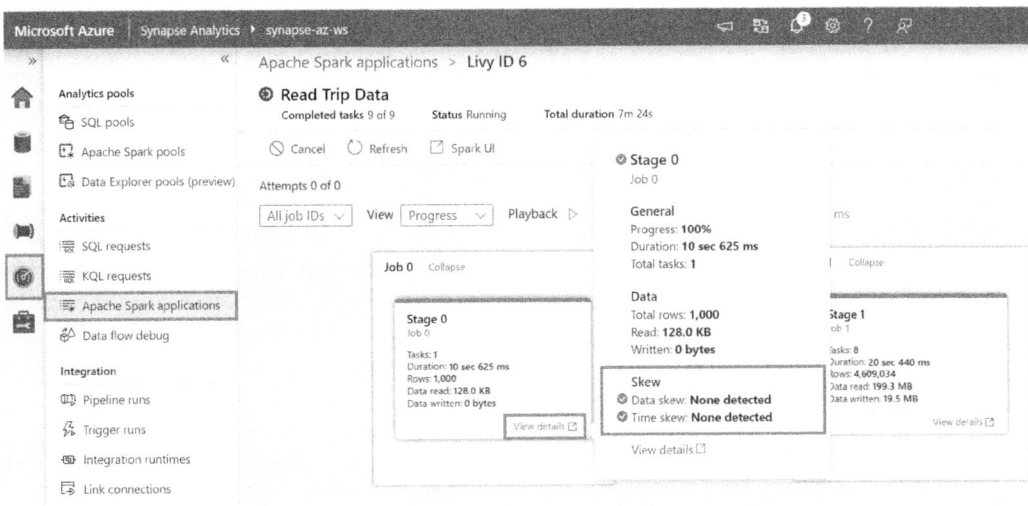

Figure 10.4 – Data skew at different stages in Synapse Spark

This way, the Synapse Spark feature makes it very easy for you to identify skew in the datasets.

This section dealt with skewness in data, which refers to an asymmetry in its distribution, which can significantly affect the outcomes of statistical analyses and machine learning models. You also learned that there are two main types of skewness, which are right (positive) and left (negative), and how identifying and correcting for skewness is crucial for unbiased model training and accurate predictions. Techniques such as data transformation normalize data and mitigate the effects of skewness. Overall, you gained knowledge about the importance of preprocessing skewed data to ensure the reliability and robustness of analytical models. Now that you know the basic techniques for handling data skew, it is time to learn about handling data spill.

# Handling Data Spill

**Data spillage** happens when a compute engine (such as SQL or Spark) cannot keep the needed data in memory while running a query and has to save some data to disk. This makes the query slower because disk reads and writes involve accessing physical storage devices, which are typically slower compared to accessing data in memory. As a result, the time it takes to read from and write to disk increases, leading to slower query performance.

Data spills can happen when the data partitions are too large, the compute resources are too small, especially the memory, and the data size grows too much during merges, unions, and so on and goes over the memory limit of the compute node.

Consider the **IAC** scenario here. You are working on generating an annual report on data collected from their trips over the past year. The data includes information such as trip dates, origins, destinations, and trip durations. After analyzing the data, you notice that the number of trips in November and December is significantly higher compared to other months. This disproportionate distribution of data can lead to data spill during processing.

If you distribute this monthly data across individual computing nodes for processing, the nodes handling November and December data may experience data spill, as the amount of data exceeds the available memory. This can result in slower processing times and potential failures in generating the report. For instance, if you are compiling an annual report where each month's data is processed separately, the nodes processing November and December data may spill data to disk, causing delays in processing and potential errors.

To deal with data spills, you can try the following solutions:

- Increase the compute resources, especially the memory if you can. This will cost more but is the simplest option.

- Reduce the data partition sizes and repartition if needed. This will take more time and effort, but it's the best option if you can't afford more compute resources.

- Remove data skew. Sometimes the data itself causes the spills. If the data is skewed, it might spill into the partitions with more data. You already observed how to handle data skew in the *Handling Skew in Data* section. You can use those methods to reduce spillage.

> **Note**
> This section primarily focuses on the **Handle data spill** concept of the DP-203: Data Engineering on Microsoft Azure exam.

You are now familiar with the general techniques for handling spills. However, to fix data spills, you need to first identify the spills in Synapse SQL and Spark.

## Handling Data Spill in Synapse SQL

Data spills happen when a query needs more memory than is available to complete the operation. When a query needs more memory, Synapse SQL has to use `tempdb` to store some data temporarily. This can degrade the performance of your queries because writing data to `tempdb` and reading it back from disk is slower than keeping it in memory, leading to longer query execution times.

The key to maximizing your performance is to follow best practices. The following are some steps to identify and handle data spills in Synapse SQL to enhance performance:

- **Knowing the query life cycle**: Comprehending the life cycle of a query can help identify where the bottlenecks are, which includes steps such as **parsing**, **binding**, and **memo compilation**. Consider the life cycle of a SQL query:

  - **Parsing**: The query is parsed to ensure it conforms to the SQL syntax rules. This step involves breaking down the query into parts. If parsing takes an unusually long time, it might indicate complex queries or inefficient use of SQL syntax.

  - **Binding**: During this stage, the query is checked for references to database objects, such as tables and columns. These references are bound to the corresponding objects in the database schema. Slow binding could suggest issues with the database schema or indexing.

  - **Optimization**: The Query Optimizer generates various execution plans for the query. It considers factors such as indexes, statistics, and system resources to determine the most efficient plan. Optimization bottlenecks might indicate outdated statistics or inadequate indexing strategies.

  - **Execution**: The selected execution plan is executed, and the query is performed on the database. This may involve reading data from disk, applying filters, joining tables, and aggregating results. Execution problems could stem from factors such as insufficient memory, disk I/O contention, or inefficient query plans.

- **Checking for warnings in query plans**: You see a warning in your query plan that reads: `Operator used tempdb to spill data during execution with spill level`. This warning message means that the query was not granted sufficient memory to complete the operation. As such, it spilled over into `tempdb`.

- **Discrepancy in estimated and actual number of rows**: A discrepancy between the estimated number of rows and the actual number of rows returned by a query usually indicates that statistics are out of date.

- **Using Synapse Analytics tools**: Azure Synapse Analytics provides tools for diagnosing data skew issues. Additionally, you can take advantage of features such as workload isolation and resource classification. By configuring resource classes, you can prioritize critical workloads and allocate dedicated resources to prevent data spills.

- **Troubleshooting slow queries**: You can use specific SQL commands to troubleshoot slow queries on a dedicated SQL pool.

> **Note**
>
> You can learn more about monitoring SQL query memory usage at `https://packt.link/cqExC`. You can learn more about monitoring SQL query `tempdb` usage at `https://packt.link/hXmWH`.

## Handling Data Spill in Spark

Data spills in Spark occur when the executor is reading shuffle files, but they cannot fit into the execution memory of the executor. When this happens, some chunk of data is removed from memory and written to disk. The following are some steps to help you identify and handle data spills in Spark:

1. **Know the spills**: When you process data, Spark uses memory for intermediate calculations. Sometimes, the data might exceed the available memory, which leads to spills.

   The following are the types of spills:

   - **Spill (Memory)**: This represents the size of data before it spills to disk. Imagine a bucket overflowing with water (data). The amount of water in the bucket before spilling is the spill (memory).

   - **Spill (Disk)**: This represents the size of data after being spilled and compressed on disk. Think of the spilled water collected in a container (disk). The volume of water in this container is the Spill (Disk). *Table 10.1* shows the metrics relating to Spark job performance, such as the total time taken to execute a task. In this case, the task took a duration of `76.0 ms` to complete. **Garbage Collection (GC)** time indicates the tasks are memory-intensive or there is insufficient memory allocated to the job. **Spill (Disk)** indicates the data was spilled to disk because it couldn't be held in memory. In this case, a small amount of data (`124` and `122` bytes) was spilled during the execution of the tasks:

| Duration | GC Time | Spill (Disk) |
|----------|---------|--------------|
| 76.0 ms  | 1s      | 124 B/4      |
| 76.0 ms  | 2s      | 122 B/4      |

Table 10.1 – Data spills from the task summary metrics

2. **Identify spills**: Spills occur when a compute engine such as **Spark** or **SQL** runs out of memory and has to write data to disk. By monitoring spills, you can learn about the resource usage and optimize your queries accordingly.

   The following are the types of spills:

   - **Spark UI**: Spark navigates to the specific stage details in the Spark UI and looks for two values: **Spill (Memory)** and **Spill (Disk)**. This allows you to monitor spill behavior.

   - **SpillListener class**: This class programmatically monitors spills. This class provides notifications whenever your Spark application encounters memory or disk spills.

3.  **Minimize spills**: To minimize spills in Spark applications, optimizing memory allocation per worker node, addressing data skew, increasing partition count, tuning Spark configurations, and controlling file sizes can effectively reduce spill frequency and impact, ensuring smoother processing and performance. The following are some strategies to decrease the frequency and impact of spills:

    - **Boost memory**: You can allocate more memory per worker node in your **Spark cluster**. This gives your processing tasks more space to breathe, reducing the likelihood of spill.

    - **Tame the skew**: If data skew is causing spills, you have to address it first. **Skew** occurs when some partitions contain significantly more data than others. Techniques such as **salting** or **custom partitioning** can help distribute data more evenly.

    - **Partition power**: Increasing the number of partitions can decrease the size of individual partitions, reducing the chance of a single partition overflowing memory and causing a spill.

    - **Tune configurations**: Adjust Spark settings, for example, configurations such as `spark.sql.shuffle.partitions` to optimize or control the number of shuffle partitions. Experiment with different values to find an optimal configuration for your workload.

    - **Fine-tune file size**: You can use `spark.sql.files.maxPartitionBytes` to limit the maximum size of individual data files within a partition. This prevents any single file from consuming too much memory during shuffles.

You are now aware of handling spills in Synapse SQL and Spark. The next section will deal with efficient resource management.

## Optimizing Resource Management

Efficient resource management is the secret formula for achieving top-notch performance, scalability, and cost efficiency in Azure data engineering. In this section, you will cover the essential strategies for managing resources in Azure environments. Mastering these will help you craft data solutions that meet your business goals while managing operational costs.

> **Note**
>
> This section primarily focuses on the **Optimize resource management** concept of the DP-203: Data Engineering on Microsoft Azure exam.

The following are some key areas you should focus on to efficiently manage resources:

- **Resource provisioning**: You need to know how to provision various Azure resources, such as **Azure SQL database**, **ADLS**, **Azure Synapse Analytics**, and **Azure Databricks**, based on workload requirements and expected data volumes. This involves selecting appropriate **Stock-Keeping Units** (**SKUs**) and configurations to meet performance and scalability needs while keeping costs in check.

- **Scaling strategies**: You need to learn about scaling strategies for Azure resources to handle varying workloads effectively. This includes the **horizontal scaling** (scaling out) and **vertical scaling** (scaling up) of compute and storage resources based on demand, for example, using Azure SQL database's **autoscaling** features or scaling **Azure Databricks clusters** dynamically.

- **Monitoring and optimization tools**: You must familiarize yourself with Azure monitoring and optimization tools such as **Azure Monitor**, **Azure Advisor**, and **Azure Cost Management + Billing**. These tools provide insights into resource utilization, performance metrics, and cost analysis, enabling you to identify optimization opportunities and make informed decisions.

- **Cost management**: You can gain knowledge of cost management best practices to optimize resource utilization without overspending. This involves knowing about the Azure pricing models, cost allocation tags, budgeting, and implementing cost-saving measures such as resource scheduling, rightsizing, and using reserved instances or Azure Hybrid Benefit where applicable.

- **Performance tuning**: You can learn techniques for performance tuning to improve the efficiency and responsiveness of your data solutions. This includes optimizing query performance in **Azure SQL database** or **Azure Synapse Analytics**, tuning **Apache Spark jobs** in **Azure Databricks**, optimizing data ingestion, processing pipelines, and minimizing data movement across Azure services.

- **High availability and disaster recovery**: Know the importance of high availability and **Disaster Recovery** (**DR**) in resource management and design solutions accordingly. This involves leveraging Azure features such as geo-replication, zone-redundant storage, read replicas, and failover strategies to ensure business continuity and minimize downtime.

- **Security and compliance considerations**: Consider security and compliance requirements when managing Azure resources. Implement security best practices such as **RBAC**, encryption at rest and in transit, data masking, and compliance certifications to protect sensitive data and meet regulatory standards.

The subsequent section will review some of the general techniques that can help you in optimizing storage and compute in Synapse SQL pools and Spark resources such as Azure Databricks and Synapse Spark.

## Optimizing Synapse SQL Pools

Optimizing resource management in Azure is crucial for cost efficiency. To optimize Azure Synapse SQL pools for cost efficiency, it is essential to manage your resources smartly. This involves selecting the right resource classes to balance memory and concurrency, pausing and scaling pools based on demand to control costs, and fine-tuning performance through query optimization and data loading strategies. Additionally, cost management can be enhanced by using serverless options, auto-pause during downtime, and data compression, as well as choosing cost-effective storage solutions. You can explore some of the following techniques to achieve cost efficiency:

- **Pause and scale for cost efficiency**: Since storage and compute are decoupled in Synapse dedicated SQL pools, consider pausing your SQL pool compute during periods of inactivity. Pausing the compute won't impact your data, but it will significantly reduce costs. To use the pool again, resume the compute resources:

  - **Right-size your compute units**: In Synapse SQL pools, compute units are measured in **Data Warehouse Units** (**DWUs**). Start with the smallest DWU configuration that meets your performance requirements and then gradually increase the DWUs as needed to strike the right balance between cost and performance. Next, monitor your workload and adjust the number of DWUs accordingly.

- **Dynamic scaling with Azure Functions**: To handle varying workloads, manually scale out or scale in the compute resources. You can also automate this process using Azure Functions. In order to optimize resource utilization, scale out when demand increases and scale in during quieter periods.

> **Note**
>
> You can learn more about resource management for Synapse SQL pools at `https://packt.link/jJSHU`. You can learn more about best practices for dedicated SQL pools in Azure Synapse Analytics at `https://packt.link/SKs51`.

## Optimizing Spark

By implementing these optimization strategies, your organization can maximize the efficiency and performance of Spark resources in **Azure Databricks** and **Azure Synapse Analytics**, enabling faster insights and better decision-making from Big Data Analytics workloads.

The following are a few suggestions for optimizing the effectiveness and performance of Spark in both Synapse Spark and Azure Databricks Spark:

- **Autoscale options**: When setting up your cluster, consider using autoscale options in Azure Databricks or Synapse Spark. Autoscaling dynamically adjusts the cluster size based on workload demand and eliminates the need for manual resource management. Make sure there is optimal resource allocation without overprovisioning or underutilization.

- **Auto-terminate clusters**: Enable the auto-terminate option in both Azure Databricks and Synapse Spark. With this setting, the clusters automatically shut down if they remain unused for a configured period. The auto-terminate option helps reduce costs by avoiding idle cluster resources.

- **Spot instances for cost savings**: Consider using Spot instances where available. Spot instances are cost-effective nodes that may be preempted if higher-priority jobs require those resources. Use Spot instances strategically to lower overall cluster costs without compromising performance.

- **Choose the right cluster nodes**: Select appropriate cluster nodes based on your workload type (memory-intensive, CPU-intensive, or network-intensive). Always choose nodes with more memory than the maximum memory required by your jobs. Selecting proper nodes will always enhance execution efficiency and resource utilization.

- **Dynamic resource allocation**: Enable dynamic allocation for Spark executors. This feature adjusts the number of executor instances based on workload demand. Executors are added or removed dynamically and optimize resource utilization.

- **Monitoring and logging**: Regularly monitor cluster performance using tools such as **Azure Monitor** or **Databricks monitoring**. Analyze query execution plans, identify bottlenecks, and fine-tune configurations.

> **Note**
>
> You can learn more about optimizing Spark jobs in Azure Synapse Analytics at `https://packt.link/52ThL`. You can learn more about best practices for Azure Databricks cluster configuration at `https://packt.link/ujlHW`.

These are a few of the best ways to optimize your resource usage. Next, you will look at how you can tune queries using indexers.

## Tuning Queries Using Indexers

**Indexers** are essential in databases, data warehouses, and analytical engines such as Spark environments as they contribute to faster data retrieval, improved query performance, optimized join operations, enhanced resource utilization, and streamlined data analysis. By utilizing indexers effectively, you can unlock the full potential of the Data Analytics workflows and derive actionable insights from the data more efficiently.

> **Note**
>
> This section primarily focuses on the **Tune queries by using indexers** concept of the DP-203: Data Engineering on Microsoft Azure exam.

In both Synapse SQL and Spark, there are various options for indexing and query tuning. To prepare for the DP-203 certification exam, it is important to know about the following indexing and query-tuning techniques:

- **Indexers in Synapse SQL**: Indexers in Synapse SQL provide a powerful mechanism for optimizing query performance by creating and managing indexes on tables. These indexes can significantly speed up data retrieval operations, especially for complex queries or frequently accessed columns. By strategically choosing which columns you want to index and utilizing different types of indexes, such as clustered and non-clustered indexes, you can efficiently enhance query performance in **Azure Synapse Analytics**. Knowing how to leverage indexers is crucial for optimizing query execution and maximizing the efficiency of data processing tasks. Dedicated SQL pools offer the following indexing options:

  - **Clustered columnstore index**: A table without any index options in a dedicated SQL pool will have a **Clustered Columnstore Index (CCI)** by default. This type of index provides the best data compression and query performance. **Clustered columnstore tables** are usually more efficient than clustered index or HEAP tables and are ideal for large tables. Use a CCI for large tables of 60 million rows or more to achieve top-level compression and faster query performance.

  As an example of this, use the IAC scenario again. Your goal is to manage information about cab drivers efficiently, so you need to create a table to store details about each driver, such as `driverId` and `name`, and apply a `CLUSTERED COLUMNSTORE INDEX` to the table to optimize the storage and querying of data for analytical purposes. You could do this using the following code:

  ```
  CREATE TABLE dbo.Driver
  (
  [driverId] INT NOT NULL,
  [name] VARCHAR(40)
  )
    WITH ( CLUSTERED COLUMNSTORE INDEX );
  ```

This creates a table named dbo.Driver with two columns: driverId and name. Additionally, it specifies that the table should have a CCI. This index optimizes data storage and retrieval for analytical queries, making it suitable for scenarios where large volumes of data need to be efficiently analyzed.

- **Clustered and nonclustered indexes**: If you need to retrieve one row quickly, you might prefer using a clustered index or a **nonclustered secondary index** instead of a Clustered columnstore table. **Clustered indexes** are efficient for this kind of query, but they only work well if you filter by the column that has the clustered index. If you need to filter by other columns, you can add a nonclustered index to them. But be careful because more indexes mean more space and more time to load the data as it consumes additional disk space, because each index requires storage for its data structure and pointers to the table rows. This can lead to increased storage requirements for the database. Moreover, when loading or modifying data, you need to update all associated indexes, which can slow down data loading and modification operations. Therefore, it is essential to carefully consider the trade-offs between query performance and the overhead of maintaining multiple indexes.

Here is an example of creating a table with a clustered index:

```
CREATE TABLE dbo.Driver
(
[driverId] INT NOT NULL,
[name] VARCHAR(40),
[customerId] INT NOT NULL
 )
 WITH ( CLUSTERED INDEX (driverId));
```

In the preceding code, the SQL code creates a table named Driver with three columns: driverId, which serves as the primary key, name, and customerId. Additionally, the table has a clustered index on the driverId column, which organizes the physical order of the rows in the table based on this column's values, optimizing retrieval speed for queries involving the primary key.

To add a non-clustered index on a table, use the following syntax:

```
CREATE INDEX customerIdIndex on dbo.Driver (customerId);
```

In the preceding code, the SQL statement creates an index named customerIdIndex on the customerId column of the Driver table. Indexing customerId can improve query performance when filtering or sorting based on this column.

- **Non-index option (HEAP)**: **HEAP** tables are an effective option for storing data temporarily in dedicated SQL pools. They have a faster loading speed than index tables and can sometimes be read from the cache, if the data is frequently accessed and stays in memory due to repeated queries or the dataset is small enough to fit in memory. This is useful when you need to stage data for further transformations. You can also use temporary tables instead of permanent tables to speed up the loading process. After loading data to HEAP tables, you can create indexes to improve query performance.

The following snippet shows how this is done:

```
CREATE TABLE dbo.Driver
(
[driverId] INT NOT NULL,
[name] VARCHAR(40)
)
WITH ( HEAP );
```

In the preceding code, the SQL code creates a table named `Driver` with two columns: `driverId`, which serves as the primary key, and `name`. The table is specified with the HEAP option, indicating that it is a HEAP table. HEAP tables are unordered collections of data rows, meaning that the physical order of the rows in the table is not defined by an index. This can be advantageous for temporary data storage, as HEAP tables typically have faster loading speeds than indexed tables and can sometimes benefit from reading data directly from the cache, depending on various factors, such as memory availability and access patterns.

> **Note**
>
> You can find the complete code in the accompanying GitHub repository at `https://packt.link/7ZwFl`.

Clustered columnstore tables are powerful for optimizing performance, particularly when you are dealing with massive datasets (thousands or even millions to billions of rows). Their strength lies in the compression of large amounts of data, which significantly reduces storage requirements and boosts query efficiency. For smaller lookup tables (under a million rows), you can choose storage options such as HEAP, or clustered indexes might be more suitable and ideal for frequently accessed lookup data.

- **Indexing your table**: Indexes serve to speed up data retrieval operations, enhancing query efficiency and overall system responsiveness. Consideration of factors such as data distribution, query patterns, and system resources is crucial in determining the most suitable indexes for a given table.

*Table 10.2* shows an analysis and breakdown of potential index candidates along with their respective suitability for the table based on your needs:

| Type | Great fit for... | Watch out if... |
| --- | --- | --- |
| Clustered columnstore index (default) | Large tables (more than 100 million rows) | It is used on a replicated table.<br><br>You make massive update operations on your table.<br><br>You over-partition your table: row groups do not span across different distribution nodes and partitions. |
| Clustered index | Tables with up to 100 million rows<br><br>Large tables (more than 100 million rows) with only 1-2 columns heavily used | It is used on a replicated table.<br><br>You have complex queries involving multiple join and Group By operations.<br><br>You make updates on the indexed columns.<br><br>It takes memory. |
| HEAP | Staging/temporary table<br><br>Small tables with small lookups | Any lookup operation requires scanning the full table |

Table 10.2 – Analysis of potential index candidates along with their respective suitability

If your CCI is running slowly because your row groups are not compressed, you can tune up by rebuilding your CCI, aiming for a minimum of 100,000 rows per compressed row group. On top of a clustered index, you might want to add a nonclustered index to a column frequently used for filtering (see the clustered and nonclustered indexes example).

> **Note**
> You can learn more about indexing in Synapse SQL at https://packt.link/P5b5l.

Next, look at the indexing options available for Spark.

## Indexers in Synapse Spark Pools

**Hyperspace** is an indexing subsystem for Apache Spark that provides efficient indexing capabilities to enable fast data access and efficient query execution. It is an open source project developed by Microsoft to design and enhance the performance of Spark-based Data Analytics workloads. It builds and maintains indexes on data stored in **Spark DataFrames** or datasets, allows for the rapid retrieval of relevant data subsets without the need for full table scans, and introduces the ability for users to create indexes on their data, such as CSV, **JavaScript Object Notation** (**JSON**), and Parquet files.

Hyperspace helps accelerate workloads or queries under two circumstances:

- **Highly selective filters**: When queries involve filters on predicates with high selectivity (e.g., selecting a few rows from a large dataset)
- **Heavy shuffling joins**: When queries require joins between large datasets (e.g., joining a 100 GB dataset with a 10 GB dataset)

Here, you can learn how to use Hyperspace to speed up your Spark queries by creating indexes on your data. You can use a sample dataset that consists of two tables: `student` and `course`. To store the data and the indexes, you need to specify the `studentLocation` and `courseLocation` paths in your storage account. These paths should point to the folders where you want to save the data and index files.

Once the paths are configured, you can create the Hyperspace indexes on your datasets. This involves defining indexes on specific columns such as `courseId` to optimize query performance and accelerate queries on your datasets.

## Preparing Data

**Preparing data** for query tuning with indexers involves organizing and structuring data to enhance its accessibility and retrieval efficiency within a database. This process is vital for optimizing **query performance**. It begins with assessing data usage to determine which columns should be indexed. Based on this assessment, appropriate indexes, such as clustered or non-clustered, are created to expedite query response times.

First, you will create sample data records for `student` and `course` tables then save them as Parquet data files. Parquet is used for demonstration in this example; however, you can also use other formats, such as CSV. Perform the following steps to create the `student` and `course` tables:

```
from pyspark.sql.types import StructField, StructType, StringType,
IntegerType

# student records
students = [(1001, "Alice", 101), (1002, "Bob", 102), (1003,
"Charlie", 103), (1004, "David", 104), (1005, "Eve", 105), (1006,
"Frank", 106), (1007, "Grace", 107), (1008, "Harry", 108), (1009,
"Ivy", 109), (1010, "Jack", 110), (1011, "Kate", 111), (1012, "Leo",
112), (1013, "Mary", 113), (1014, "Nick", 114)]

# course records
courses = [(101, "Math", "Room A"), (102, "English", "Room B"), (103,
"Science", "Room C"), (104, "History", "Room D"), (105, "Art", "Room
E"), (106, "Music", "Room F"), (107, "PE", "Gym"), (108, "French",
"Room G"), (109, "Spanish", "Room H"), (110, "German", "Room I"),
(111, "Computer Science", "Lab 1"), (112, "Biology", "Lab 2"), (113,
"Chemistry", "Lab 3"), (114, "Physics", "Lab 4")]
# Create a schema for the dataframes
# student schema
student_schema = StructType([StructField('studentId', IntegerType(),
True), StructField('studentName', StringType(), True),
StructField('courseId', IntegerType(), True)])

# course schema
course_schema = StructType([StructField('courseId', IntegerType(),
True), StructField('courseName', StringType(), True),
StructField('room', StringType(), True)])

student_df = spark.createDataFrame(students, student_schema)
course_df = spark.createDataFrame(courses, course_schema)

# customize your location path
studentLocation = "abfss://path/to/student/students.parquet"
courseLocation = "abfss://path/to/course/courses.parquet"

student_df.write.mode("overwrite").parquet(studentLocation)
course_df.write.mode("overwrite").parquet(courseLocation)
```

In the preceding code snippet, PySpark is utilized in a Synapse Spark Notebook to create two DataFrames representing `student` and `course` records. The `student` DataFrame contains fields for `studentId`, `studentName`, and `courseId`, while the `course` DataFrame contains fields for `courseId`, `courseName`, and `room`. `StructType` is used to define schemas for both DataFrames.

The data is then written in Parquet files, with `student` records saved to one location and `course` records to another. The script writes the DataFrames to **ADLS Gen2** using the **Azure Blob File System (ABFS)** protocol. The overwrite mode ensures that any existing data in the specified locations is replaced with the new data. This process effectively prepares and saves structured data in a distributed file format, enabling efficient storage and retrieval for subsequent analysis or processing tasks.

Now run the following commands in a **Synapse Spark Notebook** to see the output display the rows in the `student` and `course` DataFrames:

```
student_DF= spark.read.parquet(studentLocation)

course_DF = spark.read.parquet(courseLocation)

# Verify the data is available and correct

student_DF.show()
course_DF.show()
```

The preceding code reads the Parquet files located at `studentLocation` and `courseLocation` into Spark DataFrames named `student_DF` and `course_DF`, respectively. Then, it displays the contents of both DataFrames using the `show()` method, which allows you to verify that the data has been successfully loaded and is correct.

## Creating a Hyperspace Instance

**Hyperspace**, a performance optimization framework, allows you to create indexes on large datasets, vastly improving the query execution speed. When handling massive data volumes, traditional indexing methods may falter, which causes slow query performance. Hyperspace tackles this issue by enabling the creation of lightweight, domain-specific indexes tailored to the dataset and queries at hand. By strategically establishing a Hyperspace instance, you can leverage advanced indexing techniques to streamline query operations, minimize latency, and ultimately derive faster insights from the data.

To create an instance of Hyperspace, the first step is to import the necessary libraries into your environment. These libraries provide the tools and functions needed to work with Hyperspace. Once the libraries are imported, you can then proceed to create an instance of Hyperspace within your code. This instance serves as your gateway to accessing and utilizing the various functionalities offered by Hyperspace.

With the Hyperspace instance set up, you gain access to a range of APIs that allow you to interact with your data, and these APIs enable you to create indexes on your `student` and `course` datasets, as well as modifying existing indexes.

The following code shows an example of how to create an instance of Hyperspace in Apache Spark:

```
from hyperspace import *
# Create an instance of Hyperspace
hyperspace = Hyperspace(spark)
```

First, it imports the necessary classes and functions from the Hyperspace module. Then, it initializes a Hyperspace instance, assigning it to the `hyperspace` variable. This instance is constructed with a **SparkSession** object (`spark`), which allows interaction with the Spark environment for executing operations on data.

## Creating Index Configurations

An **index configuration** is a way to tell Hyperspace how to create an index on a given DataFrame. It has the following components:

- **Index name**: This is used to identify and manage the index.

- **Indexed columns**: These are a list of columns from the DataFrame that will be used as keys for the index. These columns should appear in the `filter` or `join` conditions of the queries that will benefit from the index.

- **Included columns**: These are a list of columns from the DataFrame that will be stored as values in the index. These columns should appear in the `select` or `project` clauses of the queries that will benefit from the index.

The following code shows the index configuration required to create Hyperspace indexes on the `student` and `course` datasets, which will be used to speed up queries on these datasets:

```
# Create index configurations
student_IndexConfig = IndexConfig("studentIndex", ["courseId"],
["studentName"])
course_IndexConfig = IndexConfig("courseIndex", ["courseId"],
["courseName"]
```

Here, the index named `courseIndex` has the indexed column `courseId` and the included column `courseName`. This means that the index will store the mapping between the course IDs and names and can be used to quickly filter or join by `courseId`.

## Creating Hyperspace Indexes

Hyperspace indexes offer an innovative approach to optimizing Spark queries. It is a specialized indexing subsystem that allows you to build indexes on various data formats, such as **CSV**, **JSON**, and **Parquet** files. This capability has the potential to significantly speed up query performance and workloads. In this section, you will go through the steps of setting up Hyperspace in your environment, preparing your data, and creating indexes that Spark can leverage for faster queries.

You will now create the indexes using the following index configurations:

```
# Create indexes from configurations

hyperspace.createIndex(student_DF, student_IndexConfig)
hyperspace.createIndex(course_DF, course_IndexConfig)
```

The preceding code creates indexes on the `student` and `course` DataFrames using predefined configurations with Hyperspace. Here, `hyperspace.createIndex(student_DF, student_IndexConfig)` initiates the creation of an index on the `student_DF` DataFrame, using the configuration specified in `student_IndexConfig`. Similarly, `hyperspace.createIndex(course_DF, course_IndexConfig)` creates an index on the `course_DF` DataFrame, following the configuration in `course_IndexConfig`.

Then run the commands to create the indexes.

## Enabling Hyperspace Indexes

Hyperspace acts as a hidden channel within Spark, a network of intelligent pathways waiting to be awakened. Here, network refers to the underlying structure of Hyperspace within Spark that operates as a system of interconnected pathways or routes that guide data processing and query execution within the Spark environment. These pathways (known as **indexes**) hold the key to unlocking the true potential of your data. By enabling Hyperspace, you become the conductor, guiding Spark's engine to leverage these hidden pathways and accelerate its data navigation.

As a result, Spark can now leverage these shortcuts, streamlining its operations and delivering results at lightning speed.

However, not all indexes are equally valuable. Indexes vary in their value based on factors such as data distribution, query patterns, and the types of operations being performed. Some indexes may significantly improve query performance by efficiently filtering or sorting data, while others may have no impact or even degrade performance.

Therefore, not all indexes are equally valuable in terms of their contribution to query optimization. It's essential to carefully consider which columns to index and how to configure indexes to maximize their effectiveness for specific queries and workload characteristics. Disabling Hyperspace gives you granular control, allowing you to selectively choose which pathways Spark should utilize. This fine-tuning ensures that only the most relevant and efficient indexes are used, thereby optimizing performance without introducing unnecessary processing overhead. Remember, Hyperspace is a powerful tool, but it is crucial to grasp its distinctions by mastering the art of enabling and disabling indexes. This can help you control the performance of your Spark queries and maximize the potential of your Spark applications.

Perform the following steps to enable the Hyperspace index and reload the DataFrames from the same file location again:

```
# Enable Hyperspace
Hyperspace.enable(spark)


student_DF = spark.read.parquet(studentLocation)
course_DF = spark.read.parquet(courseLocation)

student_DF.show(5)
course_DF.show(5)
```

The preceding code enables Hyperspace and then reads the student and course DataFrames from Parquet files located at studentLocation and courseLocation, respectively. Finally, it displays the first 5 rows of each DataFrame using the show() method.

Then start the join and view query plan, as shown in the following steps:

```
# Join

hyperspaceJoin = student_DF.join(course_DF, student_DF.courseId
== course_DF.coureseId).select(student_DF.studentName, course_
DF.courseName)

hyperspaceJoin.show()

hyperspaceJoin.explain(True)
```

The preceding code performs a join operation between the student and course DataFrames using the oursed column as the join condition. It then selects the studentName and courseName columns from the joined DataFrame.

> **Note**
>
> You can find the complete code in the accompanying GitHub repository at https://packt.link/sSrBb.

This section focused on using indexers to optimize query performance in analytical engines such as Spark. You were introduced to Hyperspace, an indexing subsystem for Apache Spark developed by Microsoft that efficiently indexes data stored in Spark DataFrames or datasets, enhancing data access and query execution efficiency. You explored data preparation for query tuning, which involved organizing and structuring data to improve its accessibility, including assessing data usage to determine which columns should be indexed and creating appropriate indexes such as clustered or non-clustered. You have also learned how to set up Hyperspace, prepare data, and create indexes in various formats such as CSV, JSON, and Parquet.

> **Note**
>
> You can learn more about Hyperspace for Spark at `https://packt.link/SjTNc`.

Now, it is time to move on to tuning queries leveraging the caching mechanism to enhance efficiency further.

## Tuning Queries Using Caching

When you are dealing with massive amounts of data, getting quick results is essential for smooth operations. Azure offers a range of tools to help speed up queries, and one powerful method is **caching**. Think of caching as keeping frequently used information close at hand for faster access. In this section, you will dive into how you can use caching in Synapse Spark and Synapse SQL to make your queries run faster and your data analysis more efficient. You will cover why caching matters, how to set it up in Synapse SQL or Synapse Spark, and how it works alongside other optimization techniques, such as indexing. With caching, you can dramatically improve query speeds, reduce delays, and make your data analysis experience much smoother.

**Caching** is an optimization technique used in both **Apache Spark** (which includes **Synapse Spark**) and **Databricks Spark** to improve the performance of iterative or interactive workloads by storing intermediate data in memory, which refers to the data generated during the execution of various transformations and computations within a Spark job. This data is produced as a result of intermediate steps in a computation pipeline before reaching the final result.

Caching intermediate data in memory allows for faster access to the data during subsequent stages of computation. By keeping frequently accessed data in memory, Spark can avoid re-computation and efficiently reuse the cached data, leading to improved performance, especially for interactive workloads where the same data may be accessed multiple times. When you are dealing with massive datasets, optimizing query performance becomes paramount for smooth operations. Azure offers powerful tools such as caching to speed up queries, ensuring quick results for efficient data analysis.

In this section, you delved into how you can utilize caching in Synapse Spark and Synapse SQL to enhance query performance. Now, you will explore why caching matters, how to set it up in Synapse SQL or Synapse Spark, and how it complements other optimization techniques such as indexing. With caching, you can significantly improve query speeds, reduce delays, and enhance your overall data analysis experience.

> **Note**
>
> This section primarily focuses on the **Tune queries by using cache** concept of the DP-203: Data Engineering on Microsoft Azure exam.

## Tuning Queries in Synapse SQL

**Caching** is a widely recognized technique for enhancing read performance in databases. Synapse SQL introduces a feature called **result set caching** that allows query results to be cached and reused when the query remains unchanged. Once the result set caching is enabled, the subsequent query executions retrieve results directly from the cache and eliminate the need for recomputing. It is important to note that the result set cache is utilized only under specific conditions.

### Result Set Caching

Imagine your dedicated SQL pool as an active library, overflowing with information. However, retrieving specific details can be time-consuming, requiring repeated searches through the vast collection. That is where result set caching comes in, acting like a smart librarian's assistant, accurately noting down frequently requested information for quick retrieval.

To enable result set caching, you can use the following command and replace [database_name] with your actual database:

```
ALTER DATABASE [database_name]
SET RESULT_SET_CACHING ON;
```

This command empowers the assistant to analyze frequently executed queries and store the results in a readily accessible cache within the database you specified.

### Benefits of Caching

Caching in Synapse SQL offers several benefits, including significantly improved query performance by storing frequently accessed data in memory. This reduces latency, speeds up data retrieval, and enhances overall query efficiency, making data analysis processes smoother and more responsive.

The following are some of its benefits:

- **Swift responses**: Subsequent identical queries can bypass your entire search process; directly fetching results from the cache will result in significantly faster response times.

- **Resource conservation**: Cached queries utilize minimal resources, so they free up valuable concurrency slots for other critical operations to improve the overall system performance.

### Important Considerations

When utilizing caching in Synapse SQL, it's crucial to consider key aspects. Ensure proper authorization and enable the result set caching. Also, you can control caching as needed for specific sessions using designated commands:

- **Authorization**: You can access the cache results as you are the cache creator and anyone else with the same level of access to the data can also access them.

- **Default state**: Result set caching is initially disabled at both the database and session levels, and you have to enable the result set to access it.

- **Session-level control**: You can also enable or disable caching for a specific session using the following command:

```
SET RESULT_SET_CACHING { ON | OFF };
```

## Handling Exceptions in Result Set Caching

When result set caching is enabled for a database, the query results are cached for all queries until the cache reaches its capacity. The following types of queries are excluded from result set caching:

- Queries containing built-in functions or runtime expressions that remain non-deterministic even when there are no changes in the underlying data or query structure, for example, `DateTime.Now()`, `GetDate()`, and so on

- Queries that utilize user-defined functions

- Queries involving tables with row-level security

- Queries returning data with a row size exceeding 64 KB

- Queries returning large datasets (greater than 10 GB in size)

## Considerations in Result Set Caching

In result set caching, certain queries may be excluded due to reasons such as non-deterministic functions or large result sets, which can impact caching efficiency. It is essential to know these considerations to optimize query performance effectively:

- **Avoid stressing the control node**: Running queries returning large result sets (>1 GB) with caching enabled can stress the control node. Before running such queries (common during data exploration or **Extract, Transform, and Load** (ETL)), **disable result set caching** at the database level.

- **Monitoring**: Check the time taken by result set caching operations using the `sys.dm_pdw_exec_requests` view. In cases where the query takes more time, you need to analyze the execution details, identify bottlenecks, and optimize query performance. This may involve optimizing data distribution, increasing resources, or restructuring queries to improve efficiency and reduce execution time.

## Optimizing Cached Results

Managing cached results in your Synapse SQL instance involves controlling the storage and automatic invalidation of frequently executed query results through mechanisms such as result set caching and data caching.

The following are the ways to manage your cache size and its automatic refresh policies:

- **Spacious storage**: Each of your databases in Synapse gets a generous 1 TB of space dedicated to storing cached results. This allows you to hold the results of frequently executed queries, so you don't need to calculate it every time.

- **Automated cache updates**: The dedicated SQL pool in Synapse takes care of updating your cache for you. Here's how it works:

  - **Timely cleanups**: Every 48 hours, the system checks your cache. If a result hasn't been used in that time or is no longer valid, then it gets removed.

  - **Maximum size threshold**: When your cache nears its 1 TB limit, the pool initiates a proactive eviction process that prioritizes less frequently used or the oldest entries to free up valuable space.

- **Manual cache reset**: While the system handles most of the cache management for you, you have the power to clear the entire cache if needed. Pausing a database won't empty the cached result set. The following are the ways to clear the cache:

  - **Toggle it off**: You can temporarily stop using the cache. Run the following command to do so:

    ```
    ALTER DATABASE [YourDatabaseName] SET RESULT_SET_CACHING OFF;
    ```

    In the preceding code, the `ALTER DATABASE SET RESULT_SET_CACHING OFF` statement turns off the result set caching for a specified database. This means that any caching of query results within this database will be disabled, which can be useful if caching is not desired or is causing issues.

  - **Direct clearing**: You can clear the cache immediately. Connect to your database and run the following command:

    ```
    DBCC DROPRESULTSETCACHE
    ```

> **Note**
> You can learn more about result set caching at `https://packt.link/pDzwm`.

## Tuning Queries in Spark

When it comes to handling data in **Synapse Spark** and **Azure Databricks Spark**, caching works a lot like it does in Synapse SQL. It's kind of like having mini storage lockers where you can stash away bits of data you might need later on. Here, the discussion pertains to things such as individual **Resilient Distributed Datasets** (**RDDs**) or DataFrames, and you can do this with methods such as `cache()` or `persist()` in Spark. It's like giving your data a little speed boost, which is especially handy when you are dealing with big chunks of information.

In the context of **RDD** and DataFrames and datasets, caching works as follows:

- **RDD caching**: In Spark, RDD can be cached using the `cache()` method. This method stores the RDD's partitions in memory across the cluster nodes. When an RDD is cached, Spark keeps the data in memory and reuses it in subsequent actions, reducing the need to recompute the RDD from its source data. The following is a simple example of a cache:

```
# Create an RDD
rdd = spark.sparkContext.parallelize([21, 88, 32, 54, 100])
# Cache the RDD
rdd.cache()
```

In the preceding code, an RDD named `rdd` is created using Spark's `parallelize` method. Then, the `cache()` method is called on the RDD, instructing Spark to cache the RDD in memory for faster access in subsequent operations.

- **DataFrames and dataset caching**: Similarly, DataFrames and datasets can also be cached using the `cache()` method. This allows intermediate data generated during DataFrame transformations to be stored in memory. The following is a simple example to cache the inputs of a DataFrame created from a CSV file:

```
# Provide path to your CSV file

sales_file_path = "path/to/csv/sales/file.CSV"
# Read the Sales CSV file into a DataFrame
Sales_df = spark.read.csv(sales_file_path)
# Cache the DataFrame
cache_sales_df = Sales_df.cache()
```

In the preceding code, a CSV file containing sales data is read into a DataFrame named `Sales_df` using Spark's `read.csv()` method. Then, the `cache()` method is called on the DataFrame to cache it in memory for faster access in subsequent operations.

> **Note**
>
> You can find the complete code in the accompanying GitHub repository at `https://packt.link/mbRBZ`.

## Caching on Azure Databricks

**Azure Databricks** and **Spark** offer caching mechanisms that allow you to optimize performance by storing intermediate results. Now you will explore how caching works in these contexts:

- **Azure Databricks disk cache**: Azure Databricks leverages disk cache (previously known as the Delta cache or DBIO cache) to accelerate data reads. When you fetch the data from remote Parquet files, copies are created in local storage on worker nodes using a fast intermediate data format.

  There is no more waiting for slow remote data; disk cache smartly caches data locally whenever you need it from a distant source. The next time you need the same information, it is right there to use at lightning speed. You can think of it as a handy local copy shop for your data, and the results speed up significantly.

  There are two different types of caching for files and folders. They are as follows:

  - **Automatic disk caching**: Automatic disk caching makes your data faster and easier to retrieve by storing frequently used data locally on the device's storage. You don't have to do anything or change anything to use it as it works well for most of the operations you perform.

  - **Manual disk caching**: This is a method used in Apache Spark to proactively control cache contents, particularly when you want to manage caching behavior more granularly. **Manual disk caching** allows you to explicitly specify which **RDDs** or DataFrames to cache and where to store them, typically on disk. This approach is beneficial in scenarios where you need to optimize disk usage or manage large datasets that may not fit entirely into memory. Manual caching is useful for scenarios where you want to control cache contents proactively.

  You can use the CACHE SELECT command to preload specific data into the cache before execution. The following is sample code to cache all columns and rows from a table:

  ```
  CACHE SELECT * FROM my_table;
  ```

  If you want to cache specific columns and apply a condition, use the following code:

  ```
  CACHE SELECT column1, column2
  FROM my_table
  WHERE column1 > 10;
  ```

- **Disk cache versus Spark cache**: *Table 10.3* summarizes the key differences between disk and Apache Spark caching so that you can choose the best tool for your workflow:

| Feature | Disk Cache | Apache Spark Cache |
|---------|-----------|--------------------|
| Stored as | Local files on a worker node. | In-memory blocks, but it depends on storage level. |
| Applied to | Any Parquet tables stored on ABFS and other filesystems. | Any DataFrame or RDD. |
| Triggered | Automatically, on the first read (if cache is enabled). | Manually, requires code changes. |
| Evaluated | Lazily. | Lazily. |
| Force cache | The CACHE SELECT command. | .cache + any action to materialize the cache and .persist. |
| Availability | Can be enabled or disabled with configuration flags; enabled by default on certain node types. | Always available. |
| Evicted | Data is cached automatically in a **Least Recently Used** (**LRU**) fashion. This means that Spark evicts the LRU data from the cache when the cache reaches its capacity limit. Eviction can trigger on any file change, manually when restarting a cluster. | Data is cached automatically in an LRU fashion. Eviction can also occur when the cached data is explicitly unpersisted manually with the unpersist method. |

Table 10.3 – Differences between disk and Apache Spark caching

- **Configuring disk usage**: Configuring disk usage in Apache Spark allows you to control how cached data is managed on disk, providing flexibility and optimization options for handling large datasets. By adjusting settings such as the disk storage level and eviction policies, you can ensure efficient utilization of disk space and enhance overall performance in Spark applications. To configure how the disk cache uses the worker nodes' local storage, you must specify the following Spark configuration settings during cluster creation:

  - `spark.databricks.io.cache.maxDiskUsage`: This parameter allows you to control the "amount of disk space allocated for caching data" in **Databricks,** helping to manage disk usage and prevent excessive caching that could impact performance or lead to resource contention. Adjusting this parameter enables you to optimize caching behavior based on your specific requirements and available resources. The disk space per node is reserved for cached data in **bytes**.

- `spark.databricks.io.cache.maxMetaDataCache`: This parameter controls the "amount of memory allocated for caching metadata," such as file metadata and directory listings, in Databricks. By adjusting this parameter, you can optimize the memory usage for caching metadata and improve the performance of file I/O operations, such as reading data from storage systems such as **ADLS**. Adjusting this parameter allows you to balance memory usage between caching data and caching metadata based on your specific workload requirements. The disk space per node is reserved for cached metadata in **bytes**.

- `spark.databricks.io.cache.compression.enabled`: This parameter in Databricks determines whether "compression is enabled" for cached data. When set to `true`, this parameter enables compression for cached data, reducing the amount of storage space required for cached data on disk. Compression can help optimize disk usage and improve performance by reducing I/O overhead when reading and writing cached data.

The following are the sample configuration settings you can use while creating your cluster:

- `spark.databricks.io.cache.maxDiskUsage 50g`

- `spark.databricks.io.cache.maxMetaDataCache 1g`

- `spark.databricks.io.cache.compression.enabled false`

> **Note**
>
> Here g stands for Gigabytes.

- **Enabling or disabling the disk cache**: When you turn off the cache (`spark.databricks.io.cache.compression.enabled false`), it does not delete the data that is already stored. It just stops queries from adding new data to the cache or reading data from the cache. The following is a simple example of how to turn the cache on or off:

```
spark.conf.set("spark.databricks.io.cache.enabled", "[true |
false]")
```

In the preceding code, the `spark.databricks.io.cache.enabled` configuration parameter in Databricks determines whether the caching feature is enabled or disabled. When it is set to `true`, which enables the caching, data can be read from external storage systems such as **ADLS** and will be cached in memory or disk for faster access in subsequent operations. When it is set to `false`, which disables caching, data read from external storage systems will not be cached, and each read operation will directly access the data from the storage system without caching it.

> **Note**
>
> You can learn more about Spark caching options at `https://packt.link/5VbZA`. You can find the complete code in the accompanying GitHub repository at `https://packt.link/SW0Jk`.

By now, you have explored **caching** techniques in **Synapse SQL**, **Synapse Spark**, and **Azure Databricks Spark**, and uncovered powerful ways to enhance read performance and optimize data handling. In Synapse SQL, you learned that result set caching eliminates the need for computation and speeds up subsequent query executions. Transitioning to Synapse Spark and Azure Databricks Spark, you found that caching works similarly to Synapse SQL but on a smaller scale. By using methods such as `cache()` or `persist()`, you can give your data a speed boost, which is especially useful when dealing with large datasets. In Azure Databricks, you discovered that the disk cache mechanism accelerates data reads by creating copies of remote Parquet files in local storage on worker nodes using a fast intermediate data format.

In the next section, you'll learn how to troubleshoot a failed Spark job.

# Troubleshooting a Failed Spark Job

**Spark** is a powerful framework for large-scale data processing, but it can also be challenging to troubleshoot when things go wrong. When a Spark job fails, the first step is to carefully examine the error messages and stack traces provided in the logs. These messages often pinpoint the root cause of the failure. If the logs are not clear, you may need to dig deeper into resource usage metrics or analyze the code itself to identify the problem.

> **Note**
>
> This section primarily focuses on the **Troubleshoot a failed Spark job** concept of the DP-203: Data Engineering on Microsoft Azure exam.

There are many possible reasons why a Spark job may fail. Some of them are as follows:

- **Resource issues**: Spark jobs may run out of memory, disk space, CPU, or network bandwidth, which may cause them to crash or slow down. You can monitor and adjust the resource allocation for your Spark jobs using the **Spark UI**, the **YARN UI**, or the health of Azure services.

- **Data issues**: Spark jobs may encounter corrupt, missing, or incompatible data, which causes them to throw exceptions or produce incorrect results. You can validate and clean your data before processing it or use error-handling techniques such as `try-catch` blocks and logging.

- **Code issues**: Spark jobs may contain bugs, logical errors, or performance bottlenecks in the code that cause them to fail or run inefficiently. You can debug and optimize your code using tools such as **Spark Shell**, **Spark SQL**, or the **Spark History Server**.

When it comes to diagnosing a failed Spark job in a cloud setting, you need to consider two primary facets: issues related to the environment and issues specific to the job itself.

The following sections will review each of these causes and walk you through troubleshooting each.

## Troubleshooting Resource Issues

Troubleshooting resource issues in Spark is essential for ensuring smooth job execution. By effectively managing resources such as memory and CPU, you can optimize performance and prevent job failures.

The following are the steps for checking resource issues:

1. Select the **Compute** option to navigate to the cluster's dashboard within your **Databricks** workspace and select Spark UI to see all the jobs that have succeeded, are running, or failed (*Figure 10.5*). You will notice that the Spark UI shows the number of stages and the duration of each job's completion:

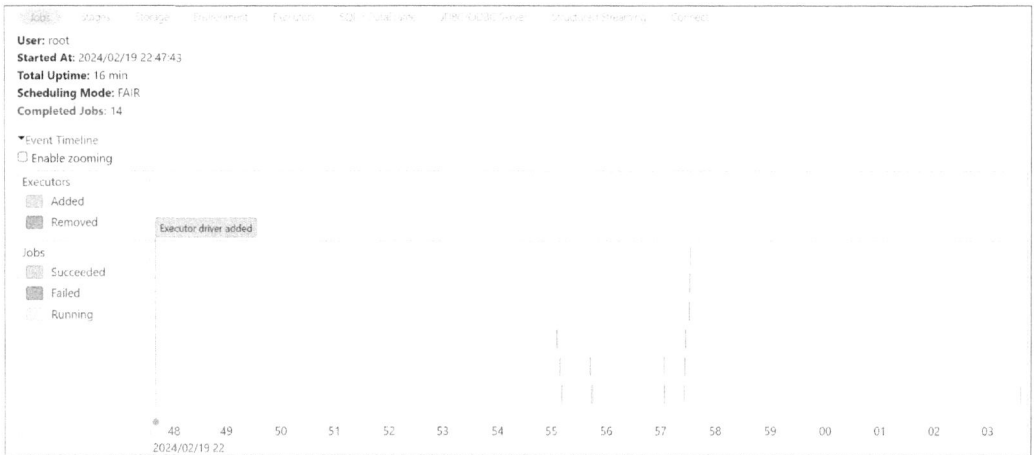

Figure 10.5 – Spark UI screen showing the status of the jobs

2. Next, click on `Stages` on the top menu. This opens the **Stages for All Jobs** screen, as shown in *Figure 10.6*:

Figure 10.6 – Checking the stages and duration of all job stages

3. Click on the cluster's `Metrics` option to check for cluster health.

You can see `CPU utilization`, `Memory utilization`, and `Network` usage. *Figure 10.7* shows the volume of memory utilized by the CPU:

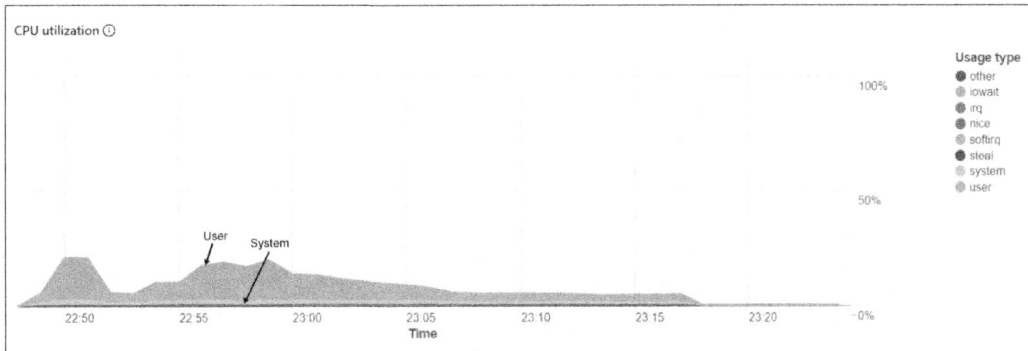

Figure 10.7 – The CPU utilization in cluster metrics

*Figure 10.8* shows the memory consumption. This is internally aggregated on average based on the total memory usage bytes for a predefined interval by each mode.

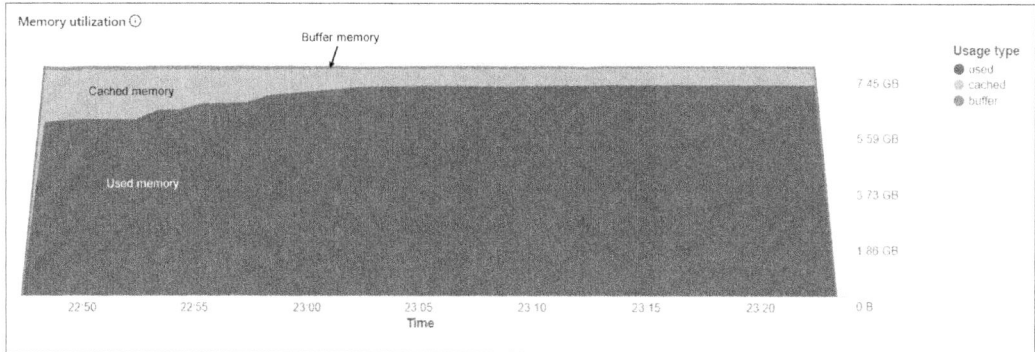

Figure 10.8 – Memory utilization in cluster metrics

*Figure 10.9* shows the network usage. This is internally aggregated on average based on the bytes received through the network by one second for each device.

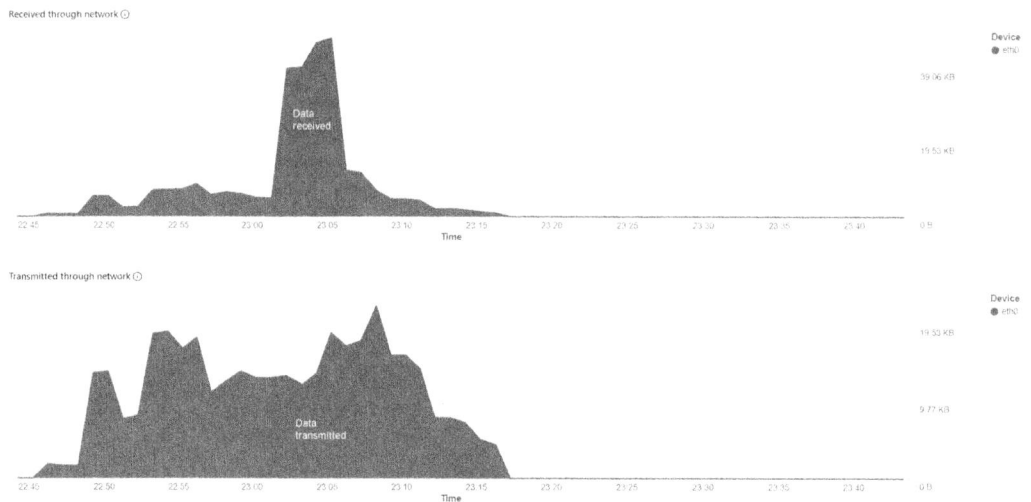

Figure 10.9 – Network usage in cluster metrics

> **Note**
>
> You can check the health of Azure services in the region where your Spark clusters are at `https://packt.link/Hv6tZ`.

By now, you have explored troubleshooting resource issues in Spark and learned that when a Spark job fails, the first step is to carefully examine the error messages and stack traces provided in the logs. These messages often pinpoint the root cause of the failure. If the logs are not clear, you may need to dig deeper into resource usage metrics or analyze the code itself to identify the problem.

Additionally, you have learned that troubleshooting resource issues in Spark is crucial for ensuring smooth job execution. By effectively managing resources such as memory and CPU, you can optimize performance and prevent job failures. Next, you will grasp the ways to troubleshoot job issues in Spark.

## Troubleshooting Job Issues

When working with Spark, troubleshooting job issues is key to keeping your data processing running smoothly. Spark's complexity and distributed nature mean that problems such as job failures or performance slowdowns can occur. Here, you will dive into common job issues and learn how to diagnose and fix them to ensure your workflows stay on track.

Checking for job-specific issues is a crucial step in troubleshooting when the cloud environment and the Spark clusters are healthy. The following are some steps you can take to troubleshoot job Spark jobs:

- **Checking job logs**: Look for any errors or exceptions that might indicate what went wrong. This could include out-of-memory errors, data serialization issues, and other potential issues that caused the job to fail or perform poorly.

- **Examining Spark UI**: The Spark UI provides a wealth of information about your Spark job, which includes a summary of task completion and details about the time spent in various stages of data processing. This can be examined in the Spark UI tab, as shown in *Figure 10.11*.

- **Looking for application details**: Check the details of the Spark application, including the Spark version, the configuration parameters, and the command used to submit the job. This helps troubleshoot by providing context and potential clues about the job's behavior and any issues encountered. For example, you might find compatibility issues with certain Spark versions or misconfigured parameters that could affect job performance.

- **Inspecting the data**: Sometimes, issues can arise due to the data being processed. Check whether the data is correctly formatted, has changed or been deleted during processing, any unexpected events occurred in the source files, or values changed in the source files.

To troubleshoot Spark job issues, checking the log files is a crucial step in debugging job-specific issues. The Spark UI is a great tool for tracking and debugging your Spark applications, as the log files provide detailed information about errors, exceptions, and other issues that occurred during job execution, helping to identify the root cause of the problem, and providing real-time insights into the job's progress, task completion, and resource usage.

- **Driver logs**: These logs check the recent logs and troubleshoot any issues with the jobs. You can launch the Driver logs from the Compute tab to see all the recent logs in the cluster, as shown in *Figure 10.10*:

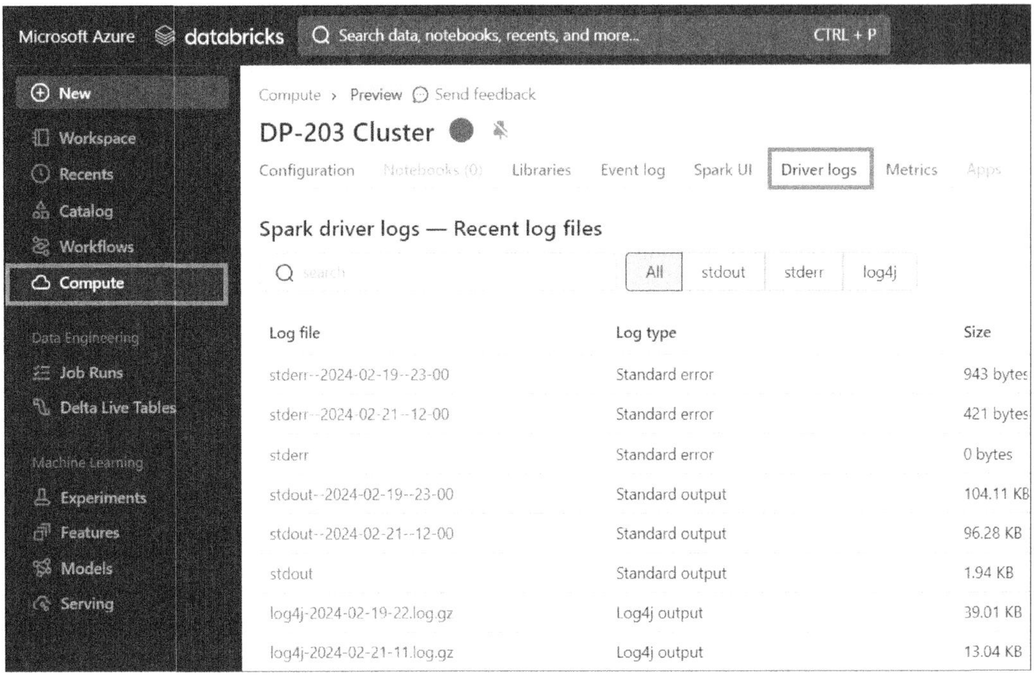

Figure 10.10 – Displaying Driver logs location in an Azure Databricks cluster

- **Spark jobs**: They check the status of each job in each stage. You will see a table of all the jobs that have been scheduled or run. It includes information about the status of the job, the number of stages and tasks, and so on (*Figure 10.11*):

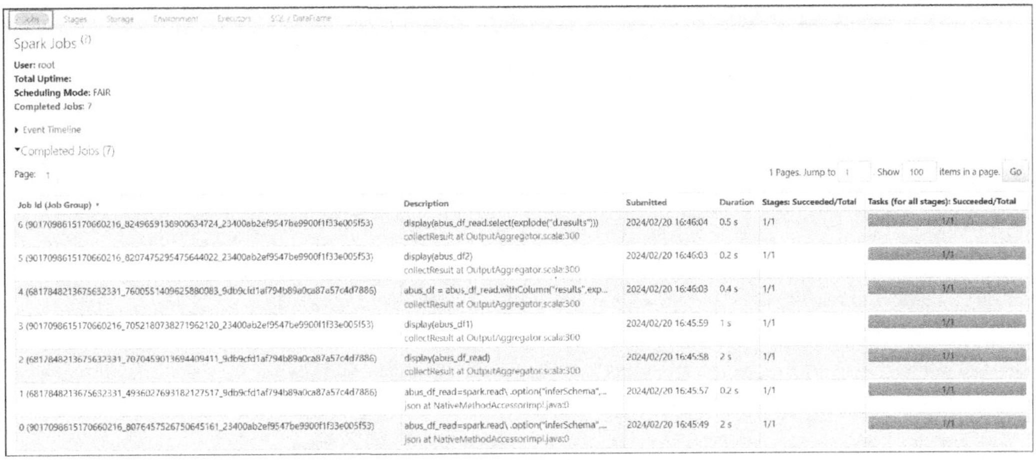

Figure 10.11 – Checking the status of a job in Spark job location within the Spark UI

- **Inspect executors**: The `Executors` tab shows details about each executor, such as the number of tasks, active tasks, and failed tasks and the amount of memory used (see *Figure 10.12*):

Figure 10.12 – Executor log location in the Spark UI

- **Stages**: A stage is a set of parallel tasks that perform the same computation on different partitions of the input data. The **Stages** tab shows the stages associated with the application, as shown in *Figure 10.13*:

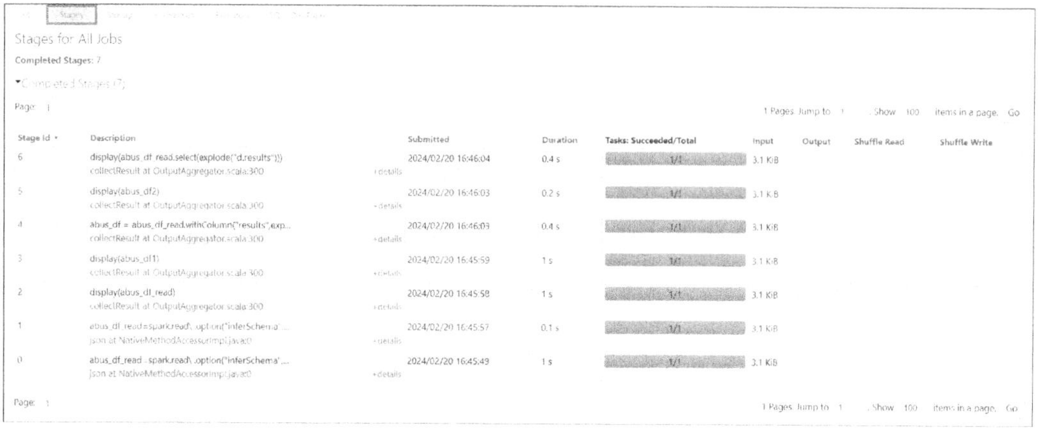

Figure 10.13 – Displaying task in each stage location in the Spark UI

Remember to start with the Driver log, and then proceed to the task jobs, followed by the executor and task-level logs to identify any errors or warnings that might be causing the job to fail.

> **Note**
>
> You can learn more about troubleshooting Spark jobs at `https://packt.link/2eRnA`.

Now you have explored common job issues and learned how to diagnose and fix them to ensure your workflows stay on track. When troubleshooting Spark job issues, you start with checking job logs for errors or exceptions that might indicate what went wrong, and these logs provide detailed information about job execution, such as out-of-memory errors or data serialization issues. Next, you explored the Spark UI, which offers insights into task completion and processing stages, tracks the job's progress, and identifies any bottlenecks affecting performance. You also looked into application details, such as the Spark version and configuration parameters, for context and clues about job behavior. This can reveal compatibility issues or misconfigured parameters that may impact performance. Next, you will look at how to troubleshoot a failed pipeline run, including activities executed in external services.

## Troubleshooting a Failed Pipeline Run

When managing complex data workflows, encountering occasional hiccups is almost expected. In Azure data engineering, troubleshooting is a critical skill to ensure the smooth functioning of pipelines—whether it's ADF orchestrating data movement and transformations or Azure Synapse Analytics handling large-scale analytics workloads. Proficient troubleshooting can swiftly diagnose and rectify issues, minimizing downtime and optimizing performance.

> **Note**
>
> This section primarily focuses on the **Troubleshoot a failed pipeline run, including activities executed in external services** concept of the DP-203: Data Engineering on Microsoft Azure exam.

The subsequent sections delve into troubleshooting ADF and Synapse pipelines, exploring best practices and proven strategies to navigate through the details of pipeline failures.

## Debugging a Failed Pipeline

ADF and Synapse pipelines offer comprehensive error messages upon pipeline failures. The following are the four straightforward steps to debug a failed pipeline:

1.  **Checking linked services**: Click on the **Linked Services** tab in ADF and then click on the `Test connection` link to ensure that the linked services are working fine and that nothing has changed on the source. *Figure 10.14* shows an example of the **Test connection** link on the **Edit linked service** screen:

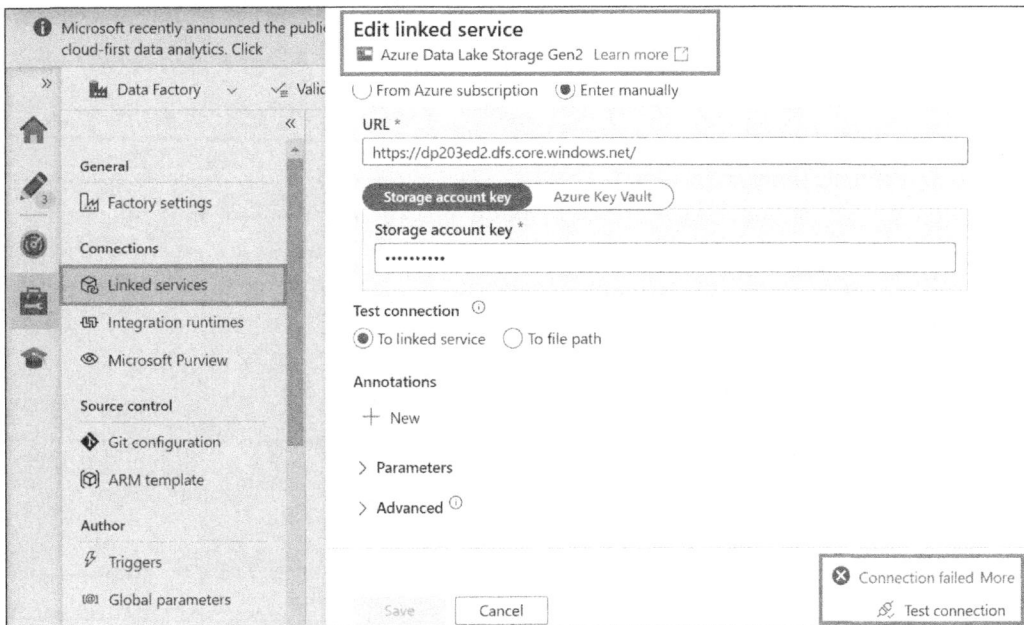

Figure 10.14 – Troubleshooting linked service connection

2.  **Checking datasets**: Verify the dataset in your pipeline as the file path may have been altered or the original file may have been replaced with new files. This is crucial for maintaining the accuracy and efficiency of your data processing tasks.

In *Figure 10.15*, the file was not located, and this invalid status of the file led to the failure of the pipeline. You can check the **Error details** screen for information on the error.

Figure 10.15 – Displaying an error when the Troubleshoot path is not found in the pipeline

3. **Files with different schemas**: Sometimes, the files in the folder you are copying are different from each other. For example, they may have a different number of columns, different ways of separating the values, different symbols for quoting the values, or any other differences in the data. When this happens, the pipeline may not be able to copy them and can give you the following error:

```
Operation on target Copy_sks failed: Failure happened on
'Sink' side. ErrorCode=DelimitedTextMoreColumnsThanDefined,
'Type=Microsoft.DataTransfer.Common.Shared.
HybridDeliveryException, Message=Error found when processing
'Csv/Tsv Format Text' source '0_2020_11_09_11_43_32.avro' with
row number 53: found more columns than expected column count
27., Source=Microsoft.DataTransfer.Common,'
```

In this scenario, you must select the `Binary Copy` option while creating the **Copy activity**. This way, the pipeline won't open the files to read the schema, treat each file as binary, and copy it to the other specified location.

4. **Pipeline queued for a long time**: The pipeline status may be queued or stuck for an extended period due to various reasons, such as reaching concurrency limits, experiencing service outages, or network failures.

- **Perceiving the delay**:

  - **Concurrency limits**: Sometimes, too many pipelines are running simultaneously, exceeding the allowed limit. This can put yours on hold until others finish.

  - **Temporary issues**: Network hiccups, credential mishaps, or even service outages can temporarily disrupt your pipeline's progress.

- **Taking action**:

  - **Check concurrency**: If your pipeline policy is set to have a maximum number of concurrent runs, you can check any old runs that are active. If there are any running from the past 45 days, consider canceling them to free up a slot for your current pipeline.

  - **Wait and see**: ADF has a built-in recovery process that monitors run and automatically restarts them if it detects temporary issues such as network problems or service interruptions. So, give it an hour and see whether your pipeline picks up again on its own. If your pipeline remains queued for more than an hour or an extended period, consider contacting Microsoft support.

> **Note**
>
> You can learn more about troubleshooting pipelines in ADF and Azure Synapse Analytics at `https://packt.link/GUhxG`.

By now, you have learned a comprehensive approach to debugging failed pipelines in ADF and Synapse pipelines. You learned to ensure the operational status of linked services by testing connections, followed by verifying datasets to maintain data processing accuracy. Handling files with different schemas is addressed by selecting the `Binary Copy` option during the copy operation. Additionally, you gained knowledge about the potential delays in pipeline execution, such as concurrency limits or temporary issues. You grasped ways to check for old runs consuming resources, cancel them if necessary, or wait for ADF's built-in recovery process to address temporary issues. Now, it is time to look at how you can troubleshoot activities executed in external services.

## Troubleshooting Activities Executed in External Services

When working with **ADF** and **Synapse pipelines**, you often have to interact with external services. Sometimes, the source files are not always readily available in Azure Storage, so you might consume the data from external sources. These external services can be anything from databases and storage accounts to other cloud services. When your pipeline run fails, it is important to consider these external service dependencies in your troubleshooting process.

Consider Databricks in this scenario. The error message in *Figure 10.16* is an HTTP ERROR 403 error, which is typically returned when the pipeline knows the request but refuses to authorize it because it is an **Invalid access token** issue that has occurred while trying to access a specific URL endpoint in Azure Databricks. This error usually occurs when the access token used for authentication is either expired or incorrect.

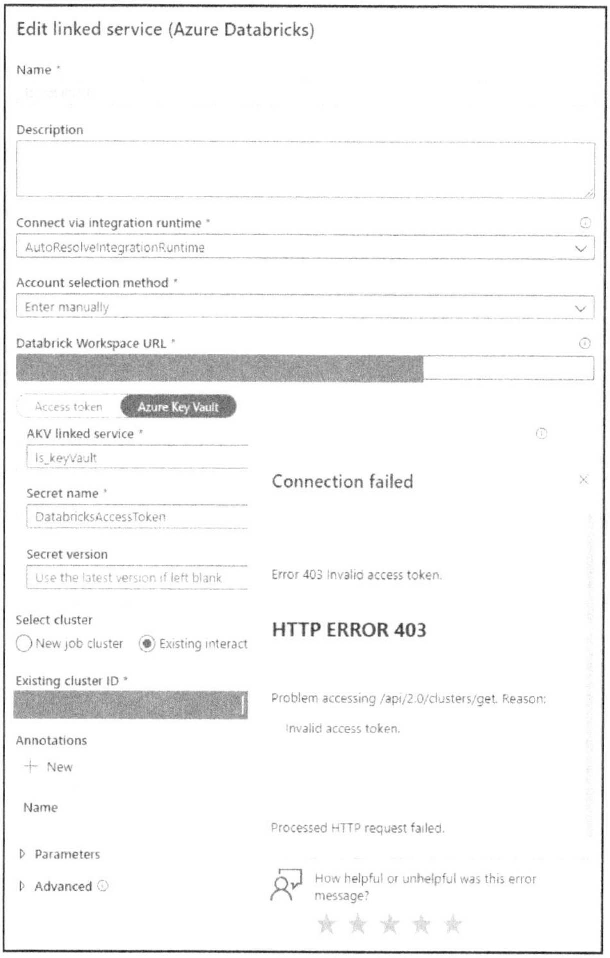

Figure 10.16 – Troubleshooting an access token issue for Azure Databricks service

The following are some steps you can take to resolve this issue:

1. **Check the access token**: You might have made a mistake while copying the token, so make sure that the access token you are using is correct.

2. **Token expiration**: Access tokens in Azure Databricks are valid for 90 days (default). If your token has expired, then you will need to generate a new one.

3. **Permissions**: Ensure that the access token has the necessary permissions to operate.

4. **Regenerate token**: If the issue continues, you might need to regenerate a new token and update the linked service in your pipeline with the newly generated token.

The following are a few other common issues and troubleshooting methods to resolve for external activities:

- **Databricks authoring issue**: The error code 3201, which is typically returned when the pipeline fails, is due to inefficient authoring in a Databricks notebook activity in the pipeline. This can be caused by the following issues:

  - **Missing notebook path**: The notebook path is not specified correctly. You should specify the notebook path in the Databricks notebook activity.

  - **Non-existent cluster**: The Databricks cluster does not exist or has been deleted. You should verify that the Databricks cluster exists.

  - **Incomplete linked service definition**: The linked service should have the workspace and access token as required properties; make sure you verify the linked service definition.

  - **Missing cluster information**: The linked service should specify either an existing cluster ID or new cluster information for creation.

- **Azure Data Lake Analytics issue**: The error code 2711 refers to the user who is forbidden from performing the requested operation due to failed **ACL** verification. This could be because the file does not exist in data lake or you are not authorized to perform the operation. Check the following causes and recommendations to troubleshoot this issue:

  - **Problem identified**: Restricted access to the file in your ADLS.

  - **Root cause**: Insufficient permissions for the service principal or certificate.

  - **Solution**: Verifying the service principal or certificate and granting the necessary permissions for the following:

    - **Data Lake storage account**: Ensuring that the service principal or certificate has appropriate access rights configured in **ADLS**

    - **File or directory**: Verifying that the file exists in the specified location within ADLS, reviewing and updating the **ACLs** on the file or folder to grant the required permissions to the service principal or certificate

> **Note**
>
> You can find the troubleshooting guide with the complete details of all the error codes and recommendations on how to fix the issues at `https://packt.link/1kKTV`.

Mastering the art of troubleshooting is a process that develops with experience. The guidelines provided in this chapter serve as an initial roadmap to navigate this complex skill. It is essential to apply these principles across a wide array of examples to gain a comprehensive knowledge. Over time, you will develop a keen eye for identifying and resolving issues to elevate your debugging proficiency. Remember, patience and persistence are key in this journey toward becoming a debugging expert.

## Summary

In this chapter, you explored several new concepts, some of which may require considerable time and effort to fully grasp. Tasks such as handling skew in data, data spill, tuning queries, and troubleshooting failed pipelines and jobs are complex enough to warrant their own books. An overview of these topics was provided, along with additional resources for further exploration.

You learned about essential concepts for efficient Big Data Analytics, by addressing the issue of small files, as well as data compaction techniques to improve storage efficiency and query performance. After that, you explored strategies for handling data skew and spills, which is crucial for optimizing SQL and Spark environments, and then examined shuffle partitions in Spark, where techniques such as indexing and caching for performance enhancement were discussed. Additionally, you saw general tips for resource management and guidelines for debugging Spark jobs.

By now, you should have a solid knowledge of various optimization and query-tuning techniques, which will prove invaluable both for certification purposes and in your journey to becoming a proficient Azure data engineer. Mastering these concepts will not only advance your career by improving your ability to work with large-scale data but also prepare you for the certification exam, validating your expertise in data engineering and analytics.

Congratulations on completing all the topics outlined in the DP-203 certification syllabus! Your dedication to seeing this through to the end is commendable. Looking ahead, you will focus on the mock exam, flashcards, and practical exercises designed to support your exam preparation on the platform.

# Exam Readiness Drill – Chapter Review Questions

Apart from a solid understanding of key concepts, being able to think quickly under time pressure is a skill that will help you ace your certification exam. That is why working on these skills early on in your learning journey is key.

Chapter review questions are designed to improve your test-taking skills progressively with each chapter you learn and review your understanding of key concepts in the chapter at the same time. You'll find these at the end of each chapter.

> **How to Access These Materials**
>
> To learn how to access these resources, head over to the chapter titled *Chapter 11, Accessing the Online Resources*.

To open the Chapter Review Questions for this chapter, perform the following steps:

1.  Click the link – `https://packt.link/DP203E2_CH10`.

    Alternatively, you can scan the following **QR code** (*Figure 10.17*):

Figure 10.17 – QR code that opens Chapter Review Questions for logged-in users

2.    Once you log in, you'll see a page similar to the one shown in *Figure 10.18*:

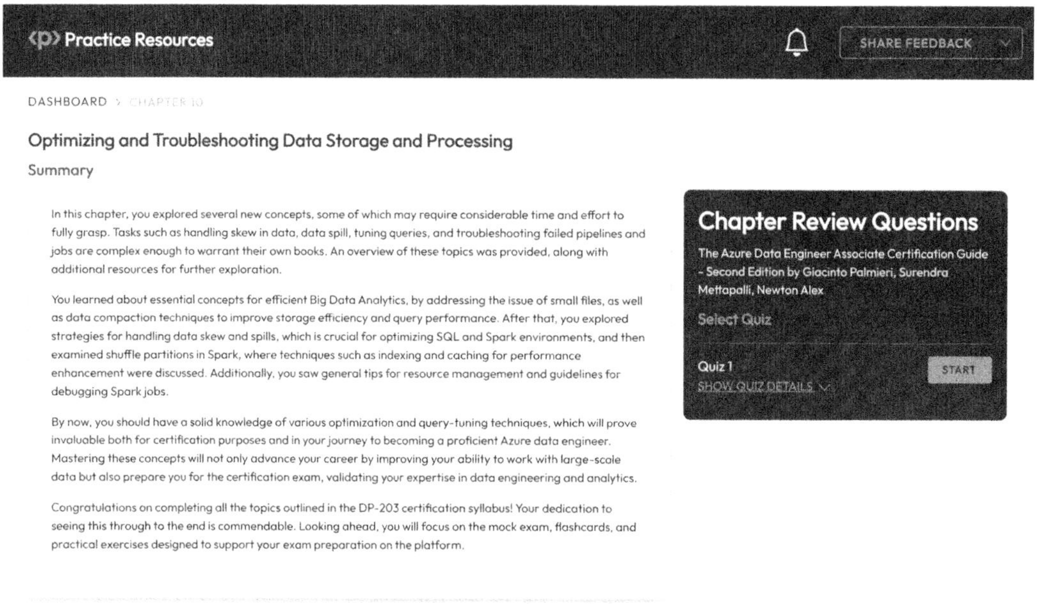

Figure 10.18 – Chapter Review Questions for Chapter 10

3.    Once ready, start the following practice drills, re-attempting the quiz multiple times.

## Exam Readiness Drill

For the first three attempts, don't worry about the time limit.

### ATTEMPT 1

The first time, aim for at least **40%**. Look at the answers you got wrong and read the relevant sections in the chapter again to fix your learning gaps.

### ATTEMPT 2

The second time, aim for at least **60%**. Look at the answers you got wrong and read the relevant sections in the chapter again to fix any remaining learning gaps.

*ATTEMPT 3*

The third time, aim for at least **75%**. Once you score 75% or more, you start working on your timing.

> **Tip**
> You may take more than **three** attempts to reach 75%. That's okay. Just review the relevant sections in the chapter till you get there.

# Working On Timing

**Target**: Your aim is to keep the score the same while trying to answer these questions as quickly as possible. Here's an example of how your next attempts should look like:

| Attempt | Score | Time Taken |
|---------|-------|------------|
| Attempt 5 | 77% | 21 mins 30 seconds |
| Attempt 6 | 78% | 18 mins 34 seconds |
| Attempt 7 | 76% | 14 mins 44 seconds |

Table 10.4 – Sample timing practice drills on the online platform

> **Note**
> The time limits shown in the above table are just examples. Set your own time limits with each attempt based on the time limit of the quiz on the website.

With each new attempt, your score should stay above **75%** while your "time taken" to complete should "decrease". Repeat as many attempts as you want till you feel confident dealing with the time pressure.

# 11
# Accessing the Online Practice Resources

Your copy of *Azure Data Engineer Associate Certification Guide, Second Edition* comes with free online practice resources. Use these to hone your exam readiness even further by attempting practice questions on the companion website. The website is user-friendly and can be accessed from mobile, desktop, and tablet devices. It also includes interactive timers for an exam-like experience.

## How to Access These Materials

Here's how you can start accessing these resources depending on your source of purchase.

## Purchased from Packt Store (packtpub.com)

If you've bought the book from the Packt store (`packtpub.com`) eBook or Print, head to `https://packt.link/dp203practice`. There, log in using the same Packt account you created or used to purchase the book.

## Packt+ Subscription

If you're a *Packt+ subscriber*, you can head over to the same link (`https://packt.link/dp203practice`), log in with your `Packt ID`, and start using the resources. You will have access to them as long as your subscription is active.

If you face any issues accessing your free resources, contact us at `customercare@packt.com`.

## Purchased from Amazon and Other Sources

If you've purchased from sources other than the ones mentioned above (like *Amazon*), you'll need to unlock the resources first by entering your unique sign-up code provided in this section. **Unlocking takes less than 10 minutes, can be done from any device, and needs to be done only once**. Follow these five easy steps to complete the process:

### STEP 1

Open the link `https://packt.link/dp203unlock` OR scan the following **QR code** (*Figure 11.1*):

Figure 11.1 – QR code for the page that lets you unlock this book's free online content.

Either of those links will lead to the following page as shown in *Figure 11.2*:

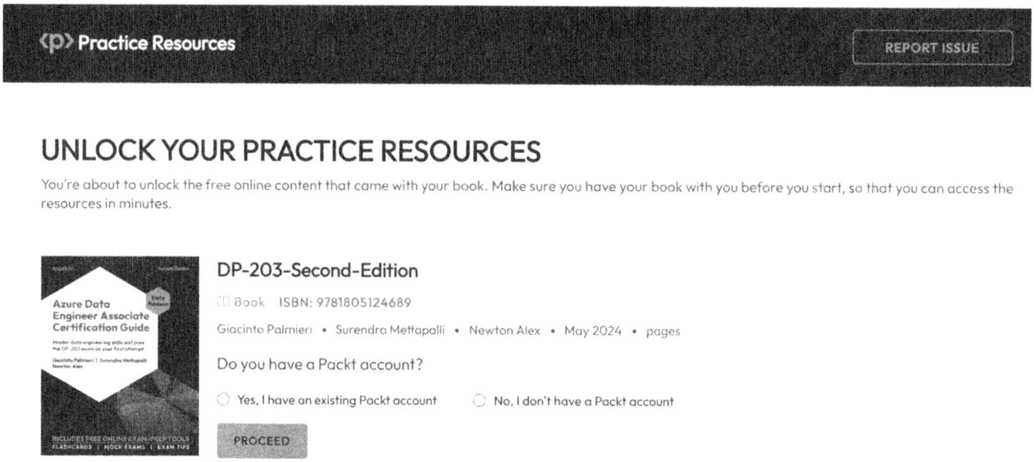

Figure 11.2 – Unlock page for the online practice resources

## STEP 2

If you already have a Packt account, select the option `Yes, I have an existing Packt account`. If not, select the option `No, I don't have a Packt account`.

If you don't have a Packt account, you'll be prompted to create a new account on the next page. It's free and only takes a minute to create.

Click `Proceed` after selecting one of those options.

## STEP 3

After you've created your account or logged in to an existing one, you'll be directed to the following page as shown in *Figure 11.3*.

Make a note of your unique unlock code:

CQG5850

Type in or copy this code into the text box labeled 'Enter Unique Code':

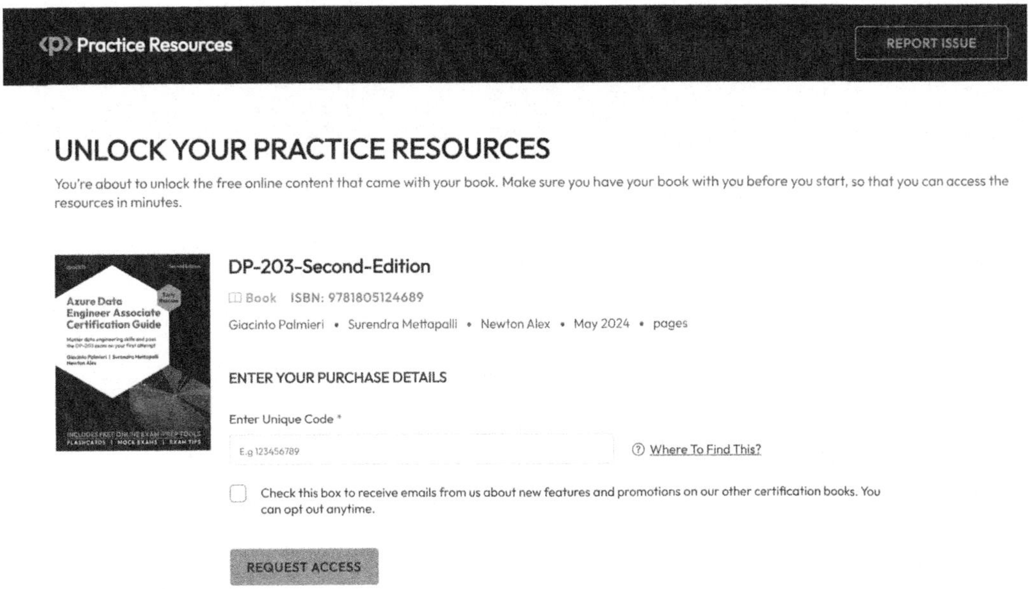

Figure 11.3 – Enter your unique sign-up code to unlock the resources

> **Troubleshooting tip**
>
> After creating an account, if your connection drops off or you accidentally close the page, you can reopen the page shown in *Figure 11.2* and select `Yes, I have an existing account`. Then, sign in with the account you had created before you closed the page. You'll be redirected to the screen shown in *Figure 11.3*.

## STEP 4

> **Note**
>
> You may choose to opt into emails regarding feature updates and offers on our other certification books. We don't spam, and it's easy to opt out at any time.

Click `Request Access`.

## STEP 5

If the code you entered is correct, you'll see a button that says, `OPEN PRACTICE RESOURCES`, as shown in *Figure 11.4*:

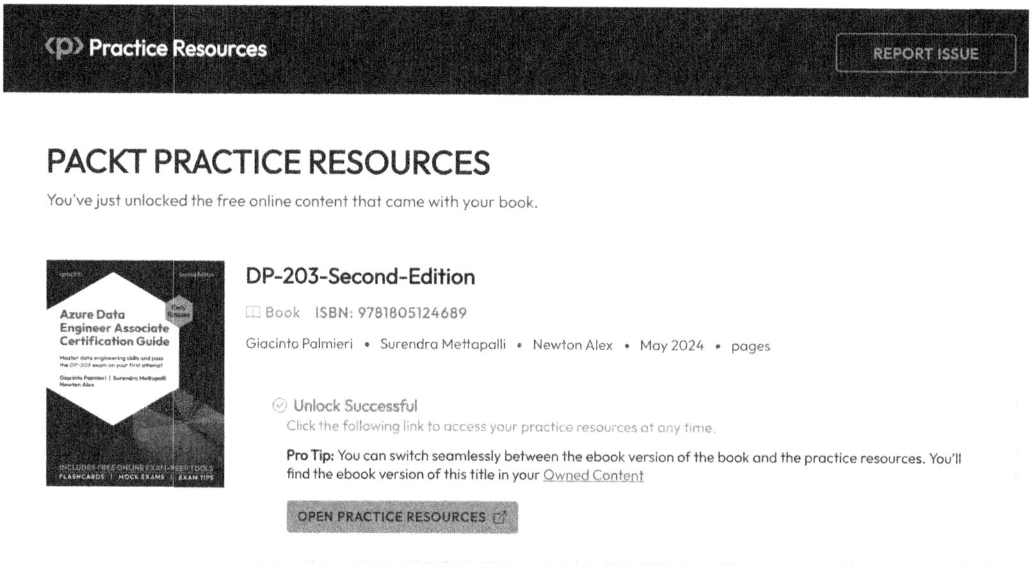

Figure 11.4 – Page that shows up after a successful unlock

Click the OPEN PRACTICE RESOURCES link to start using your free online content. You'll be redirected to the Dashboard shown in *Figure 11.5*:

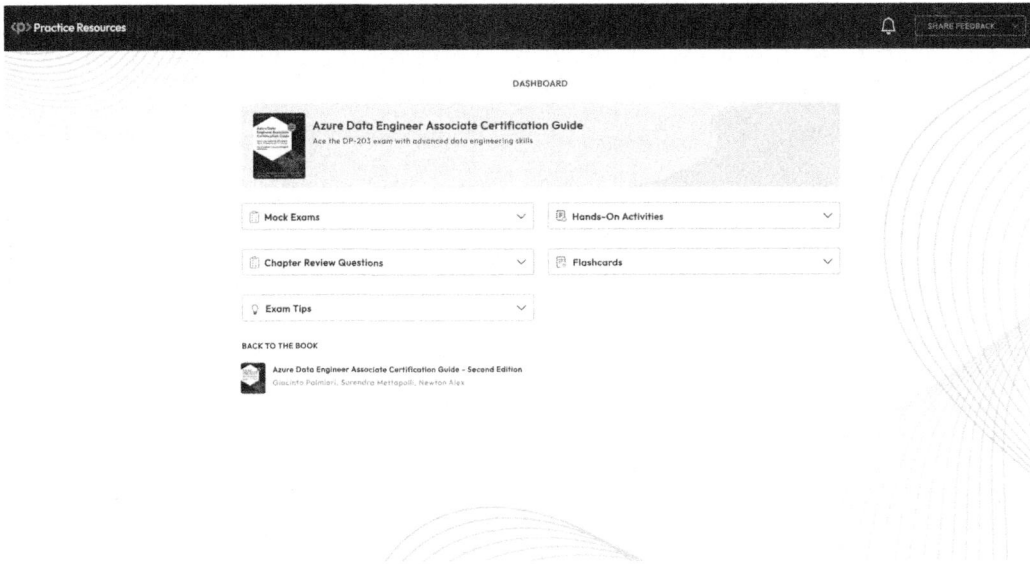

Figure 11.5 – Dashboard page for DP-203 practice resources

**Bookmark this link**

Now that you've unlocked the resources, you can come back to them anytime by visiting https://packt.link/dp203practice or scanning the following QR code provided in *Figure 11.6*:

Figure 11.6 – QR code to bookmark practice resources website

## Troubleshooting Tips

If you're facing issues unlocking, here are three things you can do:

- Double-check your unique code. All unique codes in our books are case-sensitive and your code needs to match exactly as it is shown in *STEP 3*.

- If that doesn't work, use the `Report Issue` button located at the top-right corner of the page.

- If you're not able to open the unlock page at all, write to `customercare@packt.com` and mention the name of the book.

## Share Feedback

If you find any issues with the platform, the book, or any of the practice materials, you can click the `Share Feedback` button from any page and reach out to us. If you have any suggestions for improvement, you can share those as well.

## Back to the Book

To make switching between the book and practice resources easy, we've added a link that takes you back to the book (*Figure 11.7*). Click it to open your book in Packt's online reader. Your reading position is synced so you can jump right back to where you left off when you last opened the book.

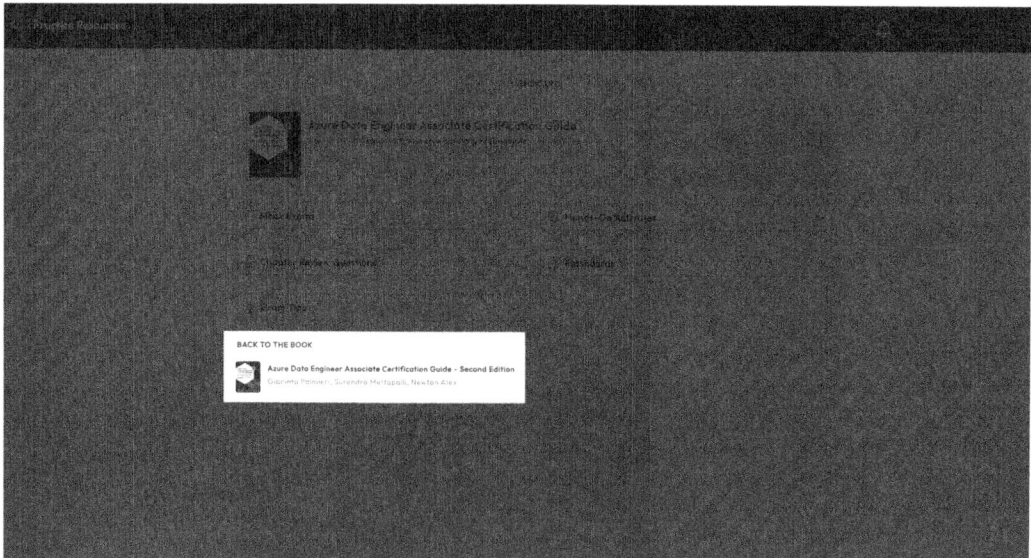

Figure 11.7 – Jump back to the book from the dashboard

> **Note**
>
> Certain elements of the website might change over time and thus may end up looking different from how they are represented in the screenshots of this book.

# Index

# ‹packt›

# Other Books You May Enjoy

If you enjoyed this book, you may be interested in these other books by Packt:

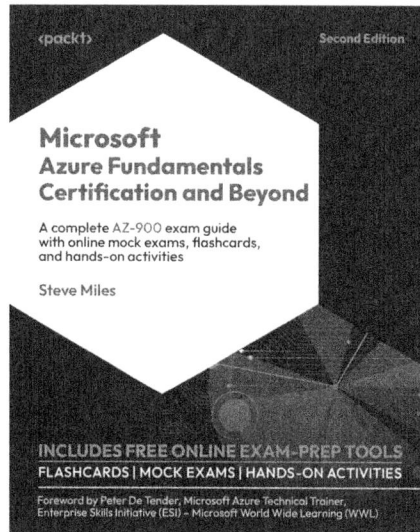

**Microsoft Azure Fundamentals Certification and Beyond, Second Edition**

Steve Miles

ISBN: 978-1-83763-059-2

- Become proficient in foundational cloud concepts
- Develop a solid understanding of core components of the Microsoft Azure cloud platform
- Get to grips with Azure's core services, deployment, and management tools
- Implement security concepts, operations, and posture management
- Explore identity, governance, and compliance features
- Gain insights into resource deployment, management, and monitoring

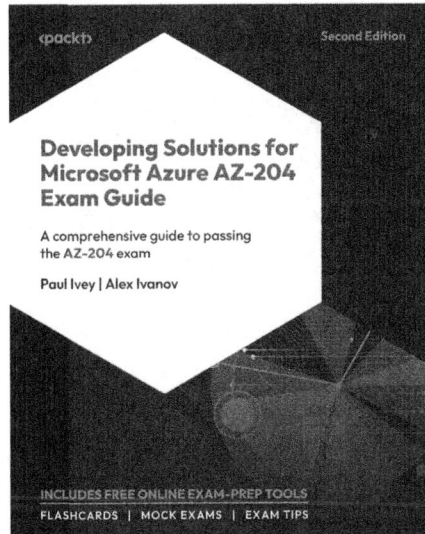

**Developing Solutions for Microsoft Azure AZ-204 Exam Guide, Second Edition**

Paul Ivey and Alex Ivanov

ISBN: 978-1-83508-529-5

- Identify cloud models and services in Azure
- Develop secure Azure web apps and host containerized solutions in Azure
- Implement serverless solutions with Azure Functions
- Utilize Cosmos DB for scalable data storage
- Optimize Azure Blob storage for efficiency
- Securely store secrets and configuration settings centrally
- Ensure web application security with Microsoft Entra ID authentication
- Monitor and troubleshoot Azure solutions

## Share Your Thoughts

Now you've finished *Azure Data Engineer Associate Certification Guide, Second Edition,* we'd love to hear your thoughts! Scan the QR code below to go straight to the Amazon review page for this book and share your feedback or leave a review on the site that you purchased it from.

https://packt.link/r/1805124684

Your review is important to us and the tech community and will help us make sure we're delivering excellent quality content.

# Download a Free PDF Copy of This Book

Thanks for purchasing this book!

Do you like to read on the go but are unable to carry your print books everywhere?

Is your eBook purchase not compatible with the device of your choice?

Don't worry, now with every Packt book you get a DRM-free PDF version of that book at no cost.

Read anywhere, any place, on any device. Search, copy, and paste code from your favorite technical books directly into your application.

The perks don't stop there, you can get exclusive access to discounts, newsletters, and great free content in your inbox daily.

Follow these simple steps to get the benefits:

1. Scan the QR code or visit the link below:

https://packt.link/free-ebook/9781805124689

2. Submit your proof of purchase.
3. That's it! We'll send your free PDF and other benefits to your email directly.

Printed in Great Britain
by Amazon